THE SHAPING
OF THE
AMERICAN
PAST

VOLUME 2

ROBERT KELLEY

University of California, Santa Barbara

THE SHAPING OF THE AMERICAN PAST

Second Edition

Prentice-Hall, Inc.
Englewood Cliffs, New Jersey 07632

**Library of Congress
Cataloging in Publication Data**

Kelley, Robert Lloyd (date).
    The shaping of the American past.

    Bibliography
    Includes index.
      1. United States—History. I. Title.
E178.1.K27 1978b   973   77-12252
ISBN 0-13-808121-2 (v. 2)

Printed in the United States of America

10 9 8 7 6 5 4 3 2 1

Design Ben Kann
Picture Research Mira Schachne
Chapter Bibliographies Joyce Baker
Cover Photo J. Alex Langley, dpi

Prentice-Hall International, Inc., *London*

Prentice-Hall of Australia Pty. Limited, *Sydney*

Prentice-Hall of Canada, Ltd., *Toronto*

Prentice-Hall of India Private Limited, *New Delhi*

Prentice-Hall of Japan, Inc., *Tokyo*

Prentice-Hall of Southeast Asia Pte. Ltd., *Singapore*

Whitehall Books Limited, *Wellington, New Zealand*

Acknowledgments

Excerpts

p. 542 from *Dusk of Dawn,* by W.E.B. DuBois. Reprinted by permission of DuBois Publications, S.A.

pp. 586 and 615 from *Hard Times: An Oral History of the Great Depression,* by Studs Terkel. Copyright 1970 by Studs Terkel. Reprinted by permission of Random House, Inc.

p. 682 from "The Sources of Soviet Conduct", by George F. Kennan, from *Foreign Affairs,* July 1974. Excerpted by permission from *Foreign Affairs.* Copyright 1947 by Council on Foreign Relations, Inc.

p. 775, copyright 1972 by David Halberstam. Reprinted from *The Best and the Brightest,* by David Halberstam. By permission of Random House, Inc. First published in *Esquire* Magazine.

p. 807 from "Supermarket or Superpower," by Anatole Shub, *Harper's Magazine,* January 1972.

p. 808 from Henry Brandon, "The Balance of Mutual Weakness," copyright ⓒ 1972 by The Atlantic Monthly Company, Boston, Mass. Reprinted with permission.

Maps

All maps except those on pp. 402 and 829 are from Rebecca Brooks Gruver, *An American History,* 2/e, ⓒ 1976 by Addison-Wesley. Reprinted by permission of Addison-Wesley.

to Madge

CONTENTS

Chapter 23   **Gilded Age Politics: Instability and Impasse**   *440*

Chapter 24   **Emergence to World Power**   *460*

Chapter 25   **The Progressive Era: New Ways of Thinking**   *482*

Chapter 26   **The Progressive Era: Republicans in Charge**   *503*

Chapter 35

Years of the Whirlwind: The 1960s   728

Chapter 36

The Politics of Turmoil: Kennedy, Johnson, and Nixon   762

Preliminary Remarks
to the First Edition

THIS book contains a personal view of the American past. Its main focus lies in the great political struggles of each era, for here, it seems to me, is where the nation shapes itself most consciously and reveals its nature most tellingly. My tendency has been to conceive of these controversies in cultural terms; that is, along the lines of what is now being called the "new political history." When we observe public affairs from this vantage, we see the conflict not only of economic interests, but also of ethnic group ranged against ethnic group, members of one religious faith lined up against those of another, even life-style pitted against life-style. As a cultural historian whose principal concern has been the comparative study of politics and political persuasions in the transatlantic community, I have found that wherever one tests the notion that such feelings between social groups powerfully shape the character and structure of nations, the results have been conclusive. In this formulation, political narrative becomes like life itself: pluralistic, many sided, a compound of emotions and mutual images, as well as of economic motives. It also becomes closely interwoven with the history of the disadvantaged and the exploited, blacks, women, American Indians, workers and farmers, European immigrants, Mexican-Americans—all receive close attention in this book.

Social antagonisms are remarkably persistent. Tactics may change, but the enemy remains the same, decade after decade. Irish Catholics have lined up massively in the Democratic party because the Republican party (and its forebears, the Federalist and the Whig parties) has been the stronghold of their ancient cultural enemy, the Anglo-Saxon Protestants, whose social preeminence has made outsiders of Catholics and other non-WASP ethnocultural minorities. Similarly, businessmen and Democrats have usually regarded each other with distrust, from Andrew Jackson's day to Franklin Roosevelt's, and with brief intermissions the same has been true for intellectuals, as a class, and the Republicans.

Against this background of long-run persistence in the social coalitions that have lined up behind each party, one can observe a remarkable continuity in their outlooks and policies, and thus an order and coherence in the controversies marking each period of American history.

Since this work focuses on the nation's public affairs, the mainstream of the narrative traces the classic themes with which every historian must grapple when his subject is the life history of an entire nation: the founding of the first colonial settlements and the sweep of population across the continental expanse: the evolution of the society, its ways of life and its institutions; the great events and crises through which America has passed, from the Revolution to the Watergate affair; and its increasingly complex relations with the rest of the world. The arguments that have raged over these issues have been crucial, and their description has much absorbed my attention. How shall the country be governed? Its currency managed? Its race relations organized? Its powerful corporations regulated? In addition, I have frequently explored the larger history of ideas. From the Puritans to the Pragmatists, from John Locke to Sigmund Freud, it is a rich story to tell.

Because the topic interests me and I find that many teachers of history share my interest, I have placed after these opening remarks an introduction, "The Historian's Task," which briefly discusses what it is historians do when they write and teach history. The main body of the book considers the major periods traditionally examined in American history. Then, since I strongly believe that we have not completed our task as historians until we show how the past flows into the present, four full chapters plus part of another one are devoted to the years from 1960 to 1977, thus giving to this turbulent period, so crucial in its effects on our lives, just as close and careful a look as was given to earlier times. Finally, to help students look back and reflect on what they have read, the book concludes with a retrospective essay (chapter 39). Designed as a spur to discussion, the essay is cast in the form of a comparison across time. It may be useful for students to read it first, since it highlights many of the work's themes.

Each chapter contains a time line, which lists, year by year, the major events discussed, as well as brief excerpts from documents and relevant historical writings. To indicate at least a part of the learning process that has lain behind my writing of the book, I have listed after each chapter three of the books that have most helped me in composing that particular part of the narrative. A longer historiographical essay follows, prepared with thoughtful care by Joyce Baker, a doctoral student and lecturer at the University of California, Santa Barbara, who has worked with me in my teaching of American history.

The writing of *The Shaping of the American Past* has been strongly affected by two influences: many years of encounter with students in classes and seminars, and a realization that, in preparing a survey of American history, one is operating within a formidable tradition. The names Charles Beard, Samuel Eliot Morison, and Henry Steele Commager only begin the list of distinguished historians who have been drawn to the task. To search for the pattern of the whole, and to describe it, seems to be perennially attractive to the historical mind. It is, indeed, perhaps our most important professional aim. For this reason I have always felt that the survey course presents the largest challenge to teacher and student alike. In it, as in this book, the goal is to form an encompassing understanding of the whole of the nation's past and thereby create a framework within which to view the present most clearly and usefully.

Robert Kelley

Preliminary Remarks
to the Second Edition

THE author of a textbook has the privilege of periodic revision, an opportunity always welcomed, for it provides an occasion for bringing things up to date and making improvements. In this case, there is an additional consideration. For the past several years I have been researching a study of the nation's political culture and ideologies, from the Revolutionary period to the present. The scholarship on these subjects is very rich now, especially in its ethnocultural aspects. As I've read through this mass of new research, I've thought of the relevant chapters in the text, for I was learning much that made me want to bring in these fresh perspectives.

This is the background for the Second Edition. The chapters which focus upon the nation's political struggles have been recast, in a number of cases extensively revised and rewritten, particularly: 6 THE REVOLUTION; 7 FORMING THE NATION; 8 THE NEW NATION: THE FEDERALIST ERA; 23 (now entitled) GILDED AGE POLITICS: INSTABILITY AND IMPASSE; and 26 THE PROGRESSIVE ERA: REPUBLICANS IN CHARGE. In others, the new material has been woven in by means of fresh passages and sections, as in, for example: 13 THE AGE OF JACKSON; 18 THE NATION SPLITS APART; 28 AMERICA AND THE FIRST WORLD WAR; and 30 THE REPUBLICAN ERA: TRIUMPH AND DISASTER.

A few comments will hint at what is new: the ideology of "republicanism" as the radical political consciousness for the Revolutionary generation and its role in later periods has been much deepened and broadened; the recent discovery by scholars of the five party systems, each about thirty to forty years long, provides a new structure for the political narrative throughout; such dynamics as modernization versus traditionalism, cosmopolitanism versus localism, take a key position in the analysis; striking new understandings of why it was that Virginia and Massachusetts, ethnically the most English of the colonies,

led in bringing on the Revolution are now explored; the existence of the "other South," as a force working against the traditionally-described pattern in the South of violence, agrarianism, and anti-Yankeeism, now has a significant place in the narrative; the Scotch-Irish role, a towering one, as the angriest anti-English ethnic group in the Revolutionary years and the next half century (the Catholic Irish taking over thereafter) is a prominent new feature, helping to explain much in the nation's public life; new understandings of the political disintegration of the 1850s, North and South, leading to secession and war, appear; the tremendous importance, as we now realize, of prohibitionism in 19th century politics and well into the twentieth century, is carefully explained; the surging of the urban Democrats which began about 1910, pointing toward the New Deal—these and many other things could be recounted at length. Suffice to say that we are in the presence of a sweeping revolution in the way scholars understand American history, and so far as I have been able, leading features of this revolution, covering wide areas of the American past, are in this Second Edition.

Suggestions which have come in from professors and students have also been of great aid, and in the new edition there are many locations in the narrative where I've responded to what has in this fashion been said to me. Indeed, the letters which the author of a book such as this one receives have led me gratefully to reflect upon the special relationship which can spring up between those who teach from a textbook, or are called upon to read it, and the person whose good fortune it has been, in writing it, to reach so many colleagues and students. This has led to a number of new sections on, for example: early explorations; colonial women; the Founding Fathers and slavery; the ethnics and the election of 1920; the Harlem Renaissance; the lasting effects of Great Society reforms; and a number of other topics, some treated in brief passages. In the book's latter sections the chapter on Vietnam (37) has been brought up to date, and a new chapter (38) entitled THE WATERGATE CRISIS AND THE FORD PRESIDENCY has been written, running through the election of Jimmy Carter and the first months of his administration. The last chapter (39), which compares American life now with what it was like a hundred years ago, now includes the latest social statistics, and it concludes with a discussion of the new "era of limits" psychology which has so swiftly emerged recently.

I have done a good deal more in this Second Edition. I have gone through every paragraph in the book, line by line, to carefully excise what we could perhaps do without—usually elaborations—to make the narrative a bit leaner and tighter. As is usually the case, this has had, I believe, a beneficial effect. We have decided from responses received that it would be better to have illustrations placed near the subjects to which they refer, rather than in separate vignettes in each chapter. Thus, I have re-illustrated the book, selecting pictures and photos from fresh sources as well as re-locating in the narrative many already in use.

In addition, the book contains four groupings of illustrations designed to highlight particular themes. Where there has been major rewriting, bibliographies have been modified.

The Second Edition remains what the First Edition was: a book I've tried to write as if speaking directly, face to face, to the students who will be reading it, talking to them through the typewriter. What I have wanted most of all is for them to *understand* their country and through that experience, themselves. There's a reason why history, as a literary form, is thousands of years old: it is because the first and most natural way we have always had of understanding ourselves has been by listening to a story about our shared past; by learning, through the medium of a human narrative, how the people who have pre-

ceded us did what they did, and brought us to where we are. If in this book, which explores all the major aspects of our past, I concentrate particularly upon politics, it is because for two centuries the country's national politics has been our national theatre, in which millions of Americans have participated in one way or another, defining who they are and what they believe in. Where better to start when, sooner or later, to tell that story, everything else has to be brought in?

For this Second Edition I have many people to thank: those in other institutions, here and abroad, who were thoughtful enough to send me comments and suggestions; my students and teaching assistants in my course in the history of American politics and culture, among the latter especially Miss Diane Nassir; my colleague Mario García, at UCSB, who kindly reviewed my sections on Chicano history and the Southwest; and particularly Brian Walker, Edward Stanford, and Marina Harrison, my editors at Prentice-Hall, Inc. Many members of Prentice-Hall's field staff, furthermore, have with their characteristic courtesy relayed to me the reactions to the book they have encountered in their personal discussions with faculty members around the country. The aids that a large and well-directed publishing house can bring to an author in this kind of enterprise are hidden to readers, but nonetheless they form a major element in what is presented for their study and benefit.

Above all, my thanks go again to my wife, Madge. Once more I had her continuing encouragement, the benefit of many conversations on the topic, and the guidance of her sensitive feeling for style and nuance. As before, I could not have carried through the task without her aid.

ROBERT KELLEY
Santa Barbara, March 15, 1977

INTRODUCTION:
The Historian's Task

ISTORY is studied for many reasons. The one most commonly advanced is that history is our social memory. Our memories tell us who we are, where we belong, what has worked and what has not worked, and where we seem to be going. More than anything else, perhaps, it is our ability to remember, to think historically, that sets us off from the animals.

For what purpose do we use history? Some historians insist that history is basically a means of helping us cope with present difficulties. Societies develop particular problems, and they ask of the past: How has it come into being, and what has been done earlier about it? When a depression occurs, economic history is turned to, and many books on this topic appear. When civil rights become the national problem, we search in the past for the background of this issue, and books on black history and race relations are written. When we awake to the fact that our nation is a world power, diplomatic history becomes an active field of study.

Other historians see the value of history in the fact that it takes us out of the present. By steeping ourselves in the history of an older time or of different peoples, we broaden the horizons of our minds. We develop a greater sensitivity to human possibilities, are chastened by the knowledge that our present culture is not the only way—or perhaps the best way—that human beings have lived, and begin to lose the present-mindedness that makes for superficial thought. In this sense, as Thomas Babington Macaulay observed, history is like foreign travel.

History serves, in short, not only specific purposes (how was the TVA built?—for we might want to build another one), but also the large purposes of giving us fundamental understandings of humanity and society: What motivates people in politics? What have our failures been, and our successes? What is it that holds us together as a people? Is life just a repetitive round, or is it evolutionary? Can we anticipate goodness or evil in humankind? In the broadest sense, history is studied because it gives us a frame of reference.

If there is a variety of ways in which history is used, one statement holds true of all historians as they go about their work: they are trying to find out as nearly as they can what the truth is about the past. They are attempting to answer the question of what happened and what it meant.

Thus the historian becomes a searcher for the kinds of documents that will bring him or her as close as possible to the events themselves. Such documents are called *primary* source materials, for they are produced by the people who participated in or observed the events. They include letters, diaries, speeches, news articles, testimonies of eyewitnesses, artifacts, photographs, and so forth. The historian will also look for all *secondary* sources that will help: books, articles, or reports prepared by someone else who has also studied the primary materials.

This search can lead everywhere, from attics to vast libraries. It also poses knotty problems: Are the letters genuine? Was the observer close to the event? Was he biased? Do other of his letters give a different picture? How soon after the events did he prepare his account? Are there other observers of the same events, and do their accounts differ? If the document is old, what did the words commonly mean at the time it was written? If it is a secondary work, how thorough was the author's research, how impartial was he, did he ask the right questions?

In short, historians test the evidence they find, using guidelines that their craft has developed over the generations. It is at this point, and largely only here, that they can be "scientific" in what they are doing. Above all, they are being properly scientific if they are guided by a judicious skepticism. If the study of history teaches historians nothing else, it teaches that people usually do not fully understand or accurately report what they see. For this reason, the evidence they leave behind does not speak for itself. It usually presents a partial or conflicting story that must be sifted, analyzed, and skeptically yet sympathetically winnowed out. The person who examines historical evidence cannot just passively pile it up; he or she must penetrate it actively and search for the truth.

The problem, of course, is that all evidence is incomplete. We see everything in the past through the eyes of others, but a great deal of information is hidden even from them. For example, direct observation of a religious ceremony will not reveal, to the onlooker, much about what the ceremony means to the participants. Direct observation of a speaker will not tell us his motivations—which even he may not understand himself.

Historians are hampered, too, by the fact that some activities produce documents while others do not, and some societies preserve documents while others do not. A committee hearing produces documents; the dinner party held the evening before in which the committee members discussed the issue does not. The Normandy invasion produced mountains of documents; the Anglo-Saxon invasion of England, so important for all future history, was carried out by an illiterate people and is therefore almost totally beyond the reach of historians. A monk's lament in a chronicle here, a confused account of a battle there, and a welter of myths and stories passed down orally for generations until someone wrote them down: this is all that is available.

In short, much that is important about the past never gets written down. Historians have been compared to astronomers, who gather light on the mirror of their telescope and try to decide what the dots and flares tell them about the universe, which they cannot visit personally. Historians, too, cannot visit the past and must search among its physical traces to elicit the story. In their case, however, many of the heavenly bodies *they* are trying to perceive never report their presence at all!

There is another problem. The historian Carl Becker reminded us that all perception of historical facts is set in the framework of the perceiver's experience. We cannot avoid our preconceptions;

they are the lenses through which we see the world. Each historian is alive to some aspects of the past, oblivious to others. Just as one person, walking into a crowded meeting, notices those individuals who are important to him and remains indifferent to the others, so historians who are by nature inclined to react to one class of evidence, while ignoring others, will assess matters differently from their colleagues. They will "see" some evidence while being blind to other materials, not through conscious bias, but simply because of the way their perceptions work. If a historian is inclined to believe that the profit motive is the key factor in what people do, then he or she will "find" money, vested interest, and wealth-seeking behind events.

In short, scientific history—that is, reproducing the past exactly as it was—is not the hope of the historian. Not only is the past too huge and complex, not only is the evidence it leaves behind too incomplete, but also we are too subjective in our views, guard against this failing as we will.

For that matter, there is a vigorous tradition that the objectivity implied in the ideal of scientific history is not only impossible but undesirable. It implies blandness, purposelessness, lack of commitment. Lord Acton insisted that the historian must sit in judgment upon past men and their actions, and that the sentences passed must be terrible and harsh. His modern disciple, Geoffrey Barraclough, insists that moral issues continue and are imperative. To seek only to "understand" in the light of circumstances— "The Nazis set out to kill off the Jews, and from their point of view did a good job"—is to be guilty of an inhuman and destructive relativism.

Most historians feel, however, that while such terrible events as the massacring of the Jews may be easily condemned, there is a vast range of human activities that is not so easily assessed. The act of preparing oneself to be a historian, they feel, does not simultaneously endow the scholar with intellect and experience and knowledge superior to that of the presidents and premiers who actually had the job to do. Making harsh judgments of past individuals may only betray the arrogance of ignorance. An event that seems simple to someone reading about it in a university library may actually have been extremely complex and intractable when it took place. One must, therefore, practice the historical art with appropriate prudence, and try in most cases not to take sides. Suspension of judgment is a valuable historical virtue.

It remains true, however, that complete neutrality is impossible, and that proceeding as though it were possible is a mistake. Carl Becker's view perhaps best sums up the spirit in which most historians work: basic in the historian's character must be a *concern* about the issues they examine, a deep involvement with the fate of the movements and ideas that they describe. There cannot be, and should not be, impartial history in the sense of indifferent history.

These remarks about the subjective aspect of history should not lead to the assumption that the cumulative work of the profession is merely a collection of personal statements. Historians who are true to their craft seek always to base their work on verified facts, and they have succeeded in searching out and validating a steadily mounting quantity of factual historical data. The main point about the problem of the historian's own subjectivity and unconscious bias is that he must try to keep these dangers in mind and achieve as much honesty as he can. He is constantly searching for the facts that beat on the question he has asked of the past and making painful efforts to put the story together as truthfully as he can.

To the extent that history is factual, it is a social science. Indeed, some leading historians have patterned their work on the social sciences by looking for what seems to be repetitive in human experience, such as the conditions that precede the outbreak of revolutions—skillfully examined by Crane Brinton—and thus eliciting data that might forecast future behavior. Others, in recent years, have sought to apply to an understanding of past events certain theories and insights of the social sciences. The fresh perspectives they pro-

vide, Richard Hofstadter has pointed out, add to "the speculative richness of history. The more the historian learns from the social sciences, the more variables he is likely to take into account, the more complex his task becomes."

Despite these tendencies, the historian's primary concern is not to create abstract conceptions about the laws of human behavior but to describe it faithfully in its actual individuality, its actual delineations, "warts and all." Taking the totality of human life as our province, we seek to portray its multiplicity, its variety, its irreducibility. Life does not fit formulas, the historian insists; meaning does not lie in universals, but in particulars. Therefore, we do not seek to cast what we describe into a rational system. It is life's unpredictability, the uniqueness of each sequence of events, the capacity life has for presenting us with inexhaustible freshness and uniqueness that history celebrates. This means that our methods cannot be entirely rational. Historians must rely on such qualities as empathy—the capacity to feel oneself into an era, to look at life from inside the other person's situation.

Reader's should not be misled, then, by the factual character of the historical account into making false analogies. The historian is not only a scientist with human perspectives but a creative artist as well. As Sir Lewis Namier has written, historians are like painters, not like photographers. They do not reproduce the past by means of an exact image. They are certainly not interested just in its surface appearance. Rather, they analyze the whole, search for its essence, and paint on their canvas that which is revealing and important. What matters in history, Sir Lewis observes, "is the great outline and the significant detail, what must be avoided is the deadly morass of irrelevant narrative."

It is in this sense that history is a branch of literature. The greatest practitioners call on the same resources of imaginative insight, grace and clarity of language, sensitivity to human experience, and concern with fundamental matters as do the great writers of fiction. It is, after all, the *human situation* that the historian seeks to describe.

So it is that some of the greatest historians have been much concerned with the problems of narrative artistry. A brilliant producer of narrative history, Thomas Babington Macaulay, wrote that "history has its foreground and its background; and it is principally in the management of its perspective that one artist differs from another." The selection of detail by which to hint at the whole is extremely important. The portraitist does not depict every pore in the subject's skin, but rather its hue; not the eye entire, but its aspect. History, George Macaulay Trevelyan insisted, is "a tale." It must therefore be as full as life. It must flow; narrative must be its bedrock.

The tale must show us past events as if they were fresh, as if we were participants. How is this achieved? By presenting the facts of the past not narrowly but in their full emotional and intellectual value. This requires that historians must have "the largest grasp of intellect, the warmest human sympathy, the highest imaginative powers."

History, then, is at once science and art. This is an ambivalent and precarious condition. Perhaps the perceptive words of the great German historian Johann Gustav Droysen strike closest to the heart of the matter. For all its faults, Droysen remarked, "History is Humanity's knowledge of itself. It is not 'the light and the truth,' but a search therefore. . . ."

THE SHAPING OF THE AMERICAN PAST

CHAPTER 20
Reconstruction

TIME LINE

1863	President Lincoln's Reconstruction plan issued
1864	Lincoln vetoes Wade-Davis bill
	Black leaders form Equal Rights League
1865	Andrew Johnson becomes seventeenth president of the United States
	Johnson attempts Reconstruction of the Union; southern white governments formed; Freedmen's Bureau established
	Thirteenth Amendment abolishes slavery
	Ku Klux Klan formed
1866	Johnson vetoes Freedmen's Bureau extension
	Civil rights bill
	Congressional elections establish large Republican majority
1867	First Reconstruction Act launches Radical Reconstruction
	The French withdraw from Mexico
	Alaska purchased
1868	Impeachment trial of President Johnson
	Fourteenth Amendment guarantees civil rights and extends citizenship to all persons born or naturalized in the United States
	Ulysses S. Grant elected eighteenth president of the United States
	Burlingame Treaty struck with China
1870s	Terrorism against blacks in the South; flourishing of Darwinism and ideas of racial inferiority
1870	Fifteenth Amendment forbids denial of vote on racial grounds
1871	*Alabama* claims controversy settled with Great Britain
1876	Rutherford B. Hayes elected nineteenth president of the United States
	End of Reconstruction

The United States at war's end

THE American nation ended the Civil War a profoundly changed country. It was now a "nation" in every constitutional sense. The defeat of secession proved in combat the legal and philosophical argument that the North had all along advanced: that the states had no reserved right to secede; that the federation which "We the people" had ordained in the Constitution was indissoluble.

Almost four million Americans who had been enslaved were freed of that condition, though no one yet understood what their new status was to be. The long supremacy of the South in the national capital, which had endured with only brief interruptions from 1800 until secession in 1860, was ended. The southern states lay shattered and powerless, while the triumphant North was wholly in command of the Federal government.

This meant that the Yankees of the upper North, with their homeland in New England and in that broad band of territory running from western New York out into the northern Middle West, now possessed that opportunity they had long dreamed of to shape the country in their image; to create the universal Yankee nation. Through the Federalists and the Whigs, and now through the Republican party, they had long insisted that the country should be thought of in the way they had since its founding thought of New England: as a cohesive, unified community, rooted in a consensual agreement upon the same values, devoted to common goals and actively led by a strong and confident common government.

Their "city on a hill" in New England had sought to provide an example to the world of an austere, classically democratic, virtuous, pious, and hardworking community in which the interests of each person were subject to the larger needs of the whole community. So, they fondly believed, it was now to be in the whole of the American nation.

During the war the Republicans had finally secured enactment in Washington of what amounted, with important modifications, to the program so long before called for by Alexander Hamilton and by Henry Clay in his "American System": a strong protective tariff to encourage the growth of American industry; lavish federal aid to internal improvements which would speed transport and tie the economy together (railroads, and river and harbor improvements); a national system of currency and banking, controlled by private interests; a network of state universities to produce the educated elite to direct the new economy; and a homestead law to encourage rapid development of resources. Thus federal power was vastly expanded, and constitutional and economic nationalism firmly established. The war had made millions of Americans in the northern states think in new ways: of the nation as a unified entity; of great and all-consuming joint enterprises; of a Union confirmed in suffering and death. They learned of the power of the national government, and how effective it could be in achieving common goals. Proud of their victory, so hard won, and of the proof it gave to the world that a self-governing republic based in the will of the majority could survive the sternest of all tests, northerners now looked around them for new challenges to master, new means of building a great and flourishing democratic nation.

Andrew Johnson and Reconstruction

In April, 1865, however, the North was stunned. Its widely loved president was brutally assassinated. Plunged in grief, the nation tried to absorb the fact of his death. Mourners filed by his casket in the Capitol rotunda and massed silently by the railroad tracks to watch his funeral train take its slow way home to Springfield, Illinois. Then all eyes turned to see what manner of man was the new chief executive. Few liked Andrew Johnson personally, for he was rigid and quarrelsome, but many respected his courage, personal strength, and vigorous administrative talents. A gifted and powerful speaker in the rough combative style of the Appalachian mountain country, from his early twenties he had won a long succession of political victories, serving in both houses of the Tennessee legislature, and as governor, congressman, and United States senator. He was a Jacksonian Democrat who hated the southern aristocrats, whom he blamed for the Civil War. The only southern senator to remain in Congress after his state seceded, he became the military governor of Tennessee in 1862, and was chosen to be Lincoln's vice-president in 1864 when the Republicans briefly adopted the name "Union party" and sought to attract Democratic votes.

In the eight months between Lincoln's death and the reconvening of Congress in December 1865, Johnson moved briskly to reconstruct the Union. He shared Lincoln's view that the southern states had never actually left the Union, since secession was an illegal act. The task was simply to reconstitute loyal governments. In a presidential proclamation in December 1863, Lincoln had offered pardon to any southerner who would swear loyalty to the United States Constitution. If a number of voters equal to one-tenth of those who cast ballots in the election of 1860 took such an oath, they could reform a loyal state government and, after abolishing slavery, secure presidential recognition as being back in operation as active states in the Union.

Leading Republicans in Congress had rejected this plan as far too lenient. In July 1864 they passed the Wade-Davis bill, which required a majority of all white males to take a loyalty oath before a new state government could be created. It also demanded "iron-clad oaths" of delegates to constitutional conventions and state office holders that they had never borne arms against the United States or held state or Confederate office under the rebel regime. Lincoln gave the Wade-Davis bill a pocket veto, much to the rage of leading Radical Republicans like Thaddeus Stevens in the House and Charles Sumner in the Senate.

Johnson accepted Reconstruction as complete in the four states that had already begun the process under Lincoln (Louisiana, Virginia, Tennessee, and Arkansas) and initiated proceedings in the other seven ex-Confederate states. He used whatever proportion of the local populations he could get to take the loyalty oath to get Reconstruction started and new governments formed. He made only three requests of them: that they declare secession null and void from the beginning, repudiate any Confederate war debts, and ratify the Thirteenth Amendment. At first the South was apathetic and submissive, expecting the North to make many demands for social change as its terms for readmission to the Union and was apparently ready to make those changes. But since Johnson demanded so little and actually urged the southern states, by many things that he said or implied, to pay little attention to northern opinion, they soon began to show much of their

This photograph of Richmond, Virginia, after the war shows the terrible devastation many southern cities suffered.
Courtesy of the Library of Congress

old-time prideful independence, to mounting irritation in the North. They either refused to ratify the Thirteenth Amendment (as in Mississippi), or quibbled about repudiating the Confederate debts (as in South Carolina), or only "repealed" their secession ordinances. Southerners elected to their constitutional conventions and new state governments the very men who led them into secession and war, and they even sent ex-Confederate generals, colonels, and congressmen (including the former vice-president of the Confederacy, Alexander Stephens) to Washington as their elected representatives.

Worse yet, the reconstructed state governments enacted "black codes" that practically reenslaved black men and women. Marriages among Afro-Americans were finally recognized as legal, and blacks were allowed to own property and to sue and be sued. But the black man's children were to be bound out as apprentices; the terms of his labor contracts were specified, including hours and wages; and servants were prohibited from leaving their employers' premises without permission. If a black man tried to be other than an agricultural laborer, he had to get a license from a white judge. He could not enter any mechanical trade without going through a closely disciplined apprenticeship. Vagrancy laws made any black person who wandered about, engaged in "disreputable occupations," or acted in a "disorderly manner" subject to arrest after which he could be hired out to a white employer to serve his sentence. Blacks were not allowed to testify in court unless the case involved other blacks. Segregation in schools and public facilities was commonly decreed. Sometimes black men could own only rural property, sometimes only urban. Most importantly, they could not bear arms or vote in elections.

The issue of equality

As early as 1863 Frederick Douglass had warned northerners that emancipation was but the first step toward real freedom for black peo-

ple. But the North in general was no more in favor of black equality than it had ever been. In recognition of blacks' courageous fighting record during the war, some of the worst anti-black laws in the North were repealed after 1860, but only seven percent of the 225,000 Afro-Americans in the northern states were allowed the vote, it being granted to them in five New England states. Blacks were segregated in public facilities, schools, prisons, hospitals, churches, and even cemeteries. Many states still had laws against the immigration of free blacks, and everywhere there were obstacles to equal employment, equal housing, and equal rights. Both political parties insisted that they were for the white man.

On the other hand, many northerners grieved for the condition of the southern black population. They heard stories of killings, the peonage of the black codes, callousness, cruelty, and lynchings, and by the end of 1865, when Congress was about to reassemble, there was a great deal of talk about doing something concerning black equality. Fundamentally, this was what the term *reconstruction* actually meant when it came into general use around 1862: some real and meaningful *reconstruction* of southern society and politics in order to give blacks a better life. To believe in this was what it meant to be a "Radical Republican." But the crucial question was, if the goal of Radical Reconstruction was equality for blacks, what was meant by *equality?* Almost unanimously Republicans believed that this meant at least equality before the law, i.e., civil rights. Black people should not be subject to legal restrictions that did not apply to whites. They should be able to testify in court, sit on juries, move freely about the countryside, take up any occupation, and give up one job for another. They should have the same punishment as whites for the same crimes, and not be told some things were crimes for them, but not for whites. They must be able to own land wherever they wished, not be imprisoned for debts and hired out, and not be subject to apprenticeship laws that limited their freedom. Special curfew laws and vagrancy statutes were to be condemned. All this added up to Lincoln's fundamental position: that the black person, while living separately in society, should be free to secure "life, liberty, and the pursuit of happiness."

Radical Republicans also agreed that there should be equality in politics and government: the right to vote, campaign on public issues, run for and hold office, and serve in governmental posts. A few Radical Republicans believed that blacks should have social equality as well: in social relationships, and in schooling, housing, and public accommodations. An even smaller number joined with black leaders in calling for economic equality. This meant providing skills and education, and, most revolutionary of all, confiscating rebel-owned plantations to give land to freed black people and make them truly independent.

The Freedmen's Bureau

Congress created in March 1865 the Freedmen's Bureau, an organization within the War Department that sent hundreds of local agents into every southern locale to aid refugees and freedmen (as ex-slaves were called). It provided emergency food and housing and built more than forty hospitals to afford medical aid. Searching out vacant lands (in some cases, in confiscated estates), it helped to settle some 30,000 people on the land. President Johnson severely cut back on this part of the bureau's work, however, by insisting that all land taken from rebels be restored after they were pardoned. The bureau found jobs for thousands of blacks, then supervised hundreds of thousands of labor contracts to secure equitable treatment by white employers. It set up its own court system, under military law, to mediate disputes between employers and freedmen and preside over cases in criminal and civil law where one or both parties were black. Its most lasting achievement was the building of thousands of schools—4,300 by the bureau's termination in 1872—to which hundreds of thousands of freedmen and their families flocked eagerly, usually to have instruction by a "teacher lady" from the northern states. Southern whites hated the bureau "more for what it stood for," as the historian George Bentley has written, "than for what it had done. . . . To most of them it was virtually a foreign government forced upon them and supported by an army of occupation. They resented its very existence, regardless of what it might do, for it had power over them and it was beyond their control."

What were Andrew Johnson's views on these matters? The president was a southerner, he had been a slaveowner, and he completely rejected the notion of racial equality. Black people, he

Freedmen's Village in Arlington, Virginia. The Freedmen's Bureau struggled manfully to carry former slaves through the difficult transition to equal citizenship.
Courtesy of the Library of Congress

believed, were inferior beings who should remain in an inferior position. He urged caution in giving votes to black men, since universal suffrage "would breed a war of races." Southern whites regarded him as standing between them and black suffrage. This, in effect, was the implication of his constant assertion that voting matters must be left to the individual states.

The crisis begins

Congress was deeply troubled when it assembled in December 1865. Every Confederate state save Texas had completed Johnson's Reconstruction procedure, and a large group of elected representatives awaited admission to Congress. To northern congressmen, the fact that many of these representatives had been Confederate leaders seemed bold and mocking. Indeed, "an uneasy conviction had spread throughout most of the North," Eric McKitrick has written, "that somehow the South had never really surrendered after all. . . . These feelings were neither focused nor organized; but they were pervasive, they seemed to ooze from everywhere and they invaded the repose of weary men who would have given much to be rid of them." It stuck in northern throats to think of readmitting southern representatives as though nothing had happened.

There was a deeper consideration. For many years Republicans had labored fruitlessly (as Whigs) to shape a new kind of American nation. Intermittently they had got brief periods of power but never enough to achieve their goals. The Civil War had given them their opportunity, and they had swiftly passed the measures needed to open the new era. The Republicans were launched upon the building of a nation with a vigorously growing industrial economy fertilized and energized by the federal government, working in close collaboration with the nation's leading entrepreneurs. With the emergence of efficiency and organization throughout the business world during the war and the creation of a strong federal government, the United States seemed about to become a strong and unified *nation* in

place of the loose aggregation of separate states that had existed before.

It was too much to ask of human nature that the Republican majority should so quickly readmit the southerners. They would bring in such a massive infusion of Democratic votes that, together with the northern Democrats in Congress, they would form a majority. Considering Johnson's views, they might be able to enact a federal black code, or even force the payment of the Confederate debt. They would certainly dismantle the economic system the Republicans had built up, the tariffs, bounties, banks, and other aids to business. Whatever happened, Republicans were determined not to go back to the old states' rights, decentralized, southern-oriented regime that had dominated the nation since Jackson's day.

A joint committee on Reconstruction was formed with members from both houses of Congress, Thaddeus Stevens emerging as its central figure. Southern representatives were refused admission to Congress until that body decided that their states were actually back in the Union. Then a long investigation of Johnson's Reconstruction program was launched by the joint committee. In February 1866 the Republicans enacted a bill extending indefinitely the life of the Freedmen's Bureau (it was due to expire in June 1868). Its powers were greatly broadened in the hope that, through military courts, it could nullify the black codes and protect freedmen's civil rights. The bill provided that anyone "who should, by reason of state or local law, or regulation, custom, or prejudice, cause any other person to be deprived of any civil right was to be liable to punishment by one year's imprisonment or one thousand dollars' fine or both."

Johnson strikes back

President Johnson exploded with rage. He sent a ringing veto back to Congress in a dramatic step that wrenched apart and polarized the politics of the whole postwar period, as Jackson's bank veto had done in the 1830s and 1840s.

Johnson condemned the Freedmen's Bureau as a monstrous intrusion on states' rights, condemned the use of military courts in peacetime as a violation of southern civil rights, and scoffed at the notion that freedmen needed help. "They are self-sustaining," he said, "capable of selecting their own employment and their own places of abode, of insisting for themselves on a proper remuneration, and of establishing and maintaining their own asylums and schools."

Three days later he publicly attacked Thaddeus Stevens, the leading Radical Republican in the House, and Charles Sumner in the Senate, as wild revolutionaries who were trying to take over the national government and were inciting others to assassinate him. "If it is blood they want," he yelled to a crowd outside the White House, "let them have courage enough to strike like men." Shortly thereafter the moderate Republican senator from Illinois, Lyman Trumball, tried to find some common legislative ground between the president and Congress that would ensure equality before the law to the southern black. (This did not include suffrage, which he opposed.) He secured passage of a civil rights bill to which, he thought, he had secured Johnson's approval. It established for the first time the status of "citizen of the United States" (formerly citizenship had been within a given state) and provided that the federal government could intervene within a state to ensure that citizens "of every race and color," save Indians not taxed, were given the same legal rights as white men. Agents of the Freedmen's Bureau would make arrests where civil rights were violated, but the federal civil courts, not the army's military courts, would hear the cases.

Once again Johnson struck back with a veto. In his message he scornfully derided a measure that would denominate as "United States citizens" the Chinese on the West Coast, Indians who were taxed, and "the people called gypsies, as well as the entire race designated as blacks, people of color, Negroes, mulattoes, and persons of African blood." This was a "grave question," he said, for the blacks had just emerged from slavery, and it had long been national policy to require people "who are strangers to and unfamiliar with our institutions [to] pass through a certain probation." Why discriminate against "intelligent, worthy, and patriotic" foreigners, he asked, who were required to wait five years for citizenship? The whole proposal, he said, was "fraught with evil," establishing "for the security of the colored race safeguards which go infinitely beyond any that the general government has ever provided for the white race. In fact, the distinction of race and color is by the bill made to operate in favor of the colored and against the white race."

Johnson's vetoes so outraged the moderates that they were driven over to join forces with the Radicals. His first veto had been upheld; his second one was overridden. From that point on, a strong and determined Radical Republican group in Congress pushed vigorously ahead to take over Reconstruction, sweep away everything Johnson had done, and, eventually, come within a single vote of impeaching the president himself.

The Fourteenth Amendment

The joint committee on Reconstruction began drafting a constitutional amendment that would place the principle of equality before the law beyond any future tampering—or so it was believed. The measure drawn up did not by any means meet Thaddeus Stevens's demands. He urged the adoption of a simple but powerful statement: that all laws, state and national, should apply equally to all persons. As Charles Sumner put this idea, "Show me . . . a legal institution, anything created or regulated by law, and I will show you [an institution] that must be opened equally to all without distinction of color." "This was true Radical argument," writes W. R. Brock. "It recognized that private prejudice could not be legislated out of existence, but maintained that discrimination could be prohibited in every activity touched by the law." There would always be discrimination in homes or private relations, "but they would have outlawed discrimination at the polls, in public places, on public transport, and in education."

The Republican majority, however, would not go this far with the Radicals. It was insisted that certain things were "privileges," not rights. The amendment should not apply, moderates said, to voting, or segregation in schools and public facilities. Its only reference to voting was to provide that a state's representation would be reduced in proportion to the number of its citizens denied the vote (this has never been applied). The amendment worked a powerful change, however, by making everyone born or naturalized in the United States a citizen and forbidding all efforts by states to interfere with each citizen's fundamental civil rights. By conscious design, the amendment was broadened to make equal civil rights national in scope, protecting the rights of "any person," and not just those of blacks. In later decades, its sweeping and powerful phrases were enormously important weapons in social reform and in giving legitimacy to the aspirations of minority groups.

Article XIV, The Constitution of the United States (ratified July 28, 1868). Section 1. All persons born or naturalized in the United States, and subject to the jurisdiction thereof, are citizens wherein they reside. No State shall make or enforce any law which shall abridge the privileges or immunities of citizens of the United States; nor shall any State deprive any person of life, liberty, or property, without due process of law; nor deny to any person within its jurisdiction the equal protection of the laws. . . . Section 5. The Congress shall have power to enforce, by appropriate legislation, the provisions of this article.

The proposed amendment was adopted by both houses of Congress in June 1866 and sent on to the states. Johnson protested against it, and recommended against ratification. The southern states defeated this first attempt at ratification, for all the former states of the Confederacy, save Tennessee (where ratification was highly equivocal) rejected it, plus Kentucky and Delaware. This drove even deeper into the northern mind

that the southern states, as reconstructed by President Johnson, were arrogant and unregenerate. In the congressional elections held in the autumn of 1866, the South's refusal to accept equality before the law became the major issue. Just as grave in northern opinion were race riots in Memphis and New Orleans in May and June 1866, in which policemen and whites murdered scores of blacks, shooting and knifing indiscriminately to "kill every damn nigger" they could find. No prosecutions were launched, and Johnson blamed it all on northern Radicals. Then he made an intemperate "swing around the circle" in August and September, speaking in many northern cities. This in itself was shockingly indiscreet. In the nineteenth century, presidents simply did not do this. They did not even campaign when they were presidential candidates. To do so, in the viewpoint of the time, would be demeaning—and Johnson was demeaned. Furthermore, he lost his temper, bandied words with hostile crowds, and destroyed whatever credibility he had left. The Republicans won a landslide victory, gaining a two-thirds majority in both houses of Congress.

Radical Reconstruction

Now the triumphant Radical Republicans could begin a genuine *reconstruction* of Southern life. They undertook this task as leaders of a victorious Yankee culture at its most self-confident. "It is intended," said Thaddeus Stevens of Pennsylvania, New England born and educated, "to revolutionize . . . Southern institutions, habits, and manners." The ruling constitutional theory under which this was to be done was Stevens's: that the southern states had in fact seceded and were no more than conquered provinces with which Congress could deal as it saw fit. In the language of the First Reconstruction Act, which it enacted over Johnson's veto on March 2, 1967, "no legal State governments or adequate protection for life or property now exist in the rebel States . . . and it is necessary that peace and good order should be enforced in said States until loyal and republican State governments can be legally established." The ten states still unreconstructed (Tennessee, having ratified the Fourteenth Amendment, was admitted in July 1866) were grouped into five military districts, each under a federal military commander whose powers were superior to those of the state governments. The states were to call elections for the writing of new state constitutions, all male citizens "of whatever race, color, or previous condition" being enfranchised to vote, while those whites who had been federal officials and later supported the rebellion were disenfranchised. The new constitutions were to guarantee black suffrage. After ratification, and after the new state governments had ratified the Fourteenth Amendment and that amendment had become part of the federal Constitution (as it did in July 1868), then the states were entitled to be represented in Congress, though readmission would still require congressional enactment in each case.

Was Radical Reconstruction designed to help black people or to help the Republican party? The question is still debated. For many years historians took the latter view. Hungry for the graft and corruption that office holding allowed and eager to maintain their protective tariffs and land bounties—so this version ran—greedy and vindictive Republicans incited southern blacks to an "unnatural" hatred of whites, gave them the vote, then enrolled them in the Republican party so as to keep themselves in power. (This assessment was exactly that of Democrats when these events were going on.) In recent years historians have accepted that many Republicans sincerely wanted to help black men; that others simply wanted to make the blacks happy where they were, so they would not flood the northern states; and that the desire to keep their own party in power, when that was the dominating motive, was not so discreditable as it has been depicted. The Republicans, after all, had a different vision of what America should be. They had been frustrated by what they regarded as a "southern

conspiracy" in the antebellum years, and now they aimed at protecting the possibility that their goal for the nation might be realized. It is clear, however, that Republican concern to help black people was limited. Thaddeus Stevens tried to get his colleagues to establish an economic foundation for black equality by allowing the confiscation of rebel estates and the redistribution of land. He was turned down. And there were no efforts to ensure social equality for black people. The dominant Republican view was that, given equality before the law and the vote, black persons were then to rise by their own initiative.

To ensure its absolute control of the Reconstruction process, Congress enacted legislation requiring the president to give orders to the army only through the general-in-chief, who was Ulysses S. Grant. Fearing that Johnson might remove Edwin Stanton, the secretary of war (who, like Grant, was sympathetic to Radical goals), Congress passed the Tenure of Office Act, which took away the president's authority to remove cabinet members without the Senate's consent. Another enactment limited the Supreme Court's authority so as to keep it from ruling on the legality of any Reconstruction legislation. Subsequent Reconstruction acts elaborated the powers of the military commanders so that any state official who should "hinder, delay, prevent or obstruct the due and proper administration" of the Reconstruction acts could be removed.

In August 1867 President Johnson tried to remove Secretary of War Stanton, primarily for failure to accept the president's directions but also in order to test the constitutionality of the Tenure of Office Act. In January 1868 the Senate refused to accept Stanton's suspension or to recognize another man whom Johnson had appointed in his place. In late February a seriocomic affair began in which the House impeached the president for violating the Tenure of Office Act and a host of other vaguely worded "high crimes and misdemeanors." For more than two months until the middle of May, an intensely dramatic trial proceeded before the Senate. (The president was represented by legal counsel and spared the indignity of being present.) When the votes were taken, conviction fell one vote shy of the necessary two-thirds majority because seven Republicans—at great cost to their political careers—concluded that no case had been made. A public outcry arose against them as traitors to the nation.

Black Reconstruction

Meanwhile, "black Reconstruction" was underway in the South. The first thing to be said of the freed slaves was that the fears which had apparently driven South Carolina and the rest of the South into secession in 1860–1861 were without foundation. The freedmen did *not* immediately rise in bloody violence against their former masters, dealing out the massacre and rapine that had hysterically been warned against for generations. The horrors of Santo Domingo and Haiti did not reenact themselves. Few more striking instances in history exist of a mass delusion leading millions of people into a needless, disastrous war. So, too, race war did not break out when the freedmen were given the vote. Indeed, massive and violent assaults against the white community and its institutions were not ever to be mounted by black Americans in the South, either in the Reconstruction years or in later generations. The massacring was instead to be in the other direction. When black Americans did in fact join in destructive outbreaks, it was to be almost a century later, and in northern cities.

Some 700,000 black men were enfranchised in the southern states as a result of the Radical Reconstruction program, while 150,000 whites lost the vote for having supported the rebellion after having held federal office. In every state except Virginia, Republicans took control. In June 1868 six states were admitted to the Union: Arkansas, North and South Carolina, Florida, Alabama, and Louisiana. The rest were admitted in early 1870. Republican regimes did not last long: one year in Georgia, two in North Carolina, four in Texas, six in Alabama, Arkansas, and Missis-

sippi, and nine in Florida, Louisiana, and South Carolina.

These years have traditionally been described as a carnival of corruption that left the South crippled by enormous debts. Hordes of ignorant and greedy blacks were pictured as taking over the legislature, rolling drunkenly in the aisles and shouting approval for huge appropriations that went into the pockets of their carpetbagger leaders (northerners come South to fish in troubled waters), or those of the scalawags (southern whites who joined the plunder). After a decade of this robbery, white "redeemers" moved in sternly to restore white dominance and careful, honest government.

This picture is now largely discredited. There was corruption, some of it spectacular, but corruption was a national phenomenon in these years. Nothing in the South compared, for example, with the luxuriant graft then going on in New York City under Boss William M. Tweed. In only one state, South Carolina, was there a black majority in the legislature, and there only in the lower house. No blacks were elected governor; few were judges; and only seventeen served in Congress. Those who held official positions served admirably in most cases. Blacks were not vindictive and often supported appeals that disenfranchised whites be given the vote and allowed to hold office. There were no attempts to overturn social relationships. Indeed, Reconstruction governments did little for the black person specifically. Heavy expenditures were made because the South had to be rebuilt after the war and because emancipation doubled the civil population. Millions of blacks formerly given nothing by state governments now were citizens who could claim services in schools, courts, and welfare agencies.

Reconstruction reforms

The Reconstruction governments enacted major reforms. They gave the South its first system of public schools (though they were segregated in fact, if not in law). Manhood suffrage free of property qualifications was enacted, and imprisonment for debts was terminated. Homestead laws guaranteed poor men a minimum amount of property safe from attachment for debts. Popular election of county officials replaced the former oligarchical system of appointment. Salaries were provided to public officials so someone other than a rich planter could serve. The number of crimes punishable by death was reduced. Taxes were rearranged so as to bear on plantation owners, rather than just on landless individuals.

The thousands of northerners who came south after the Civil War, the "carpetbaggers," were not the depraved and dissolute adventurers they have been described to be. Many brought needed capital and entrepreneurial skills; others were serious reformers who sought to democratize the South and teach the poor—white and black. The "scalawags" (southern whites who joined the Republican party, who amounted to perhaps a

quarter of the white population) were often new men from poor counties, with little former reputation in government. They were angry at the "bombastic, high falutin, aristocratic fools" who had dragged the South into a disastrous war, and been "driving negroes and poor helpless white people until they think they can control the world of mankind." They liked Republican policies of economic development, for they promised jobs where at present there was poverty, and called for social reforms.

Indeed, the "other South" still survived strong and healthy. The Whig party had died completely in the 1850s, in the South, when the whole region swung to the Democratic party, but former Whigs bulked large in the Confederate congresses. For that matter, after the first elections, which gave Democrats dominance, the Confederate congress in subsequent ballotings began to swing strongly toward the Whigs. As the war went badly, Democrats were stigmatized

Reconstruction of the South, 1865–1877

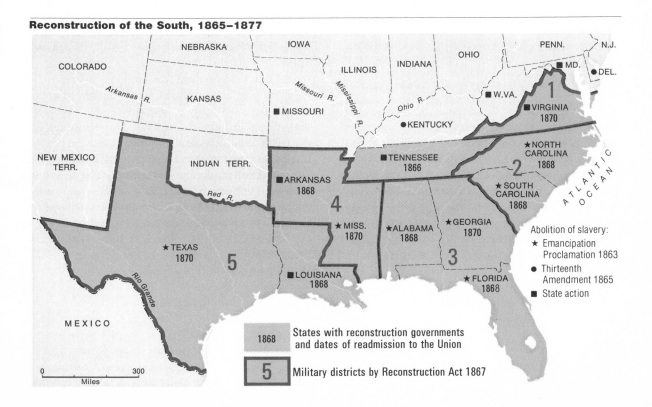

by many as "radicals," and Jefferson Davis had to turn more and more to Whigs—who seemed to know more about running industries and organizing things—to help him marshal the South's strength. At the end of war former Whigs either joined the Republican party, or formed parties like the Conservative party in Virginia, which sought to do for the South what the Republicans were doing for the North: develop its economy, foster industrialization, build railroads, encourage urbanization.

It must be understood that within what became the borders of the Confederacy, 49 per cent of those casting ballots in the 1860 presidential election had cast ballots either for Bell or Douglas, thus indicating that they did not favor secession. Thousands of white Southerners served in the Union army during the war, forming almost ninety regiments; Appalachia was a hotbed of Unionism; and the white South's return so easily to the Union after the war can be understood only by taking into account that its fundamental loyalty to that Union was always strong, only being overborne in hysterical circumstances by fear of what never occurred, a black uprising.

Economic Reconstruction in the South

Radical Republicans wanted not only to reconstruct the blacks; they wanted to reconstruct southern white society as well. Yankees had said for many years that if slavery were only eliminated, then southern whites would stop being lazy, improvident people who shunned physical labor, and would start taking up hard-working Yankee ways. Now, Radical Republicans urged southern whites to take the road to industrialization and urbanization—and were delighted with the response. The business community of the South, largely composed of ex-Whigs who had always been irritated at the languid, unprogressive rule of the plantation owners, "burst into effusions of assent and hosannas of delivery." Thousands in the South had always admired northern ways and had tried vainly to take their section in Yankee directions.

Virginia "Conservatives"—who took that name in politics to distinguish themselves from both the Democrats and the Republicans—worked consciously to regenerate Virginia's economy along northern capitalist lines. The task they took on was admittedly great and forbidding. The war had left widespread devastation behind. Thus, to break out of the depressed conditions they were in, state governments eagerly pushed the building of railroads in the South. Project was piled on project with feverish haste, and almost every state invested huge sums in private companies. The railroad system was rebuilt and a good deal of mileage added. Also, new industries were encouraged by state grants of funds and tax privileges. Immigration was encouraged, producing a heavy influx of white settlement and northern capital. Textile mills appeared in the Carolinas and in Georgia. The Richmond ironworks were rebuilt and flourished more than ever. Northern Alabama's iron and coal resources were opened, and the city of Birmingham, soon to be the Pittsburgh of the South, made its appearance. A movement of population to the cities occurred, since textile mills and other urban industries offered jobs (to whites only).

The black population was largely ignored in all this. Initially, many blacks had abandoned their plantations, refusing to remain at the scene of their humiliation and suffering. They gathered in the cities, destitute, or wandered about the countryside. Then most of them drifted back to the white-owned land. They rejected going to work for wages, however. They tried to get white owners to rent or lease land, but found few willing to do so. The result was the working out of a halfway house, sharecropping. Produced primarily by the black man's determination to gain at least a semblance of independence, sharecropping allowed black farmers to till plots of land without supervision, so long as they delivered a portion of the crop to the owner. The system often evolved into a form of peonage, for debts to the owner or to local merchants bound the black farmer to the soil. As a system for reviving production, however, it was relatively successful. The cotton crop, which had fallen from 5.3 million bales annually before the war to 2.0 million in 1865, was back to 3.0 million bales by 1870 and 5.7 million in 1880. Other crops surged also, tobacco production rising rapidly, rice and sugar more slowly.

Grant's administration

The readmission of the first group of reconstructed southern states in June 1868 was in time for them to vote in the presidential election of 1868. Horatio Seymour, Democratic governor of New York during the Civil War and a strong opponent of racial equality, ran on the Democratic ticket. The Republicans chose the military hero Ulysses S. Grant.

Samuel J. Tilden, who in the Age of Jackson had worked closely with Martin Van Buren as speech writer and political adviser, was chairman of the Democratic party in New York during the 1868 campaign. He expressed pungently the Democratic viewpoint on Radical Reconstruction, showing how strongly antiblack attitudes still dominated the Democratic outlook. If the Republicans had been "magnanimous" toward the southern whites, he said, they could have built a lasting Republican party in the southern states. But the Republican party, "which boasts its great moral ideas and its philanthropy," could not resist striking its adversary when it was down. "It totally abandoned all relations to the white race of the ten states. It resolved to make the black race the gov-

The election of 1868

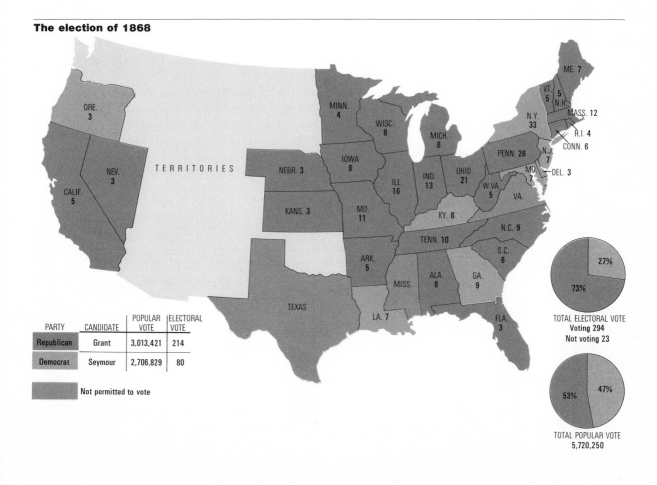

PARTY	CANDIDATE	POPULAR VOTE	ELECTORAL VOTE
Republican	Grant	3,013,421	214
Democrat	Seymour	2,706,829	80

Not permitted to vote

27%
73%
TOTAL ELECTORAL VOTE
Voting 294
Not voting 23

53% 47%
TOTAL POPULAR VOTE
5,720,250

erning power in those states, and by means of them to bring into Congress twenty senators and fifty representatives—practically appointed by itself in Washington." The Republican party had no interest in the internal affairs of the southern states; it neglected them entirely. It wanted only "to strengthen its hold on the federal government against the people of the North," so as to continue its corrupt career of handing out favors to vested interests. Southern blacks "have been disassociated from their natural relations to the intelligence, humanity, virtue, and piety of the white race, set up in complete antagonism to the whole white race, for the purpose of being put over the white race, and of being fitted to act with unity and become completely impervious to the influence of superior intellect and superior moral and social power." The three million blacks "will have ten times as much power [through their] twenty senators and fifty representatives . . . as the 4 million whites in the state of New York. . . . One freedman will counterbalance thirteen white citizens of the Empire State," and will count ten times as much as the whites of Pennsylvania or Ohio, Illinois, or Indiana. "These 3 million blacks will have twice the representation in the Senate which will be possessed by the five great commonwealths—New York, Pennsylvania, Ohio, Indiana, and Illinois—embracing 13,500,000 of our people."

Congress was taking control of the suffrage away from the states and was "systematically breaking down" division of powers in the federal government. It was becoming an "elective despotism." It must "pass into imperialism [and] . . . the destruction of all local self-government. . . . The grim Puritan of New England . . . stretches his hand down along the Atlantic coast to the receding and decaying African, and says: 'Come, let us rule this continent together!' "(John Bigelow, ed., *The Writings and Speeches of Samuel J. Tilden* [1885].)

Thus began an eight-year administration that has little to commend itself to history save noisome scandals. Grant was unqualified for the presidency, and he chose many subordinates who made free use of their opportunities. He allowed two noted stock market manipulators, Jay Gould and James Fisk, to be intimate with him until their disgraceful activities in rigging the stock market became too blatant. Companies received monopoly contracts from the New York Customs House and made hundreds of thousands of dollars in graft. During Grant's administration the massive speculations of the Crédit Mobilier, the company formed to construct the Union Pacific Railroad, came to light. Congressmen were caught profiting from the scheme, and the scandal reached upward to involve Vice-President Schuyler Colfax. Secretary of the Treasury Ben Butler was found aiding an arrangement whereby hundreds of railroads were forced to pay delinquent taxes, half of which, to the amount of hundreds of thousands of dollars, went to a henchman—and then, perhaps, to Butler himself.

These activities were mirrored at every level of American government. In city councils, in boards of supervisors, in state legislatures, wherever profitable deals could be made, grafters were there, and compliant legislators assisted them, for a consideration. Much of the history of the period, wherever it is touched, consists of little but damaged reputations. Ice-house franchises, street construction contracts, railroad land grants, bank subsidies, tax rebates, purchased jurors, judges, and sheriffs—the list is endless.

All this produced a new and consuming national concern that went far to dwarf everything else in the minds of many voters. No obsession was more central to the Democrats than the problem of corruption in the economy and in government. They believed it to be simply inherent in the way that Republicans ruled. Handing out land grants, protective tariffs, bank charters, immunities from taxation, railroad contracts, and every other kind of profitable privilege inevitably produced corruption. It was the very means, they insisted, by which the Republicans rooted themselves in power, buying up supporters by creating vested interests.

Many Republicans shared these worries. It was not long before they were disillusioned with the Grant regime. It seemed tawdry, opportunist, low in tone, and greedy. Grant was not interested in civil service reform, as they had assumed, and the spoils system flourished. Men like Lyman Trumbull, E. L. Godkin of the *Nation,* and Charles Francis Adams broke away from the "regulars" of the Republican party in 1872 and resolved to run their own candidate for the presidency in place of Grant, who was nominated for a second term. Calling themselves "Liberal Republicans," they chose Horace Greeley, editor of the New York *Tribune,* to oppose Grant. The Democrats swung in with them, nominating Greeley as their presidential candidate as well.

The result was a disastrous campaign. An eager and aggressive candidate who condemned Grant's policies, he also championed such unpopular causes as women's rights, labor unions, vegetarianism, and social reform movements such as Fourierism, a form of communalism. He was ridiculed as a crank, and Grant secured a massive 750,000 vote majority. Exhausted, brokenhearted and grieved by the recent death of his wife, Greeley died three weeks after the election.

Foreign affairs: Seward and Fish

Two gifted secretaries of state, William Seward and Hamilton Fish, directed the nation's foreign relations with notable success during the administrations of Andrew Johnson and Ulysses Grant, respectively. Seward dealt successfully with a bold adventure that Napoleon III of France undertook in Mexico while the United States was involved in the Civil War. The French emperor installed an Austrian nobleman, Maximilian, on the Mexican "throne" in 1864. But as soon as the Civil War ended, Seward placed troops on the Mexican border and informed Napoleon that the United States would never recognize Maximilian's regime. By patient diplomacy he got the French to withdraw all their troops in 1867. Max-

imilian, who foolishly refused to leave with them, was executed by the Mexicans.

Seward also responded eagerly to a Russian offer to sell Alaska. He agreed to purchase it for $7.2 million and, in the face of much amused comment about "Seward's Ice Box," secured the Senate's ratification of the treaty in April 1867. Looking to the Far East, Seward sent a gifted diplomatist, Anson Burlingame, to China to open that country to American trade. Hoping to fend off European partitioning of China, the United States formally recognized China's territorial integrity and promised no interference in Chinese affairs. In return, by the Burlingame Treaty (1868), American citizens were accorded the right of travel and residence in China and the right of freely exercising their religion there. This opened the way for an extensive involvement of American missionaries and traders in Chinese life over the next several generations.

The most explosive issue in Seward's hands after the war was the negotiation of claims against Great Britain arising from the activities of a group of Confederate commerce raiders during the Civil War—the *Alabama* chief among them—which the British had allowed to be built in their shipyards and taken to sea. These raiders sank or captured many Union merchant ships, causing huge losses to northern merchants. The first agreement Seward got with the British, which called for arbitration of the American claims, was summarily rejected by the Senate 54 to 1. Charles Sumner, chairman of the Senate Foreign Relations Committee, insisted on the British accepting the principle of "indirect losses"; that, is, that the work of the commerce raiders had lengthened the Civil War, and this meant the British should pay half the cost of that conflict, or over two billion dollars. Sumner suggested that the British cede Canada to the United States in payment.

The issue was still unsettled when Grant entered office. Hamilton Fish wisely let the controversy cool down for a time, then transferred the negotiations from London to Washington. By this time a major shift had occurred in the British government, bringing the great Liberal party leader, William Gladstone, to the premiership. He was strongly opposed to aggressively nationalistic diplomacy, quite ready to admit British wrongs where they had occurred, and devoted to the notion of arbitration. He was also much more friendly to the United States, as was traditional on his side of British politics, than were the Tories whom he had supplanted. He was eager to settle not only the *Alabama* claims, but also a whole series of outstanding issues between the two countries. A Joint High Commission composed equally of Britons and Americans began discussions in Washington in 1871. A long dispute over who owned the San Juan islands between Seattle and Vancouver Island was referred to the German emperor for settlement (he gave them to the United States). The Americans secured extensive privileges to fish in Canadian waters, and Canadian seamen were allowed to fish as far south as Delaware Bay. The *Alabama* claims were referred to a Tribunal of Arbitration in Geneva, with the result that the United States received fifteen and a half million dollars, the "indirect" claims being ignored. A counterclaim, arising from attacks on Canada by Irish-Americans in the Fenian organization, who sought in this way to free Ireland from British rule, gave almost two million dollars to the British. The crowning achievement of Grant's administration, the complete restoration of good relations with Great Britain, was successfully completed.

The Fifteenth Amendment

After Grant's first election in 1868, the Republicans took up once more the problem of the black man in the South. They moved carefully, for the northern states were still hostile to black enfranchisement. This had been shown in the first local elections held after passsage of the First Reconstruction Act in March 1867. In state after state, the Democrats won handily on antiblack suffrage platforms. The journal *Independent* sardonically

remarked that "it ought to bring a blush to every white cheek in the loyal North to reflect that the political equality of American citizens is likely to be sooner achieved in Mississippi than in Illinois—sooner on the plantation of Jefferson Davis than around the grave of Abraham Lincoln!" In Ohio a proposal to establish black suffrage went down by 40,000 votes in the autumn. "Thousands have turned against us," observed Horace Greeley in November 1867, "because we purpose to enfranchise the Blacks."

Southerners had good reason to scoff, therefore, at the stated goals of Radical Republicanism. What hypocrisy it was, they said, for Republicans to protest moral sincerity! Northerners clearly had no interest in the black man. All they wanted was to get his votes behind the Republican ticket to keep the party in power in Washington. Endlessly repeated, the charge of hypocrisy was the stock reply of southern whites to everything the Republicans attempted. An editor in Raleigh, North Carolina, ridiculed Republicans in 1867 when members of their party voted two to one in the Pennsylvania legislature against giving the vote to black men. "This is a direct confession, by Northern Radicals, that they refuse to grant in Pennsylvania the *'justice'* they would enforce on the South. . . . And this is Radical meanness and hypocrisy—this their love for the negro." Even the Republican platform of 1868 perpetuated the dual standard, insisting that "every consideration of public safety, of gratitude, and of suffrage in all the loyal [i.e., northern] States properly belongs to the people of those States."

When congressional Republicans decided after Grant's election to aid black suffrage, they had to move with care lest they offend northern sensibilities. Moderates and conservatives, not Radicals, dominated the writing of the Fifteenth Amendment. Even Wendell Phillips, a dyed-in-the-wool reformer since his days as a leading abolitionist, urged his followers, "For the first time in our lives we beseech them to be a little more politicians and a little less reformers." Radicals wanted a positive national guarantee that the vote would be permanently granted to blacks; moderates wanted only a negative statement that would deny taking the vote away simply on the ground of race or previous condition of servitude. As Oliver P. Morton put the matter, the intent was not to nationalize suffrage, but to leave it in state hands subject only to this one federal limitation. He went on to add, "They may, perhaps, require property or educational tests." Even a clause that would prohibit denial of office holding on the ground of race was rejected. Southern Republicans were understandably alarmed at these proceedings; southern Democrats were amused and unconcerned.

The historian William Gillette suggests that the real motive behind the Fifteenth Amendment was not to safeguard black voting in the South but to allow black Republican voting in the North. For moral reasons? Many men, such as Wendell Phillips and Charles Sumner, were clearly moved by such motives. Most, perhaps, were moved instead by concern for their party. The Afro-American population in the northern states was relatively small, but in key states where Democrats and Republicans were almost evenly divided, black votes on the Republican side could tip elections. State laws prohibited their voting, so federal enfranchisement seemed the only way. The amendment, of course, would need ratification by twenty-eight states, another fact that militated moderation. Passed by Congress in February 1869, it went to the states and was ratified in March 1870 (Virginia, Mississippi, and Georgia were required to ratify as conditions of readmission in early 1870). Then, and only then, did black Americans finally secure the vote in the northern states.

Counter-Reconstruction

Since 1865 an organization called the Ku Klux Klan, or the Invisible Empire of the South, had existed for the purpose of frightening blacks, usually by nonviolent means. In 1869 it was officially disbanded by Nathan Forrest, the Con-

federate general who, with others of the southern elite, had provided its leadership, because it was rapidly veering toward violence. Thereafter the Klan proliferated informally through local "dens," which began promiscuously shooting, hanging, whipping, torturing, burning, and drowning blacks, carpetbaggers, and scalawags. Mobs took proceedings into their own hands, and private vendettas were launched that soon became simple campaigns of plunder. Congress investigated and found that in only one county of South Carolina, eleven murders and over six hundred whippings had taken place. Several federal laws—the "force bills"—were enacted in 1870, which reinforced the army in the South, reserved to the federal courts exclusive jurisdiction in suffrage cases and provided troops to enforce court orders. These laws only temporarily checked terrorism.

In 1875 the state of Mississippi demonstrated what terrorist tactics used extensively and systematically could achieve. Whites began taking pledges and forming organizations to revitalize the Democratic party around the principle, as the *Democrat* put it, "that white men shall govern . . . that niggers are not rightly entitled to vote, and that when [the Democratic party] gets into power, niggers will be placed upon the same footing with white minors who do not vote or hold office. . . . Nigger voting, holding office and sitting in the jury box, are all wrong, and against the sentiment of the country." Lists of independent-minded blacks were printed in newspapers to encourage private terrorism directed toward them. Thousands of young white men and boys took it on their own to discipline the blacks. They formed militia companies, and openly practiced target shooting.

With the state elections of 1875 approaching, the unorganized, unarmed, frightened blacks of Mississippi watched as companies drilled and paraded and cannon practice produced rolling thunder. Black Republicans found their names prominently displayed in "dead books" and were warned that any further public speaking would lead to their murder. When attempts were made to register Republican voters, armed men prevented anyone from approaching.

The "election riot" was the most useful device. It simply amounted to a sudden outbreak of pistol firing and armed attack wherever Republicans gathered, sending black families and white Republicans fleeing. Many of these took place throughout the state in 1874 and 1875, when white southerners took advantage of any pretext to begin assaults. A Republican meeting in Yazoo City was invaded by Democrats, one of whom prominently carried a rope. A native white Republican was killed, the white sheriff fled the county, and then a general lynching murdered black leaders in every supervisor's district. Riots like this were frequently followed by days of terror with armed bands scouring the countryside and shooting at will.

When the election came, "It was a very quiet day in Jackson," an observer remarked, "fearfully quiet." In Yazoo City, "Hardly anybody spoke aloud." At Okolona an armed mob took over the town, the Republican sheriff locked himself in his jail, and the Democrats picked up the ballot box and stuffed it. Such fraud, however, was hardly necessary and was little used. The Democrats simply swept the state. Merciless, overwhelming, and absolutely relentless force had turned the trick.

The North's reaction

What was the North to do? The only appropriate response, if it genuinely wished to reestablish interracial government in such states, was to renew Radical Reconstruction in all its panoply and vigor. Huge sums of money must be spent for troops, the South must be flooded with agents of a revived Freedmen's Bureau, and military courts, where juries were not required, would have to be used extensively. In effect, the North would have to reopen the whole case of the white versus the black South. It was a solution that northerners could not bring themselves to un-

dertake. Their will, their sense of crusading purpose—such as it had been—was dying. The North was ready to let the southern black man and woman fend for themselves. Indeed, the passage of the 15th amendment had seemed to most northerners to close the account. Thereafter, blacks were to be on their own, like every other American—or so the whites conceived the situation to be.

Mississippi was in fact a special case, as it always was to be in later American history. In the rest of the South blacks continued for another twenty years to vote by the hundreds of thousands, schools were provided by white-dominated governments, a modicum of civil rights were guaranteed, public facilities were shared, and blacks even held office and sat on juries. It was not even necessary, in most cases, for Democrats to resort to violence in order to win elections; it was only required that they turn out and vote. Thousands of white Southerners in the old Whig regions—in North Carolina, and throughout Appalachia—continued voting Republican until well into the twentieth century. The two-party system disappeared slowly and reluctantly in the South.

Northern commitment to racial equality had been, in the best of circumstances, only marginal. Indeed, in the northern educated classes where a moral concern for the welfare of black Americans had been strongest, a new climate of opinion was forming. Science and rationalism were flooding in. Charles Darwin's *Origin of Species* (1859) acquired enormous vogue. It described nature as a system in which "natural selection" operated, dooming the less prolific and reproductive species to extinction. Count Arthur Gobineau's *Essay on the Inequality of Races* (translated 1860) classified humankind into many separate races (French, German, Welsh, Irish, etc.), each supposedly carrying ineradicable characteristics in its bloodstream. Blending races always produced, he said, offspring that took on the characteristics of the "lower" race. One alleged quality of "lower" peoples was their passionate sexuality, which made them breed prolifically, while the more intelligent races had few children. Many educated northerners of British (Anglo-Saxon) origins took a grim lesson from such "science"—that the Anglo-Saxon race stood in grave peril. Though alleged to be intelligent and gifted, it could be overwhelmed by swarming inferior races if it did not take steps to guard its superior position. Genteel northerners recoiled in distaste from the grimy, illiterate, strange-looking immigrants, with their huge families, who were crowding into the northeastern ports. Alarmed, they began to feel a new sympathy for their counterparts in the South who detested blacks.

Another widely influential writer was the British social scientist Herbert Spencer, whose book *First Principles* (1862) was being read with care. Spencer took ideas from Darwin and other scientists and applied them to social affairs, coming up with the phrase "survival of the fittest." He laid down firm principles. The "social order is fixed by laws of nature precisely analogous to those of the physical order." Therefore, "the most that man can do . . . by his ignorance and conceit is to mar the operation of social laws." In short, people should leave social problems entirely alone. Avoid public health measures, so that diseases will sweep away the unfit. Avoid even the building of lighthouses, for dangerous reefs will kill off the unfit seamen. Let the "laws of nature" operate. Strong government is a curse, for it will always be misinformed and will make mistakes, thus disorganizing nature's wise plans.

The lessons were plain. What educated people thought to be science seemed to demonstrate conclusively that the black race could never be equal to the white; and that whatever took place without government interference was best, even though it might seem oppressive. All things must be looked at coolly, dispassionately, rationally. Moral arguments were irrelevant because they were "unscientific." Let the southern whites have their way, for that was best for the Anglo-Saxon race. Government intervention would in any case be harmful.

The election of 1876

The stage was now set for the official termination of Reconstruction. Only three states were still Republican in the South: South Carolina, Louisiana, and Florida, their governments shored up by federal troops. The Republicans turned to a completely honest man whose public reputation was blameless, Rutherford B. Hayes, a former general in the Union army who was governor of Ohio. The Democrats turned to a wizened little man who was governor of New York, Samuel B. Tilden. He had led in destroying the Tweed Ring, which had taken millions from the government of New York City, and the Canal Ring, which had similarly taken huge sums from the state-run Erie Canal. Known to be "sound" on the racial equality question—he described black men as "an element of disease and death" in the body politic, to be expelled when possible—he had the priceless political advantage of being known as a successful battler against corruption. "It is not necessary for me to attempt to paint the state of political corruption to which we have been reduced," the reformer Henry George said in California as he called for Tilden's election.

It is the dark background to our national [centennial] rejoicing, the skeleton which has stood by us at the feast. Our Fourth of July orators do not proclaim it; our newspapers do not announce it; we hardly whisper it to one another, but we all know, for we all feel, that beneath all our centennial rejoicing there exists in the public mind to-day a greater doubt of the success of Republican institutions than has existed before within the memory of our oldest man.

Tilden got a popular vote majority of about 250,000 in the election of 1876, but the presidency went to Rutherford B. Hayes. When it appeared that Tilden was one electoral vote shy of election if he did not get the three states in the South still in Republican hands, those states were "delivered" to Hayes. Congress was thrown into turmoil. Should it accept the Republican votes from these disputed states, or agree with the

In the election of 1876 Republicans attacked Democrats for forcing blacks to vote the Democratic ticket.

Culver Pictures

Democrats that returns were fraudulent? Weeks of public and private negotiation took place, in an atmosphere of near hysteria, many in the South and North warning of direct military action if the "steal" were successful. Not until early March 1877 was the "Compromise of 1877" reached. The South acquiesced in the counting of Florida, Louisiana, and South Carolina in the Republican column, so long as all federal troops were withdrawn from the South.

This was the "public" agreement. Behind the scenes, C. Vann Woodward's researches demonstrate, the crucial consideration was a decision by southerners that they would actually get more economic aid from the Republicans than from the northern Democrats. Samuel J. Tilden was too

good a Jeffersonian who obviously practiced what he preached—that no government aid should be given to private business. As governor in New York he had heavily slashed all spending on internal improvements—canals, roads, and bridges. The South desperately needed its ports, rivers, bridges, and railroads rebuilt; it had not been able to get nearly enough done on its own; and the Republicans were clearly more friendly to providing federal aid to such enterprises than were the Democrats. They had constructed internal improvements all over the northern states; now, it was agreed, they would do the same in the South, if given the presidency once again. "The jobbers and monopolists of the North," said the disgruntled Montgomery Blair, "made com-

The election of 1876

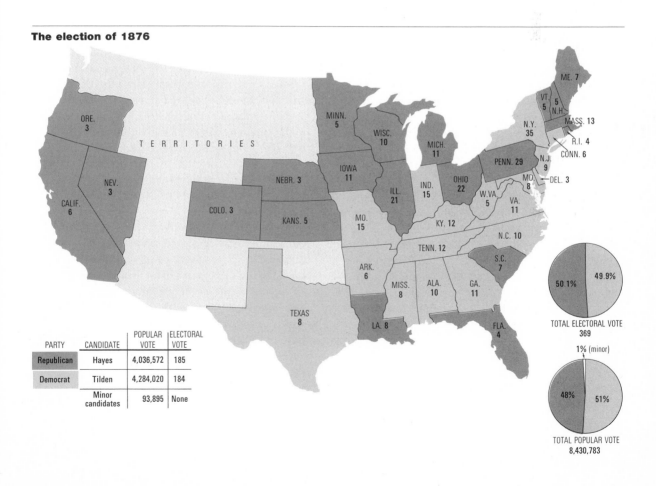

PARTY	CANDIDATE	POPULAR VOTE	ELECTORAL VOTE
Republican	Hayes	4,036,572	185
Democrat	Tilden	4,284,020	184
	Minor candidates	93,895	None

50.1% 49.9%

TOTAL ELECTORAL VOTE
369

1% (minor)

48% 51%

TOTAL POPULAR VOTE
8,430,783

mon cause with the Southern oligarchy." Whoever was to blame, and whatever were the motives, the result was the same. Reconstruction was over.

Bibliography

Three books that were especially valuable to me in writing this chapter: I found Eric L. McKitrick's *Andrew Johnson and Reconstruction** (1960) a penetrating account. Carl Degler's brilliant *The Other South: Southern Dissenters in the Nineteenth Century* (1974) opened up for me the whole non-Democratic South and its continuing role in southern life. Jack P. Maddex, Jr., *The Virginia Conservatives, 1867–1879: A Study in Reconstruction Politics* (1970) is an absorbing case study which buttresses Degler's case.

How have historians looked at the topic?

The stormy era of Reconstruction has evoked the attention of myth-makers and propagandists as well as careful scholars. The first major American film, "The Birth of a Nation" (1915), depicted Ku Klux Klansmen as the heroes of the postbellum South, a highly distorted and blatantly racist interpretation that nevertheless influenced countless millions of viewers. After a private showing in the White House, historian and president Woodrow Wilson said the film medium was "like writing history with lightning."

Unfortunately the film did not convey history. Its characters and message only vaguely resembled the actualities of Reconstruction. However, its highly sympathetic view of the South's victimization is portrayed with scholarly conviction in W. A. Dunning's *Reconstruction, Political and Economic, 1865–1877** (1907); Claude Bowers's *The Tragic Era* (1929); and E. M. Coulter's *The South during Reconstruction* (1947). Standing in direct opposition to this interpretation is W. E. B. Du Bois's pioneering, militantly pro-black account *Black Reconstruction in America, 1860–1880** (1935).

The complexities of Reconstruction are perceived from a sharply different angle in Charles Beard and Mary Beard's classic *The Rise of American Civilization* (1927). Rejecting the idea that the main actors in the Reconstruction drama were unscrupulous carpetbaggers and misled or courageous blacks, the Beards interpreted the struggles of the period as basically economic ones, primarily motivated by ambitious northern businessmen who were determined to keep the advantages they had gained during the war years. Robert P. Sharkey's *Money, Class, and Party: An Economic Study of Civil War and Reconstruction** (1959) brilliantly expands and criticizes the Beards' thesis, eliminating their bloc approach and emphasizing that northern businessmen took many positions, often mutually opposed to one another. C. Vann Woodward's classic work *Origins of the New South, 1877–1913* (1951) illustrates the affinity between northern and southern businessmen and discredits the picture of hostility.

Several significant reassessments of the Reconstruction era appeared during the 1960s. John Hope Franklin's *Reconstruction: After the Civil War** (1961) offers a host of new insights and concludes that Reconstruction was a genuine search for social justice for the Afro-American. Robert Cruden's *The Negro in Reconstruction* (1969) elaborates on black attempts to exercise power during the period while *After Slavery: The Negro in South Carolina during Reconstruction, 1861–1877* (1965) by Joel Williamson is a case study that stresses the initiative and progress of blacks in one state. James M. McPherson's *The Struggle for Equality: Abolitionists and the Negro in the Civil War and Reconstruction** (1964) explodes the theory of the abolitionists' abandonment of the black following the Civil War. A major study that examines the development of Reconstruction policy from the beginning of the Civil War is Herman Belz's *Reconstructing the Union: Theory and Policy during the Civil War* (1969). G. R. Bentley's *A History of the Freedmen's Bureau* (1970) reports the political maneuverings that led to the demise of the bureau in 1872. The activities and influence of the

Ku Klux Klan are chronicled in S. F. Horn's *The Invisible Empire* (1939).

Kenneth M. Stampp's *The Era of Reconstruction, 1865–1877** (1965), is a richly provocative analysis in which the Radical Republicans emerge as avant-garde thinkers rather than as fanatics. H. L. Trefousse's *The Radical Republicans: Lincoln's Vanguard for Racial Justice* (1969) supports and extends Stampp's interpretation. See also David Donald's massive new work *Charles Sumner and the Rights of Man* (1970).

The first year of Andrew Johnson's administration is probed with care in LaWanda Cox and John H. Cox's *Politics, Principle, and Prejudice, 1865–1866* (1963); and a British historian, William R. Brock, offers an important perspective on presidential-congressional relations from 1865 to 1867 in *An American Crisis: Congress and Reconstruction, 1865–1867** (1963). William Gillette's *The Right to Vote: Politics and the Passage of the Fifteenth Amendment* (1965) argues that the Fifteenth Amendment was written with northern rather than southern blacks in mind.

An excellent one-volume guide to the perplex-ities of Reconstruction is James G. Randall and David Donald's *The Civil War and Reconstruction* (1961). The historiographical debate over Reconstruction is skillfully synthesized in Rembert W. Patrick's *The Reconstruction of the Nation* (1967) and stated with clarity and wit in Hal Bridges's *Civil War and Reconstruction** (1962), a bibliographical essay in the American Historical Association series.

The controversial election of 1876 and the compromise of the following year are definitively assessed in C. Vann Woodward's *Reunion and Reaction: The Compromise of 1877 and the End of Reconstruction** (1966). Woodward's economic analysis is supported by John F. Stover in an unusually interesting account, *The Railroads of the South, 1865–1900: A Study in Finance and Control* (1955). Tilden's role is presented in Robert Kelley's "Samuel Tilden: The Democrat as Social Scientist," chapter 7 in his *The Transatlantic Persuasion: The Liberal-Democratic Mind in the Age of Gladstone* (1969).

* Available in paperback.

CHAPTER 21
Late Nineteenth-Century America: Growth and Development

TIME LINE

1860–1878	Indian wars
1861	Kansas admitted to the Union
1863	West Virginia admitted to the Union
1864	Nevada admitted to the Union
1865–1885	Cattle industry grows on the western plains
1867	Nebraska admitted to the Union; Alaska purchased
1873	Panic begins depression of 1870s
	In the *Slaughter House Cases* the Supreme Court rules that government may regulate business
1876	Colorado admitted to the Union
1877	In *Munn* v. *Illinois* the Court rules that states may regulate rates charged by grain warehouses and railroads
1879	Standard Oil trust formed
1880s	Big businesses emerge; wheat boom in the Great Plains
1883	Railroad companies divide the nation into four time zones
1887	Interstate Commerce Commission formed; Dawes Act establishes policies of Indian severalty and acculturation
1889	North Dakota, South Dakota, Montana, and Washington admitted to the Union
1890	Sherman Anti-Trust Act, Sherman Silver Purchase Act, and McKinley Tariff; Idaho and Wyoming admitted to the Union
1895	In *Pollock* v. *Farmers' Loan and Trust* the Court forbids unequal income taxes; in *United States* v. *E.C. Knight Company* manufacturing is ruled not part of interstate trade
1896	In *Cincinnati, New Orleans, and Texas Pacific Railway Company* v. *ICC* the Court decides ICC cannot fix railroad rates
	Utah admitted to the Union
1907	Oklahoma admitted to the Union

Late nineteenth-century America

THE years from 1860 to 1900, during which the American population grew from thirty-one to seventy-six million, present a paradoxical picture of booming growth streaked with crisis and ruined hopes. Ambitious and imaginative capitalists ranged the continent looking for new opportunities. Although business conditions lurched erratically from upswings to slumps, the country's industrial base grew rapidly. New factories were hammered together—black hulking shapes attended by swarming laborers, consuming mountains of raw materials, and sending out streams of freight cars jammed with products. Thousands of men in battered hats, talking a score of languages, drove spikes and dug through hills as the railroads expanded rapidly from the skeletal system that existed in 1865 to an intricate mesh of lines linking all parts of the nation.

Galloping cavalry and thudding .44-40 rifles swept the Great Plains brutally clean of Indian tribes and buffalo so that this tragically empty land could become a spreading empire of cattle ranches and wheat farms. The vast continental sweep between Kansas and California filled in with new states: Colorado in 1876; the Dakotas, Washington, and Montana in 1889; Idaho and Wyoming in 1890; Utah in 1896. Only Oklahoma, Arizona, and New Mexico remained territories (the first was admitted as a state in 1907 and the latter two in 1912). Watching the map in these years, Americans were filled with pride as they observed the appearance of a new, truly transcontinental United States.

But the country was also torn by crisis. Rapid changes made people feel anxious and unsettled. Hundreds of towns were swept out of their quiet isolation when railroad tracks appeared in their streets. Powerful corporations reached into every community, and prices and wages began rising and falling chaotically. Men who had worked eagerly to get railroads into their towns soon became angry critics of the "railroad monopoly." Factory owners paid low wages and worked their employees up to fourteen hours a day, thus setting off tremendous labor strikes that sent violence and disorder ripping through many communities. The cities, meanwhile, grew so fast that they could not dispose of their sewage or provide clean water. Thousands of people died annually in epidemics. So many officeholders took graft that they made a mockery of democratic government. Farmers formed the Granger movement in the 1870s to fight back against the railroads, and in the 1880s this protest spread into the Great Plains and down into the South. By this decade so grave were the nation's troubles that politicians, ministers, and writers everywhere were worriedly talking about the "social question." Grover Cleveland warned somberly that selfishness and sordidness had blighted the nation's promise. When the worst depression of the century began in 1893, the sense of crisis deepened.

Yet much that was creative and solid occurred in the new industrial age. Jobs were provided for a booming population; most people lived better as the standard of living rose significantly; isolation and rustic crudity gave way to more varied and challenging patterns of life. A bustling inventiveness created many things that eased and enriched the lives of ordinary people, among them electric lights, streetcars, steel plows, mail order houses, refrigerators, and inexpensive homes. America mistreated its immigrants, but gave them great opportunities as well. Imaginative educators built vigorous private and state universities from which came confident young men and women who took up the renovation and reorganization of American society. In the countryside, farmers gladly adopted many new conveniences and welcomed the breakdown of their country-bound isolation. They eagerly raised crops to sell in the markets that railroads opened up and used the money earned to gain a better life.

Both of these aspects of late nineteenth-century America, one ugly and the other encouraging, must be considered when assessing this complicated era. Optimism and gloom lived side by side. Generally, Republicans were the optimists, as had been their predecessors, the Whigs, while the Democrats, led by Grover Cleveland, warned of greed and corruption and looked yearningly to the past, as they had been doing since Jackson's day.

The railroad explosion and the transformed economy

Railroad expansion fueled the booming economic growth of these years. There were 35,000 miles of trackage at the end of the Civil War, composed of local lines that used different track gauge (widths). By 1910 there were some 240,000 interconnected standard gauge miles. In some years more than 10,000 miles of track were laid, the most spectacular undertakings being the transcontinental lines that reached westward to various points on the Pacific Coast in the 1880s. As early as 1890, the United States contained one-third of the world's total railroad mileage.

Now there was one vast marketplace that extended across the continent. Industrialists and farmers piled on more productive capacity to profit from their new nationwide opportunities. This led to glutted markets, overproduction, and the beginning of a long price decline that lasted until the late 1890s. The railroads overbuilt badly, for to grab off each other's trade they built parallel lines and handed out rebates and special favors. This produced loud complaints from people who lived where there was only one railroad, since such companies often jacked up their rates to compensate for losses elsewhere. Small producers also protested bitterly because the railroads refused to give them rebates while handing them out liberally to large corporations whose businesses they coveted. Hundreds of local railroad companies suffered because their builders borrowed more money than needed during the construction phase in order to skim off funds into their own pockets. With large financial debts,

railroads were forced to charge high rates to meet interest payments or to build additional mileage to compete with other roads and take away their traffic.

By the late 1870s, therefore, railroad owners began looking for some way to bring order out of chaos. They saw that if they could agree on rates and split up the traffic in some equitable way, their problems would be eased. This would also quiet the complaining small shippers by eliminating the problem of unequal rates. It would rely, however, on the adoption of a new technique: counting everything—cars, amount of freight, distances traveled, costs, wages, and every other business expense. This, in turn, required that central business offices be established where statistics concerning freight and passenger movements could be gathered, analyzed, and used to figure costs and fair rates. In this new technique lay the embryo of modern business with its reliance on centralized, analytical, bureaucratic methods.

Such "pools," were adopted with varying degrees of success in the 1880s, and they caused much resentment. Large shippers like the Pillsburys of Minnesota did not like pools because they wanted to keep receiving rebates. Others insisted that the pools exploited the public. In the late 1860s and 1870s many midwestern and other states had tried to control railroad rates by creating commissions that were charged with regulating them. Now these commissions turned to do battle with the pools. In 1886, however, the United States Supreme Court ruled that state commissions could not regulate commerical activities that extended beyond their borders.

Formation of the Interstate Commerce Commission

This made federal regulation mandatory, for only Washington had constitutional authority over interstate commerce. In January 1887 President Grover Cleveland signed legislation that prohibited rebates, declared pools illegal, and established the Interstate Commerce Commission (ICC) with power to ensure that railroad rates were "reasonable and just." Thus began a new era in American history. For the first time the government of the United States established a new kind of public agency: an independent commission given broad and unspecified powers to regulate a crucially important part of the national economy—with the proviso that its decisions could be appealed to the courts. Drawn partly from the British example, the ICC was a step in the direction of the kind of centralized control by high officials that has become an increasingly major feature of modern government. It was widely criticized at the time of its creation as an aristocratic, elitist, essentially Federalist idea.

As the first such agency, the ICC went through difficult times in its early years. Conducting investigations, gathering information, making rulings and publicizing them widely, the ICC helped stabilize railroading. The new techniques of statistical analysis and centralized management were widely adopted by the railroads, for they had to justify rates and become efficient. Step by

The solitary figure of a man standing on newly laid sleepers of the transcontinental railroad, at the 100th Meridian, October, 1866, with the roadbed dwindling off into the western distance, expresses the lonely flat expanses of the high plains country.
Courtesy of the Library of Congress

step, the new commission began teaching the owners of great railroads that they had public responsibilities as well as private rights. In the mid-1890s, however, the Supreme Court cut down drastically on the ICC's powers, and the old order of cutthroat competition and special favors—including high rates to small producers—returned.

Meanwhile the railroads continued making their operations more efficient. They adopted a standard guage of 4 feet 8.5 inches in 1886. Then they built connecting links between their systems of tracks so that cars carrying passengers and freight could pass uninterruptedly from one road to another. Then came standard freight classifications, following which railroads divided the country into four time zones in 1883 to replace the bewildering variety of local times that had formerly existed.

In other words, it was in the effort to manage effectively the continental railroad system that modern bureaucracy, both industrial and governmental, began in the United States. Regularity of operation, efficiency, the use of trained experts, even-handed treatment of people in widely varying situations, standardized regulations and rates, centralized planning and control, predictability, and promptness—all these qualities, which

The United States, 1861–1912

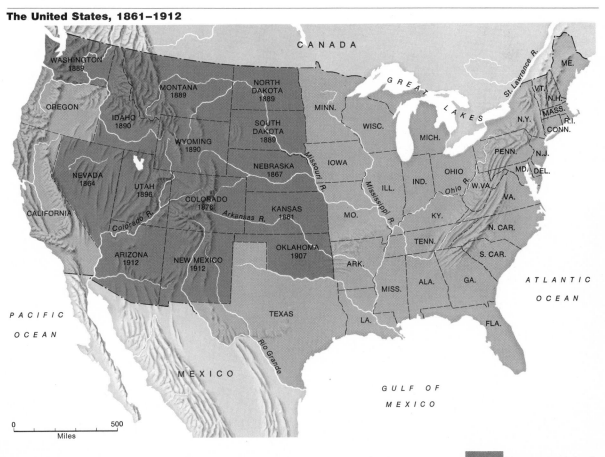

New states admitted

comprise the central characteristics of large-scale bureaucratic organizations, started here. It was impossible to run the system over such a huge expanse of territory in any other way.

The rise of big business

The national market, created by the railroad system, transformed business life. By the early 1900s the economy was no longer composed of thousands of small producers who sold to local markets; rather, it was dominated by a small number of large firms that sold nationwide and to the world at large—Standard Oil, American Tobacco, National Biscuit, United Fruit, United States Steel, General Electric, and International Harvester. Clearly, the era of big business had arrived.

A big business appeared when many small businesses came together or when a gifted entre-preneur discovered a product that would sell in the national market and organized his operation on a continental scale. Gustavus Swift took the latter road. A skillful meat salesman from New England, he went west in the 1870s and observed the huge herds of cattle spreading over the interior plains. The practice at that time was to bring large numbers of the animals to Chicago, place them on trains to eastern cities, and butcher them after their arrival. Swift saw the waste in this process, for the animals had to be fed en route, they lost a good deal of weight, and much that was unsaleable in them had to be transported east only to be thrown away at butchering. He successfully built an industry which butchered the cattle in the West, refrigerated the saleable meat, and transported only that part of the animal for sale in the East.

The lure of the national market or the excitement of periodic booms would often inflate a

Railroads, 1850–1900

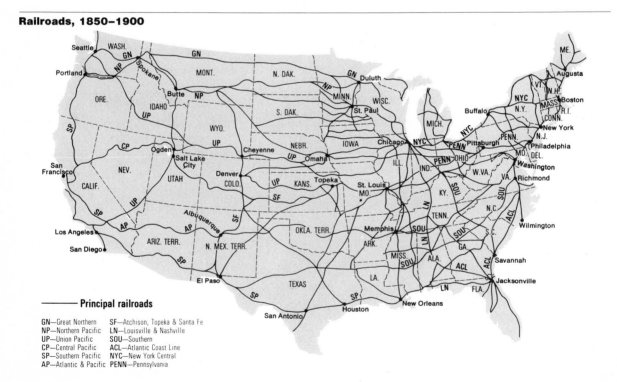

─────── **Principal railroads**

GN—Great Northern   SF—Atchison, Topeka & Santa Fe
NP—Northern Pacific LN—Louisville & Nashville
UP—Union Pacific   SOU—Southern
CP—Central Pacific   ACL—Atlantic Coast Line
SP—Southern Pacific NYC—New York Central
AP—Atlantic & Pacific PENN—Pennsylvania

manufacturer's confidence in the future. As all his mills or distilleries or stamping plants roared along in full production, he would add more productive capacity only to be met by a slump and dropping prices. It was common for factories to stand empty much of the time or for whole industries to operate at only fifty percent of capacity. The initial response was to mechanize operations more intensively, thus increasing efficiency and raising output. But this, in turn, led to oversupply and a renewed drop in prices. "It is a chronic case," said one producer in 1888, "of too many stoves, and not enough people to buy them."

The solution was for a group of manufacturers to form a pool, divide the market, and establish agreed-upon prices. But such arrangements constantly broke down. The final recourse was to place the stock of many competitors in the hands of a group of trustees. By this step the manufacturers created centralized management, though not centralized ownership. The first of these trusts was the Standard Oil Company, which was formed in Cleveland in 1879 when a group of small refineries joined forces. Its success led to the creation of many other trusts, involving such items as leather, sugar, salt, biscuits, fertilizer, rubber boots, and gloves.

David A. Wells, a nineteenth-century inventor and economist, was an early observer of the way small businesses were wiped out by mechanization: "About [1874] the new and so-called roller process for crushing and separating wheat was discovered and brought into use. Its advantages over the old method of grinding by millstones were that it separated the flour more perfectly from the hull or bran of the berry of the wheat, gave more flour to a bushel of wheat, and raised both its color and strength (nutriment). . . . The cost of building mills to operate by the roller process is, however, much greater than that of the old stone mills. . . . The consequence of requiring so much more capital to participate in the flour business now than formerly is that the smaller flour mills in the United States

are being crushed, or forced into consolidation with the larger companies, the latter being able, from dealing in such immense quantities, to buy their wheat more economically, obtain lower rates of freight, and, by contracting ahead, keep constantly running. At the same time, there is a tendency to drive the milling industry from points in the country to the larger cities, and central grain and flour markets where cheap freights and large supplies of wheat are available.

"Thirty or forty years ago the tinman, whose occupation was mainly one of handicraft, was recognized as one of the leading and most skillful mechanics in every village, town, and city. His occupation has, however, now well-nigh passed away. For example, a townsman and a farmer desires a supply of milk cans. He never thinks of going to his corner tinman, because he knows that in . . . other large towns and cities there is a special establishment fitted up with special machinery which will make his can better and 50 percent cheaper than he can have it made by hand in his own town. . . . And what has been thus affirmed of tinplate might be equally affirmed of a great variety of other leading commodities. The blacksmith . . . no longer making but buying his horseshoes, nails, nuts, and bolts; the carpenter, his doors, sash, blinds, and moldings; the wheelwright, his spokes, hubs, and felloes; the harness maker, his straps, girths, and collars; the painter, his paints, ground and mixed. . . ." (David A. Wells, *Recent Economic Changes* [1889].)

The Standard Oil Company was the model for all who aspired to "vertical" integration of an entire industry (i.e., where one firm owns or controls a complete operation, from the raw material to the finished product). The company owned its own forests for lumber, made its own barrels, manufactured its refinery chemicals, bought up oil-terminal facilities, possessed fleets of vessels and oil cars, and carried on its own retail marketing. In the 1880s it even acquired its own wells. Soon Standard Oil agents were competing actively with Russian oil producers in the markets of central Europe and teaching Orientals the value of the kerosene lamp. The five-gallon kerosene tin from Standard became a worldwide institution.

The antitrust movement

The name "trust," however, rapidly became a stench in the public nostrils. Even though prices drifted downward, the notion of monopoly, which the trusts certainly seemed to threaten,

was too much for people to bear. Both Republicans and Democrats joined in condemning such combinations as a flagrant violation of all the laws of the marketplace. In 1888 a Republican senator from Ohio, John Sherman, proposed the first version of what became in 1890 the Sherman Anti-Trust Act. It declared illegal "every contract, combination in the form of trust or otherwise, or conspiracy, in restraint of trade or commerce among the several States, or with foreign nations." Anyone who made such agreements or who "monopolize[d] or attempts to monopolize"

Industry, 1860–1890

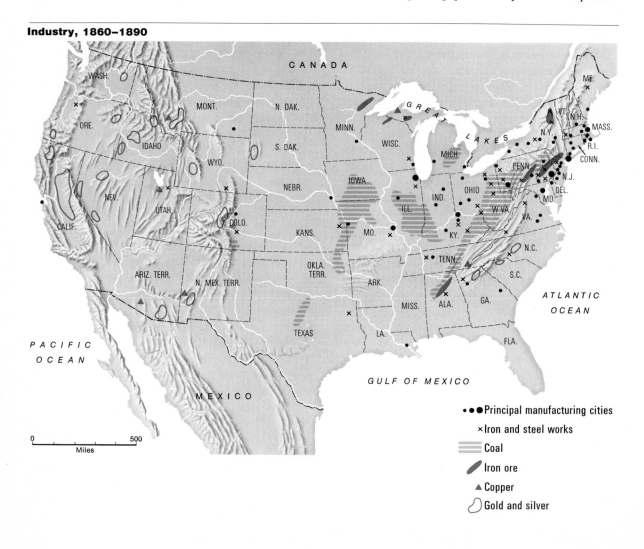

some aspect of the nation's business could be fined $1,000 and jailed for one year. Also, anyone injured by the monopolizer's activities could sue for triple damages.

Whatever Congress's intentions, the law had little effect on big business for many years after its passage. John D. Rockefeller simply converted his Standard Oil trust into a single corporation, headquartered in New Jersey and directed from his offices in New York City. Furthermore, the courts were hostile to the new law. In 1895 the Supreme Court went so far as to rule that manufacturing could not be considered part of interstate commerce and was therefore exempt from antitrust action.

Comparison of American and European industry

Europeans were astonished at the swift growth of American industry, which seemed to bound upward, soon surpassing their own industries in size and wealth. Why was this so? Was it simply because the country was large and had huge resources? Clearly this was a major factor, but there were other influences as well. From the beginning, American manufacturers had had to compensate for the small number of laborers available (since most were on the farms) by mechanizing operations to a far greater degree than abroad. When immigrants came pouring in after 1840 to provide labor, manufacturers were already used to machines. Even the most intricate processes were carried out by machines that could be tended by unskilled workers.

Businessmen in the United States were also surrounded by a friendly environment. In Europe, ancient governments dominated by land-owning aristocracies with strong powers scorned businessmen. Furthermore, restrictive laws hampered business operations, and governments favored stability rather than change. In comparison with Europe, government hardly existed at all in the United States. A county or a state would have

only a few employees whereas corporations hired thousands. Businessmen were praised and admired; young boys were trained in getting ahead; everything was assessed on strictly practical standards. At the same time, the expanse of the country and the opportunities for a huge continental market opened by the railroads encouraged a risk-taking mentality far more adventurous in the United States than elsewhere. People were convinced that if they leaped forward the future would catch them. This attitude made business efforts more wasteful but also more buoyant and productive.

Northern industry triumphant

So matters stood in the 1880s and 1890s. Northern industry dominated the nation's life. It had scattered the country with great cities: steel cities like Pittsburgh and Philadelphia; oil cities like Cleveland; Chicago with its huge stockyards, slaughterhouses, grain elevators, and spreading train yards; Peoria with its whiskey, Waltham with its watches, and Minneapolis-St. Paul with its flour.

Industrialists preened themselves on the notion that their success was good and proper. Andrew Carnegie insisted that "the millionaires who are in active control started as poor boys and were trained in the sternest but most efficient of all schools—poverty." His father had been a poor Scottish weaver; Swift's a farmer; and Rockefeller's a traveling salesman of patent medicines. Although the proportion of rich men who came from poor beginnings increased only slightly during this period (most, as is usually the case, sprang from comfortable backgrounds), the opposite view was widely believed. It was their hard work, special talents, and the American system of unfettered individualism, rich men told themselves, that explained their eminence. Without an ancient landed aristocracy around to take the limelight, American millionaires could bask all alone in public adulation. "*We* have made the

Funkville, Oil Creek, in western Pennsylvania, was one of the river towns from which flowed the raw crude to distant distilleries, setting off the explosion of the petroleum industry.
The Granger Collection

country rich," said the unprincipled speculator Jay Gould, "We have developed the country." Rockefeller, devout Baptist that he was, had the simplest answer: "The good Lord gave me my money."

The Supreme Court protects capitalism

The United States Supreme Court swung its massive weight behind businessmen in the post-Civil War years although at first it moved cautiously. The American system of law, inherited from England, is rooted in the principle of *stare decisis*, or decision by precedent. Justices rarely plant their feet very far ahead of where the law is at that moment. They may edge ahead, but always retain the option to veer off in a different direction. The issue of governmental regulation over business first came before the Court in 1873,

when in the *Slaughter House Cases* a bold defense lawyer insisted that the Fourteenth Amendment protected his clients, the owners of the slaughter houses, from such regulation. The key passage of that amendment runs as follows:

No State shall make or enforce any law which shall abridge the privileges or immunities of citizens of the United States; nor shall a State deprive any person of life, liberty, or property, without due process of law; nor deny to any person within its jurisdiction the equal protection of the laws.

The Court ruled that the amendment applied only to civil and political rights. It did not accept the lawyer's assertion that corporations were "persons" in law, and that governmental regulation amounted to taking property without due process, that is, without going through a court proceeding. In 1877 in the case of *Munn* v. *Illinois*, the Court ruled that it was constitutional for the state of Illinois to regulate the prices charged by railroads, grain warehouses, and elevators. Such institutions, it said, were "clothed with a public interest when used in a manner to [be] of public consequence, and affect the community at large."

One justice, Stephen J. Field, trumpeted his dissent. A self-proclaimed conservative who proudly quoted Alexander Hamilton and attacked the Illinois laws as wildly socialistic, he insisted that the judgment was "subversive of the rights of private property," which under the Constitution were placed "under the same protection as life and liberty. Except by due process of law no State can deprive any person of either."

Field lost this case but won the future, for the Court began swinging in his direction. Increasingly alarmed over attacks on business, it accepted the idea that a corporation was a "person" in law, and that property must be protected against governmental regulation. Until well after 1900, the Court consistently threw out state attempts to regulate any business with interstate operations. Such matters, it said, could only be regulated by Congress. Then, when the ICC was created, the Court turned around and ruled in 1896 that even the federal government lacked the power to fix railroad rates in *Cincinnati, New Orleans, and Texas Pacific Railway Company* v. *ICC*. The Commission could only make reports and issue protests. Following the same course in *United States* v. *E. C. Knight Company,* the Court ruled that the Sherman Anti-Trust Act did not give the government power to forbid monopolies in manufacturing, since that activity was only indirectly a part of interstate commerce.

In those instances where the Court accepted the regulation of railroad rates by state commissions, it assumed the prerogative of deciding whether the regulation was carried out in an unjust or arbitrary fashion. In the 1890s it repeatedly insisted that railroad rates would have to be high enough to allow the companies involved to earn a "reasonable" profit, which the Court would define in each case. In 1895 in *Pollock*

v. *Farmers' Loan and Trust Company,* it invalidated a federal income tax enacted under Grover Cleveland of two percent on incomes above $4,000 a year on the ground that the income tax was a direct tax and had to be equal and bear on everyone alike in the most literal sense. Despite criticism—much of it heated and bitterly prolonged—the Supreme Court pushed ahead confidently in this "activist" mode for many years after the 1890s. It was obsessed with the idea that its task was to protect capitalist interests and preserve what it regarded as the best philosophy for the nation—laissez-faire.

The agricultural transformation

The impact of the Industrial Revolution struck American agriculture with full force after the Civil War. Markets expanded enormously, both because of the appearance of an integrated national market and because city populations in Europe were growing rapidly and demanding American grains, meat, and cotton. Huge sums were invested in farm machinery to increase output, from expensive steel plows to the most intricate equipment for harvesting. Whether the task was planting trees, caring for livestock, or raising flowers, a flood of inventions revolutionized operations. Mechanical refrigeration and assembly-line slaughtering transformed the meatpacking industry. In the 1870s agricultural chemists began persuading farmers to use fertilizers on a wider scale than before. Inquiries into plant diseases initiated the use of pesticides in the 1880s, which vastly increased production and saved whole industries.

While the center of farm production continued to move westward, agricultural growth flourished even in the increasingly urbanized and industrialized northeastern states. Corn, wheat, potatoes, dairy products, cattle, vegetables, fruits—all mounted in production. Since their transportation costs were low, farmers in the East could invest so much in fertilizers and equipment that the yield per acre in the Northeast was higher than elsewhere in the nation, despite the fact that New Englanders were still tilling the stony soils that had plagued the Puritans.

In the southern states, as early as 1875 the cotton crop was more abundant that it had been in 1859, when 4.5 million bales were produced. By the 1890s, the output had reached more than 7 million bales. The use of fertilizers opened up older sections thought to be farmed-out and, by shortening the period necessary for growth of mature cotton bolls, allowed farmers to raise their crops at higher elevations and in more northerly latitudes. Tobacco culture slowly revived. In rice, similarly, the postwar years witnessed a vigorous revival along the coastal regions of Georgia, South Carolina, and particularly Louisiana.

From Ohio to the rich plains of Iowa and the Dakotas stretches one of the richest growing regions of the world, matched only by the pampas of the Argentine and the vast Ukrainian plains in Russia. In the Great Plains an enormous agricultural empire grew and proliferated in the nineteenth century. The fertility of its soils was incredible. Great volumes of wheat and corn, especially in the huge and productive "bonanza" farms in the northern plains—some of them encompassing tens of thousands of acres—were

Agriculture, 1860–1890

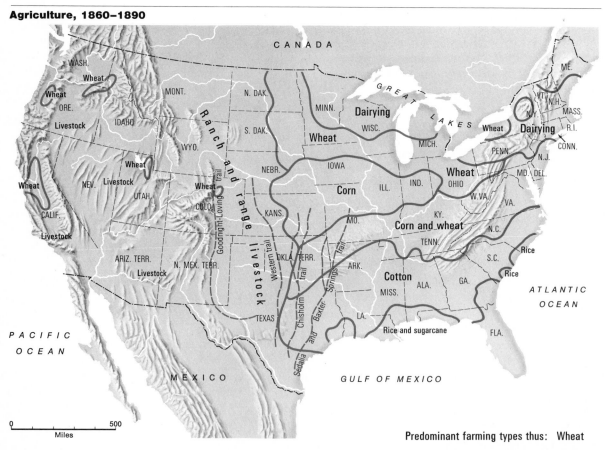

Predominant farming types thus: Wheat

Cattle trail: - - - -

harvested year after year. Thousands of migratory workers, using heavy machinery, followed the crops, producing on one North Dakota farm some 600,000 bushels of wheat in 1881. In the early 1880s, wheat prices were excellent and produced large profits. Where grasslands were abundant, as in Kansas, livestock increased rapidly. The abundance of cheap corn for hog feed produced an increase of hog production in that state from 432,000 in 1877 to 3.2 million in 1891. In the latter year, Illinois grazed 1.7 million beef cattle, there were 1.3 million dairy cattle in Iowa, and 4.5 million sheep in Ohio.

Beyond the Rockies and the deserts, California became a booming agricultural state. Hundreds of vessels called annually at San Francisco to carry off to Europe the prized hard wheat of California's Central Valley, where bonanza farms stretching beyond the horizon produced millions of bushels of grain. More than in any other region, California's farmers invested heavily in large equipment and pioneered in the use of steam-driven harvesting combines that could thresh and bag as much as 450 pounds of grain a minute. At the same time, farming entrepreneurs poured large sums of money into irrigation and reclamation works and began raising fruits, nuts, and grapes for wine. In the 1880s refrigerated cars began carrying such products to eastern states.

The mining West

Miners were early on the scene in the vast region from the Missouri frontier to the Pacific coast. Between 1858 and 1875 they explored every nook and cranny of the mountain country and the desert basins, populating a region formerly inhabited only by Indians and fur traders. After the gold rush to California, miners spread eastward and northward, discovering gold and silver in the present regions of Nevada, Idaho, Montana, and British Columbia. Other gold seekers rushed to Colorado in 1858 when they heard wild tales of

fabulous deposits in the Pikes Peak country. Steamboats ascending the Missouri River were jammed to the rails, and a parade of covered wagons headed westward over the plains, "Pikes Peak or Bust" scrawled on their sides. Scattering out all over the eastern Colorado Rockies, they created such towns as Denver, Pueblo, Canon City, and Boulder. In 1859 large gold deposits were found near Central City, followed by others elsewhere, and a permanent population settled down in Colorado to make it a major mining state.

By the 1890s, corporation mining entered the picture. Hired laborers and eastern-trained engineers took the place of the romantic prospector with his battered hat and sluice box. Millions of dollars were invested in opening up California's large hydraulic gold mines—where jets of water under heavy pressure washed down whole hillsides—and the deep rock mines of the Sierra Nevada, the ranges of Nevada, and the Rocky Mountains. In time the violence of the West no longer involved the exploits of Wild Bill Hickok but conflicts betweeen capital and labor.

The Indian

Miners in the mountain and desert country encountered Indians everywhere. Those of California's Sierra Nevada were peaceable and were soon brutally exterminated. The Snake and Bannock Indians of Oregon and southern Idaho fought back bravely, as did the Ute who occupied much of Utah and Nevada; but intermittent warfare between 1850 and 1855 broke them down, and they were eventually placed on small reservations.

The southwestern Indians (of what is now New Mexico and Arizona) were much more difficult to subdue. Apache and Navaho Indians kept the miners out until the army was sent in during the 1850s to provide protection. In 1860 major warfare erupted. For the next four years the Apache and Navaho, riding swiftly over the high deserts on ponies, fought so skillfully that they almost won. But in the campaigns of 1863 and 1864, hundreds of them were killed and thousands captured. By 1865 they were forced to submit and were placed on reservations, which some of them refused to accept until relentlessly hunted down in another decade of fighting.

The Indians of the Great Plains were first angered when California gold seekers and pioneers heading for Oregon crossed their country in the 1840s and 1850s. An unending line of wagons, stretching practically from one horizon to the other, drove away buffalo, littered trails with discarded equipment, destroyed grass, and spread disease. Cholera that raged like wildfire in the wagon trains swiftly spread to the Indians and decimated whole tribes. Indian survivors were convinced that the affliction had been purposely introduced to destroy them. Then came the Pikes Peak rush and the settlement of Colorado, which established more permanent wagon roads across the central plains. The government decided to clear Colorado of Indians, assigning them to large reservations in what are now Oklahoma and the Dakotas. Treaties to this effect were made in 1861, but the Indians resisted. Desperate for food, weakened by disease, in 1863 they began raiding wagon trains and driving off herds of cattle. Army detachments soon appeared, officered by contentious young men eager for the glory that their colleagues were acquiring in the Civil War. In 1864 warfare broke out over wide areas of the plains.

As soon as the Civil War was over, General William Tecumseh Sherman was assigned the task of bringing peace to the Great Plains. His favorite word was "extermination." Always an autocrat, he was determined that the Indians were either going to obey or be wiped out. By the spring of 1868, his winter campaigning and relentless pursuit, combined with the indiscriminate slaughter of peaceful villages (for which to do him justice, he was not responsible), brought Sherman apparent success. Chiefs of all the tribes signed treaties in 1868 accepting residence on two large reservations.

But many young Indians could not accept this indignity. By the fall of 1868, warfare was in full swing on the plains, and it lasted for ten years. Even after that time, sporadic outbreaks continued for years as small groups of Indians broke away from their reservations for brief raids. Indeed, they might be fighting still were it not for the fact that by the 1880s the enormous buffalo herds of the plains, that had given life and independence to the plains Indians, were practically wiped out.

The slaughtering of the buffalo began when the railroads were built across the plains. At that time, perhaps thirteen million buffalo roamed the grasslands in huge herds. At first white men killed them simply for sport. Then, in 1871, a Pennsylvania tannery discovered that buffalo hides could be made into commercially valuable leather. Professional hunters swarmed over the plains and began killing buffalo at a steady rate. Some of the hunters were deafened for life by the detonations of their heavy rifles. Millions of buffalo were killed every year. By 1878 the southern herds were gone; by 1883 the buffalo on the northern plains had disappeared. A museum expedition sent out to search for specimens in 1883 could find only 200 buffalo in the entire West.

The new Indian policy: Severalty and acculturation

Without buffalo the Indians were now virtually helpless. What was to be done with them? Eastern reformers who in the 1870s began clamoring for more humane treatment of the Indians insisted that the only hope for them was to become "civilized." There was no realization that the Indians could live more fruitfully within their tribes than as scattered individuals in American society. Lewis Henry Morgan, a pioneer anthropologist, believed that the only way to solve the "Indian problem" was to teach the tribesmen the white man's ways. Another noted scientific observer who was widely familiar with Indian culture, Major John Wesley Powell, urged in 1874 that the Indians be made to settle as farmers, learn English, and adopt white values. "A reservation should be a school of industry," he said. Even Helen Hunt Jackson, whose two books in behalf of the Indians, *A Century of Dishonor* (1881) and the novel *Ramona* (1884), caused a national sensation, agreed with the idea of acculturation. This would require fixed settlement, instruction by resident Indian agents, dividing tribal lands into individually owned plots (severalty), and learning the arts of agriculture.

In the Dawes Act of 1887 these policies were combined in permanent form, not to be changed until the 1920s. The Indians were forced to choose 160-acre allotments (except where the land was clearly valueless for agriculture, as in the desert Southwest). Title to each person's allotment was to be held in trust by the government for twenty-five years, so as to ward off white speculators. It could be leased, however, and this opened the door to unscrupulous whites who secured the land from unsuspecting Indians at a pittance. Altogether, most of the 135 million acres remaining in Indian hands in the 1880s was later taken from them as a result of the severalty policy. The remaining land was mostly in the mountains or arid deserts.

The attempt to provide agents to train the Indians broke down quickly, for the Indian agencies, ill-paid and isolated, usually went to political hacks who used every opportunity for graft. At the same time, off-reservation schools were established to provide education, which was hopefully regarded as the ultimate solution to the Indian problem. The schools, however, divided the Indian world further, for those who responded positively to white education met rejection by their tribes when they returned or be-

In 1869, when this photograph was taken of Heap Wolves, the Comanche, noted warriors and raiders were confined to reservations below the Arkansas River.
History Division, Los Angeles County Museum of Natural History

came a culturally disruptive influence. For the Indian in late nineteenth-century America, there was little that promised him continued identity in his own culture and on his own land.

Carl Schurz, a Liberal Republican (also an immigrant German, an intellectual, and an active reformer), was secretary of the Interior under President Hayes. He discussed the Indian problem in the *North American Review* in July 1881: The government, he said, could continue trying to maintain vast reservations, containing millions of unused acres. ''But will those who are hungry for the Indian lands sit still? It will be easy for the rough and reckless frontiersmen to pick quarrels with the Indians. The speculators, who have their eyes upon every opportunity for gain, will urge them on. The watchfulness of the government will, in the long run, be unavailing to prevent collisions. The Indians will retaliate . . . and in spite of all its good

The western Indian situation to 1890

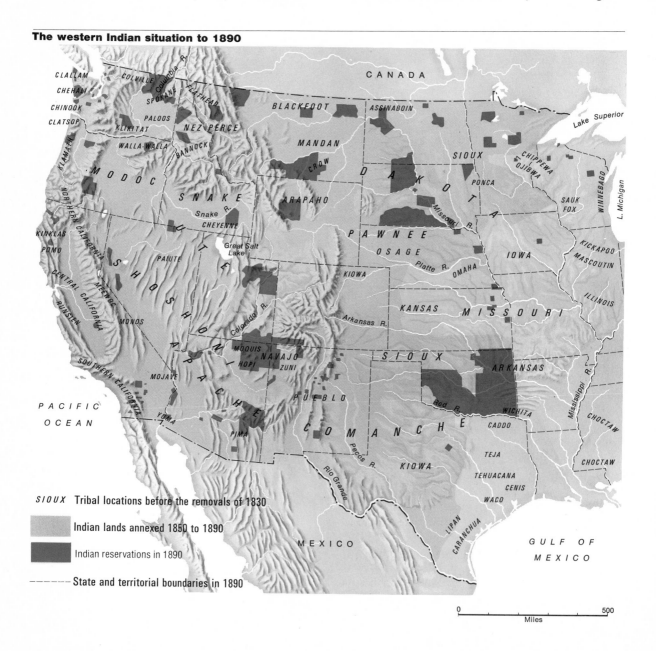

SIOUX Tribal locations before the removals of 1830

Indian lands annexed 1850 to 1890

Indian reservations in 1890

------- State and territorial boundaries in 1890

0   500
Miles

intentions and its sense of justice, the forces of the government will find themselves engaged on the side of the white man. The Indians will be hunted down at whatever cost. It will simply be a repetition of the old story, and that old story will be eventually repeated whenever there is a large and valuable Indian reservation surrounded by white settlements. Unjust, disgraceful as this may be, it is not only probable but almost inevitable. The extension of our railroad system will only accelerate the catastrophe. . . .

"What does, under such circumstances, wise and humane statesmanship demand? . . . I am profoundly convinced that a stubborn maintenance of the system of large Indian reservations must eventually result in the destruction of the redmen [for land-hungry frontiersmen will obliterate the reservations]. What we can and should do is . . . to fit the Indians . . . for the habits and occupations of civilized life by work and education; to individualize them in the possession and appreciation of property by alloting to them lands in severalty, giving them a fee simple title individually to the parcels of land they cultivate, inalienable for a certain period, and to obtain their consent to a disposition of that part of their lands which they cannot use, for a fair compensation, in such a manner that they no longer stand in the way of the development of the country as an obstacle, but form part of it and are benefited by it."

Opening the Great Plains

Pushing the Indians onto reservations opened the way for the occupation of the Great Plains from 1870 to 1890. Their most important characteristic is low rainfall. An average fifteen inches of rain falls each year, and much of that during the hot summer when it quickly evaporates into the atmosphere. Only grass could grow in this climate, not forests. Such an environment could be put to use either by introducing an industry that was naturally adapted to its peculiarities, such as cattle raising, or by developing new devices and methods that would allow farmers to till the land productively.

The cattle kingdom

The cattle industry was the first to invade the Great Plains. It began in southern Texas when Spaniards brought cattle and horses to the region in the eighteenth century, and their herds multiplied rapidly. When Americans arrived in Texas in the 1830s, the Nueces Valley was a great unfenced cattle range where thousands of steers roamed freely. Dairy cattle brought in by American farmers and interbred with the range beasts produced heavier animals whose meat was more suitable for the American market. Roaming wild, cattle drifted northward in search of more grazing land as their numbers swelled. They eventually blanketed west Texas from the Rio Grande to the upper Panhandle. Some five million animals roamed the western high plains of Texas in 1865. Ten years later the cattle kingdom had spread northward over the Great Plains clear to Montana, a swiftness of expansion unparalleled in American economic history. In effect, cattle replaced the buffalo, and in roughly equal numbers.

This process began when Texans learned at the end of the Civil War that northerners were willing to pay up to forty dollars a head for cattle in order to restore their war-depleted herds. The result was the beginning of the "long drive," in which a group of cattlemen gathered up a thousand or so cattle and took them to Sedalia, Missouri, then the nearest railhead. Soon a better location was found in Abilene, Kansas, a town far enough out on the plains to let the cattle drivers avoid wooded and settled areas. Huge stockyards were built there in 1867, riders headed south to intercept the trail herds, and thousands of beasts began to be loaded onto the cattle cars at Abilene—some 1.5 million by 1871. As farm settlement continued to push westward, the stockyards were moved to Ellsworth, Kansas, and then on to Newton, where cattle were received from 1872 to

1875. In that year the final move was made to Dodge City, Kansas, from where one million steers were shipped eastward in the next four years.

But the long drive was coming to an end. The cattle lost too much weight in their long walk, and Kansas farmers, fearing Texas cattle diseases, enacted quarantine laws against them. The only recourse was to raise the cattle near the railroads, or bring the railroads to the cattle. In Texas many lines were built, and the western part of the state was carved into huge ranches, some of them 100 miles across. Northward, railroad lines building into Colorado, Wyoming, and Montana opened that region to stock raising. By 1869 one million cattle were grazing in the Colorado territory.

A veritable "gold rush" set in for western ranch land. The road to wealth seemed ridiculously easy. A man had only to buy some animals, wait a few years while they multiplied on free government grazing land, and he was rich. By the mid-1880s, this mad rush had created a highly unstable situation. The dry Great Plains could support only so many cattle, and then when conditions were just right. Each year the pastures grew thinner. The winter of 1885 struck the industry a crippling blow, and that of 1886 completed the devastation. When spring came, cattlemen rode out over their ranches to find almost every ravine filled with bodies of steers. Heaps of dead animals were piled up against fences. Company after company went bankrupt. The open range phase of the cattle industry ended. In Wyoming alone, the number of cattle declined from nine million in 1886 to three million in 1895.

A massive readjustment followed in which grass and cattle were brought back into balance. The whole of the West was divided into huge fenced pastures, and winter feed was grown in special lots. Thereafter the cattle industry was characterized by cautious investment, careful breeding, and close attention to such things as cattlemen's associations and scientific husbandry.

Farmers invade the Great Plains

Meanwhile, the Industrial Revolution was opening the Great Plains to the grain farmer. Lack of trees made fencing prohibitively expensive, but in the mid-1870s barbed wire was invented, and practical fencing at a reasonable price was available. The lack of running streams was met by the invention of well-drilling machines that drove pipes far down into the ground. Utilizing wind power, the one perpetual source of energy on the plains, water could then be raised by windmills. This apparatus, however, was too expensive for most farmers until the 1890s.

Some other method of adjusting to the dry climate had to be found. What was needed was a system of plowing that would preserve the small amount of water that fell. The answer was "dry farming." Agricultural scientists instructed farmers to dig deep furrows (twelve to fourteen inches) that would create a deep and absorbent blotter to hold the scanty rains that fell on the plains and then would pull up subsurface water to the root zone by capillary action. The technique was hardly infallible and gave erratic results, but it did open up huge areas of the plains to agriculture.

Since farms were so large, the invention of a gang plow that opened several furrows at once was a great benefit. The grain drill was developed by the mid-1870s to speed up planting. Check rowers put down corn seeds at equal distances. Then, in 1880, came the lister, which dug a deep furrow, planted a seed, and then covered it, all in one operation. The first hay baler was invented in 1866, about the time a mowing machine became available. After this came a wide variety of harvesting machinery.

By such means, huge yields resulted. Where a farmer had formerly been able to work only 7.5 acres by himself, in the 1890s he was able to put 135 acres of land to wheat. Where an acre of wheat had formerly required over sixty hours of hand labor, now it required three. The result was the greatest movement of people in the history of the United States. Millions of farmers who had been held back for a generation in their westward movement by the barrier of the Great Plains now moved out into the open country and filled up Kansas and Nebraska, the Dakotas, Wyoming, and Montana, and finally the Indians' last sanctuary, Oklahoma, after it was opened to white settlement in 1889.

Sources of population

Where did the settlers come from? They streamed in either from the older states of the central Mississippi Valley or from Europe. So great was the exodus from the older states that most of them bordering the Mississippi lost population in the 1870s. In the following decade, more than one million people left the Middle West for the Great Plains. In the 1890s, the tide reversed because of grave economic problems encountered by the Great Plains farmers (to be discussed in the next chapter), but by then the great work of this migration had been completed: a region half the size of Europe had been brought into settlement.

Living conditions were wretched. No timber meant sod houses, which were dusty in summer and damp all winter. There was no running water and no fuel; summers blazed and winters were bitterly cold. The unending wind was a constant torment to men and women used to living in sheltered woods. Grasshopper invasions were periodical, as were prairie fires. But prices for wheat were excellent in the 1870s, and the inflow of new migrants continued heavy year after year. The American market for grain grew rapidly as its cities swelled, and the overseas market was huge. After 1875 a series of crop failures in Europe made American wheat much in demand. Then came the Russo-Turkish war of the late 1870s, when the wheat ports of Russia were closed, pushing the price of American wheat even higher. Meanwhile, the rapid invention of new

processes and new machines raised productivity rapidly, and an unusually wet cycle of rainfall produced abundant crops. The average amount of wheat acreage in the United States, which ran at about twenty million acres from 1865 to 1875, suddenly soared to almost thirty-five million acres in the ten years after 1875.

The boomers' spirit

In all sections of the nation the boomers' spirit captured the minds of millions. While the Great Plains were emerging as a region of huge cattle ranches and abundant wheat farms, the first great migrations to southern California filled that region with farms, towns, and land speculators' waving banners. A hundred towns were laid out—many of them soon to disappear—in the year 1887, when the Santa Fe railroad entered Los Angeles and promptly began a rate war with the Southern Pacific, in which ticket prices from Chicago plummeted to one dollar. In 1886, Henry W. Grady, a young and burstingly hopeful editor from the Atlanta *Constitution,* appeared before a New York audience to proclaim the existence of a New South, risen phoenixlike from the ashes of total defeat. Rejecting its ancient ways, he said, the New South was turning toward industrial development, northern habits of industry, town-building, and an abundant future in which there would no longer be a division between the North and South. Caught up instantly, Grady's message became the widely trumpeted cry of publicists, politicians, and educators throughout the South. "Never doubting the vitality of the human resources," writes Paul M. Gaston, "and convinced of the superiority of natural ones, the New South spokesmen believed that by adopting the ways of the industrial age in the same way other Americans had done their dream would be realized."

The voices of hope and optimism, however, were joined by voices of doom. The United States entered a grave time of troubles in the 1880s. In the cities, the factories, the farms of the plains, the cotton plantations of the South—wherever one looked—there were festering sores, apparently incurable, and growing ills. Along with its productivity and its enormous creative power, the new industrial order had also brought a massive social blight. The New South turned out to be largely rhetoric; thousands of defeated farmers left the Great Plains states as their dreams collapsed; each year brought more violent convulsions to the cities as labor rebelled against the industrialists; and a generation of young people turned to reform as they entered national life and found its promises illusory.

Bibliography

Three books that were especially valuable to me in writing this chapter: Thomas C. Cochran and William Miller's *The Age of Enterprise: A Social History of Industrial America** (1961), a major interpretation of industrial development through the whole of the nineteenth century; Walter Prescott Webb's bold, innovative, and still valuable book *The Great Plains: A Study in Institutions and Environment** (1931); and Gilbert C. Fite, *The Farmer's Frontier, 1865–1900* (1966).

How have historians looked at the topic?

During the past twenty years American economic history has undergone profound changes. Its special impact has contributed to a substantially different view of the booming industrial growth following the Civil War. In his *Growth and Welfare in the American Past: A New Economic History** (1966), Douglass C. North summarizes the distinctive concerns of economic history and presents an interpretation based on new quantitative knowledge. Another fine survey with insightful comments on the post-Civil War era is Louis M. Hacker's *The Course of American Economic Growth and Development** (1970).

The importance of railroads in transforming the American economy is disputed in an intriguing study by Robert Fogel, *Railroads in American Economic Growth* (1964). John F. Stover's *American Railroads* (1961) ably presents the more traditional view. Thomas C. Cochran's *Railroad Leaders, 1845–1890: The Business Mind in Action* (1966) is a fascinating analysis of railroad leaders' letters, revealing pressures for honesty and thrift within their community. Gabriel Kolko sees the railroad magnates themselves as the instigators of federal regulation in his controversial book *Railroads and Regulation, 1877–1916* (1965).

C. Vann Woodward's classic interpretation *The Origins of the New South* (1951) highlights the triumph of northern business values while Raymond B. Nixon's *Henry W. Grady* (1969) explores the role of this influential southern spokesman. *The Industrial Revolution in the South* (1968) by Broadus Mitchell and G. S. Mitchell ably examines, among other things, the cotton textile industry.

The deeper meanings of industrialization—the breakdown of a personal, community-oriented system and the beginning of a bureaucratized society geared to planning, control, and efficiency—are explored in an excellent brief book by Samuel P. Hays, *The Response to Industrialism 1885–1914** (1957), and in a more comprehensive and compelling work by Robert H. Wiebe, *The Search for Order, 1877–1920** (1968). Bastions of conservatism are analyzed in Robert G. McClosky's *American Conservatism in the Age of Enterprise** (1951), a stimulating examination of the ideas of men like Justice Stephen Field.

Gilbert C. Fite's *The Farmer's Frontier, 1865–1900*, cited above, is a fine survey of settlement in the Far West, emphasizing the stabilizing role of the farmer. Rodman W. Paul explores mining technology in his *Mining Frontiers of the Far West, 1848–1880** (1963).

*Bury My Heart at Wounded Knee** (1971), Dee Brown's graphic history of Indian-white relations told from the Indian point of view, is absorbing reading. The origins of the acculturation policy pursued by the federal government are explained in Henry E. Fritz's *The Movement for Indian Assimilation, 1860–1890* (1963), and the effects of severalty are poignantly described in Robert M.

Utley's *Last Days of the Sioux Nation* (1963). Helen Hunt Jackson's contemporary denunciation *A Century of Dishonor** (1881) remains penetrating and worthwhile.

Lewis Atherton's *The Cattle Kings* (1961) emphasizes the important role of the cattle entre- preneurs as does E. S. Osgood's *The Days of the Cattleman** (1957). Julian E. Choate and Joe B. Frantz's *The American Cowboy: The Myth and the Reality* (1955) places the cowhand in perspective.

* Available in paperback.

The Newcomers

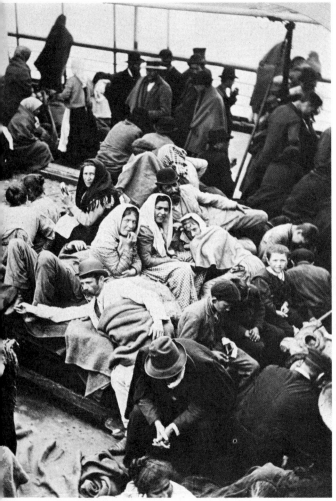

The Granger Collection

This 1902 photograph shows immigrants huddled together on the steerage deck of a liner bound for New York. Millions came in this way to the 'land of opportunity,' hoping to find a better life. Their travel aboard steerage ships was difficult. People were jammed together, and when someone became ill others were afraid of catching the illness and not being allowed to enter the country.

In the February 11, 1888 issue of *Judge,* an employer tells American laborers, ''As long as I am plentifully supplied with immigrant labor, I shall be deaf to the demands of the native working man.'' For this reason, the A.F. of L. generally opposed unrestricted immigration, especially what was called ''contract labor'' where employers, through agents, actually scoured Europe for workers. Within factories, laborers were often kept ethnically mixed so that differences of language, religion, and customs would prevent a unified stand against the employer.

Culver Picture

This Lewis Hine photograph of young boys at work long hours picking (sorting) coal reveals the conditions to which many immigrant families were reduced. Each member of the family had to work, forgetting attendance at schools, in situations where floods of cheap labor were eagerly exploited.
Library of Congress

An emigrant child, gazing wistfully out his tenement window, symbolizes in his somber, concerned expression, the quiet frustrations immigrants felt when jammed together in miserable housing conditions and with low-paid employment. Living in one-or two-room apartments, immigrant families tried to live with countrymen, so they could hear the familiar sounds of their homeland. Many older folk hardly ever left these ''little cities.''
Collection, International Museum of Photography at George Eastman House

CHAPTER 22

Late Nineteenth-Century America: The Nation in Crisis

TIME LINE

1860–1890	Ten million immigrants arrive in the United States
1867	National Grange of the Patrons of Husbandry formed: Illinois Warehouse Act
1870s	States create railroad rate control commissions
1873	Panic begins depression of 1870s; silver demonetized
1876	Greenback party formed
1877	Nationwide railway strike
1878	Knights of Labor formed; Socialist Labor party formed; Bland-Allison Silver Purchase Act
1879	Specie resumption
1880s	Mood of national crisis; thousands of strikes; rise of big business and trusts, wheat boom
1881	American Federation of Labor formed
1883–1896	Farm prices in steady decline
1885–1886	Formation of Southern Alliance, Northwestern Alliance, and Colored Farmers' National Alliance and Cooperative Union
mid-1880s	Farm rush to Great Plains; nativist organizations formed
1886	Haymarket labor riot in Chicago; public feeling turns against the Knights of Labor
1890–1920	Fifteen million immigrants arrive in the United States; "new immigration" from central, eastern, and southern Europe
1890	Sherman Silver Purchase Act
1892	Populist party formed
1893–1897	Depression and major collapse of economy
1894	American Protective Association reaches 500,000 members
1910	Half of population lives in towns and cities

Crisis in the 1880s

INCE 1865 the nation had been swept along by a mood of confidence in the future, even during the difficult depression years of the 1870s. But the mood cracked in the mid-1880s as the economy slumped repeatedly and a mounting clamor of social protest rose on every side. "Our era . . . of happy immunity from those social diseases which are the danger and the humiliation of Europe is passing away," observed a writer in the *Atlantic Monthly* in 1882. Hundreds of strikes broke out every year as angry workers left their factories, and miners with blackened faces streamed from the pitheads, to protest wage cuts and layoffs. Farm prices plummeted, and from the cotton lands of the South to the sweeping high prairies of the Dakotas, farmers crowded into Grange halls to cheer attacks on the "money trust," railroads, and commodity speculators. While the wealthy continued ostentatiously to parade their riches, bitter anarchists, eager to destroy the capitalist system, preached revolution and issued detailed instructions on bomb making. Industrial monopolies grew everywhere; graft and corruption mocked democracy; and the fetid slums of the cities grew more densely packed as immigration soared. Old-stock Americans recoiled from the flood of immigrants, who seemed to them degraded and dangerous to the American social order.

Booming cities and immigration

Over one hundred American cities doubled or more than doubled in population during the 1880s. Most of this growth was fed by one source—American farmers who had found that farm life entailed drudgery, numbing isolation, primitive living conditions, and low income, and who flocked to the cities, which to them meant neighbors, bustling streets, newspapers, theaters and saloons, and jobs with what seemed like good pay. City growth was also fueled by huge masses of immigrants from abroad. The result was that, while in 1869 less than a quarter of Americans lived in a town or city, by 1890 a third of them did, and by 1910 nearly half.

In the 1880s the United States was receiving the second of three great waves of immigration that entered the nation after 1820. The first, from 1820 to 1860, brought in five million immigrants. The second, from 1860 to 1890, brought in ten million. The last and greatest, from 1890 to 1920, comprised fifteen million people. These migrations to the United States, which have become legendary, were actually part of a larger movement in which fifty-five million Europeans emigrated overseas, only three out of five of whom went to America. Of these, perhaps thirty percent reemigrated elsewhere, usually back to their countries of origin. In brief, there was not simply a great migration across the Atlantic to America, but an enormous shifting about of European peoples throughout the western hemisphere.

Because America's native-born population grew rapidly, the proportion of foreign-born in the United States was no higher in 1910 than it had been in 1860 (about fifteen percent) even though twenty-five million immigrants had arrived since the Civil War. They concentrated in northern cities. Less than half the native American population lived in urban areas in 1910, but three out of four immigrants did so. Slum dwellers were almost wholly foreign-born. When a survey was made in 1910, hardly a single native American could be found living in a tenement.

Ethnic enclaves

Thus was created a new phenomenon in American city life, the segregated ethnic living area. Whereas the young people who poured into the cities from the American countryside melted into the urban population, the European immigrants stood out. This was especially true of those who came in growing numbers after 1890 from eastern, central, and southern Europe, bringing in strange faces and styles of life. Almost every northern city had its German quarter with its beer gardens, German newspapers, Lutheran and Catholic churches, and *turnvereins* (men's social clubs). New York's Lower East Side was the classic Jewish quarter with its thousands of sweatshops producing clothing. Grim rows of mud-flat housing, "Hunkeyvilles," in Gary or East St. Louis contained Hungarian and Slavic workers who labored twelve hours a day, sometimes seven days a week, in huge factories. The archetypical Polish section was Hamtramck in Detroit, with its large Catholic churches and neat, small homes. Clamorous Italian enclaves and Bohemian quarters were prominent features of the "new cities." Meanwhile the electric interurban streetcar, invented in the 1880s, allowed the middle class to move to suburbs ringing the inner urban core of factories and business districts. By 1910 the foreign-born were segregated in their living areas in the same way that the northern black population had been all along.

Jews in great numbers now came to America. In 1870, there were about 250,000 Jews in the United States; by 1920, there were 3.5 million. The older Jewish population, present in 1870, had been predominantly German in background, religiously liberal (Reform Judaism), and widely dispersed in the population. But then came hundreds of thousands of strongly orthodox, or conservative, Jews mainly from eastern Europe, Poland, and Russia. Their ways of life set them off sharply from the general American scene. Usually a people who for generations had lived in ghettos and worked in small shops, they formed rigidly separated urban enclaves in American cities where they could maintain their religious customs, dress, and dietary restrictions. Like those Jews already in America, they were intensely devoted to education and self-improvement. Although the first generation might labor in a cigar shop or sew coats and shirts in a loft, the carefully educated second generation frequently entered the professions. Already an urban people, the Jews brought with them—unlike the peasant immigrants from the European countryside—a richly complex and urbanized way of life.

The Catholics emerge

From 1850 to 1900, the number of Catholics in America rose from 1.6 to over 12 million people. Before 1850, they had been primarily Irish, a fact that gives to American Catholicism the Irish cast that strongly colors it even today, for most bishops were and are of that nationality. But after about 1880, American Catholicism became a church as well of Italians, Hungarians, Poles, and Lithuanians, though there was a continued inpouring of Irishmen. Catholics strikingly shunned the countryside, probably because establishing a farm was by this time costly (it required at least $1,000 in capital) and most Catholics were poor immigrants. Having become far and away the largest single religious denomination in the country, Catholicism was regarded with alarm by the Protestants. Burstingly vigorous, the Catholic church in the United States built thousands of churches, monasteries, and schools, a huge undertaking that gave Catholics a common enterprise and a strong sense of morale and identity.

There were conflicts in this new Catholic movement, however, for each ethnic group had its distinctive style of worship and separate language. Catholicism was torn by demands for separate churches, eventually forcing the church to establish ethnic parishes within the boundaries of regular parishes. Most of all, however, there was conflict with the surrounding Protestant world, a fact that built into Catholicism the fortress mentality characteristic of beleaguered social groups everywhere. Protestants saw in Catholicism a church that claimed authoritative power over the faith and morals of its members, that was ruled from abroad, relied upon a celibate clergy, and seemed to challenge the nation's basic values of individualism in faith and life style. More than anything else, the building of Catholic schools created Protestant hostility. Part of each parish and supported by it, the Catholic school was supremely a cultural instrument designed to hold Catholics together. It provided free education, both religious and secular. After 1870 Catholic leaders periodically launched campaigns to get public funds for their schools, which led to angry counterattacks by Protestants.

City problems

Huge problems faced the cities. City authorities had to build miles of streets, find and distribute clean water, drain off sewage, and clear away reeking mounds of garbage that blocked passages everywhere. To house the influx of people, a uniquely American dwelling was developed made of light, cheap lumber, the so-called balloon frame house. Inexpensive and quickly built, it gave ordinary Americans a standard of housing far above that of the average European. But in the most crowded cities, tenement buildings that housed thousands of people on each square block became standard. Erected by speculators, tenements crowded together back to back and lacked light, air, water, heat, or sanitation. Most apartments had only two rooms, often sheltering five

European immigration patterns, 1910

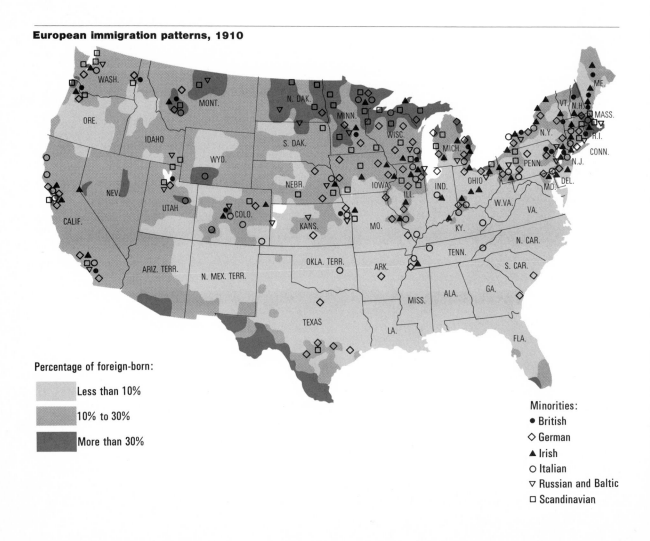

Percentage of foreign-born:

Less than 10%

10% to 30%

More than 30%

Minorities:
- • British
- ◇ German
- ▲ Irish
- ○ Italian
- ▽ Russian and Baltic
- □ Scandinavian

Two pictures of Fifth street in New York City in the 1890s show what the city looked like before a campaign was launched to get garbage off the streets, and after. By these simple public measures, health in cities was vastly improved.
Jacob A. Riis   Jacob A. Riis Collection, Museum of the City of New York

to seven people. In the 1870s New York City contained 100,000 slum dwellers, 20,000 of whom lived in cellars. This produced a congestion greater than that of any large city in Western civilization.

Disease ravaged the slums. Typhoid, smallpox, scarlet fever, and typhus continually claimed victims. Since the medical profession was as yet hardly worthy of that name, survival was simply a case of sturdier bodies throwing off disease. The only recourse was a long, laborious campaign of cleaning up every source of contagion. Major improvements in gathering pure public water enormously reduced the death rate and also allowed a flow of water to carry off wastes. By painstaking efforts, workers cleaned up the garbage that choked the streets. In the 1880s bacteria were discovered and the germ theory of disease gathered advocates. City hospitals were built, and a medical profession with a new sense of responsibility began to give attention to the poor.

Jacob A. Riis, a Denmark-born social reformer in New York City, described the city's slums: "To-day three-fourths of [New York's] people live in the tenements, and the nineteenth century drift of the population to the cities is sending ever-increasing multitudes to crowd them. The fifteen thousand tenement houses that were the despair of the sanitarian in the past generation have swelled into thirty-seven thousand, and more than twelve hundred thousand persons call them home. . . . In the tenements all the influences make for evil; because they are the hot-beds of the epidemics that carry death to rich and poor alike; the nurseries of pauperism and crime that fill our jails and police courts; that throw off a scum of forty thousand human wrecks to the island asylums and workhouses year by year; that turned out in the last eight years a round half million beggars to prey upon our charities; that maintain a standing army of ten thousand tramps with all that that implies; because, above all, they touch the family life with deadly moral contagion [produced by overcrowding and windowless bedrooms]. This is their worst crime, inseparable from the system."

Without money for transportation the poor had to live close to their jobs. For cheap housing, the rooms of old mansions were cut up into smaller ones and multi-storied "rear houses" were put up on the backs of lots. This was done "without regard to light or ventilation, the rate of rent being lower in proportion to space or height from the street; and they soon became filled from cellar to garret with a class of tenantry living from hand to mouth, loose in morals, improvident in habits, degraded, and squalid as beggary itself. . . . Neatness, order, cleanliness were never dreamed of . . . while reckless slovenliness, discontent, privation, and ignorance were left to work out their invariable results, until the entire premises reached the level of tenement-house dilapidation, containing, but sheltering not, the miserable hordes that crowded beneath smouldering, water-rotted roofs or burrowed among the rats of clammy cellars." (*How the Other Half Lives* [1890].)

By 1910 the cities were no longer more fatal to live in than the countryside, for they had largely caught up with the problem of sanitation. Municipal health codes required the selling of food under hygienic circumstances, the pasteurizing of milk, the wrapping of bread, and the use of refrigeration. In 1906 came the passage of federal pure food and drug laws. Housing laws improved tenements somewhat, and the cost of food fell as the western plains were opened and railroads brought in larger supplies at lower costs. Streetcar fares dropped, so that many city workers could move their families to the better housing of the suburbs. In sum, though the urban poor were still exploited, they at least survived, ate better, and lived in housing more suited to human needs.

Labor struggles for socal justice

The income of American workers rose in the late nineteenth century since wages increased about ten percent and the cost of living dropped almost a third—due to the persistent downward drift in prices for manufactured goods and farm products, caused by runaway overproduction. But a revolution of rising expectations was also taking place. Workers watched the wealthy few making enormous fortunes and observed the flight of the middle class to spacious suburban homes. In the face of this opulence, workers' modest gains appeared pitifully small, especially since most still labored twelve hours a day for six or seven days a week.

Great waves of protest passed over the laboring classes from the 1870s onward. There was much to make them angry besides envy of the wealthy. Employers pressed by the steady decline in prices took every possible step to cut labor costs. Whenever business slackened there were immediate and drastic wage cuts and abrupt layoffs. Employers acquired the same habit of authority that British life had bred into its middle and upper classes. Every workers' protest, however mild, was regarded as monstrous insubordination. Obedience was desired above all else. Workers, said one employer, must "submit to our orders, otherwise their places would be vacant." Unions were seen as fundamental challenges to the employer's authority, so that labor-management disputes involved much more than the issue of wages or hours. The question often became, who was master? "Yellow dog contracts," which required workers to agree at the time of employment that they would not join a union, were common. Blacklists of "disloyal" laborers were circulated. "Experience with laboring men," a shoe manufacturer once said, "has convinced me that nothing saves men from debauchery and crime so much as labor—and that, till one is tired and ready to return to the domestic joys and duties of home."

To make these hostilities more intense, employers were usually native Americans, British in descent, Republican, and Protestant, while the workers were usually immigrants from Ireland or the Continent, Catholic, and, when not socialists or outright anarchists, at least Democrats (save for many of the skilled workers, generally British or old stock American, who voted Republican). Worker protests were seen, therefore, as by definition un-American and disloyal. Giving in to their demands was widely seen as a defeat of Yankees by dirty aliens.

The problem of tactics

What were workers to do? Many argued for "pure and simple" unionism: concentrating on getting better wages and hours through bargaining with employers and utilizing the strike as an ultimate weapon. Others called instead for broad programs of social reform on the ground that only a more humane social order would create lasting improvement. This meant agitating for land reforms, new banking and currency systems, and even governmental ownership of major segments of the economy. A small minority of workmen demanded a violent war against capitalism, looking toward the creation of anarchy, in which all forms of power, including government itself, would disappear.

"Pure and simple" trade unionism dominated the labor movement during the Civil War. Then came the first nationwide labor organization in 1866, the National Labor Union, which was social reformist. Its main practical objective was the establishment of the eight-hour day, which it appeared on the verge of achieving until the organization (and practically all the trade unions that composed it) was destroyed by internal dissension and the depression of the 1870s.

In the mid-1870s, a predominantly Irish organization of coal miners called the Molly Maguires adopted the startling new tactic of terrorism. By sabotage, arson, pillage, assault, robbery, and even murder, they tried to force employers to pay desired wages. Soon a number of workers were arrested, tried for terrorism, convicted, and executed. The Molly Maguires disappeared, but the nation was left with the firm belief that miners as a class were criminally inclined.

Following this came the most enormous labor upheaval of the nineteenth century, the railway strike of 1877. Smoldering labor discontent burst into open rebellion when a number of eastern railroads abruptly cut wages. Beginning in western Pennsylvania, workers went on strike in July and began blocking trains, burning buildings, and battling openly with police and militia sent to quell them. Popular hatred of the railroads spread the disorder until it involved practically the whole nation. There were hundreds killed and uncounted injured. Property damage was estimated to run to ten million dollars. When the tumult subsided in late August, the stunned nation finally realized how massive was the feeling of solidarity among laborers—many nonrailroad workers actively joined the strike—when driven to desperation.

The overwhelmingly native American and British-descended middle classes were terrified. Not since plantation owners in the antebellum South had been frightened by fears of slave revolt were so many alarmed by the prospect of mass social upheaval. The conviction spread that not only miners but also railway and many other kinds of workers were inherently violent and criminal because composed of aliens. Aghast at the "enemy" in their midst, many cities hurriedly built large armories and staffed them with a disciplined militia. But strikes and disorders continued to flare up across the industrial scene, for workers were thoroughly aroused. Even in such a relatively prosperous year as 1881, there were almost 500 strikes, involving 130,000 workers. In 1886 over 600,000 workers participated in more than 1,500 strikes, and from then on there were at least 1,000 strikes a year, culminating in massive outbreaks in the depression-ridden 1890s. A conflict of cultures as well as of economic classes seemed to be tearing the country apart.

Labor tries the tactic of social reform

In 1878 American labor began a decade of experimenting with the tactic of reforming the whole society in order to improve the worker's lot. A secret organization, the Knights of Labor, was formed in that year. Led by a handsome and exciting Irishman, Terence Powderly, who had the conviction—bred into the Irish people by their long struggle with England—that everyone must hang together in the face of the common enemy, the Knights welcomed all workers into their ranks, whether skilled or unskilled, male or female, white or black. The Knights believed that the ultimate solution to the laboring person's problem was to end the wage system, establish cooperative factories where no one was employer and no one employee, and share the wealth equitably. In the interim, before such a sweeping goal could be achieved, trusts and monopolies should be closely regulated, the currency reformed, land made available to all, and both child labor and drunkenness swept away. Organized labor, in short, should become a great force for social reform.

The Knights, however, got nowhere with their program since to most Americans they looked like wild-eyed radicals. The coincident rise of an anarchist socialist movement, derived mainly from German immigrants, intensified national anxiety. In 1884 the socialists formed the Central Labor Union, which aimed at "emancipation of mankind" through "the open rebellion of the robbed classes." Meanwhile, a depression in 1883 brought huge numbers of unskilled workers into the Knights of Labor, for they had learned that, whatever the value of the Knights' idealistic reform philosophy, the union had begun to demonstrate that organized workers could win strikes. The organization mushroomed and contained 700,000 members in 1886. Hundreds of strikes were launched, culminating in an immense labor stoppage on May 1, 1886, in a demand for an eight-hour day. On the fourth of May, a bomb was thrown at policemen who were trying to break up an anarchist rally at Haymarket Square in Chicago. When the ensuing gunfire died down, ten people lay dead and fifty more were injured.

The Haymarket riot electrified the country. A tidal wave of labor repression swept across the United States. In Chicago, eight radicals were jailed and blamed for the bombing simply because of speeches they had given. Four of them were executed; one committed suicide; the rest were imprisoned until pardoned in 1893. State after state hurriedly passed laws restricting workers' freedom to organize, and scores of union members were tried for conspiracy, intimidation, and rioting. Employers, emboldened by public support, turned massively against the Knights; the disheartened unskilled workers began leaving the organization; and during the 1890s, the much-reduced Knights of Labor finally expired.

The American Federation of Labor

The American Federation of Labor (AFL) rose to take the place of the Knights of Labor. Its president, Samuel Gompers, was an immigrant Jewish cigar maker in New York City, who had headed a union composed of skilled Jewish workers in his craft. The experience of the Jewish people through generations had taught them tactics different from those adopted by the Irish. Living in small, scattered communities surrounded by Christian majorities, they had come to value tight organization and limited objectives, not mass campaigns inspired by soaring ideologies. Gompers believed that the working person's best hope was to build strong organizations of skilled craftsmen that would concentrate on pure and simple unionism. In 1881, the cigar-makers union joined with seven other skilled trade unions to form the American Federation of Labor.

When the Knights collapsed, the AFL burgeoned. Several influences aided this growth. The skilled workers were frightened of the unskilled. They felt demeaned by having to work in the same organization with them, as in the Knights of Labor, and they were alarmed at the unskilled workers' militance. Most of all, however, they were frightened because new machines were being invented that could be tended by unskilled and semiskilled workmen. Unless the craftsmen banded together to gain job security as well as higher wages and better hours, disaster seemed inevitable. Furthermore, many trades were monopolized by particular ethnic groups who wanted to keep exclusive control over the craft. The Irish worked in transportation, Jews in the

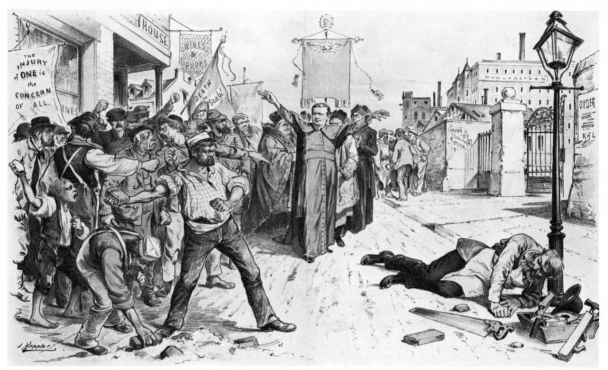

This *Puck* cartoon, in its attack upon Cardinal Gibbons's 1887 statement to the Vatican in support of the Knights of Labor, depicts middle-class hatred of unions. They were seen as composed of strong-armed thugs who prevented honest men from practicing their trade unless they joined up.
Culver Pictures, Inc.

needle trades, Italians in stone masonry, English-men in brick laying, Germans in heavy framing, and Frenchmen in artistic trades. To each of them, the principle of autonomy for each craft union was practically sacred.

The 1890s, a time of widespread labor disorder accentuated by the severe depression that began after 1893, was a time of testing for the AFL. Union after union was crushed by management, for corporations had grown far more powerful than they had been in the past. They were larger, had learned better how to use the courts against unions, principally in the securing of injunctions, and how to band together to break strikes. Gompers steered the AFL clear of involvement in disastrous strikes, and when the depression began lifting in 1897 and factories afterward resumed full production, the organization was

ready to expand. Winning a series of spectacular victories in the coal fields through one of its member organizations, the United Mine Workers, the AFL swelled to a membership of 1,675,000 in 1904.

Nativism

The Haymarket riot of 1886 fixed a specter in the American mind—the bearded, bomb-throwing, foreign radical. In its time of grave troubles, the nation was looking for scapegoats, and many Americans found them in the flood of immigrants debarking at Boston, New York, and Philadelphia and crowding into the already jammed cities.

When nativism—hostility to aliens—erupted in the mid-1880s, it did so because practically every problem afflicting the United States seemed linked to the immigrant. Growing cities, municipal corruption, urban squalor and disease, low wages, the rising "threat" of Catholicism, alcoholism, social and political disorder and radicalism—each seemed to derive from the "strangers in the land." They were "an invasion of venomous reptiles . . . long-haired, wild-eyed, bad-smelling, atheistic, reckless foreign wretches, who never did an honest hour's work in their lives . . . crush such snakes . . . before they have time to bite . . . a danger that threatens the destruction of our national edifice by the erosion of its moral foundations." Josiah Strong, a Congregational clergyman, warned in his popular book *Our Country* (1885) that the immigrants were criminal, immoral, socialistic, and corrupt. The economist Richard Mayo Smith wrote the first scholarly study of the problem, *Emigration and Immigration* (1890), in which he said that the nation's orderly ways of life, self-reliance, and freedom were gravely endangered by continued immigration. Temperance workers were alarmed by heavy-drinking foreigners. Women's rights advocates found peasants from European villages hostile to their ideas. "Every reformatory movement of the day," complained a prohibitionist, "finds [among the immigrants] its most persistent and indefatigable foe."

Aliens did in fact feed political corruption. The Irish, who dominated city government by the 1880s, freely used graft to hand out favors to their immigrant friends, especially those of Catholic faith. The ordinary European peasant, after all, had been denied any experience of democracy and the concept of the "citizen." Government to him had always been a highly personal affair, chiefly concentrating in the local landowner or nobleman. The important thing was to get on his good side, give him loyalty, and receive in return such patronage as he could bestow. Irish political bosses in the United States played this same role. The immigrant could see that they were clearly men of power in the confusing cities of America and that they had jobs, food, legal services, and other aids to give those who voted their way.

Corruption, to the poor European immigrant, functioned like social welfare, delivering jobs and food when most needed.

Immigrants were also accused of being politically radical, and, in fact, the revolutionary and anarchist movements were largely foreign-born. The Socialist Labor party, founded in 1878, was mainly German in membership, and its twentieth-century descendant, the Socialist party of America (which won more than 900,000 votes in the presidential election of 1912), drew support primarily from the foreign-born. In truth, however, the radicals formed a tiny minority of the alien influx. Most immigrants were frightened, divided among themselves by their diverse languages and customs, illiterate, and quite bewildered by public affairs. Their main concerns were getting and holding jobs.

Nativist movements

In the mid-1880s nativism became organized into societies. The Minute Men, formed in New York in 1886, campaigned against immigration. The Loyal Legion appeared in 1887 and began parading prominently through city streets. The Sons of America displayed red, white, and blue regalia, condemning "anarchists and all that class of heartless and revolutionary agitators [who come to] terrorize the community and to exalt the red flag of the commune above the States and Stripes."

Joined to the nativist fear of bombs and revolution was alarm at the huge upsurge in Catholicism. The swift rise of Catholic parochial schools in these years seemed to many people a direct attack on the heart of the American system, the public schools. Huge crowds cheered such men as the Reverend Justin D. Fulton when he shouted that the pope was plotting to destroy American education and that James Cardinal Gibbons, bishop of Baltimore and American Catholicism's leading figure, was already the ruler of the United States. A further irritant was the growing Irish stranglehold on municipal governments. To zealous Protestants this was indisputable proof that the Roman Catholic church was getting hold of the country. Many secret anti-Catholic societies appeared, such as the American League, founded in Chicago in 1886, which demanded that employers discharge all Catholics.

In the 1890s nativism grew more hysterical. The nation's troubles worsened after a severe depression began in 1893. Calamity followed calamity. Labor battled capital with unmatched ferocity, and governor after governor called out troops to quell strikers. Farm radicalism reached new heights in the Populist crusade of 1892 and in William Jennings Bryan's free-silver campaign of 1896. In these circumstances, "fear of the stranger accumulated on all sides," the historian John Higham has written, "mounting into hatred, bursting into violence, and intruding into politics." Even the AFL, long dominated by immigrants and hostile to nativism, began to advocate immigration restriction. Vast campaigns exhorting "Americanism" swept the country. Schools instituted daily flag salutes, American history became a required subject for students, and prestigious organizations such as the Sons of the American Revolution (1889) were formed. Anti-Catholicism became a giant movement. The Iowa-born American Protective Association soared to perhaps a half-million members in 1894. It announced the electrifying "news" that the panic of 1893 had begun because the pope, in preparation for taking over the country, had instructed Catholics to begin runs on all the banks. In Toledo the mayor, the police commissioner, and other citizens even bought rifles to fight off a Catholic invasion.

The "new immigration"

Americans now became aware that in recent years a "new immigration" had begun, composed of Jews, Italians, Slavs, Poles, and Sicilians who were entering the country in huge numbers. Settling in slums, they lived apart from others and aroused repugnance by their strange dress, hair styles, and swarthy appearance. When Slavic coal miners in Pennsylvania went on strike, newspapers spoke of the "wild Huns." Vigilante attacks in 1897 culminated in the massacre of twenty-one Polish and Hungarian strikers by Pennsylvania deputies. Italians were thought particularly inclined to crimes with knives. Lynching parties hunted them down in mining communities and in the Deep South. Jewish businessmen and landlords had their property burned in the South, or were stoned in northern cities.

Now there emerged a racial theme in nativist ideology. Patrician Anglo-Saxon intellectuals in the northeastern states alleged that the new immigration was bringing in inferior blood stocks that would dilute and debase the racial purity of the predominantly Anglo-Saxon American nation. Senator Henry Cabot Lodge of Massachusetts was the leading spokesman for this point of view. Morbidly sensitive to anything that threatened to cause social change, in 1888 he began calling for the end of immigration. In the 1890s his ideas spread. The issue around which he and other nativists gathered their forces was the establishment of a literacy test for all immigrants, for it would strike most severely at the new immigration.

After 1894, when the Republican party won a huge victory in the congressional elections, the literacy campaign intensified. Lodge introduced a literacy bill after making a violent speech warning that the racial foundations of America were in danger of destruction. Whooped through Congress, it was vetoed by President Grover Cleveland on the ground that it clearly violated the nation's democratic values. Congress, he remarked, should avoid the sham of a literacy test if its real intention was to exclude the allegedly inferior races of the new immigration. To the rage of men like Theodore Roosevelt, who considered Cleveland's action a disaster to the nation, Congress was unable to override the veto. Literacy advocates confidently looked forward to a Republican presidential victory in 1896, which they believed would lead to prompt passage of the restriction. As it happened, however, returning prosperity in 1897 lifted the nation's anxious mood, and nativism's strength wilted. More than twenty years passed before the American government finally enacted stringent measures of immigration restriction.

Farm discontent

Farmers everywhere were both aided and injured by the building of the railroads. By the middle of the 1880s hardly a farm in the Middle West was out of earshot of a train whistle. The result was mounting overproduction, for nearly everyone rushed to produce for the newly opened national and international markets. Farm prices fell more or less steadily from 1865 to the mid-1870s, then moved upward for a few years until 1883, when they resumed their downward fall until the mid-1890s. Angry farmers consequently agitated for aid. Their protests flared up in the early 1870s, died down through the years of prosperity, and after the mid-1880s mounted ever higher to explode in the vast Populist and free-silver crusades of the 1890s.

The farmer's immediate enemy was the railroad. Heavy debts and erratic patterns of competition led railroads to charge glaringly inequitable freight rates. When a freight war between competing roads went on between such widely separated points as Omaha and Chicago, farmers at all intermediate points would have their rates jacked up sky high to compensate. Farmers unloading at Minneapolis were forced to pay the full rate to the Great Lakes. Dakota producers learned that it cost more to ship their grain to Chicago than from that point to Liverpool, England. Short hauls were commonly more costly than long hauls, for short haulage was notoriously noncompetitive. Grain elevators were controlled by the railroads, which charged high storage prices. Where there was competition, a road would charge perhaps one cent a mile for a ton of wheat; where there was none, upwards of five cents.

The first protests came in the states surrounding the Great Lakes, where the National Grange of the Patrons of Husbandry was formed in 1867. Initially aimed at relieving the isolation of farmers by providing social and cultural activities, it soon became a militant antirailroad movement. By 1875 it contained more than 850,000 members, who gathered in local Granges from Texas to Ohio, from Minnesota to Georgia. Its greatest political strength, however, lay in the states on the upper Mississippi River. In 1867, Illinois farmers secured passage of a Warehouse Act requiring railroads to pick up grain at independent elevators. In 1871, regulation of railroad rates began in Illinois, followed by similar actions in Minnesota, Iowa, and Wisconsin. Railroads fought back in the courts, evaded compliance, and even reduced service in entire states to force repeal, sometimes successfully. In 1876, the United States Supreme Court, which had not yet swung behind the railroads, ruled that state regulation was constitutional (*Munn* v. *Illinois*). By that time foreign demand was lifting farm prices, and by the late 1870s the Grange had largely withdrawn from politics.

Through the mid-1880s a vast westward movement of farmers swept into the Great Plains, turning Kansas, Nebraska, and the Dakotas into an enormous wheat and corn region. A mounting flood of grain moved eastward to the markets of the East and of Europe. Rain was unusually abundant, and an agricultural miracle seemed underway. Farm land doubled and redoubled in value, setting off a "gold rush" to the high plains. "In one week," wrote a local historian, newcomers "became as wild as their fellows and joined the maddening crowd." Land near Abilene, Kansas, that had gone for $6.25 an acre in 1867 was sold for $270 an acre in 1887. But then came collapse. Drought struck first in 1887, followed by disastrously slumping wheat prices in the international market. Half the population of western Kansas cleared out in the years from 1888 to 1892; large areas of the Great Plains were practically depopulated. Towns emptied; extravagant streetcar systems turned to rust; abandoned houses with doors flapping stood on empty farm land stretching to the horizon. Kansas, which had raised thirty-one million bushels of wheat in 1882, produced only ten million in 1887.

The crucial issue on the high plains was debt. The newly settled plains states were still heavily burdened with mortgages, and now they were being foreclosed by the thousands. "Men and women who had been carefree and lighthearted," recalled an early settler, "were turning bitter, and there was a sudden, unheralded, spontaneous outburst of resentment over the hardships result-ing from crop failures, or from low prices." Where interest rates had been well below twelve percent, now, in the late 1880s, they soared over twenty, and sometimes reached forty percent, a savagely punitive figure. In four years unpaid

debts forced 11,000 foreclosures in Kansas. In some counties ninety percent of the land was lost to mortgage companies.

The money question

The farmer had many enemies to hate, but his greatest anger was directed at bankers and the "money conspiracy." Ever since the Civil War, Americans had argued constantly over the money system. No other issue so fascinated the age or was regarded as so crucial to every other prob-lem.

The crux of the matter may be simply stated, but its implications were enormously compli-cated. Briefly, producers who got their income in the open market, such as farmers, favored an

Rawding family sod house home in Custer County, Nebraska, about 1886, shows the bleak conditions of life on the treeless Great Plains, where wood for homes was not available save from great distances at high cost.
Solomon D. Butcher Collection, Nebraska State Historical Society

expanding money supply because more money in circulation seemed to produce rising prices and make it easier to pay off mortgages. Furthermore, those who needed to borrow money to start new factories, such as iron products and enterprising businessmen in general, also liked an expanding money supply because bankers would then have plenty of money to loan them and interest rates would be low. However, those whose income was set by someone else—such as working people, the salaried, and consumers in general—favored a stable or perhaps contracting money supply because they believed this would keep the cost of food and other necessities stable, or even cause it to drop, a critically important matter to people living close to the poverty level. Those who had lent money also tended to favor stability or deflation, since this would ensure that the money paid back to them would be worth as much as what they had lent in the first place, or perhaps even more.

There was another aspect to the question. Those heavily engaged in foreign trade, such as textile manufacturers and exporters of raw materials, wanted to keep American prices low and thus competitive in the world market. They therefore favored stability or deflation. But those who sold primarily at home and worried about competing goods coming in from abroad took the opposite view. Inflated American currency would be able to buy fewer foreign goods, so people would tend to buy from domestic manufacturers. Protective tariffs and money inflation tended to be parallel policies; free trade and money stability or deflation also went together. Republicans, as the party of the producers of manufactured goods, tended to favor the former; and Democrats, as the party of the city masses, the consumers, tended to favor the latter.

The nation ended the Civil War with several kinds of money. There were gold and silver coins as well as United States notes, or paper "greenbacks," not backed by gold, which the government had printed during the Civil War out of the pressing need to pay its debts. Over $400 million

in face value, they were worth considerably less in gold on the open market. National banknotes were another form of paper currency. They were issued by nationally chartered private banks and backed by the federal bonds owned by each such institution. This privately issued currency was limited in volume to $300 million until 1875, when all limitations were taken off. In practice, therefore, a large part of the nation's money supply was controlled by private banking corporations, who decided how much money to print and circulate.

The greenbackers

For a dozen years after the Civil War, the money argument was concerned with the question, what should be done with the greenbacks? Practically everyone in authority wanted to achieve resumption of specie payments, that is, get enough gold in the Treasury to support the greenbacks. Then anyone could get gold coin (specie) in return for his greenback if he wished. But one group of reformers strongly condemned this idea, saying that the greenbacks actually gave the country a chance to establish a permanent inflationist monetary system in which the government would simply print paper money as the economy needed it. To nearly everyone, this was a radical notion. Do away with gold and silver and rely just on paper money? It seemed monstrous. But the greenbackers went even further: they said it was wrong to allow private banks to issue national banknotes and thus control the amount of money in circulation. The currency system is so crucial, they said, that the people should control it wholly and directly through their elected government. In brief, the currency system should be nationalized, not left largely in the hands of private enterprise.

Greenbackers like Henry C. Carey, long one of the Republican party's chief economic theorists, said that relying on gold and silver to form the basis for money was absurd. The economy grows; therefore, the money supply should grow.

Let it rise abundantly, for the more money, the more productivity, and productivity was the proper objective. An abundant money supply, he said, would keep interest rates low and make debts easy to repay. In the early 1870s both the National Labor Union and the iron and steel makers of Pennsylvania joined in warmly supporting the greenback idea. Later in that decade farmers in the Granger states pitched in as well. In 1876 the Greenback party was formed to agitate the question nationwide, running presidential candidates in that year and in 1880, and electing a number of congressmen. Prosperity for farmers in the late 1870s reduced their interest, however, and in 1879, when the federal government achieved resumption of specie payments—so that greenbacks were fully backed by gold—greenbackism died away. Remarkably modern in its basic assumptions (the present philosophy of a "managed" currency supply is mainly what greenbackism called for), it was an idea whose time had not yet come.

The rise of free silver

But the money controversy was far from over. By the late 1870s new discoveries of silver changed the whole picture with regard to the metallic base of the currency system. The nation had been ostensibly on a bimetallic standard from its beginnings; that is, its currency was based on both gold and silver, their relative value being legally set at a ratio of sixteen ounces of silver equaling one ounce of gold. Since the 1830s, however, silver had been scarce and was more valuable than sixteen to one on the world market. Therefore, it was little used in the nation's coinage.

At the same time, major shifts in the international monetary situation were taking place. Most of the western European nations decided to use only gold as the basis of their money systems. This held out great hopes for an internationally unified money system to be used by all the advanced trading nations. Relying on a common stock of gold that would move back and forth

from nation to nation to pay for purchases of goods, the world's traders would, so the theory ran, share a common level of prices. If inflation began in one country, gold would flee from it because it would be more valuable elsewhere; that nation's money supply would have to be contracted; and deflation would bring prices back down to the world level. If deflation began, the opposite would occur. Both international trade and price stability would benefit.

To join into this unified international trading system, the American government took important steps. Since silver coins were practically nonexistent anyway, "gold standard" supporters in the Treasury persuaded Congress in 1873 to demonetize silver; that is, make gold the only basis for American currency. They were further encouraged to do this by the knowledge that silver was beginning to pour out of the western mines and that soon it would probably be back in circulation. At the time no one paid much attention to the shift to the gold standard, but it soon became nationally notorious as the "crime of '73." Inflationists now demanded free coinage of the white metal at the old ratio of sixteen to one, since—because it was so plentiful—its price on the open market was lower than that, and people would be glad to sell it to the Treasury and have it stamped into currency.

Under immense pressure from farmers, a Republican-dominated Congress partially agreed in 1878, enacting the Bland-Allison Silver Purchase Act. It did not remonetize silver—the gold standard remained—but it allowed the Treasury to purchase up to four million dollars monthly in silver and to coin it. It was, in effect, silver paper. The purchased silver did not itself provide a legal basis for the government to print paper currency, but was used to replace greenbacks, which were then taken out of circulation in proportion. Inflationists were thus frustrated.

The return of prosperity and good farm prices after 1879 temporarily took the issue out of national politics. By the mid-1880s, hard times returned and farmers began agitating the issue again. In response, Congress enacted another measure ostensibly designed to meet silver demands, the Sherman Silver Purchase Act of 1890—a Republican measure. In effect, it required the government to buy practically the whole output of American silver mines and store it as uncoined metal (bullion) in the Treasury (about 4.5 million ounces monthly). New paper currency was printed to pay for the silver, but the value of silver had slumped so far that this act actually produced less inflation than the Bland-Allison enactment it had replaced. Thoroughly angered, the farmers turned to politics and won sweeping victories in the South and Great Plains in 1890. Pleased by their success and with dreams of a great new future, farmers turned to the project of forming their own national political party.

The Populists appear

Kansas farmers had taken the name "People's party" in their local election victories in 1890; in 1891, the nine congressmen elected by alliance campaigns organized a People's party caucus in Washington; and in early 1892, almost nine hundred delegates met in St. Louis to form a national People's, or Populist party. Containing more than eighty representatives of the Knights of Labor (the AFL held aloof from political action), the Populists looked eagerly to a national coalition of laboring and farming men. On July 4, 1892, a nominating convention met in Omaha, Nebraska, and in an atmosphere of intense evangelical zeal chose a presidential candidate, James B. Weaver of Iowa, and issued a clarion call to the nation for a fundamental reform of its government and economy.

The Omaha platform of 1892 was the basic document of populism. The delegates met, it declared, "in the midst of a nation brought to the verge of moral, political, and material ruin. Corruption dominates the ballot-box, the legislatures, the Congress, and touches even the ermine of the bench. The people are demoralized; most of the States have been compelled to isolate the voters at the polling-places [using the secret ballot] to prevent universal intimidation or bribery. The newspapers are largely subsidized or muzzled; public opinion silenced; business prostrated; our homes covered with mortgages; labor impoverished; and the land concentrating in the hands of the capitalists. The urban workmen are denied the right of organization for self-protection; imported pauperized labor beats down their wages; a hireling standing army [hired groups of private Pinkerton detectives], unrecognized by our laws, is established to shoot them down, and they are rapidly degenerating into European conditions. The fruits of the toil of millions are boldly stolen to build up colossal fortunes for a few, unprecedented in the history of mankind; and the possessors of these, in turn, despise the republic and endanger liberty. From the same prolific womb of governmental injustice we breed the two great classes—tramps and millionaires.

"The national power to create money is appropriated to enrich bondholders; a vast public debt, payable in legal currency, has been funded into gold-bearing bonds, thereby adding millions to the burdens of the people. Silver, which has been accepted as coin since the dawn of history, has been demonetized to add to the purchasing power of gold by decreasing the value of all forms of property as well as human labor; and the supply of currency is purposely abridged to fatten usurers, bankrupt enterprise, and enslave industry. A vast conspiracy against mankind has been organized on two continents, and it is rapidly taking possession of the world. If not met and overthrown at once, it forebodes terrible social convulsions, the destruction of civilization, or the establishment of an absolute despotism." (Norman Pollack, ed., *The Populist Mind* [1967].)

What did the Populists call for, in order to save the nation from its corrupted state? The secret ballot everywhere, to guarantee electoral freedom and protect voters from intimidation; a graduated income tax, to strike at huge fortunes; restriction of "undesirable immigration" to protect American wage earners from the competition of "the pauper and criminal classes of the world"; shorter hours for labor, and an eight-hour day for government workers; abolition of hired armies ("the Pinkerton system . . . the hired assassins of plutocracy"); the initiative and referendum; direct election of senators; a one-term presidency; and an end to all subsidies or national aid for private corporations. In addition, the Populists believed that "the time has come when the railroad corporations will either own the people or the people must own the railroads," and that therefore "the government should own and operate the railroads in the interest of the people." Similarly, the telegraph and telephone systems should be nationalized. Land monopoly should be ended and alien ownership prohibited. The Populists demanded, too, a sound and flexible national currency. They maintained that silver and gold must be freely coined at the ratio of sixteen to one and that the money supply must be rapidly increased to not less than fifty dollars per capita. A special system of subtreasuries should be placed in the countryside by the government, allowing it to make direct loans to farmers, always in need of capital at reasonable rates. Private banks should no longer print currency, but only the federal government. In brief, the Populists believed that the nation should put aside the reigning notion that laissez-faire and government passivity will solve everything. The people must use their power, through government, to solve their pressing ills.

For the first time a major political party had appeared that called for positive rather than passive government and for what amounted to a sharp turn leftward in the direction of socialism. Its fate (to be discussed in the next chapter) was not encouraging. The Populists' presidential candidate carried one grain state (Kansas) and three silver states (Colorado, Idaho, and Nevada) in the election of 1892, while gaining enough votes in other Great Plains and mountain states to amass slightly more than a million popular votes.

But the party's hoped-for coalition with labor never occurred (since city workers hated inflation), and the race issue in the South kept white voters from leaving the Democratic party. In 1896 the Democrats swung to free silver, nominated William Jennings Bryan, and absorbed the Populists. The party, as such, disappeared.

Populism failed ultimately because it did not understand the city or the laborer. It could never become a genuine farmer-labor movement despite its eager appeals to workers to join up in a common alliance of the "producing" classes against the "nonproducers." The Populists never realized that inflation would hurt city consumers, nor that it could not by itself solve the problems of monopoly or poverty. Populism was, in the last analysis, a farmer movement, bound together by real economic problems, but in national politics always to be fatally weakened by its inability to expand beyond the plains and silver-producing states, or capture the white supremacist South from the Democrats. The later progressive movement of Theodore Roosevelt's day sprang primarily from the cities and not from the Populist countryside. In some important ways, the two reform campaigns were concerned with different things.

Basically, however, they were both aroused by the spectacle of unrestrained power and devoted to the notion that the time had come for the government to change the country's social order. Although the historical relationship between populism and progressivism is uncertain, it is difficult to believe that this great "pentecost of politics," this huge flame of revivalistic reform, did not play a major role in preparing for the national regeneration that began in the cities in the late 1890s and flowered in the progressive era of Theodore Roosevelt and Woodrow Wilson.

Bibliography

Three books that were especially valuable to me in writing this chapter: One of the most interesting and influential books to appear in recent years, Robert H. Wiebe, *The Search for Order*,

1877–1920* (1968); John Higham's brilliant classic on nativism, beautifully argued and written, *Strangers in the Land** (1955); and, among the numerous writings on the Populists, Walter T. K. Nugent's *The Tolerant Populists** (1963), which struck me as the most judicious account in a field crowded with controversy.

How have historians looked at the topic?

During the latter half of the nineteenth century, the nation born in the American wilderness moved to the city. Urban machinery, whether sewers or city hall, creaked and sometimes collapsed under the massive influx of foreign immigrants and people from "down on the farm." The impact of urbanization, uniquely coupled in the United States with rampant industrialization, has been until recently a lost dimension in American history. Lewis Mumford's classic works on urban life and culture spoke out early for urban planning and reform: *The Brown Decades: A Study of the Arts in America, 1865–1895** (1931); *The Culture of the Cities* (1938); *The City in History: Origins, Its Transformation and Its Prospects* (1961). Arthur M. Schlesinger was one of the first historians to underscore the importance of cities in shaping American life in *The Rise of the City, 1878–1898* (1933).

Over the last fifteen years some historians have taken the city as the major focus of their work, illuminating very significant facts of urbanization. Richard C. Wade's article "Urbanization" in C. Vann Woodward's edited volume *The Comparative Approach to American History* (1968) offers a perceptive overall view of the urban genre. Excellent excerpts that give one a sense of what urban historians have accomplished are found in Alexander B. Callow, Jr.'s *American Urban History** (1969). See also his fascinating book *The Tweed Ring** (1966). Blake McKelvey interprets the period between the Civil War and World War I in *The Urbanization of America* (1962). Two special studies are particularly noteworthy: Sam B. Warner elucidates the critical connection

between transportation and urban growth in *Streetcar Suburbs: The Process of Growth in Boston, 1870–1900* (1962); and Stephan Thernstrom analyzes the question of mobility and presents some startling conclusions in *Poverty and Progress: Social Mobility in the Nineteenth-Century City* (1964). Valuable too is a fine group of essays edited by Stephan Thernstrom and Richard Sennett, *Nineteenth-Century Cities: Essays in the New Urban History** (1969).

Herbert G. Gutman reveals the city as the stronghold of antagonism toward the unionizing laborer in a provocative article, "Industrial Workers Struggle for Power," in H. Wayne Morgan's collection *The Gilded Age* (1970). Gerald N. Grob explores the philosophy behind the labor movement in *Workers and Utopia: A Study of Ideological Conflict in the American Labor Movement, 1865–1900** (1961). Philip Taft's *The A. F. of L. in the Time of Gompers* (1970) admires Gompers as a realistic, nonpolitical moderate while William M. Dick studies American trade unions' rejection of socialism in favor of "Gompersism" in *Labor and Socialism in America: The Gompers Era* (1972). W. G. Broehl, Jr.'s *The Molly Maguires** (1964) is a thorough account, and John Laslett fills an important gap in labor history with *Labor and the Left: A Study of Socialist and Radical Influences in the American Labor Movement, 1881–1924* (1970).

Ethnic enclaves are highlighted in an outstanding collection of readings edited by Leonard Dinnerstein and Frederic C. Jaher, *The Aliens: A History of Ethnic Minorities in America* (1970). Two excellent studies in this vein are Moses Rischin's *The Promised City: New York's Jews** (1962) and T. N. Brown's *Irish-American Nationalism** (1966). Barbara Solomon explores the emergence of nativism among New England's Protestant elite in *Ancestors and Immigrants** (1956). John Higham's brilliant work on nativism is cited above.

The importance of money in American history is sometimes obscured by the difficulties of understanding concepts such as monetary standards, inflation, deflation, and foreign exchange. Susan S. Burr's *Money Grows Up in American His-*

*tory** (1964) offers a clear explanation of financial intricacies and contains a short bibliography. Irwin Unger's Pulitzer Prize-winning book *The Greenback Era** (1964) expertly probes the complex economic and ideological motives behind hard money and inflationary stances in this period of growth and crisis. Two fine books by Walter T. K. Nugent, *The Money Question during Reconstruction** (1967) and *Money and American Society, 1865–1880* (1968), are basic to the money question.

Populism has deservedly attracted much attention from historians. In addition to the works by Nugent cited above, see Norman Pollack's *The Populist Response to Industrial America** (1962), a spirited defense that views the Populists as legitimate radicals fighting economic oppression, and Robert F. Darden's *The Climax of Populism** (1965), a study of the 1896 election and the internal divisions that plagued the Populists. Raymond J. Cunningham, ed., *The Populists in Historical Perspective* (1968) is a useful overview of the argument among historians over the real nature of Populism.

* Available in paperback.

CHAPTER 23

Gilded Age Politics: Instability and Impasse

TIME LINE

1870s	Tweed Ring flourishes; widespread political corruption
1876	Rutherford B. Hayes elected nineteenth president of the United States
1880	James A. Garfield elected twentieth president of the United States
1881	Chester A. Arthur becomes twenty-first president of the United States upon death of Garfield
1883	Pendleton Civil Service Act
1884	Grover Cleveland elected twenty-second president of the United States; Liberal Republicans (Mugwumps) give him support; transatlantic Liberal-Democratic community flourishes
1886	Cleveland begins battle over the tariff
1887	Cleveland attacks protective tariff in his annual message
1888	Benjamin Harrison elected twenty-third president of the United States
1889	North Dakota, South Dakota, Montana, and Washington admitted to the Union
1890	McKinley Tariff; "Czar" Thomas B. Reed, Speaker of the House, centralizes operations; Wyoming and Idaho admitted to the Union
1892	Grover Cleveland elected twenty-fourth president of the United States
1893	Repeal of Sherman Silver Purchase Act; Wilson-Gorman Tariff
1893–1897	Depression
1894	Coxey's Army marches on Washington; Pullman strike in Chicago; Cleveland orders troops to intervene; strong Republican victory in congressional elections
1896	William Jennings Bryan's free-silver presidential campaign; William McKinley elected twenty-fifth president of the United States; gold from discoveries in South Africa, Yukon, Colorado, begins pouring in, bringing prosperity
1897	Dingley Tariff
1900	Gold Standard Act

Gilded Age politics

FOR more than fifty years, American history books have described late nineteenth century politics in just the terms implied in Mark Twain and Charles Dudley Warner's choice of the name *Gilded Age* for their novel of the era of Ulysses Grant. It has been seen as a time of hypocrisy, shallow glitter, dollar chasing, and political irresponsibility. The nation's leaders were venal, crafty, and indifferent to the public welfare. They trumped up bogus controversies over the tariff, political corruption, and the money system to divert the people's attentions from the "real" issues: the exploitation of labor and farmers, and profiteering. By this means they fended off what was actually needed: strong government intervention to reform the country's corrupt capitalist system. Gilded Age politics, in short, were little but noise and confusion, signifying nothing. Partisan divisions were meaningless, for both Democrats and Republicans were tools of the wealthy.

We are now beginning to see that this picture is fundamentally miscast. The politics of the Gilded Age, like that of every other period, have their own inner validity and reality. It is of little use, as Geoffrey Blodgett has written, to be impatient with Gilded Age leaders "for having not yet discovered the Welfare State." There were huge changes swiftly transforming American life in these decades; the people were deeply worried about them; and they argued endlessly about the tariff, money, and civil service questions because this pre-1900 generation believed that somewhere within their intricacies lay the answers to the nation's ills.

Probably no other generation has been so knowledgeable about such complex public issues. Huge crowds turned out year after year to listen closely to long, detailed speeches on the tariff and the currency system; to cheer when key points of extraordinary technical subtlety were made; and to carry away and distribute tens of thousands of leaflets which were handed eagerly from hand to hand. It is ironically true that, as economic historians have now established, the protective tariff probably had little effect one way or the other in stimulating industrialization, but people believed that it did, and this is what matters in understanding public affairs. The currency question was in fact, however, one of great importance, for the volume of the money supply is a crucial element in economic affairs. The civil service issue was also fundamental, for nothing significant could be done, by governments, about any national or local problem until their employees were honest, relatively free of political intervention, and professional. Upon this foundation, when it was finally established, were to rest all of the reforms of later years.

Certainly, at no time in American history was the national electorate more thoroughly mobilized, more directly involved in governing the country. Turnouts at the polls regularly soared over eighty per cent. There were almost continual rallies, speeches, torchlight parades, and mass demonstrations in the elections which occurred sometimes at the rate of every six months. Meticulously staffed political organizations reached into every ward and precinct. From the time the Democratic South returned to national politics in the mid-1870s, the two parties were so evenly balanced that national and state victories were won by whisker-thin margins. Thus, each party relied heavily upon "army style" politics. The objective was to keep everyone's spirits high by constant stimulation; to arouse intense feelings against the common enemy; and to get every possible voter, from one's own party, to the polls at each election. To be an "independent" was scorned.

It was the most politically active grass-roots voting generation in American history. There was, of course, a pressing immediate reason for all this. With a hundred thousand patronage jobs available in the Federal service to be handed out to the victors, and thousands more in state and local governments, each election was treated like a battle, for the rewards were enormous. In luxuriantly corrupt cities like New York, where contracts totalling millions of dollars were regularly given out to political favorites, poor men could become millionaires in short order.

Cultural politics

Most of all, however, Americans turned out in such huge numbers because these were years of intense cultural conflict. We have seen that at least since Jacksonian times the hatred that Protestant Englishmen and Scotsmen—the British—felt toward Catholic Irishmen, bred into them by centuries of hostility and warfare in the homeland, was at the core of American politics. From Jefferson's time, indeed, the Democrats had been the party of the Catholics, as they were in general the party of all the outgroups who did not fit the classic New England, Protestant model (save for black Americans): Southern whites, German and Irish immigrants, French-Canadians, Jews; the irreligious; the free living and the skeptical; those of Jeffersonian temper who strongly believed that people's morals should be their own affair, and that churches should stay out of politics. Republicans, on their part, were the party of that huge ethnic group which, widely distributed in the northern states, thought of themselves as uniquely the American people: Protestants of British descent, their homeland lying in Yankee New England and the territories to the west of it into which they migrated—western New York, and the upper Middle West. They dreamed of a unified, hard-working, pious America cast in their own image. They still carried with them their ancient Yankee notion that the moral life of the community was properly the concern of government, which should be actively used to promote purity and godliness.

Since immigration was huge in these years, the Democratic party grew rapidly in numbers. Then the spectacular upsurge of Republican-backed nativism in the 1880s welded the Democrats into a fighting host. The Republicans, too, kept alive the nation's oldest cultural antipathy by constantly "waving the bloody shirt" and accusing the Democrats of being the party of Southern disloyalty. From the mid-1880s on, Republican-oriented anti-Catholic societies demanded that employers discharge Catholics, attacked their parochial schools as an assault on Americanism, and bewailed the growing power of Catholics in the governments of such great cities as New York, Boston, and Chicago. In 1887 the Iowa-born American Protective Association appeared to lead the campaign against Catholics, alleging papal conspiracies against American independence. The Republican attack against labor unionism was also, in effect, an attack upon immigrants and their growing power in American life. German Lutherans, though a Protestant group, veered strongly Democratic as a result of these Republican campaigns for cultural uniformity, not only because they were non-Yankees who spoke a foreign language and clustered by themselves, but because they feared for their parochial schools. Such institutions, they felt, were crucially important in keeping their children in the old ways, and maintaining their identity as a people. This meant that they swung strongly behind the notion of absolute religious freedom, and in Jeffersonian terms criticized those zealous "clerics in politics" who would presume to use the power of government to change other people's morals.

Prohibitionism

Of all these issues, the most explosive was prohibitionism. As a general rule, Yankee Americans in the nineteenth century did not drink alcoholic liquors. Whiskey was known as the drink of the Scotch-Irish and the Catholic Irish; beer consumption was a German habit; and wine was what Italians and Spaniards drank. In the Southern states, with their strong infusion of Scotch-Irish peoples, bourbon had always been an important beverage. But Yankees, especially those of a strongly religious cast of mind, frowned upon alcoholic consumption as the core evil which led to all the other moral impurities of the age. In the 1850s, they had worked hard to end its use.

Now, in the 1880s, with the burgeoning rise of great cities, the flooding of young people into them from the countryside, and the streaming influx of immigrants, prohibitionism quickened. On every side, threats to true morality flaunted themselves in city streets: theatres, dance halls, houses of prostitution, and saloons. The latter seemed simultaneously connected with crime, political corruption, vice, and personal degradation. This was not a total misconception. Alcohol was in fact the anodyne of the working poor; alcoholism was a terrible scourge. Venal interests did in reality cluster around the liquor trade, and the saloons which were everywhere in the working class districts could be both convivial blessings for over-worked men, and a social curse. Republicans, as the party of Yankee puritanism, called for prohibition with the same passion with which they had earlier condemned slavery, and for similar reasons. Prohibitionists firmly believed that if the saloon were crushed, American life would be regenerated in the Yankee mold. Thrift, industry, and piety would reign. Like the

abolitionists, they prided themselves on their radicalism. They became a violent people who smashed saloon interiors with axes, blew them up and burned them down, and proudly received violence in return. Democrats, as the party of personal freedom and the immigrant outgroups, fought back with comparable bitterness. Prohibitionism symbolized, to them, the ancient habit of "minding other people's business" which they had always condemned in the Republicans (and in their Whig forebears).

Year after year Republicans launched drives to secure prohibition laws in the northern states, thus driving away the beer-drinking Germans, now an enormous part of the American population. Then in 1889 they escalated their assault against cultural divergence by enacting, in Wisconsin, a law which directly attacked parochial schools. It stated that a school would only be regarded as such if it taught the core subjects in the English language. Under compulsory education laws, Lutheran and Catholic children might have to be sent to the public schools, where Yankee Protestantism was openly taught in the form of "moral instruction." The result was a sweeping upsurge of Democratic victories nationally, fuelled by the anger of Catholics and Lutherans, that threatened permanently to put the Democrats in charge of American government.

Interior of a New York dive in the 1890s, classic symbol to millions of WASP Americans of the degradation of drink and the saloon. In fact, the saloon often was a center of crime, corruption, and vice.
Jacob A. Riis   Jacob A. Riis Collection, Museum of the City of New York

Political confusion

At the national level, politics had been highly unstable since the election of 1876. The parties were so closely balanced that during only four years did one of them control both Congress and the presidency: the Republicans from 1889–91, and the Democrats from 1893–95. In addition, the two houses of Congress were badly organized. No one had authority to direct the flow of bills to be considered; minorities could block all activity simply by refusing to vote; and many congressmen were openly corrupt. The result was that hardly anything got done.

Five men served as Republican presidents from

1877 to 1901, all but one from the Middle West: Rutherford B. Hayes (1877–81) of Ohio; James A. Garfield from the same state, who was shot within four months of becoming president in 1881 and died two months later, to be succeeded by his vice-president from New York, Chester A. Arthur (1881–85); Benjamin Harrison (1889–93) of Indiana; and William McKinley (1897–1901) of Ohio. These men brought traditionally Whiggish and Republican ideas about the chief executive with them to the White House. If Congress passed laws, they would administer them. However, it was not their place, they believed, to provide vigorous executive leadership; to be tribunes of the people in the style of Andrew Jackson. They were, instead, quiet chairmen of the board.

Much more important than these men were such Republican senators as James G. Blaine of Maine, Orville H. Platt of Connecticut, and Nelson W. Aldrich of Rhode Island. The Republicans consistently chose their presidential candidates from the Middle West, so as to tap the strength of the huge transplanted Yankee community in that region, but their party was run by its Congressional leaders from New England. Elected to Congress year in and year out from heavily Republican constituencies, dominating that body because their seniority gave them control of its key committees, and accustomed to watching presidents come and go, they set the tone of Republicanism. Such men instinctively thought sympathetically of the well-to-do middle and upper classes, overwhelmingly British and old-stock American in ethnic composition and ways of life, for such peoples comprised the core of their party. New England, furthermore, was by this time solidly industrial, making its Republican legislators ardent disciples of Alexander Hamilton and Henry Clay. Governments, in their view, should work closely with the capitalists of the country to develop its resources. This meant high protective tariffs, an expansive money supply, and government aid in the form of internal improvements, land grants, and timber rights.

By these devices, they firmly believed that they were doing the best for all Americans: creating jobs, making the nation prosperous, and providing opportunities for hard-working folk to get ahead. "I am entirely sick of this idea," said Senator Platt, "that the lower the prices are the better for the country. . . ." Competition was ruinous, not helpful. Businessmen should be free to set their prices at whatever level would return them a fair profit. What lay behind the constant anti-business attacks which came from Democrats, Populists, socialists, and from the working classes? Sour envy: little else. Republican senators warmly adopted that form of social Darwinism which insisted that the rich got their wealth because they were more able and talented; which argued that nothing should be done to help the poor because nature intended, by the rule of survival of the fittest, to keep them in that condition. Social classes, said their favorite philosopher, William Graham Sumner of Yale, owed nothing to each other. Each must look out for itself.

The rise of Grover Cleveland

By the 1880s this philosophy of government aids to business development had begun to produce a powerful counter-attack. On every hand, critics said—with abundant evidence—this simply produced massive corruption. Legislators and public officials regularly sold their votes and influence. American public life stunk of graft from top to bottom. Democratic leaders traditionally distrusted the profit motive, and regarded the booming industrialization of the country with alarm. Carried upward by this kind of public sentiment, the Democrat Grover Cleveland rocketed out of total obscurity in the early 1880s. A reforming mayor of Buffalo, New York, and then governor of the state (1882–84), he consistently vetoed proposals that would have granted funds, special privileges, and immunities to banks, railroad and subway companies, electric power corporations, and even ice houses. In 1885, he was inaugurated as President of the United States, the first Democrat to hold that post in almost twenty-five years. No one in American history had ever risen so swiftly.

The Liberal Republicans

His victory came in part because Liberal Republicans, whom contemptuous Republican regulars called Mugwumps, had swung behind him en masse. For years they had been alarmed at the close ties that were growing between their party and business interests. In 1872 they had actually broken loose to form a separate "Liberal Republican" party. With the agreement of the Democrats, they ran Horace Greeley for president against Ulysses Grant, only to suffer a humiliating defeat. Since then they had drifted uncomfortably back to their party, hoping vainly for its rejuvenation along less capitalistic lines. The nomination of James G. Blaine for the presidency, in 1884, was too much for them, because he was too openly linked to businessmen. Cleveland, on the other hand, was an honest and courageous man whose values seemed very much like their own. For as long as he was in the presidency, they were among his warmest supporters, teaching him much about the need for lower tariffs and a reformed civil service, and bringing with them the nation's intellectual classes. Primarily from the northeastern states, they were men of high moral concerns, many of them veterans of the fight against slavery.

The transatlantic Liberal-Democratic community

The Liberal Republicans looked to British liberalism for their name and ideas. Indeed, for America in general the half century from the Civil War to the First World War was the great Anglo-American age. For many reasons, Great Britain was the most prominent object on the American horizon. It was perhaps the most powerful nation in world affairs; its empire circled the globe; its industries were everywhere admired and copied; its Parliament was a "mother of parliaments"; and its wealth was an immense force in the world economy. The Bank of England was then the towering financial bastion of world capitalism that Wall Street became later on. For decades the American economy had been fueled by British investments. This created a rampant anti-British feeling in the western states, whose mines, cattle ranches, and lumbering operations were often controlled from London. The American middle and upper classes, British in descent, liked things British as they had in colonial days. The Irish hated Great Britain, and made the air ring with attacks on English misrule in Ireland.

The Cleveland Democrats and the Liberal Republicans admired the great leader of the British Liberal party, William Gladstone, and relied on the economic ideas of John Stuart Mill, the party's principal philosopher and economist. His *Principles of Political Economy* (1848), together with Adam Smith's venerated *Wealth of Nations* (1776), provided magisterial authority for the low tariff-sound money outlook. Gladstone's legendary victory in the 1840s in converting Britain to free trade, and his foreign policy, which condemned militarism and power politics in international relations, made him a world figure. At Princeton, in the 1870s, a young student named Woodrow Wilson hung Gladstone's picture over his desk and practiced the great man's ideas and style.

At the same time, American reformers read Charles Dickens and other British novelists who attacked oppression of the poor; traveled through British cities to see how their municipal authorities solved the problems that made American cities so ugly, corrupt, and filthy; and learned that a strong central government was needed to grapple successfully with social ills. Americans, in brief, continued to live and work within the orbit of British culture.

Cleveland as president

Grover Cleveland was a Jacksonian Democrat and a Presbyterian. He had been reared in western New York during the 1840s, and the ideals of

Jacksonian democracy were dinned into his ears. From this training he derived a conviction that society is always in danger of being exploited by the wealthy and powerful, whether they tried to control the currency in their interest as in Jackson's day, or to build protective tariffs as in his own. His Presbyterianism, derived from his father, a devotedly orthodox minister, gave him a brooding outlook on human affairs that carried a strong Calvinist coloration. What he saw, through these lenses, was a scene of grab and scramble, each person trying to get advantages over the rest. Greed, privilege, self-indulgence, petty graft—these were the forces which to him seemed to dominate American life. He was obsessed with the notion that the apparatus of privilege and special advantage, which in his view the Republicans had built, was bringing on national decay. The "spirit of selfishness is abroad in the land," he would say; unreasonable profits came from exploiting the masses. The key words that studded his speeches and writings were *selfish* and *sordid.* He lived in a corrupt age, and it revolted him.

His Presbyterianism gave him a strong sense of duty, and of right principles which cannot be violated without grave harm to society. Also, Presbyterian theology asserted that God is an active, intervening, vigorous sovereign, and so was Cleveland as president. He assumed that the chief executive should use his powers forthrightly, and he did so. Senators overshadowed Republican presidents, but not Cleveland. He worked fully within the Democratic tradition of the strong presidency. He had been summarily plucked from obscurity and sent swiftly to the White House, and he derived from this an unshakable conviction that the people were on his side.

Cleveland and the economy

Cleveland's main concern was to cleanse the nation's economic system. He was more worried about the spoliation of the West than by any other problem in his first administration. He

Grover Cleveland, first Democratic president since the Civil War. His stolid determination to cleanse politics, reduce the tariff to aid consumers and attack privilege, and introduce civil service, made him admired by millions.
Courtesy of the Library of Congress

stopped all land-office activity to investigate fraudulent claims, and harshly condemned the great robberies that had taken place. Cattle kings, land syndicates, railroad companies, and lumber barons had created a huge system of land monopoly. Attacking the "colossal greed" of the culprits, he forced them to return more than eighty million acres. In his second administration (1893–97) he continued his assault upon speculators, and began the process of setting aside great timbered regions as national forests.

In 1886, when the decisions of the United States Supreme Court took away the power of the states to regulate the rates of railroads, Cleveland gave his support to congressmen who wanted to establish some form of federal control. As mayor and governor, he had warned strongly against the harmful power of unchecked corporations. Now he agreed with those who wanted to follow British practice and establish a strong, independent commission. When the Interstate Commerce Commission bill came before him in February 1887, he ignored attacks on its constitutionality and signed it. Though unprecedented in American practice, it was quite in line with his belief that the sovereign power of the national government should be actively used.

Cleveland and the civil service

His first task, however, was to make civil service reform a reality. This involved him in seemingly endless labors. The Pendleton Civil Service Act, which established the beginnings of the system whereby government employees were appointed on the basis of demonstrated ability and were not removable save for incompetence, had been enacted in 1883, following Garfield's tragic assassination by a disgruntled party worker. However, President Arthur had been unable to make the new law very effective, and the situation continued one in which presidents spent months deciding on literally thousands of individual appointments. The White House halls were clogged with applicants and their politician friends. Constant pressure from all directions was applied on the president. Cleveland struggled his way doggedly through all of this, working toward the goal of a professional civil service, though often sliding backwards as he responded to party needs. The extent of his contribution is shown in the fact that, while at the beginning of his first term in 1885 it was a specific exception for an office to be under civil service regulations, by the end of his second term in 1897, it required a specific exception for such a post not to be.

The Irish fought Cleveland bitterly in this cause. Civil service reform would remove their ability to make party appointments, keep the organization strong, and as they put it, continue to open government employment to the poor. The Mugwumps, on the other hand, were absolutely obsessed by the cause. This, to them, was the nation's most important single undertaking. An efficient, educated, orderly civil service, removed from partisan control, would, as in the British example, be the chief instrument of executive action in a modernized, rationally-organized state. This kept the Mugwumps in a constant combat with the Irish. No cause, indeed, more sharply highlighted the conflict between ethnic politics, with its essentially inward-turning concern with local affairs—getting "our boys" a job—and the national outlook of a reforming, university-trained elite. The Irish believed government should be personal and direct, built upon networks of mutual obligation and relationship; the Mugwumps believed, instead, that it should be impersonal, efficient, and directed by general rules and national needs. In this controversy, as so often in public affairs, the conflict is to be understood not primarily as a partisan one, but as part of the long social transformation which has occurred, in every compartment of national and international life, from traditional to modernized forms of government and culture.

Cleveland and the tariff

It was the tariff question that became the great cause of Cleveland's presidencies. Since the Civil War it had become an accepted fact of American life, added to again and again. To Liberal Democrats, the tariff question was one of the most crucial issues of the nineteenth century, and they never lost interest in it. They regarded low tariffs as essential to social justice, a healthy international economy, and peace itself. How could the world become an open and free trading community, they asked, if protective tariffs chopped it up into mutually exclusive segments? Genuine prosperity would arrive only if the world were thought of as a single trading community, and there was an international division of labor. Each country would make the product for which it was best suited and no industry would gain unfair advantages. Consumers would not have to pay higher prices to protected home industries. Economic rivalries would give way to cooperation, and world peace would be assured.

In 1887 Cleveland startled the nation by devoting his entire annual message to Congress to an attack on the protective tariff. Thus dramatically inaugurated, a boiling national controversy over the tariff began which was reminiscent of Andrew Jackson's Bank War. Mugwumps were delighted. New York and New England intellectuals threw themselves into the campaign—one in which, happily for them, they were no longer in conflict with the Catholic Irish and the city bosses. Cleveland lost the battle for a lower tariff in 1888, but he was thoroughly aroused to his cause. It had become part of his belief that the nation had become sick to its core with special economic privilege and materialism. Just before he left the White House, at the end of his first term—Benjamin Harrison defeated him in the electoral college, if not in the popular vote totals, in the election of 1888—in his annual message to Congress he blasted the power of great corporations and the race for money and profit. Fortunes were no longer made by hard work, he said, or by enlightened foresight or sturdy enterprise; instead, they were made by arrangements in which the government discriminated in favor of the manufacturers. Unreasonable profits came largely from exploiting the masses. Trusts, combinations, and monopolies ruled the land, "while the citizen is struggling far in the rear or is trampled to death beneath an iron heel."

The Republican interlude

Benjamin Harrison's election began the Republican interlude between Cleveland's first and second administrations. The new president was thoroughly Republican. "Cheaper coats," he said in defending the wool tariff, would "necessarily [involve] a cheaper man and woman under the coat." He warned that the Democrats represented the South and its disloyalty and were responsible for the horrors of the Civil War. Bitterly hostile toward the British, as were many Republicans, strong nationalists that they were, and resentful of London's preeminence, he delighted in attacking the English, referring to the "grasping avarice" of their diplomacy.

In control of both houses of Congress and the presidency for the first time since 1875, the Republicans moved ahead quickly. They admitted a large group of new states, which promptly sent Republican representatives and senators to Congress: North Dakota, South Dakota, Montana, and Washington in 1889; Wyoming and Idaho in 1890. To dissipate the growing surplus in the Treasury, which was withholding too much capital from the national economy, and at the same time to give expression to their belief that the national government should be actively used to develop the country and its industries, the Republicans advanced on two fronts: internal improvements and an increased tariff. So costly was their program of public works that the session was called the Billion-Dollar Congress. They advanced an ingenious argument that the way to reduce the revenues created by the tariff was to raise them so high as absolutely to exclude imports from abroad. The McKinley Tariff, named for Congressman William McKinley of Ohio, did more: it gave protection to industries that hardly even existed as yet, such as tin plating (thus bringing disaster to the Welsh tin plating industry), in order to stimulate their creation; and raised the general level of rates to a new record of forty-nine percent.

Thomas B. Reed, Speaker of the House, imposed rules on that body that speeded up its deliberations by giving far more authority to the Speaker to prevent dilatory tactics. Loudly criticized, "Czar" Reed blandly held firm. Responding to national demands which came from both parties, the Republicans in 1890 enacted the Sherman Anti-Trust Act. There were few who could stomach the idea of outright monopoly. Furthermore, they reacted to western currency appeals by passing the Sherman Silver Purchase Act.

The Democrats responded to this forthright Republican program with a spectacular nationwide campaign against the tariff. Meanwhile, the prohibitionism controversy, and the parochial school battles, worked their explosive political medicine in local and state elections. The result, in the Congressional election of 1890, was a national Democratic landslide: 236 Democrats sat in the new House of Representatives, compared to only 88 Republicans.

The return of Cleveland

Now Grover Cleveland took to the hustings again, going back and forth across the northern states to hammer again and again against materialism and special privilege. The spirit of selfishness, he said, filled the air with demands for special privilege from the government. The McKinley Tariff seemed to him the highest expression of greed. "Vile, unsavory forms," he said in Boston, "rise to the surface of our agitated political waters, and gleefully anticipate, in the anxiety of selfish interest, their opportunity to fatten upon corruption and debauched suffrage." Nominated again by his party in 1892, he achieved a landslide victory. He won 277 votes in the electoral college against Harrison's 145, a popular plurality of nearly 400,000 votes, and Democratic majorities in both houses of Congress for the first time since the 1850s.

Cleveland and the currency

Now, however, a new issue was arising that swept away all of Cleveland's plans. The Populists and growing numbers of western and southern Democrats were calling for the free and unlimited coinage of silver at a ratio with gold that would result in a moderate inflation of the currency. The former legal ratio that silverites in-sisted be reestablished was sixteen to one. In the mid-1890s, silver in the open world market was valued at a ratio of thirty-two to one with gold. Clearly, if the United States established a sixteen-to-one ratio, silver would flood to it from all over the world in order to be exchanged for gold, and, under free coinage, turned into currency, thus expanding the money supply.

Cleveland's own position was clear and unshaken. All the voices he trusted, whether those of Jacksonian Democracy or of British Liberalism, instructed him in classic "sound money" principles. From the beginning of his first term to the end of his second, Cleveland never questioned them. He persistently held that the United States could not maintain a bimetallic currency alone in the world. The two metals would part company entirely as gold was drained from the Treasury either by panic or by the profit that could be made by exchanging cheap silver coin for the more valuable gold. This would be disastrous, he said in 1886, for gold was "still the standard of value and necessary in our dealings with other countries." Furthermore, bankers and speculators would inevitably get richer if the free-silver experiment were tried, for clever, powerful men could always profit from price rises and declines while "the laboring men and women of the land, most defenseless of all, will find that the dollar received for the wage of their toil has sadly shrunk in its purchasing power."

James Laughlin, a University of Chicago economist, attacked the free-silver idea: "As free coinage of silver would inevitably result in a rise of prices, it would immediately result in the fall of wages. Its first effect would be to diminish the purchasing power of all our wages. The man who gets $500 or $1,000 a year as a fixed rate of wages or salary will find he could buy just half as much as now. Yes, but someone will say, the employer will raise his wages. Now, will he? But the facts on that point are clear and indisputable. It has been one of the undisputed facts of history that, when prices rise, the wages of labor are the last to advance;

and when prices fall, the wages of labor are the first to decline. Free coinage of silver would make all the articles of the laborer's consumption cost him 100 percent more unless he can get a rise in his wages by dint of strikes and quarrels and all the consequent dissatisfaction arising from friction between the employer and employee.

"The damage runs in other directions, [wiping out savings laid aside] for old age, for sickness, for death, for widows and orphans, or by insurance. . . . No invasion of hostile armies, burning and destroying as they advance, could by any possibility equal the desolation and ruin which would thus be forced upon the great mass of the American people. [Meanwhile] the shrewd ones, the bankers, etc., will be easily able to take care of themselves; while we plain people will be robbed of our hard-won earnings without any hope of compensation.

"In conclusion . . . extraordinary as is the proposal for free coinage, it is in truth only a huge deceit. It was born in the private offices of the silver kings, nursed at the hands of speculators, clothed in economic error, fed on boodle, exercised in the lobby of Congress, and as sure as there is honesty and truth in the American heart it will die young. . . ." (*Facts about Money* [1895].)

Repeal of the Sherman Silver Purchase Act

When Cleveland began his second term in 1893, the Treasury's gold reserve was dropping rapidly below the $100 million level, which traditionally was regarded as essential to maintain confidence in the nation's credit and currency. A massive depression which began just as he was beginning his second term, the panic induced by the free-silver campaign, and the effects of the Sherman Silver Purchase Act of 1890—which allowed the free exchange of silver coin for gold—combined to produce the crisis situation. Cleveland decided that his most imperative duty, even before moving on the tariff question, was to obtain repeal of the Sherman Silver Purchase Act. What followed

was a long and bitter struggle stretching out over many months in which he exerted every ounce of his executive power over Congress, freely brandishing the patronage axe to force men to vote his way. Eventually he won. The Sherman Silver Purchase Act was repealed and the gold standard was saved. But prosilver Democrats from the South and West revolted. In effect, two Democratic parties came into being. Cleveland had insisted that the depression would end once silver purchase was repealed and people regained confidence in the currency, but this did not happen. The nation sank deeper into depression, and more and more Democrats turned away from the hapless Cleveland. Lonely, abused on all sides, he grew bitter and depressed while remaining doggedly convinced that he was right. When the young congressman William Jennings Bryan of Nebraska rose to take leadership of the silver Democrats and stump the country as the Democratic presidential candidate in 1896, Cleveland morosely described Bryanism as a "sort of disease in the body politic." The silverites had "burglarized and befouled the Democratic home."

Tariff failure

The president's fight over repeal of silver purchase destroyed any hopes for tariff reform, for he had made far too many enemies. He was able to force a tariff reduction bill through the House, but the Senate transformed it. The Wilson-Gorman Tariff emerged almost as protectionist as the McKinley Tariff it replaced. (An average of forty-one percent on dutiable goods as compared with forty-nine percent.) Cleveland condemned it as "party perfidy and party dishonor," but let it become law without his signature.

Except for saving the gold standard and greatly widening the civil service, he had failed in his major domestic objectives. Cleveland's administration now entered the endless dog days that made the rest of his term a nightmare. He knew that he had powerful interests in the business world principally to thank for his tariff failure. "The trusts and combinations—the communism of pelf—whose machinations have prevented us from reaching the success we deserved," he wrote a friend, "should not be forgotten nor forgiven." Meanwhile, the country remained sunk deep in economic collapse.

The depression of the 1890s

Millions of men were out of work in the mid-1890s. City police stations and government buildings were jammed every night with men sleeping in corridors and stairways. The resources of private charity were soon gone. Some cities dispensed aid, but the states and federal government refused. New York's governor rejected a plan of work relief, saying, "In America, the people support the government; it is not the province of the government to support the people."

Desperate men organized marches on Washington. Jacob S. Coxey's "army" from Ohio of about five hundred men was the most famous of seventeen such groups in the spring of 1894. All they got was sympathy and a strengthened determination on the part of the established authorities not to yield to "mob rule." Some 1,400 strikes were called in that frightful year, affecting almost 700,000 people, but few won restoration of wage cuts.

The most spectacular strike was that of the American Railway Union against the Pullman Company of Chicago. Some 60,000 men eventually struck, expanding a boycott against Pullman's cars nationwide. Richard Olney, Cleveland's attorney general and a former railroad lawyer, was determined to crush the strike. Using the excuse of protecting the mails, he authorized the swearing in of 3,600 deputies to "preserve order" in Chicago, though as yet no violence had occurred. Then he secured an injunction calling on the American Railway Union to end the strike. On the day it was served, a mob ditched a mail train in Blue Island, Illinois. Thereafter the con-troversy escalated. Cleveland, always determined to enforce what he regarded as rightful authority, decided to end the "reign of terror" in Chicago. Without waiting, as the Constitution requires, for the state of Illinois to request federal aid, he sent 2,000 troops to Chicago on the fourth of July, 1894. In response, mobs took over the railroad yards, burning and destroying cars and stealing property. The leader of the American Railway Union, Eugene V. Debs, was imprisoned, tried for contempt of court, and sentenced to six months in jail.

In the congressional elections of 1894, which took place soon afterward, the Democrats suffered one of the gravest defeats in American political history. The Republicans won large majorities in both houses of Congress. The Populists polled almost 1.5 million votes, a large increase over their 1892 total, sending four senators and four congressmen to Washington.

The election of 1896

As the depression worsened, the silver issue rose to overshadow all others. As against free silver, the Republicans now firmly supported the gold standard. Their inflationism had always been relatively moderate. At the same time, they urged high tariffs and nominated William McKinley, governor of Ohio, for the presidency. The Democrats were wholly at sea. Most Democrats detested Cleveland, but who was to replace him? When the party's national convention gathered in Chicago in July 1896, it was suddenly electrified by an exciting speech given by a young ex-congressman from Nebraska, William Jennings Bryan. "Upon which side will the Democratic party fight," he cried out, "upon the side of 'the idle holders of idle capital,' or upon the side of 'the struggling masses'? You come to us and tell us that the great cities are in favor of the gold standard; we reply that the great cities rest upon our broad and fertile prairies. . . . Having behind us the producing masses of this nation and the world, supported by the commercial interests, the laboring interests and the toilers everywhere, we will answer their demand for a gold standard by saying to them: You shall not press down upon the brow of labor this crown of thorns, you shall not crucify mankind upon a cross of gold." Pandemonium broke loose. Delegates cheered wildly, leapt on chairs, and wept with joy. After preliminary maneuvering, the thirty-six-year old Bryan was chosen as the Democratic nominee for president. Then the convention adopted a platform condemning Cleveland's policies, especially on the gold standard and the crushing of the railway strikers. It also called for a low tariff, an income tax, the abolition of national banknotes (those issued by private banks) and—now wholly won to the cause—for free coinage of silver.

Gold Democrats were shocked. Some with-

drew to form the National Democratic party, which nominated Senator John M. Palmer of Illinois. The Populists were equally nonplussed. Their issue had been taken from them. Should they fuse with the Democrats? If they did not, their votes for a different candidate might ruin the hopes of free silver. In their national convention they hit on the compromise of nominating Bryan while choosing their own vice-presidential nominee, Thomas E. Watson of Georgia.

Thereafter, the Populists simply faded away by merging with the Democrats. Many Populists held back, however. They had hoped that their party would persevere in the South by providing a genuine workingman's party, in opposition to the Democrats, that would unify both white and black labor. In the North, they had hoped that

The election of 1896

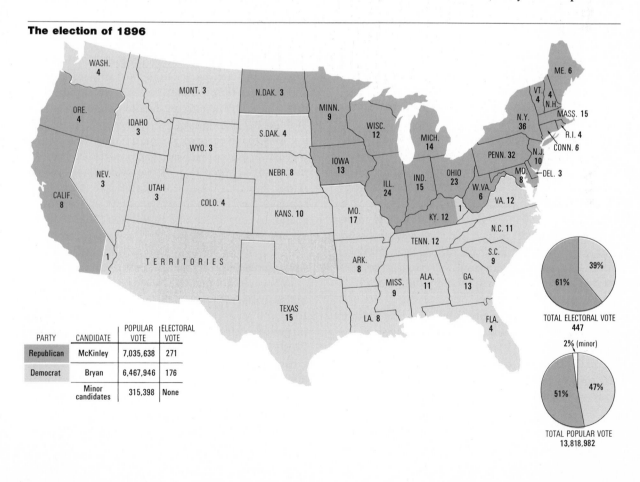

PARTY	CANDIDATE	POPULAR VOTE	ELECTORAL VOTE
Republican	McKinley	7,035,638	271
Democrat	Bryan	6,467,946	176
Minor candidates		315,398	None

TOTAL ELECTORAL VOTE
447

TOTAL POPULAR VOTE
13,818,982

populism would flourish as a broad reform movement, unifying both city and farm. Now all their goals seemed swept away in the interests of one cause alone—free silver.

William Jennings Bryan: Christian Democrat

Bryan was hated by many Republicans. Theodore Roosevelt said he and his silver Democrats were "plotting a social revolution and the subversion of the American Republic." But William Jennings Bryan was no wild-eyed radical. A deeply Christian man, he was also a Jeffersonian trying to apply the Virginian's creed in modern conditions. "The Democratic party, if I understand its position," he said, "denies the economic as well as the political advantage of private monopoly and promises to oppose it wherever it manifests itself. It offers as an alternative competition where competition is possible, and public monopoly [as in public ownership of railroads] wherever circumstances are such as to prevent competition."

He had wanted to be a minister: now he was an evangelist in politics. Bryan campaigned like no one ever had before: 18,000 miles and 600 speeches in three months, before five million people. His campaign funds were small while those of the Republicans were enormous. From Standard Oil alone the Republicans received a donation of $250,000, which was almost as large as Bryan's entire war chest. Newspapers and magazines were against him almost unanimously, but his obvious sincerity and his courage in taking on apparently insuperable odds won him widespread respect.

Bryan won only the Solid South, some of the Great Plains states, and the Mountain West. With 7.1 million votes, McKinley was 600,000 votes ahead of Bryan and won an electoral margin of 271 to 176. It was the largest total popular vote in American history and a landmark victory: the oscillation that for twenty years had taken place in Washington, first one party and then the other winning majorities in an evenly-matched strug-gle, suddenly ended. The third Civil War party system was shattered, and the fourth Progressive Era party system was forming. For more than thirty years after 1896, the Republicans dominated American political life. The Democrats held onto little more than the one-party South; the Republicans firmly held what amounted to a one-party North and West, and were almost beyond challenge. Even the election of Woodrow Wilson on the Democratic ticket in 1912 occurred only because the Republicans split among themselves and ran two candidates. His re-election in 1916 was the only straight Democratic victory in nine presidential elections. Not until the depression of 1929 struck the country was the overwhelming Republican supremacy destroyed.

Analysis

Why was this so? In the mid-1890s, the fires of cultural conflict died down. Republican leaders, recognizing the harm that the anti-immigrant crusade was doing them, pulled back, talking far less about drink and parochial schools and far more about developing the economy and providing jobs for everyone. William McKinley led the way toward the new Republican tactic of cultural pluralism. Then the massive depression which struck the country in 1893 caused tens of thousands of Democrats, in every ethnic and religious group, in country or city, in the middle and upper classes as well as the lower, to swing Republican. People looking for jobs began thinking of themselves in economic, rather than cultural, terms.

When Bryan and his western and southern inflationists took over the Democratic party in 1896, millions in the Middle West and Northeast turned away. New England had never trusted the West: its burgeoning growth had always seemed a threat to the Northeast. Neither Middle West nor Northeast was comfortable with the idea of Southern domination in the national government, as it seemed would occur if Bryan won. Furthermore, the city masses accepted the Republican argument that the silverites' campaign for cur-

The Republican press satirized William Jennings Bryan, whose open piety and many references to Biblical texts to support his cause laid him open to the charge of desecrating the Bible, while really—his critics said—being an anarchist.
Culver Pictures, Inc.

rency inflation would raise the cost of living. Conversely, they agreed that higher tariffs would start industries going again and provide jobs. In addition, Bryan's strongly Christian style of oratory and appeal repelled many immigrants, who began to fear that a Bryan victory would lead to a renewed Protestant crusade. The result was that the Republicans won the cities, long the Democratic stronghold, and with that victory secured a lasting predominance.

The Irish never left William Jennings Bryan. They remained doggedly Democratic and were thereafter, in consequence, more powerful than ever within their party. But the other non-British ethnic groups, and especially the German Lutherans, decamped to the Republicans in huge numbers. Since the Scandinavians, a firmly pietistic Protestant group from Denmark, Sweden, and Norway, had always been strongly Republican (and prohibitionist), what emerged within the Republican party after 1896 as its ethnic core was a WASP coalition (white, Anglo-Saxon—the term refers generally to persons of northern European origin—and Protestant). It contained the English, Scots, and Welsh, from Britain; the great numbers of British Canadians who had been emigrating into the country, bringing their strong anti-Catholicism with them; German and Scandinavian Protestants; and those who were, or thought of themselves as, part of the old stock Yankee tradition.

After the election of 1896, Republicans had the extraordinary good fortune to be the party in power when prosperity returned on account of the influx of enormous new supplies of gold bullion from discoveries in South Africa, Colorado, and the Yukon. Free silver disappeared as an issue, for the currency supply was expanding again and market prices rose buoyantly. At the same time, the Republicans' vigorous ideas about using national power to develop the economy, and—after the rise of the progressive Republicans—to enact major reforms, helped to consolidate for them a strong and continuing hold on the

loyalties of a majority of the nation's voters in most elections.

The new president: William McKinley

The new president, William McKinley, was a gentle and kindly man, through and through a politician, and sincerely and devotedly a Republican. He was a composite expression of practically everything that his side of American politics had always represented and believed in: its moralism, devotion to upright ways of life and organized religion, preference for the military, dislike of "southernism," and its advocacy of a high tariff—economic nationalist outlook. He was a zealous Methodist and was deeply concerned with personal morality. A courageous soldier during the Civil War, he had seemed prudish to his compatriots with his prayer meetings in camp, his avoidance of alcohol, and his chaste life. Always neatly dressed, wearing his rather formal clothes with a certain erect style, he proudly used his title of "Major" all his life, it becoming his political trademark. Believing the government should be used to regulate conduct, as a congressman he submitted floods of anti-liquor petitions from his constituents, supported temperance work, and while the anti-Mormon outcry was at its height (when Utah was seeking statehood) opposed polygamy. He and his wife, though never anti-Catholic nativists, actively supported Protestant missionary activity. He had hated slavery, fought willingly in the war, detested and condemned southern power, and supported voting rights for blacks.

William McKinley was a strong nationalist who admired Henry Clay's Whig party and built his whole career out of appeals for a new American System like that which Clay had espoused. The passion of his life was the tariff. Springing from a long line of iron makers, as a child he had heard his father complain that foreign competition made honest men close their forges. "With me," he said "[the high tariff] position is a deep conviction, not a theory. I believe in it and thus warmly advocate it because enveloped in it are my country's highest development and greatest prosperity; out of it come the greatest gains to the people, the greatest comforts to the masses, the widest encouragement for manly aspirations, with the largest rewards, dignifying and elevating our citizenship, upon which the safety and purity and permanency of our political system depend." He was impatient with those who called for free international trade. The markets of the world, he said, "in our present condition are a snare and delusion. We will reach them whenever we can undersell competing nations, and no sooner." By closing off the domestic market to foreigners, American factories would grow to the point where they could compete in the world. Meanwhile, rising prices within the national market would lead to higher wages. "Cheap goods," he said, "meant hard times. When prices were the lowest, did you not have the least money to buy with?" Academic free trade doctrines exasperated him as idle philosophy, and he was constantly irritated at the fact that "every college in the country seemed to produce tariff reformers."

McKinley came from northwestern Ohio, where a growing network of metal industries and their workers gave strong support to his policies. It was not that he was linked directly with any particular industry; he simply believed that an American System would create a prosperous and happy republic. Indeed, he was widely noted as the Republican with the closest ties with labor. Practically his first act as a congressman was to submit petitions from steel workers in his district against the reduction of tariffs. As governor of Ohio he worked for safety devices in industry to protect workers, an arbitration system to require employers to negotiate meaningfully with their employees, and laws establishing fines and jail sentences for employers who refused to permit employees to join unions. He was always firmly against violence in labor disputes, and freely used

troops to restore order, but sought to be "firm and kind."

McKinley as president

The new president broke sharply with Cleveland's haughty distance from congressmen, throwing open his doors to legislators, treating them warmly, and establishing good relations with Congress that survived throughout his administration. Noting his kindliness and sincerity, people held him in affectionate esteem. True to his Whiggish traditions, he did not threaten compulsion to get his way, and he gave his cabinet members freedom to run their own departments. He was always slow in making crucial decisions, but rock-firm thereafter.

When inaugurated in March 1897, he called for an upward revision of the tariff, an international conference to explore establishing silver coinage worldwide while maintaining the gold standard in the interim, and reciprocal trade agreements with other nations. Happily for him, prosperity was returning and the raging class conflicts of the depression years were dying away. A new day of content and plenty seemed dawning, when men could again enjoy long summer afternoons, dreaming days on the river, quiet canters through the woods. McKinley was everybody's friend, the spokesman of national unity, a genial president who refused to stir up enemies. His cabinet was made up of older conservative men with solid fortunes. Reform was clearly a topic to be shunned; the country was tired of histrionics.

McKinley now sent negotiators abroad, for he intended to pursue the notion of getting an international agreement to make both silver and gold the basis for national currencies. The British and French were solidly opposed, however, and the project died. Much more important to the president, in any event, was the tariff, and he called a special session of Congress to raise it almost as soon as he was inaugurated. The Dingley Tariff, which Congress thereupon produced, sent rates soaring to their highest level (fifty-two percent), though it included some limited arrangements for reciprocal lowering of tariffs with other nations. President McKinley then began vigorous efforts to secure such agreements, for "good trade insures good will," he told the Cincinnati Commercial Club in 1897. American industries, he said, had now been built up to the point where they needed the markets of the world.

With returning prosperity, Congress passed the Gold Standard Act of 1900. The gold dollar was declared to be henceforth the sole standard of currency, and all other forms of money were to be maintained at a parity with gold. The law also made it easier for banks to be established in small towns, thus meeting the long-standing complaint of farmers of the unavailability of local loan capital. Following this, banks were allowed to issue more currency on the federal bonds they held, and taxes on issued banknotes were reduced. As a result, the volume of banknotes doubled by 1904. Over 500 new banks were organized in rural areas. For more than a decade these two measures, the Dingley Tariff and the Gold Standard Act, held firm and introduced some stability into the nation's taxing and fiscal arrangements.

But domestic issues were not to be the dominating features of the McKinley presidency. Just a year after his inauguration in 1897, the nation went to war for the first time in more than thirty years. What led up to this fateful event? This is the question which will next take our attention.

Bibliography.

Three books that were especially valuable to me in writing this chapter: Two brilliant studies by "new political historians" who have paid close attention to ethnocultural factors: Paul Kleppner, *The Cross of Culture: A Social Analysis of Midwestern Politics 1850–1900* (1970), and Richard Jensen, *The Winning of the Midwest: Social and Political Conflict, 1888–1896* (1971). On Grover Cleveland and the concept of the transatlantic Liberal-Democratic community, reference may be made to Chapter 8, "Grover Cleveland: The Democrat as Social Moralist," in Robert Kelley, *The Transatlantic Persuasion: The Liberal-Democratic Mind in the Age of Gladstone* (1969).

How have historians looked at the topic?

The older way of looking at Gilded Age politics, as a time of unique irresponsibility in politics, the two parties being absolutely devoid of principle, and capitalists calling all the tunes, runs through practically all of the older writing on the period, and persists in some of the new. Charles Beard's great textbook, used year in and year out in college classrooms, is a classic case: *The Rise of American Civilization* (4 vols., 1927–42). Matthew Josephson's *The Politicos, 1865–1896** (1938) is another. More recent books of this persuasion are: Ray Ginger, *Age of Excess: The United States from 1877 to 1914** (1966); John G. Sproat's *"The Best Men": Liberal Reformers in the Gilded Age* (1968); and H. S. Merrill's *Bourbon Leader: Grover Cleveland and the Democratic Party** (1957), which is diametrically opposite in treatment to the account given in these pages.

Geoffrey Blodgett, author of a subtle and revealing study, *The Gentle Reformers: Massachusetts Democrats in the Cleveland Era* (1966), has recently contrasted the older and newer ways of understanding the period in an important article, "A New Look at the American Gilded Age," in *Historical Reflections* [a newly established Canadian journal], I (Winter, 1974). For others who are taking the newer tack, see: Samuel T. McSeveney's superb study, based upon quantitative analysis, *The Politics of Depression: Political Behavior in the Northeast, 1893–1896* (1972); Gerald W. McFarland, *Mugwumps, Morals and Politics, 1884–1920* (1975); Tom E. Terrill, *The Tariff, Politics, and American Foreign Policy, 1874–1901* (1973); Edward P. Crapol, *America for Americans: Economic Nationalism and Anglophobia in the late Nineteenth Century* (1973); Robert D. Marcus, *Grand Old Party: Political Structure in the Gilded Age 1880–1896* (1971); Frederick C. Luebke, *Immi-*

grants and Politics: The Germans of Nebraska, 1880–1900 (1969); Walter Dean Burnham, Critical Elections and the Mainsprings of American Politics (1970).

Many other studies are of value. They include: Rowland Tappan Berthoff, British Immigrants in Industrial America 1790–1950 (1953); Arthur Mann, Yankee Reformers In the Urban Age: Social Reform in Boston, 1880–1900 (1954); Ari Hoogenboom, Outlawing the Spoils: A History of the Civil Service Reform Movement 1865–1883 (1961); Robert H. Wiebe's seminal book, of wide importance among historians, The Search For Order 1877–1920 (1967); J. Rogers Hollingsworth, The Whirligig of Politics: The Democracy of Cleveland and Bryan (1963); Paolo E. Coletta, William Jennings Bryan (vol. 1–3, 1964–69). Essential is Robert P. Swierenga's article "Ethnocultural Political Analysis: A New Approach to American Ethnic Studies," in The Journal of American Studies, 5 (1971).

John A. Garraty's The New Commonwealth, 1877–1890* (1968), provides a fresh look at this period and avoids stereotypes; H. Wayne Morgan's William McKinley and His America (1963) gives a new look at a long-ignored president. While clearly establishing the corrupt methods used by Boss Tweed in New York City and others, Alexander B. Callow, Jr.'s The Tweed Ring* (1966) depicts city machines as peculiarly American phenomena whose creation reflected urban problems more than evil men. A solid and sympathetic account of party politics between 1877 and 1896 is his From Hayes to McKinley (1969), and the upper house of Congress receives a crucially important reassessment in David J. Rothman's Politics and Power: The United States Senate, 1869–1901 (1966).

* Available in paperback.

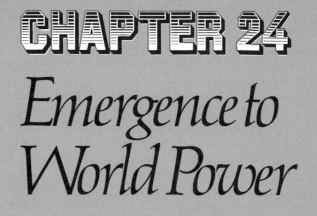

CHAPTER 24

Emergence to World Power

TIME LINE

1870–1900	Rise of Germany, Japan, Russia, and France as new world powers
1885	President Cleveland withdraws treaty giving the United States canal rights in Nicaragua
1890	Alfred Thayer Mahan, *The Influence of Sea Power upon History;* battleship navy authorized; merchant marine subsidy begins
1893	President Cleveland halts Hawaiian annexation; massive national depression begins
1895	Venezuela boundary crisis with Great Britain; Cuban Revolution begins; Senator Henry Cabot Lodge warns of British "encirclement"
1896	Congressional resolution asks recognition of Cuban belligerency; Cleveland refuses intervention; McKinley adopts more active policy
1898	Sinking of the *Maine;* Spanish-American War; Teller Amendment; Hawaii annexed; Wake Island occupied
1899	Peace treaty with Spain ratified; Philippines, American Samoa, Guam, and Puerto Rico acquired; first Open Door note regarding China
1900	The Boxer Rebellion; second Open Door note
1901	Theodore Roosevelt becomes twenty-sixth president of the United States upon death of McKinley; Platt Amendment makes Cuba a protectorate; Hay-Pauncefote Treaty with Britain allows United States to build and control an isthmian canal
1903	Panamanian Revolution; canal zone concession granted to the United States
1904	Roosevelt Corollary to Monroe Doctrine asserts right of intervention of Latin American internal affairs
1904–1914	Panama Canal built; Portsmouth Treaty settles Russo-Japanese War; American government assumes collection of Dominican customs
1906	Algeciras conference in relation to Morocco; San Francisco Board of Education orders segregation of Japanese school children
1907	"Gentlemen's Agreement" reduces Japanese immigration to the United States; Roosevelt sends "Great White Fleet" around the world
1908	Root-Takahira Agreement

A nation's foreign policy is the product of two influences—its internal condition and the world situation. When a country is remote and agricultural, it pays little heed to the outside world, especially if international conditions are not threatening. So it was with the United States for seventy years after the peace of 1815. It was concerned primarily with affairs on the North American continent, and the world was in a condition of relative stability. America was regarded by the nations of Europe as a minor power, rather on the level of Chile or Sweden today. The large navy it had built during the Civil War was allowed to molder away, and the nation clung to its traditional policy of non-involvement in world politics.

All this changed in the 1880s. The notion grew that the United States must leave behind its minor-power status and acquire the pride and dignity that comes with having an important say in world affairs. Influential voices called for an active foreign policy. In the 1890s the United States reacted startlingly to a series of incidents it would formerly have ignored: it almost went to war with Germany over a dispute concerning Samoa between 1889 and 1890; it nearly annexed Hawaii in 1893 after a rebellion by local Americans against the Hawaiian queen; it talked seriously of war with Italy and Chile over minor crises; it rattled the sword at Britain over a controversy in Venezuela in 1895; in a frenzy of national excitement it finally went to war with Spain in 1898, emerging after a brief conflict with an empire consisting of Puerto Rico, Guam, and the Philippine Islands, together with a protectorate over Cuba; and in 1898 it annexed Hawaii.

Now the United States was an audacious, ambitious, aggressive, even a covetous nation in its foreign relations. It put down a bloody insurrection in the Philippines; made the Caribbean an American lake by helping create the Republic of Panama, building a canal, and establishing protectorates over Haiti, Nicaragua, the Dominican Republic, and Honduras. President Theodore Roosevelt proclaimed America's right to intervene anywhere in the western hemisphere whenever it detected "chronic wrongdoing." Meanwhile, the United States sought footholds in Chinese markets by announcing its support of an Open Door in that country and by coming to agreements with Japan that tacitly recognized mutual spheres of influence. With unparalleled swiftness, a nation that had been of little importance in international politics became a world power.

The changed world

This came about, to begin with, because the world had changed. After 1870 Britain was no longer the dominant world power. Other nations, like Germany, Japan, Russia, and France, were challenging that supremacy. These emerging new powers equipped themselves with armies, navies, industry, and vigorous commerce. A global outburst of imperialism chopped up the map. Most of all, the rise of a united German Empire transfixed everyone. Its brilliant universities and advanced social welfare programs attracted the admiration of intellectuals and reformers; but its militarism and autocracy, together with the bellicose pronouncements of its "blood and iron" rulers, were frightening. Many in America and Britain were convinced that sometime in the future an armed conflict with Germany was inevitable. In the United States rumors went about in the 1890s that the European imperialists planned to invade Latin America. In 1895 Senator Henry Cabot Lodge electrified the Senate by a dramatic oration in which he pointed to a map showing British "encirclement" of the United States, from Canada down to Latin America and out to the islands of the Pacific. He warned that France and Germany would not be far behind if the British went unchallenged in their "plans."

Many felt demeaned by the fact that America was remaining quiescent while others were gobbling up huge empires. What glory was America winning? Progress was on the advance everywhere, it seemed, with barbarism being replaced by European law and order. How could the United States hold up its head when other nations were carrying the "white man's burden"?

Antiimperialist tradition

In the post-Civil War years, however, the antimilitarist, antiimperialist tradition remained strong. Widely shared among politicians of the transatlantic Liberal-Democratic community, its international spokesman was William Gladstone, long-time British Liberal premier, and in America its leading advocate was President Grover Cleveland. Fundamentally, these men were internationalists rather than nationalists. They believed that each country should be thought of as equal to every other, no nation overawing its neighbors. Protecting the small nations was especially important, for they were, in effect, hostages to freedom, testing points of the idea of the equality and safety of all nations. Moral values of freedom and the rights of all peoples to independence would govern world relations, not coercive force. Eventually, a system of international law would emerge that would protect everyone from oppression.

When Grover Cleveland became president in 1885 he signaled his loyalty to these ideals by withdrawing from the Senate a pending treaty giving the United States canal rights through Nicaragua. It was a coercive and expansionist document, he said. Since 1850, when America had made the Clayton-Bulwer Treaty with the British, the established policy had been that any canal constructed through the isthmus should be under international control. This idea, Cleveland insisted, should be retained. Then such a canal would "be removed from the chance of domination by any single power." In 1893, at the beginning of his second term, he withdrew another treaty from Senate consideration that would have annexed Hawaii to the United States. A group of Americans in Hawaii had recently led a rebellion with American aid against Queen Liliuokalani, and had negotiated the treaty. Cleveland thought the whole business of the rebellion and the inter-

position of American force disgraceful. All nations, whether weak or strong, he said to Congress, have the same rights. There is an international morality that governs and condemns such arrogant spoliations.

The quandary: Why imperialism?

Why was it that Cleveland and his antiimperialist followers failed to prevent America's turn to imperialism? The fact is, we really do not know. No method of historical inquiry can yield the final answer to so complex a question. We have a number of theories. Walter Millis in *The Martial Spirit* (1931) said the empire sprang from irrational militarism. Charles Beard and Mary Beard's influential *Rise of American Civilization* (1927–1942) described it as an outgrowth of capitalism. J. W. Pratt's *Expansionists of 1898* (1936) pointed to broad influences in the American population— racism, the missionary impulse, "yellow" (sensationalist) journalism, and a belief in Anglo-Saxon destiny to rule the world. After the Second World War, historians such as H. K. Beale and Ernest R. May, newly sensitized to the threat of aggression and the need for security, described imperialism as part of a larger process; that is, as part of America's rise to world power after 1890 in response to real threats from the outside world. In recent years new emphasis has been given to economic motives, as in Walter LaFeber's *The New Empire: An Interpretation of American Expansion, 1860–1898* (1963), which links imperialism to a search for markets. In brief, there were many roots of imperialism, each of which has its own historical advocate.

Roots of imperialism: The foreign policy elite

The making of American foreign policy, unlike domestic policy, is largely in the hands of one man—the president. As the war in Vietnam has demonstrated, he has enormous powers to act on his own. His advice on foreign policy comes not only from his secretary of state but also from many public groups, the most important among which is a body of men comprising what has been called the foreign policy community. It consists of those in the general population who take foreign affairs as their central concern and seek by writings and speeches to bring the president (and the general public) to its point of view. Its members include politicians, intellectuals, newspaper editors and publishers, heads of major corporations, foundation officials, international bankers, and military figures.

In its modern form this foreign policy elite took shape in the 1880s and 1890s. Most prominent

The rivalry with England many felt in the 1880s is shown in this depiction of American industry threatened by foreign imports.
The New Yok Public Library Picture Collection

were men like Senator Henry Cabot Lodge, Theodore Roosevelt, John Hay, Senator Albert J. Beveridge, Whitelaw Reid (editor of the New York *Tribune*), and the naval historian Alfred Thayer Mahan. Most of them were Republicans. Intellectual descendants of Alexander Hamilton, they were fond of talking about "the nation," "national power," and "national destiny." Democrats tended to be localists who paid little attention to the outside world, or Gladstonian internationalists who deplored power politics in world affairs. The men of the Republican foreign policy elite, however, usually had traveled much abroad, maintained transatlantic contacts, read constantly about world affairs, and as proud nationalists were dismayed that their country had so little military and naval power and carried so little weight in world politics. Elitist in their points of view, Anglo-Saxon in their lineage, they generally regarded dollar-chasing with distaste and had little interest in big business.

Great Britain played a special role in their thinking, just as it did among the Democrats. But instead of looking to William Gladstone, American Republicans looked in admiration to his great rival, Benjamin Disraeli, for many years leader of the Conservative (Tory) party. Lodge, Roosevelt, Beveridge, and others of the foreign policy elite shared Disraeli's idea that imperialism could be a great and ennobling mission for the "enlightened nations" to carry out. They certainly agreed with his basic notion, so different from Gladstone's, that the big powers of the world should run things, that a strong foreign policy based on the active use and display of a large navy would do the most to keep peace in the world and protect the nation's interests.

But these men were nationalists, and they tended to regard Britain as America's potential rival. They bristled at every indication that Britain might be encircling the United States. They also, paradoxically, possessed that same attitude toward Great Britain that had distinguished Alexander Hamilton—a respectful admiration. Britain, after all, was successfully doing in the world what they wished the United States would do—playing the role of a great nation with immense industrial and financial resources and a readiness, especially when Conservatives were in control of the British government, to take a strong hand. Americans like Lodge and Roosevelt were given to talking of "Mother England." Certainly they admired the British aristocracy and thought of themselves as its counterpart in the United States.

The foreign policy elite began talking in the 1880s of the need for a new American foreign policy. They observed that the world had changed. Growing empires and national rivalries made it a place of apparent danger. Large navies, swelling armies, threatened wars, hidden plans—to them, it all added up to one lesson: the United States must protect itself by building national power. How to do this? Alfred Thayer Mahan showed the way in his internationally acclaimed *The Influence of Sea Power upon History* (1890). National power, he said, lies in foreign trade and in the wealth it creates. An expanding foreign commerce is the key to strength and prosperity. Security lies in having that trade carried in American ships protected by a strong American navy. Taken together, these elements comprised sea power, the final arbiter, at that time, of world affairs.

The "large policy" that Lodge, Roosevelt, Mahan, and other such men began to call for would have the United States achieve these goals by a series of specific steps. American vessels, East-coast based, should be enabled to break out of the limited Atlantic basin by the construction of an American-controlled canal through Central America. This would breach the wall lying between American traders and the enticing markets of the Far East. To protect such a canal, some form of American control should be established over Cuba and the other Caribbean islands to prevent their becoming bases for hostile powers. As stepping-stones across the vast Pacific to Asia, coaling stations and naval bases were to be acquired in Hawaii, Guam, Wake Island, and the Philippines. The American government, meanwhile, should build a sizeable merchant marine—largely defunct since British steamships in the 1860s seized supremacy over American sailing vessels—and above all, a strong navy.

Senator Henry Cabot Lodge of Massachusetts, a proexpansionist, in 1895 condemned American foreign policy on the ground that it was timid and dominated by the ideas of English Liberals, who opposed imperialism. "The tendency of modern times is toward consolidation. It is apparent in capital and labor alike, and it is also true of nations. Small states are of the past and have no future. The modern movement is all toward the concentration of people and territory into great nations and large dominions. The great nations are rapidly absorbing for their future expansion and their present defense all the waste places of the earth. It is a movement which makes for civilization and the advancement of the race. As one of the great nations of the world, the United States must not fall out of the line of march.

"In the interests of our commerce . . . we should build the Nicaragua Canal, and for the sake of our commercial supremacy in the Pacific we should control the Hawaiian Islands and maintain our influence in Samoa. England has studded the West Indies with strong places which are a standing menace to our Atlantic seaboard. We should have among those islands at least one strong naval station, and . . . the island of Cuba, still sparsely settled and of almost unbounded fertility, will become to us a necessity. Commerce follows the flag, and we should build up a navy strong enough to give protection to Americans in every quarter of the globe and sufficiently powerful to put our coasts beyond the possibility of successful attack.

"[These] vast interests which lie just outside our borders . . . ought to be neglected no longer. . . . They appeal to our national honor and dignity and to the pride of country and of race. . . . [They are] something that rouses and appeals to the patriotism and the Americanism of which we can never have too much. . . . ("Our Blundering Foreign Policy," *Forum* [March 1895].)

Roots of imperialism:
The sense of mission

Could this program be achieved in an antiimperialist nation traditionally opposed to a strong foreign policy? Public attitudes were, in fact, changing. Americans were beginning to share with Europeans the idea that Western civilization had a mission to uplift the human sea of "barbarism," the term they used, that encircled them. In a certain sense Europe's outburst of imperialism was a kind of nineteenth-century Peace Corps movement. Men were proud to call themselves imperialists, for they saw their work as the spreading of civilization: law and order; sanitation; technical skills; decent standards of living; an end to slavery; even-handed court systems; and the outlawing of wife burning, mutilation, polygamy, bride purchase, and the constant scourge of native wars.

By the 1880s Darwinism was being applied to human affairs, creating the notion that the world was divided into many distinct races carrying ineradicable characteristics in their bloodstreams. Northern Europeans were thought to be inherently tall and fair and blessed with minds that equipped them to think large thoughts and exert leadership. Those of southern Europe were described as inherently short and squat, made for heavy tasks and following orders. By definition, non-Europeans were even more inferior and in need of guidance and uplift.

Linked to such racism was the belief that Britain and America, the Anglo-Saxon nations, had a unique mission in the world. As Josiah Strong put it in 1885, "The Anglo-Saxon is the representative of two great ideas . . . civil liberty . . . [and] a pure *spiritual* Christianity." Since these two ideas, he said, had done the most to elevate the human race, then "the Anglo-Saxon . . . is divinely commissioned to be, in a peculiar sense, his brother's keeper. . . ." Christian missionaries played a key role in spreading these attitudes. The Student Volunteer Movement for Foreign Missions was intensely active on American college campuses in the 1890s, and hundreds of volunteers went overseas to "carry out the Lord's tasks." They naturally assumed that they should spread the institutions of Western civilization as well as the gospel.

Roots of imperialism:
The drive for markets

As early as the 1880s some American businessmen were claiming that American industry was producing too much for the American market to absorb. The nation needed "an intelligent and spirited foreign policy" in which Washington would "see to it" that industrialists had enough foreign markets. Benjamin Harrison, with James G. Blaine leading the way as his secretary of state, made expansion of foreign trade his principal objective. As Blaine said in 1890, "Our great demand is expansion . . . of trade with countries where we can find profitable exchanges." Under Blaine's leadership in 1889, the first Pan-American Conference of all western-hemisphere nations save Canada convened in Washington, leading to new commercial ties.

Crises in the 1890s

Then came the earthquakes of the 1890s. Calamity after calamity seemed to strike the nation: agrarian radicalism, free-silver campaigns, labor violence, and then the most stunning blow of all—the massive depression beginning in 1893. Everything converged to make people believe the nation was overripe and ready for collapse. This had two results: one was a great upsurge in sentiment for humanitarian reforms; the other was the adoption of a new truculence and combativeness in foreign policy. Faced with internal weakness, many Americans seemed to feel a burning need to be reassured that their country had not lost its power and vitality. If we did not expand our energies abroad, said a Columbia sociologist, Franklin H. Giddings, our inherently active and warlike temper might "discharge itself in anarchistic, socialistic, and other destructive modes that are likely to work incalculable mischief." In this sense, imperialism was to be a lightning rod for social tensions.

The Venezuela explosion

It was in these circumstances that President Grover Cleveland unwittingly heated the fires of jingoism by setting off a controversy with Britain over Venezuela. The background to the conflict was an increasing prickliness in the United States over Britain's apparently growing role in the western hemisphere. Suspicions of encirclement and commercial rivalries heightened the tension. In 1895, the Conservative government of Lord Salisbury, then prime minister and a former close associate of Benjamin Disraeli, decided in typical big-power fashion that it would settle a long-standing border dispute with Venezuela over the location of the boundary between that country and British Guiana by simply declaring that it was taking control over the disputed region.

Cleveland was aroused. After all, this was just the kind of action that the Gladstonian, Liberal-Democratic tradition had condemned—a big country bullying a small one. As a Democrat, moreover, he had little sympathy for a Tory government. Furthermore, a storm of protest built up against Britain, traditionally hated by ethnic groups such as the Irish Catholics. At Cleveland's suggestion, Congress in February 1895 announced its opposition to British claims in Venezuela. Then Cleveland prepared and sent a private message to the British government. It condemned Britain's actions and demanded that the controversy be submitted to arbitration. Also, the message boldly restated the Monroe Doctrine: "To-day the United States is practically sovereign on this continent, and its fiat is law upon the subjects to which it confines its interposition."

Five months later the British reply found its leisurely way to Washington. It declared that the Monroe Doctrine had no standing in British eyes and certainly did not apply to Venezuela. Arbi-

tration was out of the question. In response, Cleveland and Olney prepared and issued an ultimatum that seemed to threaten war. If Britain did not submit to arbitration, the message said, the United States was prepared to resist Britain's continued retention of the disputed territory "by every means in its power." "Many still living," wrote an Englishman in 1934, "remember like yesterday with what stupefaction the Venezuelan ultimatum was received." From all over the United Kingdom shocked messages poured into the Foreign Office pleading with Salisbury to prevent war. A flood of private and governmental messages crossed the Atlantic seeking to assure Cleveland by every possible means that war was not necessary. Arbitration, on a modified basis, was agreed to, and in the ensuing months the crisis faded.

In the meantime, Americans were as startled as the British. The immediate response to Cleveland's ultimatum had been an explosion of jingoistic delight. Congress broke into almost unprecedented applause, and newspapers from coast to coast praised Cleveland. But Anglophobia was not the force it used to be. A reaction soon set in. Clergymen, university professors, businessmen, and international law specialists condemned the saber rattling and jingoistic trumpeting. A great network of ties had built up between Britain and the United States. There were commercial interests, banking houses, clergymen, eminent families that had begun intermarrying with the British aristocracy, intellectuals who traveled back and forth across the Atlantic, and politicians of all camps who admired the British example.

The result of the Anglo-American crisis over Venezuela was to inaugurate a new and much firmer relationship of friendship and cooperation. Almost overnight, the shock of the experience revealed to the two nations their mutual dependence. The British swung over to a policy of friendly cooperation, in effect recognizing American political supremacy in Latin America under the Monroe Doctrine. A form of diplomatic partnership in world affairs began to emerge, which, as it grew and strengthened in the succeeding decades, was to have great significance in the twentieth century.

The Cuban Revolution

In early 1895 a rebellion against Spanish rule broke out in the island of Cuba. Just ninety miles from the Florida coast, Cuba was intimately linked with American life. Primarily engaged in sugar culture, it sold practically all its crop in the United States. Americans, with investments of about forty million dollars in the island, had long sympathized with Cuban sentiments for independence, which had flickered and flared for decades. Americans were reared on historical memories in which Spain represented all that was destructive and oppressive about European rule. The revolt, which sprang primarily from the ordinary people of the countryside, seemed a reenactment of the American Revolution.

Rebel bands soon were roaming the countryside, and a Cuban junta set up headquarters in New York to gather funds and release a stream of news stories to the American press. Cuban Leagues emerged in the United States to aid the cause, and the AFL formally called for support of the Cuban revolutionaries. In late 1895 the insurgents formed an independent Cuban government. Meanwhile, Spain poured a force of 120,000 troops into the island and mounted an increasingly desperate campaign against the guerrillas, and the Spanish military gained de facto control over policy. As the United States has learned to its grave sorrow, guerrilla warfare with widespread support in the countryside is almost impossible to crush. Locked in combat with an elusive, skillful, and often savage enemy, the Spanish military officials chose ever more extreme methods. Finally, they resorted to a virtual depopulation of the countryside by forcing rural folk to live in concentration camps so that they could no longer aid the guerrillas. The result was an appalling loss of life due to disease and starvation.

In the United States, a new form of journalism seized on the Cuban Revolution. Young William Randolph Hearst, the son of a California mining millionaire, purchased the New York *Journal* in 1895 and began a sensationalistic race for circulation against Joseph Pulitzer's New York *World.* Every Cuban event was expanded into screaming, lurid headlines. The Spanish commander in Cuba, General Valeriano Weyler y Nicolau, was called a "human hyena" and a "mad dog." His soldiers were accused of murdering prisoners, shooting the sick, and molesting young women.

The Cuban Revolution was an ideal humanitarian crusade in which to vent the anxieties and frustrations built up in the United States by the crises of the 1890s. Generous moral passions provided most of the motivation for the Cuban frenzy; the altruism was certainly real. In early 1896 Congress passed a resolution proposing that the belligerency of the Cuban rebels be recognized, an action that set off wild anti-American riots in Spain. Newspapers all over the United States spread the same stories that appeared in more lurid style in the Hearst and Pulitzer presses. Populists viewed the Cuban issue as an example of the heartless avarice of Wall Street, for the business community generally opposed so disruptive an event as war.

Grover Cleveland refused military intervention, however, and sought genuinely to remain neutral. He is reported bluntly to have told irate congressmen that he would not mobilize the army if Congress declared war. He did, nevertheless, grow increasingly concerned over the butchery. Secretary Olney formally offered mediation to Spain, but his initiative was rebuffed indignantly. Spanish liberals called on their government to grant reforms in Cuba, but the Spanish Foreign Minister responded by saying that it was American aid to the rebels that prolonged the fighting, not Spanish misrule.

McKinley takes command

William McKinley became president in March 1897. In his party was that hard core of the activist foreign policy elite that had been leading the *Cuba libre* cry and calling for American intervention. But

McKinley was no jingo; he sincerely hoped to find some peaceful settlement. The new president, renewing Cleveland's warnings to Spain, offered to mediate. In the fall of 1897 a more liberal Spanish government came to power, the concentration camp policy was modified, and a limited form of Cuban autonomy was granted. But the rebels rejected it. The Cuban loyalists, on their side, rioted against even the possibility of limited autonomy. The Spanish army simply brushed aside compromise, for it was determined to crush the insurgents at all costs. McKinley, discouraged now by the failure of his diplomatic efforts to pacify the island, began thinking of direct intervention.

The road to war

The American armored cruiser *Maine* was dispatched to Havana harbor in January 1898 to protect Americans still in the Cuban capital. On February 15, 1898, a terrific explosion sank the *Maine* and killed over 250 officers and men. Jingoes now split the air with demands for war. "I would give anything," wrote Theodore Roosevelt, now assistant secretary of the navy, "if President McKinley would order the fleet to Havana tomorrow. . . . The *Maine* was sunk by an act of dirty treachery on the part of the Spaniards." Congress unanimously voted fifty million dollars for military preparedness. Spain was reported to be "simply stunned." But McKinley would not be hurried to war. He awaited the results of an American investigation of the disaster, which reported only that the explosion had come from outside the vessel, set off by unknown persons.

At this time one of the most important speeches ever made in the Senate was delivered. Senator Redfield Proctor of Vermont, a peace advocate who was known to be skeptical of the sensationalist reports of the yellow press, had gone to Cuba to make a personal tour. He returned to describe horrifying conditions in the concentration camps:

Torn from their homes, with foul earth, foul air, foul water, and foul food or none, what wonder that one-half have died and that one-quarter of the living are so diseased that they can not be saved? . . . Little children are still walking about with arms and chest terribly emaciated, eyes swollen, and abdomens bloated to three times their natural size.

Shocked by these disclosures from so unimpeachable a source, the nation waited gravely for McKinley's response. The president tried diplomacy again, seeking to bring peace by armistice and an end to the concentration camp system. Although the Spanish yielded in April, McKinley was under enormous pressure to declare war. Groups all over the country began offering their services. A Maine congressman said that every legislator "had two or three newspapers in his district—most of them printed in red ink . . . and shouting for blood." A Presbyterian journal cried,

"Spanish 'Justice and Honor' be darned!"
Uncle Sam's image in Hearst press, 1898, which pressed wildly for war.
Culver Pictures, Inc.

"And if it be the will of Almighty God, that by war the last trace of this inhumanity of man to man shall be swept away from the Western hemisphere, let it come!"

The Cuban revolutionaries, meanwhile, were now so encouraged by American support that they would accept nothing less than full independence, a demand the Spanish government would never accept. Word came to the president from Wall Street that financial interests that had long opposed military action as too disruptive to the just-recovering economy were finally swinging over to support intervention. In February a petition from businessmen suffering heavily from damage to their factories and other investments in Cuba had pleaded for action. The British Foreign Office informed McKinley that he need not worry that European powers might prevent American action. Lastly, Congress's appropriation of fifty million dollars for armaments was rapidly being spent to strengthen the armed forces, which, together with a recently built battleship navy, gave McKinley confidence that a military confrontation would go well. Some had feared Spanish bombardment of the East Coast, but Winthrop Chandler wrote jocularly to Lodge that if Spanish troops invaded New York "they would all be absorbed in the population . . . and engaged in selling oranges before they got as far as 14th Street." In this spirit, so strange now as to seem incredible, the nation waited confidently for war.

On April 11, 1898, two days after the Spanish had largely given in to his demands, McKinley asked Congress for authority to end hostilities in Cuba by direct intervention. Following a week of debate, Congress agreed by passing resolutions that declared Cuba free; demanded the withdrawal of Spain; directed the use of armed force to achieve these ends; and, in the Teller Amendment, announced in advance that the United States would not annex Cuba. The latter, passed unanimously, indicates the spirit of altruism and self-denial in which the crusade was begun. No one, save a few at the centers of power, had any notion that by going to war in Cuba the United States would suddenly acquire a far-flung empire.

The Spanish-American War

The war with Spain lasted only three months, but events of enormous significance occurred during that brief period. The foreign policy activists could now move boldly to secure the goals they had long sought. Theodore Roosevelt had earlier sent orders to Admiral George Dewey, commander of the Asiatic squadron, to attack the Spanish fleet in Manila Bay in the Philippines as soon as war began. Dewey was soon underway. His fleet of seven vessels entered the bay and steamed back and forth in front of a Spanish force of equal size for hours on end while the two fleets rained a torrent of shells at each other. When the battle was over, the Spanish ships were all sunk, and the Americans had lost neither a

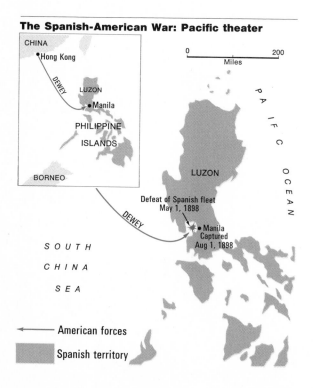

The Spanish-American War: Pacific theater

ship nor a sailor. The stunning victory electrified the United States. Many said that it was evidence that God Himself desired America to win, a sentiment that Dewey echoed in his official dispatches. The American people had been practically ignorant of the Philippines' existence before now. Suddenly no one talked of anything else. A babble of newspaper debate broke out. Should Dewey simply sail out of the bay and leave the Philippines behind? McKinley was later to remark ironically that this would have saved a lot of trouble. However, the president was strongly urged to send ground troops to protect the fleet, and in the most critical decision of the war he agreed to do so on May 16, 1898. Senator Lodge exultantly wrote Roosevelt, "the Administration is now fully committed to the large policy that we both desire." Shortly afterward, Manila was taken by American troops.

Meanwhile, a small and badly equipped army under General William R. Shafter had landed in Cuba where it fought some brief, bloody battles. Roosevelt, then a lieutenant colonel leading the volunteer Rough Riders, secured spectacular news coverage for his exploits at San Juan Hill. The Spanish fleet hid for a time in Santiago Harbor, then came out to be completely destroyed by the United States Atlantic fleet, under Admiral William T. Sampson and Commodore W. S. Schley. Just before the war ended, American troops led by Nelson A. Miles, the commanding general of the army, landed on Puerto Rico, Spain's other Caribbean possession, to take control of the island. Also, the flotilla taking troops to Manila Bay stopped by the island of Guam, fired a few shells at the surprised garrison—it was ignorant of the fact that war was underway—and left an occupying force. On August 12, 1898, the Spanish agreed to end hostilities by freeing Cuba and ceding Puerto Rico and Guam to the United States. The question of the Philippines was left to be settled by American

The Spanish-American War: Caribbean theater

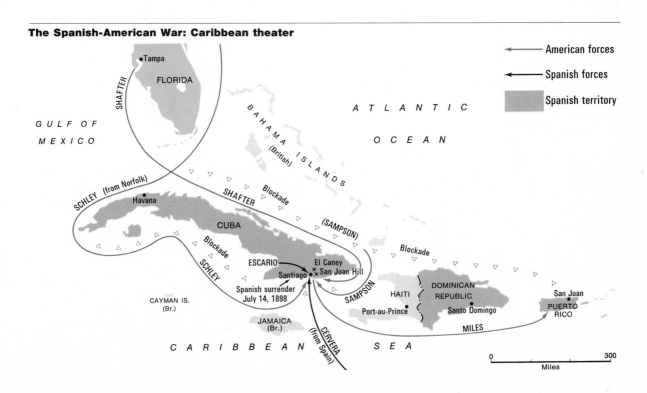

and Spanish peace commissioners, who were to meet in Paris on October 1, 1898.

What should the American government try to secure in the Philippines? McKinley seems to have begun with the simple notion of acquiring a naval base at Manila, leaving the rest to Spain. Even Roosevelt and Mahan were at first undecided as to how far the United States should go. Securing a naval base was one thing; acquiring the whole archipelago was another. Should the islands be given back to Spain, allowed to become independent, sold to Britain or Germany, or kept by the United States? In the early autumn McKinley traveled about the country making speeches carefully designed to test public sentiment. He returned to Washington convinced that the American people wished annexation. A poll of newspaper editors showed strong support for it. The president walked the floor of the White House night after night, according to his own account, pondering a decision and praying for divine guidance.

And one night late it came to me this way—I don't know how it was but it came: (1) that we could not give them back to Spain—that would be cowardly and dishonorable; (2) that we could not turn them over to France or Germany—our commercial rivals in the Orient—that would be bad business and discreditable; (3) that we could not leave them to themselves—they were unfit for self-government—and they would soon have anarchy and misrule over there worse than Spain's was; and (4) that there was nothing left for us to do but to take them all, and to educate the Filipinos, and uplift and civilize and Christianize them, and by God's grace do the very best we could by them, as our fellow-men for whom Christ also died. And then I went to bed, and went to sleep and slept soundly. . . . (*Christian Advocate* [January 22, 1903].)

So it was that the American peace commissioners in Paris were instructed to demand acquisition of the entire Philippine archipelago. Spain's negotiators resisted strenuously. After all, they said, American troops had not taken Manila until after an armistice had been formally signed. The islands could not be claimed as legitimate spoils of war. In response, the United States offered a payment of twenty million dollars—the act is reminiscent of the way in which the Mexican cession was acquired in 1848—and Spain accepted. Now the American people faced the fateful decision, should the treaty be ratified, and a colonial empire be acquired?

The antiimperialist argument

The debate over the issue went on for two years, from 1898 through the election of 1900. Hundreds of America's most eminent leaders argued loud and long against imperialism. In newspapers, magazines, pamphlets, and countless speeches, they begged Americans not to go down the fateful road. The antiimperialists were led by ex-presidents Grover Cleveland and Benjamin Harrison. With William Jennings Bryan on their side, the bulk of the Democratic party, most reformers, the leading Liberal Republicans, labor leaders like Samuel Gompers, industrialists like Andrew Carnegie, former abolitionists, prominent professors and university presidents, and a host of novelists, they condemned the annexation of the Philippines as a gross violation of American principles that was certain to destroy the nation's institutions.

American antiimperialists argued that no one should be governed without their consent, and that the fight that Philippine rebels under Emilio Aguinaldo soon began against American rule—the so-called Philippine Insurrection, 1899–1902—demonstrated how strongly the Philippines wished independence. Some antiimperialists scoffed at the notion that America's rule would be uniquely benevolent; others insisted that the whole idea of colonial possessions was unconstitutional. The Constitution would have to follow the flag; the Filipinos would have to be given full American citizenship (a fact that alarmed racists). Providence had blessed the American nation, antiimperialists said, when it had held to its traditions of liberty and self-rule; disaster would doubtless follow the abandonment of these sacred ideals. It was ridiculous to take on an expensive, remote colony just to acquire trade. The laws of commerce would create profits, not the law of imperialism.

The American Anti-Imperialist League, at its meeting in Chicago in October 1899, proclaimed that "the policy known as imperialism is hostile to liberty and tends toward militarism, an evil from which it has been our glory to be free. . . . We maintain that governments derive their just powers from the consent of the governed. We insist that the subjugation of any people is 'criminal aggression' and open disloyalty to the distinctive principles of our Government. We earnestly condemn the policy of the present National Administration in the Philippines. It seeks to extinguish the spirit of 1776 in those islands. We deplore the sacrifice of our soldiers and sailors, whose bravery deserves admiration even in an unjust war. We denounce the slaughter of the Filipinos as a needless horror. We protest against the extension of American sovereignty by Spanish methods.

"We demand the immediate cessation of the war against liberty, begun by Spain and continued by us. We urge that Congress be promptly convened to announce to the Filipinos our purpose to concede to them the independence for which they have so long fought and which of right is theirs. . . . The United States cannot act upon the ancient heresy that might makes right.

"We deny that the obligation of all citizens to support their Government in times of grave National peril applies to the present situation. If an Administration may with impunity ignore the issues upon which it was chosen, deliberately create a condition of war anywhere on the face of the globe, debauch the civil service for spoils to promote the adventure, organize a truth-suppressing censorship and demand of all citizens a suspension of judgment and their unanimous support while it chooses to continue the fighting, representative government itself is imperiled." (Quoted in Carl Schurz, *Speeches, Correspondence, and Political Speeches* [1913].)

The antiimperialists insisted that it was simply wrong for the United States to impose its rule on another people. If the Filipinos wanted independence, they must be given it, not be shot down like cattle. The savage fighting during the Philippine Insurrection gave heavy ammunition to the antiimperialist cause. More than 120,000 Americans had to be sent to put down the uprising, and the barbarities practiced by both sides were horrifying. How monstrous it was, antiimperialists said, for a war begun to free Cuba to end up as a bloody oppression of the Philippines. No republican government, they insisted, could be imperialistic and remain republican for long. Freedom was indivisible. Denying it to others would mean denying it at home. By taking colonial possessions, the United States was robbing itself of its very reason for being—to serve as an example to all the world of how a free nation could live in liberty and concern for the rights of others.

The proimperialist answer

It was a losing argument. The antiimperialists were generally older men who thought of an older America; their opponents were younger, more confident, more able to hold out alluring visions to a nation eager to dispel the specters of depression and national weakness. The proimperialists relied essentially on the theme that America had both a duty and a destiny that it could not avoid. Its uninterrupted success in battle was pointed to as proof that God had great plans for the American nation. Dewey's victory, said a religious newspaper, "read almost like the stories of the ancient battles of the Lord in the times of Joshua, David, and Jehoshophat." Senator Beveridge observed:

God has not been preparing the English-speaking and Teutonic peoples for a thousand years for nothing but vain and idle self-contemplation and self-admiration. No! He has made us the master organizers of the world to establish system where chaos reigns. He has made us adept in government that we may administer government among savages and senile peoples.

Burning the Palace of Aguinaldo, leader of the Philippine Insurrection, during the three year war (1899–1902) in which an estimated 600,000 Filipinos died.
Courtesy of the Library of Congress

Many Protestant clergymen advocated annexation because they had great dreams of missionary work. Social Darwinists argued that since life is a struggle, the United States had better gain strength while it could. Looming over all discussions was the incontrovertible fact that the United States was already in the Philippines. Administrative actions taken without prior congressional authorization had presented the nation with an accomplished fact. To leave would be to pull down the American flag, a thought repugnant to Americans in their existing state of mind. In the background was a widely stated concern that if the United States did not take the Philippines, the European powers would become embroiled in war in the subsequent scramble to get them. Exaggerated alarms concerning German intentions swept the country. And most Americans doubted sincerely that Filipinos could govern themselves after three centuries of autocratic Spanish rule. Besides, it was said, they were colored men and "backward."

To some people, the great attraction of imperialism was that it would divert America's attentions from its internal problems. The nation, such people insisted, was sick with introspection; outside challenges would once again give it new goals and new dreams. The result, they believed, would be the reemergence of national unity. Henry Watterson, nationally known editor of the Louisville *Courier-Journal* expressed this viewpoint in 1899:

From a nation of shopkeepers we become a nation of warriors. We escape the menace and peril of socialism and agrarianism, as England has escaped them, by a policy of colonization and conquest. From a provincial huddle of petty sovereignties held together by a rope of sand we rise to the dignity and prowess of an imperial republic incomparably greater than Rome. It is true that we exchange domestic dangers for foreign dangers; but in every direction we multiply the opportunities of the people. We risk Caesarism, certainly; but even Caesarism is preferable to anarchism. We risk wars; but a man has but one time to die, and either in peace or war, he is not likely to die until his time comes. . . . In short, anything is better than the pace we were going before these present forces were started into life. Already the young manhood of the country is as a goodly brand snatched from the burning, and given a perspective replete with noble deeds and elevating ideas.

Equally important was the reversal of opinion in the business community. In general, its leaders had opposed war with Spain until the last moment. But soon they had found that the war was a vigorous stimulant to business activity. Then talk began of the Philippines' providing a base from which American enterprise could finally break into the supposedly huge markets of the Far East. The beginnings of prosperity in 1897 had as yet done little to wipe away the memory of depression and overproduction. To many businessmen, the prospect of expanded overseas trade seemed the only permanent solution to the problem of glut. This opinion, communicated to legislators, doubtless persuaded many to vote for annexation.

The antiimperialists came near to victory. When the treaty came to a Senate vote in February 1899, they secured almost enough votes to prevent the necessary two-thirds approval. But then William Jennings Bryan concluded that the best way to secure the freedom of the Philippines was for the United States to annex them; that after ratification, America could turn around and grant them independence. He hoped, too, to make antiimperialism the rallying cry of the Democratic presidential campaign in 1900. In Washington, he secured enough votes for ratification to carry the day for the treaty; but in the election, he found that the nation had quickly lost interest in the imperialism question. McKinley went to the people with the golden outpouring of booming prosperity behind him. Optimism and a buoyant faith in the future was identified with the Republican party. Bryan was once again the Democratic presidential nominee, but he went

down to complete defeat in 1900. The United States had become an imperial power.

The Pacific adventure expands

During the excitement of the Spanish-American War, the administration reintroduced a treaty for the annexation of Hawaii. It could now argue, following Dewey's breathtaking victory, that the islands would provide essential bases for the support of the nation's new Far Eastern adventure. "Bridge the Pacific," appealed the Philadelphia *Press* to Congress. A joint resolution was hurried through Congress, and the islands were formally annexed on August 12, 1898.

Meanwhile, the expansionist American government was looking to China, whose trade was the ultimate objective of all this activity. That nation had recently been humiliatingly defeated in the Sino-Japanese War (1894–1895), and in the aftermath European powers began to carve up what now appeared to be the weak and backward Chinese Empire. Great Britain, meanwhile, became alarmed, for over the decades its trade with China had grown tremendously.

London turned to its new partner, the United States, for aid, suggesting a cooperative effort to keep China open to traders of all nations. John Hay, McKinley's secretary of state, was quite ready to take a strong role in world politics, but on his own. Deeply committed to the expansion of American business as a beneficent force in the world and a devout believer in Anglo-Saxon supremacy, in September 1899 he sent out the first Open Door note to the great powers. In it he stated America's loyalty to the principle of commercial equality and asked all nations to respect that principle in their own spheres of influence in China. Although he received evasive replies, he brashly announced in March 1900 that all the powers had given final and definitive approval to the principle. It was bold action, but everyone knew that it had little substance.

The occasion for confirming the Open Door policy was a violent outbreak against foreigners in North China in June 1900 by a society of fanatical Chinese patriots called the Boxers. The vast uprising resulted in many deaths and a terror-stricken flight by Europeans to the protection of foreign legations in Peking. Besieged there for weeks, they were finally freed by an international military force numbering 20,000 men—of whom 2,500 were Americans. Hay, meanwhile, moved swiftly to ensure that the Boxer Rebellion would not be used by any great power to expand its grasp on China. On July 3, 1900, he sent out another circular note declaring that it was American policy to "preserve Chinese territorial and administrative integrity," as well as to maintain an open commercial door.

This declaration was of great importance, for in it the United States, traditionally a minor figure in Far Eastern affairs, suddenly came forward as the guarantor of the vast nation of China. Hay's motives were hardly altruistic, for he had American trade interests primarily in mind. Of course, the American government had no intention of backing up its Open Door policy with military force, a fact that made its Far Eastern policy a precarious one for decades. Nonetheless, the Open Door was now fixed as one of the most sacred principles in American foreign policy.

Theodore Roosevelt takes command

On September 6, 1901, William McKinley smiled his genial way through the crowds thronging the colorfully decorated grounds of the Pan-American Exposition in Buffalo, New York. Arriving in the Temple of Music, he sent word out that he would greet the public individually. A warm and considerate man, he enjoyed nothing more than to shake hands and talk with the people. In the line was Leon F. Czologsz, an anarchist who was obsessed with a desire to kill the president. Learning that McKinley was in the city, he had taken a gun, waited his opportunity, and, draping his weapon with a handkerchief, stepped forward slowly as the line approached the president. McKinley smiled, reached out his hand, and was shot twice in the abdomen. For eight days horrified Americans hung on every word of his condition, for they genuinely loved and respected the president. They recognized in him a man of sincere warmth and honest conviction. Prosperity and world renown, it was widely felt, had come to the nation with his presidency. But on September 14, 1901, he died, saying quietly to his physician, "Good-bye, all. Good-bye. It is God's way. His will be done."

McKinley's death brought to the White House a spectacular man, Theodore Roosevelt. He loved the glory of war. Like Alexander Hamilton, he hungered for a heroic life and hoped for the same for his beloved nation. An unabashed nationalist, he thought such men as Thomas Jefferson, with their pacifist ideas on foreign policy, to be near-traitors. At the least, he was contemptuous of men who did not like power or rejoice in its use. To large policy advocates, Roosevelt was crucially important. No one came to symbolize the new adventure of imperialism more than he.

In his foreign policy Roosevelt dispensed with the careful ways of his predecessor and moved vigorously to assert America's power in the world. He has been called a foreign policy "realist" in the sense that he regarded the real forces in international life to be those of power and the consequent scramble for security. Democrats like Grover Cleveland might preach the message of international brotherhood and morality—indeed, Cleveland was shocked at Roosevelt's foreign policy and at the national enthusiasm it engendered—but Roosevelt preached instead the need to regard the world "realistically." This meant accepting the view that all nations are out to get as much power as they can and to take from others whatever they can get. He often talked as if he expected attacks momentarily from all directions, particularly from Germany. For this reason he firmly advocated—and built—a stronger navy and a well-organized and efficient army.

As a patrician, he believed in leadership by the great and the talented. Similarly, in world affairs he believed that the great nations of the world should govern international relations. Each great power should supervise that part of the world in which it was supreme. Where the interests of the great powers intermixed, as in the Far East, then the principle of "balance of powers" should be maintained; that is, America should support whatever side looked weakest so as to maintain an equilibrium.

Acquiring an isthmian canal

The large policy was only partially completed by 1901. The Philippines were in hand, and the United States possessed Guam and Hawaii. Wake Island was occupied in 1898 to provide another coaling station for the navy; and the protectorate over Samoa, which the United States had shared with Germany and Great Britain since 1889, was changed in 1899 so that the three nations divided up the little group of islands. In this step, the United States secured the island of Tutuila, with its harbor of Pago Pago. In the Caribbean, American dominance was embodied in the possession of Puerto Rico. In March 1901 Cuba's status was regularized through the Platt Amendment to the army appropriation bill of that year, which made the island a protectorate. Its key provisions were: Cuba was not to allow a foreign power to secure partial or complete control of the island; it was not to build up too large a foreign debt, which might lead to intervention; the United States was to have the right to intervene in Cuban affairs to preserve order and maintain Cuban independence; and Cuba was to agree to sell or lease to the United States appropriate sites for naval and coaling stations (which led to a large naval base at Guantanamo Bay still in American hands). Cubans were forced to include these provisions in their constitution, and when American troops withdrew from Cuba in 1903, the principles were made the subject of a formal treaty between the two nations.

However, the keystone of the large policy—an isthmian canal under American control—was not yet in place. McKinley had reminded Congress of

this fact in 1898. Negotiations then began with Great Britain to replace the existing Clayton-Bulwer Treaty, which since 1850 had provided that an isthmian canal would be jointly controlled and unfortified. In November 1901, with Theodore Roosevelt urging on negotiations from the White House, an agreement was made. The Hay-Pauncefote Treaty guaranteed equal treatment to British ships but allowed the canal to be built and controlled by the United States alone. Two years later the British signaled their acceptance of American hegemony in the Caribbean by closing down their naval stations in the West Indies.

There were two possible canal locations, one through Nicaragua, the other through Panama, then a province of Colombia. A French company had tried to build a canal through Panama in the 1880s, sinking nearly $300 million in a failing effort. The concession of the firm remained alive, however, and when Roosevelt became president the concession—including the physical works the company had built—was actively being peddled to the American government for about $40 million. Meanwhile, advocates of a Panamanian canal carried on a nationwide campaign extolling the virtues of the isthmus and publishing scare stories about Nicaragua's volcanoes. In June 1902, two months after a terrific volcanic eruption on the Caribbean island of Martinique, Congress settled on the Panamanian route. The United States proposed to buy the assets of New Panama Canal Company and give Colombia $10 million and an annual indemnity of $250,000 for control of the canal and a three-mile strip of land on either side.

Panama becomes independent

Colombian leaders were unhappy. The concession of the French company was due to expire soon, and they felt the $40 million for its assets should properly come to the Colombian government. They requested either a delay or an immediate payment to Colombia of one-fourth of the sum to be given the New Panama Canal Company. Roosevelt was angry, regarding the Colombians as a bunch of grasping bandits. Besides, he wanted his way at once. He now hit on a technicality that opened a new line of action. An old treaty made with Colombia in 1846 gave the United States a guarantee of "the right of way or transit across the Isthmus of Panama." Under this agreement, the United States had seven times landed troops on the isthmus to protect "free transit," though always with the prior approval of the government of Colombia. Roosevelt concluded that the treaty actually gave the United States the right to build a canal, and he decided to push ahead on this basis.

Then, a Frenchman named Philippe Bunau-Varilla, the American representative of the New Panama Canal Company, informed Roosevelt about a revolutionary movement in Panama that hoped to make the isthmus an independent na-

tion. If it succeeded, Roosevelt's plans might be quickly consummated. The president gave no open commitment, but there were implications in his reactions, apparently, that were unmistakable. Bunau-Varilla proceeded on the assumption that the revolutionary movement would have American support. He began working with the rebels, providing funds, a proposed new constitution, and even a code for communications. Some five hundred soldiers in the Colombian army, in Panama, were induced to take up the rebel cause.

On November 2, 1903, an American naval vessel, U.S.S. *Nashville,* arrived off the city of Colón. On the next day a practically bloodless rebellion took place in Panama. When Colombia sent troops to put it down, it was too late. Two hours after notice of the rebellion reached Washington, the American government recognized the Panamanian rebel government and received Philippe Bunau-Varilla as its ambassador. Four days

The United States in Central America and the Caribbean, 1898–1947

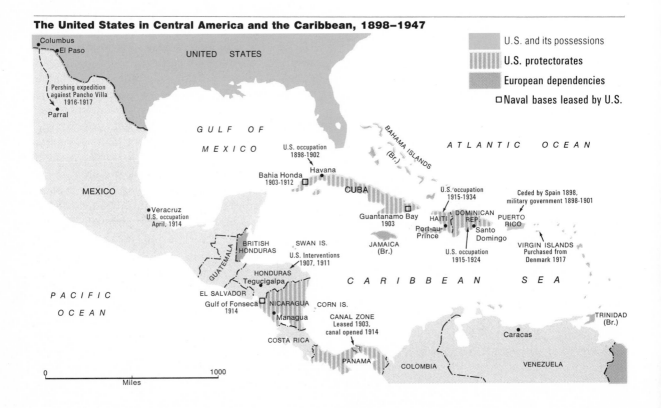

later a treaty was concluded with the Panamanian government, giving it $10 million for the right to build a canal and an anual sum of $250,000 for control (not sovereignty) over a canal zone ten miles wide. Meanwhile, $40 million was paid to the New Panama Canal Company for its assets.

This agreement aroused shock and dismay in the United States. It was "piracy," "scandal, disgrace, and dishonor," said many news editors. Most of the press approved, however, and a delighted Theodore Roosevelt proceeded with his typical vigor to get the dirt flying. Construction of the canal began in 1904 and was completed in 1914. By that time a Democratic administration was in power, and it negotiated a treaty with Colombia formally expressing American regret for the role of the United States in the Panamanian rebellion and paying Colombia $25 million indemnity. (The treaty was held up in the Senate until 1921, when interest in Colombian oil properties led to its finally being ratified.)

Roosevelt and the "big stick"

Roosevelt began a major expansion of the navy, building so many ships that by the end of his presidency the United States had become the second naval power in the world. And he proceeded to implement the principle he had expressed in 1900, "I have always been fond of the West African proverb, 'Speak softly and carry a big stick, you will go far.'" When Britain and Germany blocked Venezuela's ports and bombarded her forts in 1902 to enforce payment of debts, Roosevelt mustered a sizeable naval and military force in the Caribbean in an implied warning against more serious intervention. In 1903 he used both diplomacy and covert threats to settle a dispute with Canada over the boundary line of the "panhandle" of Alaska in a way favorable to the United States.

Then, in 1904, in order to make clear the new American role he had assumed, he announced the so-called Roosevelt Corollary to the Monroe Doctrine: "Chronic wrongdoing . . . may in America, as elsewhere, ultimately require intervention by some civilized nation, and in the Western Hemisphere the adherence of the United States to the Monroe Doctrine may force the United States, however reluctantly, in flagrant cases of such wrongdoing or impotence, to the exercise of an international police power." In brief, the United States from then on would be the western hemisphere's policeman, arrogating to itself the right to judge when the nations to the south were running their affairs badly. In 1904 and 1905 Roosevelt worked out an executive agreement with the Dominican Republic under which the American government took control of the Dominican customs so as to ensure that American and European investors would be repaid by the then-bankrupt republic. The Senate grumbled that such actions were unconstitutional, requiring a treaty to make them legal, but Roosevelt brushed aside the criticism.

Roosevelt also looked abroad to the world at large, firmly believing that the United States, as an emergent great power, should take up its proper role as one of the guarantors of world peace. This meant that for the first time American diplomats regularly attended international conferences and played an active role in them. This dramatic change caused much comment and protest at home, which Roosevelt characteristically ignored. In 1906 he sent negotiators to help settle a crisis between Germany and France over trade concessions in Morocco. The results of the conference, held in Algeciras, Spain, were widely taken as a rebuff to Germany.

In the Russo-Japanese War, which broke out in 1904, Roosevelt favored the Japanese on the ground that Russia had grown "grossly overbearing" to every other nation in the Far East, that is, that Russia was threatening to upset the balance of power. He later said that he even informed Germany and France "in the most polite and discreet fashion that in the event of a combination against Japan . . . I should promptly side with Japan and proceed to whatever length was necessary on her behalf." The Japanese won a quick series of stunning victories, and Roosevelt publicly announced that he would be happy to act as mediator to settle the conflict (though in truth he was reluctant to take on this task and did so only under great pressure). The peace conference was held in Portsmouth, New Hampshire, in August 1905, and a settlement favorable to Japan was worked out. (The Japanese people, however, had expected more and were angry at the United States for allegedly frustrating their desires.) Roosevelt received worldwide praise for his role in settling the war, and in 1905 he was awarded the Nobel Peace Prize.

Agreements with Japan

Roosevelt was now worried that in encouraging Japan he might, in fact, have upset the balance of power in the other direction. He shared the alarm that many Americans felt as they watched the swift Japanese victories over huge Russia. At the time of the Portsmouth negotiations, he worked out a secret agreement with the Japanese, the Taft-Katsura Memorandum, in which the United States recognized Japanese suzerainty over Korea, which it had recently taken over, while Japan bound itself to keep hands off the Philippines.

In 1906 a crisis erupted in California over the growing immigration of Japanese laborers. Excited over the "yellow peril," the San Francisco Board of Education ordered that the Japanese children—all ninety of them—be placed in a separate school. The proud Japanese, carried to a new pitch of national enthusiasm by their victory over Russia, protested violently at this slap in the face. By persuasive personal negotiation, Roosevelt got the order rescinded, but in return he had to agree to get Japanese immigration greatly reduced. In 1907 the Japanese agreed to halt the issuing of passports to Japanese workers and farmers, thus fending off in a "Gentlemen's Agreement" the indignity of seeing legislation passed by Congress preventing their entry.

Roosevelt decided now on a bold step designed to quiet both American fears of Japan and what

he took to be an inflated Japanese sense of power. "I am exceedingly anxious to impress upon the Japanese," he said in a private letter, "that I have nothing but the friendliest possible intentions toward them, but I am none the less anxious that they should realize that I am not afraid of them and that the United States will no more submit to bullying than it will bully." In 1907–09, he sent the "Great White Fleet," America's new battleship array, around the world. In the course of its voyage it visited Japan. Meanwhile, circumspect negotiations were underway in Washington, where in November 1908 the Root-Takahira Agreement was concluded. Another of Roosevelt's executive agreements, which bypassed the often uncooperative Senate, it provided for the following:

1. In the "region of the Pacific Ocean," each nation would maintain the status quo and respect each other's territorial possessions.
2. The two nations stated they would uphold the Open Door in China, and "by all pacific means at their disposal the independence and integrity of China."

The most important implication in this agreement was the tacit recognition by the United States that the Japanese held economic ascendancy in Manchuria, which was taken as being in the "region of the Pacific Ocean." Roosevelt, now preparing to leave the White House, had settled America's Far Eastern policy on the basis of accommodation with Japan. The Chinese might watch in surprised anger, but it was clear that the United States had pulled back from its earlier militancy on the Open Door and was ready to accept Japanese de facto dominance in the northern regions of China. Its "big stick" would be waved in the western hemisphere, but not in the Far East.

Bibliography

Three books that were especially valuable to me in writing this chapter: Walter LaFeber's provocative *The New Empire: An Interpretation of American*

Expansion, 1860–1898* (1963), a book with wide impact on the profession; David Healy's *U.S. Expansionism* (1970), the most balanced and thoughtful account; and Robert L. Beisner's study of those who opposed imperialism, *Twelve against Empire: The Anti-Imperialists, 1898–1900** (1968).

How have historians looked at the topic?

A decade of war in Vietnam has accustomed Americans to the term *imperialist,* and revived the quarrel over expansionist foreign policy that began three-quarters of a century ago. In *The Forging of the American Empire from the Revolution to Vietnam: A History of American Imperialism* (1971), Sidney Lens draws a parallel between the Spanish-American War—the first American war for empire—and Vietnam. For a provocative and controversial critique of America's "noncolonial imperial expansion," read William A. William's *The Tragedy of American Diplomacy** (1962).

Julius Pratt's *America's Colonial Experiment* (1950) concentrates on the political and strategic reasons for American colonialism and concludes that the American experiment was basically benevolent. The same author's *Expansionists of 1898** (1936) refutes the idea that the United States fought for markets, advancing evidence that American businessmen consistently opposed action that would lead to war with Spain. While still valuable, Pratt's latter work has been mostly supplanted by Walter LaFeber's *The New Empire,* cited above. This work reveals a timely swing toward war with Spain on the part of the American business community.

Walter Millis emphasized both industrialists' profit-hunger and newspaper-induced hysteria as reasons for war with Spain in *The Martial Spirit** (1931). In *The Correspondent's War* (1967) Charles H. Brown shows that the yellow press acted as though it had created the war, regardless of its authentic role. A searching and judicious examination of the United States' plunge into world politics is found in Ernest May's *Imperial Democracy: The Emergence of America as a Great Power* (1961). May's *American Imperialism: A Speculative Essay* (1968) is also thought-provoking.

A good, brief summary of the Spanish-American War is H. Wayne Morgan's *America's Road to Empire** (1965). Frank Freidel's *The Splendid Little War* (1958), titled from a letter written by John Hay, makes it clear that the war was not splendid for those who fought it. The sordid history of the pacification of the Philippine rebels is described in Leon Wolff's *Little Brown Brother* (1961).

Robert L. Beisner's *Twelve against Empire,* mentioned above, sketches a dozen Mugwump anti-imperialists and finds them sharing common assumptions about world affairs with proimperialists. Valuable too is E. Berkeley Tompkin's longer range study, *Anti-Imperialism in the United States: The Great Debate, 1890–1920* (1970). Theodore Roosevelt's enthusiastic leap to world prominence is appraised in Howard K. Beale's *Theodore Roosevelt and the Rise of America to World Power** (1956). Dexter Perkins considers the flexibility of Monroe's declaration in *The Monroe Doctrine, 1867–1907* (1966), an excellent study of American attitudes and policy toward Latin America. Dana G. Munro emphasizes American fear of European encirclement in *Intervention and Dollar Diplomacy for the Caribbean, 1900–1921* (1964). Both Charles S. Campbell, Jr.'s *Special Business Interests and the Open Door Policy* (1968) and Thomas J. McCormick's *China Market* (1967) emphasize the influence of businessmen's fear of overproduction in shaping America's China policy. Certainly one of the most influential writers in these years was Alfred Thayer Mahan. His most fundamental work, *The Influence of Sea Power upon History** (1957), provided a needed rationale for proimperialists.

*Available in paperback.

CHAPTER 25

The Progressive Era: New Ways of Thinking

TIME LINE

1879	Henry George, *Progress and Poverty*
1880	Salvation Army formed
1880–1900	Reform Darwinism and the social gospel movement emerge
1881	Oliver Wendell Holmes, Jr., *The Common Law*
1883	Lester Frank Ward, *Dynamic Sociology*
1885	Mark Twain, *Huckleberry Finn*
1886	Washington Gladden, *Applied Christianity*
1887	Edward Bellamy, *Looking Backward;* Church Association for the Advancement of the Interests of Labor formed
1889	Woodrow Wilson, *Congressional Government: A Study in American Politics*
	William James, *Principles of Psychology;* William Dean Howells, *A Hazard of New Fortunes*
1894	Henry Demarest Lloyd, *Wealth against Commonwealth;* Robert Blatchford, *Merrie England;* W. T. Stead, *If Christ Came to Chicago*
1899	Thorstein Veblen, *Theory of the Leisure Class*
1900s	Progressive movement flourishes; muckrakers active in journalism
1900	Theodore Dreiser, *Sister Carrie*
1901	Frank Norris, *The Octopus*
1903	Jack London, *The Call of the Wild*
1907	Walter Rauschenbusch, *Christianity and the Social Crisis;* William James, *Pragmatism;* Methodist Federation for Social Service established
1908	Louis Brandeis's brief in *Muller* v. *Oregon*
1911	Frederick Winslow Taylor, *Principles of Scientific Management*

Progressivism: A worldwide movement

N the 1880s and 1890s powerful reform energies built up in response to America's ills. After 1900, they exploded, producing a time of national restoration that has ever since been called the Progressive Era. So many barriers to change fell that it seemed to progressives everywhere that a new day of social justice was dawning. City governments were transformed; social workers invaded the slums; and states enacted major reforms that democratized, purified, and humanized government. The national government created potentially powerful regulatory agencies that began exerting some influence over business enterprise. Conservation had its beginnings; the financial system was reformed; tariffs were lowered; and workers began to receive legislation in their behalf. By 1917 the United States had passed through the most fundamental reordering of its national life since the Civil War.

This reorganization must be understood as part of a democratic revitalization that swept much of the globe. This was the era of the great Liberal governments in Great Britain, whose dramatic reforms turned that nation decisively toward social welfare. Even Germany and Austria, in the heart of traditionally autocratic central Europe, were shaken by waves of democracy, liberalism, and a bold drive for reforms. Russia witnessed the emergence of parliamentary institutions in 1905, followed by major social improvements. American progressives watched all this in fascination and trotted the globe to study new developments.

British reforms, as always, exerted a special appeal. Britons and Americans read the same reformist books and exchanged them eagerly across the Atlantic. Hardly would a new idea crop up in London before young Americans were trumpeting it in their own country. Was the subject city reform? Americans prepared long bibliographies of British books on the subject. Was it slum reform? Young Americans spent arduous years working in settlement houses in London, then returned to Chicago and New York to build similar institutions.

Perhaps as important as British reforms was the example of Germany. There the principle of a welfare state seemed to have reached its fullest development. Thousands of young Americans studied in German universities, bringing socialist views back with them. Simon N. Patten, who trained a generation of public figures at the University of Pennsylvania's Wharton School of Commerce, spoke for many of his contemporaries when he said he wanted to "help in the transformation of American civilization from an English to a German basis." Chambers of commerce urged German methods of industrial efficiency on businessmen; city planners drew notions of urban beautification from German cities; and advocates of vocational and technical training pointed insistently to the German example.

There was a note of fear running through these years. It was not only a world of reforming nations but a world of rearming nations as well. Countries regarded each other with suspicion as navies and armies grew and empires expanded. Much of the drive toward collectivism in Britain sprang from deep fears that the nation must pull together to protect itself from foreign threats. American and German industries were outpacing those of Britain, so industrial efficiency was needed. American and German fleets were growing, making imperial and naval efficiency essential. The British Fabians, advocates of collectivism, spread the word *efficiency* throughout the Anglo-American world. Soon after Sidney Webb first publicized the term in London in 1902, a young Princeton professor, Woodrow Wilson, began writing articles on the theme in the United States. Men like Theodore Roosevelt and Albert J. Beveridge were greatly alarmed at the "threats" from abroad and were eager to make America a strong and efficiently organized nation.

The new university

The wellsprings of progressivism lay in the American middle class. It was acquiring new ideas and new ways of doing things in the emerging "new universities," which more than any other institution were the spawning grounds of the progressive movement. They provided training and inspiration to the young Americans who led progressive campaigns.

The nation's system of higher education in the 1850s, before the changes took place, consisted of a number of small colleges, most of them dating from colonial days. They were small, church-connected institutions whose primary concern was to shape the moral character of their students. The content of their courses had been fixed for generations as the proper study for gentlemen. The faculty were clergymen, as were the trustees and presidents. Each young man took the same courses as every other; all students were drilled to learn by memory; and they were kept under close discipline. The college stood in place of the parent (*in loco parentis*), and its rule was heavy. There were many riots against strict living rules.

In Germany a different kind of institution had developed. Bearing the ancient name of *university*, which means a collection of colleges and schools under some form of common administration, it was concerned primarily with disseminating knowledge, not morals. Beginning in midcentury, many young Americans, dissatisfied with their training at home, went to Germany for advanced study, numbering more than nine thousand by the end of the century. Some of them returned to become presidents of venerable colleges—Harvard, Yale, Columbia—and transform them into modern universities. Others headed up new institutions (Johns Hopkins University, the University of Chicago) or fledgling state-chartered universities (Michigan, Cornell, California, and Wisconsin). The new presidents, such as Charles Eliot of Harvard (president from 1869 to 1909), and Andrew Dickson White of Cornell (1868–1885), broke all ties with churches and brought in a new kind of faculty. Professors were hired for their knowledge of a subject, not because they were of the proper faith, and had a strong arm for disciplining boys. The new principle was that a university was to create knowledge as well as pass it on, and this called for a faculty composed of teacher-scholars. They were to participate in the international conversation of scholars and scientists by leading creative intellectual lives outside as well as inside the classroom. Drilling

The University of Wisconsin in Madison, in the 1880s. It was one of the pioneering "new universities" which combined the search for knowledge (research), teaching, and professional training.
State Historical Society of Wisconsin

and learning by rote were replaced by the German method of lecturing, where the professor brought into class the results of his own research. Graduate training was introduced, leading to the Ph.D., an ancient German degree signifying the highest level of advanced scholarly attainment. For graduate students, the seminar system was established in which they learned to question, analyze, and conduct their own researches.

At the same time, the new university was greatly expanded in size and course offerings, thus breaking completely out of the old constricted curriculum of mathematics, classics, rhetoric, and music. President Eliot at Harvard pioneered the elective system by which students were able to choose their own courses of study. The notion of major fields of study emerged, made possible by the wide array of programs. The new universities tried at least partially to pull back from the close supervision over students' private lives that was implied by the traditional *in loco parentis* role of the American college. Many decades passed, however, before American higher education allowed students the same freedom outside the classroom that continental European schools provided. Though the new universities were no longer church-dominated, the American people continued to think of college as a place in which the character, as well as the mind, of the student was molded.

The new goal was to make the university relevant to the real pursuits of the world. Paying close heed to the practical needs of society, universities trained men and women to work at its tasks. Especially in the state universities, the atmosphere was strongly practical, with engineering students being the most characteristic expressions of the new regime. Industrialists began making large gifts to universities, even endowing them: Rockefeller the University of Chicago; Vanderbilt and Stanford the universities bearing their names; and Ezra Cornell helping by his gifts to create a state university for New York.

The old colleges had admitted students only from certain faiths, families, or social classes. The new university was open to everyone, so long as he or she had ability and the willingness to work hard. (Minority groups were excluded, however, by poverty, language difficulties, and social prejudice.) In the long run this meant that the universities became meritocratic instead of aristocratic. They divided people according to competence, interest, and achievement, rather than according to their origin. Tending to be much alike in their philosophies and curricula, since they were staffed by faculty members who interchanged ideas and moved from institution to institution, the new universities stripped away locally inherited habits and customs and made their students members of a national elite with shared life styles and outlooks. Lawyers and doctors, who had formerly been locally trained, began to go instead to the universities, where they were schooled in relatively similar curricula and urged to adopt an ethic of social service. Going out into the world with them were graduates in new, university-trained professions: economists, architects, biologists, scientifically trained agriculturists, chemists, public health specialists, social welfare workers, and teachers of all sorts.

Not only did the new university cultivate in its students the same values of hard work and getting ahead that the business community admired, but it also sent out a growing number of middle-class graduates and trained professionals who became social reformers. They were self-aware, idealistic, and equipped with a strong sense of mission. This was to have a momentous impact in the years after 1890, when the number of such graduates was sufficiently large to have an influence on national affairs.

Higher education did not change all at once. Each institution struggled through these transformations in different ways; many hardly passed through them at all. Some colleges, especially in rural areas, were alarmed by the new sciences, philosophy, and history being taught at Harvard and the University of Michigan. In conservative schools, the old ways were clung to with a determined sense of righteous justification.

Revolt against conservative Darwinism

American thought in this era, like American politics, was profoundly shaped by British influences. In the years after the Civil War a conservative social Darwinism had flourished. Derived mostly from the writings of the English engineer and social philosopher Herbert Spencer—such as his *Social Statics* (1851) and *The Man versus the State* (1884)—conservative Darwinism had preached that nothing could or should be done about social problems. As in nature at large, human societies should rely on natural evolution. Every person must stand completely alone, relying on their own capacities for their welfare and not on the aid of anyone else. "Survival of the fittest" must be the rule. Eventually, if everyone let natural forces have their way, a better race would emerge. Meanwhile, the government should do nothing but maintain order, prevent crime, and protect property. Reform should be shunned as soft-headed sentimentalism.

To compassionate young people, this negativism was terribly discouraging. They wished to serve society, to help other people, but how could they do so in the face of these ideas? Many of them turned to the new professions being taught at the universities as a way of living unselfish lives—medicine, social work, teaching, and government service. The building of hospitals and the discovery of anesthesia and antisepsis allowed medicine in particular to emerge in the 1880s as an important field for their altruistic efforts.

But the young social reformers needed and searched for a philosophy that could refute Spencerism. They received it from one of the most prodigious scholars and creative thinkers in American history, Lester Frank Ward, who made his living as a civil servant in Washington. He wrote a massive work aimed at destroying conservative social Darwinism, published in 1883 under the title *Dynamic Sociology*. It proclaimed that Spencer had forgotten humanity's unique possession—its mind. Whereas plants and animals might evolve, as Darwin had said, without conscious action, humanity had been given a reasoning brain with which consciously to improve its situation. Spencer's kind of evolution, he said, was aimless, without goals. Social movement must be planned, not left to haphazard influences.

All across the country professors at the new universities picked up Ward's ideas and began teaching them to their students. Search for the life of service, they urged. One outgrowth of this mood was the emergence of social work as a medium through which young reformers could serve society directly. Jane Addams of Chicago's Hull House became the most persuasive symbol of this new breed. At this famous slum settlement house her work taught her to turn away from the narrow, almost secretive isolation of conservative Darwinism. She saw that people were stronger and more able to deal with adversity if they immersed themselves in the life of the group and built a web of outward-reaching relationships.

By these and other means, there emerged an outlook that may be called reform Darwinism. Society certainly evolves, said Lester Frank Ward and his followers, but only if it uses its collective intelligence to work out social goals and achieves them through its collective arms and legs, the government. The welfare of the people must be ministered to by massive infusions of public services—education, regulation of minimum wages and maximum hours, and by many other social reforms. There should be a minimum standard of living for everyone.

Lester Frank Ward disputed the determinism in conservative social Darwinism that implied that people cannot change things. "It is commonly supposed that the highest wisdom of man is to learn and then to follow the ways of nature. Those dissatisfied people who would improve upon the natural course of events are rebuked as meddlers with the unalterable. Their systems are declared utopian, their laws [vain threats]. All efforts in this direction are held to be trifling and are stigmatized as so many ignorant attempts to nullify the immutable laws of nature. This general mode of reasoning is carried into all departments of human life.

"In government, every attempt to improve the condition of the state is condemned and denounced. . . . In commerce and trade, absolute freedom is insisted upon. . . . To dilute, adulterate, or even poison food and medicine for personal gain is not objectionable, since the destruction thereby of a few unwary consumers only proves their unfitness to survive in society. . . . All schemes of social reform are unscientific.

"[This] laissez-faire doctrine fails to recognize that, in the development of mind, a virtually *new power* was introduced into the world. . . . The great fact [is that man] *has,* from the very dawn of his intelligence, been transforming the entire surface of the planet he inhabits . . . [by his power of] *invention.*

"Glancing now at the ensemble of human achievement, which may be collectively called civilization, we readily see that it is all the result of this inventive process. . . . When a well-clothed philosopher on a bitter winter's night sits in a warm room well lighted for his purpose and writes on paper with pen and ink, in the arbitrary characters of a highly developed language, the statement that civilization is the result of natural laws and that man's duty is to let nature alone so that untrammeled it may work a higher civilization, he simply ignores every circumstance of his existence and deliberately closes his eyes to every fact within the range of faculties. If man had acted upon his theory, there would have been no civilization and our philosopher would have remained a troglodyte." (*Mind* [October 1884].)

Popular prophets of social action

The men who preached the need for collective action and were most listened to by the general public, however, were not scholars but popular writers such as Henry George, a California newspaperman who had witnessed labor riots in San Francisco and farm radicalism in the Sacramento and San Joaquin valleys in the 1870s. He was appalled that rich land and productive factories existed in the midst of starvation and unemployment. George concluded that it was the system, not the nature of mankind, that produced this suffering. In his book *Progress and Poverty* (1879) he noted that when civilization pushed ahead, poverty increased. There was one fundamental cause, he said, for this baffling paradox—land monopoly. Clever men had got hold of the best and most valuable city and farm land, then skimmed off the cream of society's advancing wealth by demanding high rents and prices. And yet, the landowner himself did nothing: it was the hard work of everyone else—of society at large—that made his land valuable. Businessmen had to pay high rents for their land, and they squeezed workmen's wages to compensate. Farmers were strapped by high mortgages and could not live on the price they got for their grain. The solution: replacing all forms of taxation with a single tax that landowners would have to pay on the increased value of their land, the "unearned increment." The burden of taxation would thus be dramatically lowered, and the economy would be able to grow abundantly.

George's single tax idea was too simplistic: it could never work so powerful a change. But the enormous appeal of his book was in its convincing demonstration that it was the system that was at fault and that poverty was not inevitable. *Progress and Poverty* went through a hundred editions and by the twentieth century had been read by at least six million men and women. In Britain, Australia, and New Zealand, George was "the prophet for whom they had been searching for years, the Columbus of political economy and social science." Farmers were uncomfortable with George's emphasis on land taxation, and businessmen disliked the aura of confiscation in his book, but the working class was warmly enthusiastic.

In 1887 Edward Bellamy published a utopian romantic novel called *Looking Backward.* This work described what the world would be like a century later if proper social principles were followed. At present, Bellamy said, society was like a stagecoach, with wealthy plutocrats sitting on the box above and whipping the toiling masses below, who struggled to pull on the heavy conveyance. The answer was to reorganize society until it resembled a well-arranged army. The principle of individualistic competition would be scrapped, for it led to selfishness. Combination would be the secret of the new order. Industry would be nationalized, for the brotherhood of all men required that no one should have the power of ruling over others irresponsibly. Relying on the survival of the fittest, he said, simply enthroned brutality and exploitation. There should be a strong central government to plan everything carefully and do away with waste. There would be large department stores instead of many small shops, for instance, and credit cards in place of money! Serving in the state industrial army until the age of forty-five, people would then retire to follow their own desires. Bellamy's book was a best seller in the United States and abroad. His proposals seemed to appeal mostly to the middle class, where in many circles the vision of such a regulated society directed by trained intelligence was highly attractive.

Many other such books were widely read, each of them proposing some variety of collectivism. In 1894 Henry Demarest Lloyd's *Wealth against Commonwealth* appeared, showing how Standard Oil used the laws to become a great exploitive monopoly and proposing strong governmental regulations. There was also Robert Blatchford's *Merrie England* (1894), which explained the reasons for poverty, described socialism, and advocated its adoption. In ten years, two million copies of this book were sold in England and the United States.

The churches and social action

American Protestantism was severely challenged by the new age and its problems. In the midcentury decades the response of most clergymen was to preach stern messages drawn from the Calvinism which was widely diffused in Protestant churches. The general thesis was that godliness was in league with riches. The wealthy acquired their money by hard work, and God smiled upon them. The poor earned their sufferings by their own failings. But in the 1880s a small group of young clergymen who worked in the cities and were shocked by the suffering they saw began appealing to the churches to take up social action. Charles Loring Brace pointed out that in fact the working classes were ignored almost entirely by Protestantism. Most of its churches were rural, and those in the cities turned up their noses at the dirty, stinking, teeming slums. Their stern sermons seemed to link Protestant ministers with exploitive capitalism.

One response to these appeals was the invasion of the slums by city missions and such new agencies as the Salvation Army, originally a British organization that came to America in 1880. Another response was to transform the churches in the poorer districts into "institutional" churches. Like Jane Addams's settlement houses, the institutional church was designed to minister to the whole person, rather than simply to preach a sermon at him on Sunday. The basic thesis was that a man ground down by poverty, unemployed, illiterate, and unskilled, would be too desperate to listen to sermons or practice a religious faith. The new churches provided reading rooms and classes to attack illiteracy and ignorance; day nurseries to help working women; sewing and manual-training instruction to provide skills; social clubs and gymnasiums to bring people together and build physical health; and personal counseling that went beyond theological matters. The reaction was startling. A church in New York that had only seventy-five members in

1882 acquired more than four thousand members in fifteen years after it became institutional. These experiences, repeated elsewhere, spread the institutional church idea throughout urban America.

The theological challenge of Darwinism

The churches were also in turmoil because of Darwinism's implications for biblical interpretation. If the theory of evolution was valid, what happened to the Garden of Eden? Were humans simply animals, like monkeys or cats, whose present form was arranged not by God's loving hands but by the eons-old process of evolution? The Darwinian idea seemed a monstrous assault against everything that the churches had ever preached concerning man's status in creation and his relation to God. Why pray anymore to God if everything operates according to natural laws? Common people in the churches could not understand it. What had happened to the faith of their fathers? For that matter, all of modern science seemed a threatening influence. In the 1870s clergymen and laymen began a long struggle to turn back modern science, inaugurating an argument that was to create half a century of wracking controversy.

Many clergymen, however, followed the teachings of liberal Protestantism. Darwinism, so the liberal Protestant view ran, simply told us in new ways how God works his wonders to perform. Evolution was the divine means of achieving divine purposes. Rural churches held fast to the old faith, but the liberal teaching spread in urban churches. Science and religion were not enemies, said such prominent clerics as Lyman Abbot, but were complementary sources of divine truth. This meant that the Bible was not to be interpreted literally, but to seek out its spirit.

Having turned away from orthodox biblical interpretation, such clergymen were inclined to turn away from orthodox social teachings as well. They were encouraged in this by what was going on in many northern seminaries. Influenced by German scholarship and the new universities,

seminaries like Andover in Massachusetts and Union in New York City brought young professors of sociology into their faculties who taught that the church must concern itself with solving social problems. Fundamentalist clergymen regarded such seminaries as seats of the devil, for they also taught the new ways of interpreting the Bible, but liberals regarded them as sources of strength for their cause.

Rise of the social gospel

Thus the ground was prepared for the rise of what came to be called the social gospel. Washington Gladden, a Congregational clergyman, began a widely influential career as a social gospel leader when he published *Applied Christianity* in 1886. He thought of Christianity as a fellowship of love and of the church as having a social mission. We must reach out to one another, he insisted, assist one another, and not stand back in cold impersonality while the alleged principle of survival of the fittest operated. Since capital was waging war on working people, labor should have the right to organize. There should be profit-sharing so that workers would receive a portion of the profits their toil produced. Gladden went on in succeeding years to endorse a long list of social reform measures: public control of money; regulation of corporations; the right of black people to equal educational and economic opportunities; and all the reforms of the Progressive Era.

Walter Rauschenbusch, a Baptist of German origins, similarly reacted in dismay to grim slum life in the 1880s. He responded by publishing his own newspaper, *For the Right,* in which he advocated Christian socialism. In the 1890s he supported the Populists; after 1900 he worked eagerly for the socialist Eugene V. Debs. In 1907 his *Christianity and the Social Crisis,* a landmark in social gospel history, condemned capitalism as essentially un-Christian: it destroyed people's moral growth and made them corrupt. The time had come, he said, to revive the communalism of the early Christians, who had shared all things in common; to inaugurate once again the kingdom of God.

While reforming Protestants were usually not so radical as Rauschenbusch, they still insisted that their denominations take up social reform. Church after church in the 1880s began setting aside doctrinal questions and coming to grips with the "social question." The Episcopalians were the first to do so, having been inspired to this by social reform movements within the Anglican church in England. In 1887 they formed the first social gospel organization, the Church Association for the Advancement of the Interests of Labor. It immediately began working to eliminate child labor, sweatshops, and slums, and to help labor unions get just settlements in disputes with employers. The Congregationalists soon followed, bringing in their diverse and very influential newspapers and periodicals. The Presbyterians, strongly identified with the business and corporate leadership of the country, held back, as did the Methodists and the Baptists, whose primarily rural parishioners wanted no truck with radicals. But by the turn of the century strong movements toward social action within even these denominations were underway. By that time, to demonstrate the scope of the movement, the Methodist Federation for Social Service, organized in 1907, was one of the most active of such organizations.

The social gospel movement by no means converted the great mass of churchgoers. Conservative churchmen, led by the Fundamentalists, continued to preach that their work should be directed only at saving individual souls. The social gospel was detested as simply another branch of modernism. But the movement did grow to powerful proportions during the Progressive Era, especially in the cities.

William James:
The Progressive Era's philosopher

What the reformers of the Progressive Era needed most of all was a new image of humanity and its potentialities. In this sense, the central figure in American thought from the 1890s to the First World War was the Harvard psychologist and philosopher William James. An agile, quick-witted, wonderfully tolerant man, James had served on the Harvard faculty since the 1870s. By the turn of the century his writings and lectures were reaching out to ever wider circles of Americans, making him a kind of national sage in the manner of Ralph Waldo Emerson before the Civil War. Intellectuals in Europe and the United States were deeply influenced by him, as were ordinary people in the educated public who bought and read his more popular works by the thousands. No American intellectual was so cosmopolitan, none before him so widely known and read in the transatlantic community since, perhaps, Benjamin Franklin.

Early in his career, James had struggled hard with the determinism that flourished as a result of Charles Darwin's work. He was appalled at the notion that everything is caused by physical influences; that the laws of biology, and not of the free human spirit, dominate what we are and how we think. James chose instead to believe in humanity's free will. In 1890, after years of research and writing, he summed up his vision of human nature in his first major work, *Principles of Psychology*. Gracefully written, daring in concept, it became the dominant work in the teaching of psychology. James rejected outright the idea that

The philosopher William James (with his novelist brother Henry James on the left) in the turn-of-the-century period, when William was becoming one of the shapers of American thought. He urged the need to ground ideas in actual experience, and to test them by it (pragmatism).
The Bettman Archive

people are like little machines, shaped wholly by their environment. What fascinated him most of all was human creativity. There is a self at the core of each human being's personality, James wrote, and that self has a will of its own. Clearly influenced by the external environment, the conscious self at the same time reacts upon that environment. People live in constant interaction with their surroundings. They are not passive creatures pushed this way and that by external forces.

In 1907 James published *Pragmatism,* a short work that went through edition after edition. In it he made a famous distinction between the "tender-minded" and the "tough-minded." The former, he said, are unable to face the fact that reality is enormously complicated, often confusing, and perhaps without any encompassing structure that one can see. Tender-minded people therefore put their faith in abstract, logical theories. Determined to fit themselves and their world into some kind of intellectual structure that they can hang onto, the tender-minded form an exaggerated faith in the ability of the mind to know all things by the use of reason and logic. By contrast, James said, tough-minded people are comfortable with the indeterminacy of life, content to work away in the midst of booming confusion, and interested most of all in coming to grips with how things really are in some limited area of examination. Skeptical, rather materialistic, they go by facts (empiricism) and not by theories (rationalism). "The tough," observed James, "think of the tender as sentimentalist and soft-heads. The tender feel the tough to be unrefined, callous, or brutal."

Most people, he went on, were mixtures of both, but in his belief the tough-minded empiricist seemed to be growing in dominance. This was all to the good, James remarked, for it meant that the pragmatic method was rising to ascendancy. What was pragmatism? It was "to try to interpret each notion by tracing its practical consequences." This put ideas in their proper place: they were only tools, not reality itself. The tough-minded observer considers facts, puts to-

gether an idea as a possible explanation for the facts, tests it, and tosses it aside willingly if it does not work. If a theory works satisfactorily, James said, then it is true. Experience, not logic, is the proper test. This approach, James said, "unstiffens" all opinion and opens up new possibilities. It lets men be creative, by which they actually add to what the universe contains.

Such was the message the Progressive Era received from its central thinker: examine reality directly, be quick to toss aside theories, and test everything by results. Take a kind of joyous delight in the complexity and indeterminacy of life: ride the waves, laugh at the tumbling, avoid the closed-in calms. Gather huge amounts of facts, think carefully, and then be ready to risk. Pragmatism was taken up eagerly by an age that was confident, hopeful, breaking barriers, and ready to run rough-shod over people and traditions if "results" could be achieved.

Realism in scholarship: Economics

Throughout the world of scholarship, born in the new university, there was the kind of search for fresh understandings of "reality" that James had called for. Each field had its set of constrictive established dogmas to revolt against. In economics, the reigning concept preached a formal, logical, and highly moralistic view of the business world. The men who taught it were usually philosophers or ministers. The objective was to demonstrate that competition was the iron law. If it was allowed to operate untouched by governmental interference, everyone would benefit so far as he should benefit.

Younger, college-trained economists began disagreeing with all this in the 1880s. Richard T. Ely at Johns Hopkins University and later at the University of Wisconsin said: "We regard the state as an educational and ethical agency, whose positive aid is an indispensable condition of human progress." What should economists do to make their emergent "science" a useful discipline helping to solve actual problems, instead of simply justifying in grand language what businessmen were doing? Stay away from methods of analysis that work downward from grand theories and begin studying the "actual conditions of economic life." Following this injunction, students of economics began examining institutions such as the corporation, the banking system, or the ways in which prices were set. This meant plunging into real situations and leaving the library, observing markets, financial operations, and labor negotiations.

Thorstein Veblen dispensed with the classical "economic man" of the orthodox economists in his *Theory of the Leisure Class* (1899). People simply did not operate in business life according to logical calculations of profit and loss, he said, but rather they were driven by instinctual urges inherited from the dim past of human history. As barbarians, they had fought one another with fists and weapons. They did this for emotional reasons, so as to feel superior and powerful. Evolution had changed the form, but not the spirit, of all this. Now, Veblen said, people use business life to gain their sense of power and dominance. They drain off profits so as to be able to engage in "conspicuous consumption," e.g., building great mansions that flaunt their riches and, by implication, their power and social status. The economy is not an ideal mechanism, self-balancing and beneficent. It is, rather, a product of long evolution, bearing pieces and traces of the barbaric past, and it must undergo still more changes before it can become humane.

Realism in scholarship: History

One of the features of the new university was the establishment within it of the formerly ignored field of modern history. It was a provocative field, founded on the teachings of the great German historian Leopold von Ranke. Historians at the time were tossing aside the venerable old books that provided stylized accounts of the ancient past and, instead, going directly to the sources, to the traces of the past left to us in the form of original documents, tablets, and the like to uncover the truth. Discover what things are really

like, said von Ranke; do not be content with what the old historians said. Doing so, the investigator will find a fresh story that tells him unsuspected things. Be skeptical, analytical, take nothing for granted; build from facts, not from theories.

The result was a complete rewriting of ancient history in the nineteenth century. By the end of the century historians were beginning to apply the same methods to the examination of modern history. Scholars uncovered the largely forgotten history of their individual nations, thus giving great impetus to the soaring nationalism that captured the modern mind. In the United States a young historian at the University of Wisconsin, Frederick Jackson Turner, issued an exciting challenge in 1893: stop explaining American history, he said, by means of grand panoramas that depict the United States simply as an outgrowth of Europe. Investigate instead the actual setting in which American democracy emerged, for the United States, he insisted, was a unique phenomenon in the world. Looking for what forces really operated to shape nations, he arrived at the notion that they were environmental and economic in nature. At first he pointed to the frontier, saying that out of this experience emerged American individualism, initiative, impatience with formalisms, equality, and creative drive. Later he developed also the concept that the nation is naturally divided into great physiographic sections, each of them based on different economic systems, and that United States history is a record of the conflict of these sections as they struggled for dominance in Washington.

The fundamental note in Turner's form of history, however, remained: it was a story that concentrated on lively, eruptive, conflicting forces. Struggle—this was the theme that dominated the work of the men of whom Richard Hofstadter wrote in his book *The Progressive Historians: Turner, Parrington, Beard* (1968). Older historians, as Hofstadter pointed out, had sought to present edifying stories of Washington and Jefferson that were idealistic and unifying. Progressive historians concentrated instead on change and social conflict, leading ever onward toward democracy. It was a story that inevitably led to partisanship, to tales of good guys and bad guys. The essential history of the United States, as progressive historians showed it, was a struggle against privilege, usually economic privilege. As Turner said in 1910, "We may trace the contest between the capitalist and the democratic pioneer from the earliest colonial days."

Realism in scholarship:
Political science

Keenly concerned with the public implications of their work, the progressive historians thus left their quiet studies and plunged into public con-

troversy. The same was true with political scientists, who were also engaged in establishing their field of study as a separate and distinct discipline. They, too, had to combat established dogmas and formalistic ways of thinking. The books on government that fed the nineteenth-century mind were overwhelmingly abstract and philosophical. Henry Steele Commager has commented:

They were vastly concerned with Sovereignty, or States' Rights, or the distinctions between People, Nation, and Government, with the Judicial Function or the Executive Power, with theories of Territorial Authority or of Reconstruction. They drew up admirable definitions of the Political Party whose resemblance to any actual political party was

Realism in art also emerged in the Progressive Era, forecast by the work of such painters as Thomas Eakins. In his "Agnew Clinic" (1889) he shocked the public and art critics not only by his grim subject, but by actually showing blood on the surgeon's hands.
University of Pennsylvania, School of Medicine

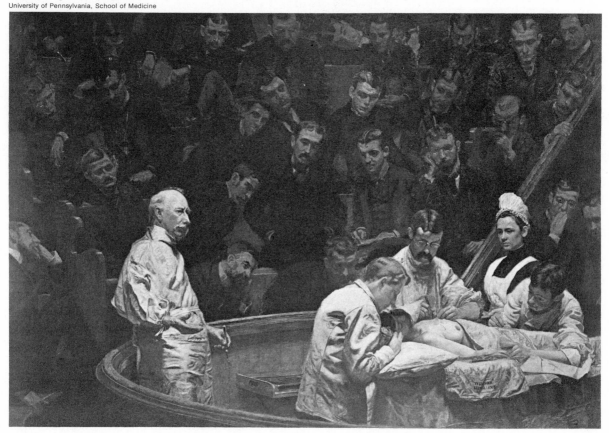

purely coincidental; they indulged in learned analyses of the nature of Law without bothering to trace the law in its actual operation; they made sweeping assumptions about federalism, the separation of powers, or judicial review which had little perceptible relation to their functioning. (*The American Mind* [1951].)

As early as the 1880s, Woodrow Wilson, then just beginning his career as a professor of political science, inaugurated a realistic way of examining political institutions. His doctoral dissertation, *Congressional Government: A Study in American Politics* (1885), firmly rejected the old mechanical interpretation of the Constitution and how it works. He showed how it functioned in real life, demonstrating that in its actual operation all its energies were so dissipated that little could get done. What was needed, he said, was a reorganized Congress that gave real power to leadership, so that the legislative system could begin solving problems instead of evading them. Four years later, in his book *The State* (1889), he again depicted government as vital, not static and machinelike. It is, he said,

. . . not a machine, but a living thing. . . . It is modified by its environment, necessitated by its tasks, shaped to its functions by the sheer pressure of life. No living thing can have its organs offset against each other as checks and live. On the contrary its life is dependent upon their quick cooperation, their ready response to the commands of instinct or intelligence, their amicable community of purpose. Government is not a body of blind forces; it is a body of men.

Political scientists now began applying these same approaches to all other aspects of public life. They studied lobbying as well as the formal procedures for passing laws; the way laws are administered as well as enacted; the relations between banks and government; the nature of political parties as social institutions; spoils systems, political bosses, pressure groups, and a host of other groupings in public life. Instead of relying on moral laws and philosophical absolutes, they based their work on huge masses of statistics drawn from census figures and on floods of facts drawn from state and federal agencies. Po-

litical theory was little discussed: what they concentrated on most of all was the impact of interest groups on public policy.

Realism in scholarship: The law

American legal theory had long been set in the same fixed, mechanical modes of thinking that had characterized other fields of thought. From about the middle of the nineteenth century legal scholars had settled on the notion that law was a science, a self-contained storehouse of rational, philosophical rules that needed not to be changed, but simply carefully applied. Finding precedents in earlier court decisions became almost the sole concern of the "black letter" lawyer, that is, the careful legal scholar who decided everything by looking in books. Such men believed that there was nothing tentative in the law, nothing growing or changing. Books were put together that carefully reduced whole areas of the law to a symmetrical pattern of legal principles, all derived most logically from two or three general philosophical beliefs.

By the 1880s a few perceptive men realized that this could not be true. Life was too various and changing to fit into a series of neat pigeonholes derived from ancient decisions. In 1881 the brilliant Oliver Wendell Holmes, Jr., who later served twenty years on the Massachusetts Supreme Court, and then thirty years (1902–1932) as one of Theodore Roosevelt's appointees to the United States Supreme Court, thrust at the heart of these formalistic beliefs. In an epochal book, *The Common Law* (1881), he said:

The life of the law has not been logic; it has been experience. The felt necessities of the time, the prevalent moral and political theories, intuitions of public policy, avowed or unconscious, even the prejudices which judges share with their fellow-men, have had a good deal more to do than the syllogism in determining the rules by which men should be governed.

This was pragmatism in the law (or, as it was called, legal realism), uttered by a man who was a close friend of William James. Legal realism was argued and debated and shouted over for decades. Holmes's words by no means settled the matter. After he joined the Court he usually wrote dissents, for the majority of the Court disagreed with him. Realists were accused of having no principles at all, of rejecting the whole idea of trying to form general principles from particular cases. Judges were offended by the view, often stated by legal realists, that court decisions that quoted precedent and philosophical rules were nothing more than after-the-fact rationalizations. Realists replied that they never wished to dispense with general principles but only to give far greater weight to practical facts in everyday life than had formerly been the case. When Louis Brandeis argued before the Supreme Court that state laws limiting the hours of labor were constitutional in the case of *Muller* v. *Oregon* (1908), he included in his argument a careful description of sociological conditions created by long hours of labor as well as citations to legal precedent. Law, realists said, was a tool for social action, a crucial instrument in a society rapidly changing. Jurists must not quote ancient principle and stand in reform's way.

The intellectual as expert

These transformations in the world of thought were important, for the time had finally arrived in America when intellectuals were gaining the public ear. The United States had always been an intensely practical nation, and Americans had regarded academics as ineffectual dreamers. But a great change had occurred by 1900. The universities formed or reorganized around 1870 had by this time been engaged for thirty years in graduating professionals in many fields who constituted, in effect, a new middle class. In business, labor, and agriculture; in social work, education, and law; in journalism, architecture, and public administration—in all these and more a steady influx of university-trained young people had been arriving on the scene and, by their work,

gaining public respect. A cultural system that was national in scope had emerged, replacing the decentralized little social worlds—the small towns and villages—where men and women had formerly received all their training.

Professional organizations, trade associations, agricultural cooperatives, chambers of commerce, leagues of small businessmen, national labor unions, manufacturers' organizations, and other such institutions provided a nationalized structure within which the new middle class worked. Essentially urban in character, the new middle class was proud of its cities, cosmopolitan in outlook, proud of its new skills, and hopeful of a shining future for the United States. Worshiping a new phenomenon called science, they were so effective in solving problems that the public formed a new notion of college graduates and academic intellectuals: they were not effete dreamers, but experts—and therefore men of power.

Their first arena of action lay in the states, where in the 1890s the initial attempts at regulation of business enterprise took place. Especially in Madison, the capital of Wisconsin, the use of a group of experts who provided trained advice to the government attracted nationwide attention. The "Wisconsin idea" was for the state government to call on the professors at the state university to serve as nonpartisan advisers on such issues as taxation, railroad problems, and the like. The young economist Richard T. Ely set up a special school at the University of Wisconsin designed to promote social science in the training of public servants. When Robert M. La Follette was elected a progressive governor in 1900, he began making extensive use of the professors, forming a kind of brain trust. Soon such people were being consulted in many states and on the national level as well.

The Progressive Era was for them an exciting and exuberant time filled with challenges and opportunities. Everything seemed open to fresh examination: industrial methods, banking systems, railway franchises, the use of political power, the nature of education, social relations, and even sexual life. Everywhere the chasm that had formerly separated the men of theory from the men of practice seemed to be bridged. The progressive political elite listened closely to the expert. Henry Cabot Lodge, Woodrow Wilson, Albert J. Beveridge, Robert M. La Follette, and Theodore Roosevelt nourished themselves on ideas and surrounded themselves with intellectuals. Perhaps no other characteristic set off progressives from their contemporaries more distinctively than their passion for ideas. Such people sat in their studies and laboriously wrote long analyses of concepts, principles, and institutions. It seemed uniquely their challenge to rethink all the old ideas that had served America for so long and had grown outworn, rigid, and useless. They responded enthusiastically to the new realism in scholarship, for it seemed to them that it was coming to grips with all that was vital and moving in American life.

Realism in popular literature

Well before the turn of the century, a new kind of literature emerged that was arrestingly realistic. The common Victorian novel had been flagrantly escapist, providing cozy tales of proper citizens who struggled high-mindedly with simple problems and went on to happy endings. But now writers turned to expose whatever was shabby, false, and shocking. Mark Twain led the way, culminating a long career as a humorist writer with *Huckleberry Finn* (1885). Twain's Mississippi valley was a sardonic, uproarious, but not happy place. There was too much casual death, meanness, selfishness, and crudity for that. It was a sly, jeering world of little men who puffed themselves up with false stories and scrambled around looking for success.

William Dean Howells, a contemporary of Twain's, was another realistic novelist. A simple man from the West who lived in New York City—in good part realism was a revolt against the eastern genteel tradition in literature—in the mid-1880s he began writing jarringly realistic stories. He chose New York, with its grim poor, as his setting and human suffering as his theme. His novels, such as *A Hazard of New Fortunes* (1890), focused on greedy capitalism, the confused life of great cities, the suffering caused by industrialism, and the collapse of morality under the pressures of modern life.

Other writers, younger than Howells, spoke in harsher tongues. They depicted a world in which natural passions had run riot. For these novelists, violence became the leading theme. Stephen Crane in *Maggie: A Girl of the Streets* (1893) described how city life could destroy a young woman, leading her through seduction and moral collapse to eventual suicide. Jack London, in *The Call of the Wild* (1903), *The Sea Wolf* (1904), and *White Fang* (1906) described a crude, Darwinian vision of nature. He glorified physical power and spoke of civilization as just "a veneer over the surface of the soft-shelled animal known as man." Throughout his writings ran an implicit appeal that the social injustice of his day needed to be swept away by violent revolution.

Frank Norris, like Jack London a Californian, came from the journalistic career that spawned so many realistic novelists. In his books *McTeague* (1899), *A Man's Woman* (1900), *The Octopus* (1901), and *The Pit* (1903), he saw his task as combating "false views of life, false characters, false sentiment, false morality, false history, false philosophy, false emotions, false heroism." Terrible forms of sadism, gore, and rampant sexuality stalked through his fiction. In *The Octopus*, a great railroad, the Southern Pacific in California, laid waste countless lives and corrupted the entire state.

Theodore Dreiser wrote similar novels. Seeing people as poor fools tossed about by forces they seemed unable to control, Dreiser centered on the theme of power exploiting weakness. Beginning with *Sister Carrie* (1900), his characters discover that "life was nothing save dark forces moving aimlessly." Powerful men learn that life

George Bellows's painting, "Cliff Dwellers" (1913) fulfilled the inherent tendencies of artistic realism by concentrating on a teeming, grimy scene from ordinary tenement life.

"Cliff Dwellers", 1913, by George Wesley Bellows, American, 1882–1925 Los Angeles County Museum of Art, Los Angeles County Funds

is a struggle for survival and push their way to the top of some social pyramid, only to spend their lives exploiting those below using any corrupt means they can find. "He had no consciousness of what is currently known as sin," Dreiser wrote of the chief character in *The Titan* (1914). "He never gave a thought to the vast palaver concerning evil which is constantly going on. There were just two faces to the shield of life—strength and weakness."

Realism in journalism

For some time before the turn of the century, a revolution had been going on in journalism, as well as in fiction. Responding to the huge new audiences of the cities, both the number and the circulation of newspapers rose spectacularly. In 1870 there were 600 daily newspapers; in 1909, more than 2,500. In 1870, 3 million papers were sold each day; in 1909, 24 million. The revenues produced by this huge sale meant that newspapers no longer needed to rely on the financial support of particular political parties. With their own sources of income, they could drop their obsessive concern with politics and turn instead to the kinds of subjects that appealed to their teeming readership. They launched sensationalist projects to build circulation—vice campaigns, sniffing or stamping out corruption in city hall, or clean-up-the-city drives.

Most importantly, newspaper publishers found that readers were absorbed by stories that concentrated on sufferers in the slums, whether they were young girls or unfortunate families. "Sob sister" journalism released latent humanitarian sentiments that the impersonality of urban life usually kept locked up. Thus, the middle class began to grow interested in the lives of the unfortunate, an interest that was to have major consequences in the Progressive Era. Similar discoveries were made by a new kind of magazine typified by *Munsey's, Saturday Evening Post,* and *McClure's Magazine,* which, unlike the genteel and sedate *Harper's* and *Century,* built large circulations on the appeal of stories that pitilessly exposed corruption and malpractice.

These changes in the press created a demand for vivid writing. A new career emerged, that of the reporter or magazine writer. Someone who was brash, moved easily in the jumbled human world of the city, and could write colorfully could claim a good salary. College graduates who went into the new profession brought the sophistication of the emerging social sciences. Journalism benefited from these new writers' high ideals,

particularly their sense of responsibility to the public welfare. And what they found was arresting enough—the "real" story, behind the closed doors or inside the smoke-filled rooms. Cultivating their contacts, they uncovered payoffs, false politicians, and the betrayal of public trusts.

These were the muckrakers, as Theodore Roosevelt dubbed them in a moment of pique. There was Upton Sinclair exposing the meat-packing industry, Ida Tarbell on Standard Oil, and Lincoln Steffens on civic corruption, followed by a host of other bold writers whose exposés met with spectacular success. Muckraking articles were particularly suitable, by their length and time of preparation, for the magazines. The writers had no great scheme for how American life should be reorganized; they simply concentrated on exposure. Again and again they appealed to the American conscience, insisting that the real cause for the malodorous goings-on they uncov-

Jack London, most flamboyant of the literary realists, poured harsh Darwinian images of violence and human brutality into his novels, as in *The Call of the Wild* (1903). His own life was a tragic blend of sudden wealth from his writings, and egoistic self-indulgence.

The Bettman Archive

ered lay in the complacency of the American people. There were all sorts of machines and systems for corruption which they eagerly described, but only an aroused citizenry, they insisted, could genuinely revitalize the nation.

Lincoln Steffens, a leading muckraker, wrote of political corruption: "And it's all a moral weakness; a weakness right where we think we are strongest. Oh, we are good—on Sunday, and we are 'fearfully patriotic' on the Fourth of July. But the bribe we pay to the janitor to prefer our interests to the landlord's is the little brother of the bribe passed to the alderman to sell a city street, and the father of the air-brake stock assigned to the president of a railroad to have this life-saving invention adopted on his road. And as for graft, railroad passes, saloon and bawdy-house blackmail, and watered stock, all these belong to the same family. We are . . . a free and sovereign people, we govern ourselves and the government is ours. But that is the point. We are responsible, not our leaders, since we follow them. We *let* them divert our loyalty from the United States to some 'party'; we *let* them boss the party and turn our municipal democracies into autocracies and our republican nation into a plutocracy. We cheat our government and we let our leaders loot it, and we let them wheedle and bribe our sovereignty from us. True, they pass for us strict laws, but we are content to let them pass also bad laws, giving away public property in exchange, and our good, and often impossible, laws we allow to be used for oppression and blackmail. And what can we say? We break our own laws and rob our own government, the lady at the custom-house, the lyncher with his rope, and the captain of industry with his bribe and rebate. The spirit of graft and lawlessness is the American spirit. . . . (*The Shame of the Cities* [1904].)

The detailed studies the muckrakers produced presented the American public with a fresh social drama, one that everyone could recognize, for it was right at their own front door. Robert Cantwell observed:

They wrote . . . an intimate, anecdotal, behind-the-scenes history of their own times. They traced the intricate relationship of the police, the underworld, the local political bosses, the secret connections between the new corporations . . . and the legislatures and the courts. . . . At the same time, the muckrakers pictured stage settings that everybody recognized but that nobody had written about—oil refineries, slums, the red-light districts, the hotel rooms where political deals were made—the familiar, unadorned, homely stages where the teeming day-to-day dramas of American life were enacted. ("Journalism—the Magazines," in Harold E. Stearns, ed., *America Now* [1938].)

This, then, was the new reality. Whatever was behind the scenes, sordid, illegal—this, the muckrakers told the public, was what America was truly like. This, the scholars told the new middle class, was what institutions were actually like. In books, magazines, and newspapers; in university extension courses, testimony before congressional committees, and public lectures; in the gatherings of professional, business, and farm associations—wherever public attention could be captured, the message of social decay was unceasingly sounded. With this image of American life before them, it is understandable that by the opening of the twentieth century the people of the United States were ready, in unprecedented numbers, to vote for men who called themselves progressives.

Bibliography

Three books that were especially valuable to me in writing this chapter: Three of Richard Hofstadter's brilliant studies of American history: *The Age of Reform** (1955), a work of major impact among historians that has helped me understand the period from the 1870s to the 1930s; *Anti-Intellectualism in American Life** (1963), which explores the rise of the expert as a major force in national affairs; and *The Progressive Historians: Turner, Parrington, Beard** (1968), a thoughtful exploration of these historians' thinking.

How have historians looked at the topic?

The various forms of conservative thought in the United States are ably discussed in Robert G. McCloskey's *American Conservatism in the Age of Enterprise** (1951). Of major importance are Richard Hofstadter's *Social Darwinism in American Thought, 1860–1915** (1944) and Arnold M. Paul's *Conservative Crisis and the Rule of Law* (1960), which illuminates the judicial aspect.

In an engrossing, lively history, *Rendezvous with Destiny: A History of Modern American Reform** (1952), Eric Goldman stresses the breakdown of conservative social Darwinism and the emergence of reform Darwinism. Donald Fleming's sensitive essay "Social Darwinism" in Arthur M. Schlesinger, Jr., and Morton White, eds., *Paths of American Thought* (1963), is of major importance. An encyclopedic coverage of the intellectual trends in diverse fields is found in Henry Steele Commager's *The American Mind: An Interpretation of American Thought and Character Since the 1880s** (1950). Also excellent are: Morton G. White's *Social Thought in America: The Revolt against Formalism* (1949), which traces the evolution of social thought by examining the seminal minds of Charles Beard, Thorstein Veblen, John Dewey, and others; and Sidney Fine's *Laissez-Faire and the General Welfare State: A Study of Conflict in American Thought, 1865–1901** (1956), a fine summary of the ideological clash between advocates of government regulation and defenders of classical liberal economic doctrines.

The role of the Christian conscience in the progressive uprising is convincingly illustrated in Henry May's *The Protestant Churches and Industrial America* (1949). The best study of the social settlement movement is Allen F. Davis's *Spearheads for Reform: The Social Settlements and the Progressive Movement, 1890–1914* (1967). Jane Addams's autobiographical *Twenty Years at Hull House** (1910) is a rich work of great value in understanding the woman who became the symbol of the new breed of reformers. For an analytical treatment, see the essay by Jill Conway, "Jane Addams: An Ameri-can Heroine," in Robert Jay Lifton, ed., *The Woman in America** (1965) and Staughton Lynd's article "Jane Addams and the Radical Impulse," *Commentary 32* (1961).

The progressive era's philosopher, William James, wrote gracefully as well as originally, and many of his works are now available in paperback. *Pragmatism** (1907) and *The Will to Believe and Human Immortality** (1898) are good introductions, but other works of his should be read as well: *Psychology: The Briefer Course** (1892); *Varieties of Religious Experience** (1902); and *Talks to Teachers* (1898). James has received biographical attention in several worthwhile publications: See Margaret Knight's *William James* (1950); Ralph B. Perry's two-volume biography *The Thought and Character of William James* (1935).

The Emergence of the American University (1965) by Laurence R. Veysey focuses in part on the struggle within the academic community over the definition of the university's intellectual and moral purposes; and Richard Hofstadter and Walter P. Metzger's *The Development of Academic Freedom in the United States,** vol. 2 (1955) highlights the importance of professional faculty in the battle against church and business control of universities. Alfred Kazin's *On Native Grounds* (1942) traces divergent tendencies in turn-of-the-century American literature while Jay Martin's *Harvest of Change: American Literature, 1865–1914* (1967) discusses several major works, placing them in historical context. Willard Bleyer's *Main Currents in the History of American Journalism* (1969) is a provocative survey that focuses on the development of the American newspaper while Frank L. Mott's *A History of American Magazines, 1885–1905* (1957) explores the beginnings of mass circulation, extensive advertising, and muckraking in this media.

The most readable book on the bold writers of exposé is Louis Filler's *Crusaders for American Liberalism** (1939), but David Chalmers's *The Social and Political Ideas of the Muckrakers** (1964) is also valuable. Lincoln Steffens's brilliant and widely influential *Autobiography** (1931) should not be missed. Steffens's *The Shame of the Cities** (1904) and Upton Sinclair's *The Jungle** (1906) are classic examples of seminal muckraker works.

Finally, the works cited in the text of this chapter are perhaps the most germane of all. They form the inner core of progressivism and offer access to the minds, motives, and actions of those who lived in the era. They should be placed first on any student's reading list.

* Available in paperback.

CHAPTER 26

The Progressive Era: Republicans in Charge

TIME LINE

1890	Yosemite National Park created
1892	Sierra Club formed by John Muir
1897	Forest Management Act
1897–1904	Merger movement creates many giant corporations
1898	Gifford Pinchot becomes chief of Forestry Division
1900	Disaster in Galveston, Texas, leads to commission form of city government
1901	Socialist party formed, led by Eugene V. Debs; Theodore Roosevelt becomes twenty-sixth president of the United States; Robert M. La Follette becomes governor of Wisconsin
1902	Roosevelt begins Northern Securities prosecution under antitrust laws, intervenes in anthracite coal strike; Newlands Act creates Reclamation Bureau
1906	Roosevelt secures Hepburn Act, giving strong powers to the Interstate Commerce Commission; Upton Sinclair, *The Jungle;* Pure Food and Drug Act
1907	Roosevelt's conservation message; Oklahoma admitted to the Union; financial panic in Wall Street; Roosevelt becomes more radical, calls for many social reforms
1908	Roosevelt convenes Conservation Congress; William Howard Taft elected twenty-seventh president of the United States
1909	Payne-Aldrich Tariff
1910	Insurgents reduce powers of Speaker of the House; Pinchot fired as chief forester; Mann-Elkins Act gives ICC powers over telephone and telegraph; many antitrust suits begun; Roosevelt gives New Nationalism speech at Osawatomie, Kansas; Woodrow Wilson elected governor of New Jersey
1911	Weeks Act empowers government to acquire forest lands in eastern states
1912	Republican party splits; Roosevelt forms Progressive party; Woodrow Wilson elected twenty-eighth president of the United States; New Mexico and Arizona admitted to the Union
1913	Sixteenth Amendment authorizing income tax ratified; Seventeenth Amendment providing for direct election of United States senators ratified
1917	Flood Control Act inaugurates federal flood control programs

Opinion mobilizes

THE muckrakers did not fictionalize. The United States they so luridly described was gravely ill. It was this realization that seized the nation's consciousness in the 1890s and inspired the Progressive Era. Now the many different reform movements which for years had tried to get the public ear—the 8-hour day, votes for women, trust busting, honest government, controlling railroads—could finally get together and sweep ahead, jointly, to exciting victories. The catalyst lay in the massive depression of the 1890s. It created so great a sense of crisis that people who had formerly avoided each other were driven together to work in close partnership.

Furthermore, a new generation of young people was arriving on the scene, eager for action. In politics, literature, and scholarship they led the urban leagues, staffed the settlement houses, wrote the slashing journalism, and won the elections. Theodore Roosevelt in the White House, Robert M. La Follette in the Senate, Jane Addams at Hull House, Woodrow Wilson taking over the presidency of Princeton, Ida Tarbell exposing Standard Oil, William Randolph Hearst inaugurating yellow journalism, and Louis Brandeis arguing his brilliant briefs before the United States Supreme Court—these were the young leaders, university-trained and hungry for leadership, who led the new era of reform.

The setting

In the cities, a social revolution seemed imminent. The lower classes in America were on the edge of starvation. Social workers who roamed the slums wrote searing accounts of degradation and disease, which the middle classes feared would spread to them. William McKinley's prosperity meant rising prices; few laborers were organized; and wages lagged far behind the cost of living. Labor-management warfare raged and

flared. The Socialist party, led by Eugene V. Debs, was organized in 1901 and grew steadily in vote-gathering power. Factory workers suffered horrifying injuries, but employers refused to install expensive safety equipment or to compensate the maimed. Hours of labor were long, hitting especially hard the millions of children who labored in the mills and industries, and the women who worked so many hours each day that their children saw them only late at night.

City and state governments were corrupt. Every kind of special interest paid graft to get charters, franchises, and other privileges. Immigrants flooding the inner-city cores were desperate for work, and they voted for the bosses who gave them jobs—who in turn sold their political power to whomever was willing to pay money to receive a service. Wealthy men flagrantly refused to pay taxes, made it impossible for assessors to examine their holdings, and forced reduced tax rates through compliant city councils. The politics of entire states was taken over by powerful railroad, mine, steel, lumber, and petroleum corporations. From 1897 to 1904, there was a sudden and startling acceleration in the formation of huge industrial combines, giving them what amounted to a stranglehold over major areas of the national economy. Financiers like J. P. Morgan rose to enormous power, for they presided over these conglomerates, and were held in awe. In 1897, there were only twelve large combinations; by 1904, there were more than three hundred. Forty percent of American industry was in their hands.

The merger movement fell off rapidly after 1904, mainly because every kind of enterprise that could profitably be combined had been taken up. But these dramatic events, watched closely by the alarmed nation, left a permanent mark on the national mind. Much of the history of the Progressive Era consists of a response to these swift transformations. A few powerful men, so it seemed, had decisively closed off opportunities to everyone else. They had gained vast powers through their control over prices; could squeeze the purses of millions of Americans and skim off huge fortunes. Some two percent of the population held sixty percent of the nation's money. Could these powerful men be trusted to use their great power, to which no one had elected them, rightly and wisely? Few believed so. The very structure of the country seemed gravely imperiled by the existence of gigantic corporate power.

The new middle class—the college-trained lawyer, engineer, economist, corporate executive, banker—wanted to reach out and get all this national confusion under control. Their inclination was to think in terms of efficiency, management, planning, and central direction. Confident that their "scientific" methods and new bodies of knowledge equipped them to take on the largest tasks, they launched bold undertakings. Physicians, confronted by slum disease, demanded nothing less than the reorganization of entire cities in order to establish effective programs of public health. Whether it was the creation of centralized systems of city government to combat urban corruption, rationalized control over natural resources to protect the forests, commissions to oversee competitive practices in business, or government regulation of the giant railroads, the predominating urge among such people was to establish national order.

Anti-partyism

Out of this came a powerful attack on the political party itself. The "army style" politics of the previous generation was looked upon as a major source of the corruption that so stained and weakened democratic government. This sentiment was especially strong in the countryside and in small and medium cities, where traditional WASP America still predominated. Because state legislatures were badly skewed to over-represent the rural areas and keep the multiethnic cities from growing in power as they grew in (alien) population, in state after state reforms which aimed at breaking the power of party bosses were

enacted. All of them were justified in the name of bringing government directly into the hands of "the People." The Australian, secret ballot was widespread by 1900, so that party agents could not keep control over voters. Ballots were printed by public authority rather than by the parties, so that voters could pick and choose between candidates rather than simply turning in the party ticket. The huge number of elective offices was reduced sharply, so that voters could have a reasonable opportunity of knowing the candidates' qualifications, and not be forced simply to rely upon party recommendations. Civil service reform at the level of local government cut back sharply upon the patronage that parties could control, and upon the funds they could raise from office holders, who, if they did not contribute, could be fired. To fight ballot box stuffing, voters were required to register a considerable period before elections, so their names could be checked off at the polls, and strict residence requirements were established.

The direct primary system, which many states adopted during the Progressive Era, badly weakened parties. Now the voters at large had the power of selecting between possible party nominees. This made conventions, which were controlled by the politicians, and provided party organizations a powerful unifying agency, much less important. Furthermore, primary elections took away the decisive meaning of general elections. Opposition could now arise *within* parties. It was no longer necessary for the populace to rely upon the existence of a strong second party to provide this vital balancing force.

Parties were weakened in other ways. City-wide election of councilmen, instead of by wards, cut down on bloc voting and the scratching of backs within council chambers to get construction contracts, and other plums, for the people in particular legislators' districts. Middle class candidates tended now to win more often, for they were better known throughout the city. School systems were taken out from under council control, and placed under specially elected school

The popular alarm over the trusts, which grew rapidly in numbers around 1900, is shown in this *Puck* cartoon calling for stronger antitrust action.
The Granger Collection

boards which in turn hired professional educators. Relief of the poor was taken over by city and state bureaucracies. Professionally directed street and highway departments, and city-owned garbage collection, took away from local politicians the staffing of these offices, and the granting of lucrative contracts. More and more, the parties found themselves with less and less to do. They functioned primarily to get out the vote, at elections frequently made non-partisan (in local government).

George Washington Plunkitt, veteran ward boss for Tammany Hall in New York City, talked of graft in a 1905 interview. "Everybody is talkin' these days about Tammany men growin' rich on graft, but nobody thinks of drawin' the distinction between honest graft and dishonest graft. There's all

the difference in the world between the two. Yes, many of our men have grown rich in politics. I have myself. I've made a big fortune out of the game, and I'm gettin' richer every day, but I've not gone in for dishonest graft—blackmailin' gamblers, saloonkeepers, disorderly people, etc.—and neither has any of the men who have made big fortunes in politics.

"There's an honest graft, and I'm an example of how it works. I might sum up the whole thing by sayin': 'I seen my opportunities and I took 'em.'

"Just let me explain by examples. My party's in power in the city, and it's goin' to undertake a lot of public improvements. Well, I'm tipped off, say, that they're going to lay out a new park at a certain place.

"I see my opportunity and I take it. I go to that place and I buy up all the land I can in the neighborhood. Then the board of this or that makes its plan public, and there is a rush to get my land, which nobody cared particular for before.

"Ain't it perfectly honest to charge a good price and make a profit on my investment and foresight? Of course, it is. Well, that's honest graft. . . . The books are always all right. The money in the city treasury is all right. Everything is all right. All they can show is that the Tammany heads of departments looked after their friends, within the law, and gave them what opportunities they could to make honest graft. Now, let me tell you that's never goin' to hurt Tammany with the people. Every good man looks after his friends, and any man who doesn't isn't likely to be popular." (William L. Riordon, *Plunkitt of Tammany Hall* [1905].)

In order further to break down the power of parties and to make government directly responsible to the people at large, voters were given many new powers (though the pattern varied widely from state to state). They could recall judges and other officials; elect senators directly, thus taking this task out of the hands of party-dominated state legislatures; enact laws directly by the initiative procedure; and nullify laws passed by legislative bodies by putting them on the ballot and voting them down in the referendum process. In many states, reformers fought for and won the right for cities to govern themselves (home rule), through their own locally-adopted charters and elected governments, thus taking control over their daily lives out of the hands of distant state capitals where corruption was often a heavy influence.

Voter drop-off and one-partyism

As parties withered, so did voter participation. The massive turnouts of the Gilded Age, and the keen and almost continuous attention voters then paid to public issues, faded. In most of the larger industrial states, and especially in the larger cities, presidential voting dropped perhaps a fifth

after 1896. About 70% of the South's eligible voters voted in the 1880s; by 1900, only about 40%; and by 1920, voting was down to 25%. In non-Southern states, the comparable figures were 85%, 84%, and 60%. (The South's figures were especially low because of the disfranchisement of black Americans around 1900, a process much advanced by the direct primary system, which, by being an internal party process, could be flatly limited to white voters.) About two thirds of the national electorate in the late nineteenth century could be termed "core" voters, who turned out regularly; a tenth were peripheral voters, casting ballots occasionally; and a quarter were entirely outside the political system. In the 1920s, the comparable figures were a third and a sixth, with half of the electorate being outside the political process altogether.

At the same time, huge one-party regions appeared. The South was, of course, solidly Democratic. The Northeast and Middle West were almost as solidly Republican, and so was much of the West. Some 85% of the total electoral college vote which went to Democratic presidential candidates from 1896 to 1928 was cast in former slave states. In states like Pennsylvania, conversely, Democratic candidates for governor were almost never elected. The upper Middle West—the states of Wisconsin, Iowa, Minnesota, the Dakotas, Nebraska, and Kansas—comprised a kind of Solid North, for these states were overwhelmingly Republican. Since a two-party competition had largely died away in large parts of the country, general elections were formalities, which further reduced voter participation.

Progressivism in the cities

These changes profoundly transformed the way American communities governed themselves. Breaking the close control of party, and professionalizing government, meant drawing centers of control away from local neighborhoods and placing them in city-wide offices. The folkish, intensely personal politics of the ethnic minorities was now challenged by WASP, middle class notions of a formal and legal social order, relying upon strong, centralized administration. The role of the local ward heeler, who sat in the ethnic kitchen and offered his services, was in many cities challenged by that of the impartial, trained city worker ministering in regulation-bound and standardized ways to individual needs. The depersonalizing of government and its services meant, to many, its dehumanization.

On the other hand, a more honest and efficient government was potentially a much more powerful weapon to use in social reform. Stronger city governments could exert controls over such utilities as gas, water, and street transportation companies, forcing them to charge just rates. Tax assessments, which had been highly skewed in favor of wealthy individuals and grafting corporations, were the subject of massive public campaigns of reform. Nonpartisan tax equalization commissions were created, and tax assessors made elective. Many cities began building municipally owned water, gas, and electricity plants. New controls over housing extended further the idea that government should involve itself deeply in social conditions. Death rates were slashed dramatically when water supplies were cleaned up, garbage regularly collected, and inoculation programs established. The Progressive Era was especially concerned about the health of the family, and of the nation's children. Now, with these new agencies of government, with their planned budgets, audited expenditures, and logical distributions of powers, there could be new schools, free milk, public health programs, parks, libraries, laws to limit hours of work, industrial safety measures (and enforcement), and workmen's compensation.

Progressivism in the states

The reform wave rose up from the cities to the states, in part because the cities learned that their problems could not be completely solved until the state governments were cleaned up. Particu-

larly in the Midwest, the South, and the Far West, a chain reaction of progressivism seemed to begin when Robert M. La Follette became governor of Wisconsin in 1901. Under La Follette's determined urgings, Wisconsin enacted a direct primary law, created a railroad rate commission that had real powers, curbed lobbying, began to conserve natural resources, established regulations over banks in the state, raised taxes on railroads and corporations, and created state civil service. Wisconsin even went so far as to enact a state income tax law.

By this time the state was being called "the laboratory of democracy," and its achievements were closely followed and copied in many other states. Governors were given more power to act on their own, thus helping to centralize authority; and commissions were formed to deal with flood control, banking systems, transportation, and industrial conditions. Corrupt practices acts were passed to cut down the influence of corporations on elections; and initiative, referendum, recall, and direct primary arrangements were enacted. The surge for direct popular election of United States senators achieved national victory when the Seventeenth Amendment was ratified in 1913.

As in the cities, the states showed a keen concern for the welfare of children, millions of whom were employed in cotton mills and on farms. After 1901, child labor laws were enacted, and by 1914, every state save one had established fourteen as the minimum age for legal employment. Beginning in Illinois in 1893, women's hours of work were also limited, in good part to make them more able to be with their children.

Progressivism in the nation: Theodore Roosevelt

Reformers had to turn to Washington, D.C., however, to assault the nation's larger problems. The railroad system, the power of great corporations, the banking system, the protective tariff, and the problem of natural resources—all were national in scope. Above all, the reform cause needed a dynamic national spokesman. Progressives found that person in Theodore Roosevelt.

There is no way to summarize Roosevelt's character. A diplomat observed that his temperament was that of a small boy, always excitable, enthusiastic, impulsive. Certainly he loved the outdoors, and glorified what he called the strenuous life. He could be an impossible clown, for as one of his muckraking friends, Lincoln Steffens, remarked, "the gift of the gods to Theodore Roosevelt was joy, joy in life." A cultivated man—he wrote many books of still-valuable history—he was eager and able to learn quickly. As an official in New York City, he had been horrified at slum conditions and began then to listen to social reformers. After his spectacular exploits in the Spanish-American War, he was elected governor of New York (1898–1900), where he battled the utility corporations and forced them to accept important public controls. He never liked people whose only concern was in making money, and

The "man of the decade," Theodore Roosevelt, said "I had a great time as president," and, in his whirlwind seven and a half years at the post (1901–1909), he catapulted the nation into the Progressive Era.
Brown Brothers

he habitually spoke of them in terms of contempt and derision. His door was open to intellectuals, poets, prize fighters, cowboys, artists, and brash young reporters.

Theodore Roosevelt, in short, fitted no one's pattern. But he *was* a Republican, and a devoted one. Why? Partly from his inherent style of life. He was a patrician, the Republicans were the party of "the best men in society," and that was that. He thought the Catholic Irish disgusting, and grieved over declining birth rates among Anglo-Saxons. A firm nativist in the 1890s, he had supported immigration restriction. Besides, he genuinely detested dishonesty in public office. The Tammany machine of New York City, with its timeless corruption, made it impossible for him to even think of being a Democrat.

But there was much more to it than this. Fundamentally, Theodore Roosevelt was a deep-dyed nationalist, a man who was intensely patriotic. He liked intellectuals, but only if they were not, in his eyes, too critical of America. The novels of Frank Norris made him fume. It was Roosevelt, after all, who in distaste coined the term *muckraker*. He thought big businessmen had gone too far in their selfishness and firmly believed the poor had a right to decent wages and living conditions, but socialists and Populists made him purple with rage.

His political impulses were classically Hamiltonian: he wanted to build a vigorous America by erecting a strong and active central government that would lead the nation confidently. Like so many in his time in Britain and America, he talked constantly of the need to solve the nation's ills by making it "efficient." The way to do this, he firmly believed, was to give real authority, real power, to strong men of good character. Roosevelt never trusted the legislative process. State legislatures and Congress seemed always to come out wrong, largely because, in his view, they were confused, leaderless, and petty. Whenever he could, he directed foreign and domestic affairs in ways that circumvented the need for congressional approval.

Roosevelt, more than anyone else, talked the nation into the idea of creating strong independent commissions, staffed by experts, that would regulate large areas of national life without congressional interference. Again and again Roosevelt sought in strong administration the solution to the nation's ills, in this mirroring what the new middle class was doing at the same time in city and state governments, farm organizations, the professions, and in commerce and industry.

It must be clearly understood, however, that the strong independent commission, though widely praised as democratic and on the side of the people, is not necessarily a democratic idea at all. It represents a great concentraton of public power in a few hands, presumably for good purposes, but how that power is actually put to use remains the question. Theodore Roosevelt was not concerned, for he had a simple answer: always make certain that men of good character are appointed to the commissions. Thus did the fundamental elitism of Theodore Roosevelt, his optimistic faith in strong leadership by the best men, create a new institutional pattern for the American government.

Roosevelt's first administration: The conservation crusade

Roosevelt had little room for maneuver when he became president. He inherited a McKinley administration, Congress was dominated by conservatives, and the Republican organization was firmly in orthodox hands. But he was restless. He immediately launched a vigorous foreign policy, as described in chapter 24. Turning to domestic affairs, he took up conservation, which became one of his favorite causes. The notion of husbanding the nation's resources appealed to him. As he said to the Conservation Congress that he called to meet in Washington in 1908, "let us remember that the conservation of natural resources . . . is yet but part of another and greater problem . . . the problem of national efficiency, the patriotic duty of insuring the safety and continuance of the Nation."

Conservation, as a problem and a cause, sprang directly out of the condition of the West, where forests had been swept away, creating national alarm. Beginning in Grover Cleveland's administration, millions of acres of forested lands had been withdrawn from public entry (that is, they could not thereafter become private property). At the same time, farmers in such states as California were struggling with flood problems while others in semi-arid regions, like Nevada, were trying to build irrigation systems.

Conservation was another issue in which centralization was competing with local control, the common people with the experts. It was an elite movement, staffed by scientists, civil servants, engineers, and far-sighted politicians, usually from the eastern states. They spoke of the planned use of resources and deplored uncontrolled exploitation. Gifford Pinchot, trained in French and German forestry practices and inspired by the possibilities of "sustained yield," pursued these goals with almost utopian zeal. He became chief of the federal Forestry Division in 1898, and immediately set out to educate the public and the lumber industry about scientific forest management. But many westerners, anxious for jobs and profits, wanted to see natural resources developed. Lumbermen, cattle and sheep ranchers, miners, men eager for farm land—all heatedly condemned the foresters, hydraulic engineers, and lawyers who urged the federal government to take control of natural resources.

Also clamoring for public attention was the preservationist movement, whose most dramatic leader was John Muir. Inspired by Henry David Thoreau's famous dictum "in Wildness is the preservation of the World," Muir had spent years living in Yosemite Valley and hiking through the Sierra Nevada, his "range of light." Nature, Muir said, was a "window opening into heaven, a mirror reflecting the Creator." It should be preserved as a restorative to jaded modern humanity. With the help of others he won an important victory in 1890 when Congress created Yosemite National Park specifically to protect a beautiful wilderness. In 1892 he helped to form the Sierra Club in San Francisco to advance the preservation idea.

For a time Muir and Pinchot were eager allies. But their aims were sharply divergent—planned use versus preservation. Muir was appalled by what happened to flowers and grasses when sheep were allowed to graze in the forests; Pinchot thought this a wise use of forested land, so long as it was controlled, for it provided essential food. In the late 1890s Muir and Pinchot contended briefly over what principle would govern administration of the new forest reserves that were being set aside. In 1897, when the Forest Management Act was passed, it was clear that Pinchot had won. Muir was an attractive figure, but he had captured the nation's mind only marginally.

Although Roosevelt loved the wilderness, he firmly agreed with Pinchot. Strong administration, centralized planning, making resources fruitful for society—these appealed to the president. With his encouragement Pinchot transformed the Forest Service from a small office that provided information to lumbermen into a vigorous corps of determined foresters who struggled to protect the forests from destructive overuse. Roosevelt expanded the area of national forests from 46 million acres to more than 150 million, despite clamors of protest from westerners, who got Congress in 1907 to take away the president's authority to establish reserves in six western states. Meanwhile, Roosevelt and Pinchot urged that the national forest idea be extended to the eastern states. This eventually led to passage of the Weeks Act in 1911, which allowed national acquisition of huge tracts of eastern forested land. The Forest Service program was thus expanded to the entire country. In the process, Roosevelt greatly broadened the concept of conservation to apply to mineral resources and power sites. He even had Pinchot withdraw 2,500 hydroelectric sites on the nation's rivers, stating that he intended to place ranger stations at these locations.

Planned use of water resources

Meanwhile, new ideas concerning water use were forming. The Constitution gives the federal government control of all navigable streams, and in a hit-and-miss way there had been occasional efforts to use the army's Corps of Engineers to maintain navigability. In the 1890s it began to be urged that the government should treat the rivers as a multiple-use resource—for irrigation, flood control, reclamation, and other purposes. Congress resisted the appeals for a long time, for the implications were enormous and extremely costly. It was one thing to remove snags so steamboats could use rivers; it was another to build levee systems, dams, and all the other apparatus of a system of controlled water use. Flooding was a severe problem, especially in the lower Mississippi and in California's Sacramento Valley. In both areas college-trained landowners joined forces with hydraulic engineers to draw up detailed plans for flood control. After years of intensive lobbying and the marshaling of public support, Congress in 1917 finally made flood control one of the federal government's responsibilities. From that beginning grew the continent-wide program in which the Corps of Engineers plans and builds flood control works in practically every watercourse in the nation.

Before 1900 many western states experimented extensively with building irrigation projects, most of which ended in financial disaster. Congressman Francis G. Newlands of Nevada proposed that the federal government establish a Reclamation Bureau to set up a fund derived from the sale of lands that would be improved by irrigation, which would be used to finance such projects. To keep the program for the small farmer, a limit of 160 acres per family was to be established, greater holdings not being allowed to benefit from federal aid for irrigation. Roosevelt gave the scheme his eager support, and in June 1902 the Newlands Act became law.

The problem of business concentration

From the beginning of his presidency, Roosevelt pondered how he might approach what to him was the country's gravest problem—business concentration. He was not in principle opposed to big corporations. On the contrary, he regarded them as an inevitable and fruitful part of the evolutionary process. They seemed much more efficient, since they could bring large supplies of capital to the development of the nation's resources, coordinate operations, and eliminate "wasteful" competition. Roosevelt always admired powerful men and was disposed to stand back and leave them alone. But the fact remained that some of these men were using their power badly, and the time had come, he believed, for him to step in and act.

Accordingly, the president revived the Sherman Anti-Trust Act and began prosecutions. His first target was the Northern Securities Company, a railroad monopoly formed by the financier J. P. Morgan in 1901 that dominated the northwestern part of the United States. In February 1902 Roosevelt startled the business community and delighted the rest of the nation by beginning suit for dissolution of the company. Within a year he won his case and opened the way for the federal government to undertake a program of breaking up the largest and most damaging combines.

Under Roosevelt more than forty corporations were brought to court, and his successor, William Howard Taft, began suits against an even larger number. In 1911 a major victory was achieved in two cases, concerning Standard Oil and American Tobacco, that had been begun under Roosevelt. This established conclusively that the federal government did in fact possess the constitutional power to break up monopolies where in the judgment of the Supreme Court the company involved had placed an unreasonable restraint on the free flow of trade.

Roosevelt's second administration: The vigorous progressive

In 1904 Roosevelt swept to a second-term victory, overwhelming Alton B. Parker, a conservative lawyer nominated by the Democrats. The president was now free to become a progressive leader in his own right.

He immediately zeroed in on national control of the railroads. The time had come, he said in his railroad message to Congress in December 1905, "to assert the sovereignty of the National Government by affirmative action." He demanded unprecedented powers for the Interstate Commerce Commission, which had become practically useless because of adverse court decisions. The ICC should be allowed, he said, to establish fair rates when shippers complained and to inspect the railroad's books in doing so in order to be certain what rates the railroad actually needed to stay profitable. A storm of abuse erupted, for Roosevelt was challenging two of private business's most sacred rights—to set its own prices and to keep its books secret. But he got his law. The Hepburn Act of 1906 made what for many years had been only a possibility become a reality. Railroad rate-making was no longer left to private enterprise but brought under the oversight of public experts and a powerful independent commission.

For many years scientists in the Department of Agriculture had urged Congress to pass laws cleaning up the food and meat-packing industry and forbidding the sale of fraudulent and poisonous drugs. The conditions of meat packing were nauseating and revolting to all who inspected them. From state food and dairy departments came similar pleas, as well as from women's clubs and young doctors of the American Medical Association. Many food and drug businessmen wanted regulation too—so long as it was in a form they approved. Large companies were gravely endangered by the operations of fly-by-night drug houses and malodorous packing houses that gave the industry a bad name. Foreign markets for American meats were being severely reduced by European complaints. In 1906 Upton Sinclair's *The Jungle* laid out in disgusting detail the filthy meat-packing conditions in Chicago. This put the fat in the fire, and the congressmen who for years had blocked legislation as an infringement on private freedoms began to fall silent. Roosevelt, shocked by Sinclair's book, sent off his own investigators, while writing to Sinclair, "I agree with you that energetic, and, as I believe, in the long run radical, action must be taken to do away with the effects of arrogant and selfish greed on the part of the capitalist."

The big companies now swung into action, working assiduously with congressional committees to get regulation made palatable. A federal stamp of purity on their meats would restore their markets, so they approved the establishment of a corps of federal inspectors. However, they refused to provide the costs of such a service, thus ensuring that a cost-paring Congress would always limit its scope. At the same time, fines against drug manufacturers selling fraudulent merchandise were set ridiculously low, reaching only $300. When millions could be made selling a ballyhooed product, the fine simply became a license. Genuine regulation of useless and often harmful substances in drugs had to wait for many years—and has not yet been fully achieved.

Roosevelt and labor

Roosevelt had a complicated relationship with the labor movement. Fundamentally, he was on the side of the employer, who was, after all, the man on the top. But as a compassionate person, the president had long been disturbed by the conditions in which workers, especially women and children, labored. Furthermore, he looked on big unions as he did on big business—as a natural and valuable evolutionary growth that brought order and efficiency to the system. Workers had economic interests: they should be allowed to organize to achieve them.

In 1902 Roosevelt intervened spectacularly in a crucial labor-management dispute. The coal miners in Pennsylvania's anthracite region, under the leadership of the United Mine Workers and its chieftain, John Mitchell, a careful and cautious tactician, went on strike. The miners' hours were long, a rising cost of living pressed them cruelly, and their work was extremely dangerous. But the owners, primarily controllers of the six railroads that crossed the region, arrogantly refused even to talk to the workers.

During the 1902 anthracite coal strike, the leader of the coal operators, George F. Baer of the Reading Railway, wrote a classic letter expressing a capitalist's view of his prerogatives: "I do not know who you are [he wrote to a Mr. Clark]. I see that you are a religious man; but you are evidently biased in favor of the right of the working man to control a business in which he has no other interest than to secure fair wages for the work he does.

"I beg of you not to be discouraged. The rights and interests of the laboring man will be protected and cared for—not by the labor agitators, but by the Christian men to whom God in His infinite wisdom has given the control of the property interests of the country, and upon the successful Management of which so much depends.

"Do not be discouraged. Pray earnestly that right may triumph, always remembering that the Lord God Omnipotent still reigns, and that His reign is one of law and order, and not of violence and crime." (Quoted in Mark Sullivan, *Our Times: The United States, 1900–1925* [1927].)

As the months passed, Roosevelt fumed. Always frightened of the possibility of social revolution, he regarded the coal operators as the kind of businessmen who, by their selfishness, would destroy the country. Panic buying pushed the cost of coal sky-high; in the fall of 1902 schools began closing for lack of fuel. Finally, in October, the president, who lacked any legal powers whatever to intervene in the strike, succeeded in bringing both the operators and the union men to the White House for a conference. The operators protested against being made to "deal with outlaws" and elaborately pretended that John Mitchell was not even present. A public commission of investigation was finally agreed to, production began again, and eventually the miners were given an approximate ten-percent increase in pay. Organized labor looked in gratitude to the president, for he was the first chief executive ever to have taken their side.

Even so, labor regarded "marvelous Teddy" warily. Sometimes they gave him warm and enthusiastic support as their first friend in the White House; but they never felt wholly comfortable with him, for his attitudes were still those of an upper-class patrician. Besides, he was a Republican, and in these tumultuous years of constant labor-management disputes, it seemed to workers that the employer was always a Republican. Roosevelt might warm their hearts, but when it came to elections they often turned to the Democrats. Whatever Roosevelt did, the core of the labor movement was still composed of ethnic minorities, and most of them found the Republicans still too much the party of nativism and Anglo-Saxon Protestantism for them to support it.

William Howard Taft: The unhappy president

In 1908, for the third time the Democrats turned to William Jennings Bryan as their presidential nominee, and he went about the country crying out, not illogically, that he was the legitimate heir to Theodore Roosevelt. But Roosevelt himself had chosen William Howard Taft as his successor, and the nation accepted that judgment. A man from Ohio—thus, the Republicans returned to the Middle West to choose their presidential nominee, as was their tradition—he had been a federal judge, governor of the Philippines (1901–1904), and for four years T.R.'s secretary of war. A thoughtful man of progressive conservative opinions, he had always supported Roosevelt's policies.

Unfortunately, he was ill suited to the presidency. Huge and slow-moving, he could hardly provide a suitable successor to the lively Roosevelt. Furthermore, when on his own, he proved deeply loyal to the belief that the Establishment should rule. Reformers set his teeth on edge, and he was soon locked in hostile combat with the "insurgents" in his party. Drawn heavily from the "Solid North"—the upper Middle West—these Republican senators and congressmen loved Roosevelt, despised the "interests," and wanted to keep the reform movement sweeping ahead. In 1909 they set off a terrific fight in the Senate to win reductions in the Payne-Aldrich tariff bill then being considered. When they failed, they regarded Taft as responsible, for he had indeed given the protectionists his tacit support even though their bill was exposed as a blatant giveaway to eastern industrial combines.

In conservation, Taft appeared to swing toward the side of those crying out, "throw open the public domain!" He appointed Richard A. Ballinger, nationally known as a fighter against conservation, as his secretary of the interior, and sided with him when Gifford Pinchot levelled charges—later shown to be untrue—that Ballinger was corruptly linked to certain coal field owners. At this, the angry Taft fired Pinchot, an act which convinced thousands that "the interests" were back in control, and infuriated Theodore Roosevelt.

Taft actually had reform tendencies of his own.

Ballinger's goal had been for the national government to cede its public lands to the states, but Taft refused. He even considerably expanded forest reserves. At his urging, in 1910 the Mann-Elkins Act was passed, which strengthened the ICC by giving it regulatory powers over telephone and telegraph companies and allowing it to revise railroad rates without waiting for complaints, after which it would be up to the railroad company to prove that the new rate was inequitable. Taft also played a role in the passage of one of the most fateful changes ever made in the structure of American institutions—the income tax amendment, which in the long run was almost by itself to transform the whole nature of government in the United States. (It became the Sixteenth Amendment when ratified in 1913.) Taft was also a determined trustbuster. In 1910 his administration began suits that eventually totaled sixty-five in number, as against forty-four under Roosevelt.

Taft and the progressives

Taft, however, became convinced that the progressive insurgents in his party were endangering the country. He and his Old Guard followers firmly believed that the people at large could not be relied upon to provide effective government. When progressives called for democratizing government, he recoiled. The initiative, referendum, and recall seemed to conservative Republicans dangerously socialistic. They feared such reforms would deliver social policy into the hands of those jealous of the rich. Especially after progressives began calling for the right of recalling judicial decisions, conservative Republicans were horrified. Taft reverenced the law (he was to serve as Chief Justice of the United States from 1921 to 1930), and was appalled at such ideas. He publicly said that they would destroy freedom and order, making everything subject to the fitful gusts of public opinion.

In August, 1910, in Osawatomie, Kansas, Theodore Roosevelt dramatically re-entered national politics by calling for a new social order in America based upon true social justice. It would be achieved by a "New Nationalism," which would see a much bigger and more powerful national government battling with the interests, and making of the presidency the "steward of the public welfare." Soon thereafter, angered at Taft, he let politicians know that if the people wanted him as president again, he would run. Taft, meanwhile, had already decided that he had to be the champion of a true and conservative American philosophy of government; that Roosevelt's wild ideas—especially his support for the recall of judges and judicial decisions—gravely threatened the health and stability of the nation.

Taft and Roosevelt now went about the country shouting angry words about each other to wildly partisan audiences. Wherever there was a direct primary system, Roosevelt won, for he was popular with the rank and file in progressive states; wherever the convention system existed, Taft swept the delegates. When the Republicans gathered at their national convention in Chicago in June 1912, a huge crowd was on the scene, excited by the knowledge that over 250 seats in the convention were being contested for by rival delegations, each claiming the other was illegally chosen. Whoever got these contested seats would get the nomination.

Roosevelt debarked from his train into a roaring crowd, teeth agleam, wearing an enormous sombrero and a Rough Rider uniform. He was practically crushed, but he bellowed to reporters "I feel like a bull moose!" Wherever he went, shouting his cries for social justice, he was surrounded by an almost religious hysteria. His followers frequently burst out singing the hymn "Onward, Christian Soldiers." Indeed, the mounting reform campaign was saturated with powerful religious imagery: *uplift, redemption, conversion, battles for the Lord, forces of evil, crusades*— these were the sonorous, powerful trumpet calls

that stirred progressive audiences in the hinterland. A progressive political campaign was like a religious revival, tongues of flame lighting prairie fires of political evangelism.

In Chicago progressive arguments were expressed in biblical quotations. The *Chicago Tribune,* which backed Roosevelt, put a banner headline on the issue that was read while the Republican National Committee pondered which delegations to seat: "THOU SHALT NOT STEAL." Roosevelt responded with a roaring speech to a packed crowd on the night preceding the opening of the convention. His crusade, he said, was directed against the "leadership of men whose souls are seared and whose eyes are blinded, men of cold heart and narrow mind, who believe we can find safety in dull timidity and dull inaction. . . . We fight in honorable fashion," he concluded in a dramatic climax, "for the good of mankind; fearless of the future, unheeding of our individual fates, with unflinching hearts and undimmed eyes; we stand at Armageddon, and we battle for the Lord!"

Roosevelt was beaten before he began. The National Committee, appointed four years before by Taft, was firmly in the president's hands. The committee seated Taft delegates, and Taft's supporters took over firm control of the convention. Roosevelt delegates finally stopped voting. While Taft was being nominated, they pleaded with Roosevelt to form a new political party. Now at white heat, Roosevelt agreed, and in August 1912 the Progressive party (nicknamed the Bull Moose party) met to nominate Theodore Roosevelt for the presidency.

The Democrats were delighted. With the Republicans irretrievably shattered, their votes in the presidential election would be divided in two, and a Democrat would finally have a good chance to win. Democratic progressives determined to nominate one of their own. They concluded that the best such figure was Woodrow Wilson, the former president of Princeton University who was then compiling a stunning record of reform as progressive Democratic governor of New Jersey. When the delegates gathered in Baltimore, the progressive Democrats won the nomination for Wilson.

The surging Democrats

The Democrats were, in fact, beginning a renewed national surging of political strength. The labor movement was still relatively small, for it had only 5.5% of the industrial labor force unionized in 1910 and only 15–20% of the skilled, but it was swinging strongly Democratic and helping to win key elections. Furthermore, the "new stock" immigrants from eastern and southern Europe who had been arriving in the country by the millions since 1890 were turning to their traditional friends, the Democrats. Cleveland, Ohio, with its large immigrant population of industrial workers, sent only Democrats to the state senate between 1911 and 1921, and, with rare excep-

tions, only Democrats to the national Congress. In New York City, new stock voters helped the Democrats win all 35 seats that city had in the state assembly, and all of its twelve senate positions as well. In Boston, where Democrats had formerly won half of the fifty legislators from that city who sat in the state legislature, after 1909 they began winning four-fifths of them, for they were now reaping heavy Italian and Jewish as well as Irish votes.

A powerful new urban liberalism emerged in this setting, which concentrated upon enacting major programs of social—not simply political—reform. In the state of New York, in the years 1911–13, a strong ethnic coalition led by the Irishman Alfred E. Smith and the German Robert Wagner enacted the most sweeping such program in American history: regulating inhuman conditions of labor; protecting women and children in factories; limiting hours of labor; creating new state agencies to enforce laws concerning industrial safety; insuring one day's rest in seven; establishing minimum wages on the state canals; and creating pension funds for widows and children, and for retired public employees. In Ohio, Illinois, Massachusetts, and other industrial states with large ethnic populations, similar programs were enacted.

The progressive movement, in short, was becoming Democratic. It had never succeeded in capturing the heart of the Republican party. Though progressive Republicans had had considerable success at the state level, especially in the upper Middle West and in California, at the national level the party remained firmly conservative. Progressive Republicans had fought against the Payne-Aldrich tariff and lost; had defended Pinchot, and he was dismissed; had tried to get T.R. nominated in 1912 as a Republican, and lost that battle too. For years William Jennings Bryan had been preaching advanced progressivism, insisting that the Democrats were T.R.'s real political heirs; the solid Democratic South was burning with anger at northern financial and corporate

After Taft and Roosevelt had lost the 1912 presidential campaign to Wilson, during which they had bitterly assailed each other as the nominees, respectively, of the Republican and Progressive parties, a cartoonist depicts them as saying exhaustedly to each other, "Cheer up! I might have won."
Library of Congress

interests; and now Democrats in many middle western and northeastern states began capturing governor's mansions. In the 1920s, the shift toward the Democrats that was now beginning in northern cities would become a landslide—and a crucial question would have to be fought out within their party: were they a Southern, rural, Protestant party, or one that was Northern, urban, and non-WASP immigrant?

The Election of 1912

The Progressive party labored manfully in the 1912 election, but Roosevelt himself had practically no hopes. "I would have had a sporting chance," he said, "if the Democrats had put up a reactionary candidate." He could have pulled out and perhaps helped Taft to win, but his passion to destroy Taft was too overwhelming. He jibed at Wilson's distaste for big government (to be explored in the next chapter), insisting that, "We propose to use the whole power of the government to protect all those who, under Mr. Wilson's laissez-faire system, are trodden down in the ferocious, scrambling rush of an unregulated and purely individualistic industrialism." Wilson, however, won in an electoral landslide with 435 votes. He did not have a popular majority behind him—he secured 6.3 million votes to Roosevelt's 4.1 million and Taft's 3.5 million—but he had a

The election of 1912

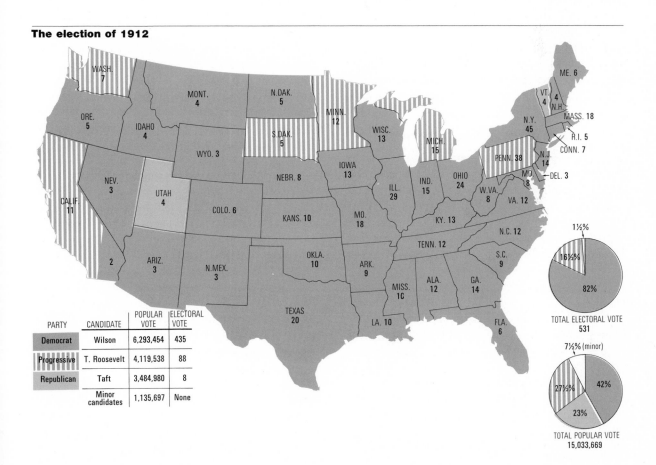

PARTY	CANDIDATE	POPULAR VOTE	ELECTORAL VOTE
Democrat	Wilson	6,293,454	435
Progressive	T. Roosevelt	4,119,538	88
Republican	Taft	3,484,980	8
	Minor candidates	1,135,697	None

TOTAL ELECTORAL VOTE
531

TOTAL POPULAR VOTE
15,033,669

large plurality. In the same balloting almost a million votes went to Eugene V. Debs, the Socialist candidate. By any reckoning, the nation wanted reform.

Bibliography

Three books that were especially valuable to me in writing this chapter: I have been instructed by Otis L. Graham, Jr.'s *The Great Campaigns: Reform and War in America, 1900–1928** (1971), a sophisticated analysis that brilliantly interweaves ideas and institutional realities; Walter Dean Burnham's *Critical Elections and the Mainsprings of American Politics* (1970), which is essential on the changed political universe after 1900, in relation to the decline of party and voter participation; and John D. Buenker's, *Urban Liberalism and Progressive Reform* (1973), which has made us understand how powerful was the role of the "new stock" ethnic voters who came into the country after 1900, and city-based reform movements.

How have historians looked at the topic?

Until the 1950s historians generally described the progressive reform movement as an uprising of the people against vested interests. Richard Hofstadter's erudite, gracefully written *The Age of Reform: From Bryan to F.D.R.** (1955) changed the focus to crucial cultural shifts within American society which created a new consciousness. Robert H. Wiebe's *The Search for Order, 1887–1920** (1961) points to the rise of the new middle class and its efforts at building centralized control wherever its influence extended. Samuel P. Hays's *Conservation and the Gospel of Efficiency: The Progressive Conservation Movement, 1890–1920** (1959) explores in absorbing detail how the progressives operated when dealing with one major national problem. Gabriel Kolko's *The Triumph of Conservatism: A Reinterpretation of American History, 1900–1916** (1963) holds that progressivism's strongest push came from businessmen wanting

to use government to solve their internal problems of order and the damping down of competition. A work of major importance is David P. Thelen's *The New Citizenship: Origins of Progressivism in Wisconsin, 1885–1900* (1972).

Important scholarship explaining the struggle between Taft and the progressive Republican insurgents lies in: Norman M. Wilensky, *Conservatives in the Progressive Era: the Taft Republicans of 1912* (1965); and Laurence James Holt, *Congressional Insurgents and the Party System, 1909–1916* (1967).

Progressivism grew out of the grave ills of the cities. Constance M. Green's *The Rise of Urban American* (1965) and Blake McKelvey's *The Urbanization of America, 1860–1915* (1963) describes this setting. Robert H. Bremner's *From the Depths: The Discovery of Poverty in the United States* (1956) treats the recognition of the urban poor, and Roy Lubove's *The Progressives and the Slums* (1962) explains what reformers tried to do about them. Frederic C. Howe's *The Confessions of a Reformer** (1967), originally published in 1925, is a personal account of a city reformer while *Plunkitt of Tammany Hall** by William L. Riordon (1963) is a lively defense of machine politics. The larger significance of city progressivism is analyzed in an excellent article by Samuel P. Hays, "The Politics of Municipal Government in the Progressive Era," *Pacific Northwest Quarterly* 60 (October 1964).

George E. Mowry's *The California Progressives** (1951) is the seminal study on state progressivism. Also valuable are Spencer Olin's *California's Prodigal Sons: Hiram Johnson and the Progressives, 1911–1917* (1968) and Hoyt L. Warner, *Progressivism in Ohio, 1897–1917* (1964).

Oscar E. Anderson, Jr.'s *The Health of a Nation: Harvey W. Wiley and the Fight for Pure Food* (1958) is useful on the Pure Food and Drug Act and its administration. The progressives' effectiveness in this area is placed in larger perspective in two splendid books by James Harvey Young, *The Toadstool Millionaires: A Social History of Patent*

Medicines in America before Federal Regulation (1961) and *The Medical Messiahs: A Social History of Health Quackery in Twentieth-Century America* (1967).

William Manners's *TR and Will: A Friendship That Split the Republican Party* (1969) is a compelling story of the changing relationship between Roosevelt and Taft, from protégé to opponent.

Henry Pringle offers a sympathetic view of Taft in *Life and Times of William Taft*, two vols. (1939). The breakup of the Republican party is discussed in George E. Mowry's *Theodore Roosevelt and the Progressive Movement** (1946).

*Available in paperback.

Equal Rights for Women

Any proposal concerning an improved situation for women, whether it has related to dress, jobs, or the vote, has always attracted ridicule, even from women themselves. An 1868 Currier and Ives cartoon emphasized the prevailing attitude that giving the vote to women was as ridiculous as men's taking over the household duties, while at the same time it would "masculinize" them and "feminize" their husbands.

A group of women in the 1910s enjoy lampooning traditionally male habits. Respectable ladies were then to appear in public only in formal situations, and certainly not to drink or to smoke. Conservatives raged that women activists were threatening the survival of the human race by becoming unattractive to men.

A major tactic adopted after 1900 by women activists was the urban parade, attended by thousands of scoffing men on the sidewalks and determined women in the floats and carriages. Here, women parade through Washington, D.C. in 1913, to demonstrate for the right to vote. On a similar occasion in 1915, 40,000 women marched up New York's Fifth Avenue, proudly waving placards and clutching enormous banners splashed with ''Votes for Women,'' and ''Equal Rights for Women.''

After passage of the Nineteenth Amendment in 1920, women, as here, were free to vote in every state in national elections. For years it had been forecast that women would be ruined as wives and mothers by the act, or, conversely, that a higher moral tone would instantly appear in national politics. Neither occurred.

CHAPTER 27

The Progressive Era: Democrats in Charge

TIME LINE

1883	*Civil Rights Cases* render federal civil rights laws ineffective
1890s	Populists try vainly to create biracial party in South
1890	In *Louisville, New Orleans, and Texas Railroad* v. *Mississippi* Supreme Court rules that states may require segregation in railroad cars.
1895	Booker T. Washington gives Atlanta address calling for black self-help
1896	In *Plessy* v. *Ferguson* the Court establishes separate-but-equal doctrine in relation to public schools and facilities
1898	In *Williams* v. *Mississippi* the Court allows Mississippi to withdraw the vote from blacks
1903	W.E.B. Du Bois, *The Souls of Black Folk*
1904	Anna Howard Shaw becomes head of National American Woman Suffrage Association
1905	Niagara Movement calls for integration and leadership education
1906	President Roosevelt discharges black troops, charging complicity in Brownsville, Texas riots; Atlanta race riot
1910	National Association for the Advancement of Colored People formed; state of Washington enfranchises women
1912	Woodrow Wilson elected twenty-eighth president of the United States
1913	Underwood Tariff; Federal Reserve System created; Wilson greatly broadens segregation in civil service
1914	Louis D. Brandeis, *Other People's Money;* Federal Trade Commission created; Clayton Anti-Trust Act
1915	Supreme Court rules Oklahoma's ''grandfather clause'' unconstitutional
1916	Wilson turns in New Nationalist directions; Brandeis appointed to Supreme Court; child labor legislation passed (later ruled unconstitutional); Tariff Commission created; Adamson Act
1917	Jeanette Rankin becomes first congresswoman
1920	Nineteenth Amendment granting women suffrage ratified

The new leader: Woodrow Wilson

N early March 1913 Woodrow Wilson arrived in Washington, D.C., for his inauguration as president of the United States. A cheering mob of Princeton students escorted him from the train, and a huge crowd filled the Capitol square to hear his moving inaugural address summoning the country to national restoration. The public was fascinated by this extraordinary man, the first intellectual in the White House since Thomas Jefferson and James Madison. A brilliant professor of political science and history at Princeton in the 1890s, he had become president of the university in 1902 and gained national attention as an educational reformer. In 1910 he burst into politics with an amazing performance as governor of New Jersey, where he overturned boss rule, created strict controls over utilities, and established the initiative and the referendum. Sweeping to the presidency, he seemed the man of the hour. Behind him the Democrats gained a majority of both houses of Congress for the first time in twenty years, and they welcomed their exciting new leader with gratitude and admiration.

In appearance Wilson was somewhat forbidding. Erect, precise in manner, long-jawed, his slim neat form contrasted markedly with that of the huge, jovial Taft. Everything about him was rigidly self-controlled. A forceful man of remarkable intellectual powers, he was contemptuous of stupidity, confident of his moral righteousness, and eager for power and authority. Wilson's passionate nature found full release when he spoke to large groups of people. His massive intellect would play eagerly over his topic, words would pour from him with fiery intensity, and his usually somber face would come eagerly alive. At Princeton his students had often broken into spontaneous applause; cynical politicians were transfixed when they listened to him; and audiences of common citizens were ignited into frenzies of cheering. Theodore Roosevelt had called the White House a "bully pulpit," and the office of the presidency was for Wilson a solemn and divine obligation. He entered the presidency firmly convinced that God had chosen him for a great mission. This conviction was to be his greatest strength and perhaps his gravest weakness.

Wilson's political attitudes

The new president, who had been born and reared in the South, was a Democrat by inheritance. Also, he was deeply rooted in the transatlantic Liberal-Democratic community. His mother was born to a Scottish family in Britain; and his paternal grandfather was a Scotch-Irishman who had immigrated from Northern Ireland first to Pennsylvania and then to Ohio. Wilson frequently went to Scotland and England for extended visits. His political ideal was that legendary Scotsman and leader of British Liberalism, William Gladstone, whom Wilson described as "the greatest statesman who ever lived." While studying at Princeton in the 1870s, Wilson pored over parliamentary debates and made British public life his model. He was a confirmed, doctrinaire free trader who regarded Adam Smith as the high prophet of political economy; a convinced supporter of sound money and the gold standard; an implacable opponent of political corruption; and a political scientist who believed that strong governments were necessarily tools of the rich and powerful.

In addition, Wilson was a romantic and a moralist. His imagination constantly seized on great epics of the human spirit. History fascinated him as a story of brave men struggling doggedly and courageously for grand ideals. Whatever he loved, he loved deeply. And whatever he despised, he despised thoroughly. His family was like a Scottish clan, bringing to America the combative, contentious life of the old country. It was infused with a feisty and almost primitive tribal loyalty in which the men seemed always to be fighting some external enemy, usually a religious one. He was more than a Democrat, he was a *fervent* Democrat. If someone opposed him on any issue, Wilson, combative Scot that he was, immediately made the opponent a personal enemy.

Shaping Wilson's whole personality was his powerful religious faith. Like Grover Cleveland, he was a Presbyterian who emphasized duty, strong government, decisive rule, moral principles, and the transcendent need for law and order. God has His purposes for the world, Wilson believed, and man's task is to be His agent. Such a faith could make one dogmatic and conservative, and through much of his life Wilson was both of these. But it could also make one radical. The God of the Presbyterians was a stern, Old Testament Jehovah who was angry at evil and corruption in human life. When Wilson, like Cleveland before him, was seized by this same anger, he became an inspired reformer.

Wilson's New Freedom

Wilson had hungered for power all his life. Now that he had it, what was he going to do with it? In the 1912 campaign, he traveled about the country giving a series of ringing addresses that set forth what he called, in contrast to Roosevelt's New Nationalism, the New Freedom. In recent years, Wilson said, a new form of social organization had taken over American life—the great corporation. Impersonal, inherently amoral, great corporations had created an almost conspiratorial network of power that enabled them to exploit the whole country. Hiding behind the protective tariff and insisting that all their affairs be conducted in secret, corporations corrupted the government into providing them with special privileges—bounties, land grants, hydroelectric power sites, legal immunities, and the aid of the courts in putting down labor strikes.

The Republican administrations, Wilson said, had listened only to the men who ran the great banks, the big industrial corporations, and the railroads. They did so because they subscribed

President-elect Woodrow Wilson, a lean and intense scholar bent upon major national reforms, stands on Inauguration Day, 1913, in sharp physical contrast to the jovial, rotund President Taft, a man who believed the nation already essentially sound.
The Granger Collection

to the pernicious philosophy of Alexander Hamilton, which was that the nation should be run by the wealthy and the powerful because they knew what was best for everyone. This idea was monstrous, Wilson insisted, for it violated the sturdy independence and manhood of the ordinary American. The whole philosophy of "government by trustee" must be thrown aside and the people allowed to take over their own government once again. Representatives of special interests could never understand the general interest.

The tariff, he said, was a throttling monster

that spawned trusts and monopolies. Take away its protective features and the whole economy would begin to multiply and diversify. Then the federal government must make a direct assault on the trusts. It was wrong, Wilson believed, to regard trusts as inevitable, as did Roosevelt, and to propose simply that the government regulate them in the public interest. This would mean a continuation of "government by trustee." Powerful bankers would sit down with powerful government officials and settle things privately, while the public waited outside. The New Freedom would strengthen the antitrust laws so that existing combinations could be broken up; transform the money trust to remove its stranglehold on credit; and specifically outlaw the ways in which trusts unfairly destroyed competition. Interlocking boards of directorates, run from the powerful banks, linked together railroads, factories, mines, and utilities in a spreading network that constricted the entire nation. However benevolent the corporations' autocracy might be, it must be broken up. The United States must experience a new flowering of individualism; the people's vital energies must be liberated.

Louis D. Brandeis, brilliant reform lawyer and adviser to Woodrow Wilson, issued a famous attack on the banking system: "The practice of interlocking directorates is the root of many evils. It offends laws human and divine. Applied to rival corporations, it tends to the suppression of competition and to violation of the Sherman law. Applied to corporations which deal with each other, it tends to disloyalty and to violation of the fundamental law that no man can serve two masters. In either event it tends to inefficiency; for it removes incentive and destroys soundness of judgment. . . . It is the most potent instrument of the Money Trust. Break the control so exercised by the investment bankers over railroads, public service and industrial corporations, over banks, life insurance and trust companies, and a long step will have been taken toward attainment of the New Freedom.

"A single example will illustrate the vicious circle of control—the endless chain—through which our financial oligarchy now operates: J. P. Morgan (or a partner), a director of the New York, New Haven & Hartford Railroad, causes that company to sell to J. P. Morgan & Co. an issue of bonds. J. P. Morgan & Co. borrow the money with which to pay for the bonds from the Guaranty Trust Company, of which Mr. Morgan (or a partner) is director. J. P. Morgan & Co. sell the bonds to the Penn Mutual Life Insurance Company, of which Mr. Morgan (or a partner) is a director. The New Haven spends the proceeds of the bonds in purchasing steel rails from the United States Steel Corporation, of which Mr. Morgan (or a partner) is a director. [And so on, through a long circular trail of transactions involving firms of which Morgan or a partner was a director: General Electric Company, Western Union, American Telephone and Telegraph, the Pullman Company, Baldwin Locomotive Company.] Each and every one of the companies last named markets its securities through J. P. Morgan & Co.; each deposits its funds with J. P. Morgan & Co.; and with these funds of each, the firm enters upon further operations." (*Other People's Money* [1914].)

In these captivating orations we hear clearly the voice of the older Democratic tradition. Wilson, like all his predecessors in the White House save Theodore Roosevelt, had never lived in big cities or near great factories; had never directly experienced their festering social ills. As a traditional Democrat, he was primarily concerned that the economy be kept open, dynamic, and fair, so that the small men could get ahead. Roosevelt's New Nationalism called for the government not only to regulate the trusts, but for it to give direct assistance to the disadvantaged: to labor, women, children, and the unemployed. Wilson, true to his Southern Democratic inheritance, distrusted big government; drew back from those who would like to use government to intervene directly and positively in the economy. He certainly did not want a "smug lot of experts" running the country from the center. He felt the whole enterprise would degenerate into more government by trustee where the wealthy and the government formed a corrupt alliance. Therefore, he turned away from social reforms. No one, he believed, really needed help if opportunities were open.

Wilson and the strong presidency

Woodrow Wilson was determined to inaugurate a new kind of presidency. He had long believed that the American president should be a kind of British prime minister. Instead of sitting at the White House and waiting to carry out such laws as Congress might in its wisdom enact, he should closely direct the work of his party members in Congress and drive legislation through by teamwork. Accordingly, Wilson's telephone line to the Capitol was constantly busy; party leaders trooped in and out of the White House for frequent meetings with the president and a stream of handwritten messages went off from Wilson to legislators that flattered, cajoled, and sometimes discreetly threatened them to support his causes.

This was, of course, in the tradition of a governing style long characteristic of the Democratic party—the strong presidency. On the Republican side only Theodore Roosevelt had been a vigorous executive who got Congress to pass major reforms and acted as a tribune of the people. In significant measure it was on this ground that he lost the loyalty of Republican regulars and had to break with his party. On the Democratic side the list of strong presidents was noteworthy, stretching back through Grover Cleveland to James Polk and Andrew Jackson. Wilson ran things directly, and like a Scottish laird demanded personal loyalty to himself in all his policies. Time and again he "went to the people." When clouds of lobbyists swarmed around Congress during the tariff battle, he issued an appeal to the public that aroused so enormous a flood of mail to legislators that tariff reform finally had its day.

Wilson and the tariff

After taking office Wilson electrified the nation by boldly calling Congress immediately into special session to reform the tariff. Going personally to Congress to deliver his message, he became the first president since John Adams to appear before that body. The Underwood Tariff that was enacted tumbled the rates down and down, back below those of the long Republican years, reaching levels that the nation had not seen since before the Civil War. The new tariff average was set at twenty-nine percent. All products produced by monopolies were placed on the free list, and the new income tax provision was put into effect in order to make up for the loss of tariff revenues, the tax being set at seven percent maximum.

Reform of the banking system

In the summer and autumn of 1913, Wilson forced Congress to remain in sweltering Washington, D.C., and tackle another huge issue—the reform of the banking system. Here at the heart of the economy was private control untrammeled and triumphant. No public agency had any voice in settling such critical issues as the volume of the money supply, discount rates (how freely credit would be available), the location of banking facilities, and what kinds of links banks should have with business corporations. Farmers complained that all the money was locked up in eastern banks, resulting in exorbitant interest rates in western regions. Progressives insisted that the money supply should be taken out of private hands and put in those of a public agency. Bankers themselves were alarmed at the condition of their institutions, for there was no central bank that could pool reserves and shift them about as needed to meet unusual demands. Perhaps most important, the supply of money was relatively static. The economy could grow, but there was rarely enough money to meet its needs.

Woodrow Wilson had no intention of destroying private banking. His primary goal was to establish some form of public supervision over limited aspects of the financial world. Going before Congress in June 1913 for another address to the two houses, he called for the creation of the Federal Reserve Board to supervise the banking system. Its membership would be appointed by the president and confirmed by the Senate, and bankers would be ineligible for such appointment. The nation would be divided into twelve Federal Reserve regions, in each of which would be placed a Federal Reserve bank. These institutions would be governed by boards elected primarily by the private banks in the region that had affiliated themselves with the system.

The Federal Reserve System would provide a means of shifting currency reserves about the country to meet demands. Also, it would take over the issuing of paper currency. From the Federal Reserve banks would come a new form of currency, Federal Reserve notes. These would be issued wholly as an obligation of the national government. It would work in this fashion: when a private bank authorized a loan to, say, a local factory, it would receive a mortgage or other form of legal indebtedness (*commercial paper* is the term usually used) from that business; with this in hand, it could go to the regional Federal Reserve bank, deposit the mortgage as security, and receive Federal Reserve notes, which it would then issue to the borrower.

An important step in this process was that the Federal Reserve bank would not issue currency up to the full value of the mortgage. In effect, it would charge some interest by "discounting" the commercial paper—issuing the money to an amount slightly less than the full value of the indebtedness. By charging the borrowing bank a certain percentage of the transaction, the Federal Reserve bank could make loans easier or harder to obtain by raising or lowering the discount rate. This gave the system the potential power of controlling the total money supply and thereby damping inflations or easing deflations.

For the first time, currency was being based not entirely on gold or some form of federal bonds, but on the value of the business and industrial system itself. This would let the currency supply grow and contract in volume in proportion to business activity. Furthermore the decentralized nature of the system, providing reserve banks in every part of the country, helped to break the Wall Street monopoly.

The nation's private bankers sent up a storm of protest. For generations they had serenely carried on their affairs with the feeling that the banking system was uniquely their private property. Now those rascals down in Washington, led by the unpredictable Woodrow Wilson, were proposing to take over, a monstrously offensive prospect to men long habituated to being in control of the nation's economic life. The New York *Sun,* voice of Wall Street, could hardly contain its outrage. "It is difficult to discuss with any degree of patience," it snorted, "this preposterous offspring of ignorance and unreason, but it cannot be passed over with the contempt it deserves." The proposal was "covered all over with the slime of Bryanism."

Nevertheless, the bill went through largely as Wilson had presented it. An overwhelming number of the nation's businessmen favored it as a major improvement of the existing situation. They too, like the farmers, resented the tight control that Wall Street had always exerted, and applauded the spreading of financial resources throughout the nation. Progressives were also pleased. "It is a communistic idea," protested a San Antonio banker, but his outburst was futile. The crowning achievement of Woodrow Wilson's domestic reforms, the Federal Reserve System was enacted in December 1913.

It was a characteristically Wilsonian reform. When all was said and done, his critics maintained, Wilson's actions did not match his rhetoric. Nothing was done about the money trust: interlocking directorates were not outlawed. Private bankers still largely controlled the money supply and its availability. The New York Federal Reserve bank dominated the system. The Federal Reserve Board was not strong enough to serve as a central bank, nor really to control the nation's bankers. It used its influence over discount rates only tentatively until after the crash of 1929. But a new and flexible currency had been created, and a system of public supervision with a large potential had come into being. The start had been made, and in the existing situation so fundamental a change was an enormous achievement.

Wilson and the trusts

The trust problem was the next item on Wilson's agenda. His attorney general, James C. McReynolds searched out a major target in the American Telephone and Telegraph Company. Threatening the company with a long drawn-out court suit, the attorney general forced it to give up ownership of Western Union Telegraph. He thus established a new procedure that became important in the Wilson administration, the *consent decree*. In this, an agreement was worked out by the government and the monopoly concerned, which was then formalized in a court decree to which the company had already given its assent.

Meanwhile, new legislation was being prepared in Congress. The Clayton antitrust bill, which Wilson supported, enumerated and outlawed a list of unfair trade practices. Soon a storm of controversy erupted. Labor unions found that the legislation did not exempt them from antitrust prosecution. Some weak provisions to that effect were inserted, but they had little impact in later years. Labor unions were still wide open to court injunctions during strikes.

More damaging to the bill was the fact that legislators were realizing how impossible it was to enumerate specifically what actually constituted unfair business practices. The list could be practically infinite, for the techniques unscrupulous businessmen could adopt were endlessly varied. Louis D. Brandeis, progressives in Congress, authorities on the trust problem—all urged Wilson to take a new tack. He should instead, they said, take up the New Nationalism idea of an independent commission with broad powers to investigate business activities and issue "cease-and-desist" orders when it concluded that unfair practices were being used.

After considerable haggling and protracted thought—for the proposal required a major shift away from his New Freedom philosophy—Wilson accepted this change. The result was the creation in 1914 of the Federal Trade Commission, charged with preventing the appearance of new monopolies by ensuring that businessmen competed fairly and openly (without specifying in detail what this meant). An independent commission modeled on the ICC, it was composed of five members appointed by the president with the Senate's consent, who would hold office for seven years. Meanwhile, the Clayton antitrust bill was mostly ignored. By the time of its passage a disgusted Missouri senator said that it had been transformed from "a raging lion with a mouth full of teeth . . . to a tabby cat with soft gums, a plaintive mew, and an anemic appearance."

Wilson now announced that the program of the New Freedom was complete. No more major reforms needed to be enacted. In truth, Wilson seemed genuinely uninterested in going any further. He was implacably opposed to special interest legislation, which meant not only that manufacturers and bankers should get no aid from the government, but also that laborers, farmers, and children were to be similarly ignored. When proposals came forward to aid them, he used his influence to quash the bills. He refused to support the idea of rural banks for farmers to provide the long-term loans on low interest that they needed. When progressives appealed for a national child labor bill, he also resisted, saying that "domestic arrangements" were for the states, not the federal government, to supervise—a position not surprising in a southerner.

Wilson turns toward New Nationalism

In 1916, however, Woodrow Wilson surprised the nation by suddenly launching out in New Nationalist directions, making the national government an agency of social reform. Why did he do this? First, in the elections of 1914 the Republicans won a series of stunning victories. T.R. had abandoned his fledgling Progressive party (which promptly expired) to return to the Republican fold. War had broken out in Europe in August 1914, and he wanted to bring the United States into it against the "beastly Hun." Where would the leaderless Progressives go, back to the Republicans with Roosevelt or over to the Democrats? Wilson now had a straight-out two-party contest ahead of him in the coming presidential election of 1916, and he needed to win them over to gain an absolute majority in the electoral college. So, too, he needed to take positive action to hold onto the emergent ethnic Democrats in the northern states, and they demanded social reforms of the newer kind.

Being an inactive president was not, in any event, Wilson's style. Power was his meat and drink, and to sit back placidly after his program was "complete" was impossible. He had learned, too, that the nation had evils that only a vigorous government could assault. Wilson, indeed, was fundamentally devoted to the belief that government must grow and change to meet society's actual needs.

So now, in 1916, he led Congress in new directions, stimulating it to enact "the most sweeping and significant progressive legislation in the history of the country up to that time," as Arthur S. Link has written. He startled the business community by proposing the reformer Brandeis for a seat on the Supreme Court. This led to a stiff fight in the Senate over his confirmation, for the action was like waving a red flag at the Wall Street bull. (There were also those who reacted against a Jew being on the Supreme Court.) Then he began pushing a bill he had earlier opposed that established twelve farm loan banks, each of

them with $500,000 provided by the federal government, in rural regions of the nation. Conservatives angrily cried "socialism," but the measure went through.

A workmen's compensation law for federal employees that had been languishing in Congress suddenly came alive when Wilson became its advocate. Following its enactment, he put strong pressure behind passage of a child labor bill, going to the Capitol personally to make his plea. (The law, later declared unconstitutional, prohibited the shipment of goods in interstate trade that were made by children under fourteen or by children under sixteen who worked more than eight hours a day.) In this landmark legislation the federal government made its first effort, in its long history, to supervise the way private employers ran their businesses. Here lay the germ of all the social reform measures that later transformed the relationship of the national government to social conditions.

Following this, Wilson secured the creation of a new independent commission, the Tariff Commission, that would provide a continuing expert study of trade conditions. Its task was to propose "scientific" tariff changes designed to equalize the cost of production domestically with that abroad, a procedure that Wilson had specifically condemned in his original New Freedom speeches. By thus providing "rational protection," Wilson had shifted startlingly away from traditional Democratic principles, and he brought along most Democrats in Congress with him.

Practically every important proposal that the Progressives had made in 1912 had now become law, with Wilson's blessing. This allowed him in the campaign of 1916 to claim that the Democratic party was also the progressive party; that social justice would now come from his side of politics, not from the Republicans. In June 1916 a massive railroad strike gave him another opportunity to demonstrate his new loyalties. The railroad workers were fighting for the eight-hour day with no reduction in wages. Wilson supported them and pressured the railroad owners to grant their demand. When they refused, he quickly got Congress to pass the Adamson Act, which imposed an eight-hour day on the railroads and made higher wages possible.

Businessmen were now furious with Woodrow Wilson. In the 1916 campaign, they threw their support wholeheartedly behind the Republican nominee for the presidency, Charles Evans Hughes of New York. Once again, as was traditional, the Democratic candidate was widely depicted as antibusiness. Meanwhile, Wilson moved vigorously about the country reminding people of what he had done for labor, farmers, and the nation's children. Progressives flocked behind Wilson's banner. Labor, delighted with its new champion, pressed hard for his victory. Progressive journalists and writers applauded Wilson's transformation of the Democratic party into an agency of social reform. Many thousands of urban, ethnic voters who had cast their ballots in 1912 for Eugene V. Debs, the Socialist candidate, now swung over to the president.

Furthermore, the peace movement was in Wilson's camp, for its leaders feared that a Republican victory would mean a rapid entry into the war then raging in Europe. Theodore Roosevelt went from city to city proclaiming that Wilson was a weak-kneed coward for not immediately going to war on the British side, and every such attack gave more strength to the Wilson following. The election itself was a cliff-hanger, for the eastern states went heavily for Hughes. But when the western returns came in, Wilson was reelected with a total of 9.1 million popular votes to 8.5 million for Hughes. For the first time since Andrew Jackson, a Democrat had won reelection for a second consecutive term.

Women in the progressive era

One of the great victories for social justice that was finally won in the Wilson years was the Nineteenth Amendment, which gave women the right to vote. In 1890 the National American Woman Suffrage Association appeared, formed by the merger of two smaller and older movements. The association concentrated on the tactic of converting individual states to woman suffrage. Hundreds of campaigns were launched in more than thirty states, but by 1896 only four victories had been won—in Colorado, Idaho, Wyoming, and Utah. Everywhere the suffrage cause encountered not only general hostility but also the determined opposition of the liquor and brewing industries, for they assumed an intimate link between the prohibition and suffrage movements.

After the turn of the century, the fact that women were increasingly moving out into factories and offices gave renewed vigor to the suffrage campaign, since it provided positive proof that women were not limited in their intelligence and personalities to the cloistered tasks of the home. Whereas some 4 million women were gainfully employed in 1890, by 1910 the figure had reached almost 7.5 million. In sweatshops and textile factories, it was clear that women had a direct interest in influencing legislation, for they needed laws to improve their working conditions.

As elsewhere in the Progressive Era, the influence of a new college-educated middle class was crucial. In 1910 almost 8,500 women received baccalaureate degrees, as compared with approximately 29,000 men. Carrie Chapman Catt and Anna Howard Shaw, both college-trained, provided the new leadership that the women suffrage movement needed, the former as the leading figure in the International Woman Suffrage Alliance, founded in Germany in 1904, and the latter as president of the National American Woman Suffrage Association from 1904 to 1915.

A transatlantic connection with Great Britain was closely maintained by the American suffrage workers, and it provided a vital spark of stimulus and example. In Britain a strong swing toward unprecedentedly radical tactics took place in 1903 when Emmeline Pankhurst, a woman of great courage, formed the Women's Social and Political Union, which held outdoor meetings and began a regular program of interrupting government speakers to ask their views on woman suffrage. Soon there were uproars leading to spectacular arrests, wide-splashing newspaper publicity, and intense national interest. The women's cause had broken out of polite and subdued gatherings to which no one paid any attention, and it was never to be the same again.

The Women's Political Union was formed in the United States also with the objective of holding public gatherings and launching active campaigns against male politicians who opposed the vote for women. Parades became a distinctive tactic of the new women's organizations. Hundreds of women also began traveling through the countryside in the Northeast, speaking to audiences of ordinary men and women wherever they could find hearers, who, in truth, were eager to gather for so remarkable a sight as a woman politician. At the same time, under Catt's leadership, members of the National American Woman Suffrage Association began a carefully detailed and executed plan of precinct organization in order to bring direct pressure on every legislator.

Then, after fourteen dry years in which no state could be induced to grant suffrage, the state of Washington in 1910 electrified women across the country by approving it by a two-to-one margin. A whirlwind of organized publicity workers then launched an incredibly varied campaign in Californa, featuring an effort at each polling booth to ward off the influences of liquor salesmen and barkeepers. The result was a narrow victory in 1911. Three more states were won in 1912—Arizona, Kansas, and Oregon.

But the state-by-state tactic was costly and wearing, and defeats in Ohio, Wisconsin, and Michigan were deeply discouraging. The women began to look toward Washington, D.C., encouraged by the fact that Theodore Roosevelt's Progressive party had made woman suffrage one of its electoral planks. Alice Paul, fresh from being jailed in Britain as a militant woman suffrage worker and the ordeal of a hunger strike, emerged to provide fresh leadership. With the aid of a small group of vigorous co-workers, she succeeded in organizing a parade of thousands of women in Washington on the day before Woodrow Wilson's first inauguration. They practically had to fight their way to the Capitol building, for hostile observers jeered at them and broke up their line of march. But with this flood of publicity behind them, they succeeded in getting Congress to pay attention and hold hearings on a constitutional amendment. A petition bearing 200,000 signatures was presented, and President Wilson began to receive visiting delegations of women. A new organization, the militant Congressional Union, began a program of nationwide activities, organizing campaigns to defeat Democrats—whom the women chose as their adversaries on the simple ground that the Democrats were in power in Washington, and therefore responsible if a women's suffrage amendment was not passed.

A long siege ensued against a reluctant Congress. The women organized spectacular national pilgrimages beginning in San Francisco and arriving in Washington, D.C., with petitions bearing hundreds of thousands of signatures. Votes were forced in key committees and on the floors of both houses of Congress, usually meeting the moral victory of narrow defeat. The White House was picketed, and hunger strikes were begun. Immense efforts were poured into voting referenda in four key eastern states—New York, Massachusetts, Pennsylvania, and New Jersey—where, again, defeat was the result. But Catt, who became president of the National American Woman Suffrage Association in 1915, never relented, and the national campaign grew, if anything, more active. Money was raised, conferences held, schools established to train organizers, and every state organization given specific tasks. Woodrow Wilson was assiduously wooed in his reelection campaign in 1916. On one occasion, when he appeared to speak at the national convention of the National American Woman Suffrage Association, Anna Howard Shaw said to him, "We have waited so long, Mr. President, for the vote—we had hoped it might come in your administration," at which point the immense audience of women rose silently and stood quietly looking at the president. Within a year, he came out formally on the side of the women's cause and called on Congress to act.

In 1917, the first woman ever to sit in Congress took her seat—Jeanette Rankin of Montana (who, after a long and honorable career in public life, principally as an opponent of both world wars, died in 1972). Enormous numbers of women were meanwhile pouring into the job market as war work made unprecedented demands on them to support the military forces. Indeed, the great wars in American history—the Civil War, and the First and Second World Wars—worked lasting transformations in the status of women in America. Furthermore, when women took up outside jobs during the First World War, they did so in an atmosphere in which democratic values of equality and individual dignity were being trumpeted around the world by the White House. Clearly, the principles being thus invoked had a great field for application in the women's cause.

State after state began to give the vote in presidential elections to women. Then in January 1918, after a massive lobbying campaign, the House of Representatives passed the women's suffrage constitutional amendment, primarily because of heavy Republican majorities in its favor. In 1919 the Senate followed, and in August 1920 the Nineteenth Amendment completed the ratification process. Twenty-six million women of voting age could go to the polls and share responsibility with male Americans for the government of the country.

Blacks in the Progressive Era

In Wilson's movement toward social justice one note jars harshly out of tune. Woodrow Wilson was a southerner, and so were most of his cabinet members. As soon as he became president, his administration began to practice segregation in government departments. Black and white work-

Woman suffrage before the Nineteenth Amendment

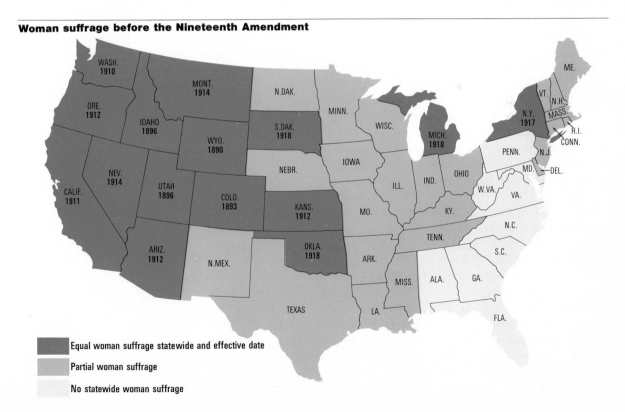

Equal woman suffrage statewide and effective date

Partial woman suffrage

No statewide woman suffrage

ers were separated "to reduce friction," it was said, and so as not to enforce "unwelcome" closeness on white workers. There was a particular touchiness about black civil servants supervising white women. Wilson, when appealed to, insisted that segregation was actually a humanitarian policy, for it would give black workers job areas of their own in which they need not fear white encroachment.

Black leaders generally accepted the fact that the president was a sincere man, but nevertheless his defense of segregation rang hollow. Wilson's father had ardently supported slavery; his wife was strongly segregationist; and Wilson seemed to do nothing but cover over the Jim Crow practices with high-flown words. More disturbing, supervisors in government offices seemed bent on discharging as many black employees as possible by putting them into specially organized offices that were then closed down.

This was not, however, entirely a Democratic matter. During the Progressive Era both parties were indifferent to the needs of Afro-Americans. Roosevelt and Taft had been so markedly anti-black that for the first time since black Americans began voting, significant numbers of them had actually switched to the Democratic ticket in 1912. Wilson, the intellectual, had seemed the man of the future, and he had issued encouraging statements. The aftermath, therefore, was very discouraging to blacks. Progressives everywhere had boasted that they were the spokesmen of the forgotten man, but they turned away from the race question. What could one do, they seemed to feel, about a problem that was so overwhelmingly difficult to solve and that was a southern one besides? (Some ninety percent of black Americans still lived in the South.)

Theodore Roosevelt gave much thought to the whole issue and finally gave up, telling blacks that they had to rely on the goodwill of the whites. Then, as if in violent reaction to a problem he could not solve, he took steps deeply offensive to the black community. In 1906 he peremptorily discharged three companies of

black soldiers on the allegation that they were involved with rioting in nearby Brownsville, Texas. He even informed Congress that lynchings were brought about because black men were raping white women. The Republican party became ever more "lily white" in its policies, giving few positions to blacks any longer. Wilson's segregation policies were actually preceded by some similar arrangements under Taft.

Black America in the North since Reconstruction

Indeed, none of this was new. Since the end of Reconstruction in 1877, northern whites had increasingly ignored black interests. The dominant concern in the northern mind was knitting the nation back together. This seemed to require leaving the race issue in the hands of southern whites, in return for which they would finally and irrevocably give up their dreams for separate nationhood. The Supreme Court confirmed these views, gutting the federal civil rights legislation of the Reconstruction era in the *Civil Rights Cases* (1883). The philosophy adopted by the Court was that individuals were free to do what they wished in race relations. In 1890 in the case of *Louisville, New Orleans, and Texas Railroad* v. *Mississippi* it ruled that a state could require, not simply allow, segregation in railroad transportation. Then in *Plessy* v. *Ferguson* (1896), the Court established the separate-but-equal doctrine in public facilities (and by implication in public schools). The court's view was that it was useless to try to change "racial instincts" by law. In practice, southern state legislatures provided less money for black schools than they did for white schools, which led inherently to inequality. Then in 1898, steps taken by Mississippi to withdraw the vote from black men (to be explained later) were ruled constitutional in *Williams* v. *Mississippi.*

Blacks in the North retained their political and civil rights but still suffered from social and economic discrimination. They usually studied in separate schools and held only the most menial occupations. Northern labor unions were strongly antiblack, especially the AFL. (The United Mine Workers was a notable exception: two-thirds of its membership was black.) The notion of racial equality was almost universally condemned. If black people fell behind, it was their own doing, said white Americans.

Black America in the South since Reconstruction

In the South, for a generation after the Civil War, two philosophies of race relations struggled for supremacy. One was that of outright race hatred, which resulted in the mass violence and intimidation described in earlier chapters. The other, held generally by the white upper class, was the concerned and paternalistic creed that existed in pre–Civil War days. Neither side, of course, even considered racial equality, but the paternalistic view taught that whites should carry out their responsibilities as trustees for blacks carefully and thoughtfully. The northern states had left the problem to the South, and southern whites should take up this task in a responsible and civilized way. Black men continued to vote in large numbers after 1877, some held public office, served as jurymen—even as judges—and sat in city, state, and national legislatures. Southern whites and blacks rode in the same compartments in railway carriages, entered hotels by the same doors, used the same public facilities. Indeed, some observers remarked that in large areas of the South black people were more fairly and equitably treated than in the North.

Even so, as late as 1900 three-fourths of the black farmers in the South were living on someone else's land. As sharecroppers and tenant farmers they had to give up a large portion of their crop for rent and depend on the local white grocer to provide food and clothing on credit, at prices usually so high that black families were perpetually in debt. In effect, a kind of peonage developed where black farmers were bound to the soil in a status somewhere between slavery

Life for most American black persons was little changed in the Progressive Era, from the 1880s scene here presented of farm laborers picking cotton in the South. With little education and a web of Jim Crow laws enacted from the 1890s onward, the situation was, if anything, worse than at any time since the Civil War.
Courtesy of the Library of Congress

and freedom. Southern states spent little on schools for blacks, so that illiteracy intensified the black man's inability to break out of his economic condition. At the same time, southern law enforcement traditionally imprisoned blacks for petty crimes that, when committed by whites, went overlooked. Those in jail were then "farmed out" to labor on white-owned farms, on the railroads, or in the frightful labor conditions of the Georgia turpentine farms. Meanwhile, lynch law rode the land. In the 1880s and 1890s more than a hundred black men were strung up by lynch mobs every year, often after the most barbarous torture.

Populism and black southerners

The uprush of southern populism in the 1890s introduced new ideas on race. As a class movement, populism took up the cause of the poor farmer, black or white, against the banks, railroads, and other businesses of wealth and power. Populists welcomed blacks into their movement, stressing the equalitarianism of the poor. "They are in the ditch," said a Texan Populist, "just like we are." This was brave doctrine, for the mass of the white population was not ready to accept any form of racial equality. This was especially true among the poor whites, who seemed the most rabidly bigoted, and yet they were the group to whom the Populists directed most of their appeals. Acts of great courage marked populism in its heyday. Populist sheriffs put black men on juries, and the party's newspaper editors took pains to laud black achievements.

The Populist campaign was doomed before it began. "Whites must stick together!" was the overwhelmingly powerful cry in the southern states. To pull whites back into the Democratic party, race agitators began preaching black hatred. Then, by all sorts of legal devices, the vote was taken away from black men—literacy tests, property requirements, "understanding" tests, poll taxes, the "grandfather clause" (a provision that illiterates could vote only if their grandfather had been voting before 1867), and even that sacred "democratic" reform of the Progressive Era, the primary election. Being purely a party proceeding, primaries could be restricted only to whites. The situation in Louisiana alone tells the story: in 1896, 130,000 black men could vote, and in 1904, only 1,300. The black man had been effectively disenfranchised.

All this took place in a hysteria of race baiting, featuring an explosion of racist novels, endless allegations that black men were raping white women, and loud attacks on black impertinence and "uppitiness." Having lost the vote and been rendered powerless, blacks began to suffer periodic mass violence. In 1898 in North Carolina, 400 white men streamed into a black residential area and burned homes, killed and wounded the frantic inhabitants, and sent hundreds fleeing. The whole city of New Orleans was taken over in 1900 by uncontrolled mobs that killed and terrorized blacks. In Atlanta in 1906, after Governor Hoke Smith had won a white supremacy victory, the city rocked to days of white rioting.

Then came a flood of Jim Crow laws. Railway cars and waiting stations, streetcars, theater entrances, boarding houses, toilets, water fountains, ticket windows, parks, circus shows, halls, auditoriums, ball parks, residential areas, textbooks, schools, even prostitutes were segregated. Atlanta courtrooms had separate Bibles for blacks and for whites; public buildings had separate elevators. The result was a massive crystallization of race relations in a pattern that was worse than anything blacks had endured for decades. In time, southern whites came to believe that segregation had always existed and was part of the natural order, forgetting, if they were aware, that Jim Crow laws did not appear until thirty years after the Civil War. Once the Jim Crow era began, all relations were transformed. Every black person, whether intelligent or stupid, well dressed or in tatters, cultivated or ignorant, was legally the inferior of every white person, no matter how crude or brutish.

Changes in the North

Discrimination against blacks in the North grew harsher from the 1890s onward. Almost none were elected to legislative seats any longer or held appointive office. Hotels, restaurants, and theaters frequently discriminated against blacks, and separate schools existed in many states. White customers stopped buying from black businessmen, and white unions and businesses refused to employ black laborers. Most trade unions excluded them, and the huge influx of immigrants took away much of their domestic, hotel, and restaurant work.

The background to the more severe discrimination was the impact of America's imperialism. In the late 1890s the United States took under its tutelage millions of Filipinos whom it had no intention of admitting to equal citizenship. The North, therefore, had a huge stake in racism. Theories that described white people as superior and pigmented races as inferior were widely preached. The *New York Times* observed in 1900 that "Northern men . . . no longer denounce the suppression of the Negro vote [in the South] as it used to be denounced in the reconstruction days. The necessity of it under the supreme law of self-preservation is candidly recognized."

Blacks turn inward

In these circumstances, the black community turned in on itself. If segregation was the order of the day, Afro-Americans seemed to say, so be it: black people would stress that they too wanted segregation; they too wanted the pride of having their own spheres. The dominant message now passed around the black world was that of self-help. This was, indeed, an old idea. As early as the 1870s black leaders had stressed the need for industrial education, by which black men could acquire the jobs needed to help themselves, rise in the community, and demonstrate that they were worthy of respect—and equality. Southern states had even established industrial schools for this purpose. Hampton Institute and Tuskegee Institute became symbols of this philosophy.

Booker T. Washington, head of Tuskegee, became in the 1890s the prophet of self-help. At the Atlanta Exposition in 1895 he captured national attention by calling on black men to accept the white man's philosophy of hard work and getting ahead in the community by material advancement. Remember, he said, that most black men must live by manual labor. The overwhelming majority of them were unskilled and therefore imprisoned on the farm. The best hope for them lay in acquiring skills and working faithfully, not in agitating for racial equality and demanding positions of leadership. "In all things that are purely social," he said, "[the white and black races] can be as separate as the five fingers, yet one as the hand in all things essential to mutual progress." Cooperate with white men, he urged Afro-Americans. Be "patient, faithful, law-abiding and unresentful." It is vitally important, he maintained, "that all privileges of the law be ours; but it is vastly more important that we be prepared for the exercise of these privileges."

By this utterance Washington immediately became, in white eyes, the towering figure in the world of black America. His was a philosophy that whites could thoroughly approve of. Though potentially explosive—what would happen when blacks *did* get ahead and expected the privileges that they earned?—its immediate significance was attractive, for it promised to keep away all radicalism. Philanthropic institutions hastened to fund Washington's programs and to get his advice on all the other projects that were proposed in aid of American blacks. Theodore Roosevelt called him to the White House for consultation. After this, the White House appointed no black men to the government without clearing them first with Booker T. Washington, a fact that gave him great power in the black community. A staunch Republican, he worked hard to get out the black vote in the northern states, though he never publicly criticized the massive disenfranchisement then taking place in the South.

Great numbers of black Americans agreed with Booker T. Washington that individual effort and striving to get ahead were the answers to their situation. Jobs and a respectable standard of living: these were what they wanted. In spite of all difficulties, there was, in fact, a small and growing black middle class in both the North and the South. Self-made, proud of their success, they approved of Washington's message. Rocking the boat was not their desire but a hope that some kind of peaceful and modestly comfortable life in twentieth-century America could be allowed to them. Such ideals were taught in black schools, in conventions of black farmers, and at meetings of black businessmen's organizations. Self-sufficiency was stressed. The ideal was an all-black town where black physicians, lawyers, bankers, merchants, and teachers would minister to the needs of black workers and farmers. Out of Hampton and Tuskegee went a stream of teachers schooled in the philosophy of self-help to work with black children throughout the South. As always, the black church was the heart of Afro-American life, and from its pulpits ministers preached the same message of self-help and racial pride and solidarity.

Emergence of black radicalism

It was increasingly difficult, however, for this viewpoint to be maintained without challenge. Southern blacks were surrounded by a rising storm of frenzied racism. The advent of Jim Crow took place to the accompaniment of screaming oratory praising white supremacy and describing blacks as ravening beasts. The black middle class, it seemed to many, was on an island of sand being eaten away by the tide. Appropriations for black school children were dropping rapidly as blacks lost the vote; race riots broke out; and in a revealing episode, the homes of the comfortable black middle class were singled out for especially savage attacks in the Atlanta riot of 1906. It was one thing for blacks to talk of hard work and patience; it was another when whites began violently attacking the homes and property that blacks had worked hard to obtain.

In this situation, some leading black Americans began to call for a new philosophy. All around them, after all, was the progressive movement, which preached high moral values of equality and social justice. After 1900 an increasingly outspoken opposition to Booker T. Washington developed, especially among northern blacks. The new dissidents were usually college-educated professionals and intellectuals who were peculiarly subject to that cruel dilemma traditionally facing black Americans who do not remain encapsulated in the world of blackness: choosing between their two identities—being an American like everyone else, and being a black. It is a dilemma, indeed, that minority groups in every country must face. As W. E. B. Du Bois, a professor at Atlanta University, explained it in 1897:

One feels his two-ness—an American, a Negro, two souls, two thoughts, two unreconciled strivings, two warring ideals in one dark body. . . . The history of the American Negro is the history of this strife—this longing to attain self-conscious manhood, to merge his double self into a better and truer self. . . . He would not Africanize America for America has too much to teach the world and Africa. He would not bleach the Negro soul in a flood of white Americanism, for he knows that Negro blood has a message for the world. He simply wishes to make it possible for a man to be both a Negro and an American, without being cursed and spit upon. . . .

Such men rejected the implicit segregation in Booker T. Washington's philosophy. Integration, which meant full acceptance on an equal basis as a human being, was their goal. Patience and submissiveness in a caste system were unacceptable. The new dissidents insisted on their civil rights, particularly the vote. They demanded that young blacks should be given not only industrial education but also training for leadership, which meant schooling in the liberal arts and sciences.

W. E. B. Du Bois

The Afro-American's "two-ness" was eloquently symbolized in the career of William Edward Burghardt Du Bois. Born in 1868 in western Massachusetts, he studied at all-black Fisk University in Nashville, Tennessee, in the 1880s.

Here he imbibed a sense of racial pride, induced in him, as he said, by association with a "closed racial group with rites and loyalties, with a history and a corporate future, with an art and a philosophy." Taking a PhD at Harvard in 1895, he began his career as a professor at Atlanta University. In these years he echoed much of Booker T. Washington's philosophy. Blacks, he would say, had themselves to blame for much of their treatment. "We must remember," he observed, "that a good many of our people . . . are not fit for the responsibility of republican government." The black man's real struggle, in his view, was to improve himself morally, to become a better and more responsible American, more hard working, self-denying, and ambitious. After that, white society would open its doors.

Already, however, he was deploring the fact that young blacks were not being given liberal arts education. Even as a student at Harvard he had begun talking about what he called the "talented tenth": those blacks with inherent leadership abilities who should be trained for the role. He remained at Atlanta University, until 1910, when he moved to the University of Pennsylvania. In these years he urged that black America adopt a policy of racial solidarity—living and working among themselves, buying from each other, and turning to black lawyers and doctors for their professional services. This would lead to a United States characterized by "cultural pluralism," in which Afro-Americans could be Americans and at the same time active members of the black community. As a race, he said in 1897, "we

W. E. B. DuBois and Booker T. Washington, the two leaders of black America whose contrasting philosophies vied for support within the black community. White Americans disliked DuBois as a radical, approved Washington for his pragmatism.
Courtesy of the Library of Congress

must strive by race organizations, by race solidarity, by race unity to the realization of the broader humanity which freely recognizes differences in men, but sternly deprecates inequalities in their opportunity of development." Separation, pride in their distinctness, yet equality—these were the touchstones. Du Bois looked to Africa as a homeland and advocated "pan-Negroism."

Gradually he began to veer more sharply away from Booker T. Washington's leadership. In 1901 he demanded that blacks protest ceaselessly against the Jim Crow system. In 1903 he published his famous *The Souls of Black Folk,* which contained an essay openly attacking Washington. His policies, Du Bois said, "practically accepted the inferiority of the Negro," ignored cultivating the mind while concentrating only on skills for the hand, and taught blacks to accept prejudiced treatment. It was not true, said Du Bois, that the backwardness and bad habits of the black people justified their treatment, as Washington seemed to say. The time now had come to adopt the tactic that Washington had deplored—open public protest. What good did it do to work hard and become prosperous, Du Bois asked, when it was precisely the middle-class black person who received the bitterest attacks during rioting? Not separation, but integration and the full rights of citizenship, should be the new objective. Black men must have the best education available, adopt the most challenging goals, and reject segregation as an insult to their manhood. "Separate schools for whites and blacks are not equal, can not be made equal, and . . . are not intended to be equal." The real result was not separation but subordination, which was what the white southerners, he said, had been after all along.

After 1904 Du Bois began to look sympathetically toward socialism. By 1911 he was a devoted member of the Socialist party and writing Marxist analyses of the ways in which both white and black laborers were being commonly exploited by white capitalists, usually by stirring up race animosities, he said, which kept the two groups from joining hands. He dreamed of a future in which white and black workers would jointly create a society based on economic and racial justice.

The Niagara Movement and the NAACP

Most Afro-Americans refused to follow Du Bois. All of his long life—he lived into his nineties—he was in the unhappy position of having to work against the mainstream of black American life, for the overwhelming majority of Afro-Americans rejected agitation and accepted the Washington values of accommodation, hard work and training, and the hope for a slow rise in status. Besides, Du Bois's essential following, which lay primarily among black professionals, was very small. Only 1 percent of employed Afro-Americans were professionals in 1900, and ten years later this figure had reached but 3 percent in the northern states and 2.5 percent in the South. Of these, furthermore, many were without formal training, being self-taught ministers or teachers without college educations.

Even so, a small nucleus of reformist blacks responded to Du Bois. In 1905 a group composed primarily of northern blacks joined him in a meeting held in Niagara Falls, Canada, at which they formed a national organization, the Niagara Movement. They issued a call to American blacks to protest continuously against any loss of political and civil rights and to agitate against unequal economic opportunities. Liberal arts as well as vocational training, they insisted, must be a part of black education. Above all, blacks should wipe away the national impression that "the Negro-American assents to inferiority, is submissive under oppression and apologetic before insult."

W. E. B. Du Bois spoke for the Niagara Movement: "Stripped of verbiage and subterfuge and in its naked nastiness, the new American creed says: fear to let black men even try to rise lest they become the equals of the white. And this is the land that professes to follow Jesus Christ. . . .

First, we would vote; with the right to vote goes everything: freedom, manhood, the honor of your wives, the chastity of your daughters, the right to work, and the chance to rise, and let no man listen to those who deny this. . . .

"We want discrimination in public accommodation to cease. . . . We claim the right of freedom to walk, talk, and be with them that wish to be with us. . . . We want the laws enforced against rich as well as poor; against Capitalist as well as Laborer; against white as well as black. We are not more lawless than the white race, [but] we are more often arrested, convicted and mobbed. . . . We want our children educated. The school system in the country districts of the South is a disgrace and in few towns and cities are the Negro schools what they ought to be. . . . We want our children trained as intelligent human beings should be, and we will fight for all time against any proposal to educate black boys and girls simply as servants and underlings, or simply for the use of other people. They have a right to know, to think, to aspire. . . .

"We do not believe in violence, neither in the despised violence of the raid nor the lauded violence of the soldier, nor the barbarous violence of the mob; but we do believe in John Brown, in that incarnate spirit of justice, that hatred of a lie, that willingness to sacrifice money, reputation, and life itself on the altar of right." (W. E. B. Du Bois, *Dusk of Dawn* [1940].)

An open rupture now took place between pro- and anti-Washington men that agitated black American life for more than ten years. A small group of white liberals was attracted to black radicalism and gave it crucially important support. Their leading figure was Oswald Garrison Villard. He had warmly assisted Booker T. Washington, but now he began turning to the Du Bois movement. In 1910 a group of white liberals under Villard's leadership joined with Du Bois to create the National Association for the Advancement of Colored People (NAACP), to which the members of the now-expiring Niagara Movement flocked en masse. Its chief concern was to fight through the courts to win legal rights for black Americans. The first victory for the NAACP came in 1915, when it won from the Supreme Court a ruling that the grandfather clause in use in Oklahoma was unconstitutional. Another crucially important organization, the National Urban League, was formed in 1911 to help blacks find jobs in the cities, and adjust to urban life.

By the time of Washington's death in 1915, the split between radicals and conservatives was healing over. All shades of active black opinion agreed, in effect, with the spirit of the Niagara Movement. Accommodation, in the Washington manner, might continue to be the dominating practical philosophy in Afro-American life, but now there lay always in the future the goal of an integrated society in which black and white lived on equal terms and had equal opportunities. By this time, too, the First World War was making a great impact on the life of black America. Now, more than 300,000 southern blacks began a great exodus as they headed for war-related jobs in northern cities. This northward movement did not cease until the 1970s. In its train have come deep and profound changes for life in the United States, which will take our attention at a later point in the narrative.

Bibliography

Three books that were especially valuable to me in writing this chapter: Arthur S. Link's numerous writings on Woodrow Wilson and his era, such as *Woodrow Wilson and the Progressive Era, 1910–1917** (1954), provide a deep encounter with this remarkable man; August Meier's *Negro Thought in America, 1880–1915: Racial Ideologies in the Age of Booker T. Washington** (1963) provides a lucid and thoughtful account of black America in this crucial generation when modern directions were being worked out; and C. Vann Woodward's milestone work *The Strange Career of Jim Crow** (1974) illuminates tellingly the rapid shift toward segregation that occurred in the South after 1890.

How have historians looked at the topic?

Arthur S. Link's monumental, multi-volume biography is the indispensable source on Wilson; *Wilson: The New Freedom,** vol. 2 (1956) and *Wilson: Campaigns for Progressivism and Peace, 1916–1917,* vol. 5 (1965) are particularly important for the president's first administration. John Blum's *Woodrow Wilson and the Politics of Morality** (1956) is a short, interpretive work that expertly captures the complexities of Wilson's personality and portrays the sense of poignancy surrounding him. Biographies of Wilson's allies and opponents include: J. M. Blum, *Joe Tumulty and the Wilson Era* (1951); R. M. Lowitt, *George W. Norris* (1963); A. T. Mason, *Brandeis* (1946); and M. J. Pusey, *Charles Evans Hughes* (1951).

Eleanor Flexner captures the anger and determination of suffragists in her thorough, scholarly account *Century of Struggle: The Woman's Rights Movement in the United States** (1959). William O'Neill offers a provocative analysis of why feminists failed in *Everyone Was Brave: The Rise and Fall of Feminism in America** (1969). Debby Woodroofe's pamphlet, *Sisters in Struggle, 1848–1920** (1971) has a similar but more sympathetic analysis. Although somewhat dated, Inez Haynes Irwin's *Up Hill with Banners Flying* (1964)—first published as *The Story of the Woman's Party* (1921)—graphically depicts the tactics and commitment of Alice Paul and other members of the women's movement. The monumental *History of Woman Suffrage,* six vols. (1881–1922) is a grabbag of source material put together over the years by Elizabeth Cady Stanton, Susan B. Anthony, Mathilda Gage, and Ida Husted Harper, all major figures in the suffrage movement.

The most definitive and impressive work on black America in the Progressive Era is August Meier's *Negro Thought in America, 1880–1915,* cited above. Meier probes the black response to increasing white prejudice and discrimination, revealing the existence of a much more complex set of alternatives than the usual protest-or-accommodation dichotomy would indicate. The background to the progressive period—aptly called the nadir in the black American's status in Rayford W. Logan's *The Negro in American Life and Thought: The Nadir, 1877–1901* (1954)—is provided in several perceptive studies. Louis D. Rubin, Jr., ed., *Teach the Freeman: The Correspondence of Rutherford B. Hayes and the Slater Fund for Negro Education, 1881–1887,* two vols. (1959) draws a connection between the actions of Hayes and other northern philanthropists and the vogue of industrial education for Afro-Americans so often ascribed to Booker T. Washington's leadership.

One of the most important books published on the segregation question, *The Strange Career of Jim Crow** by C. Vann Woodward, mentioned above, offers an insightful analysis of the development of institutional patterns separating the races. Woodward's conclusion as to the recency of southern segregation is supported in a case study by Charles E. Wynes, *Race Relations in Virginia, 1870–1902* (1961). In addition to Meier's book, black reaction can be studied in Samuel R. Spencer, Jr.'s critical biography *Booker T. Washington and the Negro's Place in American Life* (1955) and in a thoughtful selection of writings by and about the black leader, Hugh Hawkins, ed., *Booker T. Washington and His Critics* (1962).

The rise of black radicalism is best tasted in the works of W. E. B. Du Bois, most notably *The Souls of Black Folk** (1903). Two meritorious biographies of Du Bois are now available: Francis L. Broderick's *W. E. B. Du Bois: Negro Leader in a Time of Crisis* (1959), which treats Du Bois's career as a student and professor as well as his years of leadership with the NAACP; and Elliott M. Rudwick's *W. E. B. Du Bois: Propagandist of the Negro Protest* (1960), which incorporates findings from the Booker T. Washington papers.

The NAACP receives thorough treatment in Charles F. Kellogg's fine study *NAACP: A History of the National Association for the Advancement of Colored People* (1967) and an older work by Robert L. Jack, *History of the National Association for the Advancement of Colored People* (1943). Walter A. White's *Autobiography* is an invaluable source on the tribulations encountered by the interracial organization.

The way in which racist attitudes permeated other aspects of the progressive movement is clearly defined in Roger Daniel's excellent monograph *The Politics of Prejudice: The Anti-Japanese Movement in California and the Struggle for Japanese Exclusion** (1970) and in Aileen S. Kraditor's important and fascinating study *The Ideas of the Woman Suffrage Movement, 1890–1920** (1965).

* Available in paperback.

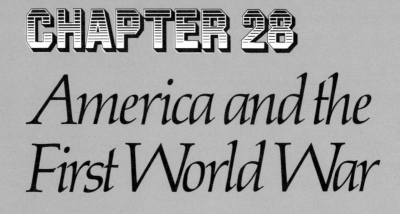

CHAPTER 28

America and the First World War

TIME LINE

1909	President Taft inaugurates Dollar Diplomacy in China and Latin America; United States intervenes in Haitian and Nicaraguan finances
1911	Sun Yat-sen leads creation of Republic of China; Francisco Madero leads revolt in Mexico against Porfirio Diaz
1913	President Wilson terminates Dollar Diplomacy; Victoriano Huerta overthrows Madero and establishes dictatorship in Mexico
1914	First World War begins; President Wilson orders occupation of Veracruz, Mexico
1915	American troops sent to occupy Haiti; Wilson recognizes Carranza government in Mexico; Germany declares unrestricted submarine warfare, sinks *Lusitania;* United States begins preparedness campaign; Shipping Board created to expand merchant marine; House-Grey Memorandum
1916	Germans sink *Sussex,* agree to warn before sinking merchant vessels; Wilson intensifies mediation efforts; American troops occupy Dominican Republic; Francisco Villa raids American town; American troops chase him into Mexico
1917	Wilson gives "Peace without Victory" address; Germans announce resumption of unrestricted submarine warfare; Russian Revolution; United States enters First World War; Espionage Act
1918	Wilson gives "fourteen Points" address, takes near-dictatorial powers over economy, utilizes central direction and planning; Treaty of Brest-Litovsk; Sedition Act; defeat of Germany
1919	In *Schenck* v. *The United States* Supreme Court confirms federal powers over freedom of speech during national emergencies; Eighteenth Amendment prohibits alcoholic beverages; Treaty of Versailles; defeat of treaty by Senate; Wilson incapacitated by stroke
1920	Nineteenth Amendment gives vote to women; Warren G. Harding elected twenty-ninth president of the United States

THEODORE Roosevelt made the United States a world power. By 1908, the last year of his administration, the nation was deeply involved in Asian politics, thrusting southward into Latin American affairs, and playing a significant role in European diplomacy. Equipped with a large and growing navy, the great Republic became a force to be reckoned with in the chancelleries of Europe. Following Roosevelt, William Howard Taft adopted programs designed to expand American investments, and therefore influence, in Latin America and Asia. Woodrow Wilson then took the nation far down the road toward world leadership. By the end of his time in office, American troops had established protectorates in the Caribbean region, made a major foray into the interior of Mexico, and by the millions had gone abroad to fight in the First World War. No other president in American history was so activist in his foreign policy, which is certainly one of the ironies of history, for Wilson came to the presidency devoted to the Liberal-Democratic notions of nonintervention and peaceful foreign relations.

Taft and Dollar Diplomacy

President Taft, a peaceful and legalistic man, turned away from Roosevelt's power politics. He believed that the United States should use its economic strength rather than military power to spread its influence throughout the world. Commerce and the interdependence of nations directed from America's Wall Street was his prescription for world order. By putting dollars in place of guns and by working cooperatively with foreign regimes to allow American businessmen favorable investment opportunities, common interests would replace the rivalries that threatened world peace.

In the Far East, Taft exercised his new Dollar Diplomacy policy by encouraging American investments in China, especially in railroad build-

ing. This, he believed, would halt Japanese expansion of influence there and also hold back the encroachment of European powers. E. H. Harriman, the railroad monopolist, pushed the project vigorously, for he had conceived the grand vision of a worldwide network of steamships and railroads under his direction. At Taft's urging in 1911, a group of American bankers joined a four-power consortium to loan money to the Chinese government for railroad construction. Then in that same year, a Chinese revolutionary named Sun Yat-sen led a rebellion in south China that eventually threw off the Manchu dynasty and established the Republic of China. This triumphantly nationalist movement was hostile to foreign influence, and American bankers withdrew from the railroad consortium.

Meanwhile, Dollar Diplomacy was pushed actively forward in the Caribbean. The basic notion was that stability in the Central American republics was vital to the safety of the Panama Canal, and that this stability would be best achieved if the United States took over their finances. Vain efforts along these lines were launched in Guatemala and Honduras. Greater success was achieved in Haiti, where a group of American bankers took control of the Haitian National Bank. Nicaragua attracted the greatest American attention because it was near the Panama Canal and contained another potential canal route. An anti-American dictator named José Santos Zelaya was overthrown in 1909 by what amounted to direct American intervention. Soon American marines landed in Nicaragua, and the United States took control of its finances. A small detachment of marines remained in the country until the 1920s to ensure the safety of American lives, property, and investments.

Wilsonian foreign policy

Woodrow Wilson came to the White House with a firm grounding in the foreign policy tradition of British Liberalism. This involved a fundamental distrust of power politics, a dislike of great empires, and a feeling that international relations should be based on moral rather than materialistic considerations. William Gladstone's ideas, which Wilson had taken up as a Princeton undergraduate, constituted an essentially religious world view stressing the family of humankind in an interdependent, global community where each country should be concerned about the welfare of all others. Wilson, like Gladstone, hated war and armaments and believed that every nation should be free from intervention by outside powers. Ultimately, some form of world parliament should provide a rule of law and order for all, in which every nation, large or small, would be equally treated. Dominating all considerations should be the moral values of the Judeo-Christian tradition.

This was far removed in ideology from the power politics of Theodore Roosevelt. He and Wilson, therefore, were bitterly opposed to one another in foreign policy matters. Roosevelt thought Wilson spineless, unmanly, a canting Presbyterian preacher who did not understand the realities of life. But the paradox was that the noninterventionist Wilson intervened far more in world affairs than Roosevelt ever did as president. A moralistic, self-denying foreign policy contains strong interventionist potentialities. Perhaps the chief difference is that a president like Wilson does things with agonizing reluctance that a president like Roosevelt does with relish and confidence.

Woodrow Wilson dreamed of a better world. He was devoted to a foreign policy of "movement"; that is, he wanted to do everything he could to foster the spread of a better way of life for the world's peoples. He was a missionary in diplomacy who felt impelled, for example, to teach the Latin American republics how to establish law and order, as he put it. What could conceivably be better for their citizenry? he would ask. The best thing for everyone, Mexicans and Americans alike, was to help encourage, directly if necessary, the growth of democracy

and the defeat of dictators. Wilson has been revealingly compared, in this, with the Communist leader Nikolai Lenin, who also conceived of foreign policy as an opportunity to spread what he regarded as a better way of life. Both men would have denied that their actions were meant just to benefit their own nations; both would have insisted that they were agents of an ennobling world mission. But to the nations in whose politics they intervened, it was difficult to tell the difference between world reformers and nationalists who grabbed as much power and influence as they could.

The central difficulty in a foreign policy of movement is that to those nations being "improved," the policy often looks like hypocrisy. Woodrow Wilson received perhaps more abuse on this score than on any other. To the Latin American nations that bore the brunt of his missionary diplomacy, he seemed to be looking out for America's power ambitions while covering his track with high-flown words. His constant habit of preaching made the situation worse, for Wilson treated Latin American governments with a paternalism that could easily pass for arrogance. His democratic faith and his religious convictions, moreover, convinced him that he was absolutely right. European prime ministers were to be just as offended by Wilson's righteous ways as were the Latin Americans.

Wilson in action

As soon as Wilson entered the White House he denounced Dollar Diplomacy as shameless financial intervention in the affairs of weaker nations. He withdrew American support for investments in China, relying instead on his hopes for a sweeping worldwide program of tariff reductions and freer trade to help every nation achieve prosperity. Part of his foreign policy tradition was to applaud the rise of self-government in other nations, and he warmly supported the Chinese revolution of Sun Yat-sen. Wilson continued American support of the Open Door policy and deplored the actions of European imperialists in China.

The president also announced a fatefully important policy toward Latin America. It was his desire, he said, to help Latin American peoples by giving American support only to "the orderly processes of just government based upon law, [and] not upon arbitrary or irregular force." The result was that he was soon deeply entangled in the internal affairs of Haiti and the Dominican Republic, where a series of bloody revolutions took place in the years from 1913 to 1915. Faced by outright anarchy and widespread suffering in Haiti, in 1915 Wilson sent American troops to occupy the country and establish a government that he believed would be more reflective of the people's wishes. A year later, the same occurred in the Dominican Republic. The two countries were then made American protectorates. Meanwhile, a treaty to the same effect was negotiated with Nicaragua. What had happened to the policy of nonintervention? It had given way to what Woodrow Wilson clearly regarded as a higher and more pressing requirement—the best welfare of the people, as he understood it, who lived in these countries.

Wilson and Huerta

Much graver events were underway in Mexico. A dictator named Porfirio Diaz had ruled the country since the 1870s. An iron-fisted executive who kept relative peace and good order, he welcomed American investors. Such men supported Diaz, for he created the conditions in which more than a billion American dollars was invested in Mexico by 1910, and some 40,000 American citizens could live there in safety and profit. In 1911, however, a liberal revolution led by Francisco Madero took over the country, calling for genuine representative government, widespread social reforms, and a curbing of foreign investment. American businessmen were hostile to Madero, and the American ambassador, Henry Lane Wilson, shared their sentiments. With his aid, one of the victorious generals in the rebellion, Victoriano Huerta, was able to overthrow Madero, who was then promptly murdered, apparently at Huerta's instigation.

This was the situation when Woodrow Wilson took office. Huerta had seized power only weeks before Wilson's inauguration. The contrast between the two regimes could hardly be more dramatic. Wilson was immediately besieged with advice from businessmen and bankers, including his own ambassador in Mexico City, that he extend diplomatic recognition to Huerta. This, after all, was standard practice. Nations did not then sit in judgment on each other, at least in the daily conduct of foreign relations. If a new government had de facto power—was in reality the effective government of a country—then it would be recognized: ambassadors would be exchanged; consuls established in various cities to ease trade relations; and all commercial interactions regularized.

But Wilson broke with this practice. He was deeply offended by the bloody-handed Huerta and hardly allowed the man's name to be uttered in the White House. The Mexican regime, in Wilson's words, was a "government of butchers," and he would have nothing to do with it that even remotely implied moral acceptance. The State Department was staffed with people of the old diplomacy, and they were shocked at Wilson's new approach. They could understand the use of high-handed diplomacy in order to open markets and protect American property, but the same tactics adopted to reform the government of another nation seemed inconceivable.

So far as historians are aware, most of the Mexican people despised Huerta, but they reacted angrily at Wilson's efforts to change their government. Whatever their problems, they wished to settle them among themselves, without the indignity of intervention by a moralistic, preaching *Norteamericano* (the term preferred in Latin America for citizens of the United States, *American* carrying the implication that only those living north of the Rio Grande can be so named).

Whatever the "Colossus of the North" does in Latin America is necessarily regarded with distrust, just as Scots distrust their larger neighbor, England, and Danes react against everything German.

Wilson decides on direct intervention

Wilson informed European governments that he intended to see Huerta removed. At first he relied on diplomatic pressure and sought to get the cooperation of the Constitutionalists in Mexico who under the headship of First Chief Venustiano Carranza were struggling to overthrow Huerta. Following this, the upper classes of Mexico, joined by the Roman Catholic church, rallied around Huerta so that by the spring of 1914 Huerta was, if anything, more strongly in control of the heart of the country than ever. In this circumstance Wilson felt forced either to give up entirely in his determined effort to remove Huerta and establish democratic government, or take up arms himself.

It was inconceivable, given Wilson's character and his beliefs, that he should back down. He believed the Mexican cause to be vital to the rise of democracy and constitutional government throughout Latin America. But he blundered terribly in the steps he then took. He seized on a ridiculously meaningless incident at Tampico, in which Huerta's soldiers and officials had apparently treated American sailors and the American flag with studied contempt. Going before Congress in April 1914, he talked grandly of American honor, inflated the importance of the Tampico and other "similar" events, and asked for authority to use American forces in whatever ways might be necessary to force General Huerta to treat Americans with due respect. His real objective, however, was to cut Huerta off from the sea, dry up his source of funds (import revenues from Veracruz), and topple him from power.

Wilson badly misled himself. He confidently believed that the Mexican people so detested Huerta that they would welcome his aid. He

U.S. Troops lined up in Veracruz, Mexico, after American forces in 1914 had attacked and occupied the city. Wilson by this means hoped to bring down the dictator, General Victoriano Huerta, who had recently seized power in Mexico.
Wide World Photos

anticipated a bloodless occupation of Veracruz, followed by a peaceful downfall of Huerta. After this, American forces, having done their deed for democracy, would withdraw. He got authority from Congress to intervene, but as soon as he landed troops to take over Veracruz, an enormous uproar broke out in the United States and throughout Latin America and Europe. The Mexican people were deeply offended at this high-handed action, and a short battle ensued in which 126 Mexicans and 19 Americans died. Mexican newspapers screamed patriotic appeals. Huertista and Constitutionalist forces joined in condemning Wilson. Mobs roaming the streets of Mexican cities destroyed American property and threatened American citizens. Riots broke out all over Latin America, Europeans furiously condemned the action, and a flood of messages poured in on Wilson from outraged Americans. Few could understand so shocking an event on so puny a justification.

These events—especially the news of the casualties at Veracruz—left Wilson shaken and ashen-faced. He was shocked that his decisions had led to such a disaster. Thereafter Wilson tried to walk a narrow line. Military leaders and bellicose Americans demanded full-scale war, but Wilson would not budge beyond Veracruz. He quickly agreed to proferred mediation by the "ABC" powers (Argentine, Brazil, and Chile), during which he insisted that the way must be cleared for the Constitutionalists to assume the government of Mexico. The Constitutionalists, however, continued proudly to spurn any diplomatic help whatsoever from the United States. As the mediation conference ended on an inconclusive note, Huerta finally had to give up the presidency in response to Constitutionalist victories, and Carranza's regime triumphantly took over the government of Mexico. Wilson received a flood of congratulations.

The crisis, unhappily, was not yet over. Francisco Villa, one of the Constitutionalist generals, wished to be president and soon revolted against Carranza. Once more, Mexico was plunged into bloody civil war. Eventually, it became clear to Wilson that Carranza represented the hope of genuine social reform, while Villa would reinstitute the old corrupt regime of wealthy landowners and American investors. Having withdrawn American troops from Veracruz in November 1914, thus allowing Carranza forces to take the city and secure its revenues, he extended recognition to the regime in October 1915.

Villa then began murdering Americans in an outright attempt to force American military intervention. In March 1916, he invaded New Mexico to sack the town of Columbus. In response Wilson sent General John J. Pershing into Mexico to search out Villa. By April 1916, Amer-

ican troops had traveled 300 miles into Mexico and were fighting at Parral with the Mexican government's troops. But Pershing never caught Villa, and President Carranza angrily demanded that American troops withdraw. Wilson finally pulled Pershing's expedition out of Mexico in February 1917 only because affairs in Europe were so threatening that the American government could no longer afford to divert its energies. A Constitutionalist regime was finally established in Mexico. The Congress installed Carranza as president, adopted a new constitution, and set in motion Latin America's first twentieth century socio-economic revolution.

Mexican-Americans swell in numbers

Immigration to the United States from Mexico began between 1880 and 1910, because the American Southwest was developing, and cheap labor was desired for railroad construction and maintenance and in mining, especially in Arizona. The political upheavals in Mexico now had a profoundly important impact on these migrations. Bloody warfare rocked Mexico from 1911 to 1920. Perhaps a million Mexicans lost their lives in the fighting, and possibly a million crossed the border, settling in the United States. What for generations had been a small minority group swelled enormously, laying the basis for the emergence of the Mexican-American as the largest American minority after the Afro-American. Texas, New Mexico, Arizona, California, and Colorado contained only about 100,000 people of Mexican birth in 1900; by 1930, the total in these states of Mexican-descended residents skyrocketed to more than 1,250,000. The most startling increase was in California, where in these thirty years the number of Mexican-born (plus a relatively small number of *Californio* descendants, whose families had been in residence since pre-gold rush days) rose from 8,000 to 368,000.

This immense immigration, pulled by the huge demand for stoop labor in the rapidly growing agriculture in these states and pushed by the civil war going on in Mexico, created large pools of unorganized, cheap labor and sizable *barrios* (Mexican-American residential areas) within southwestern cities. The immigrant workers built the irrigated farming industry of this region by providing an essential supply of laboring hands. In return they received bare subsistence wages, housing like that given slaves a hundred years before, no education, prejudicial treatment in social relations, and the status of America's most pitifully exploited workers—the migrant farm laborers. Mexicans also continued to labor in the railroads, mining, construction, and in various urban occupations. Very few became American citizens. Only 5.5 percent of the 320,000 Mexican-born living in the United States in 1930 who were over twenty-one years of age had gone through naturalization. Perhaps this was because their homeland was next door, a fact that has made the Mexican-American minority group sharply different in its attitudes from every other such group in American history. Many harbored hopes of returning to Mexico; there was always much coming and going across the border. Where Mexican immigrants did vote, as in New Mexico and in Texan border cities like El Paso, in San Antonio, and in South Texas, they were usually voted by Democratic political machines. For these reasons and those of poverty and language and cultural differences, the Mexican-American group, for all its size, has had little voting power. (Indeed, the tendency of Mexican-Americans to stay home from the polls continues to reduce their political influence.) Therefore, their ability to improve their condition—especially since American labor unions usually refused to admit them—was practically nonexistent.

Mexican-Americans went into many other lines of employment, however, besides that on the farms. During World War I they began for the first time to appear in midwestern cities such as St. Louis, Chicago, and Detroit where they labored in steel plants, automobile plants, and packing houses. (During and after the Second

World War, this movement grew tremendously.) Los Angeles, by 1925, was the second largest Mexican city, after Mexico City itself. Living in crowded ghetto conditions, urban Mexican-Americans entered at the bottom of the social scale under the Poles, Italians, and Slavs who by this time were beginning to move upward—and to look downward with dislike on the new arrivals. So significant was this movement into nonagricultural employment that in 1930 the census stated that while 180,000 Mexican-Americans worked on the farms, about 150,000 were common laborers in the railroads and other industries.

The depression of the 1930s, however, brought an end to this first huge immigration of Mexicans into the United States. Jobs were no longer available; laws were passed prohibiting the employment of aliens on public works; contractors were discouraged from hiring noncitizens; migrant American farmers displaced from the dust bowl of Texas and Oklahoma moved heavily into the farm labor market; and probably a half-million Mexicans returned to their homeland. To keep them off welfare, whole trainloads were shipped southward; some 200,000 were moved out in the year 1932 alone. This was a grievous experience for thousands of people. It confirmed the view of most Mexican-Americans that Anglo-American society could not be trusted, and that the United States government was a power to be avoided. Welcomed when their presence produced profits for employers, Mexicans were abruptly expelled when things got difficult.

America reacts to the First World War

The First World War broke out in August 1914, with startling suddenness escalating into a worldwide conflict in which the combatants fought with unparalleled ferocity. Every weapon imaginable or technically possible at the time was put to use in this unbelievably desperate struggle. Why it broke out, no one seemed able to explain satisfactorily. But the fact was that the First

World War became a total war in which millions of men rushed to arms and were flung at each other in such huge charging masses that in some battles more than a hundred thousand men died in a few hours. The planet had never before witnessed anything like it.

The Central Powers (Germany and Austria-Hungary, together with Bulgaria and the Ottoman Empire) faced the Allies (Great Britain, France, and Russia, together with Italy and some smaller states). The Germans swept into France through neutral Belgium on a broad front, being brought to a halt just short, so it seemed, of victory. Trenches hundreds of miles long, stretching from the English Channel to Switzerland, were quickly dug, and enormous armies disappeared into them for four terrible years of periodic charge and countercharge. The huge Russian front saw a confused and bloody grappling that in 1917 ended in the collapse of the Czarist government, and after a brief interregnum, the emergence of the Soviet Socialist Republic under Nicolai Lenin, who promptly made a separate peace with the Central Powers. The United States entered the war in April 1917. The million men it placed in France within a year tipped the scale on the Allied side, and with their front collapsing, the Germans asked for an armistice in November 1918.

The dead were uncountable. No one will ever know exactly how many died, but they numbered at least thirty million, including civilian deaths. All European civilization was bled white, for a large proportion of an entire generation had been swept away. No graver wound had ever been suffered by European culture save perhaps the Black Death of the Middle Ages. In 1914, it had seemed that democracy and a better life for all was on the march everywhere; at World War I's end, democracy seemed either destroyed or dying, millions were starving, and a new era of barbaric totalitarianism was emerging. The Austro-Hungarian Empire was destroyed, as were the empires of the Germans, the Ottomans, and the Russian Czars—surely no great loss to humankind. But an entire way of life, encompassing tens of millions of people and stretching over vast reaches of the earth's surface, lay in ruins. In many ways the greatest tragedy of the twentieth century is the first World War, not only for what it destroyed directly, but for what it led to.

What did Americans think in 1914 when Europe suddenly fell into this savage war? They were utterly and completely shocked. President Wilson tried from the outset to be neutral in thought and deed, and by and large the mass of the American people agreed. But at least a third of the population in 1914 was either foreign-born or the children of foreign-born, and so the war put cruel strains on everyone. Some 8 million Americans were of German or Austrian descent, about 4.5 million were of Irish heritage, and both groups were outspokenly hostile to Great Britain.

For millions more, however, Germany had long been a threatening menace on the horizon. There was the potent image of the German military caste, whose spike-helmeted visage now appearing in newspaper photographs seemed almost bestially warlike. More than this, the majority of the American people were of British lineage, and everything in the deepest chords of memory pulled them toward the British side. Democrats looked to Liberals with a sense of comradeship; Republicans looked to Conservatives in brotherly respect; and Socialists admired the Labor party. Language, culture, religion, way of life, economic and social ties, a lively and continuous interchange of books and ideas across the Atlantic, the common heritage of representative government and personal rights—these all made it a foregone conclusion that from the outset American sympathies would be primarily with the British and the similarly democratic French.

Wilson searches for peace

Wilson did not ask the nation to go to war, however, until he had spent two-and-a-half years in a futile search for some means of keeping the United States out of the combat. His first step

The First World War, 1914–1918

U.S.A.
1917

NORWAY
Oslo

SWEDEN
Stockholm

FINLAND
Indep. July, 1917
Helsinki

Lake
Ladoga

Petrograd

ESTONIA
Indep.
Feb, 1918

LATVIA
Indep. Riga
Nov, 1918

RUSSIA
1914

NORTH
SEA

Battle of Jutland
May-June, 1916

DENMARK
Copenhagen

Riga offensive
Sept, 1917

LITHUANIA
Indep. Feb, 1918

Smolensk

GREAT
BRITAIN
1914

Edinburgh

London

Kiel
Hamburg

Memel

Königsberg

Danzig

Masurian Lakes
Sept, 1914

Vilna

Minsk

BALTIC SEA

Amsterdam
NETH.

Tannenberg
Aug, 1914

Brussels
BELG.
1914
Cologne

Berlin

GERMANY
1914

POLAND
Indep. Nov, 1918

Warsaw

Pinsk

Brest-Litovsk

GERMAN INVASION
AUG-SEPT, 1914
LUX.
Mainz
Metz

Leipzig

Dresden

Lublin

Kiev

Paris

Strasbourg

Prague

Cracow

Lemberg

GALICIA

Kerensky offensive
July, 1917

Rhine R.

BAVARIA
Munich

Danube R.

Galicia offensives
Aug, 1914

Brusilov offensive
June, 1916

UKRAINE

FRANCE
1914

Berne

SWITZ.

Vittorio-Veneto
Oct-Nov, 1918

Vienna

Pressburg

AUSTRIA-HUNGARY
1914

Budapest

Graz

Odessa

Milan

Piave June, 1918

Venice

Trieste

RUMANIA
1916

BLACK
SEA

Genoa

Marseilles

ITALY
1915

Withdrew from
Triple Alliance 1914

BOSNIA

Invasion of Serbia
1914

Belgrade

Bucharest

Danube R.

SPAIN

CORSICA

Rome

Sarajevo

MONTENEGRO
1915

SERBIA
1914

BULGARIA
1915

Sofia

Constantinople

PORTUGAL
1916

SARDINIA

Naples

ALBANIA

OTTOMAN EMPIRE
1914

Salonika

Gallipoli

MEDITERRANEAN

SICILY

SEA

GREECE
1916

Dardanelles campaign
1915-1916

Athens

Smyrna

CRETE

1916 Date of entry into the war

━━━━ Maximum advance of the Central Powers

------ Maximum Russian advance

••••••• Line of the Brest-Litovsk Treaty Mar, 1918

━━━━ Armistice lines, eastern front Dec., 1917

0   500
        Miles

Central Powers

Allied Powers

Neutral nations

was to strike a neutral course, since an over-whelming percentage of the American people had no desire to enter the frightful conflict. But how to be genuinely neutral? Without the huge production of American factories and American loans to the Allies so they could buy that output, it seems probable that the Central Powers would have won. This trade soon skyrocketed to massive proportions. American exports to the Allies before the war had been valued at about $800 million annually. By 1916, they had soared to $3.2 billion. By 1917, some $2.2 billion had been loaned to the Allies to support this trade (and only about $30 million to the Central Powers).

Clearly, an economic revolution of gigantic proportions was transforming the American economy. Not only did factories all over the land boom along day and night to fill the armament orders, they also turned busily to providing goods for the worldwide markets that the British and other European countries now had to abandon in their concentration on the war. The German government urged that the United States declare an embargo on the sale of munitions, for the British navy soon effectively ended any trade between the Central Powers and the United States by clearing the seas of enemy merchantmen. Such actions on the part of the United States, however, would in fact have been unneutral, for command of the sea lanes was dictated by the facts of war, not by American actions. An embargo would have changed the outcome of the war, in all probability, as a result of conscious American actions—and most Americans did not, in any event, wish for a Central Powers victory.

The submarine crisis

The submarine was a new invention, and like the atom bomb in a later war, it transformed the whole nature of the conflict. The Germans in 1915 felt driven to use submarines for several reasons: their land armies had not won; the war had settled down into a bloody stalemate; and the British blockade would eventually win the war if allowed to go on long enough. Moreover, Ger-

many's admirals were excited over their new weapon—of which in 1915 they possessed only about twenty—and were absolutely confident that it could win the war if unleashed. (This was not the first, nor was it to be the last, time that military men, enamored of some new weapon, were to present this argument to a national government and thereby bring about unexpected results of vast importance.)

The submarine, however, involved a grave tactical problem. A small and slow craft, its hull was necessarily thin since armor plating rendered it heavy and useless. When under the sea it was lethal and usually impregnable; when surfaced, it was potentially at the mercy of the kind of small-caliber cannon that British merchantmen carried. (Actually, skillful tactics generally negated this threat, so that no German submarine was sunk by an armed merchantman before April 1917.) This made the following of cruiser rules risky. (Cruiser rules required vessels attacking merchantmen to give sufficient warning before sinking them to allow sailors to disembark and enter lifeboats.)

Therefore, the Germans announced that every enemy ship located in a huge area around Britain would be torpedoed by submarines without notice. Neutrals were warned that the mechanics of war made their vessels liable to unintended attacks. The German announcement was almost purely a bluff, for the tiny number of submarines they possessed could do little to check the streams of vessels carrying cargoes to Great Britain and France. However, few elsewhere in the world realized this. Especially in America, this startling new departure in the means of war created a shockwave of revulsion and horror at this unprecedented and apparently cowardly form of assault. Neutral nations were intensely concerned, for it seemed highly unlikely that a German officer peering through a periscope lens awash by sea and fog could accurately distinguish between enemy and neutral vessels. Furthermore, neutrals (such as Americans) regularly traveled as passengers on British liners. Acutely concerned with protecting every detail of international law, Wilson warned constantly that neutral rights had to be protected or else the entire fabric of international law would crumble. In response to the German announcement of unrestricted submarine warfare, he stated that the United States would hold Germany "strictly accountable" if any American lives were lost or American ships sunk.

In late March 1915 the first American life was lost when a British liner was sunk. Then, in an event that shocked the world, the British liner *Lusitania* was sunk, carrying almost twelve hundred persons, including more than a hundred Americans, to their deaths. An earthquake of American anger swept the nation, and President Wilson demanded of Germany that its submarines henceforth refrain from attacking any unarmed passenger liner, whether enemy or neutral. When another such ship was sunk, he took the grave step of warning that diplomatic relations might be broken off, at which point the Germans relented and agreed to make no more such attacks.

The preparedness campaign

Now Wilson reluctantly began to equip the nation with military strength, for his negotiations with Germany had demonstrated how difficult it was to achieve anything from a position of weakness. But when he asked Congress for large increases in the navy and army, every antimilitarist group in the country broke into clamorous protest. Wilson now stumped the country appealing for support. Eventually the army was expanded moderately—to about 200,000 men—the state militia was renamed the National Guard and made subject to the president's call, and a formidable array of battleships and other powerful naval craft was authorized.

In the Democratic nominating convention of 1916, speakers found that the delegates went into frenzies of cheering at any mention of Wilson's success in keeping the nation out of the war. Thenceforth, this became the Democratic battle cry: Wilson was not only a full-fledged progres-

sive, as the reforms described in the previous chapter indicated, he had also kept the nation at peace. Wilson chimed in by charging that the Republicans were the "war party." Winning his cliff-hanging victory on these issues, he then turned again to the sober business of fulfilling his pledge.

Wilson seeks to mediate

Wilson's hope was to serve as mediator between the warring parties, and he worked hard at this from the time the war began. He sent his confidential adviser, Colonel Edward M. House, on tours of the warring capitals to try to find some basis for negotiations, but to little avail. Wilson had made it clear that the kind of peace settlement to be worked out in such a conference would be one in which they had little interest—a peace of genuine reconciliation in which neither side gained or lost anything. Wilson was calling, in effect, for a new diplomacy to replace the old. Liberals in America and in the Allied countries had been arguing since the war began for a settlement that would establish a new world order in which the practice of secret negotiations would be ended, entangling alliances would be terminated, balance of power diplomacy would be replaced by an international parliament where all nations would be treated with equal consideration, and military strength would not be the dominant consideration. Massive disarmament should take place, for it was firmly believed that huge armies and navies were themselves the catalysts that brought on such horrifying conflicts. National groups ruled by alien governments (for example, the Czechs in the Austro-Hungarian Empire) should be given self-government. In the world at large, there should be freedom of the seas and an end to economic barriers between nations.

This was the kind of new diplomacy for which Wilson contended. He insisted on open negotiations, no indemnities, no punishments, no gobbling up of new territories. Making himself the leader of the new internationalism, he said repeatedly that the peace to be made should consider the people's wishes, not simply those of powerful government leaders. The British supported the notion of an international parliament, a league of nations, for the suggestion that such a body be created had, in fact, first come from them. But the rest of the new diplomacy was unacceptable to the Allies. A whole network of secret treaties had been worked out in which each nation was promised major territorial gains at the expense of the Central Powers. Furthermore, the Allied governments recognized that Wilson's real allies within the European nations were the labor unions and the reforming parties—the parties of movement—who wanted a "people's peace." They feared that surrendering diplomacy to the control of such parties would whet appetites for social revolutions, and this they abhorred.

As the war went on and became ever more bloody, discontent began welling up in the civilian populations of the Allied countries. They read the horrifying casualty lists; they saw whole generations of young men fall like wheat before a scythe; they learned of the mounds of dead that stretched for miles and miles after each "victory." There was a point during the war, Walter Lippmann once wrote, when the First World War became "hyperbolic." That is, its fantastic pressures simply burst the bounds of western Europe's institutional arrangements, and the people lost faith both in their leaders and in the systems under which they had been ruled. At this point, with mutiny threatening in the French army and the British digging deeper into the barrel of available manpower, the masses began looking to Woodrow Wilson as their new Messiah, their deliverer from carnage and death.

Europe remains belligerent

But in 1916 this point had not yet been reached. The publics of the warring nations were so embittered against their enemies that their governments could confidently reject Wilson's propos-

als for a peace of reconciliation. Everyone wanted to punish everyone else. The Central Powers had ambitious dreams of conquest (as the peace treaty they later extorted from Russia in 1918 proved), and their admirals and generals, like those on the Allied side, constantly predicted victory.

Meanwhile, the submarine problem grew more serious. In March 1916 a French vessel, the *Sussex*, was torpedoed in the English Channel with heavy loss of life. More such attacks soon occurred, and Wilson issued what amounted to an ultimatum threatening war if the Germans did not cease all attacks made without warning on enemy or neutral merchantmen. The German government still did not possess enough submarines to justify the risk of war with the United States, and in early May 1916 it agreed that its navy would visit and search all vessels before attacking them—a sharp limitation on its whole undersea campaign. It was a spectacular diplomatic victory for the president, but the agreement was precarious. Who could tell when the Germans would change their policy, and then what would Wilson be able to do? The only weapon he had left was war itself.

Wilson feared that the mounting desperation of the struggle in Europe, of which the submarine issue was only one outgrowth, might inevitably pull the United States into the war. In January 1917 in a speech before the Senate, he called for a "peace without victory." In such a peace, he said, there should be limitation of armaments, freedom of the seas, self-determination for all peoples, and security against aggression for every nation, small and large. Then a "league of peace" should be formed to enforce the peace settlement. The European masses reacted gratefully to this appeal, and even the British indicated that they were ready to attend such a conference. But the moment was too late: the Germans had decided to launch unrestricted submarine warfare; to sink without warning every vessel, neutral as well as Allied, liner as well as merchantman, that approached the British Isles or the French coast.

And the war came

Germany made this decision because it now possessed almost a hundred submarines and its admirals had persuaded the government that an unrestricted campaign would win the war. The Germans knew that it would bring the Americans into the war, but they were convinced that victory would come long before American armies could have any effect on the western front. Totally interdicting the British Isles, they believed, would swiftly starve war-weakened England into submission. It was a bold and fateful move.

Still the president hesitated. He broke relations with Germany as a minimum gesture. Then he learned that the German government (in the British-discovered Zimmermann Telegram) was trying to get Mexico to attack the United States if America entered the war by promising to give Mexico the American Southwest. This news inflamed American opinion to a fever pitch. Then ship after ship began to be sunk. Public opinion swung rapidly toward war. Prominent newspapers urged it as the only answer, and formerly impartial public figures like the philosopher John Dewey said that war was the last response left. Then in Russia a revolution took place on March 15, 1917, in which a moderately socialistic regime overthrew the Czarist government, thus eliminating the only autocracy on the Allied side. The Allied cause could now be confidently declared to be that of democracy and human rights. Thousands of Americans gathered in protests against the sinking of American ships. By mid-March, Wilson's own cabinet unanimously urged him to go to war. By this time Wilson had come to a decision: no great power could submit to its merchant vessels being destroyed day after day without losing all influence it possessed in the world. The United States must fight back, and going to war was the only way effectively to do that. He had totally lost hope that he could deal in any way with the militarists in command of German policy. Most of all, he was convinced that American entry into the war was the best means to bring the war to an end as soon as possible and rebuild a civilized world.

On April 2, 1917, he asked Congress to declare war in a speech that gave the nation high ideals to fight for—not the balance of power, nor, national interest narrowly conceived, but the future of humankind. Wilson was sufficiently a realist to know that American security absolutely depended on the continued independence and freedom of Britain, with its huge navy and its commitment to democracy. Germany, he was convinced, was an unbearable menace to the safety of any freedom-loving world. It "was a madman that needed restraining," were his own words. The prospect of the world order that autocratic, militaristic Germany would create after a victory could not be tolerated.

By temperament, however, Wilson was a moralist, an idealist, a dreamer of great dreams. His mind, as always, could be seized most warmly by noble epics of human achievement. And so he spoke to the nation in his war message not of practical considerations or of limited objectives but of the need to eliminate autocracy, and, by eliminating the methods by which autocracies carried on their international relations, make the world a safe place for democracy. America was going to be fighting for the rights of neutrals, for peace and justice, and the right of self-government by oppressed peoples. He called for a new world order, not for a restoration of the old. The American people responded wholeheartedly to this grand vision. Unhappily, they were not prepared for the fact that in the peace conference that eventually took place Wilson faced men devoted to the old diplomacy. It was, therefore, impossible for him to secure most of the things for which he had so eloquently appealed. Wilson's brilliant war speech, one of the great utterances of American history, sowed the seeds of a later massive disillusionment.

In these words, Woodrow Wilson asked for a declaration of war against the Imperial German government: "The present German submarine warfare against commerce is a warfare against mankind. It is a war against all nations. . . . Our motive [in responding] will not be revenge or the victorious assertion of the physical might of the nation, but only the vindication of right, of human right, of which we are only a single champion. . . . There is one choice we cannot make, we are incapable of making: we will not choose the path of submission and suffer the most sacred rights of our Nation and our people to be ignored or violated. . . .

''Our object now . . . is to vindicate the principles of peace and justice in the life of the world as against selfish and autocratic power and to set up amongst the really free and self-governed peoples of the world such a concert of purpose and of action as will henceforth insure the observance of those principles. Neutrality is no longer feasible or desirable where the peace of the world is involved and the freedom of its peoples, and the menace to that peace and freedom lies in the existence of autocratic governments backed by organized

force which is controlled wholly by their will, not by the will of their people. . . . [We] know that in such a Government, following [its secret, autocratic] methods, we can never have a friend; and that in the presence of its organized power, always lying in wait to accomplish we know not what purpose, there can be no assured security for the democratic Governments of the world. . . . The world must be made safe for democracy. Its peace must be planted upon the tested foundations of political liberty. . . . We are but one of the champions of the rights of mankind. We shall be satisfied when those rights have been made as secure as the faith and the freedom of nations can make them.''

America mobilizes

The United States entered the war at a critical time for, as Wilson soon learned, the British and French were at the point of total exhaustion and near defeat. Unhappily, however, the preparedness campaign Wilson had already launched was slow to pay any dividends. Conscription was enacted, but the first draftees did not begin training until the fall of 1917. Meanwhile, the nation was stumbling along trying to find some way of marshaling its economic and military energies. Early in 1918 the president, relying on legislation earlier passed by Congress, took near-dictatorial powers to bring the economy under rigorously centralized direction. The War Industries Board took over the task of coordinating the manufacture of all war goods: raw materials were allocated efficiently; production was standardized; prices were fixed; and the purchases of American and Allied armed forces were coordinated. William McAdoo, secretary of the Treasury, took over direction of the railroads, which had fallen into total confusion. Similar steps were taken with regard to food production under the direction of Herbert Hoover, an engineer who had gained worldwide fame as the man who kept food moving into Belgium during the German occupation. Since wheat prices were set at such a high level that farm production skyrocketed,

Yanks parade through London on August 15, 1917, before being shipped to France. Huge American reinforcements soon helped check German offensives and turn the tide of war.
United States Signal Corps, The National Archives

marginal lands everywhere in the nation were pressed into service. In a year's time exports of food rose from about twelve to over eighteen million tons and at the same time farm income rose perhaps thirty percent.

The war affected the economic situation of America's city dwellers in varying ways. Salaried workers found their incomes down twenty-two percent by war's end due to inflation, but on the other hand, thousands of men became millionaires. Labor benefited greatly from the war, for Wilson gave strong support to their demands for collective bargaining agreements with employers. Since some five million men were ultimately drawn into military service, working men had an unprecedented leverage in wage disputes. Wilson established the National War Labor Board, which negotiated settlements in hundreds of disagreements, usually on the side of the unions. From about two million members in 1916, the AFL grew to 3.26 million by 1920. Even the wages of unskilled workers rose while perhaps half a million black Americans left the South to take up northern jobs.

Civil liberties crushed

Wilson's liberalism, however, failed miserably in one crucial test: he could not stand criticism. Entering the war was a frightful wrench for him, and he was forced to justify it to himself by seeing the war as one fought for the highest and most crucial interests of all mankind. He therefore saw any critic of the war as an enemy of human welfare. An Espionage Act was passed in 1917, and a Sedition Act in 1918, which revived the worst features of John Adams's Alien and Sedition acts of 1798. Anyone aiding the enemy, obstructing recruiting, hampering the sale of war bonds, or even daring to "utter, print, write, or publish any disloyal, profane, scurrilous or abusive language" about the government, the Constitution, or the military, was to be harshly punished—and many were.

Furthermore, a nationwide spy system was established to search out miscreants. Union meetings, peace gatherings, and all such assemblages were honeycombed with informants. People guilty of no discernible crime were rushed off to jail, held without bail, and reportedly in extreme cases physically abused. A woman who received a Red Cross solicitor in a "hostile" manner, a socialist who wrote a letter to a newspaper charging wartime profiteering, a Californian who laughed at rookies drilling in San Francisco, a New Yorker who spat near some Italian officers—all were put in jail. *The Masses,* a socialist periodical, was shut down, for the American Socialist party had come out against participation in the war, which it condemned as nothing more than an argument between capitalists. Eugene V. Debs was given the barbarous sentence of ten years in jail for making an antiwar speech. Robert Goldstein made a movie, *The Spirit of '76,* which was hostile to British soldiers, and he too was sentenced to ten years in jail. When a woman wrote, "I am for the people, and the government is for the profiteers," the same punishment was meted to her. Worst of all, the Supreme Court upheld these actions in *Schenck* v. *The United States* (1919), in a decision in which Justice Oliver Wendell Holmes, Jr., said that no one, in the name of free speech, had the right to shout "Fire!" in a crowded theater. By extension, this apparently justified the government in doing whatever it thought best during a time of war.

Progressives respond

American progressivism had always been largely indifferent to world affairs, but now the challenge of war forced a radical shift of attention. Many were devoted pacifists, such as William Jennings Bryan, or were doubtful about the rightfulness of the cause. Robert La Follette was one of the few in Congress who refused to rise and cheer when Wilson asked for war. But the president was successful in persuading progressives that the war was vitally related to a better future for mankind, and soon most of them swung enthusiastically behind American involvement. Now their task, as they saw it, was not only reforming America but reforming the world as well. In this spirit, Bryan and La Follette left their doubts behind and supported the cause.

Many progressives were also excited by the social possibilities that the war effort opened up within the nation itself. A sense of national unity emerged, and the progressive mind seemed always eagerly to respond to anything that induced collective action. Powerful governmental agencies in Washington, D.C., demonstrated as nothing ever had before what remarkable things could be done when the nation's energies were directed into socially useful directions—and the war was thought of as socially useful. A new sense of the possibilities inherent in cooperation between business and government emerged as business leaders came to Washington to direct the new agencies.

All sorts of reforms now seemed possible. The Department of Labor built thousands of homes for working families. Social workers labored in training camps, the Red Cross, and other agencies to aid, educate, and "uplift" thousands of poor people brought in from the hills, the farms, and the slums. The drive toward prohibition of alcohol reached victory in the Eighteenth Amendment (1919), and the vote for women was achieved in the Nineteenth Amendment (1920). Government operation of the railroads transformed them into a surprisingly efficient system. It seemed a time of true national collectivism, in which the regulatory state had finally emerged.

Even Wilson was inspired by the new possibilities. In 1919, while laboring in the peace conference at Versailles, he cabled a message to Congress calling for "a new organization of industry . . . [a] genuine democratization of industry . . . [a] cooperation and partnership based upon a real community of interest and participation in control." Progressives talked excitedly about the potentialities of national planning. McAdoo recommended that the railroads remain under government direction, and Josephus Daniels,

secretary of the navy, recommended the same for the radio system. Progressive Republicans like William Allen White were enthusiastic about the possibility of national old-age pensions and public operation of the natural resources of oil, water, forests, and mines.

At war's end, such people in the United States and in Europe cherished a magnificent vision of the future. The fighting had created terrible disasters, but the experience of winning it had revealed that each nation possessed the means of taking control of its resources and making human life rich and satisfying. When everyone was dedicated to an end greater than self-gain (save for those who became millionaires), there had been a vast release of energy. Molds had been broken, lives had been shunted into new channels, and new outlooks had emerged. The world seemed swept by winds of promising change, and for a time at least it was a young man's world full of hope in the midst of disaster.

The Fourteen Points

Wilson went to war in order to win a different kind of peace from the one he knew was on the minds of the Allied leaders. For this reason he referred to the United States as an "associated" rather than an "allied" power. The United States military operation was a separate affair, and Wilson consciously steered his diplomacy clear of any association with secret treaties of annexation or demands for vengeance. Once the United States had entered the war, he repeatedly called for a liberal peace. There were moderate elements in the German *Reichstag* (legislature), and he hoped that by his appeals he would inspire these antiwar groups to take control of German policy and make peace. He was, in fact, inclined to make separate peace negotiations if the Allies refused to respond to any overtures that might come from the Germans. He even hoped that the German army would not collapse entirely, for then the Allied governments would have the Germans wholly at their mercy.

Meanwhile, a huge American army and navy were being assembled to fight Germany. The German army mounted offensive after offensive. In July 1917 the first small American units came into the fighting line. In November the war was powerfully affected by events in Russia, where the Bolsheviks (Communists) under Nicolai Lenin overthrew the moderate socialist government that had governed since the czar's fall from power and promptly asked for peace with Germany. They published the secret annexationist treaties that they found in the Russian archives, thus humiliating the Allied governments. Lenin, in a statement to the world, called the holocaust a squabble between capitalists who were using the common people as cannon fodder. He appealed to the masses of the world to rise in revolt and open the way for worldwide equalitarian communism.

Now Woodrow Wilson came forward to give, in effect, the reply of the Western capitalist democracies to Lenin's appeals. He wished to prove to the suffering peoples of Europe that the West, too, could create a liberal and humane peace settlement. In January 1918 he issued his famous "Fourteen Points" address. Essentially a restatement of the liberal internationalist hopes for a new world order, it contained in eloquent langauge an appeal for open diplomacy, freedom of the seas, general disarmament, elimination of trade barriers, a completely impartial settlement of colonial claims, and a league of nations. He was quite specific on the issue of self-determination in such territories as Alsace-Lorraine and the Balkans, and for the oppressed Czech and Polish peoples in the Austro-Hungarian Empire. Finally, the president took careful pains to assure the German people that the West intended no vengeance against them but only desired an end to the autocratic regime that had deluged Europe with blood and suffering.

The impact of the Fourteen Points was enormous. The Allied governments gave them no open endorsement, but the European peoples responded enthusiastically. Even the German people, long patiently suffering and trustful, began to grow restive. Then in March 1918 came a fateful event—the Treaty of Brest-Litovsk. By brutal uses of force, the Germans extorted an enormous region from Russia comprising almost 400,000 square miles and 50 million people. Now it was clear that Wilson's hopes concerning an overthrow of German militarism from within were groundless. In an angry outburst that amounted almost to a second declaration of war, he asserted that there was now only one answer: "Force, Force to the utmost, Force without stint or limit, the righteous and triumphant Force which shall make Right the law of the world, and cast every selfish dominion down in the dust." It was the world's tragic fate that the very use of this overwhelming force would make it impossible for Woodrow Wilson to achieve a "peace without victory." When the Allies won, the Germans were militarily crushed. They had to accept whatever the victorious powers handed down.

The final year of war

The war, however, was far from over. The collapse of Russia had freed the German army to shift forty tested divisions from the eastern to the western front, where they mounted a climactic offensive in 1918 designed to end the war. When the assaults began in the spring, there were still less than 30,000 Americans (about two divisions) in action. By July, however, their numbers had risen to 85,000; and in the immense Allied counterattack that came in August 1918, more than a quarter of a million Americans joined the assault. The buildup continued with astonishing swiftness: soldiers were flooding into France on a veritable bridge of boats from the United States. In September 1918 there were enough Americans to form the First Army, which with half a million men assaulted and overwhelmed the German lines in the Verdun region. In a few weeks, more than 1.2 million American soldiers leaped out of the trenches in a combined assault with the British and French and fought their way grimly for-

Infantrymen of the Second Division inch their way through thick smoke and fog in the Argonne Forest. These close-packed assaults into massed machine-guns and artillery on the other side produced appalling slaughters.
United States Signal Corps, The National Archives

ward for more than a month through the wilderness of the Argonne forest.

Such assaults were incredibly costly. In the Argonne campaign the Americans suffered 120,000 casualties. But the German line was now collapsing massively, and the High Command urged the German government to make peace. Appealing to Wilson for a settlement on the basis of the Fourteen Points to which Wilson got the reluctant Allies to agree, the German government signed the armistice on November 11, 1918, and the war was over. It left behind 130,000 dead Americans (by comparison, ten years of war in Vietnam produced, by 1972, 45,000 dead), and millions of slain Russians, Germans, Italians, Rumanians, Austro-Hungarians, Serbians, Belgians, French, and British.

The peace conference

At war's end Wilson was seized with the zeal not only of a peacemaker but of a prophet as well. When he went to Europe and briefly toured the Allied capitals in 1919, millions of people cheered him with almost adoring frenzy. He must have felt that he had the cause of mankind in his hands. But there were grave barriers in the way. He had already made serious errors at home. In the congressional elections of 1918, he had appealed for a Democratic victory on the ground that if the Republicans won (as they did, gaining a majority in both houses, for reasons not particularly associated with the war), the world would interpret that victory as a rejection of his ideals. Although he would need the assent of the Senate to any peace treaty he signed, he chose not one senator to accompany him to Versailles.

There, with both Germany and Russia excluded from the conference—the latter because of the separate peace already signed and its possession of a Communist regime—he stood alone as the only advocate of a liberal peace settlement. The wonder is that he won as much as he did of his Fourteen Points. France was adamant in her desire to gain permanent security against Germany, for on two occasions within living memory, in 1870 and 1914, German armies had poured across the French borders. Premier Georges Clemenceau would hear practically nothing of the Fourteen Points.

Britain and France demanded that Germany be forced to pay all the costs of the war. Endless disputes went on with Wilson insisting that Germany could never pay such a huge sum and remain economically alive. However, he finally had to accept British and French demands for reparations, which amounted eventually to the enormous sum of more than thirty billion dollars. This issue complicated all international relations for many years after the war, causing the most intricate and insoluble difficulties and helping to lead, in part, to the rise of Hitler and the outbreak of the Second World War.

What about self-determination? Wilson agreed that Germany's colonies should remain in the hands of the Allied powers that had occupied them, but he got those powers to accept the mandate principle, in which their occupation of the colonies was to be under international supervision, the eventual goal being independence for each colony. The Austro-Hungarian Empire had already collapsed, and the people of Czechoslovakia had moved ahead on their own to establish self-rule. The Balkan areas of the empire were separated into an independent Yugoslavia, including Serbia and Montenegro; Rumania was greatly expanded by the accession of large territories; and Poland, Lithuania, Latvia, Estonia, and Finland came into existence as new nations. Meanwhile, the Ottoman Empire was carved up into mandated territories by the French and British, a direct violation of self-determination.

The problem of Russia was an enormously complicated one. The French and British govern-

The First World War: Western front

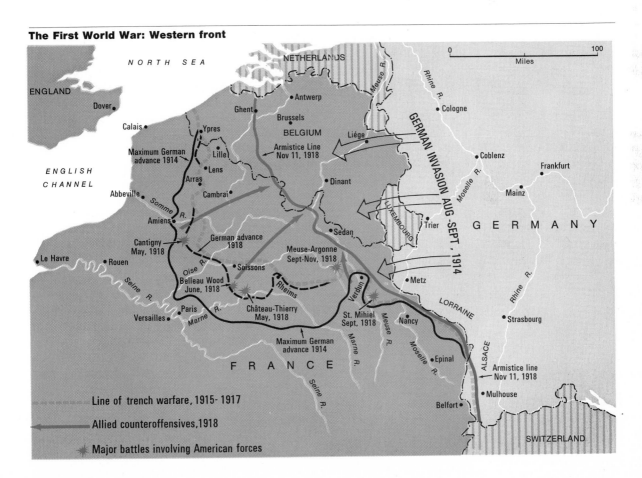

ments decided to intervene militarily in an attempt to crush the Bolshevik government and help the "White Russians" (non-Communist forces) return to power. While the war was still going on, they had even persuaded an exceedingly reluctant Woodrow Wilson to put a small force of American soldiers in Murmansk to prevent war supplies from being captured by the Germans and another in Siberia to assist a Czech army that wished to extricate itself from Russia and continue fighting on the western front. But in each of these cases Wilson scrupulously sought to take no role in internal Russian politics, and he insisted that the people of Russia be allowed to solve their own problems. All military interventions, he said at the peace conference, should be

ended forthwith. "Trying to stop a revolutionary movement by troops in the field," he said, "is like using a broom to hold back a great ocean."

In all this he kept his eye focused on his greatest objective—the establishment of a league of nations. In issue after issue he either failed or got only partial victories. The British would not agree to freedom of the seas; tariffs did not tumble; self-determination was often violated; key negotiations were usually secret, not open as he had called for; but in the end he got his league. In its final form, the League of Nations was a two-house body, composed of an Assembly representing all member nations, and a Council of nine (five of its members to be the United States, Great Britain, France, Italy, and Japan). Joined to it was a Secretariat to provide administrative functions, a World Court, and an array of special commissions concerned with specific problems. The Covenant, or constitution, of the league called for a number of admirable objectives—the reduction of arms, the arbitration of disputes, and the collective security of all members. This last was embodied in what Wilson called the heart of the Covenant, Article 10, in which each nation undertook "to respect and preserve as against external aggression the territorial integrity and existing political independence of all the members of the league." Collective security was to replace the balance of power.

The fight over ratification

Wilson returned from Versailles to the United States in a defiant mood. He had had to make so *many* compromises. His imperious soul was deeply wounded, his disappointments keen and bitter. In the United States he knew opposition to the treaty was brewing, but he had passed beyond the point of compromise. Once again he was a stern Presbyterian, a confident president, who was absolutely positive that he was right. *"The Senate,"* he said to a reporter, *"is going to ratify the treaty."* He went to that body in person to present the treaty, and insisted that its key fea-

Europe after Versailles, 1919

■ New independent nations

■ Plebiscite areas

▨ Allied occupation zone

ture, the League of Nations, was the dream of all the world's masses. "Dare we reject it and break the heart of the world?" he asked. It was God himself who had brought this great project into being.

But it was not going to be so simple. The imperious president might rumble and clench his teeth in the White House, but up on Capitol Hill a mile away, his treaty had to contend with powerful antagonistic forces. Woodrow Wilson, after all, was proposing a revolutionary change in America's relationship to the outside world. For more than a century the United States had pursued its own course in what it considered its own hemisphere, and the record of that policy seemed to many quite satisfactory. Now all of a sudden, the president was demanding that the United States become a member of a wholly unprecedented new world government that few understood and the eventual effects and power of which no one could foretell. In the best of circumstances this would be a difficult thing to carry through. But Wilson was faced by a Senate in which the majority was Republican, and that party had always contained most of those who believed that the United States should go it alone in the world. The wonder is that he got so near to the two-thirds majority that he needed.

The crucial question concerned Article 10 of the League of Nations Covenant. Under its provisions, so it appeared, the league could summon out the armed forces of the United States, whether or not Congress approved. Wilson tried again and again to allay this fear, but it would not down. Irish-Americans thundered that American boys would be sent to Ireland to put down Irish revolutionaries. German-Americans scoffed that American armed forces would soon be putting down colonial troubles in the expanded French and British empires. No matter how long the issue was debated, observes the historian Ronald N. Stromberg, "Article 10 was the stumbling block. . . . The ensuing long and bitter debate over its meaning was often obscure, yet nonetheless real. Men *felt* that a vital issue was involved."

Progressives turn against Wilson

Progressives were touchy on issues of civil liberties, and Wilson's record there had deeply offended them. Furthermore, they were repelled by a treaty that seemed to embody so little of the liberal peace Wilson had said he would create. Once again, the men of power seemed to have had their way, producing a peace that combined selfish nationalism, fear and repression. Thus, progressives regarded the treaty as a betrayal and condemned Wilson ferociously. To them, the notion that power could be built and used to good ends had turned out to be a mockery; strong government was a dangerous blunder; World War I and America's entrance into it, a terrible error.

The dreams of domestic reform that had so captivated the progressive world in early 1919 soon were dashed. Congress had no intention of going any further in the direction of collectivism. Disillusion was epidemic, and it centered on the Treaty of Versailles. Ray Stannard Baker, a veteran muckraker, gave the common opinion when he said, "It seemed to me a terrible document; a dispensation of retribution with scarcely a parallel in history."

Senator William E. Borah, a progressive Republican senator from Idaho, was a leading isolationist opponent of the League of Nations treaty. On the Senate floor in February 1919 he denounced its principles, first by quoting numerous statements of George Washington that called on America to stay free of Europe's troubles and entanglements, and then by asking: "Are there people in this day who believe that Europe now and in the future shall be free of selfishness, of rivalship, of humor, of ambition, of caprice? If not, are we not undertaking the task against which the Father of our Country warned. . . ? If a controversy ever arises in which there is a conflict between the European system and the American system, or if a conflict ever arises in which their interests, their humor, their caprice, and their selfishness shall attempt to dominate the situation, shall we not have indeed quit our own to stand upon foreign ground?

"Why should we interweave our destiny with the European destiny? Are we not interweaving our future and our destiny with European powers when we join the league of nations the constitution of which gives a majority vote, in every single instance in which the league can ever be called into action, to European powers? . . . The league nowhere distinguishes or discriminates between European and American affairs. It functions in one continent the same as another. It compounds all three continents into a single unit, so far as the operations of the league are concerned. . . . The very object and purpose of the league is to eliminate all differences between Europe and America and place all in a common liability to be governed and controlled by a common authority. [It will bind Americans to protect the British Empire, and give to that country, through its dominions, five votes to one for the United States.] Conceal it as you may, disguise it as some will attempt to do, this is the first step in internationalism and the first distinct effort to sterilize nationalism." Borah then quoted from the writings of the Russian Communist Leon Trotsky, calling for an international world order, linking his words with the recent death of Theodore Roosevelt. "I sometimes wonder, Can it be true? Are we, indeed, yielding our Americanism before the onrushing tide of revolutionary internationalism? Did the death of this undaunted advocate of American nationalism mark an epoch in the fearful, damnable, downward trend?"

Wilson's bitterest personal and political enemy, Henry Cabot Lodge, was chairman of the Senate's Foreign Relations Committee. He had first persuaded enough Republican senators to sign a letter saying they would not approve the treaty in its existing form to ensure that it would be defeated. Then he used his position as chairman of his committee to delay things as long as possible. He read the entire treaty word for word, usually to an empty committee room. Then he called in every possible enemy, particularly the

"hyphenates": Irish-Americans who hated Britain for not freeing Ireland; Italian-Americans who were bitter that their homeland had not benefited more in the peace settlement; and German-Americans who condemned the reparations and other aspects of the document.

In the face of repeated pleas that he accept reservations to the treaty, Wilson stood firm. Article 10, he said, could not be deleted without destroying the whole conception of the league. Many men, Republicans as well as Democrats, were ready to accept a treaty with a more modified approach to internationalism, but Wilson would have none of such half-way measures. When Lodge's hearings stretched on and on, Wilson decided to go to the people once more. He was a tired and sick man, he had labored almost beyond human endurance for many years, and his physician warned him against exertion. But the combative Scot and Presbyterian visionary, the messianic prophet, were too strong within him. He was determined to have his way, and this appeared to be his only hope. He left Washington in September 1919 to travel in one month more than eight thousand miles and make almost forty addresses to cheering audiences. In Pueblo, Colorado, he collapsed from exhaustion. Sped back to Washington, he suffered a stroke that largely removed him from effective executive leadership. The treaty's chances were now gravely impaired, especially since Wilson was almost completely isolated from public contacts once he had recovered enough to make his wishes known.

By this time Lodge had reported the treaty to the Senate with a long string of reservations. The most crucial of them concerned Article 10, stating that Congress would always retain final authority over the use of American armed forces. If Wilson had given the word, enough Democrats would have joined with enough Republicans to provide a two-thirds majority and ratification of the treaty. But once again he refused, instructing all Democrats to vote against the treaty with reservations. In November 1919 the vote was taken, and ratification was defeated. In response to an outcry of protest from across the nation, the treaty was brought up for a second vote; once more Wilson was adamant; and once more it was defeated.

The ethnics and the election of 1920

Woodrow Wilson, now a querulous man who seemed almost to have begun to harbor delusions, looked forward to another battle. He believed that the presidential election of 1920 would become a great national referendum on the question of the League of Nations, and that behind that cause the Democrats would win. But the political ground had profoundly shifted from how it had lain in 1916. The First World War had been an enormously explosive political event, and all alignments had shifted. For German-Americans, the declaration of war upon their homeland began a cruel time of martyrdom. They had sturdily supported the cause of the Central Powers against the Allies, as had, indeed, the Scandinavians as well. Once America was in the war, to do that was to be a traitor. Stunned, their morale shattered, on every hand subjected to harsh and violent prejudice, the Germans greeted the Armistice of 1918 a transformed people in America. Their newspapers were dying; their language was being rapidly shunned even by their own people; and the shame that they felt replaced their old soaring pride as the only large ethnic group in the United States whose homeland culture could rival that of the British in sophistication, scholarly and scientific distinction, and world stature. Children turned against parents, rejecting the traditional Germanism for Americanism. Even the mother church of German Lutheranism in St. Louis, Missouri, resolved in 1918 to change its name to "Trinity Church" and to specify English as its official language.

The Germans hated Wilson's Treaty of Versailles, and were to vote massively against his party. The Italians, too, were deeply offended that the Treaty denied long-held Italian territorial ambitions around the Adriatic Sea, and attacked

the League of Nations as a British plot. Thus the Democrats lost heavily in those urban regions in the northern states where they had been starting to gain a foothold, as well as in the heavily Germanic and Scandinavian farming states of the upper Middle West.

Also, Wilson's administration was so heavily made up of southerners and his policies during the war, especially in their favoring of cotton growers over wheat farmers, seemed so strongly colored by southern ways of thinking that many in the northern and western states recoiled. Far western states, with their rabid anti-Japanese prejudices, were alarmed at the relatively strong push that the Treaty of Versailles gave to Japanese world status and Japan's ambitions in China. Even the Irish turned against the Treaty, attacking it for its failure to give freedom to Ireland, and for the great power within the League of Nations that it gave to Great Britain.

In short, the coalition that Wilson had built in 1916 was shattered. The Democrats tried to compensate by turning, in their national convention of 1920, to the Middle West to choose their presidential nominee, James M. Cox, governor of Ohio. Franklin D. Roosevelt of New York, Wilson's engaging young assistant secretary of the navy, became the vice presidential nominee. Against Warren G. Harding, also of Ohio, Cox waged a courageous campaign for international-ism and the League. But he was absolutely crushed in the balloting. The amiable Harding, who did little more than mouth platitudes about "normalcy" during his campaign, received more than sixteen million popular votes, to some nine million for Cox. At the same time, the Republicans gained huge majorities in both houses of Congress. The nation seemed clearly to have spoken. The president-elect, within two days of his victory, announced that the League was "now deceased."

President Wilson had yet another four months to live in the White House before Warren Harding's inauguration in March 1921. He spent that cruel time sunk in gloom. The Nobel Committee awarded him its peace prize, which was some consolation, but there seemed little left of his life work. He rode to the Capitol on inauguration day with the president-elect by his side, making no response to the cheering crowds, his face drawn and haggard, and listened somberly as the oath was administered to the new president. He lived quietly on for another three years in Washington, still turning over in his mind his disappointments and thinking of himself as the symbol of international liberalism. Not long before his death, a crowd gathered before his home on Armistice

Woodrow Wilson in 1921, wan, aged, and defeated, seems to look back on the wreckage of his dreams of world order. To the end, however, he remained defiantly convinced that the future would prove him right.
The Granger Collection

Day 1923. He emerged, thanked them, and then suddenly spoke again with his old force:

Just one word more; I cannot refrain from saying it. I am not one of those who have the least anxiety about the triumph of the principles I have stood for. I have seen fools resist Providence before, and I have seen their destruction. . . . That we shall prevail is as sure as that God reigns. Thank you.

Bibliography

Three books that were especially valuable to me in writing this chapter: As in chapter 27, I must mention Arthur S. Link's magisterial volumes (see below) on Woodrow Wilson and his foreign policy. Otis L. Graham's *The Great Campaigns: Reform and War in America, 1900-1928** (1971) is a wise and thoughtful book. Important, too, is Arno J. Mayer's *Wilson vs. Lenin: Political Origins of the New Diplomacy, 1917–1918* (1964), which shows Wilson in a struggle for world opinion with the conservatives to his right and the radicals to his left.

How have historians looked at the topic?

The military transformation of the United States during the early twentieth century and Theodore Roosevelt's energetic role in the process is lucidly described in Howard K. Beale's vigorous and critical *Theodore Roosevelt and the Rise of America to World Power** (1956). Sidney Lens's recent *The Forging of the American Empire* (1971) contains a provocative and disturbing analysis. The virtues and defects of Taft's and his successor's policies are explored in Dana G. Munro's interpretative study *Intervention and Dollar Diplomacy for the Caribbean, 1900–1921* (1964). John M. Blum's *Woodrow Wilson and the Politics of Morality** (1956) contains an excellent short account of Wilson's interventionist policies in Mexico, and two admirable monographs help to round out the picture: R. E. Quirk, *An Affair of Honor: Woodrow Wilson and the Occupation of Veracruz** (1962); and C. C. Clendenen, *The United States and Pancho Villa* (1961). Also valuable is Matt S. Meier and Feliciano Rivera, *The Chicanos: A History of Mexican Americans* (1972). Manuel Gamio's pioneering work is essential: *Mexican Immigration to the United States** (1930 and 1971), and *The Life Story of the Mexican Immigrant** (1930 and 1971). Abraham Hoffman, *Unwanted Mexican Americans in the Great Depression** (1974) deals with the deportations. On Mexican labor in the United States, see *AZTLAN*, special issue, vol. 6, no. 2.

Why did America go to war in 1917? In his war message, Woodrow Wilson eloquently proclaimed one rationale that future historians would echo. "The world must be made safe for democracy." Both Burton J. Hendrick's *The Life and Letters of Walter H. Page*, three vols. (1922–1926) and Charles Seymour's *The Intimate Papers of Colonel House*, four vols. (1926–1928) substantiated Wilson's idealistic purposes.

Sharply opposing views developed swiftly. C. Hartley Grattan in *Why We Fought* (1929) held that the desire for profits was the prime motivating factor behind the American entry into World War I and that those responsible were munitions makers and financiers. Walter Millis's biting indictment *Road to War, 1914–1917* (1935) accepted Grattan's emphasis on greed but added folly and sentimentalism as causal links. In *Propaganda for War* (1939), H. C. Peterson argued that British propaganda had fooled Americans into the war and, in perhaps the most skillfully argued revisionist study, *America Goes to War* (1938), Charles C. Tansill carefully concluded that the huge trade in munitions and the extension of private loans were determining factors behind American intervention.

In his war message Wilson emphasized the importance of submarine warfare—"a warfare against mankind"—in catapulting the United States to belligerent status with Germany. In two books that scrutinize Wilson's diplomacy in great detail, *American Diplomacy during the World War* (1934) and *American Neutrality, 1914–1917* (1935), Charles Seymour advanced the thesis that American intervention was the natural outcome of German submarine warfare.

World War II gave birth to a new school of historical interpretation centering on the question of America's national security. Writing during that conflict, Walter Lippmann postulated that Wilson and his advisers had chosen to intervene in World War I because they believed that American security would be endangered if Germany won. Lippmann's influential *United States Foreign Policy: Shield of the Republic* (1943) was seconded by Hans J. Morgenthau's *In Defense of the National Interest* (1951) and George F. Kennan's *American Diplomacy, 1900–1950** (1950). The realists' position has been further fleshed out in Robert E. Osgood's *Ideals and Self-Interest in American Foreign Policy* (1953), which describes Wilson as essentially an idealist, and Edward Beuhrig's *Woodrow Wilson and the Balance of Power* (1955).

The acknowledged authority on Woodrow Wilson, Arthur S. Link, has painstakingly probed Wilson's foreign policy in several excellent and invaluable volumes: *Woodrow Wilson and the Progressive Era, 1910–1917** (1954); *Wilson the Diplomatist** (1957); *Wilson: The Struggle for Neutrality, 1914–1915* (1960); *Wilson: Confusions and Crisis, 1915–1916* (1964); and *Wilson: Campaigns for Progressivism and Peace, 1916–1917* (1965). The full complexity of Wilson's problems are apparent in Link's works, and the president's responses are depicted as more realistic and politic than often thought.

The best single volume on the many-sidedness of war issues is Ernest R. May's *The World War and American Isolationism** (1959). May analyzes the interrelations of American, British, and German policies between 1914 and 1917 and brilliantly illustrates the pressures and limitations attached to decisionmaking. May also surveys the various interpretations surrounding the United States' entry into World War I in *American Intervention: 1917 and 1941* (1960). Further historiographical insight can be gained from Warren I. Cohen's masterly study *The American Revisionists: The Lessons of Intervention in World War I** (1967).

The ethnic dimension behind these events is explored in a number of valuable works: Philip

Gleason, *The Conservative Reformers: German-American Catholics and the Social Order* (1968); Frederick C. Luebke, *Bonds of Loyalty: German-Americans and World War I* (1974); David Burner, *The Politics of Provincialism: The Democratic Party in Transition, 1918–1932* (1968); Joseph P. O'Grady, ed., *The Immigrant's Influence on Wilson's Peace Policies* (1967); Louis L. Gerson, *The Hyphenate in Recent American Politics and Diplomacy* (1964); John M. Allswang, *A House for All Peoples: Ethnic Politics in Chicago 1890–1936* (1971); Alan J. Ward, *Ireland and Anglo-American Relations, 1899–1921* (1969).

*Available in paperback.

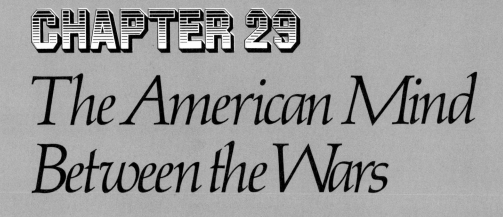

CHAPTER 29

The American Mind Between the Wars

TIME LINE

1915	Ku Klux Klan revived
1915–1940	Works of Sigmund Freud and Albert Einstein have marked impact on American thought
1916	Madison Grant, *The Passing of the Great Race*
1919	Red Scare
1921	Temporary immigration restriction law utilizes quotas based on 1910 census
1922	Sinclair Lewis, *Babbitt*
	T. S. Eliot, *The Wasteland*
	H. L. Mencken, *The American Mercury*
1924	Permanent immigration restriction law utilizes quotas based on the 1890 census and entirely excludes Orientals
1925	Tennessee outlaws teaching of Darwinian evolution; Trial of John T. Scopes in Dayton, Tennessee
	John B. Watson's writings on behaviorist psychology popular
1927	Charles Lindbergh makes first solo nonstop airplane flight over the Atlantic
1928	Advent of the "talkie" motion picture
1929	Stock market crash
	Robert and Helen Lynd, *Middletown*
1934	Ruth Benedict, *Patterns of Culture*
1935	Federal Theatre Project
1939	John Steinbeck, *The Grapes of Wrath*
1940	Reinhold Niebuhr, *The Nature and Destiny of Man*

HE two decades between the First and the Second World Wars contrast sharply. The prosperous 1920s were lively, confused, and individualistic, a time of rebellious youth and of vibrant romanticism in the arts. The 1930s concentrated on solving one great problem—the depression. This made the period collectivistic and disciplined, for people had to pull together in the face of their common problems. In the arts, realism replaced romanticism as the dominant approach. The contrast between the decades reveals one of the tidal rhythms in American public life. During times of prosperity when no single crisis such as a depression or a war focuses the national mind, a period of "cultural" politics flourishes. The issues that erupt into public controversy involve such questions as the relations between ethnic groups, the life styles being adopted by young people, changes in sexual practices, "immoral" literature, and religious beliefs. Novelists turn inward, stressing personal questions and ignoring social problems. At the same time, optimism reigns in the business community, which thrives on the national well-being. Smug in its security, the middle class trumpets the values of Main Street from pulpits and service club lecterns. In reaction to these values, alienated intellectuals cry out for self-expression at any cost, producing forms of dress, hair styles, and ways of living that antagonize everyone else.

Periods of cultural politics, in brief, are filled with contradictions, since the nation moves in many directions at once. Periods of "crisis" politics, however, see a move toward national unity and a serious attitude of mind. In the economically depressed 1930s people concentrated on such practical issues as jobs, homes, poverty, bankruptcy, strikes, and "capitalist oppression." All eyes turned to Washington, D.C., for national leadership. The arts turned away from personal questions to examine major social issues, becoming polemical and ideological.

Cultural and crisis politics are not mutually exclusive. The key fact, however, is that when the country's situation changes, the national mind concentrates upon new things and lets old ones fade. This is why the generations shaped by one period find the next so incomprehensible; why the depression-reared veterans of World War II, trained to think in sober terms of cooperation, jobs, and national security, found the individualistic, rebellious children of affluence in the 1960s so hard to fathom.

The 1920s: Seedbed of modern America

American life in the 1920s was startlingly different from that before 1914. The older America had been dominated by the life style of the small town and the countryside. Dominated by white Anglo-Saxon Protestantism, the "WASP" culture, the cultural style of the older America was genteel and moralistic. People characteristically thought and spoke in religious imagery. Cultural life was decentralized and relatively unchanging, as symbolized in the numberless traveling troupes of players who presented stock dramas in local "opera houses." There were a number of large cities, but they were tightly compacted and sharply demarcated from the quiet, older America that surrounded them. In the countryside and the smaller town, where most everyone lived, nothing seemed so settled as a way of life made up of polite periodicals, Sundays in the local Protestant church, quilting bees, and people who looked, talked, and thought alike.

By the 1920s, a series of social upheavals had changed all this. The invention of the automobile and the development of mass production provided almost everyone with a car. Hard-surfaced roads spread over the countryside with startling speed. City ways of life invaded the countryside, and farm folk found it easy to motor into town for shopping and entertainment. The radio, and most dramatically the movie, inaugurated a culture that bound the nation together as it never had been before. The new media were shaped by a few central institutions located mainly in Hollywood and New York City. Everyone went to the movies; everyone listened to the radio. What they saw and heard in that darkened movie theater in River City, Iowa, was not genteel and moralistic but earthy, flippant, and sexually liberating.

The new mass culture, in short, was urban and cosmopolitan. It was dominated by men of the recently arrived urban ethnic groups—Italians, Greeks, and especially the Jews—who had learned in the large cities how to cater to common tastes. This produced an unprecedented opportunity for such men to leap into a position of cultural leadership denied for generations to such older ethnic groups as the Irish and the Germans. Enterprising veterans of the world of New York City mass recreation, the movie makers migrated to southern California for the continuous sunlight and varied scenery. Out of their studios came a flood of fascinating new manners and morals, new heroes and heroines.

Youth and women

In this new world, young people and women behaved in new ways. Such changes never fail to alarm the general public. It was observed that young people, disgusted with the generation that had led the world into World War I, were turning to new leaders and values. They pored through the disillusioned individualistic novels of Ernest Hemingway and F. Scott Fitzgerald. Bathtub gin, "free love," erotic forms of dance springing from New Orleans jazz, the freedom of the automobile (which removed young couples from supervision), the pulsating gods and goddesses of Hollywood—these were the symbols of "flaming youth." College songs and college ways provided an alluring social model that even older people began to emulate. Irresponsibility, self-expression, a romantic flinging over of conventions, and an attack on puritanical morals—these were the attitudes that have come down to us in our picture of youth in the 1920s.

Along with prosperity came the inescapable traffic jam of riders rushing to work, or escaping for weekend pleasure outings. Narrow highways also produced fatal, head-on collisions.
From the collection of the Michigan History Division

Joined to these changes was a continuing transformation in the status of women. From far back in the nineteenth century, they had been breaking out of the home environment in search of careers. As early as 1900, a third of the students in college were women. The city home was smaller and required less labor; the size of the family was growing smaller; and machines were doing many of the tasks that had long been women's to perform, such as washing clothes and preserving food. With their new freedom, middle-class Anglo-Saxon women joined women's clubs, organized temperance crusades, and marched in women's suffrage parades. It was they who labored to change the ugly environment of the nineteenth-century city, by calling for the creation of public playgrounds, libraries, and parks. They struggled, too, against liquor and prostitution.

The most important influence on women's status was the Industrial Revolution, which provided work outside the home for many housewives. Into the mills and factories came a steady stream of women workers. After 1900, when business became more professional, communications and public relations tasks appeared, providing work for women as secretaries, telephone operators, clerks, and typists. With each year, as these growing armies of working women moved out of the home, the Victorian stereotype of the proper lady as one who never left her domestic concerns grew dimmer. Women even changed their style of dress; their hemlines rose and clothes became much simpler. By the 1920s a young woman no longer swathed herself in a mountain of cloth but dashed about freely with a few garments on her clearly revealed form, causing much alarm in traditional social circles.

Population distribution, 1920

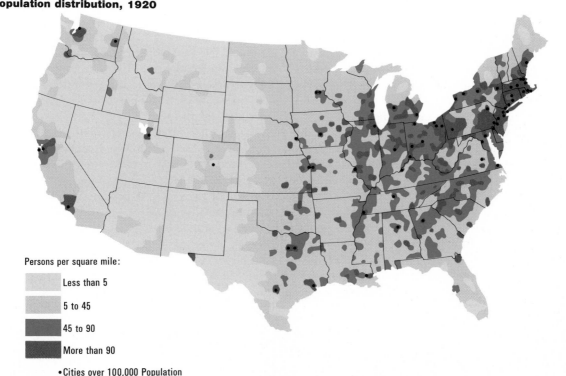

Persons per square mile:

Less than 5

5 to 45

45 to 90

More than 90

• Cities over 100,000 Population

By the time of the First World War, however, it was still true that if a woman worked outside the home, she usually had to be single. Entering a profession usually meant choosing a life of celibacy. Even in the slum districts, as late as 1900 only five percent of the wives were employed. But the First World War shattered this situation once and for all. Legal barriers against the employment of women were swept away. Women worked on railroads and in munitions factories. The Nineteenth Amendment to the Constitution finally gave women the vote in 1920. More women entered the professions in the 1920s than in any succeeding decade, for the feminist movement proudly called on women to strike out for the most competitive careers. Women began smoking in public, drinking liquor, and apparently, through wider knowledge of contraception, engaging more freely in extramarital sex. It is perhaps not a coincidence that prostitution, as a major element in the urban scene, involving red light districts and public solicitation, largely disappeared from American life in the 1920s.

After reaching these goals, the feminist movement seemed to lose steam. Indeed, the emphasis on the importance of child rearing that came with the advent of Freudian psychology (to be discussed later) gave a strong push once more to the idea of the woman as mother and home-builder. The proud young mothers of the 1940s and 1950s, with their large families and their split-level homes, bore little resemblance to the liberated flappers of the 1920s, with their boyish figures and eager entry into hitherto masculine careers. Feminists had insisted that the advent of woman suffrage would purify and elevate politics, but even this did not work out as anticipated, for women voted largely as did men. They seemed, in fact, to lose interest in politics, for the number of female legislators, judges, and other public officials waned in the years after 1930. A similar pattern appeared in the professions as well.

These developments, however, lay in the future in the 1920s. In those years the "new woman" aroused great alarm in traditional society. Hardly an issue of the popular magazines appeared that did not contain articles discussing this fascinating new phenomenon. Dancing, smoking, drinking, flinging around her long strings of imitation pearls and bobbing her hair, the flapper caught all eyes and seemed to symbolize an entire era.

The Harlem Renaissance and the "New Negro"

So too the "New Negro" startled white America. The huge migration out of the South, and the sense of pride black Americans drew from their role in the First World War, and the wartime emphasis upon democracy and human rights, flowered in a cultural explosion in the 1920s. Centering in Harlem, but eventually spreading around the country, a world of black novelists, dramatists, poets, scholars, and musicians made white America take black culture seriously for the first time. Jazz was enormously popular, moving swiftly from its New Orleans beginnings into the national youth world, both white and black. Attacked by traditionalists as scandalously sensual, it contributed to the general opening out of American daily living, breaking loose from Victorian gentility.

Meanwhile, black writers defiantly, bitterly, and impatiently explored the hypocrisy of American protestations of freedom and equality, and the reality of black life. Proclaiming that in the black soul there was a deeper humanity and a broader sensitivity to social truths than that displayed in white culture, black intellectuals experienced a soaring of the spirit, a bountiful pride and hope for black self-expression and self-realization. High culture in its traditional forms was passionately pursued, as black men and women sought to demonstrate that in the most sophisticated expressions of European and American literary and artistic performance, they could excel. James Weldon Johnson, in *The Book of American Negro Poetry* (1922) revealed the richness of contemporary black expression in this medium; Jean Toomer's *Cane* (1923) brilliantly illuminated black life; Langston Hughes, the Harlem Renaissance's leading spirit, poured out a rich miscellany of writings, and gave wide inspiration to black intellectuals. Meanwhile, black writers were appearing in many periodicals, published by white and black editors, and white intellectuals watched fascinatedly this fresh outpouring of creative achievement. Black players began appearing on the stage in other than humorous roles: in Eugene O'Neill's *The Emperor Jones* (1920), *All God's Chillun Got Wings* (1924), and other productions. The black musical, black spirituals, black painting—all of these gave voice to a rising articulateness in the black community, informing white America that the old days of silence and cultural timidity were gone.

Traditional America revolts

WASP America fought vigorously against the new ways and ideas. The adoption of prohibition in 1919 (the Eighteenth Amendment) was the greatest triumph of traditional moral values, especially those current in rural, small-town WASP social circles. In the same year, the "Red Scare" erupted and subsided almost as rapidly. The Russian Revolution had sent a shiver of fear around the world, for the Soviets sent out agents of social revolution and preached worldwide upheaval. After the First World War, waves of disorder swept over the United States. Strikes broke out everywhere as labor unions struggled to catch up with the cost of living. Bombs began exploding while radicals went about the country crying for an end to capitalism.

In the fall of 1919 Attorney General A. Mitchell Palmer, whose home had been bombed, launched raids on many radical centers. Hundreds of members of the Union of Russian Workers were summarily deported to Russia. Then, in one night, more than four thousand people were arrested as Palmer launched his most sweeping nationwide assault on the national

conspiracy which he insisted was seeking to destroy the United States. Brushing aside civil rights, his agents invaded homes, union headquarters, and meeting halls to make their arrests. Many of those detained had no discernible connection with any kind of radicalism. During the excitement, the legislature of New York expelled five legally elected members of the Socialist party. J. Edgar Hoover, head of the Justice Department's alien radical division, insisted that letting imprisoned men out to see their lawyers "defeats the ends of justice."

The Red Scare was soon over, for the raids turned up no evidence of a conspiracy and practically no arms at all. Even Warren Harding deprecated the wild talk about Communists. But one thing continued to alarm the nation: aliens seemed at the center of every radical movement. As a consequence, nativism surged upward after many years of relative quiescence. A sharp brief recession hit the country in late 1920, just when immigration from Europe, quite low during the war, suddenly grew rapidly. How could the United States go on endlessly finding room for more people, it was asked, when it could not find work for those already here? Fanning the fires of nativism even more was the fact that many immigrants, culturally conditioned to be heavy consumers of alcohol, openly flouted prohibition. Indeed, many leading bootleggers were recent immigrants. Thus the nation came to identify aliens not only with the term *radical* but with the term *criminal* as well.

The Ku Klux Klan

The Ku Klux Klan emerged as the vehicle for the fears aroused by these new influences. Revived in Georgia in 1915, it expanded rapidly across the nation after 1920. Democratic in the South, it was strongly Republican elsewhere. The Klan not only harassed black Americans—especially the "New Negro" who returned from the fighting in France with a new sense of personal dignity—it also spread accusations that Catholics and Jews were behind the breakdown in traditional America's ways of life. Fundamentalist Protestantism had exploded in the South and the Middle West, and many Fundamentalist ministers, who preached a literal interpretation of the Bible and a virulent anti-Catholicism, gave the Ku Klux Klan their enthusiastic blessing. The Klan organized boycotts of Catholic businessmen, publicly condemned Catholic office holders, and in some cases physically attacked Catholic churches and priests. It also developed an elaborate religious ritual featuring burning crosses, hymns sung to Klan verses, and kneeling prayers.

Perhaps five million Americans had enrolled in the Klan by the middle 1920s. The midwestern states experienced an enormous growth in the order, Indiana and Ohio becoming the leading states in the nation in membership. Even in Ore-

The Ku Klux Klan parades down Pennsylvania Avenue in Washington, D.C., in 1926. Then an organization with millions of members, its open flaunting of bigotry was a prominent style of behavior which in the last half century has lost its respectability.
The Bettman Archive

gon the Klan was large enough to have a strong impact on the state's politics, and burning crosses flared on California hillsides as well. By this time, however, its leadership was following the pattern classic to such organizations: excess piled on excess, financial chicanery, and internal bickering. A growing national opposition to such vigilanteism checked the Klan's growth. Never strong in the big cities, which were its particular object of hatred, the Klan was vigorously condemned by ethnic legislators from large urban centers. Eventually it began a long decline and subsided into its present role as a fringe movement in the southern states.

Hiram W. Evans, Imperial Wizard of the Ku Klux Klan in 1926, expressed the protest of his "Nordic American" organization against modern America: "The Klan . . . has now come to speak for the great mass of Americans of the old pioneer stock . . . as distinguished from the intellectually mongrelized 'Liberals.' . . .[These] Nordic Americans for the last generation have found themselves increasingly uncomfortable, and finally deeply distressed. There appeared first confusion in thought and opinion, a groping and hesitancy about national affairs and private life alike, in sharp contrast to the clear, straightforward purposes of our earlier years. There was futility in religion . . . strange ideas . . . moral breakdown . . . economic distress. . . . We found our great cities and the control of much of our industry and commerce taken over by strangers, who stacked the cards of success and prosperity against us. Shortly they came to dominate our government . . . the native Americans were constantly discriminated against, in business, in legislation and in administrative government. So the Nordic American today is a stranger in large parts of the land his fathers gave him . . . one much spit upon, and one to whom even the right to have his own opinions and to work for his own interests is now denied with jeers and revilings. . . . Our falling birth rate, the result of all this, is proof of our distress."

The war revealed how many un-American, disloyal aliens were in the United States, and Nordic Americans "decided that . . . an alien usually remains an alien no matter what is done to him, what veneer of education he gets, what oaths he takes, nor what public attitudes he adopts. They decided that the melting pot was a ghastly failure, and remembered that the very name was coined by a member of one of the races—the Jews—which most determinedly refuses to melt. . . . They learned . . . that alien ideas are just as dangerous to us as the aliens themselves.

"We are a movement of the plain people, very weak in the matter of culture, intellectual support, and trained leadership. We are demanding . . . a return of power into the hands of the everyday, not highly cultured, not overly intellectualized, but entirely unspoiled and not de-Americanized, average citizen of the old stock." (*North American Review* [March 1926].)

Nativism and immigration control

In the mid-1920s, antialien nativism reached its climax. In state after state, laws were passed forbidding the foreign-born from entering professions in medicine, pharmacy, architecture, surveying, and even from driving buses or making wills. Nativists insisted that the nation could absorb no more immigrants. The "100 percent American" groups, such as the American Legion, also condemned immigration as the principle root of radicalism. The AFL demanded immigration restriction out of fear of job competition.

A new note, however, was now entering the controversy. No longer were people interested only in cutting down immigration: what they sought was to exclude certain kinds of immigrants, while leaving the door partly open to immigrants from northern and western Europe. The writings of Madison Grant, who during the war had issued a gloomy book entitled *The Passing of the Great Race* (1916), became popular. An upper-class New Yorker of rarefied Anglo-Saxon stock, he had acquired something of a national reputation as a scientist. Disgusted by all the strange-looking immigrants from central and eastern Europe who had crowded into his city since 1890, he wrote that these people contained racial characteristics in their bloodstreams that were certain to debase the American stock. Others picked up the theme, warning that steps needed to be taken swiftly to preserve a "distinct American type" in the United States. Adherents of the theory seized eagerly on such official statements as one issued by a State Department office in 1920 that described the 120,000 Jews who had entered the nation in that year as "twisted . . . unassimilable . . . filthy, un-American."

Immigration restriction had been talked about since the 1880s and had actually been instituted during the war when a literacy test was established. But the upsurge of new arrivals after 1920 convinced nativists that much more needed to be done. In 1921 an immigration restriction law was passed that established quotas by which each European nationality could send to this country only three percent of its numbers living in the United States in 1910. A temporary measure, it was supplanted in 1924 by permanent legislation that excluded Orientals entirely, allowed free immigration to continue from Canada and Latin America, and put the quota system for European immigration in its final form. Shifting the basis of computation to the census of 1890, when the immigration from eastern and southern Europe had only barely begun, the law limited the annual inflow of each nationality to a number equal to two percent of those in the country on that date. This meant that Britons, Germans, and Scandinavians would have relatively large quotas while Italians, Poles, and the other eastern and southern European groups would have small entry quotas. Legislators from these urban ethnic groups complained bitterly against the measure, but when the crucial votes were taken in Congress, a huge chorus of "ayes" from the small towns and the countryside turned the tide. "America must be kept American," said President Calvin Coolidge as he signed the legislation.

Thereafter, the total inflow of immigrants from

Europe was limited to approximately 150,000 persons a year, practically all of them from northern and western Europe. Thus a new era in American history was begun. The country's population shifted from one strongly colored by a large contingent of immigrants or sons and daughters of immigrants to one composed overwhelmingly of the native-born. Each subsequent generation has seen a slow blurring of the differences between ethnic groups in language, styles of dress, and customs. Ethnic membership remains a prominent and persistent element in American life, especially in eastern cities and among such highly visible groups as the Mexican-Americans (who continued to immigrate into the United States in large numbers), but the long-range effects of the 1924 immigration law have tended toward a growing cultural uniformity.

Twenty-one years later, after a long decline of WASP domination of American politics, and the uprush of a multiethnic and pluralistic spirit in the 1960s, the Immigration Act of 1965 finally removed racism from national immigration policy. It ended national-origins quotas; all discriminations against Asians were terminated; and a simple ceiling of 290,000 immigrants, from whatever sources, was established. (After 1968, immigration from independent countries of the western hemisphere was to be limited to 120,000 a year.) In addition, certain exceptions were made for immediate members of families, who could be allowed entry above the limit. Thereafter, immigration from Mediterranean and Asian countries jumped significantly, that from the Orient exceeding all entrants from Europe.

Fundamentalism fights Darwinism

The climax of the fight waged by traditional America to go back to older ways of life took place in a spectacular trial in Dayton, Tennessee, in 1925. Early in the 1920s Fundamentalist Protestants had launched an attack on the teaching of Darwinian evolution in the public schools. The theory, they insisted, was a monstrous insult to God and a corrosive influence on morality. The true story of creation, they said, lay in the first two chapters of Genesis. How could young people believe in God's moral laws, laid down in the Bible, if science was allowed to challenge the Book's literal truth?

William Jennings Bryan led the campaign to outlaw Darwinism, a fact that immediately made the controversy one that was watched closely by the entire nation. The anti-Darwinist campaign was especially successful in the South, where older forms of Protestantism held firm. Kentucky's legislature fell just one vote short of passing a law outlawing the teaching of evolution in 1922, and the governor of Texas, "Ma" Ferguson, simply expunged Darwinism from the state's textbooks. "I am a Christian mother," she said, "and I am not going to let that kind of rot go into Texas textbooks." Then in Tennessee in 1925, a powerful lobbying effort led by Bryan secured passage of a law making it illegal to teach "any theory that denies the story of the divine creation of man as taught in the Bible. . . ."

The stage was set for tragicomedy. John T. Scopes, a biology teacher in Dayton, agreed to challenge the law with the support of the American Civil Liberties Union, an organization rooted in big-city ethnic minorities with particular strength among the Jews. He lectured on Darwinism and was soon hailed into court. Clarence Darrow, a brilliant, cynical defense attorney and a religious skeptic, offered his services to defend Scopes. Bryan arrived to help lead the prosecution, conceiving the trial as a "duel to the death" between true Christian belief and atheistic science. There was no question that Scopes had violated the law, and he was convicted of that act and duly fined (a higher court set aside the penalty on a technicality). But in the process Darrow put Bryan on the stand and pilloried him mercilessly on religious issues. Jonah, testified Bryan, was in fact swallowed by a big fish; Joshua made the sun stand still; the languages of the world came from the tower of Babel; and Adam and Eve were the first human beings, Eve having been fashioned from Adam's rib. Much of the nation laughed derisively at Bryan, for his statements made him appear to many like an uneducated fool. Indeed, Bryan's reputation ever since has been buried under the ridicule he received in that steaming July. He left the trial confident that he was right, and ready for renewed struggles in his battle for the Lord, but within days, apparently because of the rigors of his ordeal, he died.

The new view of humanity: Sigmund Freud

Traditional America could exclude aliens and pass antievolution statutes, but it could not keep away a flood of cosmopolitan modernism. The United States in the 1920s was eager to listen to modern science and to new ideas from Europe. None was more fundamentally important than a view of the nature of man that came from the Viennese physician Sigmund Freud. In the 1880s he had discovered that he could cure women of hysteria by getting them to talk freely about their most intimate experiences and fears. Soon he became convinced that sexual difficulties lay at the root of his patients' neuroses. For years he worked alone and despised, trying to find out through his patients' revelations why his "talking cure" seemed to work.

He concluded that beneath the conscious mind lay another layer, the unconscious, into which people thrust unbearable thoughts and experiences. Such repression often left conflicts unresolved, so psychoanalysis would release these pressures through catharsis, thus allowing the patient to gain a rational understanding of the source of his problems. Freud was fascinated by the unconscious. Dreams, he concluded, opened a window into the region, though they clothed the repressed conflicts in symbols that had to be carefully examined to disclose their real content, since dream objects often stood for other things (e.g., guns for male sexual organs). Freud came to believe that of all the forces that struggled in the

unconscious, the most powerful originated in the body and its instinctual drives. For this reason, he described the irrational side of man as often stronger and more potent that the rational.

Freud said the human personality was composed of three elements. First there was the *id*, in which all the animal forces of passion, greed, and selfishness expressed themselves. Then there was the *superego*, or the moral teachings of parents and society, embodied in the conscience; and between these two powerful entities there was the *ego*, or the conscious self, which sought to bring the conflicting forces of the id and the superego into harmony. Here was an image of humanity in which madness and sanity seemed intermixed; in which primitivism (the id) struggled constantly with civilized intellect (the ego) for mastery. Each person, no matter how proper and genteel, was capable of acting destructively toward himself and toward others. What happened to the belief that our lives could be controlled by conscious, trained intelligence? Freud's depth psychology was like the discovery of perspective in painting. No longer could one take others simply as they seemed on the surface. Now there were hidden dimensions to be considered, powerful forces that rumbled far in the interior.

Freud's way of looking at human nature was not new. The Greeks had known that people were moved by dark passions over which they seemed to have little control. The Bible is filled with similar observations. John Calvin and the Puritans had been keenly aware of the primitive flames in each person and of the precarious control that reason seems to hold over them. The romantics of the early nineteenth century believed the human personality to be primarily passionate. Friedrich Nietzsche, the German philosopher, had already written about the unconscious. But the predominate outlook in Western civilization after 1850 had been a confident faith that the human person is fundamentally a reasoning creature—had we not uncovered the secrets of the universe by science?—and a decent one as well. The long peace after the Napoleonic

Wars gave strength to the notion that civilized humanity had outgrown primitivism. But Sigmund Freud was now saying again that we are forever engaged in a struggle against clamorous inner conflicts that begin at birth and do not end until death. Human personality, he said, is best understood as analogous to a battlefield, where civilized reason battles ceaselessly to control primitive passions, much as a rider (the ego) tries to master a wild and untamed horse (the id). Even children, he said, were moved by sexual urges.

America and Freud

In America more than anywhere else Freud's ideas were picked up rapidly, beginning about 1910, and spread widely through the country. Even before the First World War, intellectuals in New York City were discussing them excitedly. By the 1920s Freudianism seemed everywhere. Word-association parlor games spread like wildfire, their professed objective being to reveal the unconscious meanings people attach to things. Young intellectuals who called Freud a liberator used his ideas to scoff at religion and morals. Freud had never preached sexual license—indeed, he was rather puritanical in his views of sex—but in popular culture this fact was forgotten, and creators of sensationalist movies and lurid stories let the sex theme run riot. Even the Sears, Roebuck catalogue began listing books on sex, including *Ten Thousand Dreams Interpreted* and *Sex Problems Solved.* Dramatists like Sherwood Anderson became obsessed with sexual symbolism. As to psychoanalysis, many seemed to take it up as a kind of new fad.

Sigmund Freud's teaching was received in the United States more enthusiastically than in Europe for several reasons. For one thing, Freudian psychology was individualistic. Europeans tended to explain things about a person by pointing to his membership in a particular social class. But Americans liked a point of view that said that each person can be explained only in his or her own terms. Look into their unique childhoods, Freud's theories suggested, and the answers will be found. Furthermore, American culture has been significantly more happiness-oriented than that in Europe. Humbled and disillusioned by centuries of suffering and wars, Europeans have tended to think that life in the best of circumstances is a difficult and unhappy business. But the innocent Americans, confronted in their national experience by an apparently unbroken string of successes and inspired by the notion that they were showing the world how to find prosperity and contentment, believed that life should fundamentally be an enjoyable experience. Running through American history, even in times of doubt and dismay, has been a sturdy, hopeful optimism. In Freud's teachings, so it seemed, a new way to happiness had been found.

The optimism of the 1920s

Nothing seemed so deeply rooted in American life in the 1920s than this national optimism, which rose high over the dark prophecies of the Ku Klux Klan and the nervous fears of traditional America. The American population delighted in the "miracles" that new inventions had brought them—electric lights, airplanes, automobiles, radios—the list seemed endless. Progress in all directions seemed inevitable. These new devices brought greater power and ease to every individual, providing a leisure undreamed-of by older generations. Automobiles and airplanes broke down space, giving ordinary people an exciting sense of mastery over distance. They watched Charles Lindbergh make the first solo nonstop airplane flight over the Atlantic in 1927 with a confident sense that it opened a new and fruitful era for mankind. The radio multiplied the power of the ear, the movie that of the eye. New amusements, comforts, and ways of life flooded in on every side.

For all of this, the business community felt a proud responsibility. Businessmen constantly proclaimed the arrival of what they called the "new era." Technology had opened many doors;

opportunities seemed endless; and the mass market had grown so huge that it seemed no earlier age of industry could compare with the current one. Industrialists and financiers believed themselves to be not conservatives, as they were usually depicted, but daring innovators. They reached a level of national popularity perhaps never achieved before in American history, and certainly never again. Calvin Coolidge worshiped business as much as he detested government. "The man who builds a factory builds a temple," he said. "The man who works there worships there." The Republican administrations of the 1920s bent every possible effort to cooperate with and assist the business community. The *Wall Street Journal* observed complacently that "never before, here or anywhere else, has a government been so completely fused with business." At the same time, a cult of success suffused popular literature. A steady stream of articles and books on how to get ahead and make a million was poured out. An almost slavish admiration of powerful industrialists and financiers emerged. Such great men as Henry Ford, it was often said, were the men to follow. If it were not for these leaders, said one business writer, "the multitude would eat their heads off, and, as history proves, would lapse into barbarism. . . . The masses are the beneficiaries, the few, the benefactors."

Optimism among intellectuals

This same optimism abounded among the social scientists. Psychology came into enormous popular vogue. Books appeared that explained everything from the psychology of golf to that of selling life insurance. Psychologists confidently used intelligence tests and other clinical devices to predict personal success and to counsel businessmen. In 1925 the writings of Dr. John B. Watson on behaviorism suddenly caught the national fancy. He predicted that by proper conditioning anyone could be transformed into anything he or she wished to be. The human person, he said, was simply a machine who responded to

Charles Lindbergh, being given a delirious ticker tape parade in New York City after his solo flight in 1927 over the Atlantic. The "Lone Eagle" became the new symbol of a hopeful America.
United Press International Photo

stimuli. In brief, there were no limits to anyone's potentialities, given appropriately "scientific" training.

Sociologists were also emerging into national prominence on the basis of another "scientific" technique, the survey. By this means, quantitative studies of all aspects of social life were made. Sociologists were confident that a point would soon be reached when trained minds, ruminating over these growing mountains of accurate social information, would distill from them the social laws that govern human life. These, then, would allow sociologists to provide guidance to politicians, who would enact appropriate legislation. A similar confidence in their abilities was exhibited by economists, who were relying on scrupulously conducted studies of business affairs to keep the nation's economy booming toward prosperity.

Ranging through this academic confidence like a presiding spirit was the philosopher John Dewey. He was convinced that people could shape the future in any way they wished if they depended on the trained intelligence of the experts and utilized central planning. At the core of everything, he believed, should be a new educational system that would train young people to test all assumptions by experience and scientific data. Ignorance and bad thinking, Dewey's teaching implied, were the only barriers to social progress. Everything old and traditional he lumped under the term *cultural lag,* an irritating stumbling block to be swept away. In the end, Dewey implied, reason would wipe away human and political tensions.

The same kind of utopianism dominated the world of liberal Protestantism. In the big-city churches and seminaries, the social gospel was triumphant. Humanity was not seen as irremediably twisted by its nature but only by ignorance of how to live a truly Christian life. The future could be made perfect. The ministers of God should work confidently in social reform to bring about "a growing perfection in the collective life of humanity, in our laws, in the customs of society, in the institutions of education, and for the administration of mercy."

Social gospelers believed that it *was* possible to follow the Ten Commandments: one need only to work at it hard enough. The Reverend Charles M. Sheldon's famous question, "What would Jesus do?" should be the guide for everyone in daily life. It would guide businessmen in their business decisions; labor in its struggles; statesmen in the issues of peace and war; bankers in their uses of other people's money. Science, in this view, would be a helpmate in building the kingdom of God on this earth. Humanity was good; the leaven of Christianity would work within society; and the principle of love would eventually rise triumphant.

Economic collapse

Then came the stock market crash of 1929 and the massive depression that followed. At first Americans regarded these events as another ripple in the business cycle similar to many in the past. But this depression was far graver than anything that had occurred before. The economy sagged lower and lower, year after year. The result was a massive loss of confidence—in the system, in the nation's leaders, and in the American dream. The optimism of the 1920s disappeared under a tidal wave of pessimism. Searching for scapegoats, the public lashed out furiously at bankers, stock brokers, and industrialists. The business community plummeted in public esteem. The confident idea of inevitable progress was deeply shaken. When Americans looked abroad, they saw another foreboding development—the collapse of democracies and the spread of dictatorships. The whole system of Western civilization seemed to be in rapid decay.

Ward James, an elderly teacher in the 1960s, reminisced on the emotional impact of the Great Depression: "There was a feeling that we were on the verge of a bloody revolution, up until the time of the New Deal. . . . I remember a very sinking feeling during the time of the Bank Holiday. . . . Everyone was emotionally affected. We developed a fear of the future which was very difficult to overcome. Even though I eventually went into some fairly good jobs, there was still this constant dread: everything would be cut out from under you and you wouldn't know what to do. It would be even harder, because you were older. . . .

"Before the Depression, one felt he could get a job even if something happened to this one. There were always jobs available. And, of course, there were always those [who said] even during the Depression: If you wanted to work, you could really get it. Nonsense.

"I suspect, even now, I'm a little bit nervous about every job I take and wonder how long it's going to last—and what I'm going to do to cause it to disappear.

"I feel anything can happen. There's a little fear in me that it might happen again. It does distort your outlook and your feeling. Lost time and lost faith. . . . (Quoted in Studs Terkel, *Hard Times* [1970].)

Deep roots to pessimism

There was one group in American life, however, who looked on the depression almost with a sense of relief. America's writers had been saying for a long time that the system was corrupt, and now they appeared to be proved correct. A remarkable literary flowering had taken place in the 1920s, the first genuinely brilliant outpouring of talent since, perhaps, the days of Emerson and the transcendentalists. Ernest Hemingway, John Dos Passos, F. Scott Fitzgerald—these were but a few of the gifted writers of the era. They had been young during the heyday of the progressive movement and had been revolted by it. The progressives had been confident, hopeful people. They had been strong on morals and filled with a faith that people can solve their problems if they apply reason and science. The confident social scientists of the 1920s were their true inheritors, and John Dewey the prophet of their philosophy.

As early as 1914, however, young intellectuals began rejecting this moralistic confidence. Listening to ideas coming from Europe, they insisted that irrationality, intuition, and passion were so strong that the dreams of the progressives would never come true. Cynical about the prospects of America's business civilization, young writers either went to live in Paris or fled to Greenwich Village. From these locations they wrote novels scorning the American way of life. Sinclair Lewis in *Babbitt* (1922) held up smalltown life to international ridicule. In 1930 he was given the Nobel Prize for Literature.

H. L. Mencken, editor of the *Mercury*, led the attack on American life in the 1920s. Democracy, he said, was a ludicrous farce enthroning the moralism and hypocrisy of the "booboisie" and the Bible Belt (the businessmen and the farmers). In such a world, Mencken scoffed, the real person of thought will always be crushed by the Rotarian and the peasant. Look at the United States, he asked, and observe its elements—prohibition, censorship of "dirty" books, and the Ku Klux Klan. He believed that progressive faith in the

people was absurd. In reality, the people were nothing but a mob—sodden, brutal, and ignorant. "Politics under democracy," he said, "consists almost wholly of the discovery, chase, and scotching of bugaboos." No gentleman could hold office in such a tawdry charade, and as a consequence vermin made the laws of the United States.

Many besides the young writers were doubtful about the long-range healthfulness of modern life and skeptical of the faith in trained reason that had sprung from the Progressive Era. For them, the most shocking fact of all was the First World War. Throughout Western civilization, thoughtful persons had had their faith in the essential goodness of mankind deeply shaken by the horrors of fighting. In Europe, theologians like Karl Barth and Emil Brunner were so horrified that they rejected almost all they had been taught and began considering a "theology of crisis." The young Reinhold Niebuhr, a pastor in Detroit (to be discussed later), felt his social gospel faith collapsing around him. For these and other such men, the war began a long search for a new way of thinking about humanity and its relationship to God.

The new view of the universe: Relativity

Great changes were taking place in the natural sciences. For more than two hundred years, educated people had believed that the scientific method would ultimately unravel all the secrets of the physical universe. They found security in the view that the cosmos was a simple affair that could be understood by common sense. One could even make mechanical models of it. The universe consisted of physical bodies (mass) scattered through measurable space, and a force called energy. Space, scientists believed, was filled with an invisible gaseous element called ether, a sort of enormous ocean through which the physical bodies of the universe moved. These beliefs were based on the fundamental assumption that the universe we look out on is as it appears to us. Linked to this was another assumption: that if we discover physical matter to act in certain ways on earth, it would act in that way throughout the universe. The laws of earthly physics, in other words, were the laws of the cosmos.

In 1905 Albert Einstein, a young European theorist and mathematician, swept these assumptions away with his *Special Theory of Relativity* (followed in 1916 by his *General Theory*). An international sensation occurred among scientists that by the 1920s spread to the general educated population, producing an outpouring of startled and fascinated editorials, popular articles, and scholarly books. Einstein began first by making famous a hitherto little-noted experiment, conducted in Ohio in 1887 by Albert A. Michelson and Edward W. Morley, that proved that ether did not exist. Physicists were shocked, for they had built all their theories about light, energy, and other radiations on the assumption that they were transmitted through the universe by ether much as water transmits waves. Michelson and Morley proved something else as well: that the speed of light is a constant 186,000 miles per second whether the person measuring its speed is moving toward the light source or away from it. How could this be?

Einstein's solution was deceptively simple, yet astounding in its implications. When we speed up or slow down, all our measuring devices change proportionately. If the earth suddenly accelerated enormously in its movement through space, people's yardsticks would become shorter, their clocks would slow down, their hearts would beat more slowly, and radioactive atoms on earth would emit electrons at a reduced rate. Things would seem to be the same, but in relation to what they had been before, they would be different. A century of earthly time, as people presently measure it, could become an instant of time to someone whose speed through the universe had been increased. A man on a voyage through space at great speed would live by his own measurements perhaps a year or two during that voy-

age, but he would return to find that a couple of centuries had passed by earthly measurements.

All measurements, in other words, are relative to the location and movement of the observer. Time is not an independent thing that exists outside the system of reference within which it takes place. The same was true of space, for distance is a function of time. This meant that scientists could no longer believe that the universe was as they observed it. To an observer situated elsewhere, on some other planet moving at a different speed, the universe would appear quite differently. People could not rely on common sense. Humankind is surrounded, in short, by a mystery that could only be described in mathematical formulas dealing with relationships, not with things as they appear. Scientists were dismayed. What can I do, asked one famous physicist, if I cannot make a model of something and look at it?

Other scientific changes

There was more. The discovery of radium in the 1890s had demonstrated that atoms are not fixed and unchanging building blocks, but in certain conditions seem to decay by spraying energy outward. What was happening, explained Einstein, was the transformation of mass into energy. These were interchangeable physical phenomena, not separate things as had always been assumed. In the most famous formula in this new kind of physics, Einstein described the relationship between energy and mass as $e = mc^2$: the mass times the speed of light squared. Thus if matter traveled with the speed of light, it dissolved into radiation, or energy. If it congealed and became inert, it was mass. Once again, Einstein had taken a stable universe with fixed elements and replaced it with flux and flow.

What was the nature of radiation? In 1900 Max Planck theorized that it was emitted in the form of little chunks called quanta. Others held to the older theory that radiation propagated itself in waves. The problem was that both theories worked. Did this mean that we would never know the right answer? For generations people had believed that the scientific method would ultimately yield final answers to every scientific question. Now it appeared that a limit had been reached, that there was a point beyond which we could not go in our search for knowledge. In 1927 a German physicist, Werner Heisenberg, put these thoughts into his "principle of uncertainty." It was pointless, he said, for a physicist to worry any longer about what a single electron was in actuality. For one thing, this was an attitude hanging over from the old physics that Einstein had destroyed—the search for the essence or substance of things. The new Einsteinian physics showed that all we could really find out was the relationship of things, not their ultimate reality, which is hidden from us. Besides, scientists dealt with electrons in streams or showers, each containing billions of electrons. To search out one and tie it down would be futile. Indeed, even if a person had a supermicroscope and could actually look at an electron, the force of the light directed on it would push it away. Thus it was absolutely and forever impossible to determine what an electron was. In short, we can never perceive ultimate certainty by the use of our senses.

One thing was certain: if Einstein was right, locked within the atom were enormous stores of energy. By the 1930s scientists were talking excitedly about what might happen if an atom were split and its energy released. Atomic physicists at Berkeley, Cal Tech, and Columbia began building atom-smashing equipment, and their early experiments demonstrated that the physical elements of the universe, long assumed to be fixed and unchanging, could actually be changed from one form to another by knocking off electrons.

Popular response to scientific changes

The popular mind was excited by these new developments. So far as Einstein could be understood, he was saying that it was no longer possible for ordinary people to comprehend the universe, and that what scientists actually did understand was strange and unsettling. Time, space, matter, energy—all these dissolved, shifted, and blurred. Everything depended on where the observer was located; relativity replaced fixity; ultimate things were hidden. At the same time, new scientific discoveries in other areas deepened the popular sense of unease. Big telescopes had been built around the turn of the century at Mt. Hamilton, California, and in Chicago that revealed strange, new things. There were other universes: galaxies like our own buried deep at unimaginable distances in space. Furthermore, everything in the cosmos seemed to be part of some massive explosion, for all the galaxies were moving away from one another at increasing rates of speed. No longer could people believe that they lived in a tidy island universe, sailing serenely and alone through space. Something far greater—and more humbling—was occurring in the cosmos.

Meanwhile, biologists were discovering that mutations within a cell nucleus could produce startling changes in plants and animals. The cells themselves, as one writer described them, were "subtle mechanisms of chemical balance, pulled now one way, now another, in endless trial and error relationships." The discovery of vitamins suggested that growth and change, even the nature of personalities, could be affected by the presence or absence of certain chemicals in the body. By the 1930s Americans had learned that they could no longer be content with the simple-minded emphasis on sexual motivations that had earlier seemed to be the ultimate explanation of human personality. Sigmund Freud himself had long since moved on from his earlier emphasis on the unconscious and its physical passions to an exploration of the conscious self, the ego. This opened up many new views of complicated relationships springing not merely out of each person's childhood but out of their current situations as well. Theory piled on theory, seemingly endless controversies developed over proper methods of treatment, and the public mind was further confused.

Meanwhile, social scientists were also losing the confidence of the 1920s. Their studies of society came under the same criticism that Einstein had leveled at the old physics—that much of what sociologists believed to be true was true only from the standpoint of a particular observer. Relativity applied to knowledge about society as well as to knowledge about the universe. From country to country, from class to class, people's fundamental ideas, their world views, change, said the sociologist of knowledge, Karl Mannheim. This is because they all have a particular location in society from which they see things, which necessarily allows them to be aware of some things and unaware of others. A laboring man has one perspective on the world, his employer another, and neither is necessarily wrong or right. Thus no one can ever know the final truth about government, society, or any large problem, for no one can ever see everything as a single fact. Such relativity in ideas was incompatible with the long-held belief that there were certain things that were true in all times and under all circumstances.

Equally well publicized was the new science of semantics. Men like Stuart Chase, Thurman Arnold, and Kenneth Burke made the educated public newly aware that thought is expressed in particular words, and the way people think is shaped by the words available to them in their particular culture. Certain Indian tribes have languages in which the concept of time hardly appears: therefore, members of such tribes would probably have little difficulty in understanding Einstein's theories of relativity. But the ordinary American is obsessed with time and unconsciously thinks in terms of a whole collection of tenses that place events in rigid time relationships. There are aspects of reality in which our kind of language is a hindrance, yet we are unaware of this and persist in trying to put things in inappropriate terminology. Americans throw around words like *democracy, capitalism, free enter-*

prise, but what do they mean? Precision in language: this was what the semanticists called for. Life changes, but people's words do not, and this leads to their constant inability to think clearly about their problems. From this the educated person drew once more the lesson that things taken for granted before—the very words that people used—could no longer be relied on with the same surety.

The new view of humanity and God: Reinhold Niebuhr

In the early 1930s a new religious voice burst on the American scene, that of Reinhold Niebuhr. Soon he became the most influential thinker in American Protestantism. Niebuhr had watched national and international developments from his pastorate in Detroit in a mood of growing disenchantment. The war had horrified him. Then the facts of industrial life in Detroit convinced him that it was fruitless to preach sermons about love and kindness, for the actual conditions of survival made it impossible for people to be always loving and kind. As early as 1927 he began criticizing the ministers of the social gospel for not realizing how evil people can be. Liberal Protestantism, it seemed to him, was fundamentally wrong in its hopefulness for humankind. Then came the depression, which conclusively destroyed the facile optimism of the 1920s and revealed deep and apparently fatal flaws in capitalism. How could anyone believe any longer in the faith of John Dewey and the social scientists: that trained intelligence could solve all problems; that ignorance alone stood in the way of utopia?

In the 1930s Niebuhr moved to Union Theological Seminary, near Columbia University in New York City, where he continued to ruminate on modern life, teach, and write his powerful books until his death in 1971. What he taught came to be called neo-orthodoxy. That is, he revived what had been the orthodox religious view of humankind—that people are inherently sinners and can never avoid the consequences of their sins. By the term *sins*, Niebuhr was concerned not with such "sins" as dancing and drinking, but with people's cruelty and selfishness.

The first thing to reject, Niebuhr maintained, was the liberal Protestant social gospel belief that the kingdom of God and this world are somehow ultimately compatible and will eventually become one and the same. Niebuhr believed that they are permanently and irrevocably separate. Furthermore, they are in constant tension. People live in history, where power and practical considerations make it impossible to live the truly Christian life of self-sacrificial love. God and His teachings stand outside the world, providing it with the standards towards which people must always strive, but which they will never, by their very nature, be able to attain. God entered history as Christ to provide proof of His love and a standard by which life should be lived. But that standard remains what Niebuhr called an "impossible possibility," for human life is ultimately paradoxical: it is a blend of warring opposites. People love, yet out of fear are driven to aggression. They sacrifice themselves for others, and yet at that very moment they are the most subject to falling into sin through the lure of self-pride. It is the human condition for a person's every action to be potentially destructive as well as creative.

In his greatest work, *The Nature and Destiny of Man* (1940), Niebuhr brought together his teachings into a powerful exploration of his belief that we are inherently sinners. He explained this by pointing to the central tension that lies at the core of life itself. Human beings possess a unique capacity: the power to stand outside themselves and observe their situation; to make themselves the object of their own thought. They even possess a capacity to stand back and view the universe and thus to become aware of their own insignificance. Knowing that they will die, people struggle constantly to save themselves. This produces an inescapable selfishness in every human personality that can never be overridden. If people had enough faith in God, they would be able

to find ease in His love and power to save them. But, being human, they never are able to muster enough faith to lose their fearful self-regard: they are inescapably selfish. This, according to Niebuhr, is humankind's original sin. All their other imperfections spring from that failing.

What, then, was the social message that Niebuhr derived from his neo-orthodox theology? First, people must sweep away all false idealism and acquire a completely realistic view of themselves and mankind. This will prevent the disillusionment that so often leads to cynical withdrawal. Search for relative justice; for "proximate" solutions; for improvements that can be achieved within a person's limited capacities. Never be utopian, or believe that anything can be done innocently. Be sober about humankind's potentialities, but be hopeful. One of Niebuhr's favorite texts was from St. Paul, about being "perplexed, but not driven to despair. . . ." Commitment, struggle, a clear-eyed view of human nature, a readiness to plunge into the contaminating game of politics and power—these were the stern strictures issued to the nation's reformers by Protestant Christianity's most powerful voice.

The arts in depression America

Paradoxically, the nation's economic collapse brought its exiled writers flocking back from Paris's Left Bank. Art for art's sake went out the window; agonized searches for personal realization faded; and literary figures suddenly found in stricken America a new focus for their creative energies. Plays, novels, articles, and paintings that stressed Marxian analyses of social strife poured out on the national scene.

Whatever the inspiration, a social consciousness emerged among creative workers that eclipsed the personalist orientation of the 1920s. Together with this went a powerful awakening to a new concept, that of *community*. Books like Ruth Benedict's anthropological study *Patterns of Culture* (1934) attained an enormous readership, for she sensitively described the myriad ways in which all mental life is shaped by the encompassing cultures in which people live. Looking about them, writers rediscovered traditional America: its farms, villages, common folk, farm implements, square dances, harvest celebrations; its sweating laborers in the steel mills, in the mines, in the automobile factories. This vast continental community exerted an enormous appeal for writers such as John Steinbeck, whose *The Grapes of Wrath* (1939) was not only a powerful novel of social protest but a loving depiction of common folk in intimate relation to the land. From Archibald MacLeish and Robert Frost came a new kind of poetry that celebrated the folkish, rural beauty of America. Civilization (technology, efficiency, science) became the enemy, and culture (ways of life, symbols, speech, and values) became the new hope. An outpouring of writings, films, recordings, and paintings depicted every aspect of American life. The common people were treated with a warmth and sensitivity quite unlike the disillusioned "booboisie" cynicism of the 1920s.

It was this new urge toward group consciousness and collective action that made the New Deal so exciting for most intellectuals. The Civilian Conservation Corps, which sent boys into the forests, the Tennessee Valley Authority, erecting vast dams throughout a wilderness to control floods and bring hope to impoverished farmers— these and many other programs seemed to revitalize the whole American community. There was despair in the depression, but there was excitement as well. To the most alienated, Marxism exerted an irresistible appeal. Few actually joined the Communist party, but a great many, in their search for social philosophies to explain the chaos, found Marxian socialism a congenial home. Until the disillusionment created by the purge trials that Joseph Stalin instituted in 1936, American intellectuals generally found Soviet Russia a fascinating and alluring example of what could be achieved by rigorous socialist experimentation.

The theater similarly swung toward social consciousness, in part through the extraordinary achievements of the Federal Theatre Project (FTP). Launched in 1935, it strove to place drama companies in cities all over the nation, thus making use of local talent and traditions. The FTP blazed up meteorically, and productions appeared in every corner of the country. Its plays were often controversial social commentaries, especially the "Living Newspaper," which dramatized current political issues. Much condemned as socialistic and anti-American, the FTP died in 1939 when Congress refused to support it any longer. Meanwhile, a left-wing theater movement following the slogan "Drama is a weapon" sprang up in New York City. In plays by dramatists such as Clifford Odets and William Saroyan, anticapitalism was the chief theme and collectivism the principal objective. The common man appeared as the hero in this kind of drama while moneyed interests were the villain. Labor unions, which seemed the epitome of group consciousness, figured prominently.

Painters and sculptors also turned away from the personalist experimentation of the 1920s to grope for a direct relation to social conditions. Turning realistic, they fell in love with the forms and shapes of the American scene. Their canvases were no longer covered with the abstract forms of modern art that ordinary Americans found incomprehensible, but with protests against capitalistic injustice. Their search was for an "art of the people." Landscapes, people at work, slum life, store windows, Coney Island bathers, farms, tractors, small towns—these were the topics of the day. Thomas Hart Benton of Missouri and Grant Wood of Iowa led an extraordinary upsurge of painting by midwesterners based on the scenes and people of their region. Benton's heroic mural of John Brown in the Kansas state capitol and Wood's austere painting of a midwestern farm couple, *American Gothic,* provided powerful symbols for the new realism of the decade. The Federal Arts Project hired hundreds of artists to paint similarly realistic

The heroic power of John Stewart Curry's mural of John Brown, done for the Kansas State capitol under the W.P.A. art program, reveals the rediscovery of American themes and American folk drama by artists and writers in the depression years. Courtesy of the Kansas Department of Economic Development, State Office Building, Topeka, Kansas

murals in post offices and other public buildings throughout the nation.

By far the most powerful art form of the 1930s, however, was the "talkie" motion picture. Beginning in 1928, the talkie struggled through a period in which technical and artistic problems produced static presentations, then flowered into an enormously flexible medium of tremendous cultural impact. Each week, eighty-five million Americans of all ages and income groups attended a movie. As studios competed to capture the largest audiences and revenues, they produced an enormous outpouring of miserable Hollywood trash. Ernst Lubitsch, a German-born

Hollywood director, commented, "The American public—the American public with the mind of a twelve-year-old child, you see—it must have life as it ain't." There were some significant movements toward social realism in the development of the documentary film, in such powerful creations as Orson Welles's *Citizen Kane,* and in the newsreel series *The March of Time.* But Hollywood producers generally shied away from controversial themes. They had had their struggles with would-be censors in Congress and in local communities, and they had no stomach for more such strife. The Motion Picture Producers and Distributors Association in 1934 fended off such efforts by establishing a production code that was particularly concerned with moral obligations. Sex was downgraded, violent FBI agents instead of violent criminals were glorified, and an endless stream of blameless movies about nice kids in nice neighborhoods—the Andy Hardy series, for example—poured out of Hollywood.

If not at the movies, the average family spent two to three hours a night listening to the radio. Primarily concerned with presenting humorous series—"The Jack Benny Show," and "Amos 'n' Andy"—the radio also began to introduce classical music into the home through broadcasts of symphony orchestras and the Metropolitan Opera. Radio theater had brilliant moments in such regular presentations as the "Mercury Theatre of the Air," created by Orson Welles, and CBS's "Columbia Workshop." Far more prominent were the soap operas that cloyed the air and filled the housewife's working day. And, perhaps most important, radio news broadcasting emerged as a powerful nationalizing influence in the 1930s. From its thin beginnings in the 1920s, the newscasts took over at least a third of all air time, bringing the entire nation news not only of national events but of crises in Europe and the rest of the world as well. Americans could now listen to Hitler speaking, a fact that made the threat of fascism seem terrifyingly close.

In sum, the American people in the 1930s were assaulted from all directions by a cultural life that was nationalizing in tone and impact. The radio seemed to make the whole nation one meeting hall; everyone went to the same movies; literature and the arts concentrated on American themes as they had not for many years. The rediscovery of America that the writers and artists experienced was the cultural counterpart of the nationalism we shall be observing in the New Deal. A new awareness of society and its needs, a fresh interest in American traditions and values, and, paradoxically in a time of economic collapse, a surging confidence in what in the 1930s began to be referred to as the "American way of life"—these were the cultural hallmarks of a turbulent decade.

Bibliography

Three books that were especially valuable to me in writing this chaper: William E. Leuchtenberg's penetrating discussion of social and cultural trends in his *Perils of Prosperity, 1914–1932** (1958); in addition to Reinhold Niebuhr's *The Nature and Destiny of Man,** two vols. (1941, 1943), one of the most profound works of the twentieth century, the valuable book edited by Charles W. Kegley and Robert W. Bretall, *Reinhold Niebuhr: His Religious, Social, and Political Thought** (1961); and L. Pearce Williams, ed., *Relativity Theory: Its Origins and Impact on Modern Thought** (1968).

How have historians looked at the topic?

For many years the decade of the 1920s was viewed as an aberration, a period of disillusionment and frivolity squeezed between the holocaust of World War I and the terrors of the depression, and characterized by expatriate literati, hip flasks, raccoon coats, marathon dances, and the ubiquitous flapper. This fascinating if stereotyped image was first presented in a lively, readable book by Frederick Lewis Allen, *Only Yesterday: An Informal History of the 1920s** (1931), and it has been preserved practically intact in other histories until recently.

The scholarship of the 1960s has revealed aspects of the Roaring Twenties that question its image of superficiality and cynicism. In *The Discontent of the Intellectuals: A Problem of the Twenties* (1963), Henry May asserted that the "lost generation" of writers and artists stood apart from the majority of Americans who continued to endorse traditional American values, a judgment supported by David A. Shannon in his penetrating volume *Between the Wars: America, 1919–1941* (1965). George E. Mowry's edited volume *The Twenties: Fords, Flappers, and Fanatics** (1963) highlights the conflicts between the caretakers of the old culture and the prophets of the new day, finding little frivolity in the struggle. In a brilliant, probing book, *The Nervous Generation: American Thought, 1917–1930** (1970), Roderick Nash reveals a "thick layer of respect for time-honored

American ways" beneath the eye-catching icono-
clasm of Mencken and others. Lawrence Levine
sees the same tensions from a different perspective in his fine article "Progress and Nostalgia:
The Self-Image of the 1920s," found in Malcolm
Bradbury, ed., *The American Novel in the 1920s*
(1971). Nathan Irvin Huggins is essential on the
*Harlem Renaissance** (1971).

The impetus of the new research marks the
1920s as a troubled decade in which fear of
change lived side by side with the fact of change.
The growing literature on women and youth
reflects this paradox. Kenneth A. Yellis probes
the condition of women following World War I in
a provocative article, "Prosperity's Child: Some
Thoughts on the Flapper," *American Quarterly* 21
(spring, 1969) while the apolitical nature of the
change in women's roles is emphasized in an
article by Beatrice M. Hinkel reprinted in Loren
Baritz's collection *The Culture of the Twenties*
(1970). David Kennedy's biography of Margaret
Sanger, *Birth Control in America* (1971), illustrates
women's continuing struggle to assert themselves
as well as the conservative uses to which birth
control was put. The first part of June Sochen's
edited volume *The New Feminism in America**
(1971) focuses on early twentieth-century feminists' analyses. William H. Chafe carefully scans
the broader scope of women's experiences in *The
American Woman: Her Changing Social, Economic, and
Political Roles, 1920–1970* (1972). Paul Carter offers
a provocative assessment of the youth cult in *The
Twenties in America** (1968).

Traditional America's postwar reaction to radi-
cals is graphically depicted and astutely analyzed
in Robert K. Murray's *The Red Scare: A Study in
National Hysteria, 1919–1920** (1955). Donald
Johnson describes the origins of the American
Civil Liberties Union in *The Challenge to American
Freedoms* (1963).

The effects of the exclusionist immigration
policy is studied in Robert Divine's *American
Immigration Policy, 1924–1952* (1957). Roger Daniels offers an excellent account of the campaign
against the Japanese in *The Politics of Prejudice: The
Anti-Japanese Movement in California and the Struggle
for Japanese Exclusion** (1970).

The persistence of the Ku Klux Klan is chronicled in a stimulating and thorough study by
David Chalmers, *Hooded Americanism: The History
of the KKK* (1965) and the strength of urban Klan-
ism is explored in Kenneth Jackson's *The Ku Klux
Klan in the City, 1915–1930** (1968).

The achievements of the business community
during the 1920s are described in a perceptive
and important study by Alfred Chandler, Jr.,
*Strategy and Structure: Chapters in the History of
American Industrial Enterprise* (1962). Morrell
Heald's *The Social Responsibilities of Business: Company and Community, 1900–1960* (1970) is a valuable overall view while business attitudes and
practices are succinctly treated in J. W. Prothro's
The Dollar Decade: Business Ideas in the 1920s (1954).
The modernizing impulses of the era are apparent in Otis Pease's *The Responsibility of American
Advertising* (1958). Allan Nevins and F. E. Hill's
*Ford: The Times, the Man, and the Company** (1954)
and *Ford: Expansion and Challenge* (1957) are indispensable on the period's leading industrialist.

The popular culture of the 1930s is skillfully
portrayed in Frederick Lewis Allen's *Since Yesterday, 1929–1939** (1940). Cabel Phillips considers
the decade one of social revolution in his journalistic account *From the Crash to the Blitz, 1929–
1939* (1969). Dixon Wecter's *The Age of the Great
Depression, 1929–1941* (1948) is also strong on
social history. Daniel Aaron's *Writers on the Left*
(1969) analyzes the effects of the depression of
literary intellectuals. The pessimism engendered
by the deepening depression is portrayed through
the words of those who experienced it in Studs
Terkel's *Hard Times** (1970).

*Available in paperback.

CHAPTER 30

The Republican Era: Triumph and Disaster

TIME LINE

1915	Non-Partisan League founded
1920s	Farm depression; business and financial boom
	Commerce Department encourages cooperation among businessmen
	Senator George W. Norris begins battle for federal operation of hydroelectric plant at Muscle Shoals and distribution of power
1920	Warren G. Harding elected twenty-ninth president of the United States
	Population reaches 106 million people
1921	Washington Naval Conference; Four-Power Pact; Five-Power Pact; Nine-Power Pact
	Farm Bloc formed in Congress
1922	Conference for Progressive Political Action formed
	Fordney-McCumber Tariff
	Herbert Hoover, *American Individualism*
1923	Calvin Coolidge becomes thirtieth president of the United States on death of Harding
1926	Revenue Act slashes income tax on wealthy and corporations
1927	McNary-Haugen bill passed by Congress, vetoed by Coolidge
1928	Herbert Hoover elected thirty-first president of the United States
	Urban-ethnic voters turn to Democrats in presidential election
1929	Federal Farm Board created to ease agricultural marketing
	Stock market crash
1930	Hawley-Smoot Tariff
	Major Democratic victories in congressional elections
1932	Reconstruction Finance Corporation established
	Franklin Delano Roosevelt elected thirty-second president of the United States

N 1920, with the election of Warren G. Harding to the presidency, the Republican party reassumed its customary position of dominance in the nation's political life. Since 1896 when it succeeded in gaining the urban vote, it had been the majority party in the sense that most people thought of themselves as Republicans. From 1920 to 1932 the Republicans reached their apogee of national power, then fell into disasters so stunning and fatal that they lost their traditionally preeminent position.

We have learned by this time to notice certain long-standing characteristics in each of the two large political parties. From the time of the Federalists, the party on the conservative, right wing side of American politics has been the most persistently nationalistic. The Federalist-Whig-Republican tradition has favored high tariffs, an independent "America first" foreign policy, and a social outlook that has thought of white Anglo-Saxon Protestants (save for those in the South), as the only "true" Americans. The Yankee heartland in New England and the upper Middle West, with strong outposts now in the Far West, was its social and territorial base. Catholics, Jews, and immigrants from eastern and southern Europe were rarely comfortable among Republicans. Strongly probusiness, the Republican party has worked in partnership with the business and financial communities and has been eager to provide them with assistance rather than critical supervision. Linked to these attitudes has been a persistent elitism. Like the Federalists before them, the Republicans tended to believe that the nation's highest goals were best served when its great spirits—its men of power and wealth—were given the widest opportunities for enterprise and leadership. Within the government, this elitism usually has led to an oligarchical style of administration (Woodrow Wilson caustically referred to it as "government by boards of trustees") in which the president is a passive figurehead and the powerful members of the cabinet and Congress cooperate in running the country in consultation with the leaders of business and finance.

Such were, in fact, the larger outlines of the Republican era from 1920 to 1932. The administrations of Warren G. Harding (1921–1923), Calvin Coolidge (1923–1929), and Herbert Hoover (1929–1933) bent every effort to free businessmen from supervision, lower their taxes, provide them protection through higher tariffs, and give them open access to the nation's resources. Harding and Coolidge were passive presidents in the traditional Republican mold (the depression forced Hoover out of this pattern). The nation and the government looked in admiration to powerful industrialists and financiers for leadership and inspiration. Rooted in WASP America, the Republican party became the instrument of an aroused nativism that condemned eastern and southern Europeans as inferior beings and led to the passage of antialien legislation. In foreign affairs, there was a conscious and determined turning away from the internationalism of Woodrow Wilson. Important reform legislation continued to be enacted by a Congress in which progressives played a major role through the decade, but it was consistently struck down by White House vetoes.

Meanwhile, the Democratic party in the 1920s was undergoing a crucial transition. On the one hand its following among the immigrant ethnic groups in the inner core of the nation's great cities was beginning to swell like a rising tide, foretelling the future. The millions of "new immigrants" from eastern and southern Europe who had been pouring into the country since 1890 had passed through their apprenticeship in democratic forms of government and were beginning to vote, following the lead of the firmly Democratic Irish Catholics. But the other great tap root of the Democratic party lay in the overwhelmingly rural and Protestant world of the southern and border states. Here were the people most alarmed at the rise of the great cities and the urban way of life. Within the Democratic party in the 1920s, therefore, a hammering conflict took place between the older America—rural, moralistic, anti-Catholic, prohibitionist—and the newer America, to be found in the great metropolises. Multi-tongued, liberal, a compound of Jewish scholarship, Roman Catholicism, and the corner saloon, the Democrats of the growing urban centers were sure to win the victory, but not until after bitter battles within the party. In the 1924 national convention it took the Democrats more than a hundred ballots to choose a nominee—the colorless John W. Davis.

The nation

In the twentieth century, the American population's growth slowed. From 1900 to 1910, the rate of increase was twenty-one percent, but from 1910 to 1920, it dropped to fifteen percent. In the latter year, when the nation held a population of 106 million people, the birth rate stood at 27.7 per 1,000. In 1930, it had fallen to 21.3 and ten years later, it had sagged to about 19 per 1,000, a replacement rate that would not be sufficient in the long run to maintain the population at a stable figure. Demographers forecast that sometime after 1960 the American population would peak and then decline in numbers.

The drop in the rate of growth was associated with a continued massive movement from the countryside to the cities and that city families tend to be smaller than those in the countryside. During these decades some 6.5 million people participated in this cityward movement, some 4.5 million of them going to the four great metropolitan centers of New York, Chicago, Detroit, and Los Angeles. This meant that in 1920, for the first time in American history, a majority of Americans (fifty-one percent) lived in communities of 2,500 people or more. At the same time, the number of workers engaged in some form of manufacturing outnumbered those in agriculture by about 5 to 4.

Immigration, which always brings in people primarily in the vigorous, reproductive years of life, came practically to a halt after the legislation restricting immigration of the early 1920s. Some three million people had flooded into the United States from 1911 to 1915, but only 68,000 arrived and stayed during the entire decade of the 1930s. A dropping birth rate also had some relation to feminism, which reached a peak in the 1920s. The same conjunction of phenomena—feminism and a lower birth rate—was to take place again in the years after 1965. Feminist attitudes may be associated with fundamental shifts in values about childbearing that lead to smaller families.

Some four out of ten Americans held membership in a Christian church in the 1920s. Of these, two-thirds were Protestant, one-third Catholic. The decrease in immigration brought about a reduction in the proportion of the foreign-born from fifteen percent in 1910—where it had stood relatively steady through many decades—to roughly nine percent in 1940. A major change was also beginning to take place in the distribution of the nation's Afro-American population. In 1865, the proportion of blacks living in the southern states was ninety-two percent. By 1920, this figure had dropped to eighty-five percent, for the First World War had seen the beginning of a heavy migration northward to industrial jobs. Thereafter, this movement accelerated, so that by 1940 nearly one-fourth of all Afro-Americans lived outside the South.

The presidency: Warren G. Harding

The election of 1920 brought to the White House a man ill-suited to his task. Warren Gamaliel Harding had been an ordinary politician who looked wonderfully like a president but who lacked any real talents save a warm and gentle demeanor that made the country like and trust him. He had been editor of a newspaper in Marion, Ohio, served as a state legislator, gave William Howard Taft's nominating speech in 1912, and in 1914 was elected to the Senate. There he supported big business, advocated high tariffs, and opposed taxes on war profits. Following

Warren G. Harding, campaigning in Ohio. A warm-hearted and devoted public servant, he was much loved, won the presidency in a huge landslide, and was mourned at his death.
Wide World Photos

Henry Cabot Lodge's leadership, he firmly resisted American membership in the League of Nations as "a surrender of national sovereignty." As he said in his 1920 presidential campaign, "Stabilize America first, prosper America first, think of America first, exalt America first!"

Harding was a devoted public servant who worked slavishly at his task. He was much too weak a personality for the stern demands of the presidency and not very bright—Woodrow Wilson said he had a "bungalow mind"—but he wanted the "best minds" around him and made some strong appointments. He chose Charles Evans Hughes as secretary of state, Herbert Hoover to head the Commerce Department, and Andrew Mellon, one of the nation's richest industrial magnates, to be secretary of the treasury. The president turned most of the nation's affairs over to these men. This credulous, simple-minded man was widely popular. He seemed to express what the nation yearned for, what he himself had summoned up in a famous word he coined for posterity—*normalcy.*

Retreat in foreign affairs

The Harding administration pulled back immediately from Wilson's internationalism. Harding's guiding slogan was "America First." The president declared that the League idea was dead, and Secretary of State Hughes refused for some time even to answer mail from that body. It was manifestly impossible, however, for the United States completely to retreat to its pre-1914 isolation. Its whole position in the world had been transformed by the war. Western Europe owed huge sums to the United States, causing Washington to be intimately involved in the complicated negotiations relating to intergovernmental debts and German reparations. American manufacturers had invaded markets all over the world, giving the United States heavy economic stakes in Latin America, China, and elsewhere, all of which required close attention. And the simple fact of America's having been massively involved in a great world war made it impossible to think any longer in isolationist terms. The world's affairs had burst irrevocably into the American consciousness.

The most pressing immediate problem at the outset of the 1920s lay in the western Pacific, where Japan, Great Britain, and the United States appeared headed for a showdown. All three nations had launched huge naval building programs during the war that were only now coming to fruition. This meant that the Pacific would soon be bristling with heavily armed ships, and there would be rising tension. The war had left behind much mutual distrust and several points of grave conflict. Would Japanese forces remain in Russian Siberia, where it appeared they were preparing to tear off a huge chunk of territory? Would Japan leave China alone and evacuate the Shantung Peninsula? What was to happen to all the new island territories she had taken from the Germans during the war? In 1920, the progressive and isolationist senator from Idaho, William E. Borah, took the crucial step: he secured passage of a resolution asking the president to call an international conference to ease the naval race.

The Washington Conference

The Washington Conference was the Harding administration's one major accomplishment. In November 1921 representatives of the nine nations involved in Far Eastern affairs gathered in Washington, D.C.: the United States, Great Britain, Japan, France, Italy, China, the Netherlands, Portugal, and Belgium. A tremendous fanfare attended the opening of the gathering, for the Republican administration hoped to make the conference their successful replacement of the much-maligned peace conference at Paris.

At the opening session of the conference, Secretary Hughes electrified the gathering by avoiding generalities and specifying an astonishingly long list of naval vessels that should be halted in construction or scrapped if already built. A total of 70 major ships would be eliminated: 15 American vessels plus 15 more under construction; 19 British battleships plus 4 under construction; and 10 Japanese ships plus 7 under construction. In addition, no more ships of the battleship class were to be built for the next ten years. The result of these changes, Secretary Hughes pointed out, would be to establish a 5:5:3 ratio in capital ships between Britain, the United States, and Japan; and Italy and France would stand at the ratio of 1.75:1.75.

No one had even remotely expected so dramatic a proposal. Hughes was suggesting, one man said, to sink more British battleships "than all the admirals of the world had destroyed in a cycle of centuries." The American people were delighted, and similar responses came from all over the world. But long and difficult negotiations ensued. The Japanese insisted that they would accept their ratio only if everyone else agreed to build no more naval bases and fortifications in the Pacific area. In the Five-Power Pact, this demand was met, and the proposed ratios were

agreed to. A Four-Power Pact was also signed by the United States, Great Britain, Japan, and France, in which these nations guaranteed the security of one another's possessions in the Pacific islands.

The end result of these agreements was to turn over military dominance of the Pacific to Japan. Recognizing that Japanese supremacy was being tacitly agreed to, Britain and the United States urged the Japanese to pledge that they would keep their hands off China. Under this pressure, they signed the Nine-Power Pact, which finally elevated America's Open Door policy to the status of international law. In this treaty, Japan and the other eight conference participants agreed to respect China's sovereignty, independence, and integrity; to maintain open commercial privileges for all nations in that country; and to avoid seeking any special rights that would impair those of other nations. Hughes also got Japan to agree to evacuate the Shantung Peninsula, give China control of the Shantung railway, and clear out its forces from Russian Siberia.

Hughes achieved in these pacts one of the great successes in international diplomacy. The United States gave up much, but what it relinquished was only a potential naval supremacy, and it was in any event doubtful that Congress would have been willing to provide the funds to complete the naval building program. The clear fact was that a frightening naval race was ended, and peace in the Far East was secured in a way that held out strong hopes for the future. Unhappily, Congress's later stupidity in totally excluding the Japanese from the United States in the immigration legislation of 1924—not even allowing them the dignity of a tiny quota—was an insulting affront going far to destroy the good feelings that emerged from the Washington Conference.

Harding's death

While his secretary of state was winning international laurels, the president was slowly becoming aware of the fact that his cronies were using their opportunities to line their pockets. "My Goddamn friends," he said to editor William Allen White, "they're the ones that keep me walking the floor nights!" The worst scandal involved the secretary of the interior, Albert B. Fall, who gave oil magnate Edward L. Doheny a lease on the naval oil reserves at Elk Hills, California, and received in return a satchel containing $100,000 in cash. Rumors of this deal were soon being passed about Washington, D.C. Then came an added shocker: another Harding appointee committed suicide rather than face an investigation.

In the summer of 1923, the worried president went on a trip to Alaska and the Pacific Northwest. Ill with incipient heart failure and unable to sleep, he played bridge endlessly, compulsively, day and night, trying to find peace of mind. But his worries and his physical weakness did not disappear, and by the time he had finished his Alaska visit he was drawn, exhausted, and at wit's end. Shortly the news went out to the nation that the president was gravely sick. On August 3, while attended by his wife, he suddenly shuddered and died, apparently from a heart attack. The public was shocked and grieved, for as yet it knew nothing of the scandals. Calvin Coolidge, as Harding's vice-president, now succeeded him, and the American people turned in relief to their new leader, a classic puritan and an honest Yankee.

Calvin Coolidge: "Puritan in Babylon"

The new president was a simple, parsimonious, tightly controlled man from a small town in Vermont who lived in an ordinary rented duplex. He was scrupulously honest, and never spent his evenings drinking and playing cards. A thorough-going, tight-laced Yankee, he seemed to carry with him the tang of maple woods and sharp winter mornings. From the beginning of his political career he had admired and firmly supported large corporations. He advocated a protective tariff, conservative money policies, and freedom for the entrepreneur. "The chief business of the American people," he said in one of his more pithy utterances, "is business." Accordingly, Coolidge felt that the government should do nothing more than aid businessmen and withdraw from every other activity save foreign relations. Reducing governmental expenditures, he said, was "idealism in its most practical form." As president, he devoted himself to a masterly inactivity. When visitors came to see him, he followed a policy of being silent. "If you keep dead-still they will run down in three or four minutes," Coolidge said to Herbert Hoover. "If you even cough or smile they will start up all over again."

He was a president, in brief, who believed the country's ills were to be solved by the silent operations of the business system. Beyond cleaning up corruption, he offered no constructive action to a country in need of leadership. Nevertheless, he was widely popular. The American people seemed most of all to want to turn away from their problems, and for such a time the new president was admirably suited.

The farmer's changed situation

By the opening of the Republican era, the American farmer had enjoyed more than twenty years of prosperity. America's growing cities provided essential markets; gold discoveries in South Africa, Alaska, and Colorado produced steady price inflation, which coincidentally raised farm prices; and the burning grievances that had exploded earlier in the Populist crusade had died down. Ironically, this transformation in the farmer's situation took place at the same time that his numbers, in relation to city people, were shrinking. The fact was that the farmer had begun to learn how to organize himself in ways similar to those used by businessmen. He had also learned to apply technology to the farm far more sweepingly, in the long run, than has been true in any other part of the national economy. By the First World War it was increasingly common for farmers to keep detailed financial accounts, learn scientific mixtures for stock feeding, concern themselves with soil chemistry, and turn to research laboratories for disease-resistant crops.

In the 1920s, however, American farmers were faced with a grave challenge. World War I had created an enormous worldwide demand for American foodstuffs that carried farmers to their highest peak of prosperity. But in 1920 an inevitable slump began. Millions of soldiers in Europe and elsewhere in the world returned to their farms, and soon world overproduction of farm crops sent prices rapidly downward. By 1921 the prices of wheat, corn, and hogs had fallen to below half their level in 1918, and they never revived very far above that point. The result was that farm income dropped from ten billion dollars in 1919 to four billion dollars in 1921. There was some recovery afterward to about six or seven billion in the later 1920s, but even so the farm depression lasted until the middle 1930s. As a result, farmers' share of the national income dropped from sixteen percent in 1919 to less than nine percent in 1929.

Such a drop in income was catastrophic. Farm people had enthusiastically moved into the mainstream of American life in the preceding twenty years, the "golden age" of American agriculture. They therefore had a much more costly standard of living. Rural roads, schools, and hospitals required heavy taxes. Electricity in the home, automobiles, trips to town, clothing and furniture like the city folk—all represented real gains in life that farmers bitterly resisted giving up. All remembered the crude living conditions of their parents and had no intention, if they could help it, of returning to those conditions, especially while the cities were enjoying prosperity.

Farm radicalism

This discontent resulted in a reawakening of farm radicalism. The Grange and the Farmers' Union came alive once more, and a newly formed organization, the American Farm Bureau Federation, took up reform enthusiastically. Meanwhile, senators and congressmen from farm areas, responding rapidly to the new crisis, met in Washington in 1921 to form a nonpartisan organization called the Farm Bloc. Pulling together legislators from both northern and southern states, it wielded great power in Congress for many years.

The most dramatic expression of the new agrarian radicalism was an organized revival of the Progressive party. The first step was the convening of the Conference for Progressive Political Action in 1922, which so successfully ignited the old fires that the candidates it endorsed in the elections of that year were strikingly victorious. Soon Senator Robert M. La Follette of Wisconsin was at the head of the movement. As in 1912, its objective was to capture the Republican presidential nomination for La Follette. When that proved unattainable, the Progressive party was formally revived and La Follette chosen as its candidate. On a platform calling for public ownership of water power and the railroads and for attacks on business monopoly, La Follette campaigned vigorously, drawing almost five million popular votes in the presidential election of 1924. (Coolidge, the Republican nominee, received almost sixteen million popular votes and 382 electoral college ballots; John W. Davis, the Democratic nominee, garnered 8.4 million popular votes and 136 electoral votes; La Follette carried only Wisconsin, receiving its 13 votes in the electoral college.)

Farmers seek aid

The chief scene of action, however, lay in Congress, where the Farm Bloc worked hard to secure legislation to aid the agrarian sector. In the Fordney-McCumber Tariff, enacted by the Republican Congress soon after Harding became president, which raised rates from the twenty-six percent average of the Underwood Tariff to thirty-three percent, they got some (ineffective) tariff protection against foreign meat and other commodities. Then for six years farmers mobilized a heavy campaign behind the McNary-

Haugen plan, which would have had the government purchase the entire farm crop at a "parity price" (one which would make farmers as prosperous, relative to the rest of the population, as they had been in the years 1910–14) for sale domestically and abroad. Sternly vetoed by President Coolidge, who believed farmers should operate as individual businessmen and take their profits and losses as they came, McNary-Haugen eventually faded from sight. Farmers were learning that their fundamental problem was overproduction, and as the 1930s approached they were beginning to think of plans for cutting back their output to match the market at home, foreign markets having been cut off by new European tariff walls.

Andrew Mellon, Treasury secretary in the Harding-Coolidge years, symbolized in his elegant, multi-millionaire person the spirit that governed 1920s economic policies.
Culver Pictures, Inc.

Andrew Mellon aids the rich

President Coolidge found his political inspiration in the writings and career of Alexander Hamilton. So did his secretary of the treasury, Andrew W. Mellon, who was fond of posing before a portrait of the great Federalist. Mellon enthusiastically preached that the country's wealthy men should be freed from taxation so that they could develop the nation's resources and create jobs by investment. He therefore appealed constantly to Congress to reduce taxation on higher incomes. At first he was unsuccessful, for the progressive-inspired tax policies of the war period, which involved heavy taxation of high incomes and corporations, were strongly supported by midwestern and southern progressives. Rebuffed by Congress, Mellon actually refunded huge sums to heavy taxpayers, reaching a total, the nation was startled to learn in 1928, of some $3.5 billion.

With Coolidge's victory in 1924, Mellon and the business classes vigorously renewed their campaign for tax reductions. By this time the country was so prosperous that Congress could no longer find much reason for insisting on high tax levels. The result was a victory for Mellon in 1926, for the Revenue Act of that year slashed corporation and high income tax rates. The end result, though unknown at the time, was to release huge sums of money that went into stock market speculation and helped to build the boom culminating in the crash of 1929.

Republicans and the regulatory commissions

The progressives had concentrated on one key objective: establishing a group of independent agencies, staffed by experts, to oversee crucial sections of the economy. The notion lying behind the commissions—the Federal Trade Commission, the Federal Reserve Board, a strengthened Interstate Commerce Commission, and other agencies—was that the public interest needed vigilant watchdogs in Washington to keep a close eye on the business community. The Republican administrations of the 1920s disagreed fundamentally with this outlook. Believing that the business community should be freed of irksome regulations, the Republican presidents filled the regulatory commissions with men friendly and cooperative to businessmen. The Tariff Commission was staffed with men who favored high tariffs. Indeed, some commissioners themselves were financially interested in the industries being protected.

Herbert Hoover's Commerce Department, eagerly supporting the new philosophy of cooperating with businessmen, swung its influence behind the formation of trade associations in each line of business. Their objective was to promote the centralized collection of information on prices, methods of production, standardization of products, and the like. Such activities made the associations perilously close to legalized monopolies, since the establishment of common prices seemed so frequently to be the result of their work. At the same time, a renewed movement toward business consolidation took place in the 1920s, with the result that by the end of the decade half of the total corporate wealth in the nation was controlled by a central core of about two hundred corporations. Monopoly, checked in the progressive years, was on the march again, and apparently with the federal government's blessing.

The power controversy

By the 1920s electrical power had become enormously important in the life of the United States. Some 6 million kilowatt hours were produced in 1902; by 1929, the number had risen to 117 million. Industry was being transformed, for the use of small electric motors allowed factories to disperse widely over the countryside since they no longer needed to rely on huge steam power plants. At the same time, electrical power was revolutionizing the home, providing light, heat, and other conveniences that eased the urban housewife's drudgery. The result was a voracious demand that stimulated a scramble for power sites. In 1920, to provide some supervision, the Federal Power Commission (FPC) was created, composed of the secretaries of war, interior, and agriculture. It was given authority to issue fifty-year licenses for the private exploitation of federal hydroelectric sites, with the government retaining the right to buy the whole operation at net cost when the lease expired. The FPC was also empowered to regulate rates, services, and financial operations if the states did not do so.

Under the Republican regimes, however, the FPC had little interest in standing as a watchdog over the private power industry. Instead, what it wanted was the rapid development of hydroelectric sites, relying on the businessmen concerned to use their leases in ways fair and equitable to the general public. The commission issued approximately 450 licenses between 1920 and 1930.

Because of the huge demand for power, great profits could be made from the building of utility networks. The result was a rush into utility investment and development reminiscent of the railroad boom of a half-century before. Small companies were merged with larger ones to rationalize the distribution of power. Then financiers created holding companies that combined the networks in order to profit from the issuance of stock. The holding companies themselves provided no major services but were primarily devices for draining off the profits made by the producing companies they owned. Imaginative entrepreneurs like Samuel Insull of Chicago piled holding company upon holding company, sometimes to the seventh level. Soon enormous burdens of debt were heaped on the producing companies, which in turn had to charge higher rates in order to meet the debt charges created by the holding companies' stocks and bonds.

When a public clamor arose against these practices, the utility companies, like the railroads long before them, boldly tried to dominate public opinion by influencing all sources of public information. They launched multimillion dollar public relations campaigns lauding private enterprise and condemning all proposals for regulation as socialism. They brought pressure to bear on newspapers, or bought them outright. The National Electric Light Association formed a textbook committee that coerced state agencies into giving up schoolbooks that criticized stock-watering and high utility rates or urged the need for public controls. A national program of public lectures was begun, and local politicians often found it financially advantageous to leave the utilities alone.

George Norris and Muscle Shoals

Many critics of the utilities began to advocate public production and distribution of electric power. It had become such a vital necessity of life, such men said, that no one should be allowed to profit from it. Electric power should be produced as cheaply as possible, distributed at the lowest possible price, and made available to Americans in all regions of the country, not only in prosperous areas where profits could be made. Many municipalities, persuaded by such appeals, established their own power production facilities that distributed electricity in the same way that municipal agencies distributed water.

The bulk of the electrical power in the nation, however, was produced and distributed by private companies. Radicals proposed that the whole system be nationalized, but for most people this was too revolutionary an idea. One device, however, remained open: for the federal government to undertake the production and distribution of power in regions up to that time ignored by private industry as unprofitable. This would allow the creation of a yardstick by which private utility rates could be judged. At the same time, the availability of cheap public power could revitalize vast areas where people lived in poverty and despair.

One location immediately offered itself—the Tennessee Valley. Where the Tennessee River dips into Alabama, at Muscle Shoals, the government had started to build a large dam during the First World War in order to produce nitrates for ammunition. This required enormous supplies of electrical power, to be produced by hydroelectric facilities at the dam. The facility was near completion when Harding took office, and the federal government immediately began looking for a private firm to lease the plant and sell power to private distribution companies.

But George W. Norris, progressive senator from Nebraska, had already taken up his great cause: making electrical power cheaply available to the masses by bringing it under public control. He had already conceived of a public corporation to control the waters of the entire sprawling Tennessee watershed for the public welfare. It would not only build many dams to produce cheap power but would also control floods, revive navigation, fisheries, recreation, and spread industry and jobs throughout an enormous region, then one of the most backward and poverty-stricken in the nation. As the nucleus for this system, he argued that the plant at Muscle Shoals should not be given to a private firm, but operated for the people of the Tennessee Valley. Republicans condemned his plan as bald socialism, but Norris was not to be dissuaded. On two occasions in the 1920s he pushed a bill through Congress to build a federal Tennessee Valley project, but both Coolidge and Hoover vetoed it. The Muscle Shoals dam was completed in 1925, and its power was sold to a local private company for distribution, but still Norris was not discouraged. He had saved Muscle Shoals, and in the 1930s under the New Deal, his dream for the Tennessee Valley was to become reality.

President Herbert Hoover's veto in 1931 of the Muscle Shoals proposal gave the Republican response to all such projects: "I am firmly opposed to the Government entering into any business the major purpose of which is competition with our citizens. . . . This territory is now supplied with power and to obtain . . . an income it would be necessary to take the customers of the present power companies [by undercutting] the rates now made by them. . . . There are many localities where the Federal Government is justified in the construction of great dams and reservoirs, where navigation, flood control, reclamation or stream regulation are of dominant importance, and where they are beyond the capacity or purpose of private or local government capital to construct. In these cases power is often a by-product and should be disposed of by contract or lease. But for the Federal Government deliberately to go out to build up and expand such an occasion to the major purpose of a power and manufacturing business is to break down the initiative and enterprise of the American people; it is destruction of equality of opportunity amongst our people; it is the negation of the ideals upon which our civilization has been based.

"I hesitate to contemplate the future of our institutions, of our government, and of our country if the preoccupation of its officials is to be no longer the promotion of justice and equal opportunity but is to be devoted to barter in the markets. That is not liberalism, it is degeneration. . . .

"The establishment of a Federal-operated power business and fertilizer factory in the Tennessee Valley means Federal control from Washington. . . . The real development of . . . Muscle Shoals can only be administered by the people on the ground, responsible to their own communities, directing them solely for the benefit of their communities and not for the purpose of pursuit of social theories or national politics."

Republican "involvement" in the world

The Republican attitude toward the outside world continued, through the 1920s, to be caught in a paradox. Fundamentally, the Harding and Coolidge administrations were isolationist and nationalistic at heart. The force of events, however, and the United States' unavoidably transformed status in the world, brought about an inevitable involvement in international politics, oftentimes in a major role. The League of Nations

was shunned; membership in the World Court was seriously discussed, for a time pursued, and then rejected. The protective tariff was re-established; the open door to immigrants was replaced with a filtering system designed primarily to admit northern and western Europeans; and the policy of refusing to make binding political commitments which would require the use of force to maintain collective security against aggressors, was continued. However, the Washington Conference and its agreements in 1921 was followed by participation throughout the decade in extended conferences in London and elsewhere which sought vainly to reduce naval armaments worldwide. Americans took major roles in complex negotiations connected with European war debts and reparations; and there was a reluctant but growing cooperation with the League of Nations in nonpolitical matters connected with the opium trade, and the "Traffic in Women and Children."

Most dramatic of all these involvements, if in the long run the effort to be most ridiculed, was the Kellogg-Briand Pact of August, 1928. In this document fifteen nations, and eventually practically the whole world, agreed to renounce war "as an instrument of national policy." For years the idea that war could be ended simply by its being outlawed by the nations of the world had circulated within the American peace movement. Senator William E. Borah first suggested it in the Senate in 1923; a Columbia professor, James T. Shotwell, urged it upon Foreign Minister Aristide Briand of France in 1927; and suddenly it exploded into prominent international discussion. Charles Lindbergh's electrifying solo flight over the Atlantic to Paris in May, 1927, created an exciting sense of revived links with America's Revolutionary-era ally. Briand proposed to the American Secretary of State Frank B. Kellogg that their two countries create such a pact between themselves. To avoid the implication of a special relationship with France, which might be taken as a kind of alliance against Germany, Kellogg expanded the notion into a universal renunciation of war by all nations. Months of complicated diplomacy followed in which Kellogg fended off efforts to attach qualifications and exemptions, dreamed of a Nobel Peace Prize (it was awarded to him in 1929), and secured the convening in Paris of a grand meeting of the representatives of fifteen nations to sign the Pact.

It was, however, purely a self-denying ordinance. No machinery whatever was established to implement it, and in time the Pact became the classic symbol of the futility of interwar diplomacy. Grand-sounding words without commitments were useless in preventing warfare; indeed, were effective only in creating cynicism and loss of mutual faith.

The emergence of Herbert Hoover

One American figure stood out with uncommon brightness at the end of the First World War—Herbert Hoover. His life had been purest Horatio Alger. A poor Quaker boy, he went to Stanford University as soon as it opened in the 1890s, became an engineer, and launched an international career that by 1914 made him a rich man. Living in London when the First World War broke out, he was asked as a neutral to direct the relief operations that brought food to the people of war-ravaged Belgium. In this enormous effort Hoover's consummate administrative skills soon made him an internationally renowned figure. When he attended the peace conference at Paris, no one else seemed to represent quite so luminously the selfless concern for humanity that Woodrow Wilson was then vainly calling on the victorious powers to exhibit.

When Hoover returned to the United States, no one knew his partisan affiliation. He had had nothing to do with politics: he was an engineer, an expert, a twentieth-century man. For him the key concepts were efficiency, strong administration, and "scientific" solutions—classic notions from the heart of the Progressive Era. When he declared himself a Republican, that party was

delighted. In fact, Quakers had always been overwhelmingly Republican, just as they had been Tory in Revolutionary times. A pious, hard-working, moralistic folk with deep English roots, they had been hostile to the Scotch-Irish and the Catholic Irish; fervently antislavery and anti-southern; and devotedly in favor of temperance. No more Republican setting could be found than the small Iowa village of West Branch where Hoover was reared. Its Quaker memories rooted it within the Protestant, "respectable" tradition, as distinguished sharply from the moral corruptions and Catholicism of Chicago, that appalling city which so fascinated the rural Middle West and symbolized the Democratic party.

Harding made Hoover secretary of commerce, a post he held until he ran for the presidency in 1928. He made the office, formerly almost ignored, the most vital and exciting center of federal activity in Washington. Hoover was a missionary of capitalism who hated both socialism and unchecked individualism. A confirmed elitist, he had a horror of mob rule. As he wrote in his book *American Individualism* (1922), "the crowd only feels: it has no mind of its own which can plan. The crowd is credulous, it destroys, it consumes, it hates, and it dreams—but it never builds." Hoover believed that American individualism, founded on the twin principles of equality of opportunity and of service, would provide the hope of the future. Although he recognized poverty in the United States, Hoover insisted that the government should not do anything directly about it, for the operations of private enterprise were progressively eliminating the problem.

As the years passed, Herbert Hoover rose ever higher as the expressive symbol and philosopher of the American business system. There seemed no end to the expansion of the economy, and the glow of national prosperity lighted him for all the nation to see and admire. When Calvin Coolidge indicated that he "did not choose to run" for the presidency in 1928, the Republican party turned almost en masse to the brilliant engineer, organizer, and publicist, Herbert Hoover.

Democrats in the 1920s:
Frustration and conflict

During the years of Republican triumph, the Democrats lurched from disaster to disaster, wounded deeply by the cultural shifts of these years. Southern Democrats disliked everything that Democrats in the northern states represented: urbanism, "foreigners," Catholics and Jews, and drinking. The Ku Klux Klan, so popular in the South, was hated in the immigrant wards. Above all, southern Democrats disliked the man who was emerging as the voice of northern Democrats, Alfred E. Smith, governor of New York. A Catholic who was reared in a tenement on New York City's East Side and in his speech and style a kind of American cockney, Smith had different memories from those held by the populistic southern Democrats. They were aroused by the threat of monopolistic corporations and the protective tariff. Rooted in Smith's remembrances, on the other hand, were the stinking slums in which he had lived, the degradation of endless labor in the foul air of crowded factories, the filth of public toilets, and the callous exploitation of child labor. He appealed for social reforms in the cities. Minimum wage laws, eight-hour days, workmen's compensation, state provision of medical services, publicly provided cheap electrical power—these were his objectives. Furthermore, as a Catholic he was keenly interested in civil liberties, revolted by the Ku Klux Klan, and inspired by the idea of a pluralistic American society that would make an equitable place for all those who were not WASP.

In 1924, rural southerners were not ready for the man with the East Side twang. He was "wet" on the liquor issue (i.e., he opposed prohibition), and they were "dry." He was Catholic, they were Protestant. The Democratic convention of that year could not even unite in condemning the Ku Klux Klan. For more than a hundred weary ballots it wrangled between nominating Smith or William G. McAdoo, Woodrow Wilson's son-in-law, who had become the hero of the rural Democrats led by William Jennings Bryan. It was this deadlock that led to the choice of John W. Davis, a lackluster Wall Street attorney of no public standing, and to the smashing triumph of Calvin Coolidge.

Four years later, in 1928, there was no doubt that Governor Smith was the only Democratic candidate of sufficient stature to challenge Hoover for the presidency. Meanwhile, too, the Democratic party had swung over vigorously to the cause of rural radicals who demanded some kind of governmental aid to agriculture and other progressive-inspired reforms such as the public control of electrical power production and distribution. With Smith supporting these causes, a political basis existed for a union of southern and northern Democrats. He was, accordingly, nominated by the Democratic party in 1928, while in New York State, the polio-crippled Franklin D. Roosevelt had been induced to come out of his semiretirement and campaign for the post of governor of that state, which he won.

Significance of the 1928
presidential vote

Smith lost by a wide margin to Hoover: the popular vote was fifteen million on his side and twenty-one million for the Republican nominee. However, Smith's showing was a critical portent

Al Smith, Democratic candidate for President in 1928. Brash, pro-drink, reared in New York City and an Irish Catholic, he represented everything that rural, WASP, and small town America was against.
Wide World Photos

of future politics. The dozen largest cities, which for years had voted Republican, swung over to the Democratic column. The "new stock" immigrants of the northern cities, which had started to go Democratic before the First World War, and had then fallen off because of their anger at Woodrow Wilson's war policies, were now swinging massively and finally into the Democratic column. Prohibitionism in the northern states was overwhelmingly a Republican policy, with its origins in small town, WASP America, and the ethnic minorities bitterly hated it as an insulting slap at themselves. In truth, WASP America drank relatively little; it was Italian wine, German beer, Irish whiskey, and other ethnic beverages, and the saloon—overwhelmingly an ethnic institution—that prohibitionism attacked. Cities like Chicago, with their huge ethnic populations, ignored prohibition en masse. Anti-Catholicism was virulent in the northern states, as was nativism, the Ku Klux Klan, and the campaign for restricted immigration, and all of these were deeply identified with the Republican party. Rural America hated the city as an evil, corrupting place. Iowa farmers thought Chicago foreign, radical, dirty, repellent, in every way a force to be battled against by the Republican party. They felt their Protestant nation was in grave danger from the immigrant hordes who occupied its great urban centers. Jews, they were startled to find, had suddenly become the second largest religious group in Illinois, taking that honor from the Methodists!

Seeing the Republicans as their enemies—in their anti-labor and pro-business views as well as in their hatred of immigrant culture—the Jews, Italians, Poles, and Yugoslavs poured in waves into the Democratic party. Most strikingly, so too did the Germans, who had got over their anger at the Democratic war against their homeland, and even the Scandinavians, a strongly ethnic group since far back in the nineteenth century (though they were to be relatively temporary Democrats).

From 1920 to 1928, seventeen million new voters passed the age of twenty-one, and the majority were from the new ethnic groups. Thus,

although Herbert Hoover was able to win some 300 counties in the South, he did so on the basis of prohibition, an issue that by 1932, with its impending repeal, would die. The Democratic party was now in the position where it would soon, with the help of the Great Depression, become the majority party.

Hoover: Triumphant president

Few presidents have taken office in such encouraging circumstances as Herbert Hoover. He was enormously popular. Everything about him symbolized and proclaimed the triumph of the "New Era," which Republicans were fond of contrasting to Woodrow Wilson's New Freedom. As for the nation, it was as rich as all of Europe. Some forty percent of the world's wealth was contained within its borders. The American business system seemed one of the wonders of the world, a compound of assembly-line production, time and motion efficiency studies, advertising, easy credit, low interest rates, and a continuing flood of new products. Its most dramatic sight was the automobile; Americans owned twenty-three million of them by 1929, an average of one per family. Henry Ford, a genuine folk hero, represented in industry the astonishing potentialities of mass production for a mass market.

Hoover convened Congress in a special session to do something to quiet the angry farmers and to revise the tariff. His party looked to him in admiration. But it was not long before the honeymoon was over, for Hoover fundamentally disliked Congress and all politicians and wanted to have as little as possible to do with either. This distaste was impossible for him to hide, for he was a tactless man. Congressional leaders, visiting Hoover at the White House, found him distrustful and pessimistic. Henry L. Stimson, his secretary of state, remarked that "it was like sitting in a bath of ink to sit in [the president's] room." Whatever happened in Congress, Hoover seemed always to interpret it as the product of some political vendetta against himself.

Hoover clearly believed that nothing was fundamentally wrong with agriculture and that it needed only a dose of business methods. Rather than provide a price-support mechanism, he secured the creation of the Federal Farm Board, whose function was to make farm marketing more efficient. The Farm Bloc succeeded in tacking onto the bill a $500 million appropriation that the board was to use in making direct purchases of crops in the market in order to stave off price declines. This step was pitifully inadequate to deal with so enormous a problem, but it represented a major breakthrough in the nation's agricultural policy.

For industry, Hoover had in mind a tariff revision that would allow him greater authority to raise or lower rates, following recommendations of the Tariff Commission. His central notion was to ensure greater efficiency by enabling the president to equalize the costs of production here and abroad. The result, after months of wrangling and back-scratching, was the Hawley-Smoot Tariff, which increased rates on more than a thousand imports, but did not give Hoover the added flexibility he requested. The general tariff level was raised to forty percent, which halted entirely the importing of a great number of foreign products. Hoover had been lauded as the expert economist who would take politics out of tariff-making, and now the nation had a bill that was more blatantly protectionist and politically inspired than ever. A thousand economists appealed to the president to veto the bill, but he signed it. This led to grave repercussions, for Britain and Germany soon retaliated by raising their tariffs against American goods, thus reducing international trade just at the time when it needed to be increased.

The great crash

There were numerous economic danger signals in 1929, though the government was ignorant of them since as yet it did not gather detailed economic statistics. In Wall Street, however, speculation went merrily onward. For a half-dozen years money had poured into the stock market from millions of investors in the United States and Europe. Profits seemed endless. The Federal Reserve Board, following Coolidge's urgings, made credit easily available. With no public supervision, the stock markets could make purchases ridiculously easy, asking investors to put down no more than ten percent on a stock (called margin purchasing), the stock brokers themselves making up the balance by issuing loans. As the speculative craze mounted, stock was "split" (divided into several shares), so there would be more for investors to buy, and "blue sky" corporations appeared that had practically no assets whatever save a stock market listing. Buyers competed so eagerly for loans that interest rates soared from about five percent to twenty percent, with the result that money poured in from abroad in order to be lent out at high interest rates. Where normally the price of a stock might stand at eight or ten times its earnings, prices now soared to as much as twenty times earnings. The mania spread everywhere. Following the stock market and making speculative plunges became as common as following the baseball scores. Almost two million Americans by 1929 were investors in American securities.

The American stock market was like an enormous vacuum cleaner sucking in capital from all over the world and draining dry every other line of enterprise. Why put your money in conservative projects when fantastic profits could be made by buying and selling on Wall Street? European nations grew gravely worried, for the siphoning off of capital severely weakened their economies. Economists in England warned repeatedly that a crash was coming if something was not done. Finally, in September 1929, the Bank of England raised its rediscount rate to 6.5 percent, thus halting the flow of gold to America. This action seemed to trigger a cascade of events, beginning with the decision by many American and European investors to pull back, sell out, and safeguard themselves. The crucial element in the whole speculative spiral had been confidence. Now it began to wane, and the result was a foregone conclusion. On Wednesday, October

The confused, dazed crowd jamming Wall Street on the day of the 1929 stock market crash expressed the mood that was soon to spread across the nation. Capitalism seemed to have collapsed.
Brown Brothers

23, 1929, a flood of "sell" orders deluged Wall Street, and since there were not as many buyers as before, stock prices began to tumble. From then on, the ghastly disaster grew more and more frightening. There were even brief periods in which nobody at all would agree to buy, no matter how low the prices. The visitors' gallery at the New York Stock Exchange was closed so that the panic on the floor would be less visible. The torrent of transactions put the stock ticker farther and farther behind, thus heightening the tension and increasing scare selling. The news spread hourly throughout the nation, and stock owners besieged their brokers' offices with appeals to sell and get out.

Bankers with enormous resources like those of the House of Morgan stepped in at once to make huge purchases and thus stop the slide. Economists, the Treasury Department, even the White House issued reassuring statements. But the fear was too widespread. After a few days quiet, on October 29 the uproar began again. Worried brokers, frantic to get their loans back, forced customers to sell. Another avalanche of sell orders descended on Wall Street, reaching an all-time high of sixteen million shares in one day. Within a month, the total value of stocks listed at the New York Exchange had dropped some twenty-six billion dollars, or forty percent of their former level. The New Era had collapsed.

Why the depression?

A recession had in fact already been underway, for businessmen in 1928 had greatly over-estimated what the American public would buy, and had produced too many manufactured goods. Thus, factories had shut down operations and laid men off, waiting for merchants' swollen inventories to drop downward again—a normal and cyclical procedure. The stock market crash suddenly wiped away enormous stores of capital, so that the whole economy was made shakier, because less able to be fed by a steady flow of investment. It also had a profound psychological impact, for it pricked the bubble of belief in ever-expanding prosperity, drained away confidence in the stock brokers and bankers who had been leading the speculation, and led distrustful ordinary citizens to withdraw their money from investments and hold it as cash.

The scene was not one, however, of potential disaster, for the economy had weathered such fluctuations before. For many years scholars have explained the great depression which actually developed as caused by what is called *under-consumption:* that is, that in the 1920s businessmen kept too much of their profits to themselves instead of paying them out in higher wages, so that ordinary Americans could not buy the huge output of the factories. Income, it has long been said, was so highly skewed, placing most of it in the hands of the wealthy—who squandered it in disastrous speculation—that fewer and fewer could buy what businessmen wished to sell. Farmers in particular were a depressed class, because farm prices had been slumping so long, and this fact made the economy even more likely to tumble into complete collapse when a triggering event like the stock market crisis occurred.

While these things had their influence, the fact is that national income was better distributed than at any earlier period; that potential demand was still very high; and that it was quite possible for the federal government within its then existing resources to have pulled the nation out of the self-feeding downward spiral which slowly began to accelerate, plunging the nation deeper and deeper into what in time became a massive depression. What we now realize happened was a grave failure of policy within the Federal Reserve Board. Before the crash, the Board had made speculation worse by responding sympathetically to the bankers' clamor for more and more funds, and making credit easier to secure. Then after the crash, in 1931 the Board grew worried that too much gold was leaving the country as Europeans, believing the American economy too weak, withdrew it. To prove conclusively that the American dollar was sound and valuable, the Board drastically slashed back all borrowing and reduced the money supply. By 1933, the nation had a third less money with which to carry on its economic life. This was tantamount to shutting off the oxygen to a man who, through over-exertion, was momentarily finding it hard to breathe. The result was catastrophic.

Thousands of banks closed; "runs" on their resources put the public in a panic. The economy now headed downward, with increasing speed. Investment in new capital plants practically ceased, falling from $10 billion in 1929 to $1 billion in 1932. Approximately 110,000 businesses closed their doors from 1929 to 1932, while the aggregate profit of all corporations declined from almost $8.5 billion to $3.4 billion. The railroads found themselves with only half their former freight-hauling trade. In 1930 industrial production was about twenty-five percent below its peak in 1929; by 1932, it had sagged to fifty percent below that figure. Within six months of the crash, unemployment stood at three million; by 1933, it had reached twelve to fourteen million. Life in industrial cities was almost indescribable. While in the nation as a whole, twenty-five percent of the working force was unemployed, in Ohio cities like Cleveland half the workers were without jobs in 1933; in Toledo, the figure was eighty percent! Huge urban areas lived in famine conditions like that in ancient times.

Hoover's response

Knowing what the stock market collapse portended, President Hoover quickly moved into action. His firm conviction was that the catastrophe was a great natural event about which the government could do little save to encourage people to be confident. The nation, he said, could no more "legislate [itself] out of a world-wide depression [than] we can exorcise a Caribbean hurricane by statutory law." If businessmen would be unselfish and if they would cooperate and keep faith in the system, recovery was certain. His own role, he felt, was to serve as "an influential advisor and well-placed cheerleader." He also briefly increased Federal spending on public works. Fundamentally, however, he regarded the emergency as one that would be soon solved by cooperative, voluntary action by businessmen. He called business leaders to the White House and appealed to them not to lay off workers or lower wages. He emphasized, meanwhile, that he had no intention of interfering in any way with private enterprise.

Hoover made it clear from the beginning that he intended to handle the depression on his own, not by appealing to Congress for legislation. In response, for a considerable period both parties in Congress were content to leave the matter in his hands. By the end of 1930, however, evidence was accumulating that the depression was very severe, and some congressional critics of Hoover's passivity began calling for enormous increases in spending for public works. The president replied testily that "prosperity cannot be restored by raids upon the public treasury." Senator Robert Wagner of New York secured passage of the Federal Employment Stabilization Act, which established a board to plan and carry through an accelerated program of public works, but Hoover made little use of it. Meanwhile, the nation became sunk with apathy. Told constantly by politicians and experts alike that the economy would right itself automatically, the public settled into a fatalistic mood.

Action begins

By the summer of 1931, however, it was no longer possible to continue in passivity. Herbert Hoover had by this time reluctantly capitulated, having found that voluntary action had grave weaknesses. Financiers everywhere were looking out for their own skins and shunning cooperation. In his state of the union address, Hoover called for the establishment of the Reconstruction Finance Corporation (RFC), to be modeled on the War Finance Corporation of 1917 and 1918, to save the collapsing banks, railroads, and insurance companies. Progressives in Congress criticized the proposed project for ignoring the sufferings of the unemployed. Fiorello La Guardia of New York called it a "millionaire's dole." A Republican congressman wailed that the RFC would be "the most decided step toward communism any civilized government has ever taken with the possible exception of Russia." Farm Bloc legislators angrily pointed out that it was only another aid to banks and railroads, long the special concern of a government indifferent to the farmers. But the emergency was patent; the bankers, impatient of political theory, were desperate for it; and the measure was enacted swiftly. Given $500 million in capital and the power to borrow additional huge sums, the RFC aided more than 5,000 companies in the year 1932 alone, practically all of which loans were paid back.

Democratic progressives revolt

The Democrats in Congress, thus far, had remained relatively quiescent. Their leaders were largely southern, and, lacking ideas of their own as to how to solve the depression, were content to leave matters in the president's hands. The election of 1930 had delivered the House into Democratic hands, but Speaker John Nance Garner of Texas prided himself on cooperating with the president, rather than serving as a carping critic. In 1932, however, all this fraternization blew apart.

A concerted drive began to force the president to agree to vastly expanded programs of relief for the unemployed, principally through federal public works. Hoover had doggedly insisted that relief was a private and local matter; that the nation's moral fiber and the vigor of its state governments would be destroyed if the federal government took up a direct role in relief. He particularly condemned all public works except those that would produce a self-liquidating revenue: toll bridges, power dams, and slum clearance projects were examples. The president was determined to keep a balanced budget and to hold down spending. Every proposal for expanded public works came under withering Republican criticism as a dole. But local governments and relief agencies had long since exhausted their funds, and they appealed for federal action. When Congress passed a bill calling for three billion dollars to be dispensed for public works, the president vetoed the measure. The man who had been the savior of Belgium and the worldwide symbol of compassion to the suffering had become "heartless Hoover." He seemed to care more for his principles of political theory than he did for the unemployed.

"I finished high school in 1930," mused Ed Paulsen, a United Nations official, in 1970, "and I walked out into [the depression]. . . . I'd get up at five in the morning [in San Francisco] and head for the waterfront. Outside the Spreckles Sugar Refinery, outside the gates there would be a thousand men. You know dang well there's only three or four jobs. The guy would come out with two little Pinkerton cops: 'I need two guys for the bull gang. Two guys to go into the hole.' A thousand men would fight like a pack of Alaskan dogs to get through there. . . .

"So you'd drift up to Skid Row. There'd be thousands of men there. Guys on baskets, making weird speeches, phony theories on economics. . . . They'd say: O.K., we're going to City Hall. . . . We'd shout around the steps. Finally, [the mayor'd] come out and tell us nothing. I remember the demands: We demand work, we demand shelter for our families, we demand groceries, this kind of thing. . . . I remember as a kid how courageous this seemed to me, the demands, because you knew that society wasn't going to give it to you. They'd demand that they open up unrented houses and give decent shelters for their families. . . . This parade would be four blocks long, curb to curb. Nobody had a dime. . . . The guys'd start to yell and there come some horses. They used to have cops on horseback in those days. Then there'd be some fighting. Finally it got to killing. . . .

"We were a gentle crowd. These were fathers, eighty percent of them. They had held jobs and didn't want to kick society to pieces. They just wanted to go to work and they just couldn't understand. . . . These fellas always had faith that the job was gonna mature, somehow. More and more men were after fewer and fewer jobs. So San Francisco just ground to a halt. Nothing was moving." (Quoted in Studs Terkel, *Hard Times* [1970].)

The election of 1932

Franklin D. Roosevelt, governor of New York, swept Herbert Hoover and the Republicans out of power with a finality that left them shattered for the next twenty years. The nation had had enough of principles; now it wanted action, which Roosevelt seemed to promise. Not since before the Civil War had the Democrats won such a great majority in the Senate, nor since 1890 in the House. They gained in every part of the United States, winning a majority of the congressional race everywhere except in traditionally Republican New England. The Democratic victories on the Pacific Coast were the most astonishing, for there the Democrats increased their percentage of the popular vote for congressman from twenty percent in 1930 to fifty-one percent in 1932. Roosevelt received almost 23 million popular votes to Hoover's 15.8 million, while winning the electoral votes of all but five states: Pennsylvania, Connecticut, Vermont, New

Hampshire, and Maine. When inaugurated in March 1933, the new president found a transformed Congress ready and eager to follow executive leadership. The New Era was gone; the New Deal now triumphantly seized the reins.

Bibliography

Three books that were especially valuable to me in writing this chapter: Robert K. Murray gives a surprising picture of a much-maligned president in his *The Harding Era: Warren G. Harding and His Administration* (1969); David Burner's *The Politics of Provincialism: The Democratic Party in Transition, 1918–1932* (1968) is fundamental on the rising power of urban ethnic groups and the cultural conflicts that ranged Democrats against each other in bitter hostility. John M. Allswang, *A House for All Peoples: Ethnic Politics in Chicago 1890–1936* (1971) illuminates these cultural dynamics in one concentrated and crucial setting.

How have historians looked at the topic?

Just as the cultural tensions of the 1920s foreshadowed divisions that have haunted American society to the present, so the decade also saw modern aspects of politics, economics, and foreign policy begin to emerge. Joan Hoff Wilson's *The Twenties: The Critical Issues** (1972) contains a perceptive introductory essay and excerpts from historians that go far toward clarifying the puzzling and contradictory 1920s. John D. Hick's *Republican Ascendancy, 1921–1933** (1960), in The New American Nation Series, is the basic account, solid and essential.

The Harding years have recently been subjected to careful scrutiny. Wesley M. Bagby explodes most of the usual myths about the 1920 electoral contest in *Road to Normalcy: The Presidential Campaign and Election of 1920** (1962) while Burl Noggle reveals the insignificant impact of the oil scandals in his *Teapot Dome: Oil and Politics in the 1920s** (1962). Andrew Sinclair offers new insights into the man who looked like a president in his scholarly biography *The Available Man: The*

Life behind the Masks of Warren G. Harding* (1965). Francis Russell's impressionistic portrait *The Shadow of Blooming Grove: Warren G. Harding in His Time* (1968) is detailed and entertaining. For almost thirty years "Silent Cal" remained a historical enigma. Donald R. McCoy's *Calvin Coolidge: The Silent President* (1967) has done much to reveal his personality, although some historians think the biography too sympathetic.

The image of the 1920s as an isolationist era was forcefully challenged in the early 1950s by William A. Williams. Positing a strong connection between the political economy of the United States and its foreign policy, Williams emphasized the expansionist nature of Republican policies during the 1920s. The latest expression of Williams's thesis is in *The Roots of the Modern American Empire: A Study of the Growth and Shaping of Social Consciousness in a Market Place Society** (1969). Joan Hoff Wilson fleshes out Williams's approach in a stimulating and scholarly book, *American Business and Foreign Policy, 1902–1933* (1971). For a different interpretation of the foreign policy of this period, see L. Ethan Ellis's balanced account *Republican Foreign Policy, 1921–1933* (1968) and Thomas H. Buckley's fine in-depth study *The United States and the Washington Conference, 1921–1922* (1970).

The prosperity of the 1920s and its abrupt end in the crash of 1929 have long been popular topics among economic historians. Herein Professor Kelley has relied upon W. Elliot Brownlee's *Dynamics of Ascent: A History of the American Economy* (1974). The institutional structure of finance capitalism is criticized in Robert Sobel's *The Great Bull Market: Wall Street in the 1920s** (1968) while capitalism as a whole is roundly denounced in *Monopoly Capital: An Essay on the American Economic and Social Order** (1966) written by the Marxist economists Paul A. Baran and Paul M. Sweezy. New light is shed on the centralizing impulse of business in Lewis Galambos's *Competition and Cooperation: The Emergence of a National Trade Association* (1966). The specific problems of labor are treated in Irving Bernstein's excellent study *The*

*Lean Years: A History of the American Worker, 1920–1933** (1960), which can now be supplemented with Robert Zieger's *Republicans and Labor, 1919–1929* (1969). The farmers' complex situation is illuminated in John D. Hicks and Theodore Saloutos's *Twentieth-Century Populism: Agricultural Discontent in the Middle West, 1900–1939* (1964) and in Robert L. Morlan's *Political Prairie Fire: The Non-Partisan League, 1915–1922* (1955).

The nomination of Alfred E. Smith as Democratic party torchbearer in 1928 has occasioned much analysis by historians. David Burner's *The Politics of Provincialism: The Democratic Party in Transition, 1919–1932* (1968), cited above, describes the changing constituency that brought Smith to national prominence while Samuel Lubell's *The Future of American Politics** (1965) emphasizes the importance of the birth rate for the Democrats.

Don S. Kirschner's *City and Country: Rural Responses to Urbanization in the 1920s* (1970) is a revealing study of cultural tensions. Fresh scholarship on Herbert Hoover is just beginning. Meanwhile, Hoover can be studied in several fine books: Gene Smith, *The Shattered Dream: Herbert Hoover and the Great Depression* (1970); Albert U. Romasco, *The Poverty of Abundance: Hoover, the Nation, the Depression** (1965); Jordan A. Schwarz, *Interregnum of Despair: Hoover's Congress and the Depression* (1970); Joan Hoff Wilson, *Herbert Hoover: Forgotten Progressive* (1975); Gary Dean Best, *The Politics of American Individualism: Herbert Hoover in Transition, 1918–1921* (1976).

* Available in paperback.

Depression Years in the Land

The grave conditions of hopeless unemployment, stretching year after year and getting worse, produced many demonstrations in 1932. Here, marchers, claiming representation from twenty-five states, stage a parade in Washington, D.C. around the White House, with banners asking for a billion-dollar appropriation and a twenty percent increase in WPA wages.

Wide World Photo

The persistence of massive unemployment into 1935 saw the jobless living in these conditions in Marysville, California, mocking the dreams of those thousands who, as in John Steinbeck's *The Grapes of Wrath,* fled from the interior to the Golden State.

Library of Congress

Migrant mother, taken in a famous photograph in Nipomo, California, in 1936. Her eyes seem to look out not just upon immediate suffering, but upon a nation stricken.
Library of Congress

Ditched, stalled, and stranded in the San Joaquin Valley, California. The old Model T Ford, left over from better years, usually carried mattresses and old chests of drawers, as tractored-out farmers from eastern states looked vainly for work.
Library of Congress, photo by Dorothea Lange

CHAPTER 31

Franklin D. Roosevelt and the New Deal

TIME LINE

1930	Norris-La Guardia Act
1933–1935	First New Deal
1933	Bank holiday and reform; the first "Hundred Days"; National Recovery Administration; labor unions grow rapidly; Agricultural Adjustment Administrations; Tennessee Valley Authority; Civilian Conservation Corps; Federal Emergency Relief Administration; Civil Works Administration; Federal Deposit Insurance Corporation; Twentieth Amendment changes inauguration day of president, vice-president, and congressmen to January from March; Twenty-first Amendment repeals prohibition
1934	Securities and Exchange Commission; gold standard terminated; London Economic Conference; large Democratic victories in congressional elections; new Democratic coalition forms
1935–1938	Second New Deal
1935	Radicals such as Floyd Olson, Charles Coughlin, and Huey Long popular; in *The Schechter Poultry Company* v. *The United States,* Supreme Court rules National Recovery Administration unconstitutional, subsequently invalidates other major parts of New Deal, such as Agricultural Adjustment Administration; Louis Brandeis and followers, hostile to centralized planning and distrustful of business, grow influential; Works Progress Administration; Federal Art Project; Federal Writers' Project; National Youth Administration; Rural Electrification Administration; Social Security Act; Utility Holding Companies Act; Federal Reserve System made much stronger; control over the money supply made a public responsibility; graduated income tax made higher on wealthy; National Labor Relations Board; Congress of Industrial Organizations formed
1937	Supreme Court "packing" battle; Supreme Court begins approving New Deal legislation; economy slumps
1938	Huge spending program launched for recovery; antitrust campaign begun; Bituminous Coal Act; Farm Security Administration; United States Housing Authority; Agricultural Adjustment Administration reenacted in new form; Fair Labor Standards Act

pledge you," Franklin D. Roosevelt had said during the 1932 election campaign, "I pledge myself, to a new deal for the American people." On inauguration day in March 1933, the tall man with the huge shoulders moved slowly on his crippled legs to the high white rostrum in front of the Capitol building. With every fourth working man out of a job, urban welfare systems out of funds, the banking system shut down, and panic spreading through an immobilized nation, his task was to jolt the United States out of despair. "First of all," he cried out in his high ringing voice, "let me assert my firm belief that the only thing we have to fear is fear itself—nameless, unreasoning, unjustified terror which paralyzes needed efforts to convert retreat into advance." The nation, he said, was in a kind of war, and now the challenge was for the president to give vigorous leadership. "This nation asks for action, and action now."

This was indeed what he provided. With his inauguration it was as if a cornet trio playing thinly in the nation's capital was suddenly replaced by huge brass bands marching in from all directions, every instrument blaring at top volume. The national government exploded into furious activity and grew rapidly in size. Tiny budgets became huge ones; Congress worked day and night, month after month; message after message arrived at the Capitol from the president, calling urgently for more and more legislation; and a cornucopia of new federal agencies opened up, cascading offices and bureaus all over Washington, each of them bringing in experts from universities, banks, labor unions, farms, and corporations to supervise some crucial sector of the national economy.

Roosevelt's New Deal passed through two phases. From 1933 to 1935, the First New Deal operated on the assumption that overproduction was the fundamental problem, and it tried to solve this by instituting massive programs of centralized planning designed to reduce output and therefore raise prices. This would help the producers of goods. After partial success, the First New Deal collapsed in a welter of confusion and impasse. The Second New Deal, which began in a rush of legislation in 1935 and lasted into 1938, adopted the idea that underconsumption was the main problem and that helping the consumer was the most important goal—a classic Democratic pattern. Aid to the unemployed was vastly expanded to boost purchasing power; labor was aided in its organizing drives; and other programs helped farmers, the old, the blind, and the helpless. Full public control over the currency was established by a major strengthening of the Federal Reserve System; gigantic utility holding companies were broken up; and income taxes were aimed at high incomes.

Franklin D. Roosevelt: Progressive Democrat

The president was a kindly man who had known personal suffering, in an encounter at age thirty-nine with infantile paralysis that left him permanently crippled, but he had never known poverty. Reared as a much-loved, only child in a gentle, Episcopalian household, Roosevelt spent his early life on his father's Hudson Valley estate at Hyde Park, New York. Then came Groton, Harvard during the era of William James, Columbia Law School, and the beginnings of a Wall Street attorney's career. In 1910 Roosevelt entered politics as a state senator in his home district, Hyde Park. His father had been a Cleveland Democrat; and at Harvard Roosevelt worked hard for antiimperialist causes at the time of the Spanish-American War. In the New York legislature he was a progressive Democrat who chiefly battled against "bossism" and Tammany Hall.

Roosevelt admired Woodrow Wilson and pushed vigorously for his election. Wilson summoned young Roosevelt to Washington and appointed him assistant secretary of the navy. Dynamic, quick to learn, Roosevelt was an eager and effective administrator. When Wilson's League of

Nations dream was killed, Roosevelt took up the cause as the Democratic party's vice-presidential nominee in 1920. In 1921, paralysis struck him down. Refusing to give in, he plunged into a years-long program of physical therapy. His courageous struggle against illness won him a national sympathy he could never have received as the handsome Hyde Park aristocrat.

Soon he was back in the political scene, nominating Al Smith at both the 1924 and 1928 national Democratic conventions and catching warm attention by his gallantry and eloquence. While Al Smith was going down to smashing defeat in 1928, Roosevelt was being elected governor of the state of New York. In this post he worked hard to make certain that the immense hydro-electric potential of the St. Lawrence River would be saved for public control, not handed over to private enterprise. When the depression struck he established the first state relief agency in the United States, tried to help workers and farmers, and provided jobs for the unemployed in state conservation projects. Soon a corps of academic experts, headed by Columbia University's Raymond Moley, gathered around Roosevelt to feed him ideas in preparation for the bid for the White House in 1932 that everyone expected. Confident, aggressive, with more than twenty years of experience in public life behind him, Franklin Roosevelt was ready for action when he finally assumed the presidential power he had long dreamed of.

What outlook would he bring to the presidency? No one really knew. Many thought him just a pleasant and smiling man, little equipped for the rigorous demands of the White House. In truth, his campaign speeches consisted mainly of bland generalities. He was certainly no radical. He had a strong sense of community, distrusted unchecked individualism, and warmly sympathized with suffering people. But he nourished no brooding rancor against the American system. He was a progressive Democrat, not a Marxian socialist. He wanted to save capitalism, not supplant it. His principal characteristic was a readi-

The jaunty F.D.R., here photographed in a typical pose, lifted the nation's morale just by his manner and ebullient optimism. Brilliant as a crisis manager, always ready to experiment, he was both loved and hated by multitudes.
Wide World Photos

ness to experiment. The theme that ran through Roosevelt's devotions was the belief that God wished men to be happy on earth, an outlook that made the goals of social reform more important to him than dogmas about laissez-faire and limited government. A product of the Progressive Era, he was a humanitarian pragmatist more interested in action than in orthodox principles. He became a president more excited by the prospect of ending child labor than worried about whether doing so violated hallowed maxims of government.

The banking crisis

Roosevelt's first challenge as president was to reopen the banks. This was a vital matter. The awesome spectacle of closed bank doors in every city in the land made people feel that in some catastrophic sense the American economy had come full stop. The president moved boldly. Assuming the mantle of commander-in-chief in time of war, he made use of First World War statutes, still on the books, to declare a bank holiday and halt all trading in gold so as to end its panic-induced flight from the country. Within a few days the president had bills before Congress empowering him to investigate the banks, allow sound ones to reopen, give loans from the Reconstruction Finance Corporation to those in need of help, and liquidate any that were hopelessly bankrupt. Congress quickly passed the legislation, Roosevelt made his first radio "fireside chat" to explain what was being done, and on Monday, March 13, banks reopened in the twelve Federal Reserve bank cities. Confidence rebounded. Deposits poured back into the banks, people talked excitedly of the decisiveness of their new national leader, and business immediately picked up. In the following two years, Treasury investigators weeded out thousands of unsound banks and thoroughly rehabilitated the national financial system.

The Hundred Days

Roosevelt now pushed forward on a broad front in the famous "Hundred Days," a three-month period in the spring of 1933 when Congress enacted the most sweeping program of reform legislation in American history. Fifteen major laws went on the books dealing with banking, the gold standard, relief, mortgages, hydroelectric power, and regional planning, the stock market, and national planning in industry and agriculture. A wartime outlook, inherited from the experiences of the First World War, linked these separate programs together. In the years 1917 and 1918, laissez-faire had been cast aside and the federal government had taken over direct supervision of the national economy. The result had been an amazing outburst of planned productivity that fascinated business leaders, public administra-

tors, and intellectuals. From then on, the dream of national planning never left the American consciousness. Academics like John Dewey looked eagerly to the building of a centralized state that would utilize planning to achieve both prosperity and social justice.

Wartime psychology creates a national pulling together. People tend to look on the country as a great team under centralized direction in which each member cooperates with every other for the good of the whole. So, now, the leaders of the First New Deal regarded national planning and social cooperation as their guiding ideals. Capital and labor should cease their strife and work together; businessmen should set aside competition and cooperate; government and business should form a mutually helpful partnership. The national economy had reached its full growth, so it was believed—was not glut and overproduction the chief problem?—and therefore the task now was that of managing a completed national estate. Ways must be found to fit production to the limited market. Everyone should be accorded his fair share of the profits available, which meant letting businessmen agree among themselves on what prices they would charge and how much each would produce.

Planning in business

Out of this atmosphere emerged the chief creation of the Hundred Days—the National Recovery Administration (NRA). Businessmen were allowed to make fair-trade codes concerning prices and production, and such agreements were to have the force of law and be exempt from the antitrust laws. In return, businessmen were to permit their laborers to organize unions and bargain collectively concerning wages and hours. For unorganized workers, employers had to agree to pay minimum wages and stay within a ceiling of maximum working hours per week. Linked to the NRA was a $3.3 billion public works spending program to be administered by a Public Works Administration.

Under the leadership of a flamboyant administrator, General Hugh Johnson, the NRA plunged into furious activity. Within weeks some 2.5 million employers had signed a standard code governing labor relations, so that 16 million workers came under the program's protection. By shortening hours and spreading the work, the NRA produced jobs for about 2 million additional workers. Some 700 detailed codes relating to particular industries were then devised, primarily by the businessmen involved. Enthusiasm soared, and a "boomlet" spurted up in the economy.

Very shortly, however, the NRA was in trouble. Progressives in Congress complained bitterly about the lifting of the antitrust laws, for they feared the emergence of massive government-sponsored monopolies. Since Johnson believed that businessmen should govern themselves, what eventuated was not central planning but a jumble of codes, each of which governed only one industry without regard to the entire economy. Since it was primarily big businessmen who influenced the writing of the codes, the result was that small businessmen felt that they were being squeezed out. They insisted that they could not pay the wages or charge the prices that big business had inserted in the codes. And what about enforcement? The truculent Johnson bristled when asked this question and barked that violators would "get a sock right on the nose." But in fact they were not prosecuted. Johnson relied only on social compulsion to force businessmen to comply with the codes, and this proved grievously insufficient. Soon the offices of the NRA in Washington were in bedlam, and protest was swelling up across the country. Faced with severe problems, businessmen by the thousands simply ignored the codes. In May 1935, when the Supreme Court unanimously ruled the NRA unconstitutional, the national reaction was one of relief.

The NRA, however, did achieve important things in its brief, meteoric rise and fall. The idea of legally specified maximum hours and minimum wages was established on a national basis, so that later, in the Fair Labor Standards Act, it became firm policy. The problem of child labor was practically eliminated, especially in the textile industries, where child labor had been used more than in any other industry. Section 7A of the NRA law made it illegal for employers to hinder the formation of labor unions, and rendered collective bargaining legal. This had a tremendous influence on the labor movement. Furthermore, for all its failings, the NRA broke the mood of economic fatalism. It accustomed people to think in terms of vigorous federal activity in regulating and stimulating the economy.

Planning in agriculture

As the NRA was being launched, the government also moved unprecedentedly into agricultural planning. The root problem was enormous overproduction, causing a disastrous agricultural depression. Farm income stood at one-third what it had been in 1929; farm prices had dropped in that period more than fifty percent; and the ratio of prices received by farmers to the prices they paid for manufactured goods (the parity ratio) had sunk from 89 in 1929 to 55 in 1932 (on a scale using the parity ratio of 1910–1914 as base 100). Mobs of farmers halted foreclosures, sometimes physically abusing judges who issued foreclosure orders.

Shortly after his inauguration, Roosevelt sent to Congress a proposal calling for strong federal control of agriculture. The producers of seven basic commodities (wheat, cotton, corn, hogs, rice, tobacco, milk and dairy products) would receive federal payments if they cut their acreage or reduced production. Congressmen Joseph Martin, a New England Republican, cried out that "We are on our way to Moscow," but the bill boomed through Congress. The task of the Agricultural Adjustment Administration, so created, was to raise farm income to 100 percent of parity by restricting production. At the same time, the law provided means of ending the farm mortgage crisis by the refinancing of mortgages through federal land banks. In 1935, a program of compulsory crop controls, voted on in each instance by the farmers concerned, was established. The sum result was that during Roosevelt's first term, gross farm income rose by 50 percent.

Unhappily, the benefits of this program did not extend to the poorest of all in the countryside—millions of sharecroppers and tenants. Landowners often expelled their sharecroppers when they reduced the acreage to qualify for benefit payments. The Farm Bureau, voice of the larger landholders, grew in power while sharecroppers, "tractored off" the land, joined the exodus of farm unemployed that swelled further the population of the hard-hit cities.

Regional planning

Another great project of the Hundred Days was to take up the long-standing issue of public power. Senator Norris and President Roosevelt toured the Tennessee Valley, paying close attention to the Muscle Shoals facility. However, Roosevelt had far more in mind than the public production and distribution of electrical power. A devoted conservationist, he wanted to use the immense physical powers of the Tennessee River to revitalize the whole 40,000 square miles of impoverished countryside that drained into that stream. In the Tennessee Valley the nation could be shown how regional planning and expert conservation could create a new design for living. The American people, Roosevelt believed, lived too much in congested cities. The countryside must be made attractive again, so that young men would stay and till the soil rather than leave for factory jobs.

Within a month of his inauguration, Roosevelt asked Congress to establish the Tennessee Valley Authority (TVA), "a corporation clothed with the power of government but possessed of the flexibility and initiative of a private enterprise." It was charged to provide a yardstick by which to judge private power rates produced elsewhere. In addition, it was to halt floods, provide river naviga-

tion, produce fertilizers, revive fisheries, provide recreational resources, reforest denuded watersheds, and lead in bringing about regional planning. In the next nine years the TVA laid the basis for a wholesale revitalization of the entire Tennessee Valley watershed by the building of twenty dams and the improvement of five already in existence. By 1960, its total investment in this and other diverse physical facilities had reached two billion dollars—and the Tennessee Valley had become a model that drew public leaders from all over the world to see how the harnessing of a basic resource could be turned to such dramatically fruitful results.

Relief programs

On taking office Roosevelt moved swiftly to help the fifteen million people who were out of work. His first effort was combined with his favorite cause—conservation of national resources. Huge numbers of young men were wandering aimlessly in city streets: why not put them to healthful and socially productive labors in the forests? Within days of the inauguration, Congress responded to Roosevelt's request by establishing the Civilian Conservation Corps (CCC). By June 1933 more than 300,000 young men were at work in more than a thousand forest camps. In the ensuing years, a total of 2.5 million CCC men planted trees, built reservoirs, erected flood control works, constructed bridges and fire towers, cleared out plant diseases, scoured beaches, and rebuilt campgrounds. Continued in existence until well into the 1940s, the CCC was easily the most popular of the New Deal agencies.

Roosevelt also got Congress to establish a Federal Emergency Relief Administration (FERA), with some $500 million to grant to the states for relief programs. "It is socialism," cried Robert Luce of Massachusetts, but the problem was too urgent for such philosophizing, and the bill was rushed through. With Harry L. Hopkins as its chief—he had run Roosevelt's relief program in New York State—the FERA urged that work relief, instead of the dole, be utilized by the states. "I have seen thousands of these defeated, discouraged, hopeless men and women," said Hopkins, "cringing and fawning as they come to ask for public aid. It is a spectacle of national degeneration." When many states lagged in their relief efforts, however, Roosevelt approved the establishment of a Civil Works Administration (CWA), under Harry Hopkins, to provide work relief directly by the federal government. By the end of 1933, so vigorously did Hopkins move, four million men were employed by the CWA. Hundreds of thousands of projects were launched: building or improving country roads, employing teachers in impoverished schools,

erecting school houses, developing playgrounds, and constructing hundreds of airports, parks, waterways, and swimming pools.

Financial and monetary reforms

The Banking Act of 1933 completely separated commercial from investment banking, thus making it impossible for unscrupulous bankers any longer to use the funds entrusted to their care by depositors for speculation in the stock market. Furthermore, the Federal Deposit Insurance Corporation (FDIC) was established to insure bank deposits up to $5,000. In order to aid the millions of homeowners who faced imminent loss of their

The Tennessee Valley Authority

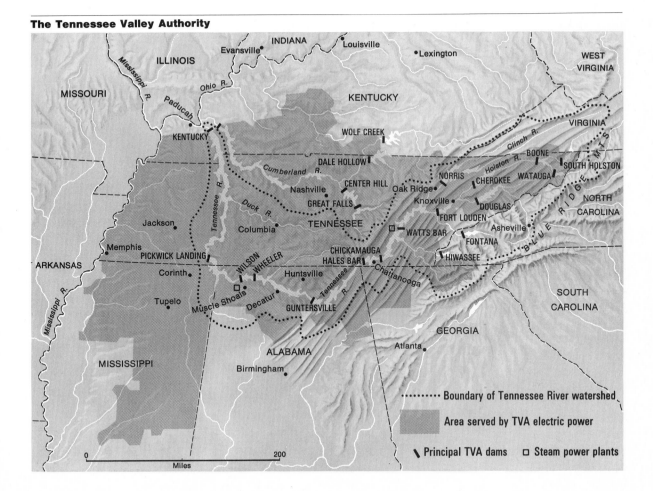

.... Boundary of Tennessee River watershed

░░░ Area served by TVA electric power

▌ Principal TVA dams   □ Steam power plants

dwellings, a Home Owners Loan Corporation (HOLC) was established that eventually refinanced twenty percent of all the mortgaged homes in the United States. On the day it began operation, distraught homeowners formed lines many blocks long, waiting for HOLC doors to open. Meanwhile, a Truth-in-Securities Act (followed by the Securities Exchange Act of 1934) put the stock exchanges under federal supervision for the first time. A Securities and Exchange Commission was created to ensure that investors were given truthful information concerning stocks and bonds and that fraudulent activities would be checked.

Roosevelt was under enormous congressional pressure from rural Democrats of Populist leanings to inflate the currency. This, they insisted, would raise the price level, aid farmers, and stimulate business activity. Responding positively, Roosevelt secured legislation taking the

Men working on a Civil Works Administration project in Central Park Zoo, New York City. This kind of program, vastly expanded later in the WPA, put millions of men to work in socially valuable projects.
Photoworld, Inc.

nation off the gold standard (so that it could directly control the volume of its own currency, rather than being subject to international influences in this regard); removed all gold from public commerce (save that used for industrial, medical, and jewelry purposes); and put it in Fort Knox to serve as a national trust for backing the currency. Then he set the price at which the American government would buy gold at a level higher than its price on the world market (eventually, $35 an ounce), so that gold began flooding into the country. By 1940, Fort Knox held more than three times as much gold as in early 1934, and the nation's money supply soared dramatically. It was this monetary expansion, observes W. Elliot Brownlee, "that seems to have been the fundamental factor in the nation's economic recovery." The country was moving strongly out of the depression considerably before the heavy wartime spending induced by World War II made its impact.

Roosevelt was not by philosophy a deficit-spending president, but this expansion in the money supply gave him what he needed: the funds to begin a wide array of social welfare programs adopted for their intrinsic importance, and not because they poured federal money into the economy and aided recovery, though that was their effect. The president talked continually of keeping the budget balanced and meant what he said, raising taxes and cutting back on spending whenever he thought he could, but the total effect was to create deficit spending. Indeed, after 1937, when he discovered the economy slumping again in a sharp recession after he cut back sharply on federal spending, he resumed his spending programs with a vengeance, accepting the need thereafter for such actions.

Roosevelt in power

By late 1934 the foundations of the First New Deal were shifting. The spirit of wartime unity evaporated rapidly. National income spurted by more than twenty percent in 1934, and people once again indulged in the luxury of carping and criticizing. The president himself dominated the whole scene. He had been in the White House almost two years, and the country had grown used to the spectacle of an endlessly active president who was not only charming and courageous, but also tough, crafty, forceful, and dominant. Hampered by his paralyzed legs, he spent most of his working days in the Oval Room of the White Houses's west wing where he regularly welcomed crowds of reporters for press conferences. His manifest enjoyment of the repartee and his gaiety and quick grasp of complex situations captivated journalists. The result was an enormous increase in the volume of news out of Washington, D.C. Roosevelt may have been hated by many big newspaper publishers, but he dominated their front pages.

It was inevitable that such an overpowering personality, who freely used the potentially vast constitutional powers of the presidency, would create an adoring following of people who loved him deeply and an implacable opposition of those who hated him. Was he a destroyer of capitalism, as many trumpeted? an advance agent of Moscow, a Jewish communist—as whispering campaigns depicted him to be? The business community has never liked Democratic presidents. The bankers were the first to recoil from the administration, for congressional committees subjected them to withering public exposures as they investigated the nation's sick financial system, and Roosevelt in his speeches seemed to give such vendettas his blessing. The president, said one wealthy man, "is a communist of the worst degree. . . . Who but a communist would dare persecute Mr. Morgan and Mr. Mellon?" Then, as the shock waves of the NRA's encouragement to labor and its policies on higher wages and shorter hours began to be felt, the dismay spread wider. Medium-sized and small businessmen were directly hit by these measures in ways the big corporations never were, for they were hard squeezed to pay higher wages, as well as personally outraged by suddenly defiant workmen. Soon all their frustrations and anger crystallized in hatred of Roosevelt.

The New Deal's style

Much of the hostility toward the New Deal, however, was a revulsion against the whole style of Roosevelt's administration. Just as conservatives had recoiled against the raffish dress and intellectualism of Thomas Jefferson, so now they did the same when they looked at Franklin Roosevelt's Washington. Everywhere there were college professors in shirtsleeves, gay parties, and brash young men of power. In an important sense every great period of reform in American history has been produced by a fresh generation arriving in positions of leadership. So it was with the New Deal. To established political leaders, the spectacle was appalling. Equally upsetting was the rather playful way in which the New Dealers tossed about ideas and refused to be humbled by traditional concepts. Frank Kent, a conservative political analyst, called the New Deal nothing but "third rate college professors and unsuccessful welfare workers." How in the world did such men ever come into such power?

In 1937 the sociologists Robert S. Lynd and Helen Lynd found the business leaders of Muncie, Indiana, convinced that "there has been 'an insane man in the White House,' with 'our best mindless thinkers advising him.' . . . 'We businessmen here aren't just a bunch of Tories,' commented a local banker heatedly, 'but we're scared to death that a lot of reckless political wild men will take everything away from us. We believe in change and know it's going on. We believe in looking ahead, but we don't believe in trying to do it all at once. It'll take two or three hundred years to get the perfect state. Change is slow and big changes won't come in our lifetime, so meanwhile we intend to go ahead and not worry too much about what these changes will be or ought to be. . . .

"We've no faith in Roosevelt—his angel wings and smiling words cover up a worse political machine than Hoover ever had. He isn't honest—he talks one way and acts another. He has no courage—or rather courage at the wrong time. He isn't fit to be President and can't hold a candle to Hoover. . . . Sure we need planning. But these bright boys that jam Washington don't know their stuff. Who's a big enough man to plan? We businessmen are afraid of bureaucrats and planners. I've walked through Washington offices, and I never saw so much loafing in a business office. . . . [The] common stockholders [of a business] control [their managers] and if they don't make money, they're turned out. But government employees don't have to make money. . . . By what God-given right do these fellows in Washington think they can do a job so big? It's the very immensity of national planning that makes it impossible. . . . You can't make the world all planned and soft. The strongest and best survive—that's the law of nature after all—always has been and always will be." (*Middletown in Transition* [1937].)

Across the country, however, millions of ordinary citizens admired and loved the president. "He has been all but crowned by the people," observed the veteran editor William Allen White after the midterm election of 1934. "There has been no such popular endorsement since the days of Thomas Jefferson and Andrew Jackson." In that balloting, historic precedent was shattered. The administration's party almost always loses seats in such elections, but instead a flood of voters pushed the massive Democratic majorities even higher. The House witnessed the election of 322 Democrats and only 103 Republicans.

Foundations begin shifting

A historic shifting of the nation's political balance was under way. In 1934, Roosevelt began reaping a harvest of solid Democratic votes based on his actual leadership. Most of all, his votes came from the nation's cities, where urban masses, much in need of a vigorous federal government, continued the strong movement into the Democratic column they had begun in the 1920s. Between 1932 and 1936, Samuel Lubbell wrote in *The Future of American Politics* (1965), "the Democratic plurality in [the twelve largest cities] leaped 80 percent, the biggest change in any single election." Furthermore, the South, which had turned away from the Catholic Al Smith, returned en masse to the Democratic ranks. No president had ever done so much as Roosevelt for that long-depressed region.

The Democrats, in short, were becoming once more the nation's majority party. Black America swung almost in a body away from the Republicans and moved to the Democrats. As tens of thousands of Afro-Americans moved out of the South (where they were effectively denied the vote), they joined the northern city masses and voted loyally for Roosevelt. Not only did he provide jobs for the city unemployed, but his administration—notably through the voices of Eleanor Roosevelt, Interior Secretary Harold Ickes, and relief administrator Harry Hopkins—also spread the notion that its sympathies were warmly problack. How substantial were the benefits that black America received from the New Deal is a matter in question, but the overwhelming majority of black voters clearly felt that the president was doing everything he could for them in a difficult situation.

So a partly familiar, partly new coalition now made up the Democratic majority. It provided the lasting, monolithic foundation for the fifth, or New Deal, party system, which endured in its basic features at least until the election of Richard Nixon in 1968, a span of more than thirty years. As in the second and third party systems in the nineteenth century, the city masses made up the core of the Democratic party, which meant consumers, laborers, and especially the Catholics, Jews, and "new immigrants" from eastern and southern Europe. There were also the intellectuals, women, the mass of the unemployed, and the South, joined by midwestern farmers—who had long voted Republican—and even some segments of the business community who chafed against

"Wall Street rule." With this revived strength in the northern masses, Roosevelt was eventually free to develop a social democratic regime oriented to the needs of the poor and unfortunate. The welfare state was the logical product of this new political balance of power. Almost never again were the Republicans to win a majority of both houses of Congress (the exception being in 1952 with the first election of Dwight Eisenhower).

Ideas begin shifting

Despite his popularity, Roosevelt knew at the beginning of 1935 that things were not so well as the nation seemed to think. The surge of the Hundred Days was over, and the economy was settling on a new plateau. Panic had disappeared, the downward spiral was halted, but there were still ten million people unemployed, and the number seemed fixed. No one was more baffled than the president himself. He kept a steady stream of businessmen, academics, and government leaders coming to the White House to talk about the state of the nation and to search for new ideas.

As the government drifted along, radical prophets spoke up. Governor Floyd Olson, Farmer-Labor governor of Minnesota, said he hoped "the present system of government goes right down to hell." He went on to demand that the "key industries of the United States [be] taken over by the government." The Reverend Charles E. Coughlin of Detroit, Michigan, built a huge radio audience out of attacks against capitalism and the "timid" New Deal. Bankers, he said, were the origin of the world's sufferings. "Modern capitalism," Coughlin insisted, "is not worth saving." He recommended that the government nationalize the banking system and take over the production of power, light, oil, and natural gas.

Most spectacular of all the new radicals was Huey Long, a senator from Louisiana. As governor of that state, he had inaugurated sweeping reforms while at the same time erecting an un-challenged dictatorship unparalleled in American history. Soon he launched a "Share-Our-Wealth" program, which called for government confiscation of all incomes above a certain level in order to redistribute the money to less affluent people. Thousands of local clubs were founded to spread his message, and millions received his mailed literature. Huge crowds fought to see him when he spoke in northern cities.

It was clear that the First New Deal could never survive this bubbling radicalism. Everywhere one listened, whether it was to Long's Share-Our Wealth campaign, or to the Marxian revolutionary talk that filled Greenwich Village cocktail parties and burst into a wide array of cultural outlets sponsored by the Communist party, anticapitalist oratory abounded. With one-fifth of the work force still unemployed and likely to remain so, it was no longer enough to preach wartime unity and centralized planning.

The Brandeisians and the spenders

In the Supreme Court building Justice Louis D. Brandeis, now an intense old man with flaring white hair, nodded his head vigorously when such things were said to him. From the beginning of the New Deal, a key group of Roosevelt's lieutenants had gathered about this fascinating old battler from the days of Wilsonian liberalism. He roundly criticized the First New Deal because it accepted and warmly cooperated with the largest business corporations. It was foolish, he believed, to say that the answer was the building of an equally large federal government, for this went beyond human capacities. The real solution, Brandeis said, lay in whittling everything down to human size; in returning control to local regions, rather than lodging it in a Washington bureau. Only then could democracy and individualism revive once more.

Brandeis's chief disciple was Felix Frankfurter, professor at Harvard Law School, who, as a close confidant of Roosevelt, had placed bright young men in major posts throughout the Roosevelt administration. As a group they had been restive under the First New Deal, condemning its fostering of monopoly and its friendliness to businessmen. Now, led by Frankfurter, they urged Roosevelt to recognize that business-government cooperation had failed, that centralized planning was a snare and a delusion, and that the real need was to take up once more the traditional Democratic assault on corporations and banks.

Frankfurter, however, believed that it was not sufficient just to renew the assault on wealth and power; that, by itself, would not bring prosperity. In search of ideas, he went to Britain in 1934, where he spent a year in close conversation with intellectuals and government leaders. He returned with the solution proposed by the English economist John Maynard Keynes—huge government spending. The essential idea was to place purchasing power directly in the hands of the consumers so that they could begin buying once more. This would require heavy spending through unemployment relief, public works construction, agricultural subsidies, and other such programs. It would also require bringing the banking system under full public control in order to make effective control of money policy possible.

Roosevelt distrusted the idea, for he was conservative in his fiscal beliefs and talked always of the need for a balanced budget. But the spending proposal dinned constantly in his ears, coming from American sources as well as from Britain. A group of American economists—chief among them Paul Douglas of Chicago—had been saying for some time that governmental spending would create lasting recovery, and the idea was spreading to such leaders of the banking community as Marriner S. Eccles of Salt Lake City, who urged it on congressional committees. Always the pragmatist in search of solutions, Roosevelt finally agreed, and in January 1935 he startled Congress with a request for the largest single appropriation of funds in American history—five billion dollars for a program of work relief.

The Works Progress Administration

Thus was born the Works Progress Administration (WPA), whose goal was the employment of 3.5 million workers. The "social conscience of the New Deal," it signified once and for all that the federal government cared for the suffering millions as well as for the organized interests. Through 1941 it spent more than eleven billion dollars on some 250,000 small-scale construction projects, building or improving more than 2,500 hospitals, 5,900 school buildings, 1,000 air fields, and nearly 13,000 playgrounds. At the same time, the WPA also employed actors, writers, and artists. Its Federal Theatre Project supported drama companies throughout the nation. The Federal Writers' Project created about 1,000 publications and sponsored myriads of local historical research projects. Artists were employed by the Federal Art Project to launch teaching programs in painting and crafts and to decorate the interiors of hundreds of public buildings with murals and other art works, "some of it good," observed Roosevelt, "some of it not so good, but all of it native, human, eager, and alive. . . ." Young people were aided by the National Youth Administration, giving part-time jobs to 600,000 students in college, and 1.5 million in high schools.

Of enormous cultural impact in the nation—perhaps more sweeping in its effects than any other piece of New Deal legislation—was the creation of the Rural Electrification Administration (REA). Designed to spread electrical lines into the countryside, it transformed country life. "Every city 'white way,'" wrote one observer, "ends abruptly at the city limits. Beyond lies darkness." Nine out of ten farms had no electricity. Farm wives labored in almost medieval conditions while their city counterparts enjoyed the delight of illumination and electric appliances such as refrigerators, washing machines, and vacuum cleaners. The REA enabled farmers' cooperatives to borrow millions of dollars from the government to dispel the darkness. Four out of ten American farms had acquired electricity by 1941, and by 1950, nine out of ten.

The Supreme Court destroys the First New Deal

Meanwhile, the basic laws of the First New Deal had been making their way upward through the courts, undergoing challenges of their constitutionality. Everyone knew that the legislation was threatened by the makeup of the Supreme Court, which contained four justices who were hard-core conservatives implacably opposed to a vigorous federal government. In 1935, the New Dealers' fears were borne out. In a unanimous decision the Court threw out the NRA as unconstitutional in the case of *The Schechter Poultry Company* v. *The United States* on the ground that Congress had wrongfully delegated its lawmaking powers to an executive commission. In addition, the justices ruled that the Schechter Poultry Company was engaged wholly in local trade, while the federal government's authority extended only to the control of interstate trade. The fulcrum of the First New Deal was broken.

In subsequent cases the Court laid waste to the rest of the First New Deal. It threw out the AAA on the ground that agriculture was a local activity and not interstate commerce, and it nullified the Coal Conservation Act which had established federal regulation of coal production, on the same ground. In sum, the Court (usually by majorities of five to four) effectively denied Congress any powers over farming, mining, manufacturing, and labor relations. Then, in *Morehead* v. *New York* (1936), it even held that states could not regulate hours, wages, and labor conditions on the principle that the Fourteenth Amendment guaranteed freedom of contract.

The second Hundred Days

In June 1935 President Roosevelt suddenly responded by sending an avalanche of major new bills to Congress, thus launching the second Hundred Days. Five pieces of legislation, he insisted, had to be passed before the legislators could leave the Capitol for their summer vacations: a social security bill, legislation on banking, a law to aid labor unions, a public utility holding company measure, and a soak-the-rich income tax law. In the succeeding months Congress bent wearily to its work and hammered through every one of Roosevelt's proposals, comprising perhaps the most far-reaching reform program it had ever enacted.

The social security bill, like most of these "must" proposals, had been gestating for some time. Frances Perkins, secretary of labor, had led a cabinet committee that worked up a social insurance system drawing directly on British practice. In Congress its leading advocate was Senator Robert F. Wagner of New York, spokesman of the poverty-stricken urban masses. A conservative senator condemned the proposal as one that "would take all the romance out of life. We might as well take a child from the nursery, give him a nurse, and protect him from every experience that life affords." But when Roosevelt swung behind the bill, it rolled through to passage by large majorities in both houses. Based on a system of taxes levied against both employers and employees, the Social Security Act established old-age pensions, unemployment insurance, and a system of federal grants to the states to support, on a matching basis, programs of relief to dependent mothers and children, the crippled, and the blind.

Called "wild-eyed socialism" by its critics, the social security program was actually a surprisingly conservative system. By taxing both employers and workers to build up the necessary central fund, it withdrew huge sums of money from circulation, while at the same time putting a heavy fiscal burden on laboring people, who were least able to pay. Farm laborers and domestic workers were given no coverage, though they needed it desperately. No aid was provided to those unemployed by reason of sickness, the most common cause of joblessness. On the other hand, it opened wide a historic door toward the social welfare state. Roosevelt and his followers knew that the programs would be expanded in later years, as it has steadily to the present. Embodying the fundamental notion that the com-

munity should aid its helpless, it fathered the enormous program of relief at the local level that has now become one of the major activities of the long-indifferent state governments. For all its faults, it was a key symbol of the new social conscience of the American governmental system.

New economic legislation

The strictly economic legislation of the Second New Deal was founded not—as in the First New Deal—on telling businessmen what to do, but on what not to do. This essentially Brandeisian idea was embodied best in the bill concerning gigantic utility holding companies. Long condemned by the public, utility holding companies—sometimes piled on top of one another to the seventh level—had seemed the expression *par excellence* of inefficient, exploitive "bigness." The goal was to restore a kind of economic democracy to the utility industry by breaking it up into much smaller and more realistic units. The electric power companies seemed like great octopuses that exploited vast regions for the sole purpose of paying stock dividends on functionless holding companies. They had corrupted state legislatures in order to escape meaningful regulation, and now they poured millions of dollars into a frantic effort to stave off federal action. But Congress was aroused, and the bill went through, empowering the Securities and Exchange Commission to break up any holding company, beyond the first level, that was not in the public interest. Within three years, practically all the great utility empires were dissolved.

The banking legislation of the second Hundred Days completed the process begun under Woodrow Wilson. His Federal Reserve System had given public authorities only limited influence on the actual supply of money that bankers issued, leaving the day-to-day operations of the Federal Reserve System in the hands of private bankers. It was time, critics said, to end this arrangement. The national government must finally take over, as a sovereign function, the crucial decision as to the size of the money supply. Then, and only then, would it be able to manage the nation's economy and prevent the onset of depressions. If Roosevelt was radical at all, it was in his inherited Democratic distrust of bankers, and he warmly supported a bill drawn up by Marriner Eccles that would transfer control over the money market from the bankers in Wall Street to the federal government in Washington, D.C. This led to a loud and turbulent struggle, for bankers had long regarded control of the money market as theirs practically by divine right. Ogden Mills cried out that the bill would "throw us back five hundred years." But Franklin Roosevelt was not to be denied. The bill as passed created a new Federal Reserve Board in Washington that had all necessary powers to put the money supply under public control. To ensure his victory, Roosevelt then appointed Eccles first chairman of the Board.

The delighted Roosevelt, excited and confident now that his new program was rolling so well, then began pushing for a soak-the-rich tax bill. The Democrats gave the bill a standing ovation in the House when they heard it read, but an outcry of rage welled up from the rich and from the business community (Roosevelt had also proposed heavy taxes on corporation income). William Randolph Hearst called the proposal "essentially Communism." The struggle over the bill went on all summer, with the result that the final measure was fairly mild. Corporations were taxed very little; inheritances were left alone; but rates on high incomes were raised. Ironically, however, the "wealth tax" bill did little in the direction of redistributing wealth. By the end of the 1930s upper-income groups were still commanding the same share of the national income that they had received before the depression.

The rise of labor

Perhaps the most significant law of the second Hundred Days was the one creating the National Labor Relations Board. The federal government had always taken either a hostile or a relatively passive attitude toward organized labor. In the 1920s, the national administration had been pro-employer, and the courts had actively hindered labor's efforts by issuing hundreds of injunctions. Capital was powerful; entire industries—such as those of automobiles and steel—were unorganized; and the union movement declined steadily, dropping from a membership of more than 5 million in 1920 to less than 4 million by 1930. The depression was an even more disastrous blow, for as the average weekly wage dropped from twenty-five to seventeen dollars and unemployment mounted, workers shied away from the unions in fear of losing their jobs. By 1933, fewer than 2.5 million workers belonged to a labor union.

Under President Hoover, labor won a major victory in the passage of the Norris-La Guardia Act in 1930. After forty years of struggle, this law finally gave labor recognition of its right to organized existence: court injunctions could no longer be used to prevent the formation of a union. Then under Roosevelt came Section 7A of the NRA law, which required that employers allow their workers to join a union. The result was a massive awakening of long-dormant unions. Organizers rushed about proclaiming the news. John L. Lewis of the United Mine Workers told miners that the president wanted them to organize. From 60,000 members in 1932, the United Mine Workers soared to 300,000 in a few months. While other older unions grew in similarly explosive fashion, the mass production industries were invaded by unions practically for the first time. Not since the days of Terence Powderly and the Knights of Labor had unskilled and semiskilled workers been enrolled in such numbers.

Employers, however, fought back, by refusing outright in some cases to admit the principle of unionization into their NRA codes or by forming hundreds of company unions to keep out the AFL and other independent unions. NRA officials stood back, often allowing an employer to bargain with a small union and ignore another that represented the majority of his workers. Nowhere was there any effective agency with power

In 1937, Chicago police beat strikers, revealing the attitude of local governments around the nation to the growing union movement. Years of such near-warfare rocked the nation well into the 1950s.
Chicago Historical Society

to enforce the right of unionization. Labor soon began striking to get what it was entitled to be granted. In the automobile industry, on the docks, and especially in the textile industry, hundreds of thousands of people refused to work, leading to violent conflict between strikers and strike-breakers. As usual, local authorities were eager to call out National Guard troops to help employers. Industry, growing confident through reviving prosperity, launched a determined campaign to roll back the labor movement.

NLRB created

The fact was that the federal government was still holding back. Roosevelt had never been more than mildly friendly to organized labor. Section 7A had only *allowed* organization; it had not actually forced employers to accept the unions. For some time Senator Wagner had been proposing that the federal government move in directly to assist labor in its organizing efforts,

but his bill languished in Congress, bereft of the president's support. But in 1935, when Roosevelt switched directions and launched the Second New Deal, everything changed. The creation of the National Labor Relations Board (NLRB), through enactment of the Wagner bill, inaugurated a historic change in the relation between Washington and the labor movement. The government now moved vigorously to help labor in its unequal struggle with capital, to ensure not only the right of organization but also the right to bargain collectively in fair and equitable conditions. The NLRB was given power to order employers to bargain with the unions that represented the majority of their workers, after elections that it supervised. It could also prevent employers from utilizing "unfair" practices designed to coerce employees away from the union, force them to join a company union, or discriminate against complaining workers. No similar prohibition of unfair practices was established against the unions.

Labor was now free to push ahead on all fronts. Within a few months John L. Lewis led a movement that split the AFL wide apart, forming the Congress of Industrial Organizations (CIO). Its goal was to build industrial unions in mass production factories where, as yet, the craft-oriented AFL had made little impression. Early in 1937 Lewis won a stunning victory in the steel industry when United States Steel recognized the CIO union as the employees' bargaining agent. Like other large employers, "Big Steel" was ready to accept the new labor-management relationship that the Wagner Act called for. The auto industries resisted, leading to massive labor outbreaks in 1936 and 1937, but in time labor won. By 1938, the CIO contained 3.7 million members. Meanwhile the AFL was stung to new activity, amazed at the CIO's astonishing successes. It, too, began organizing unskilled workers in large numbers, so that by 1938 it had 3.4 million members.

John L. Lewis, head of the United Mine Workers and president of the CIO, put labor's case in September 1937: "Five of the corporations in the steel industry elected to resist collective bargaining and undertook to destroy the steel-workers' union. These companies filled their plants with industrial spies, assembled depots of guns and gas bombs, established barricades, controlled their communities with armed thugs, leased the police power of cities, and mobilized the military power of a state to guard them against the intrusion of collective bargaining within their plants.

"During this strike eighteen steel workers were either shot to death or had their brains clubbed out by police, or armed thugs in the pay of the steel companies. . . . The murder of these unarmed men has never been publicly rebuked by any authoritative officer of the State or Federal government. . . .

"Labor does not seek industrial strife. It wants peace, but a peace with justice. . . . The United States Chamber of Commerce, the National Association of Manufacturers, and similar groups . . . are encouraging a systematic organization of vigi-

lante groups to fight unionization under the sham pretext of local interests. They equip these vigilantes with tin hats, wooden clubs, gas masks, and lethal weapons and train them in the arts of brutality and oppression . . . financed under the shabby pretext that the C.I.O. movement is communistic. . . . Do those who have hatched this foolish cry of communism in the C.I.O. fear the increased influence of labor in our democracy? Do they fear its influence will be cast on the side of shorter hours, a better system of distributed employment, better homes for the underprivileged, social security for the aged, a fairer distribution of the national income? . . . Labor has suffered just as our farm population has suffered from a viciously unequal distribution of the national income. In the exploitation of both classes of workers has been the source of panic and depression. . . ." (John L. Lewis, *Vital Speeches* [1937].)

Black Americans and organized labor

These events produced epochal changes for blacks in the organized labor movement. In general, most AFL unions had excluded black Americans for decades, the United Mine Workers and the Longshoremen being major exceptions. They were essentially industrial unions, though affiliated with the AFL, and this type of union has always tended to be more egalitarian and racially tolerant, since it enrolls all workers in a given industry rather than just a select skilled group. In 1917–19, white workers, who hated blacks not only on racial grounds but as competitors for unskilled jobs and as strikebreakers, had set off huge race riots in Chicago and other midwestern cities. The great migration of blacks out of the South to work in the North, during the First World War, had doubled the black population in Chicago from 50,000 to over 100,000. In 1910, blacks made up only six percent of the work force in that city; in 1920, thirty-two percent. They often regarded the white employers as their natural allies, not the racist unions.

An extraordinary black leader, A. Philip Randolph, brought the first all-black union with a national base into existence in 1925: the Brotherhood of Sleeping Car Porters. By "all the gods of sanity and sense," he said, "Brotherhood men are a crucial challenge to the nordic creed of the white race's superiority. For only white men are supposed to organize for power, for justice and freedom." Against enormous odds, both within and outside of the black community, he built it into a powerful and nationally-recognized body by the late 1930s.

Then came John L. Lewis's Congress of Industrial Organizations, which was of great aid to the cause of black laboring men. It was not completely successful in suppressing racial segregation and discrimination within its ranks, especially in the South, but it nonetheless made an incalculable contribution to opening the ranks of organized labor to black men and women. A militantly progressive organization on the whole range of social issues, the CIO espoused racial justice as one of its central concerns. Then when the acute labor shortages of World War II occurred, CIO affiliates capitalized on this need to gain major concessions for black workers from employers. In 1939, median income among non-white workers was 41 percent that of whites; by 1950, it was 60 percent, wages for black persons during this period having risen much faster than those for whites. Indeed, during the years 1942–45, the most important income changes occurred for black Americans since the Civil War.

The election of 1936

When Roosevelt began touring the country for his 1936 electoral campaign, enormous crowds turned out to cheer him. He had, in truth, impressive accomplishments to report to the nation. Six million jobs had been created since his inauguration, and national income was fifty percent higher in 1936 than it had been in 1933. The output of factories had almost doubled. Corporations had lost two billion dollars in 1933, but in 1936 they made a profit of five billion dollars. In

the same time period, the net income of farm operators grew almost four times. There were still eight million people unemployed, but prosperity seemed clearly on the way. Gone were the long soup lines, the apple sellers, the pathetic "Hooverville" shanty towns outside every city.

The result was one of the most sweeping victories in American history. Only Maine and Vermont cast their electoral votes for Alfred M. Landon, the Republican nominee. Republicans in Congress were reduced to practically a corporal's guard. Landon received 16.7 million popular votes, but an avalanche of 27.7 million votes went to Franklin Roosevelt. Without question, the American people wished to see the Second New Deal continued.

Second-term disasters

Roosevelt began his second term with a speech clearly signifying that he intended to push ahead on the social welfare front. "I see one-third of a nation ill-housed, ill-clad, ill-nourished," he said. But what he actually began with was a proposal that the Supreme Court be reorganized. The nation was stunned. Nothing had been said of this in the previous campaign; no congressional leaders had been warned; and Roosevelt's argument for his proposal was obviously a deception. The court system was clogged with work, he said, because the judges were too old to cope with the work load. His only desire, he told Congress, was to make the system more efficient. He asked for power to appoint up to six more Supreme Court justices (and forty-five justices in lower federal courts) to supplement the work of those judges who refused to retire at age seventy. Everyone knew this was not his real motive. The fact was that the Supreme Court was dominated by a conservative majority, and he wished to give it a New Deal coloration. Even liberal Democrats in Congress rose up in rebellion, and public opinion swung strongly in their support. Perhaps no leading American politician had made so disastrous a miscalculation since 1854 when Stephen A. Douglas wrote the Kansas-Nebraska Act.

Roosevelt clung doggedly to his request, frittering away months of Congress's time and further alienating the public. Meanwhile, Justice Owen Roberts swung over to the liberal side and began providing a majority vote in favor of New Deal laws. When the National Labor Relations Act was ruled constitutional, it was clear that Roosevelt would have no further resistance from the Court. In effect, that body had made a historic decision: it was going to give up its decades-long struggle to impose its own economic beliefs on Congress and the president. Thereafter, until it took up the issue of civil rights in the mid-1950s, the Supreme Court consciously turned away from the activist philosophy that had motivated it from the days of Grover Cleveland.

The Second New Deal revives

In April 1938, after a severe economic slump in 1937 caused by a drastic cutback in federal spending, Roosevelt began moving decisively again. He returned to the spending philosophy, securing from Congress close to four billion dollars for public works and huge increases for the WPA. At the same time, he gave warm support to an antitrust campaign begun by Thurman Arnold in the attorney general's office. Whereas Theodore Roosevelt had employed five attorneys in his antitrust campaign, Arnold had almost two hundred searching out business wrongdoing. The chief objective was to break the "managed price" stranglehold that great corporations seemed to exert on the economy; that is, instead of lowering prices when demand dropped off, they kept prices high and simply reduced production. This, it was said, was a fundamental reason why the national economy could not recover from the depression. If big corporations were broken up, as the Brandeisians urged, then they could no longer ignore the market, but in response to competition would be forced to lower prices and keep production high, thus creating jobs.

Meanwhile, Congress enacted the last major reforms of the New Deal. It had refused to allow Roosevelt to "pack" the Supreme Court, but it approved a number of procedural changes that greatly expedited the Court's work. The Bituminous Coal Act reviewed the centralized planning arrangements that the industry had had under the NRA, making it in effect a public utility. The Farm Security Administration was established to help migratory farm workers secure better housing and assist tenant farmers in buying their land. By 1946 it had helped 870,000 farm families rehabilitate their properties and lent funds to 41,000 farmers for the purchase of their land. The United States Housing Authority was created to begin the task—which is still a long way from being completed—of cleaning up the slums. By loans to public housing agencies, it brought more than 160,000 new housing units for low-income families into existence by 1941.

AAA revived

The New Deal's farm program was revived in February 1938 by the passage of a new AAA statute. Based on the principle of soil conservation, it authorized the secretary of agriculture to decide how much acreage should be planted each year in the staple crops so as to meet the nation's needs while providing compulsory quotas that stringently limited production (after approval in each case by a vote of two-thirds of the farmers producing the crop). The principle of parity price supports thus became permanently established as national policy. Production, however, continued to rise mountainously despite acreage limitations. To ease the problem, the Agriculture Department was empowered to purchase and store surpluses to be distributed to the needy, sold abroad, or released in time of shortage. The huge supplies of food thus stored were of inestimable value during the Second World War.

In May 1938 Roosevelt secured his last major reform from Congress, the Fair Labor Standards Act. Designed to aid those who did not have the protection of a union, it sought to make permanent the wages and hours standards that had been established in the now-defunct NRA codes. Southerners vigorously opposed the measure, for it would establish a nationwide floor under wages, and southern leaders insisted their only hope was to maintain a wage differential by which labor would be cheaper in their region than in other parts of the country. The law, as passed, established a forty cents per hour minimum wage (no southern textile worker had reached that level yet) and a forty-hour maximum work week (time-and-a-half to be paid for overtime). It also made illegal the use of child labor in any industry that shipped across state lines, a provision that finally won the long fight in this cause. Some thirteen million workers were protected by the law, many of them receiving immediate pay raises. Many exemptions at first weakened the program, but in succeeding years they were eliminated.

The New Deal in retrospect

What balance sheet may be struck concerning the New Deal? It did not solve unemployment completely. Primarily because Roosevelt could never bring himself to spend enough, there were still six million people out of work in 1941. Only the Second World War swept away this deep scar, though it now appears that recovery was building enough momentum eventually to have achieved this goal without this aid. Was it a revolution, as conservatives then and later alleged? Liberal historians like Arthur Schlesinger, Jr., have been saying so for decades, though calling it a desirable revolution that moved America toward social justice. In recent years dissent has risen. Columbia historian William E. Leuchtenburg, after an extensive examination highlighting the New Deal's limitations as well as its accomplishments, carefully concludes that it was only a "halfway revolution." Its accomplishments never matched its rhetoric. Massive aid went to business in the form of loans, to organized labor in the form of

an active NLRB, and to millions of commercial farmers in the form of price supports. But the assistance given to the really helpless was tentative and incomplete. Tenant farmers and sharecroppers lost heavily under the AAA program and belatedly received only the limited assistance of the Farm Security Administration, which aided but a small proportion of those in need. Millions of farm and domestic workers were excluded from the social security program, and the WPA employed only a minority of the jobless. Much of the New Deal depended on the state governments, which were notoriously lackadaisical. The noble ideals of the federal laws relied on the readiness of local county supervisors and welfare departments to implement them, and too often their hostility negated the legislation. "Unemployables" were specifically left to state governments to aid—the sick, crippled, old, and helpless—and in many regions this meant no aid at all.

Historians like Barton Bernstein and Howard Zinn have maintained that the failure of the New Deal went deeper than Leuchtenburg indicated. They believe that it sprang from a fundamental ideological conservatism. Roosevelt could have created, they insist, a truly humanitarian socialist system that could have equalized incomes and eliminated economic exploitation. But being a liberal and not a radical, he was subservient to capital. Instead of nationalizing the banking system, he refurbished it and handed it back to private bankers. Instead of really taxing wealth, Roosevelt talked loudly and then allowed Congress to leave the rich alone. While he could have nationalized the great steel and automobile industries, he simply gave them enormous loans from the RFC. Wherever one looked, say these historians, the New Deal was interested solely in the middle class and its economic security, not in the poor and helpless. Even in its loud antitrust campaign, little was accomplished. To those who had much—the skilled laborers, wealthy farmers, powerful bankers, industrialists—much was given; to those who had little—tenant farmers, blacks, unorganized workers, slum dwellers, the poor, the "unemployable"—very little was given. At the end of the New Deal decade, the rich had just as much money as before, and "the one-third ill-fed and ill-housed, and the two-thirds alienated and desperate," writes Paul Conkin, "still existed." If anything, the business classes were more secure than ever—more free of the threat of socialization, more confident that when in trouble the government would help them out.

Difficulties and achievements

The historian Otis L. Graham, Jr., has judiciously remarked that these criticisms ignore too much. They give the New Deal too little credit for the enormous changes it wrought and the opponents of the New Deal too little credit for the powerful weapons that they could and did use against change of any kind. Consider the barriers to major reforms: the Supreme Court; the southern oligarchy that dominated congressional committees; the great difficulty in getting major legislation through Congress, with its antiquated and obstructive rules, even in the best of times; the fundamental conservatism of the American population; the massive anti-Roosevelt campaigns carried on constantly by most of the newspapers; the fact that almost no one knew enough to be more than confused about most of the great problems of the day, leading to constant division in counsel, disarray, and bickering within the ranks; the deep-rooted individualism of the whole society; the fact that the poor were then, and almost always have been, so weak, so uneducated, so unskilled in the ways of politics, as to be politically inert and apathetic. "The full context," Graham writes, "has not been supplied." Considered against the full range of the ideas and possibilities current in America in the 1930s, "the New Dealers appear well toward the innovative and daring end of the spectrum, with stronger democratic instincts and a stronger commitment to racial justice and a more steady humanitarianism than all but a scant minority of their contem-

poraries." Considering the obstacles against which they worked, the remarkable fact lies not in the New Dealers' failures but in their achievements.

So warned and chastened, contemporary historians now draw up the balance sheet of the New Deal with less unquestioning enthusiasm than in the past, but at the same time with a consciousness that it constitutes a crucially important transformation in American history. The federal government experienced a vast expansion in its authority over the nation's economy, and since then it has used that authority vigorously. The list is almost endless: farm prices supported, and farm plantings centrally planned; the money supply made a federal responsibility; stock exchanges regulated; bank deposits insured and banking practices supervised; the relations between employers and employees made a matter of public concern, and closely controlled; whole regions provided electrical power by government facilities; utility systems given public direction; and economic recessions subject to ever-vigilant federal attention with increased public spending lying in wait to prevent the onset of another depression. For the mass of the population, New Deal legislation established a basic minimum standard of living. Minimum wage and maximum hour limitations; old-age and disability pensions; unemployment insurance; monthly payments to mothers living alone who had dependent children; direct assistance to the blind and crippled; insured bank deposits; higher wages through organized unions; and the sense of security that comes with the knowledge that in times of disaster the federal government will step in to provide essential aid.

The New Deal and the Democratic party

A major theme throughout this book has been to describe the deep and continuing contrasts of the two major political parties. In the previous chapter, for example, we observed that the 1920s display patterns we have come to expect of Republican eras. In similar fashion, the 1930s demonstrate how persistent is the style and outlook of the Democratic party. Franklin Roosevelt was a strong executive in the Democratic tradition. Power, as in Grover Cleveland's day, seemed to gravitate from Capitol Hill down to the White House, sitting a mile away on Pennsylvania Avenue. Henry Clay used to complain at the top of his voice about the "autocracy" of Andrew Jackson, and Republican senators did the same when they looked at Roosevelt and observed the stream of messages and directives that issued forth daily from the oval office. Here was no "government by boards of trustees"; no group of oligarchs in which the chief executive was little more than a chairman. Herbert Hoover's mail could be handled by one man; it took fifty to handle Franklin Roosevelt's. The president became the center of every consideration; he took care to see that his advisers were never able to gang up on him; he consulted anyone and everyone; and he always made the ultimate decisions himself. From the time he made his first radio address, most Americans came to regard him with a sense of close, trusting reliance.

Behind him appeared that constellation of ethno-cultural outgroups that we have come to associate with Democratic regimes. Once Roosevelt became president, Catholics began to be appointed to judicial posts in extraordinary numbers, and so, too, were Jews. A predominantly WASP national government became multi-ethnic and pluralistic. Black Americans received little, due to the power of southern committee chairmen in Congress, but they clearly believed that the Roosevelt administration was doing as much for them as it could in a difficult situation, and they swung massively into the Democratic column. At the same time, Roosevelt made Italians, Poles, and other ethnic groups feel that he cared. It became a standing joke that no Protestant minister was ever photographed in connection with a New Deal program unless he was flanked by a Catholic priest and a Jewish rabbi. In the same way, the New Deal attracted America's intellectuals, as had the Democrats in the days of Andrew Jackson, Grover Cleveland, and Woodrow Wilson. New Deal opponents were horrified at all the professors in Washington. Artists, writers, poets, economists, political scientists, most working journalists—these and the rest of the intellectual community admired and approved of Roosevelt, his programs, and his entourage.

The New Deal's moralism

The Republicans had always been concerned with personal morals, but the Roosevelt administration sang no hymns and chased no "wicked" influences. It was a consciously hard-headed, skeptical, pragmatic administration that concentrated on jobs, power, and political brokerage between contending groups. The progressive of Woodrow Wilson's day had tried to preach to the urban masses, seeking to teach them proper ways of dress, drinking, and life style. But Roosevelt's New Dealers were willing to take the ethnic minorities on their own terms; to work with them, rather than preach to them. The president was not much concerned about Tammany Hall and the political bosses who flourished in the ethnic politics of the cities. He was content to receive their votes in return for providing services to the urban populations.

While Roosevelt was not concerned with private morals, he was, however, very much a social moralist in the style of his Democratic predecessors. He was aroused by social evils rather than by private ones. His co-workers were similarly indifferent to traditional moral issues—the picture of a jaunty Harry Hopkins going off regularly to bet at the races is typical—but they, too, were inspired by Roosevelt's genuine concern for the downtrodden and his anger at exploitation. It was this powerful inner tendency that drove Roosevelt inevitably leftward. Everything in his political tradition made him move in humanitarian directions. The New Deal, moreover, was a consumer-oriented administration in the classic

Democratic mold, especially after the demise of the First New Deal. It inveighed against bankers, taking control of the money supply out of their hands. Internationalist in its economics (as we shall see in the next chapter), the New Deal steadily lowered the tariff through reciprocal trade agreements with other nations. The "enemy" was the business community, which, for its part, seemed to regard every New Deal reform as nothing short of communism.

Indeed, as has so often been true of the Democrats since the days of the Alien and Sedition acts, Roosevelt's New Dealers constantly faced the charge that they were un-American, disloyal, and lackeys of an alien subversive power. They, on their side, reciprocated by chattering endlessly of economic conspiracies in the Republican camp, thus duplicating the obsessions that had similarly agitated their own forebears. Democrats painted a picture of greedy industrialists and financiers who schemed behind closed doors and spread instructions via their network of country clubs and opulent cocktail parties. Roosevelt himself believed that the slump of 1938 was caused by an organized strike of capital against the New Deal. Monopoly was the traditional Democratic bugbear, and sooner or later Roosevelt would launch an antitrust campaign, as in fact he did in 1938. Competition, said the Brandeisians—echoing Adam Smith and his Democratic disciples through the generations—must be relied on to discipline the businessman. Thus, economic "littleness" must take the place of "bigness."

What was new in the New Deal?

Was the New Deal, then, simply a replay of the past? In a major sense, it was not. Wilson and Cleveland had been little interested in giving direct aid to the poor and the helpless, yet it was precisely the social conscience of the New Deal that gave it its distinctive cast. The urbanism of Roosevelt's regime created a social democratic government more in the style of such European governments as those in Scandinavia and the British Isles. Earlier Democrats had condemned strong government as necessarily an instrument that would be corrupted by the wealthy and powerful so that it served their interests and exploited the poor. Roosevelt's generation of Democrats had clearly come to the conviction that strong government, at least in Democratic hands, was precisely what was needed in order to achieve the goal that Thomas Jefferson had so long ago set forth—a society of economic and social justice. Unless the nation made its government powerful, the wealthy would be too free to exploit everyone else.

Later generations of reformers have wondered whether the New Dealers' faith was properly placed. Massive bureaucracies seem to get out of control and exert their authority inflexibly. Strong government agencies appear, in time, to be easily taken over by the very interests they were designed to control. Huge corporations continue to flourish, receiving bountiful government aid, while the poor still live in stinking slums and have to go to court to force bureaucracies to provide legally ordained assistance. Most of all, the experiences of the Vietnam War and the Watergate crisis have led to grave and searching doubts about the wisdom of creating a strong presidency. How could this have occurred? it is asked. Were the New Dealers genuinely concerned with aiding the poor, or were they really concerned with helping the already wealthy and powerful? Were they willfully blind to the dangerous potentialities of a strong presidency?

The ambiguity is irresolvable, for all large political ideas contain contradictory tendencies. A strong president could well become a tribune of the people, protecting them from the powerful, but he could also become a danger to democratic government. Social philosophers have long observed it to be the human condition that what is apparently good has within it the seeds of its own corruption; that each principle, as each person, possesses in the same instant both destructive and creative potentialities that are often at work at the same time. There is no reason, therefore, to doubt the sincerity of the Franklin Roosevelts and the Harry Hopkinses; and there is also no reason why their ideas should have been uniquely free from human paradox. As observed earlier in this book in relation to the accomplishments of the Jacksonian era, each reformist ideology, when it becomes an established and traditional pattern, presents features that later reformers find repellent. If the laissez-faire dreams of the Jacksonians eventually turned sour, creating not only economic freedom for the adventurous but also gargantuan corporations that gravely worried following generations, it is hardly surprising that in our own time the strong government mystique of the New Dealers is beginning to attract searching doubts and create a wondering question: where does reform go from here?

Bibliography

Three books that were especially valuable to me in writing this chapter: The best balanced and most thoughtful book now available on the New Deal is William E. Leuchtenburg, *Franklin D. Roosevelt and the New Deal, 1932–1940** (1963); helpful, too, is Arthur M. Schlesinger, Jr.'s *The Age of Roosevelt,** three vols. (1957–1960), although the author's friendliness toward Roosevelt must be borne in mind; the president's complex character is best discovered in Frank Freidel's biography *Franklin D. Roosevelt,* four vols. (1952–1973), which is as yet uncompleted.

How have historians looked at the topic?

How revolutionary was the New Deal? In the 1930s Franklin D. Roosevelt's enemies considered it a veritable earthquake, and for many years criticism of the New Deal came basically from the angry right. E. E. Robinson, *The Roosevelt Leadership* (1955) and former brains-truster Raymond Moley, *After Seven Years* (1939) are representative accounts of erudite conservative criticism. More recently Milton Friedman has kept the old con-

servative position alive and vigorous in his *Capitalism and Freedom* (1962).

Conservative hostility to the New Deal generated a liberal defense of it. Arthur Schlesinger, Jr.'s volumes, cited above, offer the most comprehensive explication of this view. By the mid-1960s, the attack-defense syndrome seemed fruitless and exhausting. William E. Leuchtenburg's excellent *Franklin D. Roosevelt and the New Deal, 1932–1940**, mentioned above, described both the mental fuzziness of the Roosevelt regime and its energy and imagination. The New Deal, Leuchtenburg said, was a "halfway revolution."

The past few years have witnessed New Left historians questioning even Leuchtenburg's judicious evaluation. Mercilessly probing New Deal failures, scholars such as Barton Bernstein in "The New Deal: Conservative Achievements of Liberal Reform," in a volume he edited, *Towards a New Past** (1968), and Paul Conkin in *The New Deal** (1967) stress Roosevelt and company's political and intellectual ineptitude and find little of lasting value in their "chaos of experimentation." The most cogent reply to New Left criticism is in Otis L. Graham, Jr.'s provocative essay "New Deal Historiography: Retrospect and Prospect," found in the same author's edited volume, *The New Deal: The Critical Issues** (1971).

While historians debate the merits and deficiencies of the New Deal, research continues on the man who stamped his initials on the era. James M. Burns balances praise and criticism in his scholarly, two-volume biography *Roosevelt: The Lion and the Fox** (1956) and *Roosevelt: The Soldier of Freedom, 1940–1945** (1970). Journalist William S. White's *Majesty and Mischief: A Mixed Tribute to F.D.R.* (1961) is generally stimulating while Richard Hofstadter drew a penetrating sketch of Franklin Roosevelt in *The American Political Tradition** (1948).

The New Dealers' primary concern was in healing a sick economy. The effectiveness of the NRA is assessed in Sidney Fine's important monograph *The Automobile under the Blue Eagle*

(1963) while Ellis Hawley's wider study *The New Deal and the Problem of Monopoly* (1966) expertly probes the relationship between the business community and the federal government. Harmon Zeigler offers a penetrating analysis of a discontented group in *The Politics of Small Business* (1961). Grant McConnell's *The Decline of Agrarian Democracy** (1969) depicts the frustration of the liberals in the AAA while the plight of poorer farmers is described in David E. Conrad's *The Forgotten Farmers* (1966). Thomas K. McGraw draws from fresh sources in his *TVA and the Power Fight, 1933–1939* (1972).

New Deal efforts in one area are judged weak and ineffectual in Michael Parrish's *Securities Regulation and the New Deal* (1970). Monetary policy is analyzed in Milton Friedman and Anna Schwartz's *A Monetary History of the United States, 1867–1960* (1963). Robert Lekachman's *The Age of Keynes** (1966) is immensely valuable. Elliot W. Brownlee's *Dynamics of Ascent: A History of the American Economy* (1974) contains a provocative interpretation of the New Deal years in which the economic setting of institutional reforms is stressed.

The years in which labor came into its own are described in Irving Bernstein's masterful study *The Turbulent Years: A History of the American Worker, 1933–1941* (1970). A case study of volatile labor tensions is Sidney Fine's *Sit-Down: The General Motors Strike of 1936–1937* (1969).

The conservative nature of the bill that for many symbolized the welfare state is revealed in *Social Security: Perspectives for Reform* (1968) by Joseph A. Pechman et al. The internal history of the agency is brilliantly delineated in Charles McKinley and Robert W. Frase's *Launching Social Security: A Capture-and-Record Account, 1935–1937* (1970). The most imaginative relief programs devised by the New Deal are studied in Paul Conkin's *Tomorrow a New World* (1958) and William F. McDonald's *Federal Relief Administration and the Arts* (1969).

For an intriguing view of the differences between progressives and New Dealers, see Otis L. Graham, Jr.'s *Encore for Reform** (1967).

* Available in paperback.

CHAPTER 32

America and the Second World War

TIME LINE

1928	Hoover announces Good Neighbor policy to Latin America
1930	Clark Memorandum terminates Roosevelt Corollary
1932	America announces nonrecognition policy regarding Japanese conquest of Manchuria
1933	Adolf Hitler becomes chancellor of Germany
1934	Roosevelt ends protectorate status of Cuba; Tydings-McDuffie Act; Trade Agreements Act
1935–1937	Neutrality Acts
1936	At Inter-America Conference in Buenos Aires, Roosevelt declares end to idea of military intervention by the United States in Latin American affairs
1937	Japan invades China
1938	Pogrom against Jews in Germany; Hitler takes Austria; Munich Agreement
1939	Second World War begins; America repeals arms embargo
1940	Roosevelt makes destroyers-for-bases deal with British
1941	Lend-Lease Act; Battle of Britain; Hitler invades Greece, Yugoslavia, North Africa, and Russia; Roosevelt freezes Japanese funds in America when Japan takes over southern Indochina; Roosevelt and Winston Churchill meet off Newfoundland, issue "Atlantic Charter"; attack on Pearl Harbor; America enters Second World War
1942	Year of disaster for Allies; American government removes Japanese-Americans and Japanese nationals from West Coast to internment camps; Arcadia Conference forms United Nations against Axis powers; Coral Sea and Midway Island naval victories halt Japanese advance; American forces invade North Africa
1943	Tide turns against Axis; Russian victory at Stalingrad begins German retreat; Roosevelt and Churchill meet at Casablanca, announce that unconditional surrender to be demanded of Hitler at war's end; Allied forces invade Sicily and Italy; island-hopping campaigns in Pacific
1944	Bombing of Japan begins; Allies invade France; Russians sweep westward into central Europe; Battle of the Bulge; Philippines retaken
1945	Yalta Conference; Harry S. Truman becomes thirty-third president of the United States on death of Roosevelt; Potsdam Conference; atom bombs dropped on Japan; end of Second World War

THE Great Depression ended the precarious peace of the 1920s. When the world economy collapsed, spreading misery and dismay among millions, explosive forces were set off that eventually erupted in the Second World War. The Western democracies responded to the sufferings of the depression by setting up programs for internal reform; but Germany, Italy and Japan reacted by launching campaigns of external aggression. The American people wanted to be free of foreign wars, and Congress passed a series of neutrality acts to ensure noninvolvement. The horrors perpetrated by Adolf Hitler, however, steadily eroded isolationism. Both President Roosevelt and the American people finally concluded that they could not survive as a nation if Hitler gained dominance over Europe. Desperate to ward off this prospect by preventing Great Britain's defeat, Roosevelt led the nation away from neutrality to armed belligerency in order to give Britain every aid short of war. At the same time, on the other side of the world he sought by strong nonmilitary actions to halt Japan's aggression. On December 7, 1941, Japan responded by attacking the American fleet at Pearl Harbor; Germany and Italy honored their treaty commitments to Japan by declaring war on the United States; and America was catapulted into the Second World War.

The isolationist temper

The isolationism that dominated United States foreign policy in the 1920s and 1930s was a traditional habit of mind to Americans. The First World War deepened the separatist outlook. There was a giant recoil from intervention after the Versailles Peace Conference, when Americans became disillusioned. For a brief time the country had followed the soaring dream of Wilsonian idealism, but soon it all seemed a bloody and foolish mistake. In the 1930s scholars examining the origins of the First World War alleged that the nation had been dragged into the conflict by munitions makers and British propaganda.

Furthermore, war had lost its glamor. The boyish enthusiasm with which men joined the colors in 1917 had been followed by the shock of trench warfare, machine guns, enormous artillery barrages, and poison gas. Gallant cavalry charges had disappeared; brutish clanking tanks took their place. War became another name for mass butchery. The invention of the movie camera brought home to millions of Americans, sitting appalled in darkened cinema theaters in the 1930s, the horror of warfare.

For generations, a peace movement had existed in the United States. It had always been relatively ineffectual; but now it grew to heights of unexampled influence. One wing argued strongly for the United States to prevent war by acting on the principle of collective security; that is, by banding together with other nations, to present a common front to the aggressors. Other groups, more radical—like the War Resisters' League—preached isolationism. The League of Nations, they said, was weak, thus proving collective security delusory; militarism was taking over everywhere; and the only answer was to refuse to build armaments and follow totally noninterventionist policies.

Americans were puzzled and angry that European nations resisted paying off the loans they had secured from them during the First World War. (The debts totaled some ten billion dollars, which with interest over a projected repayment period of more than sixty years came to twenty-two billion dollars.) Calvin Coolidge put the matter simply: "They hired the money, didn't they?" Europeans pointed to their own millions of dead and countered that America should write off the money owed as its contribution to the common cause. Besides, there was little possibility that the European countries could pay the debts off anyway, since their economies were shattered by the war. The question embittered all transatlantic relations and contributed much strength to the isolationist movement. President Hoover proposed a year-long moratorium on war debt payments in 1931 in an attempt to ease the international financial crisis, and from then on the European nations defaulted.

Withdrawal from Latin America

In the 1920s it was clear that the United States no longer had to fear European aggression in Latin America. In consequence, new policies began to be instituted. Secretary of State Charles Evans Hughes withdrew American troops from the Dominican Republic in 1924. In 1928 the newly elected president, Herbert Hoover, made a tour of Latin America before his inauguration to spread the idea that America intended to be a "good neighbor." In 1930 the Clark Memorandum, named for a State Department official, terminated the Roosevelt Corollary to the Monroe Doctrine, in which Theodore Roosevelt had declared it America's right to ensure that western hemisphere nations paid their debts. The marines were withdrawn from Haiti in 1932, and from Nicaragua in 1933.

Franklin Roosevelt carried on and strengthened the Good Neighbor policy. In late 1933 he sent Cordell Hull to the Montevideo Conference to support the declaration that no nation had the right to intervene in the affairs of any other. In May 1934 he signed a new treaty with Cuba that finally ended the protectorate status maintained since the Spanish-American War. In 1936 the American government formally gave up its legal right to intervene in Panamanian affairs, and the president traveled to the Inter-American conference in Buenos Aires to declare to a cheering assemblage that the United States had given up entirely the principle of military intervention in Latin America. Henceforth the American government was committed to the principle that any differences between western hemisphere nations were to be settled by joint consultation, not by an overbearing Colossus of the North alone.

The Far East in crisis

When the depression hit Japan, sending the export of raw silk from Japan tumbling by half and putting millions out of work, military expansionists began pointing to Manchuria. They urged that Manchuria become a settling place for surplus Japanese, as well as a vital economic underpinning for Japan's sagging commerce. In late 1931 Japanese army officers in Manchuria took the matter in their own hands. Declaring that their soldiers had been attacked by the Chinese, they launched a campaign to take all of Manchuria by force.

The officer's action openly violated the Open Door policy and the Nine-Power Pact. European nations held back while the United States urged action. In January 1932 the United States declared that it would not recognize any Japanese action that impaired "the sovereignty, the independence, or the territorial and administrative integrity of the Republic of China or . . . the open door policy." This refusal of recognition was designed to bring pressure on the Japanese by making American financiers reluctant to invest in affairs regarded as illegal by American authorities, but all it did was to stir up Japanese anger. United States' nonrecognition also excited national and international derision, for the American government clearly had no intention of backing up its policy with force. Unchecked thereafter by any power, the Japanese were free to do as they wished in China.

Lowering tariffs

With the Democrats back in power, a concerted drive to lower the tariff was soon begun. This was a particularly urgent need because the high rates of the Smoot-Hawley Tariff, created under Hoover, had set off a chain reaction of international reprisals. Indeed, a rage of economic nationalism was sweeping the world. Each country was seeking to keep out all foreign competition, erecting walled-off trade areas within their boundaries open only to their own producers. Democrats preached the message of low tariffs and open international trade. This approach, they insisted, would help bring the world out of its economic slump, for it would open up markets and lower prices for consumers. Roosevelt's secretary of state, the venerable Tennesseean Cordell Hull, had come to believe during Woodrow Wilson's administration that lowering tariffs would not only spread prosperity but would also aid in buttressing world peace by reducing economic rivalries.

In June 1934, at Hull's urging, Roosevelt secured passage of the Trade Agreements Act, a law of historic importance. Reformers had insisted for decades that true tariff reform could never be achieved if tariff legislation was always subject to the back-scratching and bargaining of congressional sessions. Only if the president—presumably an impartial judge—was given authority to raise or lower tariffs as appeared most helpful to the whole nation would an intelligent trade policy finally be established. The president was now empowered to negotiate bilateral agreements with other nations (i.e., agreements between the United States and one other country) by which he could raise or lower the tariff up to fifty percent if he could get similar adjustments in foreign tariffs. Once made, such reductions would be applied to everyone under the most-favored-nation principle, thus achieving major tariff changes across the board. This led to negotiations that produced agreements with twenty-one nations by 1940, affecting two-thirds of all American foreign commerce.

The rise of fascism

Five weeks before Franklin Roosevelt became president, Adolf Hitler was installed as chancellor of Germany. Nothing like Hitler had appeared on the stage of Western civilization for centuries. Benito Mussolini had become dictator of Italy in 1926 behind the banner of his *Partito Nazionale Fascista,* thus showing the way for the later rise to dictatorial power of the Germany leader. (The term *fascist* has become generally applicable to both Italian fascism and German Nazism, the latter being the abbreviation used for Hitler's movement, the *Nationalsozialistische Deutsche Arbeiterpartei.*) But Mussolini's political murders and foreign aggressions fade in comparison to the monstrous genocides practiced by Adolf Hitler. His pathological drives—an earlier age would have called them demonic—plunged the world into a succession of horrors so overwhelming that a war of global dimensions was inevitable.

Fascism is often described as the philosophy that is created by driving the beliefs of the political right wing to their extreme, while communism—from this point of view—is produced if the beliefs of the left are similarly pushed to their extreme. An alternative theory is that fascism and communism, both being founded on authoritarian methods, are two sides of the same coin. Certainly it is true that, in the same years that Hitler was killing millions of Jews, Joseph Stalin was killing millions of Russian peasants who resisted his agricultural collectivization. The butcheries associated with both the communist and the fascist movements give each an appalling historical burden to bear.

There are, however, fundamental differences between fascism and communism. Fascism glorifies the "race" of a given nation, preaching its superiority to other peoples. Communism glorifies a particular class—the proletariat—around the world, asserting its superiority to the middle and upper classes. There is a tribalism about fascism that draws its strength from deep, instinctual emotions, primarily those of fear and hatred of other peoples. It was not, therefore, an exportable political philosophy. How could non-Germans accept Hitler's principle that the German people were superior to all others? Communism, by contrast, proclaimed the universal equality of a particular stratum of all peoples, and could therefore flow across national boundaries and have movements within practically every country. While fascism described mankind as a pyramid the apex of which was composed of the superior race, communism described mankind as comprising some form of horizontal entity in which everyone was to be equal to everyone else. Whereas fascism enjoyed flamboyant uniforms and badges of rank that clearly demarcated superiors from inferiors, communism adopted plain dress and styled everyone "comrade." Hitler screamed to his huge, cheering audiences that the essential reality of the German race lay not only in its blood but also in its spirit. The communists taught that material forces, not spiritual ones, were history's driving influences. Anticapitalistic, they insisted that all productive property must be owned by the state and that no person should be directly employed by any other person. Fascism, on the other hand, emphasized the rights and prerogatives of private property so long as all power resided ultimately in the state. It has often been called a dictatorship of the upper class, whereas communism has been described as a dictatorship of the lower class.

Fascism glorifies irrationalism

There was a brutal kind of tribal masculinity about fascism. Mussolini enjoyed being photographed either bare-chested or stomping around in a huge, beetling steel helmet. Hitler adored the spectacle of marching masses of jack-booted troops. Physical strength was idolized, and every problem was to be solved by the mailed fist. Political enemies were simply killed. Any talk about mental difficulties was squelched, for it hinted at weakness. Sigmund Freud was hounded out of Vienna, and psychiatrists fled by the thousands. Indeed, it was distinctly unsafe to be an intellectual of any sort in a fascist country, for dissent and thoughtful reflection were not allowed. Fascism lauded instinct and distrusted rational intelligence. Absolutely crucial was obedience. Hitler would rise to towering rages at any suspicion of resistance. Throughout his life he had a pathological aversion to anyone telling him what to do. He was the führer (leader), who had

Adolf Hitler and top Nazi officials attend a 1934 party rally. Ahead of him were brutal aggressions against many nations, millions of deaths, and world catastrophe.
Wide World Photos

always to be complete master of every situation and circumstance. Whatever he said was, by definition, absolutely correct.

Hitler had many hatreds. He hated political democracy, for it guaranteed argument and criticism, making dictatorship impossible. Marxian communism was another enemy; of all political philosophies it seemed to him the most dangerous. But most of all, he hated the Jews. "Wherever I went," he wrote of his early life, "I began to see Jews, and the more I saw, the more sharply they became distinguished in my eyes from the rest of humanity. . . . Later I often grew sick to the stomach from the smell of these [people]." They seemed foul and corrupt to him. He had wild sexual fantasies about Jews, writing of the "nightmare vision of the seduction of hundreds of thousands of girls by repulsive, crooked-legged Jew bastards." It was a hatred that he fed on to the moment of his death. His last testament, written in 1945 just before he reportedly committed suicide, contained a final accusation that the Jews had caused the Second World War and were destroying Germany.

Hitler's regime, from its beginning, tried literally to eliminate the Jewish people of Europe. As soon as he became chancellor, Hitler dismissed all Jews from government service, the universities, and the professions. Two years later, all marriages between Jews and people of "German blood" were prohibited, and all civil rights were taken away from the Jewish population. In the fall of 1938 there was an indiscriminate killing of Jews, during which SS (Schutzstaffel) troops, Hitler's secret police, confiscated most Jewish property. Survivors were thrust into ghettos. When World War II began, they were systematically murdered, usually in huge death camps. In the part of Europe occupied by the German army, six million out of a prewar total population of 8.3 million Jews were put to death or died from starvation and disease. The genocide was so barbaric that, like the size of the universe or the dimensions of an atom, the mind loses its power to comprehend the phenomenon. No other single crime challenges the monstrosity of this violation of humanity even in a century as filled with horrors as our own.

Hitler's aggressions begin

Hitler announced in 1935 that henceforth he intended to ignore the restrictions of the Treaty of Versailles. He began building up a military system and in 1936 moved boldly to remilitarize the Rhineland—the district between the Rhine River and France—despite the warnings of his general staff that if the other powers resisted his action, Germany was unprepared to respond successfully. The French, however, limited themselves to written protests, and the British government, which had long considered the Versailles treaty unfair to Germany, acquiesced.

Convinced that Britain and France would never oppose him, the Germany dictator began looking toward his ultimate objective—conquest of east-

ern Europe and Russia. As he declared in his last political statement, the conquest of Russia was "the be-all and end-all of nazism." His secret plan was to destroy the Russian government, clear away or enslave half the inhabitants of the country, confiscate their land, and make the fruitful Ukrainian region a vast territory of German settlement. First he had to acquire Austria, then Czechoslovakia, and finally Poland. In March 1938 his troops took over Austria, which he incorporated into the German nation. Six months later at Munich he got the British and French to agree that the large section of western Czechoslovakia, the *Sudetenland,* containing German-speaking peoples, should be granted to Germany. After another six months passed, in March 1939, he occupied the rest of Czechoslovakia.

Now Hitler worked assiduously to neutralize the Russians before moving into Poland. In secret talks, he agreed to divide Poland with the Russians and to let them take over the Baltic nations of Estonia, Latvia, and Lithuania. The world was therefore astonished to learn in August 1939 that the former enemies had signed a nonaggression pact. This event destroyed any hopes for continued growth that might have been entertained by Communist parties in the Western democracies, for all radicals save the inner core of dedicated Communist party members were revolted by the pact with Hitler. Within days, Hitler's armies were flooding across Poland's borders, and the desperate British and French declared war, having given up the belief that the German leader could be contained by anything other than force. The Second World War had begun.

The Neutrality Acts

In the mid-1930s the American Congress reacted to the rising international storm by determinedly turning inward. The disenchantment over the First World War had struck so deep that people could no longer believe that anything but further harm would come to the nation by trying to solve international crises. The very notion of collective security was rejected. On top of such an attitude, furthermore, was the towering congressional anger against the European "chiselers" who would not pay their war debts—ironically, the very nations threatened by Hitler's Germany—Britain and France.

The Senate created a committee under progressive Gerald P. Nye of North Dakota to explore the reasons why the United States had become involved in the First World War. A sensational show featuring accusations against war industries was put on, stretching over two years, which never actually proved anything, but nevertheless left firmly implanted in the public mind the belief that bankers and arms manufacturers had dragged the country into war. This led to the First Neutrality Act, passed in August 1935, which charged the president, during a time of international war, to impose an arms embargo on all belligerents, thus making it impossible for him to discriminate between aggressors and victims. In 1936, the Second Neutrality Act prohibited the making of any loans to a country involved in a war. In the Third Neutrality Act, passed in 1937, Americans were forbidden in time of war from traveling on ships owned by belligerents; no American merchant vessel was allowed to be armed; and the sale of arms was put strictly on a "cash and carry" basis. In sum, Congress legislated out of existence all of the factors that, it was believed, had dragged the United States into the First World War. The result was to immobilize the American government in a time of grave world crisis.

America retreats from the Far East

When Franklin D. Roosevelt came to the White House, he held back from further action in the Far Eastern crisis. Meanwhile, the government proceeded on another withdrawal from the Far East—giving independence to the Philippines. Antiimperialists had called for this for many years, and Filipino nationalists had agitated for

the same objective ever since the First World War, when Woodrow Wilson's appointee as governor general, Francis B. Harrison, had encouraged feelings of self-sufficiency by granting considerable power to the Philippine legislature. By the 1920s, American producers of sugar, tobacco, and similar products were beginning to support the independence idea, for they wanted to exclude the growing importations from the Philippine Islands, based on complete free trade established in the Underwood Tariff of 1913. The Republican presidents of the 1920s, however, firmly opposed independence. Under Franklin Roosevelt, the Tydings-McDuffie Act was passed in March 1934. Tariffs were to be raised only gradually against Philippine goods, and full independence was to be granted in 1946.

In China there was a brief calm following Japan's conquest of Manchuria. But then, in July 1937, a newly militant Japanese government began the Second Sino-Japanese War, the objec-

The Second World War: Alliances

Allied nations

Axis nations

Neutral nations

tive this time being the conquest of all China. Roosevelt refused to invoke the First Neutrality Act, thus allowing arms to reach the Chinese, though the lines of communication had to wind from India through Burma.

Roosevelt turns outward

By his second term, Roosevelt could no longer remain quiescent in his foreign policy. The "community of the damned"—Japan, Germany, and Italy—was forming. The deepest values of Western civilization were clearly at stake. The kind of world that Hitler was plunging toward would be a world based on nothing but jungle law. Increasingly, the president was convinced that the United States had to play a major role in the world to defend basic human values. This meant, to begin with, initiating rearmament, and in early 1938 he obtained funds from Congress to build the navy up to a strength allowing it to defend both ocean frontiers. Later in the year, Hitler's pogrom against German Jews horrified the American public. When Hitler sent his troops into Austria, forcibly joining that country to the Third Reich, a turning point was passed. From then on, isolationism was on the defensive, for the German dictator's actions made that philosophy increasingly absurd. When Poland was struck from east and west by German and Russian armed forces in September 1933, Roosevelt was able to secure a repeal of the arms-embargo feature of the First Neutrality Act, allowing the American government to begin selling goods on a cash and carry basis to its friends while denying them to Germany, since that nation would find it difficult to get to American ports. (Loans, however, were still prohibited, as was travel by Americans in the war zones.)

Several months of quiet followed after the defeat of Poland. Americans breathed easier, for they were confident that the British and French would eventually defeat Hitler, thus making it unnecessary for the United States to do more than sell arms to the western Allies. Then in several lightning campaigns begun in April 1940, Hitler conquered Denmark, Norway, Luxembourg, Holland, and Belgium. Hardly pausing to catch their breath, his armed forces then poured into France, administering a swift defeat. On June 22, 1940, the führer secured a total French capitulation.

America becomes an armed belligerent

The fall of France set off a wave of panic in the United States. Mayor Fiorello La Guardia of New York cried out that the American government could not even defend Coney Island. In May, Roosevelt had already gone before Congress to give a sensational speech that described how bombers could fly from West Africa to Omaha, and asked funds—speedily granted—for the building of 50,000 war planes. Only Britain now stood between America and Hitler's total victory in western Europe, and the American government immediately came to one fundamental decision: the British must be saved at all costs. By various means, using go-between private companies, Roosevelt rushed thousands of aircraft and guns to Britain to replace the equipment their armies had had to leave behind as they fled out of France. A Gallup poll revealed that seventy percent of the American people now believed that a German victory would directly imperil the nation. With this tidal wave of opinion behind him, Roosevelt persuaded Congress to establish in September 1940 the first peacetime draft in American history. Meanwhile, everyone watched in horror as Hitler launched a bombing campaign against Britain's cities in preparation for an expected invasion.

The supply lines crossing the Atlantic between North America and British ports were under unremitting attack from German submarines. The American government gave the British fifty destroyers of World War I vintage, in return for which the United Kingdom gave ninety-nine-year rent-free leases of sites for naval bases on eight British possessions in the western hemisphere, running from Newfoundland through the Caribbean islands to British Guiana. By this time, it was apparent that the "cash and carry" law was not aiding the British, since they had begun to run out of money and did not have the ships to carry to their islands all the war materiel they needed. In January 1941 Roosevelt asked Congress for authority to lend or lease war goods to the British, thus taking "the dollar sign," as he put it, out of the transaction. This would effec-

tively prevent any recurrence of the festering war debt problem that had poisoned the interwar decades. Speaking to the press, he made use of a brilliantly chosen parable. Neighbors are always happy, he said, to lend their hoses to a man whose adjoining house is on fire, for it will reduce the danger to their own dwellings. All they ask is that he return the hose when the emergency is over, if it is still usable. "We cannot and we will not tell [Great Britain and her Allies]," he

The Second World War: European theater, 1939–1942

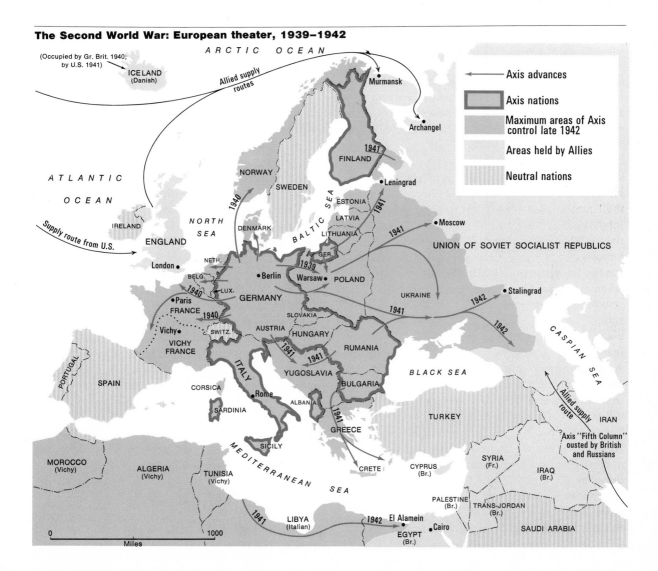

said, "that they must surrender, merely because of present inability to pay for the weapons which we know they must have."

Every anti-British, isolationist, or antiwar group split the air with protests. All recognized that the lend-lease proposal would be a crucial turning point, making the United States, in effect, a nonfighting partner in Britain's struggle against Hitler. Republican Senator Robert A. Taft of Ohio snorted that "Lending war equipment is a good deal like lending chewing gum. You don't want it back." Burton K. Wheeler of Montana made the most violent attack: lend-lease, he said, was the "New Deal's 'triple A' foreign policy—to plow under every fourth American boy." Debate raged throughout the land, in every grocery store and stock market board room. This was no administrative fiat: it was a decision reached after the fullest possible national discussion among the people. The national decision was clear: even at the risk of war, Britain must be saved. With letters expressing this viewpoint deluging them, congressmen came to their final vote after weeks of debate in mid-March 1941. They passed the Lend-Lease Act by heavy majorities in the two houses. Roosevelt immediately secured an appropriation of more than seven billion dollars and began making the United States into what he called the "arsenal of democracy."

Battle of Britain

During the following months the pressure mounted higher and higher. Great plumes of smoke rose over the British Isles as clouds of German bombers rained explosives on the civilians below. In the Battle of Britain, British fighter planes mounted a heroic and eventually successful struggle against the bomber attacks. Meanwhile, German submarines sunk scores of merchant vessels, and Roosevelt set up naval convoys that sought to protect munitions-carrying vessels as far eastward as Iceland, where the local authorities granted rights for an American military occupation. American destroyers and aircraft ranged over the North Atlantic searching out German submarines and radioing their location to British naval forces. When the destroyer *Greer* engaged in a shooting encounter with a German submarine (which the *Greer* had actually instigated), Roosevelt ordered the navy thereafter to "shoot on sight [these] rattlesnakes of the Atlantic." He secured congressional authority to arm American merchant ships and to allow them to enter war zones, boon to the hardpressed British.

Meanwhile, Hitler sent German armies racing into Greece and Yugoslavia. Then his *Afrika Korps* thrust swiftly to the Egyptian frontier, threatening to drive the British out entirely and seize the Suez Canal, which would have snapped crucial supply lines. On June 22, 1941, Hitler stunned the world by suddenly sending an armed force of hundreds of divisions into Russia. Dizzied by his swift successes, he did not prepare his troops for winter campaigning, since he expected to defeat Russia before cold weather set in. As Hitler's armies plunged rapidly into the depths of Russia, the Nazi occupation officials began systematically killing off tens of thousands of Russian village officials. Hundreds of thousands of Russian troops were captured and sent to prison camps where they were allowed to starve to death. European Russia was to be cleared out for German settlers.

This astounding event transformed American opinion toward Russia. From being hated as Hitler's accomplice in aggression, Russia overnight became a much-valued and much-praised ally. Americans watched the progress of Hitler's armies in tense alarm, for clearly a Hitler victorious over the limitless resources of the Soviet Union would be practically unstoppable in his career of world conquest. Roosevelt soon promised aid to Stalin, and in November 1941, allocated one billion dollars in lend-lease aid, which was followed by many billions more.

The Atlantic meeting

In early August 1941, Roosevelt and Churchill met off the Newfoundland coast in a gathering of British and American naval vessels. Churchill had come to plead for greatly increased aid. Roosevelt, on his side, was determined to win some agreements that looked toward the kind of world that would be constructed after the war. From his days as a Harvard student, he had been a determined anticolonialist (save for the period when he supported Woodrow Wilson's intervention in the Caribbean). He wanted to do everything possible to get the British (and the French, for that matter) to free their colonies. "I can't believe," he said to Churchill, "that we can fight a war against fascist slavery, and at the same time not work to free people all over the world from a backward colonial policy. . . ." Later on he brought pressure to bear on the French, trying to prevent their return as colonial masters to the countries of Indochina—Vietnam, Laos, and Cambodia. He also hoped to see protective tariffs lowered worldwide, thus inaugurating the world of open trading that, like Wilson before him, he had long envisioned and worked for. Of highest importance, to cap off this structure and maintain peace, would be the construction of a new international body to replace the League of Nations. In its final version, the president's and the prime minister's joint statement, the so-called Atlantic Charter, was a cautiously worded hope expressed to the world that on the defeat of the aggressors, trade barriers would be lowered, no nation would make territorial acquisitions, the peoples of the world would be allowed to govern themselves, and a "permanent system of general security" would be established. The two leaders also called for a world blessed by freedom from want and fear.

Japan moves southward

In September 1940 Japan, Germany, and Italy signed the Tripartite Pact, which pledged each nation to come to the aid of the other if attacked by the United States. This faced President Roosevelt with the sobering fact that war with any one member of the Rome-Berlin-Tokyo Axis would lead to war with all. And yet any thrust southward that Japan made to capture French,

British, and Dutch colonies—and sources of raw materials—would weaken the Allies in their struggle against Hitler. When France fell, thus opening its colony of Indochina to Japanese incursions, the last and most fateful chapter in Japan's movement toward war with the United States began. When it became apparent that Tokyo was planning to move into Indochina, preparatory to moving on the resource-rich islands of the Dutch East Indies, Roosevelt took steps to warn off the Japanese. He put the export of oil and scrap metal to Japan under a licensing procedure, which allowed him to choke off supplies should he decide to, and ordered that aviation fuel be sold only in the western hemisphere. This was a great shock to the Japanese, for about eighty percent of the scrap iron, steel products, and oil needed for their armies and navies came from America.

Militant expansionists in Japan now moved to take over greater power in the Japanese government. The new foreign minister, Yosuke Matsuoka, said that Japan was going to go "hell bent for the Axis and for the New Order in Asia." In September, the French government agreed to let the Japanese move into northern Indochina, where they controlled sea ports, built air bases, and ran the railroads. The Japanese government then began a long series of negotiations with the United States to secure American acquiescence to the "New Order." Briefly, the American government was to cease giving any support to Chiang Kai-shek, the Chinese Nationalist leader, accept Japan's dominance over China and the Far East generally, and drop its embargo against the sale of strategic goods to Japan.

Roosevelt's response

President Roosevelt refused to accept these demands. This was a crucial point. The United States could have had peace if it had agreed to give up its decades-old policy of trying to keep China an independent nation open to the trade of the world. But Roosevelt firmly believed that he could make the Japanese halt their aggressions by keeping the pressure on. He therefore told the Japanese that the only acceptable settlement would be for Japan to get out of China, respect the Open Door once more, and give up its military expansionism. Given the state of Japanese opinion, this demand was impossible for the Japanese to meet. Many in the Tokyo government believed that Japan would lose if it went to war with the United States (a view held by the Japanese emperor Hirohito, himself). But they could not bring themselves to accept so total a national humiliation. Hoping that the United States would give in, the Japanese continued negotiations until the very end. Meanwhile, on July 2, 1941, a momentous conference of all Japan's leaders, with the emperor in the chair, considered the whole matter afresh and resolved to continue to push southward. Shortly afterward, Japanese troops occupied southern Indochina, in preparation for an attack on Malaya and the Dutch East Indies.

Roosevelt responded by freezing all Japanese funds in the United States and halting the shipment of oil and war supplies to Japan. Now the Japanese war minister, Hideki Tojo, soon to be prime minister, warned that war was the only answer. It was essential, he said, to "break through the military and economic barrier" that the United States had erected. Beginning in September 1941, the high command held war games preparing for an attack on America's fleet at Pearl

The U.S.S. *West Virginia* and the U.S.S. *Tennessee*, both battleships, lie burning on Pearl Harbor's floor after the surprise Japanese attack of December 7, 1941. These pictures were long kept from the nation.

80-G-32414 in the National Archives, Navy Department

Harbor. This, it was believed, would give Japan sufficient temporary military superiority to take a vast ring of islands in the western Pacific Ocean, from which it would thereafter maintain an impregnable defense of the "Greater East Asia Sphere of Co-Prosperity." When it became clear that the United States would not retreat from its policies, a great fleet set out from the northern Japanese islands. Soon it reached the vicinity of the Hawaiian Islands, and on December 7, 1941, executed a massively successful bombing and torpedo attack on the American fleet at Pearl Harbor. When the planes ceased their wheeling and diving on the stricken vessels below and disappeared from view, heading back to their untouched aircraft carriers, they left behind five battleships sunk of the eight then at Pearl, fourteen more ships sunk or disabled, and almost 2,400 dead soldiers and sailors. Amazement and anger struck the United States. On the following day Congress declared war on Japan; three days after that, Germany and Italy honored their treaty pledges by declaring war on America. Thus was the United States finally catapulted into World War II.

The effects of Pearl Harbor

While the attack was certainly a tactical victory for the Japanese, in a larger sense it was perhaps their gravest strategic defeat. The bombing absolutely destroyed isolationism and unified the American people as they had never been in any of their previous wars. Massive unanimity welded the nation into a fighting force of unparalleled power. "My convictions regarding international cooperation and collective security for peace," said one Republican isolationist senator, Arthur H. Vandenberg of Michigan, "took firm hold on the afternoon of the Pearl Harbor attack."

From a longer viewpoint, it can be said that Pearl Harbor shaped all of America's responses to foreign policy crises in the next quarter of a century. A generation of American leaders went into the Second World War convinced that in the future the only way to secure world peace would be to maintain armed vigilance and a readiness to strike at aggression in its earliest stages. Furthermore, Hitler's barbarities and Japan's ruthless attacks on China and finally on America's own young men, hammered into the national consciousness an unquestioned belief that America represented, then and afterward, the forces of good; that its use of the mailed fist was morally right. That flaming Sunday morning in Hawaii began America's involvement not only in the Second World War, but in the Korean War and the long Vietnam agony as well.

The Second World War: Pacific theater, 1941–1942

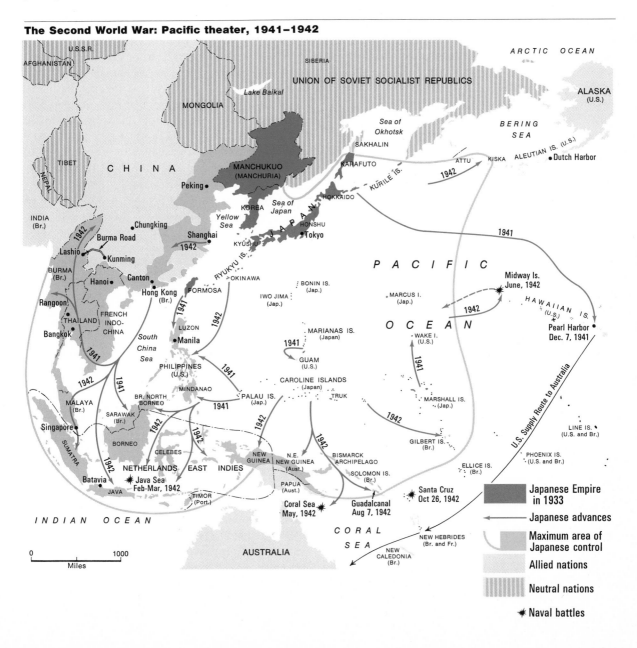

One outgrowth of the Japanese attack was the forced removal of 70,000 Japanese-Americans and 42,000 Japanese-born (by law denied citizenship) from their West Coast homes to be relocated in bleak concentration camps in the interior. Lieutenant General John L. DeWitt offered this justification: "The area lying to the west of the Cascade and Sierra Nevada Mountains in Washington, Oregon and California, is highly critical not only because the lines of communication and supply to the Pacific theater pass through it, but also because of the vital industrial production therein, particularly aircraft. In the war in which we are now engaged racial affinities are not severed by migration. The Japanese race is an enemy race and while many second and third generation Japanese born on United States soil, possessed of United States citizenship, have become 'Americanized,' the racial strains are undiluted. To conclude otherwise is to expect that children born of white parents on Japanese soil sever all racial affinity and become loyal Japanese subjects, ready to fight and, if necessary, to die for Japan in a war against the nation of their parents. That Japan is allied with Germany and Italy in this struggle is no ground for assumption that any Japanese, barred from assimilation by convention as he is, though born and raised in the United States, will not turn against this nation when the final test of loyalty comes. It, therefore, follows that along the vital Pacific Coast over 112,000 potential enemies, of Japanese extraction, are at large today. There are indications that these are organized and ready for concerted action at a favorable opportunity. *The very fact that no sabotage has taken place to date is a disturbing and confirming indication that such action will be taken.*" (United States Army, *Final Report: Japanese Evacuation from the West Coast, 1942* [1943].) [Italics added.]

Overall strategy

The first military decision made at the war's outset was to concentrate on defeating Hitler while fighting a holding action in the Pacific. The next was to form an alliance with Britain so close that even military commands were jointly staffed. It is doubtful that any two nations have ever created so intimate a partnership in time of war. No such intimacy could be achieved with Joseph Stalin, however. His distrust of the western Allies was too deep. He could well remember when British and French forces had tried to bring down the Soviet government by direct intervention following the First World War. He had witnessed Britain and France seemingly engaged in pushing Hitler eastward, and cheering on his anti-Communist activities. More important, however, were the suspicions all Communist regimes have entertained toward any capitalist government, and the deep-rooted feeling of Russians for many generations that they were surrounded by hostile forces. Although Roosevelt and Churchill tried again and again to break through Stalin's massive distrust, they rarely succeeded.

The very closeness of the Anglo-American relationship heightened that distrust. The fact, too, that the western Allies were too weak until 1944 to mount an invasion of Hitler's Europe, thus delaying the opening of the Second Front for which Stalin clamored, made him even more disbelieving. Of course, the Russian dictator was hardly a man of normal sensibilities. As later disclosures made horrifyingly clear, he had built a regime that had murdered millions of Russian citizens in order to clear away all obstacles to his will. The whole Russian government, however, joined him in his inability to believe in the West's good intentions. Although billions of dollars of American war materiel were rushed to the Soviet front (without it, it is doubtful that Russia could have remained in the war), an American observer in Moscow commented that the Russians "cannot understand giving without taking, and as a result even our giving is viewed with suspicion." Roosevelt worried constantly over this situation. He was convinced that a peaceful post-war world would be impossible unless the Russians were somehow led to adopt new attitudes of trust and cooperation. This point of view lay at the roots of his wartime diplomacy.

Meanwhile, he led in the creation of a "Grand

Alliance." At the Arcadia Conference, convened in Washington at the outbreak of the war, the "Declaration by the United Nations" was issued to the world. Signed by twenty-six nations—and twenty more signed before the war's end—it pledged acceptance of the Atlantic Charter's principles and bound the signatories not to enter into any separate armistices or peace treaties with the common enemy. In the same month of January 1942, a meeting of the foreign ministers of the American republics was held at Rio de Janeiro. Out of this meeting came the declaration that an attack against one nation in the western hemisphere was an attack against all. Following this unprecedented act—a fruit of Roosevelt's long-standing efforts at wooing Latin American friendship—all Latin American countries broke relations with the Axis (Chile not until 1943, and Argentina in 1945). Brazil even dispatched a combat division to the fighting in Italy, when the Allied campaign against Hitler reached that point.

Year of disaster: 1942

In 1942, however, the war went from disaster to disaster. The United States was unprepared for an all-out conflict. German submarines sunk vessels by the hundreds, at a pace far greater than they could be replaced. German armies fought to the outer defenses of Alexandria, Egypt. The Japanese took Singapore and sunk practically all the British fleet in the Pacific. Guam and Wake Island were swiftly overrun, and after a long struggle on the Bataan Peninsula, American forces in the Philippines were defeated. The American commander, General Douglas MacArthur, fled to Australia. Before long Japanese forces had taken the Dutch East Indies, with their immense resources of petroleum and other raw materials, and were mounting threats to India (through Burma) and Australia (through New Guinea). In May and June of 1942 the American navy suddenly halted this seemingly unstoppable advance by winning naval victories in the Coral Sea and near Midway Island. In the summer of

1942 American troops began the tortuously slow business of rolling back Japanese power by landing on Guadalcanal, which was wrested back from the Japanese army after a difficult campaign. Thereafter the American campaign in the Pacific consisted of a series of steppingstone operations in which the enemy was dug out of island after island. Shaking with malarial fever, sapped by dysentery, plucking off leeches, fighting often hand to hand in jungle slime or over sharp coral, thousands of Americans fought a kind of war of which few in the United States had ever dreamed.

Meanwhile the Russian front was on the verge of total collapse. During 1942 the huge German army renewed its offensive and struck deeper into Russia's vitals, reaching perilously close to the point of sweeping up all of the nation's industrial and petroleum resources. In response, American military planners worked desperately hard to open a second front in Europe sometime in 1942. But it was impossible: the British were not strong enough and the United States was far from ready. However, an attack had to be made somewhere: Roosevelt had pledged this to Stalin. Therefore, in early November 1942, a large Allied force, primarily American in makeup, arrived off the northwestern coast of Africa and launched an invasion. The objective was to move eastward and catch the German forces, then concentrated mainly between Tunisia and Egypt, in the rear.

Dwight D. Eisenhower

This campaign brought swiftly to international notice an American general of rare qualities, Dwight D. Eisenhower. Commander of the North Africa invasion, he had been plucked out of relative obscurity early in the war by America's chief of staff, General George C. Marshall. A career officer who had served since the First World War (in which he supervised noncombat units), Eisenhower displayed a remarkable capacity for leading large organizations and inspiring trust in his subordinates. Warm, open, unpretentious, he was a peaceful man who seemed to look on warfare not as a glorious opportunity for renown but as a painful necessity pursued only to protect innocent people against aggressors. In this new kind of warfare, in which gigantic armies of millions of men needed to be gathered together and skillfully coordinated, he was a genius at planning and administration.

Although Eisenhower's North African invasion went well at first, his troops were painfully inexperienced. The Germans knew this. In a bold counterattack they administered a severe defeat to the eastward-rushing American forces at Kasserine Pass. This had the effect of forcing a much more cautious pattern of advance on the Allied armies. Not until months had passed were the Americans and British able to converge on the German armies, basket them in Tunisia, and in May of 1943, totally defeat them.

The tide turns: 1943

By this time, the Russians had been able to mount huge counterattacks against the Germans. In January 1943, in a bloody struggle to capture Stalingrad, Hitler had pushed his forces into such an extreme position that the Russians were able to encircle and capture over 200,000 German troops. At this moment, Roosevelt and Churchill were meeting in Morocco at Casablanca to coordinate their war plans. They resolved to pour every possible resource into winning the crucial battle of the North Atlantic, for unless the flow of ships and supplies to Britain grew easier, no invasion of continental Europe was possible. Similarly, they decided on a day-and-night bombing campaign against Germany. The barbarities wreaked on Britain by Germany—and on other European countries—in the bombing of civilians, were now to be the fate of Hitler's Reich. Then, to expand the victory in North Africa and open the Mediterranean Sea completely, Roosevelt and Churchill agreed on an invasion of Sicily, to be followed by an invasion of mainland Italy.

At the conference's end, President Roosevelt announced to newsmen that the conferees had agreed that the war with Hitler was to be fought until "unconditional surrender" was won from the dictator. This set off a long-lasting controversy. Senator Burton K. Wheeler called the policy "brutal" and "asinine." Many agreed with him then and afterward that the plan would make the war longer and bloodier, for the Axis governments would fight to the end if the only terms were to be complete and abject surrender. Furthermore, if the German government was to be completely wiped out, a power vacuum would be created in the center of Europe into which Russian power would flow. In truth, however, this was the only policy on which both the western Allies and Russia could reach agreement. Anything less than that would lead to endless haggling over terms and intensified mutual distrust. Furthermore, the president was deeply impressed by the fact that Hitler had always insisted that the First World War had never really been lost; that traitors high in the German government had agreed to an unnecessary armistice. Roosevelt was determined that the powerful German people be confronted with final and unarguable defeat; that no voice could ever again say that in another aggressive war a German victory might be grasped.

In July 1943 the Allies invaded Sicily. Soon afterward the Italian people threw off their dictator, Mussolini, and signed an armistice with the Allies. German armies now flooded the Italian peninsula to take up the fight against Allied troops, with the result that a long and terribly wasting campaign had to be fought, Allied lines inching slowly northward after landings were made near Naples in September. One result, however, was to draw off large bodies of German troops from the Russian front, which helped to make it possible for the Red Army to initiate a sweep westward that began rolling the German armies back toward their homeland.

The Pacific campaign thrusts westward

Though denied highest priority by the Germany-first decision made at the war's outset, the American forces in the Pacific found means by skillful campaigning to thrust westward into the island ring Japan had conquered. Operating out of Australia, General Douglas MacArthur aimed at the Philippine Islands. His soldiers leapfrogged through the Bismarck islands, utilizing the northern coast of New Guinea and the islands of the Solomons. At the same time, far to the north, a combined naval and land force under Admiral Chester W. Nimitz fought through the islands of Micronesia in the Central Pacific, on to the Marianas, and then northwestward toward Japan itself. MacArthur's attacks, being confined to the heavily forested regions of the southern jungles, were slow and foot-slogging. Nimitz's force, by contrast, struggled through brief and bloody battles on the beaches of heavily defended small islands. Hundreds of aircraft pounded the islands in preparation for invasions, and powerful flotillas of battleships followed up with storms of bombardment. Even so, the Japanese were entrenched within strong fortifications, and they fought almost literally to the last man. When the marines waded onto Tarawa's coral beaches in November 1943, they went through a roaring four-day's hell in which 1,000 Americans were killed and 2,300 were wounded. In February 1944, Kwajalein was stormed, then Eniwetok, followed in June 1944 by the conquest of Guam, Saipan, and Tinian. The Japanese fleet struck back, but in the battle of the Philippine Sea (June 1944) was disastrously defeated, losing practically the last of its aircraft carriers.

The impact of these cumulative Japanese defeats wrought chaos in Tokyo. General Tojo and his cabinet were dismissed, and the government began preparations for a last-ditch stand. The Americans were now inside the inner defenses of the Japanese Empire, and they seemed irresistible. Late in 1944 the first B-29 Superfortresses flew off the newly captured airfields of the Marianas—on Guam, Saipan, and Tinian—to begin the bombing raids that eventually reduced the great cities of Japan to rubble.

The invasion of Europe

Millions of men, thousands of aircraft, and tens of thousands of tanks, halftracks, and artillery had been gathered in Britain by June 1944. This huge army, as Eisenhower later wrote, was like "a great human spring, coiled for the moment when its energy should be released and it would vault the English Channel in the greatest amphibious assault ever attempted." The main landing was to be made on the coast of Normandy, while another force was to enter the south of France from the Mediterranean somewhat later. On the evening of June 5, hundreds of vessels left a series of ports on the English southern coast and headed for France, carrying an assault force of 150,000 Americans, Britons, Canadians, and Free French. Thousands of fighter planes and bombers raced in over the French coast to strafe and bomb all approaches leading to the invasion beaches, while

American B-17 "Flying Fortresses" of the Eighth Air Force drop bombs on Europe. With relatively accurate bomb-sights, they tried in daylight to hit military targets, as against the night-time area-bombing of the British Royal Air Force.
United Press International

an armada of ships stood offshore and lobbed heavy shells into fortifications. The terrible fighting of D-Day, June 6, ended with the troops securely lodged in their beachhead. A hectic month of buildup followed during which thousands of troops and tanks were poured into the Normandy beaches preparatory to sweeping across France. In July the German ring around the beaches was broken. General George Patton took command of the Third Army then racing through the holes torn in the German lines, and led a lightning advance that soon spread chaos within the enemy forces. Having suffered its worst defeat since Stalingrad, the German army began reeling back, and the liberation of France was underway. In August 1944, the German command holding Paris surrendered, and General Charles de Gaulle walked down the Champs Elysées in triumph, having led the Free French forces through every kind of travail to this soaring hour.

Counterattack

It was now the autumn of 1944, and Hitler's empire was crumbling. The Soviet armies were moving rapidly westward: they were deep within Poland, had taken Rumania and Bulgaria, and were approaching Hungary. The Italian campaign was in its last stage. During three months of disastrous fighting, Hitler had lost over a million men. Clouds of bombers rained destruction on German cities. At this moment, Hitler decided on one last, bold counterattack. Choosing the forested Ardennes region in France, he planned to pull together his last reserves, break through the Allied lines (which were lightly defended at this point), race to the English Channel, and win an armistice with the western Allies. Then he could turn to deal with the hated Russians. It was a plan born of madness. The terrible bombing of Berlin had left Hitler with trembling hands, partial paralysis of one leg, and a feverishly hysterical manner of thought and speech. Three full armies and thousands of planes and tanks were gathered

for the great thrust. Then in the bitter snows of December 1944, when the Allied armies had settled down for a brief respite, he launched his attack.

The Battle of the Bulge in the Ardennes Forest frightened the western world. Everyone had thought Hitler beaten; now he suddenly came tearing out of his dark forests sending a torrent of tanks and heavily armed men westward. A hole forty-five miles wide was torn in the Allied lines. However, a crucial crossroads town, Bastogne, was held by an airborne division; the Allied forces north and south of the gap wheeled to crush off the attack; thousands of aircraft struck the German supply lines; and by early January the thrust was blunted and beginning to be turned back. Within a month, the Bulge was straightened out, and Eisenhower was free to take up his advance once more.

However, the war's end had been profoundly changed by the Battle of the Bulge. Just as the struggle was being won, Roosevelt, Churchill, and Stalin were meeting in Yalta. Their decisions at that crucial gathering (to be discussed later) were vitally affected by the fact that the western armies had just suffered a stinging rebuff and were still 400 miles from Berlin, while the Russian forces were sweeping magisterially westward and were only 30 miles from that city. Hitler's preparations for the Ardennes offensive had led to this eventuality, for he had drawn away large forces from the eastern front. Punching through Hitler's thin lines, the Soviet armies had been able quickly to take the rest of Poland and to race on into Germany. At this point, when future zones of occupation were being agreed on at the Yalta Conference, it was impossible for the western Allies to insist that Berlin belonged to them.

In February 1945, Eisenhower's armies hammered through the Siegfried Line, Germany's concrete fortifications just within its borders, and crossed the Rhine. By April, his troops were at the Elbe River, a hundred miles from Berlin. There they halted, awaiting the arrival of the Russian armies, for the Elbe was the agreed-on dividing line for occupation by the two armies. The war in Europe effectively came to an end on April 29, 1945, when Hitler, surrounded in his Berlin bunker by a holocaust of Russian attack, is reported to have raised a pistol to his mouth and shot himself. On May 7, a German delegation led by Field Marshal Alfred Jodl, chief of the German general staff, surrendered unconditionally to the Allies in a brief ceremony held in a schoolhouse in Rheims, France.

Victory in the Pacific

Meanwhile, the Japanese were being hammered inward in the western Pacific. A joint British-American campaign began driving them out of Burma in early 1944, thus opening up transportation routes to China so that Chiang Kai-shek's armies could be resupplied for assaults against the Japanese forces. General MacArthur's troops continued making long jumps of about 200 miles

The Second World War: European theater, 1942–1945

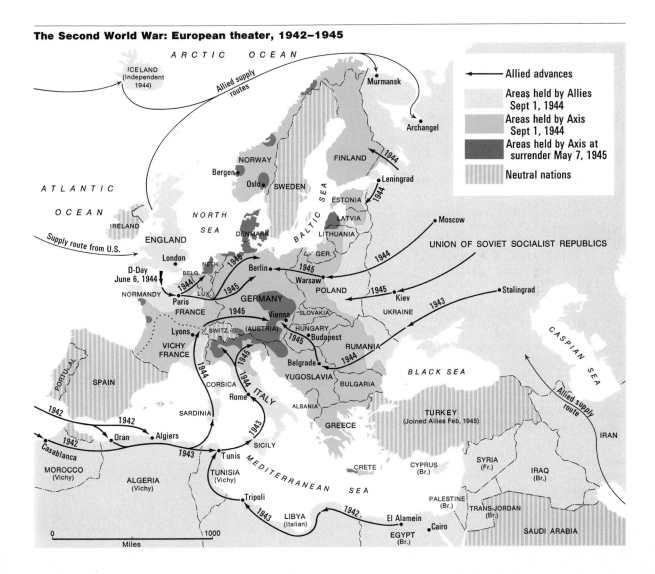

each, leapfrogging through the southwestern islands to the Philippines. In October 1944 he invaded those islands, wading ashore on the beaches of Leyte to issue a dramatic broadcast to the Philippine people: "I have returned! Rally to me!" Then the battle of Leyte Gulf, the largest naval battle in the history of warfare, led to the almost-total destruction of the rest of the Japanese fleet. In January 1945 the American army invaded Luzon, the principal island of the Philip-

The Second World War: Pacific theater, 1942–1945

pines, and drove the Japanese out of Manila. By July of that year, the Philippine Islands had been completely reconquered.

Northward, Admiral Nimitz's forces fought a bloody battle to take Iwo Jima in February 1945 in order to provide a closer air base for the bombing of Japan. In the following month, Tokyo was fire-bombed in the most horrible air raid of the Second World War, killing more than 80,000 people and rendering a million more homeless. Then came the biggest land battle of the Pacific war, the invasion of Okinawa. A force of 100,000 Japanese waited when, on April 1, 1945, American troops landed to begin their assault. Hundreds of suicide pilots, called *kamikaze,* dived in massed attacks on the American naval forces, subjecting them to a searing ordeal rarely experienced by any battle fleet in history. More than thirty ships were sunk, and hundreds were damaged. In the process, however, the Japanese air force was largely eliminated.

A new president: Harry S. Truman

Eleven days after the invasion of Okinawa began, Franklin Roosevelt was seated in a little house at Warm Springs, Georgia. For many months he had been in poor health, worn down by the burdens of war. In 1944 he had accepted his party's nomination for a fourth term and had defeated Thomas E. Dewey of New York, as in 1940 he had defeated Wendell Willkie. He had met twice with the Russians in the previous year and a half, at Teheran in December 1943 and at Yalta in February 1945. The photographs of him at Yalta were a shock to the public, for the gay, smiling president of former years had been replaced by a shrunken, weary, haggard man who stared somberly at the camera. His visit to Warm Springs was made in search of a renewed vitality. But now, suddenly, as an artist sketched his portrait, he grasped his head and said, "I have a terrible headache." He lost consciousness and two hours later died of a massive cerebral hemorrhage. The nation and the world were stunned. To the end of their lives, millions remembered the exact moment when they learned that Franklin Roosevelt died, for the news came with so sharp an impact that it seemed to shake the firmament of their accustomed world.

Equally shocked was the vice-president, Harry S. Truman, for a great weight now fell on his shoulders. A peppery, scrupulously honest man who had served as senator from Missouri, he brought little but courage and common sense to the White House, for he knew almost nothing of what had been going on in the executive branch. The world was still in flames, Hitler's Reich was going down in its last volcanic agonies, and the Russian armies were streaming westward. Complex negotiations awaited him in San Francisco where in less than two weeks fifty nations would gather to form the United Nations. After that would come a crucially important conference with Joseph Stalin and the British in Potsdam, just outside of Berlin, where fundamental decisions about the postwar world would be made. Equally grave was the news brought to the president within days of his entering the White House that for years the United States had been developing an atomic bomb and that it might need to be used to achieve the final conquest of Japan.

Japan surrenders

By July 1945 the Japanese home islands were practically defenseless. The imperial battle fleet was gone, and submarines had sunk most of Japan's merchant vessels. Cut off from food supplies, the Japanese people were nearly starving. American bombers ranged over the cities, burning out vast urban areas. An American naval force cruised up and down the Japanese coast untouched, bombarding at will. Okinawa had fallen in June; nothing was left to provide an outer defense. The military leaders, however, were filled with a fanatic zeal to fight until the end, and they had never been under the jurisdiction of the civilian government. The generals kept talking of one last battle in the homeland, where by the superior spirit and sacrificial courage of their own soldiers, the Japanese people would defeat the Americans. The loss of life on both sides would be astronomical, but Japan and its honor would be saved.

From the Potsdam Conference, the western Allies and China issued a declaration on July 26 saying that unconditional surrender would be demanded only of the Japanese armed forces, but no mention was made of the fate of Emperor Hirohito, which led high Japanese officials to fear that he would be tried as a war criminal. This strengthened the military's determination to fight on. Now, however, there was a powerful new factor in the equation. Early in the morning of July 12, 1945, a group of scientists and technicians had stood transfixed in the New Mexico desert watching a dazzling ball of flame, erupted by the world's first nuclear explosion, rising and swelling steadily larger. The fear flashed through them that it would not stop growing until it had swallowed up the earth and the heavens above. As he watched, the scientist Robert Oppenheimer suddenly found these words from the Hindu holy book, the Bhagavad-Gita, racing through his mind:

If the radiance of a thousand suns
were to burst into the sky
that would be like
the splendor of the Mighty One—
I am become Death, the shatterer of worlds.

General Leslie R. Groves, director of the atomic bomb project, had an utterly different kind of response. Turning to a military colleague, he exulted, "The war's over. One or two of those things, and Japan will be finished."

By August, a B-29 was on Tinian Island ready to carry an atomic bomb to drop on Japan. President Truman was warned that unless some great demonstration of America's overwhelming power was made, the war could be ended only by an invasion that would cause the deaths of untold

thousands. We now know that this may not have been true. Emperor Hirohito had already decided that the war had to be ended somehow. The Japanese government had sent out peace feelers, and intense discussions were taking place within the highest imperial circles on how best to respond to the Potsdam declaration. "Had the Allies given the Prince [Konoye] a week of grace in which to obtain his Government's support for acceptance of the proposals," the historian Robert J. C. Butow has written after a close examination of Japanese archives, "the war might have ended—without the atomic bomb and without Soviet participation in the conflict."

Truman's decision

To the new American president, halfway around the world, there seemed no alternative. Over and over again the Japanese had shown that they preferred death to surrender. Even their women and children had run off the cliffs of Saipan to die on the rocks below, choosing to join their slain husbands and fathers rather than suffer shame of capture by the Americans. Accepting the view that dropping the bomb would actually save lives by making an invasion unnecessary, President Truman authorized an attack on Hiroshima. On August 6 the entire city, with its 80,000 people, was destroyed. Two days later, the Russians declared war against Japan, eager to join in the booty before it was too late. When no surrender came from the Japanese, a second bomb was dropped on Nagasaki on August 9.

Soon after the Hiroshima bombing, President Truman issued a statement: "Sixteen hours ago an American airplane dropped one bomb on Hiroshima, an important Japanese Army base. . . . It is an atomic bomb. It is a harnessing of the basic power of the universe. The force from which the sun draws its power has been loosed against those who brought war to the Far East." It was developed, he said, in a race against the Germans, involving over a hundred thousand workers, scientists, and engineers. "What has been done is the greatest achievement of organized science in history. . . .

"We are now prepared to obliterate more rapidly and completely every productive enterprise the Japanese have above ground in any city. . . . If they do not now accept our terms they may expect a rain of ruin from the air, the like of which has never been seen on this earth. Behind this air attack will follow sea and land forces in such numbers and power as they have not yet seen and with the fighting skill of which they are already well aware.

"The fact that we can release atomic energy ushers in a new era in man's understanding of nature's forces. Atomic energy may in the future supplement the power that now comes from coal, oil, and falling water. . . . I shall recommend that the Congress of the United States consider promptly the establishment of an appropriate commission to control the production and use of atomic power within the United States. I shall give further consideration and make further recommendations to the Congress as to how atomic power can become a powerful and forceful influence towards the maintenance of world peace."

During these frightful days, the Japanese government was stunned into a series of nonstop crisis discussions. The militarists still vowed a fight to the death, but when the news finally reached Tokyo of what had happened to the two bombed cities (the violence of the blasts had destroyed communication lines), Emperor Hirohito convened the Supreme War Council to debate anew the fate of Japan. From this gathering a message went to the United States saying that if the emperor were left at the head of his people and not tried as a war criminal, Japan was ready to accept unconditional surrender. When told that the emperor would be subject to the orders of General MacArthur as supreme commander, the Japanese again began arguing among themselves. At this moment the emperor rose before his council and for the first time intervened di-

Thousands of feet high, a cloud of smoke mushrooms over the vaporized Japanese city of Nagasaki after American airmen dropped the second atom bomb, August 9, 1945. This specter has hung over the world ever since.
Wide World Photos

rectly. "We demand that you will agree to it," he said. "We see only one way left for Japan to save herself. That is the reason we have made this determination to endure the unendurable and suffer the insufferable."

Peace was made. On August 15, American forces ceased fire, and on September 2, 1945, surrender documents were signed on the deck of the battleship *Missouri,* swinging at anchor in Tokyo Bay. The greatest war in history was ended. In the major fighting countries some seventy million men had been mobilized (not counting Russia, where the figures are unavailable). Counting civilian casualties, perhaps thirty million people had died. Germany and Japan lay in smoking ruins. The same was true of large areas of Russia, and throughout Europe and Asia. The task now ahead was less exciting and perhaps more difficult than fighting the war—building a new world order on the ash heap of the old.

Bibliography

Three books that were especially valuable to me in writing this chapter: Above all else one must understand Hitler and Nazi Germany to understand this era, and, among other sources, I found Alan Bullock's *Hitler: A Study in Tyranny** (1953) essential. A. Russell Buchanan's *The United States and World War II,** two vols. (1964) is thorough and judicious. And for the crucial question of the dropping of the atom bombs and their effects on Japan's war plans, I relied on a fascinating book based on research in Japanese records, Robert J. C. Butow, *Japan's Decision to Surrender* (1967).

How have historians looked at the topic?

Was the entry of the United States into World War II justified? What alternatives, if any, did President Roosevelt and his advisers have? Two reporters, Forrest Davis and Ernest K. Lindley, praised American intervention as just, wise, and realistic in *How War Came* (1942), a tract that emphasizes President Roosevelt's attempts to keep the United States out of war. Early opposition to this view came from the venerable historian Charles A. Beard, whose *President Roosevelt and the Coming of the War, 1941* (1948) synthesizes his condemnation. According to Beard, Roosevelt and his aides misled American public opinion, manipulating the United States into an undeclared war with Germany and provoking Japan into its attack on Pearl Harbor. Charles C. Tansill agreed with Beard's criticisms in his *Back Door to War* (1952).

A cadre of Roosevelt defenders appeared. With the appearance of Herbert Feis's judicious *The Road to Pearl Harbor** (1950), Roosevelt's diplomacy in the Far East seemed vindicated, although Paul W. Schroeder raised disturbing questions in his *The Axis Alliance and Japanese-American Relations, 1941* (1958). The best current analysis of the fateful Japanese attack is in Roberta Wohlstetter's *Pearl Harbor: Warning and Decision** (1962), a balanced history that probes the effects of the rivalry between the American army and navy. William Langer and Everett Gleason's massive volumes *The Challenge to Isolation, 1937–1940** (1952) and *The Undeclared War, 1940–1941* (1953), emphasize the Axis powers' insatiable ambitions and find little space for maneuvering on the part of the United States government. A recent, scholarly book that promotes the noninterventionist viewpoint is Bruce M. Russett's *No Clear and Present Danger: A Skeptical View of United States Entry into World War II* (1972).

Many questions have been raised about American actions during the Second World War. Did the policy of unconditional surrender prolong the war? No, said Herbert Feis in his major work, *Churchill, Roosevelt, Stalin: The War They Waged and the Peace They Sought* (1957). Gabriel Kolko was less positive in his provocative and detailed, *The Politics of War: The World and United States Foreign Policy, 1943–1945* (1968), which raises queries about many aspects of American strategy. Was the use of the atomic bomb a reluctant but necessary action? Gar Alperovitz challenged this view in his controversial *Atomic Diplomacy: Hiroshima and Potsdam* (1965). Franklin Roosevelt's skill as a wartime leader is assessed in Robert A. Divine's *Roosevelt and World War II* (1969) and in James M. Burns's remarkable study, *Roosevelt: The Soldier of Freedom, 1940–1945* (1970).

The United States' reaction to Japan's strategy and internal Chinese political developments is illuminated in Dorothy Borg's *The United States and the Far Eastern Crisis, 1933–1938* (1964). Barbara Tuchman's brilliant biography *Stilwell and the American Experience in China* (1970) depicts the Chinese war and revolution with rare skill and insight.

Paradoxically, while fighting Hitler's racism abroad, the United States perpetrated its own brand at home. Audrie Girdner and Anne Loftis told the painful story of the Japanese detention camps in *The Great Betrayal* (1969). The story that emerges in *Uprooted Americans: The Japanese Americans and the War Relocation Authority during World War II* (1971), written by Dillon S. Myer, director of the authority, is a tragic one of confusion, rumors, and squashed humanitarian impulses. Allan R. Bosworth characterizes the Japanese detention as a "story of racist hysteria and abuse of government power" in *America's Concentration Camps* (1968).

* Available in paperback.

CHAPTER 33

The Cold War

TIME LINE

1946	Stalin declares need for buildup of strength against capitalist world; Churchill gives "iron curtain" speech; Truman stiffens policies toward Russia
1947	Cold War begins; Truman Doctrine; European economy in crisis; Marshall Plan announced; George Kennan describes containment policy against Russia
1948	Organization of American States created; Congress approves Marshall Plan
1948–1949	Berlin Air Lift
1949	North Atlantic Treaty Organization created; Russia explodes atom bomb; Chinese Communists gain control of mainland China
1950–1953	Korean War
1950	China enters war as United Nations force approaches Chinese border
1952	Dwight D. Eisenhower elected thirty-fourth president of the United States
1954	Southeast Asia Treaty Organization established as bulwark against Communist advance; United States forms alliance with Nationalist Chinese government
1957	Eisenhower Doctrine announced; Russians launch *Sputnik 1;* Khrushchev trumpets superiority of Russian technology
1958	United States occupies Lebanon under Eisenhower Doctrine; United States puts small satellite in orbit, fires first intercontinental ballistic missile; Russia joins America in halting atomic tests in atmosphere
1959	Khrushchev meets with Eisenhower in America; Fidel Castro establishes anti-American Communist regime in Cuba
1960	American U-2 airplane shot down over Russia; Communist China breaks with Russia; John F. Kennedy elected thirty-fifth president of the United States
1961	Peace Corps established; Alliance for Progress; Bay of Pigs disaster; Kennedy announces goal of placing a man on the moon; Berlin crisis intensifies, leads to partial United States mobilization and increased spending for conventional arms; Russia resumes testing of atomic bombs in atmosphere
1962	Trade Expansion Act; Cuban missile crisis results in deescalation of Cold War
1963	Test Ban Treaty agreed on; John F. Kennedy assassinated; Lyndon Baines Johnson becomes thirty-sixth president of the United States

THE American people greeted the end of the Second World War with a carnival outburst of joy and release. Crowds poured through city streets laughing and singing; men in uniform danced wildly with girls from the munitions factories; and a cacophonous symphony of happy sounds—car horns, train whistles, trumpets and brass bands—greeted the hopeful new world of peace. Within a year, however, a chill was falling, for the suspicion was spreading that a new world conflict was coming, one as ominous as that which had just ended. A year after that, and the Cold War between Russia and America had been launched. Stocky Winston Churchill, bulldog-faced and scowling, told a college audience in Fulton, Missouri, that "from Stettin in the Baltic to Trieste in the Adriatic, an iron curtain has descended across the Continent." From Joseph Stalin, Russia's prime minister, came the foreboding announcement that communism and capitalism were inevitably fated to clash. On March 12, 1947, Harry Truman faced the assembled houses of Congress and grimly announced what is known as the Truman Doctrine: the United States would support free countries in resisting Communist take-over. The immediate challenge, he said, was to protect Greece and Turkey from imminent collapse by pouring millions of dollars into their economies and armed forces. Congress quickly approved. The Cold War, gestating for almost two years, was now in the open.

It came as a stunning shock to the American people. As soon as the Second World War had ended, the nation's huge military system had been demobilized in a tearing rush: millions of young Americans were brought home and released to civilian life; ships were mothballed; tanks were dumped into the sea; cannon were spiked; and aircraft by the thousands were put out to rust in western deserts. In a brief time the world's most powerful nation, confident that its wartime allies were friendly and that the United Nations would ensure a peaceful future, put away its arms and turned in on itself. Now, inexplicably, came a new threat and the beginnings of a long and frustrating confrontation with a seemingly brilliant adversary who appeared skillfully to exploit every world problem to America's disadvantage. Americans were startled to learn that millions of people regarded them not as kindly liberators but as capitalistic exploiters. "Yankee Go Home" was scrawled on the walls of buildings around the globe.

The psychological effects of this plunge from a peak of exultation to the depths of anxiety were deep and profound. Americans were convinced that they were a good and moral people. Had they not defeated the bloody fascists and brought liberty to the world? they asked themselves. Had they not spread their treasure freely to their friends and asked nothing in return? They were massively bitter, therefore, toward the Soviets and their international coworkers. Americans took up the Cold War with a grim obsessiveness and self-righteousness that produced a near-wartime national atmosphere. Used to thinking of great crusades, they hated this new "enemy" and thirsted for his complete destruction in the same way they had concerning Mussolini and Hitler.

At the same time, they were afraid. The map seemed to show the red of communism spreading over ever larger regions of the world: into eastern Europe, erupting in violent upheavals in western Europe, flowing over China, and bursting across the borders of South Korea in a flood of Russian-made tanks. Given the American tendency to think in simplistic terms, they came to believe that every world controversy was another outcropping of the Cold War. Wherever they looked, the wily Russian hand seemed to be manipulating the strings that made the puppets dance. A paranoid fear gripped so hard on the minds of many Americans that they believed communism had secretly taken over the schools, colleges, and churches. Most frightful of all, to such people, was the thought that Communists had seized control of the State Department and perhaps even the army. For years, because of such anxieties, the nation was rocked by a national witch hunt that put the Red Scare of the 1920s to shame. What else could one expect of a people unversed in the complexities of world politics? The total victory Americans had always been led to expect in all their former controversies seemed mystifyingly to elude them. Someone, it was believed, must be traitorously selling the nation out.

Crisis followed crisis, and billions of dollars poured out of the Treasury to rebuild the military system, as well as the economies and armies of scores of the "free world" allies. From the Marshall Plan, the Communist takeover of Czechoslovakia, and the Berlin blockade in the Cold War's early years (1947–1949), through the Korean War in the 1950s, to the orbiting of *Sputnik 1* (1957), the building of the Berlin Wall (1961), and the Cuban missile crisis (1962), the Russian-American global confrontation kept the world in an uproar. Not until almost fifteen years of this continuous friction and intermittent warfare had passed were the American people, seasoned and disillusioned, ready to put aside their anger and accept the idea of peaceful coexistence with Soviet Russia, which on its side had also decided to deescalate the terror. Largely ignored in the general relief was a bubbling crisis in remote Indochina where before long a new and, for the United States and Vietnam, far graver conflict would soon begin.

The Yalta Conference

This complicated chain of events had its beginnings shortly before the end of the Second World War when in February 1945 Roosevelt, Stalin, and Churchill gathered in the Black Sea resort of Yalta on the Russian Crimean peninsula to work out the postwar settlement. In the background was the massive sweep of Russia's armies into the Balkans and central Europe. Furthermore, in four bloody years of fighting off Germany's invading

armies, the Russians had suffered hideous civilian losses, reaching twenty million deaths.

The fact that Russian armies already occupied Rumania, Bulgaria, Hungary, Poland, and other vast reaches of eastern and central Europe horrified Winston Churchill. "Good God," he exclaimed to an associate in late 1944, "can't you see that the Russians are spreading across Europe like a tide?" Franklin Roosevelt arrived at the conference convinced that through gestures of friendship he could persuade the Russians that they need not fear western aggression, and that they should relax their grip on the small nations their armies occupied. But he found Stalin adamant when the most important eastern European country, Poland, was discussed. Stalin's armies occupied it, a Moscow-trained Communist government had been put in control, and he would not even allow western observers to be present at the free elections that he finally promised (and never held). All Roosevelt and Churchill could do was to argue with Stalin, finally getting him to at least approve the Declaration on Liberated Europe, which pledged democratic governments for the nations freed from Hitler.

Most of all, Roosevelt carried to Yalta his Wilsonian faith that world peace would be safeguarded if all nations were brought within an international organization, the United Nations. He was, therefore, eager to persuade the Russians to come to the projected San Francisco conference at which the United Nations was to be formed. By this means he hoped to do away with the kind of sphere of influence that the Russians seemed to feel compelled to erect in eastern Europe. The United Nations would provide the ultimate protection for small nations by ensuring world peace and easing the fears that made great powers aggressive. What he really aimed at, in short, was the creation of a new world order that would end the need for balances of power. Crucial to Roosevelt's goals at Yalta was the establishment of a good relationship with the Russian leaders, for such an internationalist world order could only function on the basis of mutual trust.

A harsh treatment of the Soviets would destroy at the outset the kind of trustful postwar relationship he was trying to create. He has been much criticized for this attitude since things did not work out as he had hoped; but he was playing for big stakes and the long haul.

The Russians were frightened that Germany might once again rise from the ashes to launch a new war, and they got the western Allies to agree, in principle, that that country would be dismembered. They also asked for reparations. Roosevelt seemed as anxious as the Russians to punish Germany by dismemberment and the extraction of reparations, but the British retained vivid memories of the postwar period after 1919 when an economically sick Germany, borne down by reparations demands, dragged all of Europe into depression. The only final agreement concerning Germany made at Yalta was to settle on zones of occupation by the various armies.

America's military leaders had warned Roosevelt that Russian help would be desperately needed in the final campaigns against Japan. At Yalta, Stalin volunteered his desire to enter that war as soon as possible after Germany was defeated. In return, Roosevelt agreed that Russia should be allowed to take back what that nation had lost to Japan in the Russo-Japanese War of 1904 and 1905: the Kurile Islands and southern Sakhalin, together with control over Manchuria's railways and its ports of Darien and Port Arthur. All of this Roosevelt made conditional on the approval of Chiang Kai-shek's government. (When the Chinese discovered that the Russians in the Yalta agreement were ready to recognize China's complete sovereignty over Manchuria, they hastened to approve enthusiastically.)

Lastly, the Americans won approval for the project they considered most crucial—formation of the United Nations. At first the Russians argued closely on the matter of voting: they were openly scornful of small nations and recoiled from the prospect of being outvoted by them. When they learned that the great powers—to include France, China, Russia, Britain, and the United States—would have the right of veto over any actions by the United Nations Security Council, they dropped their objections. Stalin regarded the Assembly with amused indifference, for even though every nation in that body was accorded equal voting power, the Assembly would have no power to do anything other than talk and pass resolutions.

Good relations break down

The Americans left Yalta pleased with the results of their work. But within two months Franklin Roosevelt was writing Stalin of his "astonishment," "anxiety" and "bitter resentment" that the Russians were refusing to install a democratically based govenment in Poland. In a few days after that, he was dead, and the new president Harry Truman, was listening to W. Averell Harriman, American ambassador to Moscow, say that the United States was faced with a new "barbarian invasion of Europe." Truman bluntly demanded of Stalin that the Polish government be reorganized, but Stalin flatly refused. Poland, he said, was vital to Russian security. "The Soviet Union," he went on, "has a right to make efforts that there should exist in Poland a government friendly toward the Soviet Union."

The breach widened steadily. Charge and countercharge went back and forth, Russia and America interpreting the other's actions in the worst possible light. In July 1945 Truman, Stalin, and the new British premier, Clement Attlee, gathered in Potsdam, a suburb of Berlin, to discuss their differences. They were able to agree on little. The new Russian threat made American planners decide that Germany should be unified, rebuilt in democratic form, and given a healthy economy so it could serve as a bulwark against Russian expansion. On this issue there was no possibility of compromise with the Russians. Their fears of Germany and hopes for the spread of communism made them hold fast thereafter to their zone in Germany and turn it into a Communist state. They wiped out the Prussian landlord class, nationalized east Germany's industries, and forced all parties to accept Communist control. At the same time, they would agree to no arrangements that would merge their eastern zone either economically or politically with the western zone. The division of Germany was complete.

The atom bomb and Russian-American relations

When the atom bombs were dropped on Japan in August 1945, the whole balance of international power suddenly shifted, and a psychological earthquake occurred in Russia. If the Russians' tendency was to distrust the capitalist West in the best of circumstances, now their fears escalated sharply. In Washington, conversely, the bomb seems to have given men a sense of power advantage. Truman remarked to Henry Stimson, who had been secretary of war under Roosevelt, that it "gave him an entirely new feeling of confidence." However, when Secretary of State James Byrnes went to a meeting with Russia's foreign minister, Molotov, in September 1945, delighted with "the presence of the bomb in his pocket, so to speak, as a great weapon to get through the thing," he found the Soviets more truculent and unyielding than ever.

The American government went almost immediately to the United Nations (in October 1945) with a warning that some international means of

Occupation zones in Germany and Austria, 1945–1950

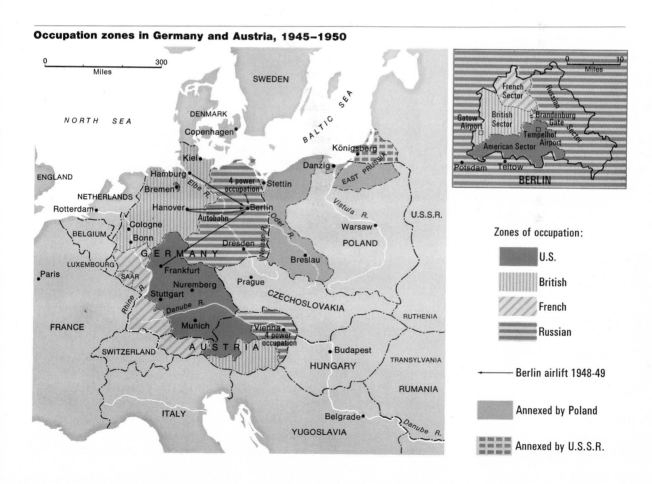

Zones of occupation:

U.S.
British
French
Russian

Berlin airlift 1948-49

Annexed by Poland

Annexed by U.S.S.R.

control over atomic energy had to be worked out. In March 1946 it proposed that all atomic production be placed under an international agency; that international inspectors be given free access to every country to ensure against violations; and that the big-power veto in the Security Council be abolished in all matters pertaining to violation of atomic agreements. The Russians had never trusted the United Nations, for in all of its deliberations they were clearly in a minority. They totally rejected the American plan. Instead, they wanted the United States to destroy its stockpile of weapons and halt all nuclear production, after which a program of international control would be established. In response, Truman observed, "We should not under any circumstances throw away our gun until we are sure the rest of the world can't arm against us. If we accepted the Russian position, we would be deprived of everything except their promise to agree to controls." The impasse was total; another deadlock had occurred.

President Truman found the world scene in January 1946 deeply alarming. The Russians were mounting intense pressure against Turkey to give them control over the Dardanelles; their armed forces were still in northern Iran, where they seemed busily to be establishing another puppet regime; and after a brief period in the fall of 1945 when they had relaxed their grip in eastern Europe (they had allowed elections in Hungary, which went smashingly against them), they had clamped down hard. Millions of refugees fled to western Europe to get away from the Russians. Truman now told Byrnes to drop conciliatory gestures. "Unless Russia is faced with an iron fist and strong language," he wrote Byrnes, "another war is in the making. I'm tired of babying the Soviets."

In February 1946 Stalin made a speech in Moscow that chilled the non-Communist world. There could never be any lasting peace with capitalism, he insisted. Soviet Russia must prepare itself for many years of austerity while it built the necessary industrial strength to meet the capitalist challenge. Justice William Douglas echoed the feelings of many when he said this speech was "the declaration of World War III." Shortly afterward, when Winston Churchill made his "iron curtain" address in Fulton, Missouri, he pleaded with Americans to use their possession of atomic strength to create "a unity in Europe from which no nation should be permanently outcast." Stalin trumpeted that Churchill's words were "a call to war with the Soviet Union," and scoffed that it was "the law of historical development" for all Europe to become Communist. Soon an intense ideological campaign was begun within Russia to drive out Western influences, deify Stalin, and inculcate the purest Stalinist dogma. The Cold War was in full cry.

Who started the Cold War?

Until recent years American historians accepted without much question that the Cold War was begun by the Russians. There seemed little reason to doubt the purity of American motives. The United States had long since acquired the fixed notion that it was the warrior for freedom in the world. The nation had fought bitterly to defeat a dictatorship that had gobbled up small countries, and now Russia seemed to be doing the same thing. That President Truman and his associates were sturdily holding back an arrogant and brutal tidal wave of force appeared beyond question.

The Vietnam War has severely shaken this view. In that conflict American motives have indeed been harshly condemned. Thus prepared, the historical mind has been more ready to listen to a group of "revisionist" historians—William Appleman Williams, Walter LaFeber, and Gabriel Kolko chief among them—who maintain that the Cold War was produced by a global American drive for power and markets. In their view, the Russians were only trying to protect their own security by building a ring of friendly buffer states between themselves and the Germans. The United States, meanwhile, tried to push into eastern Europe to secure its markets. Gar Alperovitz, in a controversial book, *Atomic Diplomacy: Hiroshima and Potsdam* (1965), has even charged that President Truman dropped the atom bomb on Japan in order to frighten the Russians and cause them to retreat from eastern Europe.

As observed at the beginning of this book (in "The Historian's Task"), a scholar's underlying view of life shapes his interpretations. Since no one has had access to Soviet records, Stalin's motives may only be surmised. Conversely, no evidence of a capitalist conspiracy may be found in President Truman's files or in his memoirs. Thus the revisionist argument must be based fundamentally on a preexisting belief that capitalist systems are inherently corrupt and that their leaders are hypocritical men who mouth democratic platitudes while serving the interests of Wall Street.

Most contemporary historians, however, strike a more middle ground. Although no longer so ready to accept the American role unquestioningly, they tend to regard power struggles as practically inevitable in world affairs, especially in the confusion following a global war. They believe that mutual distrust, once unleashed, hardened into fears on both sides that led each country to overreact. Where revisionist historians see conscious conspiracy, others see blunders made by leaders well and sincerely motivated. Furthermore, in the last analysis it is impossible for most historians to regard Joseph Stalin and his regime

tolerantly. As the Russians themselves revealed after his death in a spectacular outburst of self-criticism, under Stalin atrocities were committed both inside and outside the Soviet Union. Millions of people, including Russians, were killed in mass purges by Stalin's secret police. It is hard to believe that Moscow's sphere of control expanded only because it felt American actions threatened its security. Recent studies indicate that tremendous pressures toward expansion existed within the Communist party apparatus in Russia. Party leaders had a vision of remaking the world, and it is reasonable to assume that they intended to make the most of their opportunities.

The crisis of 1947

By 1947 the United States stood face to face with a great fact: Europe was in a state of collapse. Its railroads, factories, electrical systems, banking houses, supplies of capital, farms, markets—all had been utterly devastated by the Second World War. The governments of each European country staggered from crisis to crisis, overwhelmed by millions of refugees, desperately trying to feed starving populations and unable to find capital anywhere. American production and prosperity soared as European countries clamored for our goods—they could produce very little themselves—but soon they began running out of dollars. They tried borrowing, but were unable to

Hamburg, Germany, lies devastated after wartime bombing. In such conditions lay the economic and social plight of much of stricken postwar Europe. Quonset huts provided temporary housing.
Wide World Photos

make payments. Famine, unemployment, and black despair spread everywhere. Communist parties flourished in France and Italy, asserting that the only solution was to jettison capitalism entirely and turn to the Soviet system.

Great Britain teetered on the edge of total economic disaster. Its empire lay in ruins, trade disappeared, currency reserves were depleted, and its factories were both overworked and obsolete. Its millions of city dwellers, who made up most of its population, were desperately in need of food and raw materials from abroad, but they could not produce enough to pay for them. For two years Britain's armies had occupied Greece, helping its government fight off a Communist-inspired rebellion. In February 1947, however, London's ambassador officially informed the American government that the British could no longer carry this burden. Unless the United States took their place, Greece would have to be abandoned.

Here was the turning point. Was the United States going to cast off its traditional policy of peacetime isolation and move massively into Europe with direct aid to its faltering governments, or was it going to hold back and—as it was almost universally believed—watch communism take over? The loss of Greece to the Communists would not be a grave matter in itself, but the psychological impact of this event on the staggering nations of western Europe would be enormous. Washington buzzed with meetings. Emergency gatherings were held in the State Department and the Pentagon, and a steady stream of advisers came and went from the White House where President Truman discussed the crisis with his new secretary of state, General George C. Marshall. To the president, the question was fundamentally a simple one: the United States had fought to crush totalitarianism; the new Russian menace "facing us seemed every bit as grave as Nazi Germany and her allies had been"; and the time had come "to align the United States of America clearly on the side, and the head, of the free world." He went before

Congress on March 12, 1947, and not only asked for $400 million in economic and military aid to Greece and Turkey but also announced the Truman Doctrine: "I believe that it must be the policy of the United States to support free peoples who are resisting attempted subjugation by armed minorities or by outside pressures." Thus, before a cheering Congress, the American president called not simply for action in a limited sphere but for a policy of global scope as well: that we would assist "free peoples" anywhere who were in danger of overthrow by the Communists.

The Marshall Plan

Secretary of State George Marshall was an austere and forbidding man whose magisterial leadership of the American armed forces during the Second World War as chief of staff had made him one of the giants of the age. Revered in Washington and throughout the country, he had the kind of moral authority that enables men to lead nations into historic actions. He knew that aid to Greece and Turkey was not enough; that all of Europe was desperately sick. He therefore summoned in George F. Kennan, the State Department's brilliant and experienced expert on the Soviet Union, and instructed him to prepare a comprehensive plan for meeting the Soviet challenge and saving Europe. "He then added characteristically," Kennan later wrote, "that he had only one bit of advice for me: 'Avoid trivia.'"

The proposal that Kennan and his planning staff drew up became the bold and imaginative program known as the Marshall Plan. Promising immense gifts of money to rebuild the European economy, it caused excitement in the chancelleries of Europe. The plan was based on three premises. First, it was offered to everyone in Europe, Communist and non-Communist alike. George Kennan put the reason for this succinctly: "We would not ourselves draw a line of division through Europe." Secondly, it assumed that communism's basic appeal was economic; that a healthy Europe, able to offer jobs and hope to everyone, would not voluntarily choose the Communist system. As the secretary of state said when he announced the proposal in a speech at Harvard in June, the plan would fight "hunger, poverty, desperation, and chaos."

Third, it was hoped through this means to push Europe away from nationalism and toward internationalism. At least since the days of Woodrow Wilson, and especially under Democratic presidents, foreign policy planners in America had believed that the long-range solution to the world's problems lay in building an international structure of institutions that would allow nations to make their plans and decisions jointly. A multilateral world should replace one in which nations acted unilaterally, that is, entirely on their own. Franklin Roosevelt had placed enormous faith in the United Nations. Under Truman this same internationalist tendency persisted. Washington poured huge sums into the United Nations and vigorously supported its specialized agencies: the Economic and Social Council, the World Court, the International Labor Organization, the Food and Agriculture Organization, the International Monetary Fund, the World Health Organization, and the Educational, Scientific, and Cultural Organization. During the Second World War the United States had required all recipients of lend-lease to commit themselves to the principle of lower tariffs, and in 1947 the government led in the creation of the General Agreement on Tariffs and Trade. This agency worked worldwide to effect bilateral negotiations that progressively reduced tariff barriers. Thousands of commodities were affected by these agreements, in which more than sixty countries, accounting for four-fifths of the world's trade, participated. Similarly, in Latin America the Truman administration worked steadily toward the formation of a hemisphere-wide international body, the Organization of American States, which finally appeared in March 1948.

In this spirit, the Marshall Plan assumed that

nothing would work in Europe that rested simply on a series of uncoordinated economic programs developed within each nation. Therefore, Secretary Marshall told the Europeans that the United States would help them only if they jointly decided what their needs were and how they could be solved. "By insisting on a joint approach," Kennan wrote, "we hoped to force the Europeans to begin to think like Europeans, and not like nationalists." Responding enthusiastically, delegates from sixteen European nations gathered quickly in Paris, formed the Committee of European Economic Cooperation—the beginning, people said hopefully, of European federation—and plunged into intensive studies of their economic requirements. By September, a two-volume report was sent to Washington, D.C., and Congress began deliberations on this historic change in America's foreign policies.

America grapples with dilemma

Republicans controlled Congress—having won it for the first time since 1930 in the 1946 off-year elections—and they reacted warily to the proposal. They were even more implacably hostile to the Soviets than Truman, and continually urged harsh policies. Before long they began attacking Truman as "soft on communism." Moreover, they had little patience with economic aid as a proper response to the Communist challenge. They tended to favor military strength and constantly hammered for a bigger army, navy, and air force and a foreign aid program that would concentrate on building up the armed strength of the non-Communist governments. Senator Robert Taft of Ohio, Republican leader in Congress, scoffed at the Marshall Plan as a kind of "European TVA," which for an economic conservative of his rigorous views was the ultimate curse. Furthermore, conservative Republicans have traditionally leaned toward nationalist, unilateral approaches to world affairs—in the tradition of Alexander Hamilton and Theodore Roosevelt—and the prevailing internationalism of Truman's administration made them angry. Had they not condemned America's entry into the League of Nations and scoffed at the World Court in the interwar years? Now that they were finally in control of Congress again, they had a chance to make their views influential once more.

This presented, indeed, a grave dilemma for the American people. Was the Soviet threat mainly a military one, or did it feed primarily on misery and privation? On this assessment rested crucial differences in policy. Throughout the Cold War and after, the American government wavered on the issue. The argument went on endlessly in Washington and in the press, sincere people on both sides calling their opponents fools, militarists, or even traitors. In good part the issue was partisan. Republicans—particularly the hard-lining anti-Communists on the right wing—looked at the Communist insurrection in Greece and said: put it down by swift military force. But the Democrats had a more complicated response. Southern Democrats, with the strong martial culture of their region behind them, often agreed with the Republicans. But liberal Democrats thought in terms of social reform. (In addition to which, they traditionally distrusted the military—a distrust the military heartily returned.) Their answer to a Communist movement was: take away its appeal by economic aid and social reform; foster land reform, build schools, and give hope and opportunity to the common people so that they will lose interest in communism.

Policy of containment

The Second World War, however, had hardened many of the liberal Democrats. It was no longer possible, they believed, to get along in the world solely by peaceful methods. Reinhold Neibuhr, now at the peak of his influence among liberal Democrats—George Kennan called him "the father of us all"—criticized the optimism that led liberals to reject armaments and rely simply on international organizations to maintain peace. Liberals, he said, had foolishly ignored the side of human nature that is selfish, distrustful, and aggressive. There is an inveterate will-to-power created by fear that makes international tensions inevitable. In such a world, Neibuhr maintained, every nation must be tough-minded and meet threats by counterstrength.

In this spirit George Kennan published in *Foreign Affairs*—under the pseudonym "X"—the philosophy of "containment," which became the basis of American policy toward Russia. The Communists, he said, would unendingly press outward, taking advantage of every weak spot in the non-Communist world. Moscow did this both because it believed the world should be Communist (its version of "missionary diplomacy") and because repeated invasions of Russian territory over the centuries had made Russians fearful and insecure. Negotiation would gain very little. America should instead build "situations of strength" around the vast Russian perimeter so that the Soviets' outward thrusts would be met by effective resistance. Since the Communists believed that the capitalist system was in any event doomed to collapse, they would draw back from actually going to war. If the United States was strong, vigilant, and patient, this "duel of infinite duration" would eventually end in a peaceful stalemate.

Kennan explained his containment policy in these words: "The first of [Moscow's beliefs] is that of the innate antagonism between capitalism and Socialism. . . . It means that there can never be on Moscow's side any sincere assumption of a community of aims between the Soviet Union and powers which are regarded as capitalist. . . . If the Soviet Government occasionally sets its signature to documents which would indicate the contrary, this is to be regarded as a tactical maneuver. . . . [Thus] the phenomena which we find disturbing in the Kremlin's conduct of foreign policy: the secretiveness, the lack of frankness, the duplicity, the war suspiciousness, and the basic unfriendliness of purpose. . . .

"But we have seen that the Kremlin is under no ideological compulsion to accomplish its purposes in a hurry. Like the Church, it is dealing in ideological concepts which are of long-term validity, and it can afford to be patient. . . . Thus the Kremlin has no compunction about retreating in the face of superior force. And being under the compulsion of no timetable, it does not get panicky under the necessity for such retreat. Its political action is a fluid stream which moves constantly, wherever it is permitted to move, toward a given goal. Its main concern is to make sure that it has filled every nook and cranny available to it in the basin of world power. . . .

"In these circumstances it is clear that the main element of any United States policy toward the Soviet Union must be that of a long-term, patient but firm and vigilant containment of Russian expansive tendencies. [But we must] remain at all times cool and collected and . . . demands on Russian policy should be put forward in such a manner as to leave the way open for a compliance not too detrimental to Russian prestige. [Containment will be achieved] by the adroit and vigilant application of counter-force at a series of constantly shifting geographical and political points. . . ." ("The Sources of Soviet Conduct," *Foreign Affairs 25* [July 1947].)

Success in Europe

The Russians condemned the Marshall Plan as a capitalist plot to create war, refused to permit iron curtain nations to participate, and established the Cominform (Communist Information Bureau) to instigate revolutions. France and Italy were brought to the brink of civil war by Communist-led violent strikes and sabotage. In February 1948 Moscow obliterated the non-Communist parties in Czechoslovakia—the last iron curtain country with a vestige of democracy—and installed full Communist control. In April 1948 Congress finally approved the Marshall Plan and provided the first six billion dollars to get it rolling. (In all, twelve billion dollars was eventually

spent in carrying it out.) In response, the Russians closed off surface access to Berlin. President Truman's reply was the Berlin Airlift, which for almost a year (June 1948 to May 1949) flew mountainous supplies of food and other necessities to western Berlin. Truman thus demonstrated conclusively to western Europe that it could count on the United States in a crisis. Meanwhile, he ran for reelection against Governor Thomas E. Dewey of New York and won a stunning upset victory.

The Truman administration now moved ahead to build a system of collective military security that would make Europeans confident that they could rebuild their economies without fear of a Russian attack. In April 1949 the North Atlantic Treaty, leading to the creation of the North Atlantic Treaty Organization (NATO), was signed. It aimed not only at linking the United States militarily to western Europe (eventually including Greece and Turkey) but also at providing a matrix out of which, many hoped, some larger transatlantic federation might emerge. In the NATO treaty a council was provided for, as well as an agreement that "an armed attack against one or more of [the members] in Europe or North America shall be considered an attack against them all." An elaborate military system was built up, deployed throughout Europe, and set in readiness for any eventuality.

The Marshall Plan and NATO were remarkably successful policies. This was so for several reasons: they were in pursuit of objectives clearly vital to American interests; the goals and methods adopted were within America's means to achieve; and what Americans did had the support of those they were trying to protect. With infusions of American capital and the adoption of cooperative methods, the European economy began booming. A basis was established for a stalemate that eventually allowed East and West to live together. In 1949 the Russians exploded their own atomic bomb, thus moderating their fears of American atomic weaponry and creating a "balance of terror." Having found through their joint efforts in the Marshall Plan how successful cooperation could be, the western European nations during the 1950s launched a series of multi-national agencies that pointed toward a federated Europe: the Common Market, the European Coal and Steel Community, and the European Payments Union.

The Far East transformed

After 1945 Asia was transformed. The huge British, French, and Dutch empires crumbled away, allowing such countries as India and Indonesia to become independent nations. American power

was consolidated in the Pacific, taking over as United Nations trusteeships the former Japanese-mandated islands swept over by United States armies, as well as Okinawa. Having conquered Japan practically unaided, Washington made certain that it ruled that country without interference (a fact the Russians pointed to, asking why they were criticized when they exercised the same powers over Poland). General Douglas MacArthur became supreme commander over the occupation of Japan and thus over its way of life. A sweeping social revolution was ordered as the Americans sought to remake Japan in the United States image. Political democracy was

Postwar alliances: Europe, North Africa, and the Middle East

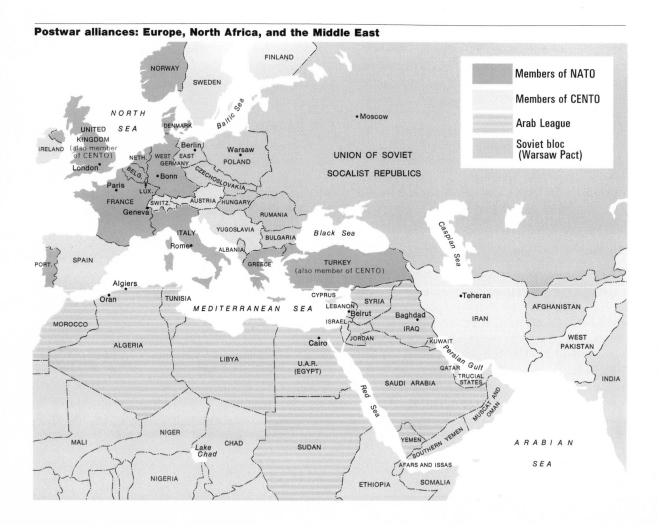

instituted, women being given the vote. War was renounced as an instrument of national policy, and the Japanese military system was scrapped. The economy was rebuilt, monopolies were broken up, and soon the Japanese standard of living spurted upward. Labor was encouraged to organize in hopes of providing a counterbalance to the power of the great industrial and near-feudal families. The Shinto religion was disestablished (i.e., no longer taught as the state religion), and freedom of religion and speech were decreed. Land reform made tenants into owner-farmers, affecting more than two-thirds of Japan's farm lands.

The total result? Difficult to assess, most experts agree. Japan has an ancient and powerfully rooted culture, and clearly it could not be remade during a brief occupation by foreigners. Americans were naive to think they could transform Japan into a Far Eastern United States. The Japanese took what they wanted and rejected the rest. At the least, however, American reforms instigated an opening up of Japanese life that released floods of social change within the family, the factory, and the nation. Japan remained an elitist nation bound together in habits of deference toward those above, but one profoundly shaken by the new values of individual freedom and self-expression.

In China, Chiang Kai-shek lost little time after 1945 beginning an all-out attack against the Communists. But his regime was riddled by corruption, indifferent to the rural masses, worn down by long years of war, and unable to inspire the Chinese people. The American government sought vainly in 1947 to bring peace between the two factions, but in a civil war compromise is impossible—as the war in Vietnam was later to demonstrate and as earlier civil wars in the United States, France, England, Greece, and elsewhere had abundantly shown. Soon the Communists were surging out of their base of power in Manchuria into North China. The Nationalist army rapidly collapsed. Many of Chiang's generals changed sides, taking their American-equipped armies with them. Following a desper-

ate retreat, the Nationalist government fled to the island of Formosa (now Taiwan). In October 1949, the "People's Republic of China" was proclaimed over the Chinese mainland, with its capital at Peiping.

The American people were shocked. Almost immediately a storm of protest blew up concentrating on one endlessly reiterated theme: the Truman administration, influenced by traitorous influences, had "lost China." Such critics brushed aside the counterargument that 800 million Chinese were beyond the control of any American policy, right or wrong. Great numbers of Americans believed that there was no limit to the power of the United States to work its will in the world. This notion, built into the American mind through generations of domestic success and by victories in two huge world wars, was called "the illusion of American omnipotence" by Denis Brogan, a perceptive British observer. Illusion or not, it was to be a major force behind United States foreign policy at least until the late 1960s, when years of failure in Vietnam began to teach the American people a new lesson about the limits of power.

The Korean War

On June 24, 1950, the Soviet-equipped army of North Korea flooded over the border into South Korea, using hundreds of tanks sent by Russia within the previous two months. Word was flashed to President Truman while he was visiting his home in Missouri. It was his habit to think historically, and now he looked at the Korean invasion not by itself, but in a historical continuum beginning in the 1930s. Then, the western democracies had held back and allowed Manchuria, Ethiopia, and Austria to be taken, only to find that the appetite of aggressors was increased rather than diminished by such victories. Now, he believed, the time had come in demonstrate that collective security could in fact work.

President Truman believed in the United Nations and in multilateralism, and he immediately

Postwar alliances: The Far East

BERING
SEA

UNION OF SOVIET SOCIALIST REPUBLICS

Sea of Okhotsk

(U.S.S.R.)
(U.S.)
ATTU

KISKA

Lake Baikal

• Irkutsk

SAKHALIN I.
(U.S.S.R.)

• Ulan Bator

MONGOLIA

MANCHURIA

KURILE IS.
(U.S.S.R.)

• Vladivostok

Peking •

NORTH
KOREA

*Sea of
Japan*

• Pyongyang

Seoul • SOUTH
KOREA

J A P A N

• Tokyo

C H I N A

Shanghai •

• BONIN IS.

TIBET

NEPAL

MATSU I.

TACHEN
IS.

QUEMOY I.

RYUKYU IS.
(Jap.)

OKINAWA

• IWO JIMA

MARCUS I. •

P A C I F I C

E. PAKISTAN

Calcutta •

BURMA

TAIWAN
(FORMOSA)

PESCADORES
IS.

INDIA

Hanoi •
Hong Kong
(Br.)

NORTH
VIETNAM

*PHILIPPINE
SEA*

MARIANAS IS. •

• WAKE I.
(U.S.)

O C E A N

Vientiane •

LAOS

Rangoon •

THAILAND

*South
China
Sea*

• Manila

GUAM
(U.S.)

M   I   C   R   O

BAY OF
BENGAL

Bangkok •

CAMBODIA

SOUTH
VIETNAM

• Saigon

PHILIPPINES
(also member
of SEATO)

MARSHALL IS.
(U.S. trust)

CEYLON

CAROLINE ISLANDS
(U.S. trust)

N   E   S

BRUNEI
(Br.)

GILBERT IS.
(Br.)

Kuala Lumpur •

MALAYSIA

SARAWAK

I   A

SUMATRA

• SINGAPORE

KALIMANTAN

SULAWESI

M   E   L   A   N   E   S   I   A

I N D O N E S I A

IRIAN
(To U.N. 1962,
Indonesia 1963)

NEW GUINEA
(Aust.)

• Djakarta

JAVA

TIMOR
(Port.)

PAPUA
(Aust.)

SOLOMON IS.
(Br.)

ELLICE IS.
(Br.)

I N D I A N

O C E A N

CORAL
SEA

NEW HEBRIDES IS.
(Br. and Fr.)

FIJI IS.
(Br.)

NEW
CALEDONIA
(Fr.)

A U S T R A L I A

Brisbane •

T A S M A N

S E A

• Perth

• Sidney

Canberra •

Melbourne •

NEW
ZEALAND

TASMANIA

Wellington •

Members of SEATO

Nations having bilateral treaties with the U.S.

Communist bloc

appealed to the United Nations Security Council for joint action. Since the Russians were then boycotting its proceedings, the Council was able quickly to pass a resolution condemning North Korea and calling on that nation to withdraw. When that failed, the United Nations asked its members to "furnish such assistance to the Republic of Korea as may be necessary to repel the armed attack and to restore international peace and security in the area." Following this step, which no world organization had ever taken before, a United Nations Command was created, and the United States was asked to appoint its commander.

Within a short time American forces were battling in South Korea, to be joined later by thousands of troops from Britain, Turkey, Australia, France, and the Philippines. (Eleven more nations helped out in lesser ways.) Under the leadership of General Douglas MacArthur the United Nations force held onto Pusan, in the southeast corner of South Korea. With typical boldness, MacArthur then decided on an amphibious invasion far up the peninsula behind North Korean lines at Inchon, the harbor for Seoul, South Korea's capital. In September, almost three months after the war had begun, he sent tens of thousands of marines and army soldiers splashing ashore. By intense fighting they quickly thrust their way to Seoul. Meanwhile the United Nations forces had burst out of their Pusan perimeter, and in a brief time more than a hundred thousand prisoners were taken, the shattered North Korean army fleeing northward back across its borders.

General MacArthur now appealed to the United Nations for authority to cross the thirty-eighth parallel and drive the Communists out of the entire Korean peninsula. After a highly charged debate, the General Assembly called on him to do so, despite warnings from Communist China. As the U.N. force approached the Chinese border it was suddenly assaulted by hordes of Chinese soldiers who caught MacArthur's troops awkwardly spread-eagled across the peninsula.

In the disaster that followed, the United Nations army suffered shocking casualties. Large units had to fight their way back into South Korea to get behind lines hastily thrown up far south of Seoul, which had once again fallen to the Communists. The Korean War, on the verge of being so brilliantly won, was now doomed to grind on for three more years.

The "Great Debate"

During the bloody seesaw warfare that ensued, Republican leaders like House minority leader Joseph Martin demanded that the war be expanded by bombing China, blockading its coast, and "unleashing" Chiang Kai-shek to begin an

Soldiers of an American army unit advance in attack formation during the Korean War, under fire from Communist forces. Many months of trench warfare across the middle of the peninsula eventually ended in a cease-fire in 1953.
U.S. Army photograph

invasion of China from Formosa. (President Truman had put the Seventh Fleet between Formosa and the mainland to prevent either side from invading the other.) But Truman was determined to keep the conflict a limited war for limited objectives. At all costs he wanted to prevent its escalation into World War III. General MacArthur chafed bitterly under this restriction, insisting that there was no substitute for total victory. In April 1951, when he publicly lined up with the Republicans by allowing Congressman Martin to read in the House an appeal by the general for total victory over the Chinese, Truman dismissed him for insubordination.

This set off a tremendous national furor, for the general was admired and adored by thousands. Congress immediately began a "Great Debate" over the issue of the war's strategy. The debate raged nationally through every media, producing, eventually, a consensus: that the military must not be allowed to challenge civilian authority, and that a major land war in Asia would be, as General Omar Bradley put it, "the wrong war, at the wrong place, at the wrong time, and with the wrong enemy."

In Korea, the United Nations Army, now under the command of General Matthew Ridgway, massacred whole armies of Chinese with its superior fire power (China lost well over a million men in Korea) and pushed back northward. By the time Ridgway had succeeded in establishing a line across the peninsula in the general vicinity of the thirty-eighth parallel, the weary Chinese proposed an armistice. Negotiations over its terms dragged on for two years, beginning in July 1951, while the deeply entrenched armies continued their bloody raids and counterraids.

The election of Dwight Eisenhower

The Truman administration was destroyed by the Korean War. The endless, inconclusive fighting; the "limited war" concept, which grated against the nerves of a nation long habituated to total victory; the very existence of the Chinese Communist regime, for which Truman was blamed—these controversies created a massive loss of confidence in the government. The Republicans chose the luminous war hero, Dwight D. Eisenhower, as their presidential nominee in 1952. Against the Democratic nominee, Adlai E. Stevenson, witty and cerebral governor of Illinois, Eisenhower swept to a landslide victory. (He massively defeated Stevenson again in the election of 1956.)

Eisenhower entered office having pledged to end the war in Korea. Fortunately for him and for the world, Joseph Stalin soon died, and in the ensuing "thaw" in the Cold War, the Chinese proved cooperative about armistice terms. In July 1953 an armistice was signed, setting the truce line along the existing line of entrenchments. (A formal peace treaty has never been settled on, and the northern border of South Korea is still heavily fortified against a renewal of hostilities.) After 150,000 American casualties (54,000 dead) and hundreds of thousands of casualties in the other armies, the Korean War was over.

The new foreign policy

Under Eisenhower and his secretary of state, John Foster Dulles, the Republicans reintroduced into the conduct of America's foreign policy some attitudes long traditional on their side of American politics. There was no return to "Fortress America" isolationism, as might have happened had an old-line Republican like Robert Taft gained the presidency, but there was, nevertheless, a shift toward a unilateral, nationalistic foreign policy. President Eisenhower admired wealthy industrialists and financiers, and he appointed a cabinet of millionaires. Consequently, there was no move to lower tariffs. Aid that would strengthen the industrial systems of foreign nations was largely shelved, and a much stronger emphasis was placed on purely military assistance. In the underdeveloped countries, the administration relied on the influence of American business and showed little patience with proposals that the United States foster social reform. Republicans had always believed that the best results for everyone, rich and poor alike, flowed from opening up resources and opportunities to modern business, thus creating jobs and a rising standard of living.

The Democratic administration had worked endlessly to maintain close relations with its allies, making sure that great decisions were arrived at after prior multilateral discussions, but John Foster Dulles had little patience with this difficult, time-consuming process. He tended to announce United States foreign policy from Washington, expecting the nation's allies to follow along and defer to his leadership. European governments were offended. The result was a steady deterioration of the NATO alliance as the foundation of American foreign policy.

Dulles was a devout Presbyterian, a Wall Street lawyer for more than forty years, and a moralist who saw the world as a battleground between good and evil. The American system of free capitalism was, to him, practically divine in origin, and communism was pure evil. As he said in 1953, the Soviet system "believes human beings are nothing more than somewhat superior animals . . . and that the best kind of a world is that world which is organized as a well-managed farm. I do not see how, as long as Soviet Communism holds those views . . . there can be any permanent reconciliation. This is an irreconcilable conflict." In this view Truman's containment policy, which aimed merely at holding the line, was fundamentally immoral. The eastern European countries must be liberated, and the Soviet system itself destroyed. How did he propose to do this? By a constant drum fire of moral outrage to bring such unrelenting pressure on the Soviet Union that—he believed—it would crumble from within.

Meanwhile, he believed that all nations must choose sides between good and evil. To be neutral, in Dulles' opinion, was to be on the Soviet side. India chose a neutral course; therefore the American government regarded the Indians as

enemies and formed a lasting alliance with Pakistan instead. Heavy shipments of military equipment were sent to governments that declared themselves anti-Communist even if, as critics asserted, their policies within their own countries were reactionary and oppressive. Time and again this form of anticommunism lined up the American government behind regimes that were undemocratic, as in Spain, Pakistan, and Brazil. Horrified at the Communist victory over the French in North Vietnam in 1954, Dulles insisted adamantly that the patched-together government of South Vietnam be maintained in power, even though repeated Central Intelligence Agency analyses warned that it was corrupt, unpopular, prolandlord, and oppressive. The Seventh Fleet, which Truman had placed between Formosa and China, was ostentatiously removed so that Chiang Kai-shek's army would be "unleashed" for an invasion (which it was never strong enough to mount). An intense propaganda campaign was beamed toward the iron curtain countries that all but promised them direct aid if they rose in rebellion against Russia.

The new defense posture

At the same time, the Eisenhower administration stated that never again would the United States get involved in a conventional, Korean-type war against Communist aggression. The Kremlin was warned of "massive retaliation"; that is, if another such invasion began, the American government would attack Russia itself with nuclear weapons. The army, the tactical air force, and other such conventional military systems were allowed to dwindle to almost token levels, while the jet bombers of the air force were relied on as the striking force. Great emphasis was placed on creation of a full range of nuclear weapons. Secretary Dulles described the American strategy in the Cold War with Russia as "brinkmanship," i.e., going to the brink of war to force compliance, without actually tumbling over the edge. The world was horrified at this tactic. It provided another reason for western European disenchantment with American leadership and for the success of those who urged Europe to take its own independent course in the world.

The Dulles alliances

Secretary Dulles decided to complete a ring of military alliances around the Soviet Union and China. In September 1954, following the defeat of the French in North Vietnam, he had taken steps to "shore up" Southeast Asia by the creation of the Southeast Asia Treaty Organization. It included Britain, France, Australia, New Zealand, the Philippines, Pakistan, Thailand, and the United States. Three months later, he completed a defensive treaty with the Nationalist Chinese government and pledged America to defend Formosa and the Pescadores (a group of small islands between Formosa and mainland China). Following that, Congress passed a resolution authorizing the president to fight if need be to protect Formosa.

In February 1955 he succeeded in forming the core of a hoped-for regional defense arrangement when he got Turkey and Iraq to sign a defense alliance called the Baghdad Pact. Soon Britain, Pakistan, and Iran joined in. Gamal Abdel Nasser, Egypt's ruler, was quickly able to take advantage of the resentment this pact created in Russia by making a huge arms aggreement with Moscow in September 1955. From this point on, a special relationship burgeoned between Egypt and Russia, greatly strengthening the military power of the Arabs. Nasser nationalized the British-owned Suez Canal in order to get its revenues, thus taking a potential stranglehold over essential supplies of oil to Europe. When Israel suddenly invaded Egypt in October 1956, the British and French joined in, seeking to regain the canal. (At almost the same time, the Russians were putting down the 1956 Hungarian rebellion, largely shielded from world attention by the attack on Egypt.)

The Atlantic alliance was practically destroyed by the Suez incident. Britain and France had gone ahead without consultation with Washington, and Eisenhower immediately drew back from their undertaking, calling on the United Nations to halt the fighting and establish a peacekeeping force in the area. The British and French were totally humiliated—and angered at the United States. Trying to salvage some order out of chaos and to fend off the Communists, in March 1957 Dulles secured congressional approval of a new policy, known as the Eisenhower Doctrine. It proclaimed that the American government would use its armed forces against any Communist or Communist-dominated aggressor in the Middle East if the attacked country sought American help. In mid-July 1958 Lebanon appealed for assistance under this doctrine, alleging Syrian-supported Communist insurrection, and American troops landed to prevent the collapse of the government. (They were withdrawn in late 1958.) In the midst of this crisis, Secretary Dulles virtually pledged American membership in the Baghdad Pact, later renamed the Central Treaty Organization (CENTO) when Iraq withdrew.

The Sputnik crisis

In October 1957 the world was electrified by a spectacular event: Russia launched *Sputnik 1*, the first globe-circling satellite. Hundreds of millions of people around the globe stood next to their dwellings and watched in fascination as the tiny gleaming satellite appeared over the horizon and then pursued its serene, inexorable path across the heavens, carrying with it the triumphant message of Russian technological brilliance. Khrushchev boasted delightedly that this dramatic event demonstrated the superiority of the Communist system, and he launched an intensive propaganda campaign designed to persuade wavering neutralist nations to join the Soviet side.

The Soviet Union's dramatic achievement began a year of national crisis in the United States. Eisenhower urged a speed-up in defense spending, especially for missiles—formerly given little attention—and nuclear submarines. He vigorously pushed through a centralization of the Defense Department, giving the secretary of defense vast new powers to unify the efforts of the military services and control the joint chiefs of staff. In January 1958 the tension was eased when the army successfully placed a small satellite in orbit, using a World War II-type rocket. The culmination of this phase was the successful firing of the first Atlas intercontinental ballistic missile in November 1958.

Renewed tensions in Europe

The most persistent problem in Europe during Eisenhower's years in office was the status of Germany. Largely through Dulles's insistence, the German Federal Republic (West Germany) was accorded independence in May 1955, given the right to rearm, and brought into NATO. The spectacle of a rearmed Germany outraged the other European nations, especially France. In late 1958 the Soviet Union suddenly reopened the long-quiescent question of West Berlin, Khrushchev calling for it being declared a "free city," the expulsion of western occupation forces, and the placing of its contacts with the west wholly under the control of the East German government.

Eisenhower, now bereft of Secretary Dulles, who died of cancer in early 1959, responded boldly. Seized with the conviction that he could bring the world back to peaceful conditions by direct acts of personal diplomacy, he invited Pre-

President Dwight Eisenhower, in search of eased relations with Russia and a damping down of the Cold War welcomes Soviet premier Nikita Krushchev to the United Stated in 1959.
Bob Henriques, Magnum Photos

mier Khrushchev to the United States for a visit and face-to-face talks. When this went well, the president embarked in December 1959 on a spectacular tour of eleven nations, from France to India, where he spoke to immense, enthusiastic crowds about the American ideals of peace and friendship in freedom. Then, in February and March 1960, he journeyed through Latin America where once more tumultuous crowds cheered him. There he proclaimed a "Hemisphere Crusade" for economic development and reaffirmed American aims of hemispheric political and economic stability. Hopes rose throughout the world that this extraordinary man might be able to reach a lasting friendly relationship with the Soviet Union and end the Cold War.

In May 1960 the president left for Paris, where he met with the British, the French, and Khrushchev. At this moment occurred one of those events, relatively minor in themselves, which deflects world history. An American U-2 reconnaissance plane, flying high over Russian territory and deep within its borders, was shot down. Eisenhower refused to take refuge in the customary denial of responsibility. The Soviet premier exploded into a rage, gave a frightening tirade, broke up the conference, and returned to Moscow where he soon revived the Cold War by threatening talk and gestures. Much of the free world blamed Eisenhower for the timing of the flight. During the rest of Eisenhower's administration, the bitterly disappointed president stayed home in the White House, watching a political storm build up in which his conduct of the presidency came under unending attack.

The world scene changes

By 1960 the world was significantly different than it had been in 1945. The British, French, and Dutch empires had disappeared, opening up an extraordinarily fluid situation in the non-Western world. Both Russia and the United States competed for the loyalties of the many new African and Asian nations. China made its momentous

break with Russia in April 1960. Thereafter Peking too began preaching support for Communist rebellions in the non-Western world and vying with the Soviet Union for leadership of the world Communist movement.

Meanwhile, western Europe was heading in new directions. Offended by America's tendency to ignore the wishes of its European allies, emboldened by the booming success of the Common Market, and convinced that the Soviet Union no longer posed a real threat, Europeans listened to leaders, like France's Charles de Gaulle, who urged that Europe become an independent "third force" in the world. This involved a turning away from what de Gaulle called the Anglo-Saxon powers (Britain and the United States) and a downgrading of NATO. The French, indeed, were soon to pull their military forces out of the NATO system. The world of 1960, in other words, was in disarray as it searched for a new kind of international order.

John F. Kennedy

In 1960 a new figure began rising rapidly in American politics, that of John F. Kennedy, a young Irish-Catholic senator from Massachusetts. Harvard trained, a historian, cool, crisp, intelligent, and wealthy, he was gifted with a wry wit and a flair for exciting, hard-driving oratory. He swiftly became a charismatic figure, inspiring adulation in millions at home and around the world. He seemed to express all the hopes of a world led by old men for a fresh leadership of vision, hopefulness, and vigor. Skeptical and—he hoped—realistic, he did not regard the world as a place in which the West was all good, and the East was all evil. Rather, he conceived of it as a chancy and untidy place in which it was important to operate from strength, but in which it was possible and desirable to live in peace and mutual helpfulness with the Russians.

An endlessly active man eager for accomplishment, he campaigned for the presidency against Eisenhower's vice-president, Richard M. Nixon, on the theme of "getting the country moving again." Recessions had hobbled the national economy during Eisenhower's years so that its growth rate lagged far behind those of Russia and western Europe. The stunning rocketry exploits of the Soviet Union seemed to reveal a perilous missile gap (later shown to be illusory). Throughout the world the new and underdeveloped nations were shunning what appeared to be the business-dominated foreign policy of the United States and welcoming the Communists. After a narrow victory over Nixon, Kennedy took office with an inspiring inaugural address calling his countrymen to a long, self-sacrificial struggle in which they should "ask not what your country can do for you—ask what you can do for your country."

Kennedy's policies

Everywhere was heard the drumbeat of fear that perhaps Khrushchev was right, that communism was the wave of the future. In the month of Kennedy's inauguration an exultant, truculent Khrushchev gave a major address in Moscow in which he boasted of Russia's industrial growth, missile exploits, immense hydrogen bombs, and growing success in underdeveloped countries from Vietnam to Cuba. History and communism, he said, were partners; "there is no longer any force in the world capable of barring the road to socialism." World wars were to be condemned, the Soviet premier maintained, but "wars of liberation or popular uprisings" were to be fostered "wholeheartedly and without reservation." In this context, peaceful coexistence meant "a form of intense economic, political and ideological struggle between the proletariat and the aggressive forces of imperialism in the world arena."

These words cast a chill over Washington. Reading them, the new president observed that "we must never be lulled into believing that either [Russia or China] has yielded its ambitions for world domination. . . ." Kennedy became fascinated by the new military doctrine of coun-

terinsurgency. "We must be ready now," he said, "to deal with any size of force, including small externally supported bands of men; and we must help train local forces to be equally effective. . . ." He began poring through books written by the leading world spokesmen for guerrilla warfare—Che Guevara and Mao Tse-tung. Spurred by his interest and support, the army developed new concepts, equipment, and training to produce military units on the order of the "Green Berets." With Dean Rusk as secretary of state, Robert McNamara running the Defense Department, the president's brother Robert Kennedy as attorney general, McGeorge Bundy and Walter W. Rostow as White House advisers on foreign affairs, the Kennedy team began vigorously to respond to Khrushchev's threats.

The best and the brightest

It is important to understand the spirit of the Kennedy administration. They were proud men who were confident that, whatever the challenge, they could solve it. "A remarkable hubris [i.e., overweening pride or self-confidence] permeated this entire time," David Halberstam has written in his brilliant study of the Kennedy and Johnson administrations, *The Best and the Brightest* (1972). "Nine years earlier Denis Brogan had written: 'Probably the only people who have the historical sense of inevitable victory are the Americans.' Never had that statement seemed more true; the Kennedy group regarded the Eisenhower people as having shrunk from the challenge set before them." The revolutionary upheavals sweeping through such countries as Vietnam and Cuba were seen merely as the newest editions of a series of "problems" that Americans had been successfully solving generation after generation.

Insurgency was thought of as something which could be fended off with organization and technology. The men of the Kennedy administration liked to think of themselves as tough-minded; they wore the popular nickname of "the Irish Mafia" with some pride. The president himself was fascinated by power in whatever form, and he liked using it. Combating the new challenge of guerrilla rebellions in Vietnam and elsewhere seemed an exciting kind of military chess in which dash, intelligence, and professional skill would be rewarded with inevitable victory. This is where the Green Berets—the United States Army Special Forces—would play their special role.

At the same time, however, John Kennedy was a liberal Democrat, heir to the tradition of Adlai Stevenson, and he carried with his fascination for power a lively belief that the United States could win no victories unless it worked for social reform abroad. He knew that the root cause of world turbulence lay in what Stevenson had called the "revolution of rising expectations," the realization by millions in the non-Western world that a better life was possible and their growing readiness to throw off what they had for a way of life more like that of the wealthy countries. Therefore, from the beginning he revived the social idealism expressed in the Marshall Plan and the concept of economic aid.

Throughout his administration ran this central conflict between a tough-minded, prideful military response that could lead the nation (and did) into overseas adventures of great potential danger, and a sensitive concern for human suffering that understood social turbulence as an outcry that would not stop until the revolution was completed. When John Kennedy was assassinated in Dallas in November 1963, this complex and subtle blend of policy was passed into the hands of Lyndon B. Johnson, a man far simpler in his motivations; more inclined to drive hell-for-leather either in one direction or in the other—characteristics that were to have grave consequences for the nation and the world.

Kennedy and the Third World

Some forty countries, holding nearly a billion people, had achieved independence since 1945 in Latin America, Asia, and Africa—the Third World. The United States had had a strange relationship to this process. On the one hand the American government was traditionally anti-colonialist and cheered it on; on the other, its NATO ties with imperial powers (France, Britain, Holland, Portugal) made it worried about doing anything that would unduly offend them. During the Eisenhower years, moreover, the Cold War psychology demanded that the new nations choose up sides, and condemned those that were neutralist—the great majority. Added to this was the predominantly business-oriented foreign policy of the Republican regime, which in each new country linked America with those of wealth and power against upwelling socialist movements.

President Kennedy was determined to transform this relationship. For some years before his election he had spoken publicly against colonial rule, especially with regard to Algeria, which was then caught up in a raging, bloody rebellion against French dominion. Often in his campaign he had referred to the Third World in terms of sympathy and understanding for the awakened hopes of millions of Africans, Asians, and Latin Americans for a better life. His election as president was cheered enthusiastically in these countries. To the White House came a steady stream of Third World leaders who were enchanted by the new president's knowledge of their problems and his genuine concern to offer American aid. They left the United States with the feeling that they had a special relationship with what they called Kennedy's America.

The most dramatic expression of Kennedy's outlook toward the new countries was his creation of the Peace Corps. Descendant of Franklin Roosevelt's Conservation Corps, which also aimed at putting young people to work in ways that served the country, it was condemned by Eisenhower as a "juvenile experiment." The response of young people throughout the United States was so enthusiastic, however, that soon the program became one of the shining lights of the new administration. Under Sargent Shriver, Kennedy's brother-in-law, it was in motion by the spring of 1961. Within three years, some 10,000 young Americans were at work in forty-six countries, laboring to bring such self-denying assistance as they could to the impoverished of the world.

Latin America

The new president was especially interested in Latin America. With 200 million people, half of them illiterate, multiplying faster than any other in the world and living in the grossest extremes of poverty and wealth, it was a vast region at once exciting and appalling. In 1959 Fidel Castro set up a violently anti-American Communist government in Cuba, and American attentions were suddenly forced southward. Cuba's quickly burgeoning ties with Russia transferred the Cold War to this hemisphere. "Operation Pan America," which was designed to raise income levels, stimulate land reform, and pull the Latin American countries together, had already been approved at a hemispheric conference in Washington in 1958. In 1960, Eisenhower pledged $500 million to underwrite development programs.

Kennedy seized on these initiatives swiftly, broadening them into a bold appeal for an "Alliance for Progress." In March 1961 he urged "the American Republics [to] begin on a vast new 10-Year Plan for the Americas, a plan to transform the 1960s into an historic decade of democratic progress." Conceived directly on the model of the Marshall Plan, the Alliance for Progress included the demand that Latin American countries work out their plans together before the United States would provide the necessary capital. At Punta del Este in Uruguay in August 1961, the Alliance for Progress was transformed into a multilateral program. At this meeting, the United States pledged at least twenty billion dollars in aid over the next ten years in private and government funds, provided the Latin American countries made fundamental social reforms. Launched with soaring fanfare, the Alliance for Progress

disappointed Kennedy. Entrenched privileged groups in Latin America, divisions among reformers, hostility from many Latin American countries, the almost constant eruption of military coups—these combined to hamstring the program, which limped along until, by the mid-1960s, it was heard of but rarely.

Even so, the Alliance was a catalyst for long-range change: governments began working out development plans; cooperative efforts developed into free-trade regional agreements; land reform pushed ahead; schools were built and teachers trained; water supplies were purified; roads opened up remote regions; and hopes were stimulated. Food production was at least keeping up with explosive population growth, and for the first time wealthy Latin Americans began investing in their own economies instead of sending their money to Swiss banks. By 1966 investment had soared to a level ten times the amount of financial aid coming in from abroad. Although terribly hampered by galloping inflation, economic growth rates, especially in the countries along the Andes, were astonishingly high.

The Bay of Pigs disaster

One of President Eisenhower's last actions had been to break diplomatic relations with Fidel Castro's Cuba because appropriate compensation for nationalized American sugar-producing facilities had been denied. Then, as Kennedy learned to his surprise on taking office, the Eisenhower administration began to train an invasion force composed of 1,200 Cuban exiles. The American government assumed that Castro, a Communist, was unpopular among his people and would be overthrown in a national uprising if outside assistance was provided. This faced President Kennedy with a crucial decision: should he remain true to his liberal Democratic heritage and keep faith with Franklin Roosevelt's policy of strict nonintervention, or would he be "tough-minded" and support an undertaking in line with his oratory about the need for a vigorous, active response to the Communist challenge? He chose a middle ground: he ruled out any involvement of Americans in the invasion itself. The 1,200 Cubans then training in the Guatemalan jungles would have to fight without the aid of the United States navy or air force. Kennedy's military advisers assured him categorically that this would work.

But it failed, utterly and completely. The invasion force was quickly smashed when it struggled onto the beaches of the Bay of Pigs in April 1961. The people of Cuba did not rally to its support. A massive miscalculation had been made that disgraced the Kennedy administration within three months of the inauguration. Military derring-do, CIA-trained guerrillas: it had all proved a miserable mistake. It was a profound shock. The president, said one of his aides, "showed his fatigue for the first time. He looked sad. The exhilaration of the job was gone. He was no longer the young conquering hero, the first 43-year old president . . . the young man smoking his cigar with his friends and telling them how much fun it was. All that was gone. Suddenly it became one hell of a job."

The space race

While the Kennedy administration was struggling to rise from this disaster, it was making a full investigation of the nation's exciting space programs. The president had concluded that it was absolutely essential for the United States to gain supremacy in space technology, both for its immediate effects on national security and for its immense psychological importance in rebuilding American confidence. Finding the space effort understaffed, underfunded, and uncoordinated, he decided to choose one great objective that would inspire the whole nation and allow everyone, scientist and technologist alike, to pull together. The objective? Placing a man on the moon. In the year 1961 this seemed an impossible visionary conception, but the very grandness of it caught his imagination.

In June 1961, therefore, he called the Congress into joint session and, in a personal address, appealed for immense funds to be devoted to the project. "Now it is time to take longer strides," he said, "time for a great new American enterprise—time for this nation to take a clearly leading role in space achievement, which in many ways may hold the key to our future on earth." Responding enthusiastically, Congress began pouring out billions of dollars to finance an enormous exploit in space technology and space science that has extended far into the 1970s.

Kennedy and Khrushchev

The president's main concern in foreign policy was to break the rigid Cold War and ease relationships with Russia. In June 1961 he flew to Vienna to meet with Khrushchev in hopes that a face-to-face encounter would create better communication. He tried hard to convince Khrushchev of the folly of missile-rattling, pointing out that one miscalculation could destroy civilization. To his dismay, he found Khrushchev unyielding. The Soviet premier lauded internal revolutions as "holy wars" that would carry communism around the globe. He would come to no agreements concerning Indochina or Berlin or any other world hot spot. Following American initiative, the Soviets had halted the testing of nuclear bombs in the atmosphere in 1958, and Kennedy had pushed insistently for a test-ban treaty to make this arrangement permanent. However, Khrushchev would not listen to Kennedy's appeals. The two leaders emerged from their last discussions grim and unsmiling.

Khrushchev returned to Moscow to make more threatening speeches, boast of his missiles and bombs, and order a thirty percent increase in military spending. He was adamant on Berlin: control over access to West Berlin was to be given by Russia to the East German government. At Vienna he had bluntly warned Kennedy that he was prepared to go to war to end the existing situation: West Berlin was to become a "free city," and western forces would be allowed to remain there only if East Germany agreed.

To Kennedy, the Berlin challenge amounted to a crucial test of the American will. If defeat were accepted, the word of the United States, he believed, would become valueless. In response to the challenge, he took a fateful step: on national television in July 1961 he called for a partial mobilization of the armed forces and a major increase of more than three billion dollars in military spending. The time had come, he said, for the United States to regain flexibility by rebuilding its conventional forces: ground armies, air transport, air tactical units, support naval craft. Eisenhower's military posture of "massive retaliation," which relied largely on delivering bombs on Moscow, had made the country unable to respond to lower-level challenges. Most of his buildup, therefore, went to the long-starved army: an addition of some 875,000 men. Meanwhile, draft calls were greatly increased, reserve units were called up from civilian life, ships and planes were reactivated, and a tremendous sum was spent on nonnuclear weapons.

Khrushchev's response was to send another huge missile around the earth and to talk about a Soviet nuclear bomb equivalent to 100 million tons of TNT. In August the Soviets built a wall across Berlin to halt the flood of refugees that for many months had poured into West Berlin. They also resumed exploding atom bombs in the atmosphere, an action that the United States eventually copied. The world was once more faced with the horror of radioactive fallout saturating the atmosphere and causing unimaginable damage to human beings below.

The "Grand Design"

President Kennedy watched the growing strength of the European Common Market and concluded that the time had come to build a revived and strengthened Atlantic community. If this was not done, the tariff walls around the Common Market would rise ever higher, trade between North America and Europe would languish, and the world would fall back into the old divisive international trade wars. The answer lay deeply rooted in Kennedy's Democratic tradition: slash tariffs all round so as to ensure a steadily growing world of multilateral trade in which the resources and skills of the world would be openly shared to everyone's benefit. In early 1962 he asked Congress for revolutionary authority to reduce greatly American tariffs across the board, in whole categories of commodities and manufactured goods, by as much as fifty percent—in some cases to abolish them entirely—provided similar concessions could be gained from Europe.

President Kennedy was a practical-minded man who did not like dealing in ideologies and soaring dreams, but this was a cause he pursued with evangelical zeal. Throughout 1962 he spent endless hours in mobilizing a nationwide educational campaign designed to persuade Americans that in his "Grand Design" there was a real hope for a better world. "The two great Atlantic markets," he said, "will either grow together or they will grow apart." In farm regions, among businessmen, in labor unions, anywhere he could reach listeners, the president preached his message. The result was the passage in September 1962 of the boldest trade legislation in American history—a bill that alone, in more peaceful eras, would have marked out the Eighty-seventh Congress for an important niche in history. The victorious president exulted, "the age of self-sufficient nationalism is over. The age of interdependence is here. The Atlantic partnership is a growing reality."

Ahead, however, lay years of careful, hard-driving negotiations. The "Kennedy round" of tariff reduction talks, convened under the authority of the General Agreement on Trade and Tariffs, did not begin until after the president's death. Negotiations among fifty-three nations from around the world (outside the Sino-Soviet block) began in Geneva in 1964 and ground on for three years, ending in May 1967 with the largest and widest tariff cuts in modern history.

Thereafter, tariff barriers posed only a minor obstacle to world trade (though other administrative hurdles, such as import quotas, remained to be dealt with).

The Cuban missile crisis

The Cold War reached its frightening climax in October 1962. American reconnaissance planes flying over Cuba discovered a startling fact: the Russians were placing intercontinental missiles on the island. The president was startled and shocked. With Soviet missiles sited within ninety miles of the southern American coast, the elaborate network of radar warning systems and military bases that the United States had built abroad would be short-circuited. It would be impossible for the United States ever to intercept a missile rising from Cuba since the warning time would be too short. In such an intensively charged international atmosphere as then existed, Kennedy felt that the implications of this move were enormous. The balance of power would shift massively to the Soviet side.

President Kennedy regarded this as the ultimate test of his administration. For two years he and his advisers had been learning how to manage crisis. They had bungled badly in the Bay of Pigs disaster. Would they do better this time? For ten days the White House bustled with secret meetings round the clock as every possible response was proposed, discussed, argued over, and balanced against alternatives. The most important condition Kennedy imposed on the debate was that Khrushchev was never to be backed into a corner. Options were always to be left open that would allow him to escape total humiliation. Meanwhile, aerial photos continued to pour in so that the conferees could watch almost hour by hour as the missile sites were rushed toward completion. At the same time, it was learned that more than a dozen Russian vessels were on their way to Cuba, some of them with suspiciously shaped on-deck cargo boxes that could contain missiles.

On October 22, 1962, the president went on national television to inform the nation of these developments and announce his decision. This "sudden, clandestine decision to station strategic weapons for the first time outside of Soviet soil," he said, "is a deliberately provocative and unjustified change in the status quo which cannot be accepted by this country, if our courage and our commitments are ever to be trusted again by either friend or foe." He declared a blockade around Cuba that would allow everything but missile-bearing vessels through. At the same time, he ordered that a small army of more than sixty thousand men be rushed to Florida, thus making use for the first time of the new military flexibility that he had called for during the 1961 Berlin crisis.

Khrushchev's response

The world was electrified with fear. What would be Khrushchev's response? Would the war that all had dreaded finally break out between Russia and the United States? To demonstrate solid hemispheric support behind Kennedy's actions, the Organization of American States met and voted 19 to 0 (even Kennedy was surprised at this unanimous action) to authorize the use of force to maintain the blockade. After an agonizing wait, the Russian ships began, one by one, to swing in wide arcs and head back to their ports.

President Kennedy and Secretary of Defense Robert S. McNamara in a tense executive committee meeting during the Cuban missile crisis of 1962. Its resolution seemed finally to end the threat of world atomic war, at least as an immediate possibility, and the Cold War.
John F. Kennedy Library

Soon a secret correspondence, initiated by Khrushchev, sprang up between the Soviet premier and the American president. It was a frank interchange in which the Americans were relieved to see Khrushchev finally expressing horror at the prospect of nuclear war. The crisis was over: the Russians withdrew their missiles, and the world began to breathe again.

President Kennedy's actions in the missile crisis have been harshly criticized by those who believe that the president was wholly unjustified in taking the world to the brink of nuclear war. At the time, Adlai Stevenson and Walter Lippmann had urged a different course: that the United States offer to remove America's long-established missile sites in Turkey in exchange for the elimination of Russian sites in Cuba. American possession of intercontinental ballistic missiles had by this time rendered such overseas launch sites as those in Turkey of minor importance. In truth, there was a hollow ring to American protests about Russian missiles within ninety miles of Florida when Turkey was even closer to Russian soil, sharing a common border.

The end of the Cold War

In retrospect, however, the seasoned journalist Walter Lippmann, who had been analyzing world events since the days of Woodrow Wilson, called this the turning point of the twenty years since the end of the Second World War. The world had been living in continuous fear of an atomic holocaust. Now it knew that when the two superpowers were faced by a naked showdown, they would pull back from the brink. The atomic bomb was defused. All world history has been different since the missile crisis of October 1962.

Russia and the United States moved steadily into a new and relaxed relationship in which each accepted the stalemate. Talk of the Berlin crisis vanished, and in early January 1963 Khrushchev wrote a letter to Kennedy saying that "the time has come now to put an end once and for all to nuclear tests. We are ready to meet you halfway."

In June at American University in Washington, D.C., President Kennedy gave a speech hailed around the world. Americans should drop their conspiratorial fears of the Russians, just as the Russians should stop believing terrible things of the United States. "No government or social system is so evil that its people must be considered as lacking in virtue." There must be "increased understanding between the Soviets and ourselves . . . increased contact and communication." Responding to the spirit of these remarks, Khrushchev made it possible for the Test Ban Treaty to be concluded. In October 1963 the treaty was initialed in Moscow. The president was jubilant. This, he felt, was his most important gift to the world, his greatest achievement. For years, he said, the world has struggled "to escape from the darkening prospects of mass destruction." Now, he went on, "a shaft of light cut into the darkness."

At American University Kennedy appealed to Americans to rethink their attitudes toward Russia: "Let us reexamine our attitude toward the Soviet Union. It is discouraging to think that their leaders may actually believe what their propagandists write. . . . But it is also a warning—a warning to the American people not to fall into the same trap as the Soviets, not to see only a distorted and desperate view of the other side, not to see conflict as inevitable, accommodation as impossible, and communication as nothing more than an exchange of threats.

"No government or social system is so evil that its people must be considered as lacking in virtue. As Americans, we find communism profoundly repugnant as a negation of personal freedom and dignity. But we can still hail the Russian people for their many achievements—in science and space, in economic and industrial growth, in culture and in acts of courage. . . . Let us reexamine our attitude toward the cold war, remembering that we are not engaged in a debate, seeking to pile up debating points. We are not here distributing blame or pointing the finger of judgment. We must deal with the world as it is, and not as it might have been had the history of the last 18 years been different. . . . Above all, while defending our own vital interests, nuclear powers must avert those confrontations which bring an adversary to a choice of either a humiliating retreat or a nuclear war. To adopt that kind of course in the nuclear age would be evidence only of the bankruptcy of our policy—or of a collective deathwish for the world. . . . We are unwilling to impose our system on any unwilling people—but we are willing and able to engage in peaceful competition with any people on earth. . . .'' (*Public Papers of the Presidents of the United States: John F. Kennedy* [1964].)

The Vietnam crisis

However, there was a growing crisis in another part of the world—Vietnam. In the pressures of 1961, when Khrushchev was rattling his rockets and threatening war over Berlin, President Kennedy had made crucial decisions concerning America's involvement in South Vietnam. By the fall of 1963 the results of these decisions were becoming known. The deeply troubled president watched and worried over the mounting troubles in that country and sought in puzzlement for answers to an increasingly confused situation. When he was killed in Dallas on November 22, 1963, the solutions he might have proposed died with him.

Bibliography

Three books that were especially valuable to me in writing this chapter: Of the many books on the Cold War, such as those by Walter LaFeber, Gar Alperovitz, and Adam B. Ulam, I found George Kennan's *Memoirs, 1925–1950** (1967) a most remarkable book to which I kept returning. Of the flood of Kennedy books, Theodore C. Sorensen's *Kennedy** (1965) and Arthur M. Schlesinger, Jr.'s *A Thousand Days: John F. Kennedy in the White House** (1965) are still basic, filled as they are with large stores of information.

How have historians looked at the topic?

Who was responsible for the beginning of the Cold War? During the 1950s the answer seemed obvious. The Soviet Union, ideologically committed to world domination, had taken advantage of the exigencies of war and, following the pattern of fascist states, sought to gobble up the nations of Europe and Asia. Eric Goldman's colorful *The Crucial Decade—And After: America, 1945–1960** (rev. ed., 1960), tells the story in these terms, emphasizing the Truman administration's surprised and bewildered reaction. Herbert Agar's *The Price of Power** (1957) takes a similar approach, criticizing the federal government for its weak, nonmilitary response to Soviet aggression in eastern Europe.

While still lingering in the minds of many Americans, this simplistic view of the origins of the Cold War has been rigorously challenged by two schools of historical thought. In *The Cold War as History* (1967), Louis Halle suggests a "realistic" assessment of postwar Soviet actions. Stressing the Russians' need to protect their borders from further invasion, Halle insists that the American emphasis on self-determination prevented an acceptable, balance-of-power settlement following World War II. Americans, not Soviets, were straightjacketed by moralism and ideology. In *The Beginning of the Cold War* (1966), a study of the months between Yalta and the Potsdam Conference, Martin F. Herz fleshes out the realist position by taking the view that the Soviet Union had no plans to expand into western Europe in 1945. George F. Kennedy's *American Diplomacy, 1900–1950** (1951) one of the most erudite and lucid statements of the realist school, criticizes the United States for its legalistic moralism.

Recently, a revisionist school has developed in Cold War historiography. Emphasizing the devastated condition of the Soviet Union following World War II, the revisionists tend to see the United States as a dynamic, pushy nation at war's end. Denna F. Fleming's comprehensive *The Cold*

War and Its Origins, two vols. (1961) concentrates on the Russians' historic fear of Western encirclement and labels American actions in eastern Europe in the months following Germany's capitulations as unreasonable and probably inspired by the strength born of its monopoly of atomic power, a theme relentlessly pursued by Gar Alperovitz in *Atomic Diplomacy: Hiroshima and Potsdam** (1965). William A. Williams suggested in *The Tragedy of American Diplomacy** (1959) that the United States was driven into an aggressive stance by the needs of an expanding economy that required foreign markets. Walter LaFeber has written a sophisticated and provocative book, *America, Russia, and the Cold War, 1945–1966** (1968), which explores the economic theme in depth. In *The Politics of War: The World and United States Foreign Policy, 1943–1945** (1968), Gabriel Kolko maintains that the pattern of the Cold War was established in earlier years by a conservative Roosevelt administration bent on containing the leftist impulses set loose by the collapse of the old order.

Several memoirs are especially helpful in understanding the origins of the Cold War and its progress: Dean Acheson, *Present at the Creation* (1969); George Kennan, *Memoirs, 1925–1950,** cited above; and Harry S. Truman, *Memoirs,* two vols. (1955–1956). An indispensable treatment of the origins of the Cold War, noted for its thoroughness and even-handedness, is Herbert Feis's *From Trust to Terror: The Onset of the Cold War, 1945–1950** (1971).

Although historians dispute why, how, and when the Cold War started, they agree that by 1947 it not only existed but was threatening to become "hot." The establishment of the Truman Doctrine and the Marshall Plan is told by a participant in Joseph M. Jones's *Fifteen Weeks, February 21–June 5, 1947* (1955). A key crisis is described in W. Philips Davison's *The Berlin Blockade* (1958). The Korean conflict is explored in David Rees's *Korea: The Limited War* (1964); and, from a personal vantage, in Matthew B. Ridgway's *Memoirs* (1956).

The rebuilding of West Germany is covered in Harold Zink's *The United States in Germany* (1957) while the importance of the North Atlantic Treaty Organization is analyzed in R. E. Osgood's *NATO: The Entangling Alliance* (1962). The views of Eisenhower's secretary of state are discussed in Richard Goold-Adams's *The Time of Power: A Reappraisal of John Foster Dulles* (1962). Herman Finer is critical of Dulles's policies in *Dulles over Suez* (1964). Dulles's own account, *War or Peace* (1960), is enlightening on the Eisenhower era, as is R. J. Donovan's *Eisenhower: The Inside Story* (1956).

In addition to the works on Kennedy cited above, H. B. Johnson's *The Bay of Pigs* (1964) and David Halberstam's *The Best and the Brightest* (1972) are valuable. The tensions of October 1962 come alive in Elie Abel's *The Missile Crisis** (1966) and Robert F. Kennedy's *Thirteen Days: A Memoir of the Cuban Missile Crisis** (1969). For a critical assessment of the Kennedy administration during the missile crisis, read relevant passages in William O'Neill's *Coming Apart: An Informal History of the 1960s* (1971).

*Available in paperback.

CHAPTER 34

Complacent Years: Truman and Eisenhower

TIME LINE

1945	President Truman proposes Fair Deal reforms; Full Employment Law; Council of Economic Advisers established
1945–1953	Massive labor outbreaks
1946	Atomic Energy Commission established; Republicans win majority in Congress
1947	Taft-Hartley Act; Truman Loyalty Program launched
1948	Truman orders end to segregation in military and civil service and unsuccessfully proposes other reforms for black Americans; major industries agree to give automatic "cost of living" increases; Communist leaders put on trial under Smith Act; Oklahoma forced to admit black students to its university
1949	Farm prices slump; Agricultural Act sets ninety-percent parity price supports; Russia explodes atomic bomb
1950	Soviet spy ring uncovered at Los Alamos; McCarran Internal Security Act
1950–1954	Era of Senator Joseph McCarthy
1951	Twenty-second Amendment limits presidents to two elected terms
1952	Dwight D. Eisenhower elected thirty-fourth president of the United States
1953	Major industries agree on guaranteed annual wage; Earl Warren appointed chief justice of the United States; House Concurrent Resolution 108 terminates federal services to Indians and places tribes under state supervision
1954	In *Brown* v. *Board of Education of Topeka* Supreme Court strikes down the separate-but-equal doctrine in public schools and facilities
1955	Merger of AFL and CIO
1957	Violence mounts against blacks in South; First Civil Rights Act; Little Rocks crisis; *Sputnik 1* launched by Russians
1958	National Aeronautics and Space Agency created; first intercontinental ballistic missile launched; National Defense Education Act gives federal aid to education
1959	Landrum-Griffin Act regulates internal governance of labor unions; Alaska and Hawaii admitted to the Union
1960	John F. Kennedy elected thirty-fifth president of the United States

THE Japanese had hardly surrendered when President Harry Truman called on Congress to fire up the banked coals of the New Deal and enact a long series of major domestic reforms. But Congress was not interested. Three years later, after he had won a stunning reelection victory in 1948, Truman tried once more, but again with no success. From 1945 to the latter 1950s, the nation worried about the Russians and about Communists at home, but it was fundamentally complacent about the nature of its own society. Problems rumbled under the surface—urban decay, festering race relations, tragically costly health crises among the poor—but they were largely ignored.

After all, most Americans were riding a crest of affluence such as they had hardly dreamed of during the 1930s. Tens of millions of people found themselves moving upward into a middle-class way of life, including golf, split-level homes, luxurious automobiles, trailers, boats, land and gardens, recreational weekends, and costly hobbies. The war had poured wealth into countless homes, and now people wanted to spend and enjoy. Millions of soldiers came home with attitudes that accentuated this national mood. In jungles and remote deserts, in farthest Asia and in sandy army barracks on the Texas plains, men and women had whiled away months of tedium and moments of frightening combat by daydreaming of the good life to come. They were not critical of America, they wanted to share in it. Their dream was to put together what most of them had never had before—a secure life in comfortable circumstances.

The United States yearned for quiet, not for radicalism. Protest met with massive disapproval. The old political cries for socialism, communism, or liberal reformism had lost their appeal. The predominant mood was of disenchantment with ideologies of any kind. The status quo: this was what people idealized, called "Americanism," and elevated to the status of a folk religion. The

fears aroused by the Cold War heightened this conservatism. Anyone politically left of center risked being stigmatized as a Communist. The national mood of suspicion laid the basis for the Second Red Scare, which began in 1950 when Senator Joseph McCarthy walked the land like a new Caesar.

The Truman-Eisenhower era was fundamentally complacent, but it was a turbulent time as well. From the nationwide eruption of labor agitation in the late 1940s, through the Red Scare of the early 1950s, to the burgeoning outbreak of race hostility thereafter, problem after problem thrust themselves forward. A tide of reformism grew, held back by the determined resistance of the Eisenhower administration until it erupted in a tumbling flood of social change in the kaleidoscopic 1960s. And underneath the complacency was a deep anxiety, produced by the frightful blood bath of the Second World War, and the existence of the atomic bomb.

Harry S Truman: Jacksonian Democrat

From 1945 through 1952, Harry S Truman presided over this inward-turning nation, seeking vainly to spur it to renewed domestic reform. A peppery, combative, courageous man, Truman brought Jacksonian qualities to the White House. He was unpolished, small-town in background—Independence, Missouri, was his home—largely self-educated, and proudly a "man of the people." Certainly his personal style had overtones of the truculent prickliness of the general from Tennessee, and like Jackson he distrusted powerful corporations and worried about the common man. Furthermore, he quickly became an active chief executive in the Democratic tradition. Not for him were the long, droning afternoons of Calvin Coolidge, taking his many naps. In domestic affairs he worked hard to push Congress toward social reforms, and in foreign relations he led the nation out of its traditional isolationism into the role of world leadership it has tried to carry on ever since.

In domestic matters Truman fell far short of his goals. He was faced with an informal coalition of southern Democrats and northern Republicans who halted practically all his efforts at social and economic reform. Southern whites wanted no part of his efforts at aiding black people, and conservatives in the North opposed his attempted revival of the New Deal. Truman's personal qualities also gravely hampered him. Although courageous, he somehow never attained the kind of moral leadership that presidents need to bring the country along with them. A nation accustomed to the majesty of a Franklin Roosevelt could not take seriously a president who surrounded himself with small-time political cronies, burst out pettishly at opponents, and once scribbled off an angry letter to a music critic who had written slightingly of his daughter's singing voice.

But Harry Truman saw where the nation's ills lay, and long before the national mind was prepared to do something about them, he was raising warning flags and calling for action. In his first major message to Congress in September 1945, his "Fair Deal" program urged, not only the expansion of social security and an increase in the minimum wage, but such far-sighted measures as national health insurance, a major assault on slum housing, federal aid to education, guarantees of equal access to jobs for Afro-Americans, support of scientific research, and vigorous new conservation programs that would spread TVA-like regional systems across the United States.

Major achievements

Truman got little of these reforms, but he did get major pieces of legislation passed. One was the Full Employment Law, which permanently committed the national government to intervene continuously in the economy to ensure that a depression would never occur again. To imple-

ment the law, a three-man Council of Economic Advisers was established to provide the president with professional expert knowledge. The second act concerned atomic energy. There was no question that this powerful new force could not be turned over to private enterprise; it was too important for that. But should it be controlled by the military, as it was during the war, or placed under civilian direction? President Truman was adamant that civilians be in charge, and against strong Republican opposition—but with the country behind him—he won his battle. The Atomic Energy Act of August 1946 created a five-man Atomic Energy Commission, which had exclusive control over research and production. At the same time, the law made certain that the president possessed the sole power of ordering the use of atomic bombs in combat.

On his reelection in 1948, Truman tried once again to launch his Fair Deal, this time with a bit more success. The National Housing Act authorized the building of over 800,000 public housing units for poor families, as well as the provision of subsidies to renters, slum clearance, and rural housing. More money went into the building of power facilities in the West, for reclamation, and for aid to tenant farmers who wanted to buy their land. The minimum wage was raised from forty cents to seventy-five cents an hour, and the Social Security System was vastly expanded, bringing 10 million more people under its protection. Truman also got Congress finally to allow 400,000 Europeans, displaced by the war, to immigrate to the United States. But this was the sum of it. The major events of the Truman administration lay not in legislative victories but in crises in the nation and the world.

The war's effect on the national economy

While Asia and Europe lay in ruins, the Second World War transformed the United States into a boomingly prosperous nation. In a population of 135 million, about 300,000 soldiers died in the war, as compared with over half a million in the

British Commonwealth, almost 3 million in Germany, and 7.5 million in Russia. Put another way, America lost 1 in 450 of its population, Britain 1 in 150, Germany 1 in 25, and Russia 1 in 22. Even in the Civil War the United States had suffered far more heavily: there had been 600,000 deaths in a population of 30 million. When civilian casualties, which ran to the many millions, are added to the losses of other nations in the Second World War, America's remarkable good fortune stands out even more.

The national economy grew explosively. The United States produced $91 billion worth of goods in 1939; by 1945, the total had soared to $167 billion. Per capita disposable income (stated in the value of 1960 dollars) grew a third, reaching $1,669 for each man, woman, and child in 1945. Together, individuals and corporations had saved more than $48 billion; state and local governments $10 billion more. The result was a boom that began as soon as the war ended, instead of the depression widely feared. The gross national product continued skyrocketing, rising

beyond the $300 billion level in 1950, the $400 billion level in 1955, and reaching over $500 billion in 1960. By that time per capita income stood at $1,969, an increase of two-thirds in twenty years.

Never before had the ordinary American been so affluent. Population rose about twenty-eight percent from 1945 to 1960, reaching 180 million, but since the gross national product had leaped fifty-six percent during the same period, individual incomes could soar. All this took place while the number of working people grew enormously, from 55 million in 1945 to almost 67 million in 1960. The income of workers in nonagricultural occupations rose steadily. In the late 1950s, however, an old problem—unemployment—returned and persisted as recession after recession frustrated economic planners in the Eisenhower administration.

Population trend

Fueling the upward rise of the economy was the dramatic reversal in population growth that took place after 1940. For twenty years the birth rate had declined sharply, but the war changed all this. The abundance of jobs and high pay sent marriage rates soaring. Furthermore, servicemen were eager to marry before leaving home or going overseas. An intangible but probably important influence came from the full impact of Freudian ideas concerning child rearing, which brought a powerful new sense of the crucial importance and value of motherhood. The feminism of the 1920s now faded almost completely, while a new ideal of the young woman surrounded by three or four children and a busy home captured the national mind. Not since the Progressive Era had American families had so many children. From 19.4 births per 1,000 in 1940, the rate leaped to 25.8 by 1947 where, with minor reductions, it remained throughout the 1950s. The result was that between 1940 and 1950 the American population grew more rapidly than in any prior decade in the nation's history (by 14.5 percent). In the 1950s even this surge was passed

The explosion of new families with many children in the postwar years, affluence, low-interest government housing loans, and freeway-building sent housing tracts marching over fields and hillsides, as here in Los Angeles in 1953.

J. R. Eyerman, Life Magazine, © Time Inc.

as the total population reached almost 180 million, or some 18.5 percent over its mark in 1950.

More marriages and children meant an insatiable demand for the many needs of these new households: washers, dryers, furniture, clothes, automobiles, homes, roads, schools, fire houses, new residential areas, lawn sprinklers, radios, televisions, rugs—the list is endless. This, in turn, brought a swift expansion in the industries producing these products. There was also a tremendous mobility in the growing population. People migrated to the places where jobs were most plentiful or to the "sun states" of Florida, Arizona, and California, where a new way of life could be taken on. The movement from country to city continued; the nation's farming population of thirty million in 1940 became less than twenty-one million by 1960. In the prior year fifty-six percent of Americans lived in cities; in the latter, seventy-five percent. This growth was primarily in suburban areas. The "white flight" from the city core was well launched, leaving behind growing slum regions with rapidly increasing minority-group populations whose reduced incomes could not provide the necessary taxes for schools and other services. The largest American cities actually declined in population as the suburban communities, supported by the widespread ownership of automobiles, higher incomes, and a federal policy of home loans, spread over the surrounding countrysides.

Black America continued to flee from the South. In 1940 three million Afro-Americans lived in nonsouthern states; by 1960 the number had grown to seven million. At the same time, only seven percent of Americans were foreign-born in 1950, and by 1960 the figure had dropped to five percent. In urban areas across the country whole ways of life disappeared as third generation ethnics, now thoroughly removed from the ways of life of the old country, adopted styles of living closely resembling those of their Anglo-Saxon countrymen.

Since immigration from western hemisphere nations was unrestricted, the hundreds of thousands of Mexican-born who after 1910 had begun moving into Texas, Arizona, and California to work as agricultural laborers led to a total of 2.5 million Mexican-Americans living in the United States by 1945. Furthermore, the opportunities of wartime employment brought a flood of Puerto Ricans to the northeastern states (New York City primarily), where approximately 750,000 lived at war's end.

The new farm crisis

While the income of urban people rose, that of farmers fell alarmingly in the Truman-Eisenhower years. In the years between 1952 and 1960, farm income dropped twenty-three percent. For this reason farm families continued their flight to cities; in 1956 alone, one-eleventh of the farm population left the land. The basic cause was overproduction, caused by soaring mechanization and greater efficiency. In 1949 the Agricultural Act of that year set parity price supports at the ninety-percent level. The result was governmental purchase of billions of dollars worth of crops, skyrocketing production and bulging federal warehouses.

Ezra Taft Benson, Eisenhower's conservative secretary of agriculture, shifted the government away from rigid to flexible price supports, his belief being that lower subsidies would cut production and force farmers to become more businesslike, efficient, and self-reliant. The Agriculture Act of 1958 reduced price supports to a general level of sixty-five percent of parity. At the same time, a program was adopted in 1956 whereby farmers would be paid for taking land out of production and putting it into a "soil bank" from which the nation could draw in future emergencies. Millions of acres were thus withdrawn, especially by "agribusinessmen" who owned large holdings.

Explosive labor

The war had hardly ended when organized labor erupted in its last major outburst in American history. The war had brought millions more workers into nonagricultural jobs, the total number of workers rising from 27 to 38 million, and the increasing efficiency of the machinery they used made each worker increasingly more productive. By 1945 the nation's factories produced 100 percent more than they had in 1939, but man-days of labor had increased by only half. At war's end there were 6.8 million workers in the AFL, 6 million in the CIO, and over a million in other unions.

Everyone was worried, however, that the nation was going to collapse into another depression. Union leaders looked at the 12 million men and women in the services who would soon be flooding the labor force, searching for jobs, and they feared disaster. When Washington's labor statisticians reported that unemployment was rising, labor's fears seemed confirmed. Union leaders decided that the best way to ward off a depression was to keep wage rates at a high level, so that there would be plenty of purchasing power in the general population. Pointing to capital's huge wartime profits and to increased productivity per worker, they insisted that employers could raise wages without raising prices.

Then a different kind of demand came from John L. Lewis, head of the United Mine Workers. He called not only for higher wages but also for employers to finance "fringe benefits," consisting of health and welfare services. This led to a coal strike that soon created heating and industrial crises through a shortage of coal. In May 1946 the railroad workers began a strike that threatened to paralyze transportation. Then, in the spring of 1946, wartime price control legislation was allowed to lapse, and the cost of food and other necessities rose with breathtaking suddenness. All the raises that labor had won were cancelled out in a brief few weeks, while corporate profits boomed upward to their highest point in history—and more strikes began.

The public, however, was angry at the unions. The national economy staggered along from day to day through a seemingly endless series of crises: strike votes; bold pronouncements by

union leaders; decisions to withhold essential services; and apparently dictatorial demands. Furthermore, this controversy tapped once more that deep-running force in American life: the habit of using and respecting authority. Protests by those below often produce enormous anger in those above. We have seen this anger stirred up in the British mind by the protests of American colonials, in southern whites by the protests of southern blacks, in Anglo-Saxon Protestants by the protests of Irish Catholics. Employers were massively offended by the demands of labor that they open their books, pay higher wages without raising prices, and "submit" to the union. Millions of unorganized Americans, running their small shops or living on restricted incomes, identified with the employers and shared their outlook. Where do the "damned unions" get off trying to tell their employers how to run their businesses? So ran the argument, as a nation still devoted to individualism, and sentimentally in tune with established authority, condemned organized labor.

The Taft-Hartley Act

In November 1946 the Republicans won a sweeping victory in Congress, taking control of both houses for the first time since 1928. Now they had their chance to turn the tables on labor. The Wagner Act of New Deal days, they said, had made the unions far too strong. They could halt production by jurisdictional strikes (where two competing unions struggled for membership), secondary boycotts (refusal by other unions to handle the goods of a factory or business under strike), violation of contracts, refusal to bargain, and open coercion of employees to join a union.

The resulting Taft-Hartley Act, which primarily expressed the ideas of the National Association of Manufacturers, listed for the first time a group of "unfair" labor practices of which the unions were guilty and henceforth declared them illegal: the closed shop (the requirement that a worker had to be a union member before he could get a job); any coercion of nonunion workers; secondary boycotts and jurisdictional strikes; demanding pay for work not performed; and refusal to bargain in good faith. Employers could now sue for breach of contract. And where a strike threatened the national health or safety, the president could secure court injunctions that would provide 80-day "cooling off" periods before the strike could begin. To reduce possibilities for union graft, all unions were required to register with the secretary of labor and provide regular financial reports.

Labor fought back hard against the Taft-Hartley Act (which Truman vetoed, only to be overridden). But southern congressmen were as implacably opposed to the unions as were northern Republicans. They adamantly protested any force that might raise wage rates in the factories which had been moving to the South because labor costs were cheaper. Furthermore, no part of American society is more devoted to the habit of authority than the South. Factory owners were respected and admired in the South as captains and generals had been in the Civil War. Union "dictation" was not to be abided. The Taft-Hartley Act, therefore, withstood all assaults.

The annual wage and cost of living principles

As inflation continued pushing prices higher, labor fought round after round of wage increase battles with employers, one hardly ending before the next one began. Then in 1948 Walter Reuther got General Motors to agree to automatic "cost of living" pay raises, which would be granted in accordance with rises in the consumer price index as measured by the federal government's Bureau of Labor Statistics. This principle spread rapidly through the economy, affecting even government workers.

In 1953 the United Automobile Workers began another campaign with crucial implications: a demand for a guaranteed annual wage. The first national response was the traditional one: the notion was rejected as absurd. For many months the issue was debated intensively. Finally, Ford agreed to such a contract, which quickly became standard in similar industries. It provided that when qualified workers were unemployed, the company would pay them about two-thirds of their normal earnings for a period of six months (to be received on top of any government unemployment benefits). These measures eased the buildup of annual pressures within the economy for wage increases, so that the vast turbulence of the late 1940s, when millions of workers struck for long periods, died away.

Except in the South. Here lay the core of anti-union sentiment, for the South was the last unorganized region in the United States. In the early 1950s when labor pushed unionization throughout the South, local officials and self-appointed labor haters openly took the side of employers and used violence against the organizers. Scenes occurred that were reminiscent of those in Detroit during the depression. The difference, however, was that the unions were now powerful national organizations with vast resources at their command. They persisted in their drive; in 1951 alone, some 1.5 million new members, mainly in the South, joined the unions. By the mid-1950s union membership had reached some 16 million nationally (8 million in the AFL, 7 in the CIO), or about one-third of all workers in nonfarm industries.

Labor merger: Formation of the AFL-CIO

The time was now ripe for the AFL and the CIO to join forces. The lines that formerly divided them had blurred, for the AFL had already swung far over in the direction of industrial unionism. In 1955 long negotiations ended in the creation of the AFL-CIO, bringing more than eighty-five percent of all union members under one administrative roof. George Meany became president, and Walter Reuther vice-president.

The last major piece of legislation concerning

organized labor was the Landrum-Griffin Act, passed in 1959. By this law, the federal government in effect recognized that unions had arrived as permanent elements in the national economy, and that—like railroads, banks, and other public utilitylike institutions—their internal organization needed careful public supervision. The law governed the way in which unions conducted their elections, held strike votes, and administered their funds, which by this time had grown enormous through pension and welfare receipts.

The threat of automation

The gravest problem remaining to labor lay in automation. The gross national product, it was pointed out, had grown forty percent from 1954

In a climactic moment for organized American labor, ending twenty years of feuding, George Meany and Walter Reuther celebrate the merger of the AF of L and the CIO in 1955. The labor-management scene henceforth became much more stable.
Wide World Photos

to 1964, but employment had risen only twelve percent. The United Automobile Workers once numbered 1.5 million workers; by the mid-1960s, this work force had dwindled by a half-million. In 1947, it took 1,300 man-hours of labor to produce 1,000 tons of coal; in 1962, the figure had dropped to 500. Employment figures in the coal mines, therefore, dropped from 400,000 to 123,000. Because of these influences, the organized labor movement reached its peak in 1956 and began declining in numbers thereafter.

The significance of automation, however, has yet to be proved. It was increasingly true that unskilled workers found it more difficult to find jobs and that such men were becoming permanently unemployed. Out of this factor has come, in good part, the persistent problem of poverty in the midst of affluence. However, automation has had another major effect: it has created hundreds of thousands of new jobs in wholly new industries, such as computers and computerization, electronics, and the like. Furthermore, the national economy has been steadily moving in a new direction where the largest proportion of its workers is engaged not in the production of goods but in the provision of services: soft water, clean diapers, health, education, landscaping, interior decoration, accounting, government, and myriads of other occupations. This has made old-time swings in the business cycle less likely to occur, for the market for services is not subject to abrupt changes.

The Democrats and disloyalty

Since Thomas Jefferson's day a conviction that the Democrats are disloyal to the American way of life has circulated among important sections of the American population. Jefferson's critics called him a French radical; Cleveland had been called a tool of the British free traders; and Franklin Roosevelt had been labeled a Moscow-inspired Communist. Democratic foreign policy has traditionally been internationalist in tone and methods, and "100 percent Americans" of strongly nationalistic views have bitterly distrusted the Democrats on this ground. Add to this a tendency on the Democratic side to distrust the military and to rely on "soft" methods of economic aid and painstaking multilateral diplomacy, and the combination was one that infuriated many people. Often such critics were curiously unconcerned with combating communism abroad: what they feared day and night was communism at home. They were ready to explain the nation's ills by saying that subversive "pinko" radical intellectuals from Harvard had taken over Washington, D.C.

In ordinary times these kinds of people have had little leverage on the American public. Like those on the left wing of American politics who constantly trace every national problem to alleged conspiracies among the wealthy corporations, right wingers who constantly preach the message of disloyalty are usually given small attention. But when the nation is struck by great fears, much of the public is swayed by these delusions.

The world, after all, was a terribly disordered place in Truman's years. It rang with the chilling threat of atomic war, of huge armies still marching, and of young Americans still dying. No one could relax for years on end. For this reason the Second Red Scare, unlike its predecessor from 1919 to 1920, went on and on. It spread throughout the country, affecting Seattle and Birmingham, Boston and Los Angeles. Librarians were terrorized by bookburners, teachers were hounded by reactionaries who condemned any mention of Russia or the New Deal, and liberal ministers were driven from their pulpits. The national mood made these goings-on seem legitimate; the violent haters were relatively free to give vent to their wild theories of subversion and treachery. Right-wing vigilantes in local communities were exhilarated to find themselves regarded as front-rank soldiers who could do no wrong in their "battle for America."

The first phase: 1938–1950

As long ago as 1938 the House had established the Un-American Activities Committee, which shortly was sending out to the alarmed populace the grave news that the Boy Scouts were Communist-infiltrated. In 1940 Congress passed the Smith Act, which made it a crime for any person in the United States to urge the violent overthrow of any government, or to organize or become a member of any group that taught such goals. Designed primarily to combat fascism, when the Cold War began it was soon revived for use against suspected Communists. In 1946 Americans were startled to learn of a Soviet espionage ring in Canada. Demands were soon made that the federal government flush out any employee whose general attitudes and affiliations made it reasonable to suspect that he or she might be a security risk. The Republican-controlled Congress prepared to enact necessary legislation, and President Truman sought to defuse the issue by establishing a rigorous loyalty program by direct executive order.

Begun in 1947, Truman's program subjected every government employee to a searching review. The procedures paid little attention to civil rights. On the bare ground that no one had a right to be a government employee, the loyalty review boards made a travesty of courtroom procedures, despite the fact that dismissal as a security risk would blot a person's entire career. They entertained any and all accusations, accepted Federal Bureau of Investigation reports as beyond question, refused to let the accused confront their accusers or even know their identity, freely condemned people on the basis of associations with other people often unknown to the accused—and spread dismay, alarm, and timidity throughout the government service. This program went on from 1947 to 1951 and resulted in the discharge (not for actions, but for supposed tendencies) of 212 employees out of about 2.5 million.

Long lists of supposedly disloyal organizations

were published by the United States attorney general in 1947, without prior hearings or even an explanation of why each organization was so named. In 1948 the government charged eleven leaders of the American Communist party under the Smith Act. All were eventually found guilty, fined heavily, and put in jail for terms of three to five years.

Hiss case

In August 1948 a former State Department official, an Ivy League graduate named Alger Hiss, was accused before the House Un-American Activities Committee of having been a Soviet spy. Congressman Richard M. Nixon, a member of the House Un-American Activities Committee, would not let the case die. A sensational trial of Hiss in 1949 for perjury ended in a hung jury, but an equally dramatic one in 1950 resulted in his conviction. The jury decided that he had actually been part of a spy network within the government in the 1930s—and right-wingers pointed with alarm to the fact that he had been on Franklin Roosevelt's staff at Yalta. The stunned country was now willing to listen to charges that the Democrats were soft on communism.

Then came a series of shocking events, piled closely on one another, that seemed to confirm the nation's hysteria. A young woman in government service, Judith Coplon, was charged with giving the Soviets crucial information on how the Federal Bureau of Investigation organized its counterespionage system. Then the Russians exploded their first atomic bomb in September 1949. How could they have so rapidly achieved the nuclear expertise to have done this? Spies in the government, said the Truman haters—and sure enough, in February 1950 a Soviet spy ring was uncovered in the Los Alamos atomic installation, leading to the eventual execution of Julius and Ethel Rosenberg in July 1953. Hard on the heels of Russia's atomic bomb exploit came the collapse of the Nationalist government in China,

widely explained as produced by the Truman administration's alleged lack of concern about Communists.

Joseph McCarthy transfixes the country

In February 1950 an obscure young senator from Wisconsin, Joseph R. McCarthy, said in a public address in Wheeling, West Virginia, that the Department of State was crammed with Communists; that he and the secretary of state knew their names; that he had, in fact, a list of them in his possession (which he never produced). These Communists were "still working and making policy," he said, and the government refused to get rid of them. For almost four years after this speech, the United States grappled with one internal problem almost to the exclusion of everything else: was Senator Joseph McCarthy telling the truth? Committee after committee of the United States Senate examined this question and reported that he was not—but huge audiences continued to shout and cheer when McCarthy spoke. He received vast sums of money from right-wingers, for in their eyes he was the new savior.

The Catholic church in Europe was locked in an unrelenting struggle to maintain its freedom from Communist control in countries such as Poland and Hungary, where the Russians had taken over. For this as well as for deeply religious reasons, the Catholic church in America and millions of its faithful were passionately hostile to "godless Communism." They were joined in this by Fundamentalist Protestants—especially in small-town, rural, "Bible Belt" regions—who had long equated radicalism with the devil. Furthermore, Irish-Catholic Joe McCarthy, in his attacks on the eastern, Ivy-League-trained, intellectual elite that for decades had run the nation's foreign policy, was assaulting the very fortress of the Anglo-Saxon Protestant ascendancy whose status had long been resented by the outgroups. For people who nourished old hatreds and an ancient sense of being excluded, the McCarthy campaign was a way of declaring that they, not the Anglo-Saxon elite, were the true patriots.

McCarthy brought the Truman administration practically to a halt by massively eroding its credibility. He destroyed the careers of State Department officials by unproved charges and smeared the reputations of both Dean Acheson and George Marshall, the secretaries of state who had shaped Truman's Cold War policies. "The Democratic label," he said, "is now the property of men and women who have . . . bent to the whispered pleas from the lips of traitors . . . men and women who wear the political label stitched with the idiocy of a Truman, rotted by the deceit of an Acheson. . . ."

McCarran Act

Out of this atmosphere came the McCarran Internal Security Act, passed over Truman's veto, which required Communist and "Communist-front" organizations to register with the federal government (so they could be prosecuted, apparently) and authorized the government in times of national emergency to gather up and imprison suspected subversives. As soon as the Eisenhower administration was installed in January 1953, it got busy rescreening all government employees under the loyalty program, and a year later it proudly stated that 2,200 workers had been fired—though not one of them was a proven Communist.

But for McCarthy, this was not enough. After a brief silence following Eisenhower's inauguration, he was soon at it again. He accused the new president of running a "weak, immoral, and cowardly" foreign policy composed of "appeasement, retreat, and surrender." The president was furious, but he refused to demean himself by openly contesting the senator. People of great standing and authority were horrified by McCarthy's lurid career and enormous sway over the public. "When I think of McCarthy," said President Eisenhower's banker brother, Arthur, "I automatically think of Hitler." He was, indeed, an

unlovely sight. He liked to be thought of as a tough guy, cultivated a reputation as a heavy drinker (which he was) and a terror with women, and swaggered forward in a lowering, heavy-shouldered way when he walked. "McCarthy," wrote an unadmiring veteran Washington reporter, Richard Rovere, "was surely the champion liar. He lied with wild abandon; he lied without evident fear; he lied in his teeth and in the teeth of the truth; he lied vividly and with a bold imagination; he lied, often, with very little pretense to be telling the truth."

But McCarthy died, politically and literally, by his own excesses. In the fall of 1954 his wild charges that the army was harboring Communists were subjected to a long series of committee hearings that fascinated the nation, for they were the first such dramatic occasions ever to appear on national television. Millions watched and found to their disdain that the senator was a rather repellent figure, a bully who twisted facts, bulldozed his way rather than let others speak, tried to smear an innocent young lawyer simply to get at the other side, and made himself ludicrous by his heavy-jowled, endlessly reiterated bellow, "Point of Order! Point of Order!" Soon the television comics were making fun of him, and, almost as swiftly as it had risen, his national reputation collapsed. The Senate censured him, relieved now that the frightening ogre had been made into a petty politician. He spent his last days hurrying through the Senate's corridors, trying to get reporters to listen to some new "sensation." In May 1957 he died of cirrhosis of the liver. Although fallen in the general public's eyes, he was mourned by many. He remains a martyred hero to thousands.

Dwight Eisenhower and Republicanism

Dwight Eisenhower was swept into the White House over Adlai Stevenson in 1952, for the nation was sick of the Korean War, thoroughly tired of the Democrats, and eager for a president it could trust and admire. This good-hearted man, whose warmth and dignity attracted grateful support from millions of Democrats as well as Republicans, could give the country what it most needed: calm and unity in place of the McCarthyite hysteria. Indeed, Dwight Eisenhower was to be a president who soared high above his party in the people's estimation, for only in 1952 were the Republicans able to gain a majority in Congress behind him. For six of his eight years in office, the nation persistently put Democrats in control of that body.

He was a Republican, however, and it is important to understand what this meant. In both foreign and domestic affairs he fell toward the liberal side of his party, but he was still incontestably a man of the right wing in national politics. He remained firmly committed to the global leadership role that Truman had built for America—thus rejecting isolationism, which many in his party espoused—but within that role he and John Foster Dulles were more unilateral and nationalist in their mode of operation than Truman and far less concerned with sponsoring social reform abroad. Within the nation he made one historically important liberal contribution: he would have nothing to do with any campaign to repeal the New Deal, thus permanently fixing its reforms in the American system. Indeed, he even broadened the coverage of social security, supported federal aid to the schools, and approved the creation of the Department of Health, Education, and Welfare.

Nonetheless, he built a thoroughly Republican administration. The Democrats had traditionally stressed ideas in their administrations, which tended to be rather confusingly organized; the Republicans, on the other hand, stressed neat and businesslike methods, while paying much less attention to intellectuals and reform proposals. The new president installed a symmetrically organized staff system in the White House, like that of a military organization, in which discussions and decisions flowed upward to him through an ascending pyramid of officials who refined the issues so that he, as president, had mainly to say only yes or no. As a commander, he had scrupulously delegated responsibilities to subordinates, and now he did the same, largely turning over the direction of the great departments in the government to his cabinet members.

Differences in governing style

This was what presidents on the right wing of national politics had been doing since the days of the Whigs and the Federalists. Republican administrations, unlike Democratic ones, traditionally rejected the idea of the strong executive who runs the government with a firm hand, keeps close tabs on internal departmental affairs, and provides active leadership to Congress and the people. Republican administrations, too, place a considerable emphasis on decorum, modes of dress, and stately procedures. Not for them the shirt sleeves of the Democrats, the party atmosphere, informality, and general raffishness of the New Deal. Homburgs were carefully chosen for the new president's inauguration; and the style of entertainment in Washington, always shaped on the model displayed at 1600 Pennsylvania Avenue, became well mannered and subdued.

Dwight Eisenhower had a strong admiration for the great men of the business and financial world, and he formed his cabinet principally of millionaires. Wherever he could, as president, he turned things over to private enterprise: government-built rubber plants; hydroelectric sites; and control of natural resources. He spoke of the Tennessee Valley Authority as "creeping socialism," and in the Dixon-Yates controversy of 1954, tried to arrange for the Atomic Energy Commission to buy electric power from a private plant rather than from TVA sources. To the federal government's independent regulatory commissions—such as the Federal Communications Commission (radio and television), the Federal Trade Commission (advertising and marketing), and the Securities and Exchange Commission (stock markets)—he appointed new members who were friendly to the businesses they were supposed to regulate, rather than critical of them. Hostile toward government spending, he spent his eight years slashing budgets and battling inflation.

He believed deeply in the separation of powers and abruptly terminated the practice of trying to shepherd laws through Congress by the daily and painstaking influence that his Democratic predecessors had sought to apply. He felt that his duty as president was to present his proposals as logically and persuasively as possible and leave the disposing to the wisdom of Congress. He did not use the White House as a "bully pulpit," as Theodore Roosevelt called it, nor did he give any presidential leadership to the Republican party, for which many of its members harshly criticized him. His was to be a quiet term in office, a time of healing, moderation, and settling down. This was his intention, and so, in large part, did it turn out. Convinced that the business community was the proper source for national leadership, that most people would do best to solve their problems without government help, and that the country was fundamentally healthy and needed only good administration, Dwight Eisenhower rarely, if ever, tried to lead the country in new directions.

The revolutionary Warren Court

Eisenhower's most important single appointment was that of Earl Warren, governor of California, as chief justice of the United States Supreme Court. Ironically, in this action the president devoted to inactivity helped to create one of the most amazing phenomena in American life: a Supreme Court that suddenly seized so bold and active a role that it was widely called revolutionary. The president is rumored to have called Warren's appointment the "biggest damfool mistake I ever made." Thousands of Americans who emblazoned "Impeach Earl Warren!" signs about the country agreed. No Supreme Court since John Marshall's, 150 years before, matched the Warren Court in the breadth and sweeping importance of its decisions, and even the Marshall Court pales by comparison, for its decisions related just to the powers of the federal government, while the Warren Court plunged deep into social and political life.

Earl Warren, like Eisenhower, was a generous, simple, and courageous man whose mind worked with fundamental considerations of decency and fair play, rather than with the fine intellectuality of the law. But unlike Eisenhower, he had been a political leader of a large and populous state and had acquired an appetite for actively grappling with large problems. He had begun in California politics as a regular Republican who attacked "communistic radicals," wanted to force school children to salute the flag even when conscience forbade them, and in wartime led the clamor to uproot all persons of Japanese ancestry and send them to concentration camps. Perhaps this last experience shook him, for ever after he showed an acute sensitivity for the rights of individuals. Three times governor, he astonished his conservative supporters after 1945 by proposing major social reforms, including prepaid medical insurance.

Appointed chief justice in late 1953, he held the post for sixteen years. During his long tenure, the Court swept away the legal basis for racial discrimination; wiped out "rotten boroughs" in the states by ruling that everyone must be represented equally in state legislatures and in the House of Representatives; rewrote practically all procedures in criminal justice by ensuring crucial rights to the accused; broadened the artist's right to publish works shocking to public taste; and in major ways made it less possible for the government to penalize individuals for their beliefs or associations. All these decisions were controversial; all were denounced as destroying the nation. But long before his term as chief justice ended, Earl Warren had become a world-famous figure symbolizing the decent humanitarian values that, many hoped, lay at the core of the American system.

The black revolution begins

No decision of the Warren Court was more famous than that in *Brown* v. *Board of Education of Topeka* (1954), when racial segregation in the schools was unanimously ruled unconstitutional. This great decision, followed by others that struck down segregation in public parks, buses, trains, and airlines, at public golf courses and other recreational facilities, in libraries and public buildings, in elections and marriage laws, amounted to a historic revolution in race relations law. Prior to this, black Americans could only appeal to moral considerations and the consciences of white people—notoriously weak reeds. This was so because the legal system was based on the separate-but-equal principle laid down in *Plessy* v. *Ferguson* (1896). Now, however, black Americans could point out that the statutory discriminations that tied them down and kept them in a secondary caste were *illegal*. This enormously important transformation poured hope and vast energies into the struggle for black equality. The Supreme Court had time and again in past generations hammered at the principle that a constitutional right, such as free speech or freedom of religion, is something that is "personal and present"; that is, it resides in the individual, and it is a permanent, continuing possession that is not created or affected by laws passed in some local city council or state legislature. After *Brown* v. *Board of Education of Topeka*, that "personal and present" quality applied to the right to freedom from any form of public discrimination that was based on or supported and maintained by law. Now the "Second Reconstruction," the sweeping change in the position and role of black Americans in national life that took place in the 1950s and 1960s, could begin.

Roots of the Second Reconstruction

The Second Reconstruction had actually been in preparation for many years. The steady migration of Afro-Americans out of the South had brought them much closer to the power centers in national life, which are located in the northern cities. In 1910, about ninety percent of black Americans lived in the southern states; in 1920, eighty percent did; and by 1960, the figure had declined to sixty percent. In the years from 1940 to 1960, almost three million blacks left the South: some 600,000 of them went to California, 500,000 to New York, 370,000 to Illinois, and nearly 190,000 to Michigan. Even within the South blacks have shifted away from rural areas, where they were isolated and powerless, to the cities (a third lived in cities in 1940; more than half did in 1960). By the time John Kennedy was elected in 1960, seventy-three percent of all black Americans lived in cities, a slightly higher proportion than that among whites. For many blacks the change has meant moving from rural misery to urban misery, but it has also meant that they have gathered in compact masses and thus have acquired much more potential leverage on public policy than they ever had living in isolated rural areas.

The Second Reconstruction sprang in part from the long-range impact of the system of segregation, which was adopted around the opening of the twentieth century. On this segregated basis, for the first time Afro-Americans were finally given a large system of schools—if limited in educational scope. On this basis, too, separate black communities emerged within major cities. Examples include those centered around such thoroughfares as Beale Street in Memphis and Auburn Avenue in Atlanta, and, of course, Harlem. Such communities had their own black doctors, lawyers, bankers, businessmen, and ministers. This meant that the segregated schooling system could greatly expand what, in fact, it had never lost—instruction in the liberal arts and sciences. The basis of every black child's education had been training in literature, geography, the sciences, and history. Even in the rural schools the traditional curriculum survived, vocational arts never being given more than secondary emphasis. Segregated colleges grew in number, reaching more than a hundred by the 1930s. They met the daily needs of the black community by offering courses in business, economics, journalism, medicine, teacher training, and theology. Indeed, black education duplicated in substance—though certainly without anything like similar resources and public funds—the kind of education given white youngsters. By Franklin Roosevelt's presidency, therefore, a new middle class was emerging among Afro-Americans that was preparing itself for leadership. We have seen that a "new middle class" trained by the universities of the late nineteenth century produced the progressive movement among white Americans in the years after 1900; so, too, the creation of a similar group among black Americans had the same effect in the mid-twentieth century.

Impact of war and depression

The two world wars and the Great Depression provided quickening stimuli. The First World War brought huge numbers of blacks out of the South and excited them with the dreams of democracy and equality that Woodrow Wilson spread to the world. Soon they found that this was a white man's dream in which they were not to share, for the image of a new democratic order was destroyed by race riots, lynchings, and continued discrimination.

During the 1920s, black America turned in on itself, producing the remarkable flowering of the Harlem Renaissance. The depression of the 1930s, however, broke open the mold again. When black voters flooded into Democratic ranks, they acquired a political power they had not had before. Since the New Deal programs were dominated by segregationist whites at the local level, blacks never shared equally in benefits, but even so the change in their situation was remarkable. At least they knew that the government meant for them to share equally. There were great disappointments for blacks in the depression decade, but their hopes had been stimulated.

Then came the Second World War. Afro-Americans entered it without the illusions they had held in 1917. Many openly called it a white man's war, and a few even supported the Japanese cause. The way blacks were treated during the conflict confirmed their cynicism. War industries gave them only menial jobs, rigid segregation existed in the services (the marines excluded blacks entirely), and even the Red Cross blood program refused to mix blood from whites and blacks. Once more, however, this was a war fought for widely trumpeted humanitarian values of equality and decency, and this intensified the Afro-American's conviction that his place in American life should be upgraded. Many agreed with the black columnist George Schuyler who said, "Our war is not against Hitler in Europe, but against the Hitlers in America."

Rising militancy

White Americans reacted in anger. Black newspapers were barred from military camps, and Franklin Roosevelt was even asked to approve the prosecution of some black editors for sedition and harming the war effort, which he refused to do. Racial tensions escalated, and riots broke out in 1943. But black militancy continued to rise. Hope and cynicism existed side by side. "What an opportunity the crisis has been . . . for one to persuade, embarrass, compel and shame our government and nation . . . into a more enlightened attitude toward a tenth of its people!" said the Pittsburgh *Courier*. Protest against discrimination mounted.

In 1945 Walter White, the executive secretary of the NAACP wrote that "World War II has given to the Negro a sense of kinship with other colored—and also oppressed—peoples of the world. . . . [He] senses that the struggle of the Negro in the United States is part and parcel of the struggle against imperialism and exploitation in India, China, Burma, Africa, the Philippines, Malaya, the West Indies, and South America. . . . [There will be] world-wide racial conflict unless the white nations of the earth do an about-face on the issue of race. . . .

"Will the United States after the war perpetuate its racial-discrimination policies and beliefs at home and abroad as it did during the war? . . . Will decent and intelligent America continue to permit itself to be led by the nose by demagogues and professional race-hate mongers—to have its thinking and action determined on this global and explosive issue by the lowest common denominator of public opinion? . . . The United States, Great Britain, France, and other allied nations must choose without delay one of two courses—to revolutionize their racial concepts and practices, to abolish imperialism and grant full equality to all of its people, or else prepare for World War III. . . . A wind is rising—a wind of determination by the have-nots of the world to share the benefits of freedom and prosperity which the haves of the earth have tried to keep exclusively for themselves. That wind blows all over the world. Whether that wind develops into a hurricane is a decision which we must make now and in the days when we form the peace." (*The Rising Wind* [1945].)

A. Philip Randolph pointed out in January 1941 that all the efforts by committees and isolated black leaders sponsored by the NAACP and other black organizations had failed to change governmental policies. Mass action was needed. Out of this recommendation quickly came a plan for an all-black march of 50,000 people on Washington to force action by the president and Congress. Alarmed, Franklin Roosevelt agreed to establish the Fair Employment Practices Committee, the first national agency that explored discrimination in jobs and worked for equal employment. This concession halted planning for the march, for it was regarded as a great victory—through it fell far short of the March on Washington Movement's stated goals, which called for massive direct action to throw open jobs to blacks and end discrimination against them in unions, government employment, and

the military services. By war's end, however, discrimination in war industries and in unions connected with them had greatly declined. Whereas in 1940 every third black worker was on a farm, in 1947 the situation had so drastically changed that the figure had dropped to one in six.

Postwar race relations

After the war, several disturbing trends became apparent: when factories slowed down during recessions, blacks were the first to be fired; blacks were rigorously excluded from management positions and sales jobs; they were given limited opportunity in the professions and were treated only a little better in skilled and clerical positions. These conditions, together with continued legal discrimination in public facilities in the South and adjoining states and the increasing congestion and dreariness of slum life, kept black militance from waning.

At war's end the battleground was initially the struggle to keep the Fair Employment Practices Committee alive, despite unending attacks against it by southern congressmen. President Truman took actions that were unusually helpful to the black cause. He eliminated discrimination in the armed services by executive order in 1948, working a revolution that many said would bring chaos but was accepted with surprising—and significant—acquiescence. From then on, the military services became an often-chosen means for young black Americans to break out of poverty (though their chances of becoming officers were low in the army, lower yet in the air force, and practically nonexistent in the navy).

In 1948 Truman also established a program to eliminate discrimination in the federal civil service and in factories and businesses supplying the government. What the program did, of course, was to push discrimination into the realm of extralegal, informal measures, but some important gains were made, especially in government employment. At the same time, President Truman urged another program on Congress that called for laws against lynching, protection of voting rights (long denied to blacks in the South), and continuing efforts against discrimination in employment. He got none of this legislation. In the election of 1948 Strom Thurmond led a bolt of southern Democrats from the party, running for the presidency in that year as the States' Rights candidate and winning four southern states in an attempt to prevent Truman's reelection.

The drive for equal education

Black America, however, put its greatest hopes in education, as, indeed, all Americans had done since Andrew Jackson's era. The first campaign led by the NAACP after 1945 was to break open segregated higher education. In 1948 Oklahoma

was forced to admit a black student to its university by court order, and then similar edicts were issued elsewhere in the South and border states: Kentucky in 1949; Louisiana, Missouri, Texas, and Virginia in 1950; North Carolina in 1951; and Tennessee in 1952.

Conditions were now ripe for the emergence of a determined and persistent mass movement. Hundreds of thousands of blacks belonged to the NAACP, and it had funds to pour into the necessary legal battles. Furthermore, the rise of new independent nations in Africa and the Middle and Far East quickened the whole community of black America. Why, it was asked, should blacks continue as a secondary caste when everywhere black and brown men were throwing off white rule and proudly ruling themselves? The "revo-

In an eloquent tableau, three men seated in a public location in a Southern town, in the 1950s, symbolize the state of race relations.
Henri Cartier-Bresson

lution of rising expectations" that was sweeping oppressed peoples around the world from China to French Canada, Brazil, and Ghana had seized the Afro-American mind as well. Also, the fact that the United States trumpeted itself as the protector of freedom in the Cold War accentuated the aspirations of black Americans for an equitable share in that freedom.

In 1952 a group of cases on school segregation awaited adjudication in the Supreme Court. Of these, that begun by Oliver Brown of Topeka, Kansas, and supported by the NAACP, was first in order. Brown's eight-year-old daughter, because she was black, was kept from a school just five blocks from her home and forced to travel two miles to a black institution. Clearly, a decision based on this case would be of national importance. Initial arguments were heard in late 1952 and then renewed in the fall of 1953 when the Court had a new chief justice, Earl Warren. On May 17, 1954, Warren read his decision, in which the Court concurred unanimously: the Fourteenth Amendment requires the equal protection of the laws for all citizens. "Does segregation of children in public schools solely on the basis of race, even though the physical facilities and other 'tangible' factors may be equal," he asked, "deprive the children of the minority group of equal educational opportunities? We believe that it does." This practice "generates a feeling of inferiority as to their status in the community that may affect their hearts and minds in a way unlikely ever to be undone." The chief justice observed that, whatever people knew about psychology in the days of *Plessy* v. *Ferguson* (1896), modern scholarship amply demonstrates this fact. "We conclude," he said, "that in the field of public education the doctrine of 'separate but equal' has no place. Separate educational facilities are inherently unequal."

White resistance

This ringing, now classic statement was followed by endless frustration for blacks. A year later, when the Court ordered school districts to proceed with all "deliberate speed" to implement this principle, the South stubbornly resisted— and northern school districts did so only slightly less rigidly. Segregation in law was now illegal, but segregation in practice continued. As late as 1965 black children in the South had been admitted to white schools in less than twenty-five percent of the school districts. Indeed, in actual numbers only a little more than six percent of the black students in the old Confederacy were attending schools with white students.

In 1956 southern senators and congressmen issued a "southern manifesto" prepared by Senator Richard B. Russell of Georgia: "The unwarranted decision of the Supreme Court in the public school cases is now bearing the fruit always produced when men substitute naked power for established law. . . . We regard the decision . . . as a clear abuse of judicial power . . . [the separate-but-equal principle] restated time and again, became a part of the life of the people of many of the States and confirmed their habits, customs, traditions, and way of life. It is founded on elemental humanity and commonsense, for parents should not be deprived by Government of the right to direct the lives and education of their own children. . . .

"This unwarranted exercise of power by the Court, contrary to the Constitution, is creating chaos and confusion in the States principally affected. It is destroying the amicable relations between the white and Negro races that have been created through 90 years of patient effort by the good people of both races. It has planted hatred and suspicion where there has been heretofore friendship and understanding.

"Without regard to the consent of the governed, outside agitators are threatening immediate and revolutionary changes in our public-school systems. If done, this is certain to destroy the system of public education in some of the States. . . .

"We commend the motives of those States which have declared the intention to resist forced integration by any lawful means. . . . We decry the Supreme Court's encroachments on rights reserved to the States and to the people, contrary to established law, and to the Constitution."

Eisenhower and the black revolution

President Eisenhower was favorably disposed to the Afro-American cause and appointed the first cabinet-level black federal official, J. Ernest Wilkins, assistant secretary of labor. He even brought a loyal black Republican, E. Frederick Morrow, into the White House as the first presidential assistant of that race. But Morrow was constantly frustrated in his efforts to get the White House to take any leadership role. Eisenhower and his advisers believed that the blacks were pushing too hard. Furthermore, they were extremely worried about offending white southerners and believed that government action could not seriously affect race relations.

By early 1957 black homes and churches in the South were being bombed by whites determined to frighten off black attempts to make the Supreme Court decision an actuality. Meanwhile, the Eisenhower administration was filling the international air with protests against the way the Russians were treating the Hungarians, and welcoming Hungarian refugees to America. Why, asked black newspapers and leaders across the country, did Eisenhower not give the same solicitude to his own black countrymen?

In August 1957 the first civil rights law since 1875 was passed by the Democratic Congress, creating the Commission on Civil Rights to study and report on the equal protection of the laws. The law also prohibited interference with the right to vote (including primary elections), and provided new procedures for securing federal protection of this right. This provision was based on the fundamental belief that if blacks in the South could secure the vote, all their other problems would eventually be solved. Shortly afterward, however, Governor Orval Faubus of Arkansas sharply escalated the crisis by using the state's National Guard to prevent the enrollment of blacks in a white high school in Little Rock, Arkansas. The president was now forced to take action, for Faubus's action directly violated a court order. In a profoundly important step, he took control of the National Guard away from the governor, utilizing legislation passed decades before (ironically, with southern support) to strengthen the Guard by linking it to the federal government. Then he used troops to ensure that black students could peacefully enroll in the white high school. Thus, at the hands of a reluctant president, the federal government took direct action for the first time in almost a hundred years to aid black Americans in the South.

Eisenhower remained deeply convinced, however, that state and local authorities should handle the race problem, and he took no steps beyond ensuring compliance with specific court orders and stating publicly in the strongest terms, as he did on September 26, 1958, that racial segregation was contrary to American ideals of equality. His assistant, Fred Morrow, could only sadly report, after all his efforts to swing blacks behind the Republican banner, that "the Republican leadership [around the country] was aloof, still looked upon Negroes as a lower class, and talked down to them rather than giving them any chance of equality." At the same time, northern Democrats were very effectively "making it possible for Negroes to share in party councils and in appointing them to jobs of influence and prestige in northern states and cities." At the end of the Eisenhower years, the black vote was still solidly in the Democratic camp, despite the presence also within that party of the white Solid South.

The forgotten minority: American Indians

The last time the history of the American Indian was discussed in these pages was in relation to the Dawes Act of 1887. White Americans then believed that they had solved the Indian problem. Indeed, for half a century the Dawes Act remained basic national policy. American Indians faded from national consciousness, becoming a forgotten minority. In fact, however, much was going on, even if it was obscured from view.

In 1889 the Indian tribes possessed 104 million acres of land, an expanse of territory equivalent to the state of California. But the principle of the Dawes Act of 1887 had been to divide this immense holding into allotments and require each Indian family to live on a small homestead, usually 160 acres. On homesteads, it was believed, Indians would learn the habits of the white majority—pride in individual property ownership, labor by the clock and calendar, and the production of articles for commerce. After allotment, surplus tribal lands would be sold. Off-reservation boarding schools were built for young Indians so as to complete the process of destroying Indian culture. Traditional Indian religious practices were suppressed.

In a decades-long tragedy, Indians had their land taken from them in return for pieces of paper that most did not understand. Many, indeed, retreated to remote woods, refusing to sign anything at all, even when it meant a total loss of all property, for the whole process was anathema to them. In some places—notably in Oklahoma where the immensely valuable oil lands of the Five Civilized Tribes were located—county courts peremptorily declared adult Indian men and women in need of guardianship and assigned control of their lands to whites. Despite all Indian protests, huge areas were opened to white settlement, save in such inhospitable land as that of the Navaho and Hopi of the southwestern states. The Five Civilized Tribes of Oklahoma had owned almost 20 million acres in 1898; by the 1930s their land had dwindled to about 1.5 million acres. Overall, America's Indians possessed only some 47 million acres in 1934, most of which consisted of empty desert land. As the Indian Task Force of the Hoover Commission was to say in 1948, "The practice of allotting land and issuing fee patents obviously did not make Indians 'competent.' It proved to be chiefly a way of getting Indian land into non-Indian ownership." Most Indians faced a wretched future. They were illiterate, lived in shacks and hovels, suffered from malnutrition, and gave way to complete hopelessness.

New spirit toward Indians emerges in 1920s

By the 1920s the white generation that had most exploited the Indians had passed on. The wars of the plains were over; most of the good Indian land was gone anyway; and a new spirit began to take the place of the old vindictiveness and contempt. The rampant abuses began to be noticed. What earlier administrations had proudly reported as "progress"—the rising proportion of allotted land—was now seen to be instead a story of poverty and suffering. The Hoover administration began to spend funds for agricultural assistance, better schools located near the tribal settlements, and a more professional Indian service.

In the 1930s Indians were further benefited when Franklin Roosevelt appointed John Collier commissioner of Indian affairs. A gifted man wholly devoted to the idea that Indian culture and ways of life were unique and valuable, to be preserved and strengthened, Collier was the moving spirit behind the passage of the Indian Reorganization Act of 1934. A landmark in Indian history, the act scuttled all past policy and for the first time since 1887 recognized the existence of the tribal system and empowered the tribes to govern themselves. Allotment of land was halted, and funds were appropriated to help the tribes buy back land they had lost. (The funds actually spent were limited but crucially helpful, especially in the form of revolving loans.) Meanwhile, Collier fostered pride in what he called "Indianhood" by encouraging ethnologists and historians to write books about the Indian past and culture. Indian religious practices, condemned as superstition by Christian missionaries, were allowed to flourish again.

Some ninety-five tribes drew up constitutions, and most formed corporations for conducting their business affairs in common. Incredible though many found it, the spirit of tribal membership and the culture that had given it life and reality for centuries still lived. Indeed, from various sources tribal lands actually grew by some four million acres in the next twenty years. Unfortunately, the problem of increasingly complex fragmentation of ownership, as successive heirs of allotted land received ever smaller fragments of property, could never be solved. In general, such land was leased by white farmers and cattlemen for nominal sums. For thousands of Indians, therefore, even the new regime meant little. They continued to live in poverty on their reservations, or they drifted to cities to work as unskilled laborers.

Post—1945 "termination policy"

After 1945, the humanitarian spirit waned. Farmers, lumbermen, and stock grazers, whose operations had been greatly expanded by the Second World War, looked covetously at the Indians' remaining land. Congressmen agitated for a repeal of Collier's Reorganization Act and the breaking up of tribal governments. In 1950 the man who had been in charge of Japanese internment camps during the war, Dillon S. Myer, became Indian commissioner. He immediately began a policy of terminating all federal services to selected tribes and placing them under state supervision. His work was formally approved in 1953, when the Congress passed House Concurrent Resolution 108, which stated national policy to be "to make the Indian . . . subject to the same laws and entitled to the same privileges and responsibilities as . . . other citizens . . . and to end their status as wards of the United States, and to grant them all of the rights and privileges pertaining to American citizenship." Indian Bureau administrators dating from the days of John Collier resigned or were fired. The keynote, once again, was "development" of Indian lands under the guise of "freeing the Indians."

These new policies sent a wave of anxiety through the Indian world. Every year the National Congress of American Indians and most intertribal councils petitioned Congress for an end to the policy, but with little success. In the years from 1952 to 1956, the government "freed" 1.6 million acres of land for sale to whites; the revolving loan fund established in New Deal days to allow expansion of Indian lands was frozen; and members of the bureau talked of migration to the cities as the final solution to the Indian problem. Thousands of Indians were recruited by the bureau for city jobs, given moving costs, and aided in finding housing. Relocation centers were established in major cities such as Chicago, Denver, and Los Angeles. The overwhelming majority of these Indians left their tribal locations because their land was being pulled out from under them. The busiest office in the Indian Bureau was the "Realty" branch, which labored steadily at working out terminations and putting Indian land up for sale. By the 1960s, about forty percent of America's Indian people had become city dwellers.

Federal aid to education begins

In 1957 the Russians launched their first orbiting satellite, Sputnik, and thereby created a storm of controversy. Everywhere there were meetings, talks, discussions, and proposals on what should be done to make up for the apparent failure of the nation's educational system in the areas of science and technology. Public educational institutions throughout the country began radically changing curricula, particularly in the direction of providing specially enriched programs for "gifted" students. Suddenly there was a new emphasis on "excellence" and high performance. High school and college students found themselves in a much more intensive academic environment, and a new seriousness—some called it overemphasis—concerning grades emerged.

In August 1958 Congress enacted the first general education law since the Morrill Act of 1862, entitled the National Defense Education Act. It authorized the spending of more than one billion dollars over the ensuing four years in federal aid to education at every level from elementary school through graduate training. The act also established funds for loans and fellowships to college students; for strengthening science, mathematics, and language teaching; for testing and counseling programs; and for the dissemination of scientific information. Thus began a massive federal program that has continued ever since.

The "new" Eisenhower

By the beginning of 1959, a "new" Eisenhower had appeared, convinced at long last that his passive conception of the presidency had been wrong. Now he began using the vast powers of his office vigorously. He spoke regretfully of the proposals he had let die in Congress in previous years through a distaste for politics and began cajoling and threatening congressmen to secure favorable votes. Out of this atmosphere came his bold new approach to foreign relations, including personal tours around the world and face-to-face talks with Nikita Khrushchev. He was able to preside over two historic events in 1959 that changed the shape of America: the opening of the St. Lawrence Seaway, which made the whole Great Lakes waterfront, in effect, an extension of the seacoast; and the admission of Alaska and Hawaii as the forty-ninth and fiftieth states in the Union.

Despite the president's new dynamism, however, Republican chances in the up-coming presidential election of 1960 looked dim. Eisenhower was still loved and could possibly have been reelected despite his age—a possibility ruled out by the Twenty-second Amendment, passed in 1951, which limited a president to two terms—but that popularity had never rubbed off on his party. Besides, his long years of studious inactivity in the face of the nation's growing problems had driven deeply into the American mind a feeling that these problems were coming to a crisis while the Republicans did nothing. Recession after recession hobbled the economy, probably induced by the administration's tight money policies; in 1960 yet another one began. Although the American economy's growth rate had never risen above three percent a year in the Eisenhower era, the economies of Russia, China, Germany, and Japan were bounding upward. Race

relations were growing worse; Eisenhower's diplomatic campaign had collapsed in confusion and embarrassment when the Soviets shot down an American U-2 reconnaissance plane over their territory in May 1960; and John Kennedy was arousing wide excitement by his promise that he would "get the country moving again." In November this arresting young man, the first Catholic ever to enter the presidency, won a dramatic victory over Richard M. Nixon—though by a narrow popular vote margin.

So it was that in January 1961, Dwight Eisenhower sat on the white inaugural platform in front of the Capitol building, the oldest president in the nation's history, and listened while John F. Kennedy, the youngest man to be elected president, gave his inaugural address. An older order now passed off the stage with Dwight Eisenhower, as he left Washington for his Gettysburg farm. The turbulent 1960s had begun.

Bibliography

Three books that were especially valuable to me in writing this chapter: Harry Truman's own memoirs provide a fascinating glimpse into his character: *Memoirs by Harry S Truman*, two vols. (1958). Richard H. Rovere's *Senator Joe McCarthy** (1960) is a compellingly graphic account of that strange man. *The Warren Court: A Critical Analysis* (1969), ed. Richard H. Sayler, Barry B. Boyer, and Robert E. Gooding, Jr., provided me with judicious accounts of the Court and its great decisions in this era.

How have historians looked at the topic?

Although contemporaries did not always recognize it, the character of American society was vastly altered by World War II. In *Don't You Know There's a War On? The American Home Front, 1941–1945* (1970), Richard R. Lingeman describes the myriad changes produced by the war. In *War and Society: The United States, 1941–1945** (1972), Richard Polenberg defines and analyzes the nature of these changes. Keith L. Nelson's fine edited volume *The Impact of War on American Life: The Twentieth-Century Experience** (1971) assesses the effects of the Second World War on all aspects of American society.

The demobilization policies of the peppery man from Missouri are praised by Cabell Phillips in *The Truman Presidency: The History of a Triumphant Succession* (1966). A more critical tone suffuses *The Politics and Policies of the Truman Administration** (1970), a collection of brilliant and provocative essays edited by Barton J. Bernstein. Bert Cochran's insightful *Harry Truman and the Crisis Presidency* (1973) illuminates the president's policies after reelection. Margaret Truman's memoirs of the White House years, *Harry S Truman* (1973), furnish a special dimension.

The labor turmoil of the late 1940s is analyzed from a political perspective in R. Alton Lee's *Truman and Taft-Hartley: A Question of Mandate* (1966). Allen J. Matusow offers an excellent study of the farm crisis in *Farm Policies and Politics in the Truman Years* (1967), and the problem is placed in wider perspective in Edward C. Higbee's challenging *Farms and Farmers in an Urban Age* (1963). In a key interpretation, *American Capitalism: The Concept of Countervailing Power** (1952), John Kenneth Galbraith viewed the trend toward large-scale business organization as a healthy one, a theory challenged by Bernard D. Nossiter in *The Mythmakers: An Essay on Power and Wealth* (1964). John Kenneth Galbraith's *The Affluent Society** (1958) has also been widely influential in understanding the 1950s. The economic question is perceptively explored in a comparative framework in Andrew Shonfield's *Modern Capitalism: The Changing Balance of Public and Private Power* (1969).

The Red Scare of the early 1950s is seen as another chapter in the growth of anticommunism as a basic American ideology in Michael Parenti's *The Anti-Communism Impulse* (1969). A more judicious analysis, which nevertheless finds the seeds of McCarthyism in the Truman administration's loyalty program, is Alan D. Harper's *The Politics of Loyalty: The White House and the Communist Issue, 1946–1952* (1969). In *The Communist Controversy in Washington* (1966) Earl Latham finds the political influence of the American Communist party practically nonexistent even at the height of its numerical strength. A prize-winning, exhaustively researched, and well-written account of Joseph McCarthy's rise and fall is Robert Griffith's *The Politics of Fear: Joseph R. McCarthy and the Senate* (1970). Richard Hofstadter's brilliant *The Paranoid Style in American Politics and Other Essays** (1965) is essential on McCarthyism and may be compared with a stimulating book by Seymour M. Lipset and Earl Raab, *The Politics of Unreason: Right Wing Extremism in America, 1790–1970* (1970).

The black revolution following World War II was predicted in Gunnar Myrdal's landmark *An American Dilemma*, two vols. (1944), completed with the assistance of Richard Sterner and Arnold Rose. William C. Berman's *The Politics of Civil Rights in the Truman Administration* (1970) is a highly competent discussion of these years. The effects of the epochal Supreme Court decision of 1954 are weighed in Benjamin Muse's *Ten Years of Prelude: The Story of Integration since the Supreme Court 1954 Decision* (1964) and B. M. Ziegler's *Desegregation and the Supreme Court** (1958). *Portrait of a Decade* (1964) by Anthony Lewis covers the struggle for black liberties, and the tone of the movement is captured in Louis E. Lomax's *The Negro Revolt** (1962). The tragic reality of a black's existence in America is poignantly and forcefully told in *The Autobiography of Malcolm X* (1965), written with the assistance of Alex Haley.

*Available in paperback.

The Black Revolution

Mrs. Rosa Parks, the courageous black woman whose refusal to move to the back of the bus in Montgomery, Alabama in 1955, inspired a 382-day boycott by the black community. In November, 1956, the Supreme Court declared Alabama's state and local laws requiring segregation on buses unconstitutional. Black militance now spread throughout the southern states, leading to a wholesale collapse of Jim Crowism.

Martin Luther King, Jr., the minister who, inspired by Gandhi's doctrines of nonviolence, led black southern America— and eventually black northern America— out of its legally-suppressed condition to the civil rights triumphs of the 1960s. Here, he is arrested and photographed for leading the bus boycott in Montgomery.

Malcolm X, shown here addressing a Harlem rally in 1963, expressed a philosophy which seemed to run counter to King's integrationist non-violence: the need for black self-defense, self-help, and perhaps black separatism. In 1965, he was murdered in New York City by three blacks.

United Press International

Don Cravens

United Press International

A quarter of a million people of both races demonstrated for black liberation and equal civil rights during the 1963 March on Washington. They converged on the national capital in seemingly endless streams of buses from as far away as New England and the Far West. Here, around the reflecting pool at the Lincoln Memorial, they listened to Martin Luther King, Jr., and other national leaders call for a nation of inter-racial equality.

Bruce Davidson, Magnum Photos, Inc.

CHAPTER 35

Years of the Whirlwind: The 1960s

TIME LINE

1945–1960	Huge migration of southern black Americans to North
1948–1953	Birth rate increases fifty percent
1955	Bus boycott in Montgomery, Alabama; emergence of Martin Luther King as black leader
1960	John F. Kennedy elected thirty-fifth president of the United States; Students for a Democratic society formed; Second Civil Rights Act; lunch counter sit-in in Greensboro, North Carolina; Student Nonviolent Coordinating Committee formed; black nonviolent protests against segregation spread widely in South
1961	Student Nonviolent Coordinating Committee and Congress of Racial Equality lead freedom rides to desegregate interstate transportation; Twenty-third Amendment gives the District of Columbia the right to vote in presidential elections
1962	University of Mississippi forced to admit James Meredith; Kennedy orders end to racial or religious discrimination in federally financed housing
1963	Birmingham police crush black nonviolent protestors; Kennedy makes national appeal for first-class citizenship for black Americans; March on Washington; President Kennedy assassinated
1964–1969	Period of massive turmoil in black ghettoes in northern and western cities and on hundreds of university and college campuses
1964	Free-speech student protest at University of California at Berkeley; Twenty-fourth Amendment outlaws poll tax; Third Civil Rights Act
1965	Malcolm X assassinated; Watts riot; Fourth Civil Rights Act
1966	Stokely Carmichael creates Black Power slogan
1967	Detroit riot; National Conference on Black Power
1968	Democratic National Convention scene of massive police attacks against antiwar protestors; Martin Luther King assassinated; Black Panthers organize; women's liberation movement becomes prominent; Poor People's Campaign; Fifth Civil Rights Act; Robert F. Kennedy assassinated
1970	Kent State University massacre of student protestors

WE have seen before that American public life swings back and forth between periods of crisis politics and periods of cultural politics. The thirty years encompassed by the Great Depression, World War II, and the Cold War crisis gave the people of the United States a team spirit psychology. The nation had a common objective—the need to restore the economy, or to fend off a foreign enemy—and for most people it was natural to pull together. There was a strong emphasis on following the president loyally. In the depression years, people worked together in Roosevelt's New Deal programs. During the Second World War, millions of Americans joined ranks and obeyed marching orders. In the Cold War, another time of threat, the common task was, as Americans saw it, the salvation of the world from tyranny.

From their experiences in these years, the people of the United States derived a strong sense of community, of national belonging and purpose. Furthermore the postwar presidents—Truman, Eisenhower, Kennedy, Johnson, and Nixon— were all shaped by this long era of crisis. They unconsciously learned to think of their country in the imagery of the football team, the army platoon, and the naval vessel. Joint effort against a common enemy, orderliness and sobriety, self-sacrifice and the supremacy of group goals—such were the elements of their generation's life style.

But after 1960, when prosperity and relative security returned, a period of cultural politics, like that of the buoyant 1920s, began. People broke away from established patterns and began doing their own thing. The media, as forty years before, were filled with excited arguments over such cultural issues as the way young people dress, behave, and relate to older people, the role of women, the status and temper of minority groups, changes in sexual practices and attitudes, and new styles of living. The sense of community faded. Romanticism shaped the new mood, with its emphasis on instinct and impulse rather than reason, joyous release rather than restraint, individualism and self-gratification rather than group discipline. And now there were millions of college students, instead of only thousands as in the 1920s, so that when the revolt of college youth came, it rocked the entire nation. The revolt was rendered even more explosive by the outrage of the war in Vietnam. By beginning and doggedly pursuing this war, the older generation, and with it the nation's governing structure, destroyed its claim to moral authority—or so it seemed to thousands of young people.

Aspects of the new mood

The new national mood was created by torrents of swift cultural change that flooded in after the waning of the Cold War in 1962. The excitement of John Kennedy's brief presidency and his calls for self-sacrifice in the service of the nation had created an uprush of hope. But his assassination in 1963 shocked and dismayed Americans, especially the young, and in reaction a series of near-revolutionary outbreaks took place. The "quiet generation" of college students became the "wild generation" of student radicals and "hippies" who rebelled against political and cultural authority. The measured, disciplined mass protests of black Americans that the Reverend Dr. Martin Luther King, Jr., had been leading since the mid-1950s exploded in 1966 into "Black Power" riots, fire and destruction in the ghettoes, and pitched battles with National Guardsmen.

Styles of life changed swiftly. "The Pill," "nudie flicks," *Playboy* magazine, and crucial Supreme Court decisions made the United States, long one of the world's most puritanical nations in sexual matters, one of its most liberated. The drug culture mushroomed. Communal living groups of "drop-outs" who rejected mass culture and offended their neighbors became prominent. Feminism burst into new flower at the end of the decade after thirty years' quiescence. Older folk were shocked to see beards suddenly sprouting on millions of young faces, men growing their hair long, and girls wearing men's clothing. People over age thirty reacted angrily against the flamboyant youth (always a small minority of the population, in truth) who flouted traditional standards, glorified self-indulgence, and scorned discipline.

Meanwhile, the economy reached a rate of $900 billion a year in gross national product in 1969, and passed the mind-boggling figure of $1 trillion in 1972. In 1971 the annual median income of American families passed $10,000, a dollar increase of almost 80 percent since 1960, or a rise of 33 percent in real buying power (i.e., allowing for inflation). The average American, in other words, was one-third wealthier than a decade before. More automobiles and motorcyles than ever before choked the already overcrowded streets and were joined by flotillas of campers and motor homes. So many Americans bought powerboats and sailboats that there was a national epidemic of water accidents created by inexperienced sailors.

Persistence of poverty

Millions of Americans, however, still lived in poverty. While a fourth of the nation's families had annual average incomes above $15,000, another fourth received less than $6,000. The number of families below the government's official poverty line (set at $4,137 in 1971) dropped by a third in the 1960s, but at the end of the decade there were still 5.3 million families (a tenth of the total) below that line. Black Americans were much worse off than whites: though eleven percent of the population, they made up twenty-nine percent of the poor.

Meanwhile, factory and automobile pollution increased. Rivers turned into stinking sewers from industrial wastes; fish and plant life in lakes died; and city populations choked and gasped in smog. Fueled by the need of growing numbers of drug addicts for money, crime rates soared. En-

tire sections of great cities displayed empty sidewalks at night. Candidates for political office could ride to victory on the law and order issue almost by itself. Twisting and warping every other problem, and producing massive protest and disillusionment, was the seemingly endless war in Vietnam.

In this setting, it was a rare public figure who tried any longer to preach the old platitudes about endless progress. The United States seemed finally to have lost its optimism. Now, instead, it shared with European nations their ancient disenchantment and pessimism. Many Americans had earlier believed that the mission of America was to provide a beacon light of freedom and an example to the world; now many wondered if this traditional ideal had passed forever into extinction. The cult of success, pride in industrial growth, and joy in technological achievement that had inspired earlier generations gave way to a reluctant belief that such ideas had had much to do with propelling the nation into grave crisis.

The age of anxiety

The complacency of the years from 1945 to 1960 has been explored in the previous chapter; here it remains to point to the fact that the Truman-Eisenhower era was also an age of anxiety. The horrors of the Second World War, the awful nightmare of the atomic bomb, which seemed to hang suspended over a frightened world—it was these influences, that, as we have seen, helped make the Cold War such a tense confrontation and the Second Red Scare led by Joseph McCarthy so enduring a national hysteria.

The age of anxiety produced a nationwide revival of religion much like the great awakenings of the past. By the mid-1950s church membership was rising twice as fast as the general population. A hundred million Americans were members of churches and synagogues, and there was a huge increase in church-building and the giving of funds to churches. There was also a profound revival in theology. Protestant, Catholic, and Jewish seminaries were crowded with young clerics who searched ancient and modern theological writings with an intensity unknown since Charles Darwin's work had cast doubt on the Bible. The war and the atomic bomb had destroyed the social gospel faith that humankind is good and may be counted on eventually to build a kingdom of God on earth. Since the 1930s, Reinhold Neibuhr had been insisting that men are irretrievably selfish and sinful, and now he became a kind of national sage and prophet.

The writings of the nineteenth-century Danish theologian Sören Kierkegaard attained enormous vogue among intellectuals, as did those of two Frenchmen whose books appeared after the Second World War—Jean-Paul Sartre and Albert Camus. The works of these writers presented the philosophy of existentialism. Life, they wrote, is a terrible riddle that can only produce fear and anxiety. Each person is totally alone, forced to choose between things he does not and can never understand. All of our purposes end in death, said Sartre; people must live for themselves. Existentialists like Sartre lost faith in God and became atheists; others followed Kierkegaard's religious version of existentialism and accepted the leap of faith to a belief in Christ.

Intellectuals disillusioned about reform

During the years from 1945 to 1960, the mood among those intellectuals who were concerned with politics and public affairs was reflective, disenchanted, and disengaged. They had lost the happy reformist optimism of the 1930s and had come to see life as complicated, ironic, and paradoxical. Indeed, intellectuals in the 1950s came to feel that reform movements of any kind, for all their noisy laborings, produced but small results. The historian Richard Hofstadter, in his widely read *Age of Reform* (1955), stressed how large a part of politics consisted simply of the discharging of feelings, rather than of realistic grapplings

with social problems. He saw public life as primarily a great socio-drama in which the masses expressed their fears and anxieties and were satisfied by symbolic actions—gestures and words—that constituted merely verbal attacks against their enemies. It appeared to Hofstadter that throughout American history the people explained their problems, not by realistic analysis, but by relying on the simple-minded belief that conspiracies lurked behind the scenes, either in the financial world or in the government. Soon scholars were finding the "paranoid style" behind every ideological movement from the Jacksonian Bank War to the free-silver movement.

Much of this attitude was shaped by the appalling spectacle of McCarthyism, which taught the intellectuals of the 1950s new lessons about the mass of the people. It seemed that nothing was so powerful among Americans as a mindless hunger for simple solutions. The Progressive Era's faith in the intelligence and goodness of the common people, which these scholars had inherited, now died away. For the first time in many years there was much talk about the wisdom contained in conservatism. There was a revived interest in the ideas of John Adams and Edmund Burke, great conservative thinkers of the 1790s (the first, America's president, the second an eminent British parliamentarian). The true conservative, it was said, knew that people reason badly, are swept by passions, greedily look after their own self-interests, and need to have their energies tempered by living within strong institutions of law and order.

Thus a strain of elitism ran through the thought of the 1950s. So, too, a kind of weary and sophisticated disenchantment colored what older scholars told younger ones. Political and social wisdom, they said, lay in recognizing that evil cannot be wiped away; people cannot escape tragedy and despair. Tension and uncertainty, together with shrunken hopes, are ineradicable parts of life. "In the Western world," wrote Daniel Bell in *The End of Ideology* (1960), ". . . the ideological age has ended."

The search for passion

But a new generation was coming to power around 1960, flooding into every area of public life. John Kennedy, like Theodore Roosevelt before him, was only the most dramatic exemplar of this new generation, which in drama, literature, scholarship, politics, and in the leadership of minority groups filled the stage with urgency and new dreams. The youngest of them had not had the chastening experience of depression and war. All they knew was that the world was filled with unsolved problems and they, themselves, with the impatient confidence of youth. In the late 1950s they were restless. They felt cheated of the brave adventures of the past that their grizzled and sardonic mentors described to them in university lecture halls. It was not the temper of the new generation to ponder history and its complexities; they hungered for a cause to believe in.

For a few heady years they found it in John F. Kennedy. Few young people who heard or saw him could forget his driving voice, the stabbing finger accentuating taut, cutting phrases. He was the cool hero, born to wealth, brave in wartime combat, witty, cerebral—and yet he seemed to *care.* Kennedy was impatient with a world grown sluggish with wealth and bewildered by its ills. As he went back and forth across the country he criticized the slack immobility he saw around him and insisted that he could light a fire where ashes smoldered.

Young people responded to the Kennedy leadership in a mood of hope and faith. Social scientists felt their time had arrived. As in the days of the New Deal, the Kennedy administration reached out to the universities and brought in scores of academics to help lead the government departments, advise the president, and write speeches. At the same time, funds began flowing to universities and research institutes to apply intelligence to all sorts of domestic and world problems, from methods for combating guerrillas to educational programs for breaking the cycle of poverty in the slums.

John F. Kennedy, here in Seattle during the presidential campaign of 1960, excited millions of Americans with a new sense of national vigor and purpose, only to be tragically assassinated in November, 1963.
Ted Spiegel, Black Star

Vast hopes, however, collapse easily into vast disillusionment. It was Kennedy's ironic fate that, though a nonideological man, he stirred up great hopes among the ideologically inclined. He was to reap the inevitable fruits of this kind of leadership. Even before his shocking death in late 1963, many young radicals were turning away from him, saying that little was being achieved—as indeed, given the obstacles Kennedy faced, was the case. Then his assassination, followed by Johnson's escalation of the Vietnam War, cut young whites and blacks loose from whatever psychological moorings they had had in the Establishment. Young activists turned toward a utopian, soaring romanticism not seen in the

United States, perhaps, since Ralph Waldo Emerson and the transcendentalists in Andrew Jackson's day. The revolutionaries of the 1960s were passionately convinced that humanity possesses enormous emotional and spiritual powers that lie untapped. Release them, they believed, and a new consciousness will emerge that will make all things possible. Revolutionary ideologies, the cry of "liberation," the use of drugs, and (later in the 1960s) the pursuit of Hindu mysticism to explore inner worlds—these became the characteristics of the "counter culture."

The new romantics rejected the religious revival of the 1950s. Norman Brown's *Life against Death* (1959) and Herbert Marcuse's *Eros and Civilization* (1962) were the new inspirations for the culturally alienated. These works attacked industrialism as repressive, explained man's predicament in sexual, psychoanalytic terms, and preached liberation. But most of the new romantics found their meaning in concrete action, primarily by joining the rebellion occurring among black Americans.

The black revolution

The event that catalyzed the black movement occurred late on a December day in 1955, when Mrs. Rosa Parks boarded a bus in Montgomery, Alabama. She was a black, middle-aged seamstress, and she was tired. Without much thought she sank down on a seat in the front part of the bus traditionally reserved for whites. Normally, when asked by the bus driver to move to the rear, she would have assented. But this day, when he demanded she do so, she could not bring herself to obey. Thus, Mrs. Rosa Parks inspired a revolution.

A year-long boycott of the bus system in Montgomery, led by the young black minister Martin Luther King, Jr., ended in victory in November 1956 when the Supreme Court ruled that segregation on buses was unconstitutional. King then founded the Southern Christian Leadership Conference and crisscrossed the South preaching

Mahatma Gandhi's philosophy of nonviolence. Oppressed peoples, King said, achieve their goals most successfully by appealing to the conscience of their oppressors. He looked toward an integrated, interracial America; toward that "beloved community" in which blacks and whites would recognize their bonds of human unity.

In 1960 a civil rights act was passed that allowed the appointment of federal referees to aid blacks in registering for and voting in federal elections. Before this, only twenty-eight percent of voting-age blacks had been registered in the South, compared to seventy percent in the North (roughly the proportion among the white population). In the states of the Deep South, the percentage of registered blacks was the lowest in the nation. In Mississippi, for example, the figure was four percent.

The sit-ins and the SNCC

In 1960 a group of young black college students in Greensboro, North Carolina, refused to leave their seats when denied service at "white" lunch counters. Sitting doggedly in their places, serenely facing verbal and physical abuse, they provided an inspiring example for a nonviolent army of thousands of southern blacks. With the backing of the Supreme Court, thousands of demonstrators marched in southern cities, demanding and usually winning open access to movie theaters, restaurants, hotels, and bowling alleys, and enduring tear gas, fire hoses, and mass arrests.

In the midst of rising turbulence, Martin Luther King in late 1959 renewed his call for nonviolent tactics: "Token integration is the developing pattern. . . . There is reason to believe that the Negro of 1959 will not accept supinely any such compromises. . . . It is axiomatic in social life that the imposition of frustration leads to two kinds of reactions. One is the development of a wholesome social organization to resist with effective, firm measures any efforts to impede progress. The other is a confused, anger-motivated drive to strike back violently, to inflict damage. Primarily, it seeks to cause injury to retaliate for wrongful suffering. Secondarily, it seeks real progress. It is punitive—not radical or constructive. . . .

"There are incalculable perils in this approach. . . . The greatest danger is that it will fail to attract Negroes to a real collective struggle, and will confuse the large uncommitted middle group, which as yet has not supported either side. Further, it will mislead Negroes into the belief that this is the only path and place them as a minority in a position where they confront a far larger adversary than it is possible to defeat in this form of combat. . . . It is unfortunately true that however the Negro acts, his struggle will not be free of violence initiated by his enemies, and he will need ample courage and willingness to sacrifice to defeat this manifestation of violence. But if he seeks it and organizes it, he cannot win. . . .

"In the history of the movement for racial advancement, many creative forms have been developed—the mass boycott, sit-down protests and strikes, sit-ins—refusal to pay fines and bail for unjust arrests—mass marches—mass meetings—prayer pilgrimages, etc. . . . There is more power in socially organized masses on the march than there is in guns in the hands of a few desperate men." (*Liberation* [October 1959].)

In April 1960 the Student Nonviolent Coordinating Committee (SNCC) was formed. In 1961, SNCC joined with the Congress of Racial Equality (CORE) to mount "freedom rides" into the South on interstate buses in order to implement a Supreme Court decision that outlawed bus, train, and air travel segregation. Mobs assaulted the freedom riders, sheriffs arrested them, and their buses were set aflame. When blacks entered white waiting rooms, white youths threw coffee cups at them, chased them outside, and unmercifully beat and kicked them. The Kennedy administration rushed in federal marshals to keep order and got rulings from the Interstate Commerce Commission directing the removal of

"white only" signs. In 1962, President Kennedy dispatched troops to Mississippi to force the state university to admit James Meredith, a black student. At the same time, he issued an executive order forbidding racial or religious discrimination in federally financed housing.

Now SNCC workers, with the aid of white students from the North, funds from northern white foundations, and the encouragement of the federal Justice Department, moved into Mississippi in force. Their demand was for equal political rights for the masses, chiefly through voter registration drives. Voting registrars used every kind of device to prevent black registration, making the procedures so complicated that often only one voter could be registered per hour. Long lines of blacks stood outside voter registration offices in the burning sun to be hooted at and abused by roaming bands of whites. Meanwhile, SNCC workers endured a ghastly succession of physical assaults and illegal jailings in laboring toward their goals.

Birmingham: The civil rights movement peaks out

In the spring of 1963 the nation was presented with the shocking spectacle on television of Police Chief Eugene "Bull" Connor and his men assaulting thousands of nonviolent black men, women, and children in Birmingham, Alabama. Some 150,000 black citizens had marched on the city hall protesting against segregation in public facilities and in job hirings. When police arrested them, they fell to their knees and prayed. Powerful streams of water from fire hoses sent them sprawling; bricks and bottles were thrown from onlooking crowds; but day after day the protest marches mounted. Thousands of young and old black people were soon in custody, chanting "Freedom! Freedom! Freedom!" Everywhere the question was raised, how could southern blacks continue to follow Martin Luther King's nonviolent approach? In the face of "Bull" Connor's attacks, would they not themselves turn violent?

Malcolm X—a leader of the Black Muslims, a black nationalist movement—denounced Dr. King, telling a black audience, "You need somebody who is going to fight. You don't need any kneeling in or crawling in."

At this point President Kennedy made one of the most extraordinary speeches ever uttered by an American president. Speaking over national television with great intensity and often extemporaneously, he explained in graphic terms how far white Americans were ahead of black Americans in such crucial matters as jobs and income; attacked segregation and the denial of votes; and asked, "Are we to say to the world . . . that this is the land of the free, except for the Negroes; that we have no second-class citizens, except Negroes; that we have no class or caste system, no ghettos, no master race, except with respect to Negroes? Now the time has come for this nation to fulfill its promise." He then asked Congress to enact a law to guarantee equal access to all public accommodations; empower the attorney general to sue for enforcement of the Fourteenth and Fifteenth amendments; and forbid discrimination in any state programs—such as schools, welfare, and highway construction—receiving federal aid. In particular, he asked Congress to outlaw discrimination in employment and voting.

In August 1963 Martin Luther King led 250,000 protestors in an enormous March on Washington, gathering at the Lincoln Memorial. There he electrified his audience by a speech in which he cried out again and again, "I have a dream!"—of a new America in which there would be freedom and equality for all, in which black and white would be reconciliated. Southern congressmen blocked Kennedy's civil rights bill, however, until after his assassination in November. The new president, Lyndon Johnson, was able to drive it through in July 1964. In March 1965, he called Congress into special session to ask for a voting rights bill that, as enacted the following August, eliminated all qualifying tests for registration that had as their objective limiting the right to vote to whites. Thereafter, the proportion of registered blacks in the South spurted rapidly upward, reaching fifty-three percent in 1966 (thirty-three percent in Mississippi). In the elections of 1968, over three million black Americans were registered to vote in the southern states. The civil rights phase of the black revolution had reached its legislative and judicial summit.

The revolt moves northward

By this time, however, black America's revolt had spread to northern and western cities. At its peak, from 1964 to 1968, more than a hundred American cities were swept by riots, dynamitings, guerrilla warfare, and huge conflagrations, creating scenes resembling the bombed-out cities of Europe after World War II.

What had brought on this upheaval? Was it because the status of black Americans was growing steadily worse? By all the major indices, this was not true. Black Americans had been on a steady rise since the Second World War. Hundreds of thousands had left the red-dirt farms of the South for northern and western cities. By 1970 almost 11 million (forty-seven percent) lived outside the South. With better access to medical facilities their death rate dropped rapidly (as much from 1950 to 1960 as in the previous fifty years). In 1940 the median education of blacks in the 25–29 age bracket was seven years; by 1959, it was eleven years, the same as that of the general American population. College attendance by Afro-Americans doubled from 1940 to 1960, then spurted rapidly: from 234,000 in 1964 (fifty-one percent in predominantly black schools) to almost 400,000 in 1971 (a third in black institutions), or more than the total of young people attending college in Great Britain.

In 1960, some sixteen percent of working blacks held white-collar jobs; by 1970, the percentage had risen to twenty-eight. Those in service occupations (cleaning and domestic work primarily) dropped from thirty-two to twenty-six percent, while employment as craftsmen, foremen, and operatives rose from twenty-six to thirty-two percent, exactly reversing the former proportion. In 1950, the annual median income among black families was approximately $2,500; it rose seventy-three percent in the next ten years, reaching slightly more than $4,000 in 1960; and after a further increase of more than fifty percent, it had reached $6,191 by 1970. Indeed, among young married couples at the end of the 1960s, there was little difference in income between blacks and whites. Showing the growth of a sizeable black middle class was the fact that every fourth black family earned more than $10,000 a year in 1970.

The revolution of rising expectations

The ironic fact, however, is that when the mold is broken and things begin moving upward, hopes and aspirations move upward even more rapidly. Revolutions do not occur among the totally oppressed, but among those whose status is improving and who are thereby emboldened to dream great dreams. Wartime studies demonstrate that morale is much better in organizations where promotions are slow than in those where they come rapidly. Black Americans lived in a country that professed high ideals of democracy and equality; for generations most of them had quietly accepted the fact that they were not to share in these ideals; but the hopes now being created resulted in a swiftly rising impatience with the status quo.

Conservatives in former times had insisted that education would make the poor discontented, and they were right. Education *is* subversive; it teaches people to be discontented if only a small and unequal portion of life's opportunities is offered to them. With more schooling, Afro-Americans were learning far more about the possibilities of life and acquiring skills they naturally wished to use. When great numbers of educated blacks found that many jobs and professions were still closed to them, alienation was intensified. Then there was the impact of the mass communications system, which daily taught

black Americans, through television, that whites had fine houses and many comforts while they did not.

Most of all, however, there was the inescapable fact that, whatever their advances, black people were being left behind by the whites. The yearly median income of white families was over $10,000 in 1970, making for a larger dollar gap than had existed ten years before. Whites were moving more rapidly above the poverty line than blacks: every third black lived below that line, while only every tenth white did so. Afro-Americans held but a tiny fraction of managerial and professional positions, and their rate of movement into them was at a crawl. On the national level in 1970, white unemployment averaged about six percent, and black unemployment about nine percent, but within the slums it was frequently true that twenty-five to fifty percent of the employable black males were unemployed. Housing conditions were incomparably better for whites. While the slums were being flooded by an oceanic impouring of blacks, white Americans made a mass exodus to the suburbs where abundant federal loans allowed them to buy new homes. In 1970, only fifteen percent of black Americans lived in the suburbs, which were ninety-five percent white.

The city changes black attitudes

Urban life had profound effects on Afro-American attitudes. Just making the move from an isolated farm house in Georgia to the teeming streets of Harlem was a profound psychological shock, similar to that made by millions of European peasants when they immigrated to America. Everything was changed. Most importantly, the ingrained pattern of submission to and dependence on whites, inherited from slavery and perpetuated on white-dominated southern farms, gave way. Young blacks could cheer a galaxy of heroes, from Willie Mays and Jimmie Brown in sports, to Sidney Poitier and Aretha Franklin in entertainment. Increasingly they realized that they were not inferior in talent, only in opportunity. The leaders of the black rebellion showed how to leave behind Amos 'n Andy and become Martin Luther King or Stokely Carmichael. The ghetto itself made blacks a community in a way they never were when they were scattered over the southern countryside.

These huge new black communities in the North had the potential of becoming a fresh and vital civilization. First, however, blacks faced the fact that the inner-city regions, within which they lived, were too often foul, decaying slums. The plumbing did not work, and rats ran in the walls. Because the tax base was dwindling, schools were bad and garbage collection spotty. Stair wells, vacant lots, and side streets were choked with refuse. Rents were as high as in white residential areas, on the average, and often higher. Bored, unemployed, and embittered residents often made a shambles of their living areas and preyed on one another by burglary, robbery, or drug peddling. For the last hundred years, crime and violence had been steadily dropping in American cities; despite common myths, they were much safer and more peaceful places to live in than ever before. But in the 1960s, this trend reversed itself, and blacks were everywhere held to blame.

Since there was little money in the ghetto, there were few jobs. Factories were far away; employment was generally out in "white country." This required long rides on deteriorating, costly bus lines, if they even existed. Since it was often impossible for black men to find jobs and support their families, many drifted aimlessly here and there, with disastrous effects on family life. In the New York area alone, in 1960, one-fourth of the black families were headed by women, as against one in ten for white families. The harried mothers were miles from potential jobs, frequently had little education, and lived in hand-to-mouth desperation on welfare.

When Martin Luther King began to lead the black revolution in the South, the tinder was dry in northern cities. Faced with degrading lives, young black men were desperate for a means of realizing their manhood. Fascinated by the rise of new black nations overseas and shamed by the fact that their southern brethren, whom they had long looked down on as crude country cousins saying "yas suh" to the white boss, were standing up with massive courage against white attacks, they sought to join in. Pulled by their own version of the "revolution of rising expectations," northern and western blacks were ready to set off the greatest social explosion in American life since the Civil War.

The flaming cities

The beginning rumbles occurred in 1963, when 200,000 persons marched in Detroit to protest discrimination, 3,000 students boycotted Boston public schools to protest segregation, and half the black children in Chicago—more than 200,000 —did the same. Then, in the summer of 1964, came the first huge riots in northern cities. For hours on end roaring multitudes smashed through the center of Harlem, shattering windows, frightening policemen, and looting stores—attacking the symbols of white domination within the ghetto. Then riots erupted in Brooklyn, Jersey City, and Paterson, then in Philadelphia and out west in Chicago. Everywhere the same deep feelings were displayed: despair, alienation, fierce anger—and, paradoxically, hopes for a better future. But these outbreaks were not religious in tone. Martin Luther King could lead a nonviolent crusade in the South, inspired by hymns and the Christian message of love; but northern cities held few "believing" blacks. Particularly among the young—and later studies found young male blacks, usually school drop-outs and unemployed, the leaders in the riots—there was little memory of what had been left behind in the South, only a consciousness of present unemployment and despair.

In the summer of 1965 the flames mounted higher. In August an enormous riot raged for five days in Watts, a suburb of Los Angeles. Thirty-five people were killed, 600 buildings were looted

The massive Detroit riot of 1967, like that earlier in Watts, California, and other cities, left large areas of this central city area looking like bombed-out Europe after the Second World War.
Detroit Free Press from Black Star

and burned, and thousands were arrested. Then came three days of violence in Chicago's West Side, and another riot in North Philadelphia. In the summer of 1966, riots flared up again: in Atlanta, Chicago, Waukegan in Illinois, Lansing in Michigan, Omaha, Cleveland, New York City, and Dayton, Ohio. Then in Detroit, in July 1967, came one of the most massive of all the riots, lasting for weeks. More than forty people died. (As in all the riots, the dead were mainly black Americans, shot down by police or National Guardsmen.) Following this came more uprisings in Michigan, Indiana, Illinois, Wisconsin, and Connecticut.

A change of mood

White Americans outside the South swiftly changed their outlook when the riots began. Sympathetic to blacks while the disorders were confined to the South, they now began to pull back. Terrified by the vast insurrections, they were much less inclined to support reform legislation. Then, in the summer of 1966, a crucial shift in opinion surfaced among young black reformers. Young SNCC workers turned away in anger from the American political system, and from the whole notion of integration, liberal values, and nonviolence. Inspired by the writings of Malcolm X, who had been murdered by hostile Black Muslims in February 1965, some preached black nationalism: complete withdrawal from whites and the establishment of a separate black nation within the United States. In the summer of 1966, while on a march of protest into Mississippi, Stokely Carmichael, leader of SNCC, suddenly began a chant that swept the nation: "Black Power! Black Power!" Thousands of blacks chanted it in city after city, while white America recoiled in fear. No one knew precisely what it meant; Carmichael was never able to explain it; and moderate black leaders condemned the slogan.

Together with Black Power came the slogan, Black is Beautiful. Indeed, much of the black movement now devoted itself to a nationwide campaign to change the self-image of blacks by introducing new themes in the arts, especially in the theater, literature, and television. Black men and women began prominently appearing in movies and television programs, not in the old stupid stereotypes immortalized in the 1930s, but as real people. Fiction and nonfiction by black authors flooded bookstands and magazine pages. Universities established programs of black studies and searched nationwide for black professors. The stigmata of black cosmetics (hair straighteners and lighteners) disappeared, and natural, "Afro" hair styles swiftly became popular.

White America, however, was frightened by the extreme rhetoric used by black militants. Just as the words used by northern abolitionists in the 1850s had frightened southerners into extreme actions; just as Chicago anarchists had convinced Americans in the 1880s that revolution was imminent, leading to nationwide jailings and scare legislation—so, too, did Black Power advocates stir up an avalanche of white overreaction by their use of such violent words as "Burn, Baby,

Burn." "It's time we stand up and take over," said Stokely Carmichael. "Move on over, or we'll move on over you." In a National Conference on Black Power in Newark in July 1967, H. Rap Brown, Carmichael's successor as head of SNCC, said, "go and get your guns, then lead the march." In 1968, the Black Panthers organized. They made a great show of being heavily armed and ready to battle the police in order, as they described it, to protect black communities from police lawlessness.

A change in directions

Terrible events rocked the nation in 1968. By this time, Martin Luther King, Jr., winner of the Nobel Peace Prize in 1964, had carried his campaign to the northern states, where he no longer worked only for equal civil rights, but for better housing, schools, and jobs as well. Preparing plans for another march on Washington (of poor black and white people), he went to Memphis, Tennessee, in April to support a strike of city garbage collectors. A riot broke out, more than a hundred buildings were burned, thousands of National Guardsmen were called in, and then King himself was assassinated as he stood on a motel balcony. This senseless act angered all black America. Riots erupted in more than a hundred American cities; some fifty people died (forty-five of them blacks); fire and looting destroyed tens of millions of dollars in property; and more than 20,000 arrests were made.

In May 1968 the Reverend Ralph Abernathy, King's successor as head of the SCLC, led the Poor People's Campaign to Washington, where for a few months protestors camped at "Resurrection City" near the Lincoln Memorial. Congress responded by passing the 1968 Civil Rights Act, which rendered illegal any discrimination on racial grounds in the sale or rental of eighty percent of the nation's private housing, or some thirty-five million housing units.

In November 1968, Richard Nixon was elected as president of the United States. He was not in sympathy with the use of federal power to implement such major reforms as the integration of public schools. Soon after taking office he dramatically signaled the end of an era by firing James Allen, forthright spokesman for integrated schools, as commissioner of education. The new "southern strategy" in the national government was to build strong relations with the white South and leave black America to the Democrats. Fundamentally, Nixon adhered to the traditional Republican doctrine that the advancement of individuals would take place by their own efforts—a doctrine that, critics charged, paid little attention to the assistance that his administration lavishly poured into the nation's business community.

Race relations in the 1970s

The 1960s were years of vast changes in race relations in the United States; the 1970s began as a time of consolidation. No more reform proposals emerged from the White House. In thousands of local situations, however, the drive was still underway for the continued integration of black Americans into all phases of life. There had apparently emerged a new consensus among white Americans who, at least in good part, accepted the notion that it was right for blacks to become first-class citizens. Entrance requirements for schools and colleges were changed; hundreds of communities tried hard to work out equitable arrangements to end de facto segregation in the schools (usually with limited success); graduate programs searched for black applicants; and integration in jobs and in the professions continued to expand and widen. The influence of radical black moments waned, and the voting rights enactments of the 1960s transformed national politics. Blacks now moved into the mainstream of the party system. Thurgood Marshall had been appointed the nation's first black Supreme Court justice by President Johnson, and in the nation at large, black elected officials increased rapidly in numbers. In 1967 there were 475; in 1971, 1,860;

in 1974, 3,503 (though this figure still represented less than one percent of all elected officials). The daily impact of television, where black Americans appeared regularly in shows and commercial advertisements, made them seem more a normal part of a pluralistic nation.

However, white resistance to mixed schooling and mixed neighborhoods continued, fueled by a widespread conviction that blacks were violent and crime-prone. Though desegregation went reasonably smoothly in most communities, thousands of white parents placed their children in white schools, or moved to the suburbs. In Atlanta, where in the years 1970–73 segregation was reduced by almost half, 51% of the white school children disappeared from the public schools; in Dallas, where segregation was cut by a quarter in these years, 26% of the white children shifted out of its school system. Cities like Boston and Detroit were in turmoil over court-ordered mandatory busing.

An ever more powerful groundswell of opinion was rising that the courts should concern themselves only with de jure discrimination (segregation in schooling brought about by the specific actions of public authorities), and not with de facto segregation (caused by patterns of residence by differing ethnic groups). The Supreme Court, increasingly dominated by a conservative group of justices appointed to that body by President Richard Nixon, appeared strongly to be swinging in this direction.

Black gains and losses

From 1970 to 1976, black enrollment in colleges went up 56% (white enrollment 15%); of those 18 to 24, 18% were enrolled in a college (whites were at 25%); and among youths 16 or 17 years of age, both whites and blacks had the same percentage in school (about 88%). The proportion of five-year-old black children in school was 87% (90% for whites); and those completing high school was 72% (85% for whites). Therefore, it may be seen that in education, as in election to public office, black Americans experienced important gains after 1970.

However, black families still made 40% of all food stamp purchases in 1974. The black jobless rate was 13.7% as against 7.6% for whites, and among black teenagers it often reached as high as 50%. Many of these young Americans were so discouraged that it appeared that they were becoming a permanent under-class within the economic system: under-educated, idle and adrift, with few if any marketable skills or job prospects. Perhaps the massive unemployment among black teen-agers was in part reflected in the fact that 42% of the nation's entire prison population in 1972—which traditionally consists heavily of young, single males—was black, even though blacks in general made up only 11.4% of the nation's population. Actual purchasing power for black families, adjusting for inflation, declined 3.2%, their median income being $7,808 in 1974 (that of white families was $13, 356). The dream of a promised land outside of the South apparently dissipated, for as many black Americans moved into the South in the 1970s as moved out of it. Thus, the black population stabilized at about half southern, half northern and western.

New day for the Indians

The 1960s saw a heartening national turnaround on Indian policy. Both Richard Nixon and John Kennedy proclaimed in their presidential campaigns that there would be an end to the campaign to break down Indian culture and "Americanize" the Indians, as embodied in the termination policies of the Eisenhower years. These words had been preceded by a rising national chorus of criticism of these policies. Congress freed loan funds; the Federal Housing Authority began actively helping Indians build their own homes; and so successfully were businessmen urged to build plants on Indian lands and thus establish employment opportunities, that in 1968 alone their total investment was almost $100 million.

In 1968 Lyndon Johnson became the first American president to send Congress a special message asking aid for the Indians: "An opportunity to remain in their homeland, if they choose, without surrendering their dignity; an opportunity to move to the towns and cities of America, if they choose, equipped with the skills to live in equality and dignity." Creating the National Council on Indian Opportunity, headed by Vice-President Hubert Humphrey, he channeled large funds into community improvement, the training of workers, youth activities, and health services.

Richard Nixon continued these progressive policies. The Bureau of Indian Affairs began to shift its emphasis to the issuing of grants to the tribes for the economic development of their resources. In 1969, however, the shape of the future was startlingly revealed when a group of Indians took over Alcatraz Island in San Francisco Bay (no longer in use as a prison facility) and demanded it be returned to them in compensation for the countless treaty violations and land steals that stretched back through American history. After this, young Indian militants in almost every major American city began seizing federal property, demonstrating that the future location of the "Indian problem" was to be in the cities, no longer in the trackless immensities of the western states. Vine Deloria, Jr., author of the best-selling *Custer Died for Your Sins: An Indian Manifesto* (1969) estimated that three-fourths of the Indian population had become both eastern and urban.

A revived concern with tribalism has swept the Indian peoples, paradoxically opening a new chain of problems. Through steady population growth, tribes with only a few hundred living on the reservation often had thousands of members listed on their tribal rolls, most of them scattered in distant cities. With their increasingly complex and mobile inner social structure, such groups could experience bewildering shifts and changes in internal policy as first one and then another group won brief voting triumphs in tribal elections. Thousands of young Indians entered the nation's colleges as a new ethnic consciousness swept the academic world. But, where programs of Indian studies were launched, the immediate question arose: what is the Indian identity? Traditional or modern? Reservation-based or urban? Could tribal culture, for centuries taught only by the elders on tribal lands, become an academic discipline without losing its validity?

Education, material advancement, and urban living seemed inevitably to destroy the Indians' ancient culture, or at least gravely to endanger it. But clearly the new urbanized Indian youth still nourished the ancient grievances. In late 1972 hundreds of them, members of the American Indian Movement, took over the Bureau of Indian Affairs building in Washington, fortifying themselves within it for almost a week and rifling—indeed carting off—its files. In 1973 a long and wearing occupation of Wounded Knee in South Dakota by Indian activists almost led to a shooting encounter with federal forces reminiscent of the nineteenth century. When it was over, the question still remained: what was the real shape of the Indian future? As urban Indians all over the nation continued seeking one another out and forming city organizations, it was ever more clear that whatever its form the Indian future lay in the metropolis. A tremendous awakening is underway that is quite unlike anything that has ever occurred in the Indian past.

Political awakening of the Spanish-speaking

Wherever John Kennedy went, when he visited the southwestern states and California in his presidential campaign of 1960, he was greeted by wildly cheering Mexican-American crowds. The "Viva Kennedy" organizations urged traditionally nonpolitical Mexican-Americans to the polls, with the result that they voted in record numbers. Some 85 percent of the Spanish-speaking vote went to Kennedy, providing the crucial margin in Texas and New Mexico, and probably even in Illinois, where the 91 percent majority he gained

among the thousands of Spanish-speaking voters in the Chicago area helped put him barely in the victor's camp—and therefore in the White House. One of the nation's largest ethnic groups, the nine million Americans of Spanish surname seemed finally to have come politically alive.

They had real and pressing grievances. From the economic standpoint, they were far behind Anglo-Americans. In 1970 the average Puerto Rican family (Puerto Ricans comprise 1.5 million of the Spanish-speaking) had an average income only three-fifths that of the United States median, or about $6,000 a year. Mexican-American families were not much better off, averaging about $7,000 a year. Latin Catholics worked in the lowest-paid jobs, either in the fields as stoop labor, or in blue-collar employment. Their jobless rate was high, and managerial positions, save in their own businesses, were generally closed to them.

Deeper than these considerations, however, were the cultural distinctions that marked them. Mexican-Americans were sharply unlike any other minority group in that their home country was next door (the same is true for Canadians, but they fade effortlessly into the general population). This fact keeps their separateness alive in a special way—as it would for, say, the Italians if Italy were next door. Family ties are immediate and direct, and there is a significant degree of coming and going. Furthermore, the immense region of the southwestern states and California carries a Spanish overlay in its place names and, in regions like southern California, the cult of a "Spanish" past which expresses itself in architecture and festivals. It is possible for intense young Mexican-Americans to speak of an "Aztlan," a legendary homeland running from southern Mexico far up into the American high plains. And yet in this huge area they are kept in second-class status, occupying the *barrios*—the ghettolike residential sections where Mexican-Americans congregate—where housing is deficient, jobs ill-paid, and public services often inadequate.

Language problems

Because of a continual heavy influx from the mother country, in recent decades it has remained true that only one-fourth of the Mexican-American population regards English as its first language. This means that the most powerful cultural distinction that sets off a people from the majority, that of language—entailing a separate culture and different ways of thinking—has intensified a special status for Mexican-Americans. It also means that the dropout rate from high school of Mexican-American youths has been very high, running at a steady 75 percent through the 1950s, for a separate language can make Americanized schooling a fatally discouraging experience.

Mexican-Americans share with black Americans and Indians the fact that the old days, in which most lived and labored in the countryside, are gone. Eighty percent now live in cities. Los Angeles holds a million people of Spanish surname. Puerto Ricans in the United States have always been an urban people, now numbering at least a million in New York City. Together, the two Latin Catholic groups number more than 400,000 in the Chicago area.

The political clout of this immense ethnic group, however, has always been limited, for Latin Catholics have not turned out so well at the polls as other minority groups. Only six out of the more than 500 members of Congress are Spanish-speaking in descent. The 1960 voting performance, when Latin Catholics flooded out to cast ballots for John Kennedy, was a high point. After that, the Latin Catholic vote steadily eroded. Puerto Ricans in New York City cast less than half the number of votes in 1968 than they had in 1960. Where labor unions are growing, as among the Spanish-speaking of Texas, the trend is upward, but in general the Latin Catholics are still not as politically alive as their numbers and importance warrant.

Partly this is so because they are not only poor, thus sharing in the traditional political apathy of the poverty-stricken, but they are also relatively young as an ethnic group, and thus not eligible to vote. Half of the Mexican-Americans are under eighteen years of age, and the same is true for those of Puerto Rican descent. Enhancing the factors of poverty, youth, and under-education is the reluctance, on the part of those Mexican-Americans among whom studies of political attitudes have been made, to be identified with black Americans, whose turbulence and political protest during the 1960s made the tactic anathema to many Spanish-speaking Americans. Nonetheless, they learned many political lessons from the black civil rights movement.

1960s militancy

A true militancy arose for the first time among Mexican-Americans in the 1960s, the decade in which "Chicano"—a shortened form of *Mexicano* generally taken up by younger, more ethnically conscious and activist Mexican-Americans— appeared as a new ethnic identification. There was much to fire this militancy. Since the depression-ridden 1930s, when perhaps 500,000 Mexicans were deported, the Mexican-American situation had vastly changed. It was during the 1930s that Mexican-American farm workers first began fighting back against their degraded living and working conditions by organizing unions and strikes—most of which failed to improve their situation. Then, during the Second World War, Mexican-Americans went into the fighting forces with the same hope that, almost a hundred years before, had inspired free black Americans in the northern states during the Civil War: to demonstrate their manhood and their rightful claim to equal status in American life. More than 300,000 served, primarily in the army, in which a higher proportion of them belonged to combat divisions than was the case with any other ethnic group. An especially high proportion volunteered for hazardous duty in the paratroops and marines. Of fourteen Texans who won the Medal of Honor, five were Mexican-Americans.

The whole experience during wartime—both in the service and in war industries—energized the Mexican-American community. For the first time, great numbers of them worked directly with Anglo-Americans and earned high salaries. Then *la raza* veterans (the term *la raza* refers to the entire community of the Spanish-speaking) were aided in going to college and starting businesses by the G.I. Bill, which provided extensive aid to all veterans. But despite their achievements, *la raza* found that the Anglo-Americans still treated them in the old, prejudicial way. In a spectacular incident in 1948, town authorities refused to allow the remains of a Mexican-American soldier to be buried in a Texan cemetery. (Lyndon Johnson, then senator from the state, secured his burial in Arlington National Cemetery.)

Braceros and wetbacks

During the Second World War, a great need for farm labor in the southwestern states led to the *bracero* program, by which the governments of Mexico and the United States supervised the recruitment of Mexican nationals who were brought across the border to labor for a year in the fields, then returned to their homeland. About 250,000 *braceros* were recruited from 1942 to 1947. Allowed briefly to lapse, the program was revived in 1948 to run for sixteen years to 1964, during which period 4,500,000 Mexican nationals participated in temporary periods of agricultural employment in American farms. (Because race prejudice has traditionally been more prominent in Texas, where from the beginning Mexicans were linked to blacks in Anglo-American eyes, the Mexican government did not allow *braceros* to be sent to that state.)

The program had sharply contrasting results. The average Mexican who participated came to it eagerly, since he could earn far more in the United States than at home. But job conditions were often demeaning, and American laborers claimed, usually with good reason, that employ-

ers used *braceros* primarily to keep wage rates down. Far worse, however, was the status of the *mojados,* or "wetbacks," so called because thousands of these illegal entrants swam the Rio Grande to get to the United States. Totally unable to appeal to the authorities for aid against their employers, they were paid the lowest wages of any manual laborers, lived in the worst housing, and were preyed on by everyone. They made an enormous contribution to the immense expansion of southwestern agriculture during and after World War II, but received little in return. Wetbacks, indeed, may well have been the principal source of cheap farm labor in the decade after 1945. In 1954 the Immigration Bureau began a large campaign of deportation, rounding up wetbacks—many of them only alleged to be wetbacks—and summarily hurrying them out of the country with little regard for due process. In 1953 some 875,000 illegal entrants had been arrested and returned to Mexico; in 1954 this figure swelled to more than a million. Altogether, from 1950 to 1955, 3,700,000 people alleged to be wetbacks were deported, only some 60,000 by means of formal proceedings. The rest left "voluntarily." Families were disrupted; people who had been living in America for longer than ten years were suddenly expelled. This experience left the same lastingly bitter feelings that had remained after the similar expulsion in the 1930s. In this case, however, those remaining behind noticed how wage rates jumped upward by as much as a third. Despite all efforts, the wetback problem has remained, however. In the 1970s, there were still estimated to be between 500,000 and a million *mojados* in the United States.

Chicano activism

In the 1960s a new generation of young Mexican-Americans began for the first time to make the Mexican-American voice heard on the national scene. They had earlier formed a number of organizations, notably the G.I. Forum, which has been strongly political in its tactics, and the

Mexican American Political Association, largely responsible for the immensely popular Viva Kennedy clubs, which helped to place John Kennedy in the White House. More and more Mexican-Americans were moving into cities; significant numbers were rising to middle-class status in income and professional position; and increasingly they were no longer ready to accept the inferior roles they had long played in American society. It was now that "Chicano" became a popular term that spread swiftly through the Mexican-American community. The older generation had counselled a passive role, but the newer leaders urged activism. As so often has been true in the history of American ethnic groups, the new world prominence of leaders and movements drawn from their own cultural tradition inspired a sense of emulation among Chicanos. Fidel Castro and Ernesto "Che" Guevara seemed eloquently to demonstrate that the Spanish-speaking need no longer be passive toward Anglo-America. Especially among Chicano students, cultural identity and cultural pride led to demands that prejudiced teachers and administrators be discharged and course offerings be changed to emphasize the Chicano past, present, and future. The Brown Berets were organized in the 1960s, consisting primarily of high school and

One of the great changes of the 1960s was the emergence out of passive quietism of the Mexican-American peoples of California, the Southwest, and many American cities. The term "Chicano" was widely adopted by the more activist among them.
Wide World Photos

college age Chicanos in the southwestern states. Their goal was to unite the Chicano community by their own example of brotherhood and self-sacrificial discipline. While for black Americans the adversary has been, within their own community, the Uncle Toms who would acquiesce in second-class status, for activist Chicanos the adversary was the *tio taco:* the Mexican-American who clung to the old stereotype and role.

The most activist Chicanos came from among Mexican-Americans in rural areas, where living conditions were the most pitiable. One Chicano leader, Reis Lòpez Tijerina, led a demand for the reversion of millions of acres of southwestern land to direct heirs of those who, under the Treaty of Guadalupe Hidalgo (1848), had their land rights guaranteed but subsequently taken away by American courts. A true visionary (and a convert to evangelical Protestantism), Tijerina formed in 1963 the Alianza Federal de Mercedes (Federal Alliance of Land Grants), which envisioned the recapturing of immense lost territories for Chicanos and the building of a confederation of free city-states based on utopian principles. In 1967 he led an occupation of a courthouse in the New Mexican town of Tierra Amarilla. During the ensuing brief warfare with local authorities, men were wounded, and a massive manhunt with tanks and helicopters finally captured the fleeing Tijerina. Jailed in 1969 after an unsuccessful appeal following conviction for various crimes, Tijerina served two years and emerged to find his movement fading.

César Chavez

Far more lastingly effective was the campaign launched by César Chavez for the organization of farm workers. The first Chicano to achieve a truly national standing and to become a unifying symbol for Mexican-Americans in the manner of Martin Luther King for black America, he was also, like King, an apostle of Gandhi's nonviolence policy. Deeply spiritual in his motivations, a gentle and thoughtful man, since 1962 he had been working in Delano, California, to form a union among grape workers. Director of the AFL-CIO United Farm Workers Organizing Committee, he had himself emerged from the extreme poverty of a family caught in the migrant farm worker cycle of constant movement, illiteracy, and low wages. Keenly aware of the need to mobilize the support of national opinion, he attracted students, ministers, and civil rights workers to Delano and by 1968, during which year Robert Kennedy gave his cause prominent support, had successfully organized a nationwide boycott of table grapes. In 1970 his long struggle came to an apparent end when the grape growers signed a three-year contract with his union. Later on, however, the growers began signing contracts instead with the Teamsters Union, apparently an organization more palatable to them in its objectives, leading to a new eruption of turmoil and protest in 1973. In 1977, a landmark agreement was finally struck between Chavez and the Teamsters. The former henceforth would organize field workers, the latter those in packing houses. However, in the background for Chavez was the sobering fact that the increasing cost of farm laborers was stimulating landowners to turn to machines for the cultivation and picking of row crops. In the decade of the 1960s, migrant farm workers in the United States as a whole dropped in numbers from 400,000 to 250,000. Whatever the outcome, however, the figure of César Chavez provided lasting inspiration to the Chicano community.

Urban Chicanos

Meanwhile, urban Chicanos, notably through the Brown Berets, were joining in the mass uprisings of the late 1960s. When some were jailed in Los Angeles in 1968 for staging a demonstration, Joanne Gonzales in *La Raza Yearbook* proclaimed their cause as "seeking Chicano Power for our people so that we can have control over our environment; control over our schools so that our children can receive a better education; control over the agencies which are supposed to be administering to the needs of our people; control over the police whose salaries we pay but who continually brutalize our people." Mexican-American leaders demanded an educational process that was both bilingual and bicultural, thus reviving the equality of treatment guaranteed in the Treaty of Guadalupe Hidalgo. Teachers of Mexican ancestry were urged to retain and emphasize, with pride, their "Mexicanism," and authentic Mexican arts experienced widely enhanced prominence. The image of the Mexican-American in Anglo-American eyes, long summed up in the figure of a somnolent peasant under a large sombrero, was beginning to be replaced with a fresh understanding of Latin civilization as urban as well as rural, progressive as well as traditional, sophisticated as well as uncomplicated. By 1972, younger Chicanos were even seeking to found a new national political party: *La Raza Unida*. At its El Paso, Texas, convention, it resolved to support neither Nixon nor McGovern. In 1976 the party held no convention, but won a few elections in South Texas. Chicanos were also heavily involved in the anti-war movement of the 1970s.

Nevertheless, Mexican-Americans found it hard to achieve unity. Their very identity was difficult to crystallize. "To start a long discussion among los Angelenos of Spanish-Mexican descent," observed Paul M. Sheldon in *La Raza: Forgotten Americans* (1966), "simply introduce the . . . question, 'Who are we?'" Spanish, Mexican, or completely Americanized? Chicano culture, he wrote, carried with it an individualism that discourages unity; a family consciousness that places the focus of concern elsewhere than in politics; and traditional values often opposed to the hard-driving success ethic of the American urban world. However, the very entrance of Mexican-Americans into the mainstream of American life made it increasingly difficult for them—as for the American Indians who had also become increasingly urban—to retain a hold on ways of life that for many had become remote.

Without question, the days of a quiet rural past, in which passiveness and political quiescence was the distinguishing mark of Mexican-Americans, had irrevocably disappeared.

The decade of youth

Together with continental upheavals caused by militant black America, the nation experienced in the 1960s a revolution in the relations between old and young. Indeed, the United States became a country practically obsessed by its young people. Everywhere one looked, or so it seemed, there were "flower children" begging in the streets, mobs of young activists storming through university campuses, drug enthusiasts, antiwar demonstrators, beads, long hair, bare feet, and communes. This was not, of course a wholly unprecedented phenomenon. But the scale of the turmoil in the 1960s—the "decade of youth"— sets it apart as a phenomenon the like of which we may rarely see again.

Census figures tell the tale. Between 1948 and 1953 the annual baby crop increased fifty percent, the biggest increase in births ever recorded in this or any other country. In 1957 the birth rate started a decline that has continued into the 1970s, but the die was cast. In 1959 about twenty million Americans were children under the age of five; about eleven million were between fourteen and seventeen years old; but thirty-two million were aged five to thirteen. In that year the center of the nation's population gravity was still in the thirty-five to forty age group, but within four years it plummeted to the late teens. In the year 1964, seventeen-year-olds became the largest single age group in the country, and they increased in numbers for the succeeding seven years—and so did those aged eighteen to twenty-two, the classic college years.

No time of life involves greater changes than the ages between seventeen and twenty-two, unless it be around retirement (for working men and women), or when the children leave home (for housewives). This is the time when young-

sters traditionally move out from under the wings of their families, try out new cultural styles, rebel against authority, and begin building their own identities. Special conditions in mid-twentieth-century America intensified this process for the nation's young. Many no longer went right to work after high school graduation at age seventeen, as in the past. Now at least half went on to college, thus stretching out their period of adolescence—their time of freedom from family and job responsibilities. Because of the large increase in graduate training, created by the growing complexity of the economy and its need for higher skills, the period of preadult life was stretched even further for many young people, reaching into the late twenties.

Read everywhere in the 1950s and 1960s by those interested in understanding young people were the writings of Erik Erikson, including *Childhood and Society* (1950) and *Young Man Luther* (1958). "I have called the major crisis of adolescence the *identity crisis;* it occurs in that period of the life cycle when each youth must forge for himself some central perspective and direction, some working unity, out of the effective remnants of his childhood and the hopes of his anticipated adulthood; he must detect some meaningful resemblance between what he has come to see in himself and what his sharpened awareness tells him others judge and expect him to be. . . . In some young people, in some classes, at some periods in history, this crisis will be minimal; in other people, classes, and periods, the crisis will be clearly marked off as a critical period, a kind of 'second birth,' apt to be aggravated either by widespread neuroticisms or by pervasive ideological unrest. . . .

"The need for devotion . . . is one aspect of the identity crisis. . . . The need for repudiation is another . . . a sharp and intolerant readiness to discard and disavow people (including, at times, themselves). This repudiation is often snobbish, fitful, perverted, or simply thoughtless. . . . The outstanding quality of these [young people] is *totalism*, a to be or not to be which makes every matter of differences a matter of mutually exclusive essences; every question mark a matter of forfeited existence; every error or oversight, eternal treason. . . . I have called this the 'rock-bottom' attitude, and explained it as . . . an attempt to find that immutable bedrock on which the struggle for a new existence can safely begin and be assured of a future.'' (*Young Man Luther.*)

The term *identity crisis* was picked up and applied in countless connections in the 1960s, becoming one of the key concepts of the era. Like Freud's and Darwin's ideas, which were picked up and applied indiscriminately, Erikson's were expanded to encompass the ''identity crisis of Europe,'' or that (allegedly) of the aerospace industry, of President Johnson, and of the Black Panthers. More importantly, Erikson provided his age a means for understanding the vast upheaval of young people in the mid-1960s.

Inevitably, this flood wave in the population moved on, and in the early 1970s entered the twenty-to-thirty age group. This fact by itself helps explain the dying away of the youth rebellion at the opening of the decade. Young adults are often more conventional in their habits than people of any other age group, for they are often supporting young children, making their first house payments, and working hard to begin careers.

If young adults are involved in public affairs—as many, inspired by the turbulent 1960s, continued to be—it is usually not as rebels but as participants in ''the system.'' This meant that party politics at the local level across the country would receive an inundation of youth, as in fact happened. Perhaps the most dramatic expression of this trend was the unprecedentedly swift passage in 1971 of the Twenty-sixth Amendment (less than three months from congressional enactment to ratification by the states), which gave the vote to all between the ages of eighteen and twenty-one.

Youth life styles

It is misleading to fashion a picture of young people in the 1960s exclusively around the college-based activist. Most young people go to work more or less directly from high school, and are often culturally and politically conservative. The proportion going to college, however, has grown greatly: in 1946 about twenty-five percent of the young people went to college; by 1970 it was about forty-five percent. Research studies by social psychologists indicate that there is a wide range of cultural styles among those in college. For vocationally oriented students with a specific occupation in mind, college is a place of practical training. Such students show little interest in being culturally sophisticated or socially and politically active. They are concerned with working hard and building traditional lives. ''Professionalists'' head toward law, medicine, and executive positions in business and government. Though wealthier and more culturally adventurous than vocational students and more likely to get high grades, they too are usually uncritical of the American system and ''stay cool.'' The ''collegiate'' student is the classic Joe College who regards studies as a necessary but boring evil, plays the social game of sex, drinking, or drugs, and pursues long, fun-filled weekends. Then there are the ''ritualists,'' who go to college simply because it is the ''thing to do,'' and they do not know what else to do with themselves.

The ''academics'' are students seriously committed to scholarly achievement, usually in the sciences. Talented and hard-working, they like learning, follow politics only incidentally, and though sympathetic to reform causes are usually too busy studying to participate. The ''intellectuals'' are similar, but their interests—in the 1960s, usually ranging into the humanities and social sciences—are wider than those of the academics. They are headed toward some form of public service, but as generalists their objectives are not specific. They are interested in ideas and seriously concerned with getting an education. Almost always of a liberal turn of mind, they give warm support to political and social causes, though usually not as leaders.

"Leftists" and "hippies"

Then there is a small minority of students, the "leftists" and "hippies," that alarms the public far out of proportion to its size. Constituting in the 1960s probably no more than two percent of the college population, activists and hippies populated the fevered imaginations of millions of older Americans, who conceived of college campuses as overrun with them, as well as with "wild-eyed radicals" on the faculty who supposedly encouraged them in their destructive activities. These two types of students differed sharply. Leftist activists believed that the system was worth saving, that it could be saved, and that personal involvement was the highest goal of life. For the most part highly intelligent, often concentrated in prestige schools that demand high grades for entrance, and springing from affluent, well-educated families, they called themselves the "New Left." They were outraged young people angry at what they regarded as hypocrisy, mistreatment of others, and public evil. They operated from the fundamental conviction that American society is corrupt—certainly the oldest motivation among reformers in the modern centuries. In a sense, they were reincarnations of the seventeenth-century Puritans, who were also outraged at corruption and consumed by an ambition to cleanse the (English) nation by radical measures.

The hippie, on the other hand, was so culturally alienated from American life that he withdrew from it. Almost always white, hippies were also from affluent families and had little sense of the need to succeed at anything at all. Like the puritanical activists, they present to us a familiar, though different, picture. As far back as the Adamites in the second century, there have periodically been highly self-conscious groups of people who feel that they have found the road to innocent, pure lives: withdrawal from society and a total rejection of its ways. Hippies, like their predecessors, denied reason and exalted feeling; detested restraints; searched in Oriental mysticism for a means of transcendence, or in drugs of various kinds; and dispensed with the ideas of work, production, and achievement. The senses were to be freely deluged with "experiences," either ecstatic or manic; everything was to be "naturally" done; and laws and principles were to be discarded. Like the communitarian experimenters in the Age of Jackson, they established what they believed would be innocent communes of mutual love and sexual freedom.

They made the tragic discovery, however, that they could not be innocent merely by wishing to be. In San Francisco, where the hippie movement began, they took up residence in the Haight-Ashbury district in 1967. They soon found that their life style too easily degenerated into a world of drugs, liver diseases (from infected hypodermic needles), filth, malnutrition, and crime. Widely hailed as prophets of the future, the flower children movement faded rapidly, leaving behind, like the Shakers of old, quiet little pockets of gentle people who turned away from publicity and sought to live noncompetitive simple lives.

"The Movement" and the universities

In the 1960s young college radicals launched a campaign to transform America, calling it "the Movement." The roots of this crusade lay in the late 1950s when white students joined Martin Luther King, Jr., in his nonviolent programs for black equality. In 1960, Students for a Democratic Society (SDS) was formed; soon its very initials haunted ordinary Americans. Its "Port Huron Statement," which seems relatively mild in hindsight, appeared then as a veritable communist manifesto. It called for black dignity and equality; condemned wars and "anticommunism"; attacked as dehumanizing and irresponsible the power of bureaucracies in government, corporations, universities, and labor unions; and, in the part of the statement that set off the most turmoil, demanded that universities be used as bases for political assaults on "the system."

The tactic of nonviolence, as practiced by King and his followers, demanded enormous patience, and it soon became intensely frustrating to white student activists who went into the South and were beaten, burned, shot, jailed, and murdered for their pains. In 1964 Mario Savio, a veteran of such efforts in Mississippi, turned his anger on higher education when he led a free-speech uprising at the University of California at Berkeley. Set off by the university's attempt to deny the distribution on campus of political leaflets, it erupted into a tumultous confrontation between students and institutional authorities that went on for months.

This pattern was repeated in varying degrees across the country. University administrations and faculty were subjected to abuse from the public, which was outraged that young people should be "dictating" to anyone, anywhere. Ordinary Americans still thought of colleges as acting in loco parentis—a role that had generally disappeared in the 1950s. Students, on their side, found the colleges easy marks for disruption, for the academic world was liberally oriented and reluctant to be punitive, while at the same time it was physically weak and practically indefensible. It was a grave business for students to risk their lives in the South or in direct assaults on military bases (where, presumably, the war in Vietnam could be most directly affected); it was much easier to smash college windows and disrupt classrooms, using the excuse that as part of the Establishment the schools were implicated in the repression of blacks and the Vietnam War.

The universities enacted many reforms to make their curricula more relevant to student interests and the nation's affairs, but they refused either to hand over control of the institutions to the students, or to let them be converted into bases for political action. President Lyndon B. Johnson's escalation of the war in Vietnam in

1965, however, made students far more angry against their society than before, and universities continued to bear the brunt of their assaults. The slogan they had shouted in 1964 was Power Now! In 1968 it was Revolution Now!

"The Movement" and revolution

So matters stood in 1968, the year of the assassination of Robert Kennedy: people everywhere were seriously discussing whether or not a revolution was possible or desirable. The Movement preached it with evangelical fervor; serious scholars like the sociologist Peter Berger felt moved to write whole books to establish the point that *"Revolution is not a viable option in America, either practically or morally"* (*Movement and Revolution* [1969]). Tactics now verged on terrorism, for "The Weathermen" and other extremist factions were shouting over and over the message, "tear it down." At San Francisco State College, Columbia, Harvard, Berkeley, Wisconsin, and scores of other institutions, arson and hit-and-run bombing created a steady stream of incidents that often brought education practically to a halt in the years from 1968 to 1970. Around the world the turmoil spread, from universities in Germany and France to those in Japan. It reached a climax on May 4, 1970, when students demonstrating against the invasion of Cambodia, at Kent State University in Ohio, were fired on by National Guardsmen, four students falling dead. At this point almost five hundred colleges and universities were on strike or closed down—and even Secretary of the Interior Walter J. Hickel was telling President Nixon that "youth in its protest must be heard."

The Movement, however, was more than a campaign to reform universities or end the war in Vietnam: it was a search by thousands of young Americans for a community to which they could feel a sense of belonging. They dreamed of an America based on love and openness, not on the technological, "rationalized," bureaucratic, centrally controlled, and militarized style of life that they were convinced dominated their country. The conduct of war was drifting to genocide; nature and the environment were being mindlessly polluted; and corporations were dominating everything. They were revolting against a society that they saw as overdeveloped, gargantuan, strangling in the coils of its immense power structures. Everything seemed moving toward depersonalization: automation and cybernation, computers and numbers, ascending pyramids of authority that insulated the decision-makers from the people, and a rise in affluence that so deadened the ordinary person's sensibilities that he was willing to put up with being made a small cog in a huge machine.

Frustration mounts

These ills, however, were much too pervasive for a student movement to affect. As their frustration mounted, activists retreated into a special world where they could convince themselves that the tactics of shock alone could somehow bring about the revolution they desired. By assaulting the sensibilities of the middle class, they hoped to overcome it; thus the ritualistic use of obscenities, the indulgence in violence, the apocalyptic preachings that the nation was on the verge of some unimaginable calamity. The reigning belief among activists was that absolute personal integrity—"authenticity"—had to be maintained at all costs, making compromise impossible, indeed degrading.

By late 1970 this irrational destructiveness was repelling the general student body. After years of massive protests on hundreds of campuses, involving countless incidents of "trashings" (window breaking), police-student conflicts, mass arrests, and the burning of buildings, the turmoil suddenly subsided. Almost as if by common decision, college students ceased turning out when the activists called for them to do so. The Vietnam War was being deescalated; the draft was ending; students were weary with immense disorders that produced little change; and, most

important, the black revolution was dying down. As student activism had been born in that movement, so, perhaps, it subsided because, for a time, black America had ceased its protest.

The reemergence of the "woman question"

What the nineteenth century called the "woman question" reemerged in the late 1960s as "women's lib." The crux of the matter was the same: were women an exploited and oppressed class? and if so, what should be done about it?

The fact was that the American woman of the 1960s occupied basically the same role she had won by the 1920s. Little change had occurred since then save, ironically, for a shift in attitudes that idealized and revived the role assigned to Victorian women: the homemaker, spending all her time raising her children and making her husband happy. Whereas the Victorians had justified this role on moral and religious grounds, it was explained in the 1960s by Freudian psychology. In major ways, however, the post-World War I American woman was indeed liberated from the restrictions that had hemmed in her forebears. She had the vote, job opportunity outside the home, light clothes and simple hair styles, the right to take a role in public life without ridicule, the opportunity of sharing men's recreations, such as smoking and drinking in public, and the freedom to engage in sexual activity, and to enjoy it.

Perhaps it was for this reason that the steam seemed to go out of feminism after the vote was won in 1920. More and more women could find jobs, and possibly this was all most of them desired. By 1960 two out of every five women were employed outside the home. The spurt in the percentage of employed wives was even more dramatic: in 1900 about one in twenty worked at a job; by 1940 about seventeen percent; and by 1960, about thirty-three percent. The Second World War profoundly accelerated this movement, particularly into metals, aircraft, and electronic industries. In no other country save the

Soviet Union did women make up so large a part of the work force.

Women's movement recedes

But in important ways women fell backward after the feminist peak of the 1920s. Some forty percent of the college student population was female in that decade; but in the 1960s, they comprised only thirty-five percent. In proportion, there were fewer women in the 1960s taking graduate degrees, or becoming mayors, governors, judges, physicians, and lawyers. Women invaded the business world as secretaries, and there they remained: management was male. On an average, women received two-thirds of the wages paid to men, which was explained by the fact that like blacks of both sexes, women were confined largely to the lower-paid jobs. Having made teaching and nursing feminine preserves, they made almost no further inroads into other professions. (Indeed, more and more men took up public school teaching after 1945, a fact that had much to do with rising salaries and labor union militance in that field.) In short, the sexual division of labor, which on the farm had been so clear—the men working in the fields, the women in the kitchens—remained still evident in modern urban employment. Furthermore, to anyone looking at American society, it was clear that the authority structure outside the home was still male.

In the post-1945 years, American women seemed overwhelmingly content with their role. The floods of little children who inundated the streets and playgrounds, in the baby boom of these years, eloquently testified to the fact that most women were powerfully attracted by the Freudian image depicting them as happiest and most creative when engaged in running a busy home and surrounded by bevies of children. The new emphasis on proud motherhood, gourmet cooking, and the challenge of rearing confident and well-trained offspring brought the average American woman far from the liberated flapper of the 1920s who flattened her bosom and praised the single life.

Betty Friedan

In 1963 a rather solitary voice was raised by Betty Friedan in her widely read *The Feminine Mystique.* She assaulted the woman-as-mother concept, maintaining that the endless chores of homemaking and the overwhelming concentration on children prevented women from fully realizing their potential. Domesticity, plus sex, plus a split-level house and a station wagon full of youngsters, she said, did not amount to happiness. The barriers that held women back from a fully equal position in employment outside the home should be swept away.

Her book aroused the ridicule that has traditionally greeted all feminist proposals, but its ideas continued to nag at the American conscience. Then there took place the same conjunction of events that the history of the women's movement has displayed before. As in the era of the abolitionist movement before the Civil War, and in the time of the progressive movement, the women's movement caught fire from the conflagration of reformism that was going on throughout the society. Furthermore, just as the women's movement of the mid-nineteenth century was a spin-off of the abolitionist crusade, created by the fact that activist women were revolted to observe that even within the abolitionist organizations they were kept in secondary status, so that of the 1960s was born in the same anger. Activist Robin Morgan observed in 1970:

The current women's movement was begun largely . . . by women who had been active in the civil-rights movement . . . and in the Left generally. . . . Thinking we were involved in the struggle to build a new society, it was a slowly dawning and depressing realization that we were doing the same work and playing the same roles *in* the Movement as out of it: typing the speeches that the men delivered, making coffee but not policy, being accessories to the men whose politics would supposedly replace the Old Order. But whose New Order? Not ours, certainly.

Especially within the radical-hippie world, it was standard practice for women to be cast in a kind of Earth Mother role. In the romantic search for whatever was "natural," there was not only the return to long straight hair, bare feet, and freely swinging breasts, there was also an almost tribal reversion to a bovine pattern of female submissiveness.

The rise of women's liberation

President Kennedy, responding to Eleanor Roosevelt's urgings, had already given the revived concern with women's problems a crucially important boost when, in 1961, he had established the Commission on the Status of Women. From its work came the Equal Pay Act of 1963, which covered all occupations except those of professional, executive, or administrative stature. Then the word *sex* was put in the 1964 civil rights bill, whose main concern was to outlaw job discrimination against black Americans and other minority groups. The Equal Employment Opportunities Commission, thus created, at first ignored the existence of the word, but when forty percent of the complaints pouring in about job discrimination came from women, it began to take action.

In 1966 small groups of women activists began

As in the pre-Civil War years, when the rise of abolitionism stimulated a similar upsurge in the women's rights movement, in the late 1960s the "women's liberation" movement suddenly exploded, catching national attention. This reversed quietist, traditional trends dominant for decades.
Wide World Photos

to form "consciousness raising" talk sessions to awaken women to the full dimensions of their secondary status. The National Organization for Women (NOW), with Betty Friedan as president, appeared late that year, its purpose being "to take action to bring women into full participation in the mainstream of American society now, exercising all the privileges and responsibilities thereof in truly equal partnership with men." In 1967 President Johnson ordered that the thousands of firms doing business with the federal government no longer discriminate against women, and, on quite another front, the state of California enacted a path-breaking law that, following later court decisions, made it possible for women to secure abortions practically on request, thus realizing an objective long sought by feminists—freedom from unwanted pregnancy.

The women's movement split off in many directions. Betty Friedan's NOW was essentially concerned with gaining equality in employment—economic and political—outside the home; that is, with equality within the system. But women of a more radical outlook said that what was needed instead was a profound social revolution. Out of their writings, indeed, came a debate among women that went to the heart of male-female relationships. Activists insisted that what was needed was the wholesale destruction of the "sexist" organization of society. Referring to their condition as one of slavery, they insisted that it sprang from the male-dominated nuclear family, allegedly formed thousands of years ago in order to keep women in subjection. Kate Millett, in *Sexual Politics* (1970), praised female homosexuality as the true route to freedom from male domination. Radical women's organizations suddenly appeared, ranging from the "cells" of Female Liberation to WITCH (Women's International Terrorist Conspiracy from Hell). In the women's lib precincts where feelings were strongest, there was a determined drive to prove that the two sexes were essentially alike; that a new "unisex" style of life in which women and men wore the same clothes and performed the same tasks, was desirable.

Women's lib attracted a storm of abuse, from men, predictably, and from a majority of women, who found its goals strange and bizarre. Among women intellectuals, after the first surge of radical women's lib writing had passed, there were many voices of enthusiastic support and equally enthusiastic dissent. "At the root of liberation's determination to disintegrate the sexes," observed Anne Bernays (in the *Atlantic* in 1970), "is the disabling anxiety that *different* means the same thing as *inferior*. . . . Why is this palpable fact [i.e., the differentness] so hard for so many women to swallow? Are we as confused as all that?"

Broader changes affecting women

Women's lib was far more than an argument over sexuality, however. It was also (like the feminist movement before 1920) a demand that male monopolies be broken: in the professions, in executive positions in government and business, even in social clubs. This, indeed, became the most enduring aspect of the movement, attracting the widest support among both men and women. The surge of bitterness about roles in the sex act faded fairly soon; what remained was a broadly based drive for social and economic equality. Women looking for employment as college professors found themselves for a time in demand. Law schools and medical schools established quotas for the admission of women, and even Congress began to hire girls as well as boys for pages. In August 1970 the House of Representatives resurrected and passed a proposed amendment to the Constitution, buried in committee for more than twenty years, that would outlaw any form of discrimination on account of sex. The so-called equal rights amendment had far to go before becoming the law of the land, however. Even women were among its critics, since it threatened many laws that discriminated in favor of women, such as those relating to child custody and hours of labor.

Many court cases were filed that attacked issues such as differential rates of pay and promotion and the denial of jobs to mothers with small children. Everywhere demands were made that the government provide child care centers, so that women could escape the limitations of the home and find jobs. That the economic problem required persistent action was revealed in 1974, when the California Commission on the Status of Women reported that the gap between men's and women's incomes was increasing. This was so because women were still stuck in lower paying jobs, while men, who continued to monopolize managerial and executive posts, benefited from rising incomes. Some forty-three percent of American women of working age held jobs, as against thirty-seven percent in 1960, but while their average annual earning in 1960 was only $2,600 behind that of men ($3,600 as against $6,200), in 1974 they were $4,000 behind ($5,000 as against $9,000). California made divorce much simpler and less expensive by eliminating the question of fault. The fact of incompatibility, testified to by one party, became sufficient grounds for action. Laws preventing abortions were challenged in many states, and some were made so liberal that the number of abortions soared into the tens of thousands, thus becoming a significant factor in the continuing decline in the birth rate.

The sexual revolution

In these and scores of other ways, a new life for women had clearly been inaugurated, just as it had for blacks and young people. No fact operated more powerfully in this regard than the introduction of "the Pill," an oral contraceptive. While not leading to instant promiscuity, as many feared (studies demonstrated that young women continued overwhelmingly to restrict sexual activity to men with whom they had a serious relationship), the Pill eliminated the fear of pregnancy and was believed to have a profound impact on sexual behavior. The women's lib movement insisted that sexual appetites on both sides were equal and that, accordingly, women should have equal access to sexual experience. This combined with the availability of the Pill to inaugurate a new era filled with unexplored uncertainties and dilemmas for women. The "real truth about the sexual revolution," wrote Midge Decter in the August 1972 issue of the *Atlantic,* "is that it has made of sex an almost chaotically limitless and therefore unmanageable realm in the life of women." Given a sexual freedom undreamed of by their sisters in former generations, Decter went on, the question that haunted these pioneers in a new way of life was, what shall be done with this freedom? What were its limitations, its prices, its opportunities? No one knew. Old codes of conduct seemed cast aside, and young women were forced to make up their own minds "at a time of life," wrote Decter, "when [they] feel the greatest need for the protection of a fixed set of manners."

One clear result of the new attitudes among women was a changed notion about child-bearing. Consternation among demographers—and those who planned public facilities, such as schools—occurred when the "war baby" crop of young girls decided not to have so many children as their mothers when they reached child-bearing age in the mid-1960s. Polls showed that women wanted an average of 2.5 children in 1971, as contrasted with 3.03 in 1965, and about 3.7 in the era of the baby boom. During the 1960s, the number of children born to twenty-four-year-old women just out of college dropped by fifty-five percent. Furthermore, the number of young women remaining single rose significantly. Thus, though the number of possible mothers was at an all-time high, the actual number of births declined sharply. The sum result was that the birth rate reached the level of replacement in 1972, a fact that created reactions of both approval and alarm.

The new industrial state

Deep-running changes were taking place also in the nature of the American economy. An ever smaller group of great corporations was taking over the national economy. In the 1960s the 500 largest corporations provided half the goods and services that the nation used. In 1962 some twelve percent of all manufacturing resources was owned by five large corporations; the 50 largest held over one-third. There were approximately 2,000 firms in the country with assets of over ten million dollars each, and they controlled eighty percent of all manufacturing. Three corporations—General Motors, Standard Oil of New Jersey, and Ford—together took in more dollars than all the farms in the country combined. Each of these companies had higher gross revenues than any single state in the Union; General Motors alone took in eight times as much money as the state of New York, and a fifth as much as the federal government. The corporate form of business had swollen so gigantically that in communications, electric power, a large part of transportation, most of manufacturing and mining, even in much of entertainment and merchandising, the corporation had become dominant.

And it was quite a different kind of organization than in Theodore Roosevelt's time. To make a Model T had been a simple business of ordering some steel from a local warehouse, and hiring a group of men to put together simple parts. Thus one man at the head of the business could run the show. But automobiles are now fantastically complicated; their designs must be worked out by teams of highly skilled specialists; and corporation presidents cannot possibly understand these intricacies, nor can their boards of directors or stockholders. Thus the "brains" of these immense firms are no longer in the head of a Henry Ford. They have instead descended deep into the organization, where the engineers, technologists, cost analysts, and marketing specialists are located. Only these men can know enough to make the crucial decisions—and then only when working together in groups. In *The New Industrial State* (1967), the economist John Kenneth Galbraith has called these staffs of specialists, who do all the planning and designing for the great corporations, the *"technostructure."*

Consumers ask for higher and better perform-ance from every one of their products—surgical tools, television sets, water softeners, light bulbs, clothes washers, and scores of other manufac-tured things. To make these more precise and complicated articles, however, takes years longer than in the past. The auto manufacturer cannot simply go to a local steel warehouse and buy whatever happens to be in stock; he must search the world for special metals—molybdenum, tita-nium, aluminum—and prepare them in special ways. Contracts with thousands of suppliers must be negotiated, and the inflow of parts and mate-rials closely coordinated.

The need for close coordination of the manu-facture of complex products means that a long "lead time" is now built into the industrial proc-ess. Years can pass from the time a given product is conceived of until it rolls out on the assembly line. An immense investment in expensive equipment is required, as are large planning staffs, to ensure that the thousands of separate procedures and items all get thought out and brought together. Only very large corporations have the necessary funds and technostructure to plan and carry through such costly and long-range operations. But even they cannot afford to make a mistake; the investments are too enor-mous. The result is that these gargantuan firms have done everything they can to gain control of all the factors that might influence their chances for success.

Major corporations control all factors

Modern corporations have largely eliminated the influence of bankers by making certain that corporation profits are high enough to generate their own investment capital—surely one of the most epochal changes in the history of capitalism. By becoming huge, and therefore one of the few buyers for particular kinds of supplies, corpora-tions like General Motors can be certain that their suppliers, eager for their trade, will charge stable and acceptable prices. Then, by being one

of the few producers, giant corporations are largely in control of prices, since their competi-tors are not likely to engage in much price-slash-ing, for they also desire a stable pricing structure on which they can base their planning. The con-sumer, for his part, can make little complaint, for he has not the foggiest idea of what it actually costs to manufacture, say, a bun-warmer. Then, to ensure that the products will actually be bought at the prices they set, the large corpora-tions maintain large research, advertising, and sales organizations to control the market. The corporations of the new industrial state are in fact far more bureaucratic, centralized, and remote from outside control than they had ever been in the past.

The sum result of these developments is that the classic picture of American capitalism as being controlled and disciplined by competition, in the free and uncontrolled marketplace, is no longer true of the big corporations. Wherever the product is most complicated, and therefore the technology is most advanced and the investment of capital the heaviest, there the marketplace as a factor in the corporation's success is the most completely removed. How to reestablish compe-tition and thus lower prices? No longer can the ancient antitrust laws be applied to break up the huge corporations if the same kinds of products are still to be manufactured. Smaller corporations cannot produce them since they are too costly, in the need for lead time and a large planning staff, to carry out design and coordination. To end bigness, it would be necessary to do away with the kind of sophisticated products that the public now consumes and wishes to go on consuming.

The technostructure

We have now, then, a new phenomenon in American life—the technostructure. It is impor-tant to ask, what are the motives of this new class of people who together plan and direct the oper-ations of the great corporations? Unlike a blue-collar worker who puts together the products someone else designs, and belongs to an externally based union, the white-collar worker tends to regard the corporation much as a football player does his team: its success, since he is part of its "brain," is his to bask in. The white-collar workers of the technostructure, therefore, necessarily put highest value on high productivity and booming sales, as signs of success.

The technostructure also seeks to reduce the number of manual workers, for their wages, being largely controlled by unions, constitute another uncontrolled element in the total picture. (White-collar workers tend to remain unorganized.) Seeking certainty, the technostructure designs and buys machines to replace manual laborers. For this reason, blue-collar employment (craftsmen, operatives, laborers, aside from farmers and miners) decreased by 4 million jobs from 1951 to 1964, while total employment grew by about 10 million. White-collar employment (professional, technical, managerial, office, and sales workers) reached 45 million by the mid-1960s, but blue-collar employment dropped to 37 million. This was why the labor union movement peaked in the 1950s and then began dropping from 16.6 million members in 1956 to 14.9 million in 1962 (or about twenty-seven percent of

the labor force, a proportion that has remained stable since the early 1960s).

The corporations and the government

One extraordinary result of these complex changes is to render obsolete a great deal of traditional political ideology. Decades of reformers answered the crisis of industrialism with one simple answer: let the government take over, either by regulation or by outright ownership. Modern technology, which requires highly skilled planners, makes this impossible. The British Labour party nationalized major industries after 1945, but it discovered that this approach did not produce what was anticipated. Great industries cannot be run by politicians, even civil servants; they are too complicated. Only the technostructure can control them and make them work; they must have autonomy from public control. And instituting civil service rules eliminates flexibility, i.e., the easy constitution and reconstitution of groups.

For groups now have the power that individuals used to have. The remarkable progress that has been achieved in science, scholarship, and industry has resulted from the process of taking ordinary men, training them very intensively in limited bodies of knowledge, and then putting them to work together. Large areas of the national economy are still being run by individual entrepreneurs or small groups of them, such as in farming, small mines, the world of the arts and professions, small merchandising firms, and most personal services. But by far the greatest economic power lies in the great corporations, located at the heart of the economy where huge supplies of capital, expensive machines, immense work forces, extensive marketing and advertising establishments, and—most of all—heavily staffed research and development operations, are required.

The huge industrial assembly plant at McDonnell Aircraft, St. Louis, producing Phantom jets, symbolizes both the complexity and impersonality of modern industry and its close links to government.
St. Louis Post Dispatch from Black Star

Business-government links

However, it cannot be said that the corporations are entirely independent of the state. In extremely high cost industries like aerospace, it needs the government to carry on, or finance, the necessary research and development. The sixty billion dollars that the Defense Department was spending annually in the 1960s supported an astonishingly large portion of the industrial system. Literally thousands of large and small firms depended on a large annual defense outlay—and still do. Furthermore, such outlays are usually on a "cost-plus" basis, ensuring profits. While the corporations depend on government support, the government, of course, depends on the corporations to supply it with its necessary goods. Firms like Boeing Aircraft, General Dynamics, Raytheon, Lockheed, and Republic Aircraft, which in the 1960s sold anywhere from two-thirds to all of their output to the government, were actually seminationalized industries. It is important to point out that, once again, the technical issues are far too complex for Congress, the government's "board of directors," to understand, and it therefore cannot exert much control over weapons procurement.

If even the government cannot effectively control the corporations, what answer can be given to protests that they have become too remote from the public's needs; that they have, in fact, created terrible problems for modern society such as pollution and overconsumption of limited natural resources? We are only beginning to grope toward the answers. Galbraith has suggested that the very educational system that was built to help meet the needs of industry may in the long run provide solutions, for only in higher education is there a potential for working out new ideas that will create social innovation. The corporations look only to their own needs, and they are wonderfully successful in meeting them. It is instructive to realize that such firms as United States Steel simply do not lose money anymore; that, indeed, the ancient business cycle of boom and bust that operated until 1940 seems to have been suspended. Furthermore, firms like General Motors are equally successful in meeting consumer demands. Who could possibly complain that the nation's industries have not sufficiently deluged us with a veritable blizzard of artfully designed and fascinating things to buy?

For all the corporations' successes, however, they seem unable to consider or to solve the very problems of endless expansion of output and consumption they have created. Perhaps Galbraith is right in his view that from the academic community will come the kinds of people who can solve such massive problems as environmental pollution. This, one gathers, was what the student radicals of the Movement were trying to do: provide, from the university setting, a program of social action that would reassert control over the great corporations. The radicals' destructive methods, however, and their taste for sweeping ideologies and grand solutions, gave them but a brief career. More and more it seemed that the scholars of the 1950s, the disillusioned intellectuals of the "end of ideology" era, were right. Simple solutions never work; demands for instant revolution are doomed to frustration. Only close and patient concentration on seemingly ordinary details could lead to the cumulative, piecemeal improvements that constituted Reinhold Niebuhr's "proximate" solutions, in themselves all that one reasonably could expect in human affairs.

Bibliography

Three books that were especially valuable to me in writing this chapter: As in all the post-World War II chapters in this book, it is almost impossible to pick three books that stand out, first because the characterizations and analyses I have made rely heavily on contemporary materials in periodical and newspaper form, and second, because there are so many books that deal with fragments of problems and so few that present the kind of matured historical narratives that are available for earlier decades. Peter L. Berger and

Richard John Neuhaus's *Movement and Revolution** (1970) is perceptive on the youth movement. John Kenneth Galbraith, in his usual witty, irreverent, but trenchant style, is fundamental on *The New Industrial State** (1967, rev. ed. 1972). Matt S. Meier and Feliciano Rivera, *The Chicanos: A History of Mexican-Americans* (1972), is superb.

How have historians looked at the topic?

Those Americans who grew to awareness during the 1960s may well be an estranged generation marked by the violence of the decade. Not surprisingly, few attempts have been made to put the decade of "future shock" in historical perspective. The most ambitious effort thus far is William O'Neill's brilliant, candid, and often irritating *Coming Apart: An Informal History of America in the 1960s* (1971).

Different aspects of the 1960s have been subjected to close scrutiny. The passion John F. Kennedy evoked and the political network he built are described in Theodore H. White's *The Making of the President, 1960** (1961). The changing emphasis of the black revolution is skillfully analyzed in Benjamin's Muse's *The American Negro Revolution: From Nonviolence to Black Power** (1970). *The Mind and Mood of Black America: Twentieth Century Thought* (1969) by S. P. Fullinwinder offers brilliant and useful insights. Charles E. Silberman's *Crisis in Black and White** (1964) is a thoughtful and penetrating assessment of the price racism exacts. Samuel Lubell's impressionistic *White and Black: Test of a Nation** (1966) includes illuminating comments and sobering conclusions. Howard Zinn's *SNCC: The New Abolitionists** (1964) is a revealing portrait of student leaders that criticizes the Kennedy administration for its lack of concerted action.

Lerone Bennett, Jr., has drawn a sensitive picture of the charismatic black leader of nonviolence in *What Manner of Man: A Memorial Biography of Martin Luther King, Jr.* (1968). King's own words are essential, both for their insights and for the commitment they express: *Stride toward Freedom** (1958); *Why We Can't Wait** (1964); and *Where Do We Go from Here: Chaos or Community?** (1968).

The explosion in Watts is graphically depicted in Robert Conot's *Rivers of Blood, Years of Darkness** (1967). The National Advisory Commission's *Report on Civil Disorders** (1968) thoroughly probes the divided society that produced the racial outburst of the late 1960s. Stokely Carmichael and Charles Hamilton explain the emerging philosophy of black nationalism in *Black Power: The Politics of Liberation in America** (1967). Several political prisoners record their firsthand experiences in Angela Y. Davis et al., *If They Come in the Morning** (1971). The black separatist movement is seen in its varying forms in Philip S. Foner's *The Black Panthers Speak* (1970), Theodore Draper's *The Rediscovery of Black Nationalism* (1970), and C. E. Lincoln's *The Black Muslims in America* (1961). Penetrating insights into black Americans' experiences can be gained by reading James Baldwin's evocative essays in *The Fire Next Time** (1963), Ralph Ellison's literary masterpiece, *Invisible Man** (1952), and Claude Brown's fierce and beautiful *Manchild in the Promised Land** (1965). Eldridge Cleaver's *Soul on Ice** (1968) is a powerful and gripping statement of a black man's anger at the white world.

Racism and its effects are comprehensively exposed in Paul Jacobs and Saul Landau, eds., *To Serve the Devil: A Documentary Analysis of America's Racial History and Why It Has Been Kept Hidden,** two vols. (1971). For an appraisal of the second largest minority in America, read Peter Matthiessen's excellent biography, *Sal Si Puedes: Cesar Chavez and the New American Revolution** (1970) and Patricia B. Blawis's *Tijerina and the Land Grants: Mexican-Americans in Struggle for Their Heritage** (1971). Manuel P. Servin's edited volume, *The Mexican American: An Awakening Minority** (1970) is also valuable. On the bracero question, see Ernesto Galarza, *Merchants of Labor** (1964). On illegal aliens, see Julian Somora, *Los Mojados** (1971).

Hal Draper's *Berkeley: The New Student Revolt*

(1965) probes the deeper meanings of the free-speech movement while Robert Kahn's *The Battle of Morningside Heights* (1970) focuses on the Columbia University disruption. A perspective critique of the entire movement is found in Daniel Bell and Irving Kristol's *Confrontation: The Student Rebellion and the Universities* (1969) and in *Students in Revolt* (1969), ed. Seymour M. Lipset and Philip G. Altbach. Essential to understanding the phenomena of the counterculture are: Kenneth Keniston's *The Uncommitted* (1965), which focuses on the bankruptcy of technological values; Theodore Roszak's *The Making of a Counter Culture* (1969) and William Braden's *The Age of Aquarius* (1970), both of which comment on the tensions between radical activists and hippies; and Philip Slater's perceptive look at a "soulless" society, *The Pursuit of Loneliness: American Culture at the Breaking Point** (1972). Keith Melville's *Communes in the Counter Culture: Origins, Theories, Styles of Life** (1972) is a careful, scholarly study of the recent attempt to create an alternate family style.

The discontent of American women was brilliantly articulated by Betty Friedan in her remarkable and scholarly *The Feminine Mystique** (1963). Friedan addressed herself to the problems of the affluent white housewife, but as women activists in the civil rights, student, and peace movements found themselves relegated to "making coffee rather than policy," an organized women's liberation movement was born once again. Several excellent collections convey the

philosophy and tone of the movement: Robin Morgan, ed., *Sisterhood is Powerful: An Anthology of Writings from the Women's Liberation Movement** (1970); Vivian Gornick and Barbara K. Moran, eds., *Woman in Sexist Society: Studies in Power and Powerlessness** (1971); Michele H. Garskof, ed., *Roles Women Play: Readings toward Women's Liberation** (1971); and Toni Cade, ed., *The Black Woman: An Anthology** (1970). Carolyn Bird's *Born Female: The High Cost of Keeping Women Down** (1970) reveals the sexist nature of society's work patterns, and Cynthia Fuchs Epstein's *Woman's Place** (1970) comments on the obstacles professional women face. Sylvia Plath's *The Bell Jar** (1972) and Alix Kates Shulman's *Memoirs of an Ex-Prom Queen* (1969) are powerful novels of special force and immediacy.

The intimate relationship between the government and the technostructure is elaborated in Carroll W. Pursell, Jr., ed., *The Military-Industrial Complex** (1972). The current thrust of interpretation was advanced in the 1950s by C. Wright Mills in *The Power Elite** (1956). Arnold Rose speaks for pluralism in *The Power Structure** (1967), a theory which G. William Domhoff assaults in *Who Rules America?** (1967). Other important studies include Richard Barber's *The Politics of Research* (1966), which analyzes the dependence of corporations and scientists on the federal government, and Gabriel Kolko's *Wealth and Power in America** (1962).

*Available in paperback.

CHAPTER 36

The Politics of Turmoil: Kennedy, Johnson, and Nixon

TIME LINE

1961–1963	Congressional opponents block most of Kennedy's reform proposals
1961	Housing Act; Area Redevelopment Act
1962	Medicare defeated; in *Baker v. Carr* Supreme Court establishes one-man to one-vote principle in legislative apportionment
1963	Higher Education Act and other enactments funnel funds to colleges and schools; Accelerated Public Works program; Kennedy proposes tax cut to stimulate economy; President Kennedy assassinated; Lyndon Baines Johnson becomes thirty-sixth president of the United States
1964	Third Civil Rights Act; War on Poverty program launched with creation of Office of Economic Opportunity; tax cut passed; Wilderness Act
1965	Johnson announces Great Society program; federal aid to education greatly broadened; Medicare enacted; Fourth Civil Rights Act; Water Quality Act; Appalachian program of redevelopment; Economic Development Administration established; Department of Housing and Urban Development created; Johnson escalates Vietnam involvement
1966	Republicans make strong gains in congressional elections
1968	Senator Eugene McCarthy almost defeats Johnson in New Hampshire presidential primary; Johnson withdraws from race; police and antiwar protestors clash at Democratic National Convention; Richard M. Nixon elected thirty-seventh president of the United States
1969	Nixon adopts conservative economic and social policies and a prowhite "southern strategy"; antiballistic missile authorized; Vietnamization announced; Neil Armstrong lands on moon; Warren E. Burger appointed chief justice of the Supreme Court; Nixon proposes family assistance payments to replace welfare system; Nixon proposes New Federalism
1970	Nation becomes widely concerned over pollution crisis; Nixon establishes Environmental Protection Agency, Council on Environmental Quality, and National Oceanic and Atmospheric Agency; Cambodian invasion leads to renewed turbulence on campuses; Democrats make good showing in congressional elections
1971	Nixon calls for "New American Revolution" in domestic policy, proposes family assistance payments and revenue sharing plans; Laos invasion fails; My Lai massacre revealed; Nixon opens talks with China in historic reversal of policy; Nixon devalues dollar, raises barriers to imports, removes gold as basis for dollar in international trade, and establishes wage-price controls to battle inflation
1972	Nixon visits China and Russia; intensive bombing of North Vietnam

A S the nation plunged into the turbulence of the 1960s, John Kennedy entered the White House with a narrow victory behind him and a crowded list of reforms that he called the New Frontier. Hampered by the thinness of his electoral margin and faced by an immobile Congress, he was forced to spend his time in building up public opinion for his proposals. Shot down before he could reap the results of his efforts, in Lyndon Johnson he was succeeded by a consummate master of congressional relations.

Joining his political skills to the momentum that Kennedy had built up and given an enormous vote of public confidence in the presidential election of 1964, Johnson was able to push through all the legislation that Kennedy had asked for, and more. In 1964 and 1965 Johnson displayed presidential leadership as masterful as that of Woodrow Wilson or Franklin Roosevelt at their best. One after the other the great reforms marched through Congress: inauguration of massive federal aid to public schools and for housing, urban redevelopment, the War on Poverty, mass transit, and the arts and humanities; medical care for the elderly and the indigent; the civil rights laws; revision of the immigration laws; a concerted drive to solve the problems of Appalachia; and the first steps toward controlling pollution.

Few presidents have stood at such a peak of national acclaim as did Lyndon Johnson in 1965; and few have fallen so far, so swiftly, as did Johnson thereafter. In that same year he escalated the Vietnam conflict into a full-throated war that destroyed much of Vietnam and took thousands of Vietnamese and American lives. Soon the war issue tore the nation apart and ended Johnson's popularity. This extraordinary man, who had been so powerful, was reduced to announcing— to a relieved nation—that he would not run for reelection in 1968.

With the advent of Richard Nixon, the turmoil slowly subsided. American troops were with-

drawn, bit by bit, from Vietnam (though the president nonetheless held on grimly for a "peace with honor" by shifting to a lavish use of air and naval power). The flow of reform proposals from the White House dwindled to a trickle, and the stress moved to reduced government spending, federal passivity on race questions, and escalated attacks on suspected criminals and radical agitators. Nixon lowered the world level of tension by initiating surprisingly bold new approaches to China and Russia. Indeed, foreign affairs were what fascinated and absorbed him, not the problems of the cities, the minorities, and the poor. These matters, he insisted, should be handled by state and local governments and by individuals solving their own difficulties. The president effectively ended the "Supreme Court revolution" by appointing four conservatives to the bench, and he built an administration notable for its sober tone. The campuses and cities slowly quieted, the turbulence died, and a measure of orderliness returned to national life—until the scandal of Watergate broke in 1973 and, in 1974, Nixon was driven from office (events to be discussed in the next chapter).

John Kennedy: Urban Democrat

At age forty-three, John Kennedy was the youngest man ever elected president, and the first to be born in the twentieth century. Except for Theodore Roosevelt, he would have been the first, too, to be reared in big cities: in his case, Boston and New York. An Irish Catholic, he was far removed from the stereotype of the Boston Irish as poor, uneducated, and patiently submissive to the church. He was a wealthy and sophisticated Harvard man, author of two books on history and politics, with his wife a member of the transatlantic social elite, and hardly a dogmatic Catholic. Indeed, most of the church's prelates distrusted him, for he was skeptical on religious matters, surrounded himself with such liberal Protestants as the Unitarians Theodore Sorensen and Arthur

M. Schlesinger, Jr.—White House advisers—and firmly opposed state and federal aid to parochial schools.

A Democratic president, he quickly built a traditionally Democratic administration. As in the days of Grover Cleveland, Woodrow Wilson, and Franklin Roosevelt, the center of gravity in Washington moved from the Capitol building to the White House. The president's office once more became the turbulent hub of everyone's attention, and a stream of messages calling for urgent national reforms came forth from it. The new president was a master of television, and he established frequent press conferences. Catholics, Jews, intellectuals, men sprung from urban politics, liberal internationalists, southerners, and blacks—these were the kinds of people brought to Washington to staff the new administration. Businessmen across the country drew back in alarm, and the Business Advisory Council, made up of wealthy bankers and industrialists, broke off its longstanding ties with the Department of Commerce. The familiar Democratic political style—irreverent, self-consciously brainy, and confident—pervaded Washington social life. An influx of young people to the capital stirred the public's hopes that the country's vital energies would be released and bold adventures launched.

Kennedy, however, faced serious obstacles. His very youth meant that congressional leaders, mainly older men deeply rooted in positions of power, felt he could be ignored. Preeminently men of small-town and rural America, they lacked his concern with the problems of big cities and of the young. Kennedy, after all, had won only a thin victory over Nixon; and the same coalition of southern, white Democrats and northern Republicans that had hamstrung Harry Truman's reform proposals was still in operation. Even Catholic Democrats from big cities often ranged in opposition to him, for they disliked his opposition to aid for parochial schools. Kennedy had to search for a broad middle ground where he could find general support; the policies

of his administration were therefore relatively moderate.

The basic strategy he and his advisers adopted was to lay out a series of proposals, whether or not Congress could immediately be brought to pass them; bend every effort to "educate" the country so as to stir up popular support; and then hope for a big reelection victory in 1964. As the first four years would sow the seeds in preparation, so the second four years would reap the harvest. Although an assassin had other plans for Kennedy, his program did, in effect, follow this course.

Kennedy's domestic reforms

In the first three months of office, Kennedy sent thirty-nine messages and letters to Congress asking for legislation. Some of them had to do with reviving the economy, but most were concerned with changing the quality of life in a wondrously abundant, but seriously ill, society. There were messages on health and hospital care, education, natural resources, highways, housing and community development, farm needs, the reforming of independent commissions such as the ICC, and others on civil rights, transportation, consumer protection, and for aid to the mentally ill, the poor, and the elderly.

Kennedy followed the advice of his trusted secretary of agriculture, Orville Freeman, and supported basic new legislation for farmers. The problems were severe: mountainous overproduction due to skyrocketing mechanization; bulging government warehouses; low farm income (in the 1960s only one farmer in nine earned as much in a year as a skilled worker in the cities); and yet millions of starving poor here and abroad. Characteristically turning to scholarly experts in the field—the Eisenhower administration had preferred instead to listen to agricultural businessmen—Freeman was able to put together a new national framework for farming. The Food for Peace program sent surpluses abroad, while the Food Stamp plan enabled poverty-stricken

Americans to join in the benefits. To farmers who would keep strict controls on production, the government made direct payments. Food prices, meanwhile, were allowed much more freedom to find their own level in the marketplace. Each year farm income rose a billion dollars while surpluses were pared down to what constituted a reasonable national storage.

Kennedy and education

The issue that Kennedy cared about most of all was that of education. He would often reel off disheartening statistics about the young: only six children of every ten in the fifth grade would finish high school; only nine out of every sixteen high school graduates would go on to college; a million young people were out of school *and* out of work; and school drop-outs were a constant drain on public resources. In 1963, Kennedy ob-

On May 25, 1961, President Kennedy went before Congress to call for a landing of man on the moon before 1970. Astronauts John Glenn, Gus Grissom, and Alan Shepard here train for the first manned space flight.
NASA

tained passage of the Higher Education Act, which produced more aid for colleges in five years than they had received in a century, since the Morrill Act of 1862. Hundreds of classrooms, community colleges, graduate centers, technical institutes, and college libraries were constructed under the act.

Then Kennedy pursued the theme of "specialized" aid to the elementary and secondary schools, getting grants for vocational education, providing literacy training to the unemployed, launching efforts to halt the drop-out and delinquency problems, and building libraries. Educational television also received important assistance. In sum, about a third of President Kennedy's main proposals to Congress had aid to education as one of their central elements. The Office of Education, surveying the record, described the Kennedy years as the most significant for education in its hundred-year history.

The Medicare proposal

In 1945 Harry Truman had asked Congress to establish universal publicly supported medical insurance for all Americans. Members of the American Medical Association rose up in massive wrath, condemning his plan as "socialized medicine," and Truman never got his proposal enacted. After that, little was heard of the notion. But the issue did not die. Rising medical costs and the low incomes of the elderly (who were growing every year more numerous) created unavoidable social distress. The tragedy was that the old could usually not get, or even retain, medical insurance, while at their time of life they needed medical care most of all. The savings of entire lifetimes could be wiped away in one illness, after which self-respecting men and women who had taken pride in being independent all their lives would have to accept the shame of being charity patients.

Within the offices of the Federal Security Agency, where it was well known that the aged were in a cruel situation, studies on the problem proceeded. Based on research by the agency, a bill was proposed in Congress that would give some aid to the elderly, but for years it was little noted. In 1957, however, the AFL-CIO got behind the measure, which then swiftly rose to become a great national issue, figuring prominently in the presidential campaign of 1960. But President Kennedy lost another of his crucial battles when he tried to get a Medicare bill through Congress that would have provided coverage to those over sixty-five under the social security system. The American Medical Association condemned it as socialized medicine, and its opponents were able to keep the bill locked up in the House Committee on Ways and Means for three years.

Aid for the cities

The president was deeply aware of urban ills. His administration sought to help cities by aiding the long court fight to redistrict state legislatures so that rural areas would have their influence decreased and cities would be able to claim their proper share of legislative power. Under the existing system, overrepresentation for rural areas was extreme. In California, a county with 15,000 people had the same representation as another with 6 million people. Attorney General Robert Kennedy helped bring the crucial cases—*Baker* v. *Carr* (1962) and *Reynold* v. *Sims* (1964)—before the Supreme Court. The Court ruled that the national House of Representatives and all state and local legislative bodies had to be apportioned on a one-man to one-vote principle, a revolutionary decision in American government.

Congress enacted a $6.1 billion Housing Act in 1961, which was of great potential value to urban families—a large proportion of them black—in low- and middle-income levels. The president failed to get approval of a job corps to train unemployed young men and women, who were then just roaming the streets. He established vocational schools, and launched the Area Redevelopment Act of 1961. The act's objective was to concentrate on the most depressed communities,

provide job retraining, and stimulate the building of new industry. In the fall of 1963, Kennedy read Michael Harrington's brilliant book *The Other America,* was shocked to learn from it about the suffering of millions of forgotten poverty-stricken citizens, and ordered that plans be prepared for a "war on poverty." He had already secured passage of an Accelerated Public Works program to employ the jobless, the first such enactment since the New Deal.

In 1962 President Kennedy, struggling hard to turn an unfriendly Congress into a cooperative one, went to St. Paul, Minnesota, (as he did to other cities) to speak for the election of Democratic congressmen: "One of the favorite bromides in the world," he said, "is that there is no difference between our two political parties. I'm going to show you what the difference is this year. Last year we had a bill to increase the minimum wage for workers . . . to $50 a week, $1.25 an hour. Do you know that on this not very drastic piece of legislation 100 percent of the Republican Congressmen from Minnesota voted against it? Do you know on a bill a month ago that was killed, to provide assistance for higher education, by 1970 twice as many boys and girls are going to be applying for admission to our colleges as in 1960—they are our most valuable resource—on a bill to assist higher education in this country, 67 percent of the Republican delegation from the State of Minnesota voted 'no.' On a bill to provide for assistance to depressed areas, those with long-term, chronic unemployment . . . 81 percent of the Republican Congressmen in the House of Representatives voted 'no.'

"That's the issue in this campaign. On a bill to provide medical care for our older citizens . . . seven-eighths of the Republican members of the Senate voted 'no,' just as their fathers before them had voted 90 percent against the social security in the 1930s. . . . We have won and lost vote after vote by 1 or 2 or 3 votes in the Senate, and 3, 4, or 5 votes in the House of Representatives, and I don't think we can find jobs for our people, I don't think we can educate our younger people, I don't think we can provide security for our older citizens, when we have a party which votes 'no.'" (*Public Papers of the Presidents of the United States: John F. Kennedy, 1962.*)

Stimulating the economy

Rising over all other immediate domestic considerations, in Kennedy's mind, was the stagnant economy and its lagging rate of growth. His principal economic adviser, Walter Heller, insisted that many other national problems would disappear if only jobs and profits became abundant once more. Black people, city people, farmers, the unemployed, those too poor to move elsewhere to find jobs, those badly housed, poorly schooled, ineffectively policed—all would benefit by renewed prosperity.

Equally important, in Kennedy's view was the international rivalry with Russia, which could not be won, he believed, if the Russians had a flourishing economy and the American system fell farther and farther behind in its growth rate. Furthermore, the United States could not maintain its position in world trade if stagnation at home meant a reduced ability to compete. With Britain, France, West Germany, Italy, and especially Japan more productive than ever before, the American dollar had lost its old-time power.

Kennedy came to office with traditional ideas about economic policy, mainly revolving around the belief that the national government should at all times work for a balanced budget. Within two years, he had dug deeply into modern economic theory by quizzing economists across the country as to how he could boost the economy from its two percent annual rate of growth to at least five percent a year. He emerged from this experience the nation's first Keynesian president: that is, he adopted the basic economic theory of the Englishman John Maynard Keynes, who a generation before had written that the way a government revives a national economy is to spend more than it receives in taxes (deficit spending). Franklin Roosevelt had toyed gingerly with the idea, but Kennedy was the first to adopt it as policy and, in a time of relative prosperity, propose a sweeping reduction in taxes. He proposed a national budget that would *purposely* wind up twelve billion dollars out of balance in 1964.

Since at the time this idea was heresy in the eyes of congressmen and the general public, the president had to set about painstakingly persuading people of its value. Removing taxes, he said, would unleash the economy. As it boomed upward, it would eventually produce *more* revenue than before, even at the lower tax rates. In a major address at Yale University in June 1962, he laid out these concepts and attacked the nation's tendency to doggedly hang on to outworn, obsolete economic ideas. He sent his cabinet members and advisers around the country to lecture to public groups and business gatherings, and released a stream of news stories from the White House dealing with the new economic plan. Then in 1963 he announced his program for a planned national deficit, which began a long series of congressional hearings and national debate that ended—after his death—in the tax reduction he had called for. Thereafter, the national economy took off on the longest uninterrupted boom in the history of the United States—which, ironically, eventually produced so affluent a nation that by the end of the 1960s it was choking on its wealth, gobbling up natural resources at a frightening rate, and lurching into inflation.

The Kennedy presidency

So matters stood in November 1963, when John Kennedy rode through the crisp, sunny streets of Dallas in an open car. The shots that took his life stunned and bereaved the nation. After the shock had worn off, what could the nation say of this presidency? The beginning of a new era, as its devotees insist? Or more gallantry and style than substance, as its critics allege? Without question, the Kennedy presidency promised more than it achieved; but then, the president was only in the first stages of his struggles with Congress. He had gone a long way toward his goal of educating the nation to its new needs. In fact, while doing so he actually carried more substantial reform legislation through Congress than any president since Franklin Roosevelt. What made this record look relatively modest was not its reality but the large hopes he had created.

But the contrast remains between his legislative record and the astonishing list of major reforms his successor, Lyndon Johnson, was able to pass. Was it because Kennedy had prepared the way, or because Johnson knew how to make the system work? The question has not been finally answered, and it probably never will be. What is evident, however, is that Kennedy transformed the spirit of the country. The mission of America seemed brought to life again. A sense of movement and of challenge, of being once more the admiration of the world, briefly reunified the country. A feeling of national purpose and pride is a rare sensation for a nation that had lost its optimism in the dark years after 1945. The aching void that millions felt after John Kennedy's death was grief not only for the loss of their leader, whom they had loved and admired, but for the loss of this new spirit, which Kennedy had instilled in them.

Lyndon Johnson:
The president of national unity

As soon as Lyndon Johnson arrived in Washington from the terrible event in Dallas, he began swiftly pulling the country together. He was a man superbly equipped for the task: strong, confident, a veteran of almost thirty years in Washington, and for much of that time close to presidents. The momentum of Kennedy's program was not allowed to die—especially in the crucial area of civil rights where, since Johnson was a southerner, the nation had understandable doubts. It was one of the peak moments in the history of the United States when in July 1964 the third civil rights act became law. Under its provisions, law suits begun by the attorney general over voting rights were expedited; all discrimination in public accommodations—hotels, restau-

rants, theaters, drinking fountains, swimming pools, parks, or any other such facility—was declared illegal; the atttorney general was authorized to bring suits to desegregate schools; the Equal Employment Opportunity Commission was created; and discrimination was barred in any state or local program that was supported by federal funds (public works, schools, agricultural research, hospitals, welfare programs, and the like).

At the same time, Johnson got Congress to enact the tax cut bill that Kennedy had proposed; secured a renewal of the National Defense Education Act, sending a billion dollars to the colleges for construction and scholarships; and proclaimed in January 1964 the War on Poverty program, which he sought to make uniquely his own. When the Republicans made the error of nominating Senator Barry Goldwater, a dedicated right-wing conservative, for the presidential election in late 1964, Johnson overwhelmed him. The president won the largest vote of any candidate in United States history (61.1 percent as compared to the former record, Franklin Roosevelt's 60.7 percent in 1936). Some forty-three million people voted for Lyndon Johnson, and twenty-seven million for Goldwater, who took the electoral votes only of Arizona, his home state, and a few states in the Deep South. Behind Johnson the Democrats won huge, lopsided majorities in both houses of Congress. The stage was set for one of those rare historical periods when the traditional deadlock in the national government was broken, and a host of reform proposals that for years had been battering fruitlessly against the legislative barrier could suddenly find the necessary majorities and become law.

The Johnson presidency

Lyndon Johnson had great virtues as a president: he was exceptionally intelligent, energetic almost beyond belief, and eager to be another Franklin Roosevelt. Reared in near-poverty in the west Texas countryside, he was sympathetic to suffering people and wanted to help them. The first president to come from that huge and venerable denomination, the Disciples of Christ (Christian Church), founded in Thomas Jefferson's day as an offshoot of the Presbyterian faith, he was always stressing, like his church, the essential unity of all peoples. It was his greatest virtue that, though reared a southerner, he was able to take a national outlook on the race question. Over and over his eloquent words calling for equal rights—uttered, on crucial occasions, before southern white audiences—helped to move the nation far toward racial justice. From the beginning, Johnson wanted to give something to everyone, and thus to have liberals, middle-of-the-roaders, and conservatives all believe that he was on their side. For three years the word *consensus* was his key term, and during much of that period, the consensus strategy worked.

Most of all, however, he was a social reformer. He never forgot the Great Depression, during which he served as a young New Deal administrator, congressman, and protégé of Franklin Roosevelt. Government, to Lyndon Johnson, meant building dams and spreading irrigation waters to make the countryside green and flourishing; finding jobs for the unemployed; building schools and hospitals; helping the aged; healing the sick and uplifting the downtrodden. When he talked about compassionate government (while proposing the War on Poverty) and decent government (while signing civil rights laws), he meant what he said. Johnson wanted to be the guardian of his people, striding over the land like a kindly colossus and building what he called the Great Society.

The War on Poverty

He had already long since launched his War on Poverty, announced with great fanfare in January 1964, less than two months after John Kennedy's death. Learning of the plans that were already underway in the White House staff, he had remarked, "That's my kind of program. . . . Move full speed ahead."

The fundamental problem, only recently discovered, was that there was a hard core of millions of poverty-stricken people, perhaps a fifth of all American families, who were being left behind as everyone else soared upward in income. The economy was becoming increasingly sophisticated and mechanized, and these people were without skills. Indeed, most of them were functionally illiterate and could not be retrained. The manpower retraining programs that Kennedy's New Frontier had already begun had run head-on into this fact. Being poor, for these people, meant staying poor. It meant being weakened by illness most of the time because medical care was too expensive; being too poor to move around to find jobs; being so uneducated as to be unaware of basic information concerning the availability of jobs. The children of such families grew up in stunted surroundings, becoming themselves chronically sick and uneducated, entering the same cycle of low motivation, hopelessness, and lack of incentive that their parents were trapped in. The result was a culture of poverty that existed in the rural South and in city slums. The result, too, was a steady rise in crime rates, for the hard-core unemployed were prominent law breakers because of their frustration at having to live empty, boring lives in the midst of a bustling, prosperous America.

The War on Poverty concentrated on children and on youth. Aid was given to the older poor, but salvaging the young, the hope of the future, by improving their health, schooling, training, and general welfare was the greatest concern. Head Start programs were established to give preschool children literacy training; the Job Corps was created to provide training and remedial education to city youth, both within slum-located centers and in forest camps where conservation was the objective. The Neighborhood Youth Corps provided experience for young people in serving those around them, and another program helped college students earn income. Funds were given to support work programs under the direction of local welfare departments, by which unemployed adults were given a chance to earn money. Loans were made available to small farmers, and to men who would like to start small businesses in the cities. And then a domestic peace corps, the Volunteers in Service to America (VISTA), was created, so that middle-class young people from all over the United States could use the skills they had learned in their homes and schools to aid the poor. Controversial federal grants were given to hundreds of public and private local organizations whose concern was in some way to uplift the poor. These "community action programs" were to be run in good part by the poor. This led to endless controversies in thousands of communities, for the poor lacked managerial experience and handled funds in ways that angered the middle class, bringing charges of corruption and social radicalism.

Critics attack War on Poverty

The fact was that the critics of the War on Poverty were legion. Sargent Shriver, who as head of the Office of Economic Opportunity was in overall direction of these many separate programs, had constantly to struggle with the fact that middle-class America distrusted the undertaking. State and city governments disliked the community action groups, which were not under their control. Republicans were adamantly opposed to them as a waste of public money. Barry Goldwater put the Republican view most simply by saying that there will always be poor people in American society and that their only problem is that they are too lazy to work. Southern Democrats were often hostile, since the Office of Economic Opportunity was deeply involved in helping black people, who were then rioting. Given organizations of their own, the poor were often militant and very loud-voiced—and Congress was enraged.

Funds, therefore, were always hard to extract from Congress. The first appropriation was only one billion dollars, hardly enough for a full-scale

"war." When the swing of the political pendulum in later elections put more conservatives back in office, the War on Poverty was one of the first casualties. Unlike such great reforms as the social security system, it had no solidly based and well-organized public support behind it. Furthermore, poverty was terribly difficult to root out. The fact that the economy was booming meant that millions did in fact move above the poverty line: from 1964 to 1968, almost six million succeeded in doing so. But huge sums were spent without any dramatic effect. Head Start did not fulfill its hopes, largely because the schools that children went into after Head Start were not equipped to keep them moving along at an enriched level. Organizations of the poor rose and faded, leaving hardly a trace. In time, President Johnson made little mention of the War on Poverty, and the many separate programs run by the Office of Economic Opportunity settled down into an almost random collection of routine operations, rather than a committed national effort to eradicate poverty. It was true, however, that the total expenditures of the federal government in all programs to aid the poor, including such operations as social security, rose from about ten billion dollars in 1960 to thirty billion dollars in 1968.

Aid for the schools

After his massive victory over Goldwater swept huge Democratic majorities into Congress, President Johnson was able fully to inaugurate his Great Society program. The first measures he proposed concerned medical aid and educational assistance, both of which had tremendous stores of accumulated national support behind them. Johnson, indeed, liked to say that he was "the education President and the health President."

What he now proposed was to concentrate on grants designed to aid disadvantaged children, whether in public or private schools. Large sums were given to the states in proportion to the number of children in families with annual incomes under $2,000. Publicly purchased materials used in private schools would be ostensibly on loan. Nothing was to be provided, however, for general expenses, such as those for faculty and buildings. Rather, the money went for libraries, special training programs for teachers, laboratory facilities, learning aids, and other special services. At the same time, Johnson pushed through another higher education bill that provided billions of dollars to colleges and universities for scholarships, loans, buildings, libraries, dormitories, and other facilities.

By 1968, Johnson had carried twenty-four major pieces of legislation through Congress that dealt with education, and federal expenditures had risen from $375 million (in 1958) to $4.2 billion. Thus a new kind of federal-state relationship had been opened, changing in major ways the venerable constitutional system. The most important area of government action formerly controlled by state and local governments was henceforth to be shared with Washington, now the source of ten percent of all national expenditures on education.

Enactment of Medicare

The Johnson landslide of 1964 poured scores of congressmen into Washington who favored Medicare; Johnson made it one of his top priority items; the American Medical Association continued to fight desperately; but even the Republicans were giving in. In July 1965 the Medicare bill went through, providing millions of elderly Americans over the age of sixty-five a kind of security they had never known before. Under the social security system, funds were set aside to provide payment of doctor's and hospital bills, nursing home fees, and the cost of necessary drugs. A "revolution" had been finally concluded—one that, in the long run, the medical profession found to be extremely profitable for its members. Medicare, so violently condemned, soon became one of the pillars of American social life that no one, any longer, would propose taking away.

The Great Society rolls on

In March 1965 national television displayed before the horrified nation the state troopers of Alabama bombarding hundreds of praying blacks near Selma with tear gas, and then beating them with clubs, whips, and ropes. The eruption of national outrage sent President Johnson before Congress to ask for passage of a fourth civil rights act, which gave the federal government the power to send officials into the South to register black voters. Black registration in the states affected by the law swiftly rose from thirty to forty-six percent of those eligible.

In his Great Society speeches, Johnson had made the environment a principal concern. John Kennedy had presided over passage of the Clean Air Act of 1963, which enabled the federal government to begin exploring the problem of aerial pollution. Johnson now launched a series of White House conferences on pollution, out of which came the Water Quality Act of 1965. It gave the federal government powers bitterly resisted by industries for years: to establish standards as to the purity of the nation's rivers (if the states did not do so, or if their standards were adjudged inadequate), and to levy penalties for pollution. Then a $3.5 billion program was established whereby the federal government assisted hundreds of communities in the building of improved sewage facilities. Following this, the clean air program was greatly broadened by empowering the federal government to set standards for the exhaust emissions of automobiles and accelerate necessary research.

Changing the quality of life

Johnson continued to pursue the main objective of his Great Society program: changing the *quality* of American life, now that bountiful affluence had demonstrated that, for most Americans, the question of *quantity* had been solved. At his urging, nine new national park and recreation areas were established (making a total of fifteen since 1961). This constituted the first major addition to the nation's park system since the days of Franklin Roosevelt. The Wilderness Act, which the Sierra Club and other environmentalist organizations had been pushing for years, had moved forward with President Kennedy's support and was passed under President Johnson in September 1964. By its provisions, some nine million acres of wilderness were to be kept in that condition, and another fifty million acres examined for inclusion in the system.

Meanwhile, an ambitious program for the revitalization of the depressed and despoiled Appalachian region swept through Congress in March 1965 with a $1.1 billion authorization. Since the area redevelopment program of the Kennedy administration had come to a halt because its efforts were too thinly spread, in August 1965 the Johnson administration secured creation of the Economic Development Administration. Its task was to locate those centers of economic activity that, if given a boost upward, could reawaken the business life of entire regions. With some $500 million authorized for the building of crucial public works that would stimulate economic growth, it became the new national agency for regional development.

For the big cities, with their masses of ill-housed and restive poor—and their frightening riots—Johnson secured establishment of the Department of Housing and Urban Development. Robert C. Weaver became its first secretary and the first black American to serve in the cabinet. Some $7.8 billion was provided for urban redevelopment and public housing, added to in 1966 by another enactment that provided rent supplements to poor families so they could live in better quarters.

Did it all help?

In the late 1960s and into the 1970s, it became politically fashionable to say that these many reforms of the Kennedy-Johnson years "threw money at problems," but did not solve them. Welfare was a mess; retraining did not retrain; medicare became just a corrupt rip-off. By 1976,

The need for a national anti-pollution effort displays itself, in 1966, in a panorama of polluted air hanging heavily over New York City. Such palls led to sharply increased deaths.
Neal Boenzi, NYT Pictures

however, the dust was settling, and scholarly studies revealed these views incorrect. The system as it had evolved was admittedly complex, but then, the problem of caring for the unfortunate was complex. The combination of improved Social Security System aid, covering practically all workers, with benefits linked to the cost of living; unemployment compensation; public assistance to the aged, blind, and disabled; Aid to Families with Dependent Children (fatherless families), the most controversial; and food stamps, a near-cash program for the needy, functioned reasonably well, bringing practically all citizens at least up to the poverty threshold.

The Medicare and Medicaid programs of the Great Society went far toward ending the aged's main worry, and one of the great problems of the poor. More medical care was in fact provided, and it was genuinely re-allocated so it reached people formerly ignored. The housing programs, both by direct construction and rent subsidies, helped bring low-income minority families out of ghettoes and into better residential areas. Retrained persons actually improved their wages, and began to acquire a much higher level of job stability. The higher earnings they received far exceeded the average cost of the programs, profiting both individuals and the whole society. Civil rights laws vastly improved the political and social situation of minorities. Federal aid for higher education greatly expanded the availability of such resources, and made it possible for tens of thousands with low incomes, especially among minorities, to secure the benefits of college study. In short, while the Great Society did not end racial inequality, eliminate poverty, equalize income, or establish full employment—achievements beyond the reach of any human government, in any reasonable time span—it did bring about very substantial improvements in the national standard of living by lifting the poor to a minimal standard of living, and opening new doors to a better life for multitudes formerly ignored.

The tragedy of Johnson

Despite these massive gifts to the nation, Lyndon Johnson was forced in 1968 to concede that his popularity was so low that he could not run for reelection. Part of the reason for the collapse of his popularity lay in his almost pathological passion for secrecy. He frequently made statements to reporters they knew were not true, covered his tracks with small lies, and denied taking steps that were publicly known. He would state categorically that no one wrote speeches for him, though everyone knew who his speechwriters were; he had more than a hundred scholars studying national problems for him and making recommendations, but he never publicly admitted this, revealed their names, or released their reports. He wanted people to think that everything came from *him.* Distrust of what he said spread among reporters in his first two years in office, and then out to the larger public, until it stained everything he undertook. The war in Vietnam became one massive deception. Even when he announced, in 1968, that he would not run again for the presidency, many did not believe him.

The irony is that the president never understood the public's distrust. He regarded it as created by a conspiracy among eastern intellectuals and newspaper reporters. Johnson was always prickly about being a Texan and a graduate of San Marcos State Teachers College. If he were only a Harvard man, he would acidly say, they would all treat him well. As a self-professed "country boy," he recoiled from the big cities and the suburbs; their way of life he neither liked nor understood. Northeasterners in general seemed to him arrogant and conceited. These, of course, have been the classic feelings of outsiders whether they were Scotsmen rankling at the snobbery of Englishmen, Boston Irishmen resentful at the condescension of old-line Yankees, or Mexican-Americans in California angry at being talked down to by Anglo-Saxon school teachers. And, in truth, cultivated Londoners never laughed more readily at the clotted accent of a Glasgow Scotsman than New Yorkers at the broad west Texas drawl of Lyndon Johnson. Their attitude hurt the president deeply. "Want to know what's wrong with Lyndon?" asked John Connally, the president's shrewd and intimate friend. "He's ashamed of being a Texan." It made him an obstinate braggart, a big man who felt compelled to put up a small man's boastful front.

The Johnson ego

Urban Americans had liked John Kennedy's lightness, his wry taste for understatement, and for not always taking himself seriously. But there was little wit about Johnson: his manner was heavy and pontifical; his humor coarse and earthy. Many Americans were offended by his immense ego, which had him spreading the initials *LBJ* on everything—from his shirts and his ranch to his wife and daughters. Always absorbed in himself, after he had undergone an abdominal operation the president thought that certainly the nation would be eager to see his scar, but when he yanked up his shirt to display it to photographers, the public shivered in distaste. Then came the horror of Vietnam.

"Johnson's almost desperate need for loyalty was the other half of the coin of insecurity of this great towering figure . . . [who] in so many important sections of [Washington] felt himself an alien, the Texas ruffian among the perfumed darlings of the East. It was a profound part of him; his sense of being alien, of the prejudice against him, was never assuaged. In October, 1964, when George Ball handed in his first memo against the [Vietnam] war, Johnson turned to an aide and said, 'You've got to be careful of these Eastern lawyers. If you're not careful they'll take you and turn you inside out.' He was haunted by regional prejudice. . . . Later, after he left office, he became convinced that it was his Southern origins, not the war, which had driven him out, that they had lain in wait for an issue, any issue, and had used the war, which was their war in the first place, to drive him from office. . . . He had triumphed over one area of Washington, the doers, the movers, men of the South and West, shrewd insiders, but he had always failed in another area, the tastemakers, so much more Eastern, more effete, judging him on qualities to which he could never aspire. . . . (David Halberstam, "Lyndon," *Esquire* [August 1972].)

The tragedy of Lyndon Johnson was very real. He loved America, and he hungered for its people to love him. But beginning in 1966 the bottom fell out; in fact there was no bottom there. The congressional elections of that year were disaster for the Democrats. In time, the president took to cloistering himself in the White House, peering distrustfully at the sightseers gathered at the fence, and muttering that he could count on no one. Always resentful of criticism, he consulted with a smaller and smaller group of people within the administration. Johnson, in truth, was that man of whom Hamlet spoke:

> So, oft it chances in particular men
> That for some vicious mole of nature in them
> . . . Carrying, I say, the stamp of one defect
> . . . His virtues else—be they as pure as grace
> . . . Shall in the general censure take corruption
> From that particular fault.

This enormously egocentric man, caught in the pitiless eye of modern television and in the total exposure of modern communications, could build no reservoir of affection and trust in mid-twentieth-century America, the country he wanted so much to serve and to lead.

The nation swings to the right

In 1968 the United States was swinging rapidly to the right. This movement could be easily explained as a reaction against a bitterly unpopular war and a characteristic and traditional turn toward conservatism after the great outburst of reform in Johnson's first two years.

Deeper and more fundamental, however, was a crucial shift that had taken place in American politics. The massive aid given to black Americans in the 1960s, the first such boost in a century, had come from the Democrats. This meant that that party had become identified with black America in the same way that, in the nineteenth century it had been identified with Irish America. The "Irishness" that had radiated from the Democrats in that time had offended Anglo-Saxon Protestant Americans. Now the "blackness" that seemed equally to characterize the Democrats caused white America—or substantial portions of it—to recoil. The burning cities of 1968 led many whites to believe that blacks were an ungrateful, inherently violent, and "uppity" people whose rise to power would gravely threaten the nation. The United States as a whole, in other words, was becoming in a certain sense "southernized." As never before, politics in the northern and western states began to throb to the same white supremacy beat that for generations had provided the fundamental rhythm in southern public life. Rocked by massive disorders and frightened at the swiftly rising crime rate—for which black America was everywhere blamed—the white majority turned toward the law-and-order appeals of the Republicans.

In addition to this, the classic cultural issues that have traditionally aided the Republicans were dinning into everyone's ears: rebellious youth, women's liberation, the drug scene, and new styles of life. Many Americans were uneasy because the whole nature of national culture had shifted in non-WASP directions. For generations Anglo-Saxon Protestants had run the nation's cultural life. We have seen how, in the 1920s, the new movie industry had introduced a strong Jewish, Italian, and Greek influence into cultural life, but even then the movie moguls and the stars they hired Anglicized their names and built their plots around predominantly small-town WASP themes. The novelists, historians, lawyers, and social scientists whom the historian Henry Steele Commager discussed in his widely read book *The American Mind* (1951) were practically all WASP: F. Scott Fitzgerald, Ernest Hemingway, Carl Sandburg, Sinclair Lewis, John Dewey, William James, Henry James, Charles Beard, Edmund Wilson, Oliver Wendell Holmes, and Lester Frank Ward. Intellectual life was expressed in *The Atlantic* (edited by Edward Weeks), and *Harper's* (edited by Frederick Lewis Allen). *The Saturday Evening Post, Collier's, The Country Gentlemen, The American Magazine*—these were the popular magazines, filled with stories and articles redolent of WASP interests and values, which sold in the millions of copies in the 1930s and 1940s. If someone was a black, a Mexican-American, a Jew, or an Italian, a Pole, a Greek, or a Russian, and he wanted to make it in American cultural life, he had to learn the style, the accent, and the value system of the dominant culture. Whatever was "American" was WASP.

Decline of the WASP

But by the late 1960s, even though WASP America still ran the Establishment—the corporations, country clubs, foundations, universities, the military, and the government—in cultural life a transformation had taken place. The names themselves tell the story: novelists Norman Mailer, Philip Roth, Bernard Malamud, Saul Bellow, James Baldwin; the scientists Robert Oppenheimer and Edward Teller; reformers Ralph Nader, Cezar Chavez, and Saul Alinsky; the sociologists David Riesman and Lewis Feuer; social philosophers Paul Goodman and Robert Marcuse; the psychologist of youth, Erik Erikson; the historian Richard Hofstadter. Scott Momaday, an American Indian, won the Pulitzer Prize for fiction in 1969, and the prize for nonfiction was split between Norman Mailer, a Jew from Brooklyn, and René Dubos, an immigrant from France. Aided by the flood of immigrant intellectuals who had fled Hitler's Europe in the 1930s, American cultural life had become pluralistic, ethnic, black, and anti-WASP. *The Saturday Evening Post* was dead (later partially revived), and the black ghetto, rock music, Hindu gurus, Zen philosophy, Jewish anarchists, even Chairman Mao Tse-Tung, were the new lodestones. Obscene words long excluded from ordinary conversation by traditional standards became commonplace utterances. The old mainstream of culture had lost its magnetic attraction; there were many strands, accents, hair styles, and audiences.

The fact that many whose parents had come to America in the great migration from 1890 to 1920—Italians, Greeks, Jews—were prosperous and successful by the 1960s, introduced a new complication. They and the older outsiders, like the Irish Catholics, had become country-club members, owners of suburban homes, and college graduates. For them there was no revolt from WASPdom, but acceptance into it. Identifying with the values and life style of traditional America, they, too, recoiled from the new cultural confusion. Often the most militant spokesmen for WASP values have been these new recruits to that world, for whom Spiro Agnew became a chief advocate, the symbol of the shift rightward.

The ethnic vote

Even so, it remained true in the 1960s, as from the beginning of American history, that the bulk of the ethnic outgroups continued to vote Democratic, though the pattern varied significantly. During the reign of the popular Dwight Eisenhower, the Republicans had made heavy inroads (at least in balloting for the president) into the immense European Catholic bloc, which had for so long voted as high as four-to-one for Democrats; that is, among the Irish, Italian, and Slavic (Polish, Czech, Russian, and Hungarian) voters. John Kennedy pulled most of them back in 1960—especially the Slavic voters, consistently the most liberal and pro-Democratic among the European Catholics—but, at that, his majorities among the Irish and Italians were not of the top-heavy variety, nor were they among the Jews and black Americans. Only the Latin Catholics, particularly the Mexican-Americans, turned out in unprecedentedly high numbers for him, producing the classic four-to-one vote that Democrats had always relied on among the ethnic outgroups to overbalance the huge WASP support Republicans could anticipate.

But by 1964 the tide was running strongly in traditional directions again. Kennedy's presidency, Lyndon Johnson's reformism for all groups, and the caustic right-wing conservatism of the Republican candidate in 1964, Barry Goldwater, unified the ethnic groups behind the Democratic banner. Blacks, European and Latin Catholics, and Jews trooped en masse behind Johnson. The massiveness of the black vote, both North and South, set the stage for the continuation of major reforms for blacks in Johnson's second administration. It also began a quiet revolution in the southern states, where the emergence of a large black voting bloc put Afro-Americans in a crucial balance-of-power position. From this point on, as later events made clear, the support of black voters for a white candidate in local southern politics would practically assure his election.

The accession of Richard M. Nixon

Senator Eugene McCarthy of Minnesota caused a political sensation when, in March 1968, he nearly defeated President Johnson in the New Hampshire primary after a campaign attacking Johnson's Vietnam policy. When the president shortly announced that he would not run for reelection, a hectic Democratic race began. Soon Senator Robert Kennedy of New York, the martyred president's brother, was in the lead for the nomination, but his shocking murder in June sent all into confusion again. When the Democrats gathered in Chicago, Vice-President Hubert Humphrey was able to win the nomination, but only after the Democratic party had been ripped apart by a mini-war that Chicago policemen launched against anti-Vietnam War protestors outside the convention hall. Through the summer and early fall, Humphrey's campaign limped along through a nightmare of howling obstructionism—the candidate could hardly be heard—mounted by hostile young war critics, who lumped Humphrey with the Johnson policy on Vietnam.

Meanwhile, the Republicans had turned to "Mr. Republican," Richard M. Nixon. Although he had not won an elective office on his own since 1950 (when he was elected a senator from California) and had lost narrowly against John Kennedy in 1960 and disgracefully against Pat Brown when he ran for governor of California in 1962, Nixon was still an amazingly potent and lively public figure. For more than twenty years he had been at the peak of national political life; only Johnson could match him in his long experience of closeness to power. Freshman congressman in 1946 (with John Kennedy), a household familiarity since the days of Alger Hiss, always controversial, intensely disliked and rarely loved, he was the kind of career politician who had no roots anywhere but in public life.

Campaign of 1968

Keying his presidential campaign to the law-and-order theme and giving the impression that he intended to get the nation out of Vietnam, Nixon went about the country speaking of the "crime crisis" and of the need for a reestablishment of authority in American life over young people and the turbulent cities. Spiro Agnew, the Republican vice-presidential nominee, called Humphrey "squishy soft" on communism. Confident, well-organized, heavily financed, the Republican campaign was far ahead of the Democrats in the national polls, and seemingly on the verge of a landslide. But then George Wallace, former governor of Alabama who was the presidential nominee of the American Independent party, came up to slice away huge volumes of votes on the right wing, since Wallace was recognized as an openly antiblack candidate who advocated a hard line in Vietnam. In the balloting Nixon won only a small popular vote plurality of 500,000 votes in a total of 74 million cast. With 43.4 percent to Humphrey's 42.7 percent and Wallace's 13.5 percent, Nixon had the smallest victory margin since Woodrow Wilson's in 1912. Indeed, for the first time since Zachary Taylor's election in 1848, a newly elected president went into office with both houses of Congress in the hands of the other party, for the Democrats retained control in the Capitol.

There was a shaking, however, in the traditional European Catholic and Democratic voting bloc. While blacks, Latin Catholics, and Jews continued in 1968, as in 1964, to turn out almost unanimously for the Democratic candidate, Nixon and Wallace together achieved a significant invasion of the European Catholic group. (Also, it should be pointed out, the numbers of Latin Catholics and northern blacks who actually went to the polls and voted continued a slide begun in 1964.) The Irish and the Slavic voters remained firm, casting about two-thirds of their votes for Humphrey, but among the Italians he was able to garner only a bit more than half the ballots. Perhaps it was among this ethnic group, still heavily rooted in the inner cities, that the factor of backlash against black rioting was strongest. For that matter, there have always been enclaves—such as New Haven, Connecticut—where Italians, much less devoutly Catholic than the Irish, have voted strongly Republican. Indeed, Nixon actually won a majority of the Italian vote

in New York in 1968, the *first* time any Republican presidential candidate had ever carried any of the six major ethnic groups in any state. In state politics, Republican candidates found themselves pulling ever larger groups of Italians away from the Democrats, though only if they were liberal, not conservative, Republicans.

Nixon as Republican

President Nixon sprang from a classically Republican background and exhibited classically Republican outlooks. He believed America to be a good land where a life of comfort and self-respect was available to all who would work for it. Reliance on government for aid would be unmanly. The nation's leadership should come from its business community; the "enemy" consisted of agitators and law-breakers. The American system, if allowed to operate freely—that is, without the intrusion of government—would solve the country's social ills. Richard Nixon was the first chief executive to come from California, but his identity, indeed, was not sectional but social and cultural: he sprang from the mainstream of WASP America. He was small town and lower middle class in his origins, reared in a world of sober coats and ties and consciously well-bred manners. In his world, bold expansiveness in personal style or sophisticated and worldly habits were frowned on. Neat and close-cropped hair styles, efficiency and order, closely buttoned vests—these were the hallmarks of Nixon's milieu.

The Nixons, like so many Republican families before them in American history, were zealously religious and moralistic. They were part of that classically Republican faith, Quakerism. English in ethnic origin, Tory in the Revolution, and Whig in Jackson's time, Quakers helped found the Republican party and traditionally disliked Democrats as drinkers, racists, and non-WASP Catholics. The Nixons were a family of true believers: in religion and politics they knew exactly who they were and where they stood.

Doubt and skepticism had little standing. Nixon's father was a hot-tempered and argumentative man who laid down strict rules in his household and reached quickly for the strap to enforce them. The aura of the Nixon family was one in which team spirit and the importance of following orders were primary values.

Nixon's enemy fixation

It is not surprising, therefore, that the president who came from this setting was a self-righteous man given to preaching moralistic sermons to the nation; an intensely combative and partisan man who for years carried the reputation of resorting to low blows in attacking his political opponents. What he enjoyed most of all in politics, he once observed, was the "battle itself." Richard Nixon knew who the enemy was; he had absolute confidence in his views; and had long suspected (and said) that the other side must somehow be disloyal to America. No belief, indeed, is more characteristically Republican. From the days of the Federalists to those of the mid-twentieth century, the cry of "subversion" and "un-American" has been the most instinctive cry of the political right wing when attacking Democrats. The WASP party has traditionally felt itself to be uniquely American, the minority outgroups behind the Democrats to be ineradicably "foreign," and the party itself given to un-American ideas.

Team-spirit Americanism was strong in Richard Nixon. He wanted to see the United States "number one" in the world—in everything. He was fascinated by football, a notably military-style sport, and gave the generals and admirals far more prestige and influence in his administration than they had under the Democrats. Veterans organizations uniformly applauded the president, as they had former Republican chief executives, for they recognized in him a kindred spirit in his intense patriotism, dislike of liberals, and preference for men in uniform. Police forces, fire departments, and National Guard organizations looked on him as their natural leader, for he preached law and order, was unsympathetic to blacks and rioting youth, and believed that authority and a strong hand, rather than social reforms, were what was needed to bring peace to the country.

The Nixon presidency

The Nixon presidential style, too, was in the traditional Republican mold. Here was a chief executive who would go months on end without a press conference; who secluded himself daily for many hours while, alone in a small office, he ruminated his policies. The active president, working assiduously with Congress, educating and inspiring the nation by frequent addresses, and driving through domestic reforms—this model disappeared, to be replaced by the remote and silent Nixon, regarded as hermitlike even by his staff. Shy and retiring anyway, a terribly private man, and one who believed America is fundamentally sound, he once observed, "I've always thought this country could run itself domestically, without a President. All you need is a competent Cabinet to run the country. . . . You need a President for foreign policy." Within the White House great stress was placed on orderliness and efficiency.

Congress receded, as is usually the case in Republican administrations, for the president made little use of it. There was an almost studious ignoring of the congressional barons, who fumed that they could not get through to the president: his huge staff of assistants (larger than that of any former chief executive) refused to let them have access. Nixon put much emphasis on the dignity of the presidency and toyed for a while with the idea of rather florid, European-style uniforms for the White House guard—until dissuaded by public ridicule. He was deeply impressed by France's Charles de Gaulle, the majestic president of the French Republic who insisted that a national leader must maintain distance, aloofness, and mystery to establish effective rule. All this was to have serious reper-

Lyndon Johnson and his successor, Richard M. Nixon, on inauguration day, 1969. Veteran Washington figures, they carried the "imperial presidency" to new and appalling heights, the one in a tragic foreign war, the other in both that war and in the Watergate conspiracy.
Elliott Erwitt, Magnum Photos, Inc.

cussions later on, for the Watergate scandal that erupted at the outset of his second term—an event unprecedented in the history of the presidency for its extensiveness and grave moral implications—was widely attributed to the secretive, conspiratorial air that such presidential isolation produced.

Nixon's assistants

The president and America's intellectuals regarded each other with mutual distaste. Save for Daniel Moynihan, for two years (1969–1970) his adviser on urban affairs, and Dr. Henry Kissin-

ger, his adviser on foreign relations and, from 1973, secretary of state, few were on his staff. Most of his assistants were men with long experience in advertising and skilled in projecting images and appearances—in "managed" news and packaging—not in generating ideas. Indeed, they had little practical political experience of the kind that involved walking precincts and talking with constituents. They thought of government as a power to be used, rather than as a democratic instrument in close touch with the people. Nixon's was a strangely unusual Republican administration in that it had few ties even with corporate America, though the president certainly followed policies aiding big business. The president's two principal aides—until they had to resign in 1973 because of the Watergate scandal—were H. R. Haldeman, a crew-cut, well-mannered, well-organized advertising man from California who served with great loyalty as Nixon's chief of staff, and John Ehrlichman, a hard-driving, supremely self-confident lawyer from the state of Washington, who contrasted sharply in style and character to Haldeman. Counselor to the president, and then from 1970 the aide in charge of domestic affairs, Ehrlichman brought to his post a biting, caustic arrogance that rubbed most of Washington raw, a fact that bothered him not at all, since he felt Washingtonians had only an amused contempt for patriotism and moral virtue.

The veteran reporter Stewart Alsop, reflecting on the tone of this administration, wrote that the president "is not just square—he is *totally* square. His political strategy is based on the assumption that a majority of the American electorate consists of people like himself—middle-class squares." There was no humor, no jauntiness; there were no Jews (save Kissinger), blacks, or big-city ethnics; it was the evangelist Billy Graham who had the president's ear, not some liberal intellectual. The White House was light years removed from the booming earthiness of Lyndon Johnson or the folksy Jacksonianism of Harry Truman.

The first two years: Time of troubles

In domestic affairs the president entered office without any great goals in mind save to fight crime and disorder, pull the white South into his party by sharply slowing down desegregation, and turn the federal government back into older, more conservative patterns. The economy was suffering from inflation, caused principally by the fact that Lyndon Johnson had poured billions into Vietnam and into social reform while refusing to raise taxes and dampen purchasing power. Like Eisenhower before him, Nixon listened to those economic advisers who told him that inflation must be halted at all costs, primarily by tightening up on interest rates and reducing government spending. This would mean higher unemployment, for high interest rates would mean less money available for the economy, but the president was willing to accept that prospect. Since he was determined not to reduce military spending, the cuts in government expenditures would have to come in social services.

Slashes in social services went along with his overall political strategy in any event, since the president was seeking to attract the conservative, antiblack Wallace vote by throttling back on social reform. The cities, low-income housing, the War on Poverty, welfare programs—these would receive only minimal attention in the Nixon years. At the same time, the president revived the venerable Republican tradition of keeping hands off the daily operations of the national economy. The Johnson and Kennedy administrations had constantly jaw-boned industrialists and labor leaders, exhorting them to keep the rise in wages and prices within guidelines established by the White House. But Richard Nixon, devoted supporter of the classic laissez-faire American business system, abruptly ended this practice. The market was allowed to operate freely without hindrance from the White House. The result was a swift rise in prices. When Johnson had kept the pressure on, prices in a key group of industries had risen by less than two percent, but in 1969 alone they rose by six percent. At the same time, the president got Congress to end (in stages) the ten percent surtax on incomes that Johnson had established in the hope of reducing spending power and thus inflationary pressure. This, too, helped to put more steam in the economic boiler. By the end of 1969 inflation had risen to the highest rate since the Korean War, even though the squeeze on credit (the tight money policy) was so severe that national productivity was slowing rapidly and unemployment was soaring.

Landing on the moon

In July 1969, the twenty-four billion dollar space program achieved its most breathtaking success when astronaut Neil Armstrong descended to the moon from his *Apollo 11* spacecraft, saying "That's one small step for a man, one giant leap for mankind." The whole world was astonished by this incredible event (which, in later missions, quickly came to seem commonplace), and jubilant President Nixon called Armstrong on the moon by telephone to communicate his delighted congratulations. But this was a rare unifying event for Americans in this troubled year. There had already been a long, acrimonious fight in Congress over whether to continue spending on the anti-ballistic missile system. The president had won a limited victory in March 1969, but there was a rising tendency to condemn a scale of national priorities that poured billions into fantastic weapons and a fruitless war, while ignoring the country's domestic ills.

The president had come to office a stern critic of the way in which the Supreme Court, under Earl Warren, had steadily broadened the rights of accused criminals. In May 1969, Warren retired, and the president promptly nominated Warren E. Burger, a law-and-order advocate, to replace Warren as chief justice, receiving Senate confirmation in June. Nixon was determined to place conservatives on the bench, and, in May 1970, Harry A. Blackmun, a relatively conservative and thoroughly competent jurist from Minnesota, was approved as his next appointment. He quickly joined Chief Justice Burger in a decision limiting freedom of the press in obscenity matters. In 1971, the president was given a remarkable opportunity to change the whole character of the Court's outlook within one presidential term when John Marshall Harlan and Hugo Black retired. Choosing Lewis Franklin Powell, Jr., a respected Virginia lawyer, and William H. Rehnquist, a young (age forty-seven) and talented assistant United States attorney general, the president thereby completed a group of four conservatives on the bench who would profoundly affect later decisions. The predictably liberal justices remaining in the Court were William J. Brennan, Jr., William O. Douglas (who resigned in 1975 to be replaced by John Paul Stevens of Chicago, a centrist), and Thurgood Marshall; Potter Stewart and Byron White were regarded as "swing men."

Domestic reform

In 1972, Congress enacted the nation's first federally guaranteed minimum income by making major changes in the social security system. Beginning in 1974, those over sixty-five years of age (together with the blind or permanently disabled of any age) were to receive payments sufficient to maintain their incomes at $130 a month ($195 for couples). Furthermore, an escalator clause was built in so that benefits would rise automatically to keep pace with the cost of living, while the social security tax would rise as wages, nationwide, rise.

Using the slogan New Federalism, the president said that the time had come to reverse the long-term trend toward a more powerful federal government. State and local governments should be revitalized by channeling to them large quantities of the revenue received by the federal government. Such governments were buried in endless fiscal crises because their sources of revenue (property and sales taxes) were limited and regressive. Property owners across the nation protested against higher taxes on their land, and sales taxes always hit hardest those with modest incomes (who must spend a high proportion of their income on the necessities of life). The federal government had the seemingly bottomless cornucopia of the income tax at its disposal. Revenue-sharing, therefore, was established in 1972, when Congress enacted a program that would grant $30.2 billion to the states over a five-year period.

Antipollution measures

The president took major steps to help stop environmental pollution, a problem that in 1970 seized the nation's consciousness with great force. He reorganized all federal agencies dealing with environmental issues, putting them under the Environmental Protection Agency, which was given power to enforce federal laws concerning pollution. The Council on Environmental Quality was to advise the president on national policy and coordinate all planning. A third agency, the National Oceanic and Atmospheric Agency, pulled together all government research agencies and concentrated scientific efforts dealing with pollution. Then Congress, heeding environmentalist arguments concerning massive aerial pollution (and economists' arguments concerning profitability) cut off all funds supporting the development of a supersonic transport plane, thus ending the project.

A major advance came in the passage of the Clean Air Act of 1970, which required the establishment of national emission standards for all "significant new pollution sources," to include the automobile. In June 1971, the Environmental Protection Agency ordered such stringent standards for the emission of hydrocarbons, carbon monoxide, and nitrogen oxides that, if they had fully implemented, would have cut automobile pollutants by ninety percent by 1976. In response, the huge research programs that automobile manufacturers had already begun into types of engines that would reduce pollutants were accelerated.

The Environmental Protection Agency seized on a long ignored statute, the Refuse Act of 1899, that gave the federal government power to control all discharge of polluting substances into the nation's navigable water courses. Scores of criminal actions were begun against polluters of navigable waterways in 1971, and injunctions were secured to halt discharges. Thus heartened, the state governments moved ahead on their own.

The federal government in 1971 began reasserting its power to prevent pollution of waterways, typified here in West Virginia. Huge industrial processes empty waste products into the Monongahela River.
Bruce Davidson, © 1969 Magnum Photos

California had long led the nation in its extensive program of research and public controls on aerial pollution. Now, in 1971, the state of Delaware enacted a law banning all heavy industry along its entire coastline and severely controlled tanker-loading operations. In Maine, an environmental commission began reviewing all developments involving twenty acres or more, and other states adopted strong regulations on pesticides, notably DDT. The phosphate content of detergents similarly came under close public attention, for this material, washed into rivers and lakes, killed fish and plant life. New Jersey ordered that sewage sludge and industrial wastes were not to be discharged within 100 miles of its coastline, and other states moved ahead to control the discharge of solid wastes. Everywhere, environmentalists were able to take advantage of the provision in the National Environment Protection Act that required that environmental impact studies be made before any federally funded project could be built.

In 1972 Congress enacted a massive program to clean up the nation's polluted waterways by 1985. President Nixon vetoed the bill on the ground of cost, but Congress repassed the bill over his veto (and Nixon immediately impounded the funds). Controls were also established over pesticides, and antinoise legislation aimed at all noise producers, especially airports, was enacted.

Year of political crisis: 1970

The year 1970 was one of growing national political crisis. The president had announced in June 1969 his "Vietnamization" policy, which entailed the progressive withdrawal of American troops, but the nation had sickened of the whole affair, and pressure for more rapid withdrawal mounted. In April 1970 the president announced that 150,000 men would be brought home within a year; but almost immediately (on April 30) he launched a massive invasion of Cambodia in an attempt to cut down the Communist buildup of arms and troops. This touched off equally massive protests across the campuses and throughout the country.

Then came the crucial congressional elections of November. Nixon chose to make this election not a national discussion of his accomplishments but a smear campaign against the Democrats. The nation, by now, was haunted by the law-and-order issue. Violent radicals on both the right and the left—but mostly on the left—were reaching a bloody summit in their mindless attacks upon society. The Weathermen and other revolutionary and anarchist extremist groups did not confine themselves to words: they threw bombs everywhere. By the end of the year the Federal Bureau of Investigation counted 3,000 bombings and 50,000 threatened bombings that cleared important buildings of their occupants over and over again. It was a frantic time of constant disorder and terrorism. And across the nation, people blamed it all on young people and blacks.

Now Richard Nixon turned to the "square majority." Mounting an unprecedented three-week campaign (presidents rarely intervene in the off-year congressional elections), he hammered over and over again on the classic cultural themes that Republicans for decades have concentrated on: law and order, the breakdown of authority, the arrogance of youth, the spreading blight of permissiveness, pornography and obscenity, and the new curse of drugs. Sounding like the Nixon of the 1950s, he accused the Democrats of adopting soft tactics toward the Communist menace.

The Democrats were able to take advantage of *their* classic issue—economics. The country was sliding deeper into recession. The number of unemployed was moving up toward five million, and by election time the rate of unemployment stood at nearly six percent. Inflation continued spiraling upward. In short, the country had entered an almost unprecedented situation in which prices were rising while millions were losing their jobs. The country was in grave economic crisis while the president, as one leading Republican was heard to say, was "running for sheriff." It was a repellent spectacle, and Nixon suffered for it: the Democrats largely held their own in Congress and swept to victory in most of the state gubernatorial elections.

The years 1971 and 1972, however, were almost completely dominated by the president's bold ventures in foreign relations. We shall now, therefore, turn our attention to the great issue that destroyed the Johnson presidency and wholly absorbed President Nixon's first term: the war in Vietnam.

Bibliography

Three books that were especially valuable to me in writing this chapter: I learned a great deal from James L. Sundquist's scholarly and remarkably comprehensive book, *Politics and Policy: The Eisen-*

hower, Kennedy, and Johnson Years (1968). Hugh Sidey's A Very Personal Presidency (1968) is a brilliant analysis of Johnson by a veteran White House reporter. I have relied strongly, too, on Mark R. Levy and Michael S. Kramer's detailed study, The Ethnic Factor: How America's Minorities Decide Elections* (1973).

How have historians looked at the topic?

Robert Frost wrote a poem for the 1961 inauguration in which he spoke of "young ambition eager to be tried." The man whom Frost celebrated—John F. Kennedy—had been groomed for a political career, and many Americans hoped with Robert Frost that he would initiate "a golden age of poetry and power." Kennedy's background may be studied in Richard J. Whalen's fascinating biography, The Founding Father: The Story of Joseph P. Kennedy (1964), in Robert J. Donovan's story of his naval career, PT 109: John F. Kennedy in World War II* (1961), and in James M. Burns's balanced account of the prepresidential years, John F. Kennedy: A Political Profile (1959).

The difficulties involved in translating ideas into laws are skillfully revealed in Theodore C. Sorenson's Kennedy* (1965) and Arthur M. Schlesinger's A Thousand Days: John F. Kennedy in the White House* (1965). Tom Wicker's JFK and LBJ: The Influence of Personality upon Politics* (1968) also probes the defeat of President Kennedy's domestic program. The economic policies of the Kennedy government are illuminated in Hobart Rowen's The Free Enterprisers (1964) and James Heath's The Kennedy Administration and the Business Community (1969). Aida DePace Donald's John F. Kennedy and the New Frontier* (1967) is a valuable collection of appraisals of the former president.

Lyndon Johnson's earthy Texas style is emphasized in Alfred Steinberg's Sam Johnson's Boy (1968), which contains a great deal of political gossip about Johnson's "ruthless drive for power." An astute analysis of Johnson's public career that highlights his years in the Senate is found in Rowland Evans and Robert Novak's

Lyndon B. Johnson: The Exercise of Power* (1966). Theodore White explains the origins of a lopsided election in The Making of the President, 1964* (1965) and a vivid account of the Republican National Convention of that year is a part of The Presidential Papers of Norman Mailer (1964). Johnson's performance as a mandated president is criticized by historian Eric Goldman (briefly a White House adviser) in The Tragedy of Lyndon Johnson* (1969).

President Kennedy's troubled response to Michael Harrington's The Other America* (1962) set the War on Poverty in motion. Other graphic accounts that stirred public attention include Harry Caudill's Night Comes to the Cumberlands* (1963), Oscar Lewis's La Vida: A Puerto Rican Family in the Culture of Poverty—San Juan and New York* (1969), and Daniel P. Moynihan's The Negro Family: The Case for National Action (1965). Moynihan presents the case against community action in Maximum Feasible Misunderstanding (1968). The best analysis of Johnson's ill-fated poverty program is in John C. Donovan's The Politics of Poverty* (1967), an excellent book that explains why exposés of poverty continue to be written—for example, Robert Coles's Still Hungry in America (1969) and Kenneth Davis's The Paradox of Poverty in America (1969).

The urban crisis that the Johnson administration sought to resolve is described in Jane Jacobs's powerful study The Death and Life of Great American Cities* (1962) and in Robert L. Branyan and Lawrence H. Larsen's Urban Crisis in Modern America* (1971). The issue of environmental decay attained national prominence with Rachel Carson's The Silent Spring* (1964) and is further illuminated in George Laycock's The Diligent Destroyers (1970), Paul Ehrlich's two books The Population Bomb* (1968) and How to Be a Survivor* (1971), and in Robert M. Chute's Environmental Insight* (1971). Clark C. Havighurst explores public policy in Air Pollution Control (1969).

The swing to the right in the election of 1968 is reported in Theodore H. White's The Making of the President, 1968* (1969). Joe McGinniss describes the Nixon victory in different terms in his *The Selling of the President, 1968** (1969). The best book on the entire subject is Lewis Chester, Godfrey Hodgson, and Bruce Page's *An American Melodrama: The Presidential Campaign of 1968* (1969). Third party candidate George Wallace is the focus of a brilliant study by Marshall Frady, *Wallace* (1968).

The Nixon strategy is outlined in Kevin Phillips's *The Emerging Republican Majority* (1969). Always valuable for insight into Richard Nixon is his own *Six Crises** (1962). Paul Hoffman presents a critical and skeptical analysis of the president in *The New Nixon** (1970).

* Available in paperback.

CHAPTER 37

The End of American Innocence: The Vietnam War

TIME LINE

1954	France defeated at Dien Bien Phu; Geneva Conference divides Vietnam
1957	Rebellion underway in South Vietnam against Diem; Vietcong rises
1961	President Kennedy expands commitment to South Vietnam, sends in 16,000 advisers, and calls on Diem to democratize his regime
1963	Buddhists in South Vietnam rebel against Diem; Diem assassinated
1964	United States begins covert military operations against North Vietnam Gulf of Tonkin incident
1965	President Johnson begins Operation Rolling Thunder, enormously escalates war, sends in ground troops; Johnson sends troops to Dominican Republic to quell revolt
1966	France withdraws from NATO; Johnson liberalizes travel rules and trade with Russia; treaty with Russia bans placing nuclear weapons in orbit; Johnson goes to Manila to help launch massive program of economic development in Southeast Asia; Senate "doves" criticize war; Nguyen Van Thieu elected president of South Vietnam
1967	American policy in South Vietnam condemned around world; Secretary of Defense Robert McNamara states bombing is useless; immense peace demonstrations in the United States
1968	Vietcong Tet offensive devastates South Vietnam, humiliates Johnson's policies; Johnson suffers national loss of faith in his leadership, forced to announce halt to escalation and bombing, withdraws from presidential race; negotiations for peace in Vietnam begin in Paris
1969	President Nixon adopts deescalation and Vietnamization policies; Nixon and Henry Kissinger formulate balance-of-power foreign policy; Guam Doctrine announced
1970	Strategic Arms Limitation Talks with Russia begin; Cambodian invasion
1972	North Vietnam makes massive conventional invasion of South Vietnam; United States revives aerial bombing; Thieu establishes dictatorship in South Vietnam; Nixon wins massive election victory over Democratic candidate, George McGovern; bombing attack on North Vietnam follows breakdown in negotiations
1973	Cease-fire in Vietnam; American forces withdraw; exchange of prisoners of war

N the day before his inauguration in 1961, John Kennedy sat in the cabinet room of the White House listening to Dwight Eisenhower talk worriedly about the Indochina situation. South Vietnam was on the verge of being overrun by a Communist-dominated insurgency, and in remote Laos, the rightist government and left-wing forces were at war. In the conflict between communism and democracy, Laos, Eisenhower said, was the key to all of Southeast Asia: if it went to the Communists, the other countries of that vast region would fall one by one like a string of dominoes. The United States, he remarked, might have to fight. From 1946 to 1954, America had poured billions of dollars into a French effort to put down Ho Chi Minh's Communist regime in North Vietnam. In 1954, the Geneva Convention gave the northern half of Vietnam to the Communists; and the United States, regarding this settlement as a disaster, pushed the French aside in South Vietnam and took over, buttressing and preserving its non-Communist government. Now that government was collapsing.

After his inauguration, President Kennedy secured the neutralization of Laos but felt impelled to pour major resources into South Vietnam (plus 16,000 noncombat troops as advisers) to stave off a Communist take-over. In 1965, when a Communist victory was again very near, Lyndon Johnson decided to take America to war. He sent into South Vietnam what became a force of more than 500,000 American troops and began a bombing campaign against North Vietnam. In 1968, after three years of growing protest in the United States and the failure of his military tactics, Johnson was forced to recognize the limits of American military power and cease the war's escalation.

In 1968 Richard Nixon became president of an American nation that was chastened at discovering that, like the ancient nations of Europe, it could be guilty of wrongfully using power. Nixon now changed the whole direction of American foreign policy. The new trend was toward withdrawal and a "low profile." While slowly pulling American combat troops out of Vietnam, Nixon drew back also from old commitments elsewhere, telling allies that henceforth they would need to rely much more on their own efforts for self-defense and economic development. As he thus disengaged the nation from old relationships, he startled the world by suddenly opening a Peking-Washington dialogue in 1971, traveling to that country for extensive discussions in the following year. With this shift, all power relationships in the world changed. In effect, the world order that had lasted since 1945 came to an end, and a new one was born. American military operations in Vietnam ceased in 1973.

Traditionally, a war once ended fades quickly from the national mind, unless it is one fought within the country's own territory and leaves visible scars. While the fighting goes on, the whole nation is wholly caught up in it, watching the terrible events with appalled fascination and a persistent anxiety about their outcome. When it is over, this fascination is replaced by a disinterest in what is felt to be merely military history, especially if the conflict took place abroad. The American dead are remembered primarily by their family members; the foreign dead, and the devastation left in their countries, are hardly thought of at all.

Following this rule, the United States' war in Vietnam, though it was the longest conflict in American history, left the American mind with almost startling celerity once it was over, perhaps speeded to this oblivion by the fact that it was in every way so doubtful an enterprise, and in many ways so shameful in its execution. All that remained was a shuddering conviction that it had been a great mistake, not ever to be repeated. It was a war, however, which perhaps above all others in the American past should not be allowed to be so conveniently set aside and forgotten. It was a searing learning experience of the profoundest importance, paid for by the lives of many thousands of young Americans, and many more thousands of Vietnamese. It is necessary to consider what happened, and to reflect upon it.

The Vietnamese background

Vietnam is a country 1,200 miles long. Placed on the American West Coast, it would stretch from Los Angeles to Seattle; on the East Coast, from Boston to Florida. Like rice baskets at the ends of a pole, two huge deltas occupy each end of the country: the Red River delta in the North, with its two major cities of Hanoi and Haiphong; and the Mekong delta in the South, with its nearby city of Saigon. The interior is mostly heavily forested hill country, thinly scattered with tribal peoples. Totaling some thirty-eight million in 1970, the Vietnamese population was divided almost equally between North and South. Europeans first arrived in Vietnam in 1615 when a French Catholic mission made its appearance. The Catholic fathers had a profound cultural influence on the country, installing Catholicism as a flourishing religion and putting the Vietnamese language into a Western-style alphabet. In 1885 Vietnam formally accepted French protectorate status.

The Japanese occupied Vietnam during World War II, though allowing the French (now defeated by Hitler) to continue governing the country and maintain military forces there. In 1945 the Japanese went to Hue, the old Vietnamese imperial capital, and informed Emperor Bao Dai, who had been the constitutional figurehead, that his country was independent. The emperor thereupon repudiated the old protectorate treaty of 1885, and French rule was legally ended. In August 1945, Ho Chi Minh, who for thirty years had worked to make his country independent, established a Communist-dominated government in Hanoi, received the official imperial seal from Bao Dai, and established the Provisional Government of the Democratic Republic of Vietnam.

But the French were determined to recapture their former colony. Soon they helped non-Communist nationalists establish a separate government in the South, based in Saigon. Now the French and the North Vietnamese government both made a grave miscalculation: each believed that they were strong enough to defeat the other in a short war. But when fighting broke out between them in late 1946, it did not end for eight years.

By this time the Cold War between America and Russia had long since begun, and the United States started giving its support to the French. Americans saw the conflict as a Communist—Free World struggle. From this point on, indeed, the United States intervened in Vietnam not because of any importance it attached to Vietnam itself, but because the unfortunate country had become linked in American minds with a larger global confrontation between democracy and communism.

The French were doomed to failure. Indeed, Communist General Vo Nguyen Giap had already explained what would happen. No democratic society such as France or the United States, he insisted, could ever fight endlessly an indefinite, inconclusive war unless its own survival was at stake. In time, public opinion in the democracy would demand an end to the "useless bloodshed"; the legislative body would demand explanations for the astronomical expenditures; and the democracy's military leaders would desperately promise a quick end to the conflict. This would prove impossible, their credibility would be ruined, and eventually the political leaders would accept any kind of settlement in order to end an otherwise endless guerrilla war. In May 1954 Ho Chi Minh's armies inflicted a catastrophic defeat on the French in the battle of Dien Bien Phu, and the war was over, for Giap was right: the people of France would no longer support a fruitless war. In the Geneva negotiations of July 1954, Vietnam was divided at the seventeenth parallel; the French withdrew from Indochina, having suffered 172,000 needless casualties; and the American period of dominance in the South began.

The American background

The American government took over as South Vietnam's protector in 1954 with little premonition of the tragedy that would follow. In fact, few people in the United States believed that America could *ever* suffer defeat. For generations, Americans had believed that theirs was such a good country, so pure and so right, that it could escape failure. Disasters, disappointments, irretrievable failure, they thought, happened to other countries, but America was exempt. At the beginning of the country's history, the Puritans had considered themselves the righteous fragment of mankind, and this conviction was as potent in the American mind in the 1950s as it had ever been before.

The Second World War, the primary learning experience for all American political leaders from 1940 on, powerfully strengthened this attitude. In that huge conflict the United States stood forth as the protector of human freedoms against tyranny. Then came the Cold War, capped by the Korean conflict, which made the United States even more a crusading nation bent on saving the whole world from evil. In this task, Americans assumed without question that whatever they did was morally good. Their mission in the world was to battle for freedom.

The Second World War also gave Americans confidence that whatever they set their minds upon, they could do. Such a notion was not new to them, for occupying a continent and building a great industrial system had long trained them to think in these terms. But the Second World War was such an enormous undertaking that American self-conceit mushroomed. A nation that could send tens of thousands of aircraft into the enemies' skies, cover the seas with ships, and send huge armies of men into battles around the globe, then top this incredible display by releasing the cosmic power of the atom, could only believe that its capabilities were boundless. In this frame of mind, the United States took on the role of international policeman. Assuming that it could "solve" the problem in Vietnam just as it was "solving" a multitude of conflicts elsewhere in the world, the American government entered a crucial stage in its self-education. It was to learn that there are indeed limits to its power. And it was also to learn the ancient lesson taught by Greek drama: no one escapes tragedy, for no one is innocent.

The two Vietnams

The two Vietnams made a disturbing contrast after 1954. The northern regime had immense advantages. For years on end it had fought bravely to throw off the hated French colonial power, a heroic achievement that had won it the abiding trust and loyalty of its people. Spartan, simple, autocratic, blooded in a long patriotic war, the North Vietnamese government could call endlessly on its citizens for further sacrifice in the holy cause of throwing out the foreigner and unifying all of Vietnam. Leading it was the venerable and honored Ho Chi Minh, who in North Vietnamese eyes blended in his person the roles of George Washington and Thomas Jefferson: father of his country and chief philosopher. Ho wore simple dress, stressed his links with the humble common people, and preferred to be thought of as "uncle," rather than as the awesome "father" of Vietnam culture. A devoted Communist, he believed in a sweeping social revolution aiming at equality of social and economic status. In Hanoi he presided over a clean, quiet, and simple city and a government notably free of corruption. North Vietnam, in short, resembled a well-run military post, unified from top to bottom by strong morale and a belief in its cause.

The South, on the other hand, was confused, spiritless, filled with dissension, and without any sense of national purpose. Its government was run by non-Communist nationalists who for years had been upstaged by the Communists. The southern nationalists were elitists, representatives of traditional Vietnam with a French overlay. Whereas Ho Chi Minh wore a simple peasant outfit, the southern leaders appeared either in mandarin dress or in the snowwhite business suits of the French colonial tradition. An upper-class regime through and through, the nationalist government based its power on the small urban population, looked down upon the farming people with contempt, and sided with the landlords. From the beginning, therefore, it was regarded with indifference by ordinary South Vietnamese.

American intelligence persistently warned Washington that the southern regime was unpopular. Ngo Dinh Diem, its president, was a devout and puritanical Roman Catholic who had been, throughout his career as a Vietnamese nationalist, just as anti-French as Ho Chi Minh. But he was "authoritarian, inflexible, and remote," the CIA observed, and quickly alienated practically everyone by his oppressive rule once he took office (with strong American support) in 1955.

Rebellion begins in the South

When the Geneva Convention had divided the country, in South Vietnam there was a tiny Communist cadre of perhaps 5,000 to 10,000 men, whom Ho instructed to work only peacefully for a changed regime in the South. They were to wait for the elections to be held in 1956, as provided in the Geneva agreement, which the Communists confidently expected to win. Diem, however, refused to hold the elections. Believing, too, that the Communists would win a nationwide election, Washington made no attempt to dissuade Diem from his decision.

By 1957 the Communists in the South had decided to take up armed struggle, for peaceful measures appeared useless. Indeed, in that year anti-Diem pressure was building up all over South Vietnam, among non-Communist as well as Communist groups. Massive disaffection was widespread among politicians, intellectuals, military officers, the country people, journalists, and

government officials. In 1959 the Hanoi regime responded by authorizing armed struggle in the South and sending a few thousand ex-southerners over the border to help out. The task of the Vietcong (as Diem labeled all insurrectionary forces) was to take over the villages. In 1959, the Vietcong felt strong enough to begin attacking large South Vietnamese Army units, and on July 8 of that year the first American died, victim of a terrorist bomb inside a military base in Bienhoa.

John Kennedy considers Vietnam

When John Kennedy came to the White House, he was trapped by his own rhetoric. He had campaigned on the theme of "getting the country moving again," injecting "vigor" into its operations, and taking quick action to solve the world's problems. It was the "Grand Design" for Europe, the "Alliance for Progress" for Latin America. What would it be for Laos and Vietnam? A retreat? It was impossible for the president to contemplate such an action, sure to be thunderously condemned by the Republicans and many Democrats as timid appeasement. The John Kennedy who had written *Profiles in Courage* must be bold in the face of the enemy, or else look like a fool. Furthermore, he and his associates were confident men, proud of their intelligence and "toughness," who believed they could crush Communist uprisings in countries like Vietnam by the use of such special counterguerrilla forces as the army's Green Berets.

This confidence was undergirded by an unquestioned faith in the existing Washington foreign policy elite. During twenty years of international leadership and the supervision of wide-flung global operations, the American government had built up a gifted corps of men whom the foreign policy analyst Richard J. Barnet has termed national security managers. Usually trained in law, engineering, or banking, these men in the State Department, the Pentagon, the National Security Council, and the CIA thought of themselves as practical, hard-headed problem solvers. Having come to power during the Second World War, they had formed the conviction that the basic problem in the world was military aggression, which occurred because of the existence of instability and weakness. Thus, America's fundamental task in the world was to build "situations of strength," which usually meant military as distinct from social strength. Control of the Third World of Africa, Asia, and Latin America was the new Communist objective; aggression in these areas, therefore, was to be countered with power.

Dean Acheson, Harry Truman's secretary of state and still a major figure in Washington in the 1960s, symbolized in his elegant, brilliant self this breed of national security managers. His followers were scattered through John Kennedy's government, among them Dean Rusk, secretary of

state, Allen Dulles, director of the CIA, W. W. Rostow and McGeorge Bundy, advisers to the president, and Robert McNamara, secretary of defense. Together they formed a compact circle of men whose pride in themselves and in their considerable achievements over the previous twenty years gave them courage and confidence. These honorable and devoted men had also developed the habit of seeing world problems as abstractions, not as human tragedies. As *The Pentagon Papers* reveal, in the thousands of memos, studies, and analyses that these men wrote on the Vietnam problem, there was an almost complete absence of any soul-searching or moral questioning about their actions. Vietnam was thought of as a practical problem to be solved by well-trained people, using statistics and immense physical resources. Two disenchanted men who were high in government councils during the

President Kennedy decided in 1961 to shore up the collapsing South Vietnamese regime. Here, in a televised press conference, he explains his reasons to the nation.
Cornell Capa © 1961, Magnum Photos

Johnson and Nixon administrations, Anthony Lake and Roger Morris, have given us a graphic picture of the atmosphere in which national security problems were handled:

We remember, more clearly than we care to, the well carpeted stillness and isolation of those government offices where some of the Pentagon Papers were first written. The efficient staccato of the typewriter, the antiseptic whiteness of nicely margined memoranda, the affable, authoritative and always urbane men who wrote them—all of it is a spiritual as well as geographic world apart from piles of decomposing bodies in a ditch outside Hue or a village bombed in Laos, the burn ward of a children's hospital in Saigon, or even a cemetery or veteran's hospital here. It was possible in that isolated atmosphere, and perhaps psychologically necessary, to dull one's awareness of the direct link between those memoranda and the human sufferings with which they were concerned.

Reasonable, decent men around tables in those quiet, carpeted rooms simply cannot imply that the other fellow, who supports a ''tougher'' policy, is a heartless murderer. Subordinates do not wish to tell superiors that they will be acting immorally if they choose the ''tougher'' option. Policy—good, steady policy—is made by the ''tough-minded.'' To talk of suffering is to lose ''effectiveness,'' almost to lose one's grip. (*Foreign Policy* [fall 1971].)

These men gathered reports on the rapidly worsening situation in South Vietnam and warned President Kennedy that Ngo Dinh Diem was on the verge of collapse. One of Kennedy's advisers, W. W. Rostow, provided a new theoretical underpinning for the notion of intervening in South Vietnam. The process of modernization, he said, was inherently revolutionary. Countries experiencing it inevitably undergo much internal turmoil. The role of the United States was to maintain the security of such a nation, like South Vietnam, so as to prevent another power from sending guerrillas across the border and, under cover of the turbulence, taking over. Once beyond this disorderly stage, the modernizing state would become internally unified and able to govern and defend itself effectively.

Kennedy expands the commitment

In 1961 President Kennedy concluded that the situation in South Vietnam was salvageable and, on this ground, decided to expand considerably America's commitment, though he was determined to keep it limited. He was convinced that the Communist insurrection could be defeated, in the last analysis, only by the local people themselves. It was essential, therefore, that President Diem be pressured to make democratic reforms in order to build support among the people. Meanwhile, the American government would help Diem "build a nation" by massive programs of social and economic reform in the countryside. This would involve building schools, distributing land, providing pure water and good roads, fostering elections, and assisting farmers to apply modern agricultural techniques.

Thereafter, the few hundred American advisers then in Vietnam were joined by 16,000 more who worked with the South Vietnam Army and moved into the villages to encourage the formation of antiguerrilla units. At the same time, President Kennedy authorized the beginning of undercover warfare against North Vietnam, carried out by specially trained South Vietnamese agents. If North Vietnam was sending secret agents southward to blow up bridges, damage power plants, and terrorize officials, so the reasoning ran, then the vigorous, courageous Kennedy administration could do no less in return.

These measures constituted Kennedy's "shot in the arm" for South Vietnam, designed to spark a "real transformation" of its government and army. If this did not work, the joint chiefs of staff assured the president that it would be necessary only to start bombing North Vietnam and that country would cave in and halt its guerrilla warfare. Thus was President Kennedy given advice that ranks, certainly, with that given King George III by Lord North when he informed his monarch that the American revolutionaries could be quickly put down. In both cases policy was formed on the basis of many years of success, on a habit of authority so bred into the nation that the prospect of its will being frustrated was hardly even considered. In both cases, too, the planners were blind to the power of a revolutionary independence movement widely supported by the mass of the population.

Optimism and disaster: 1961–1963

Meanwhile, in South Vietnam the Vietcong offensive against Diem's government went on. There were thousands of assassinations of village officials, terror bombings in the larger cities, bridges and roads destroyed, and immense destruction reaching to the gates of each provincial capital. It was impossible to travel out of Saigon save by air or with a large military convoy. Vast reaches of the South Vietnam countryside were abandoned to the Communists, and thousands of villages came under their control.

Since the American generals in South Vietnam strongly supported President Diem and were anxious to prove that they could win, the fact of mounting failure was covered up. Floods of encouraging statistics were sent off to Robert McNamara, the computer-oriented secretary of defense. Time and again he went to South Vietnam to examine the situation, but he never went outside the itineraries arranged by the American generals or challenged the elaborate briefings they prepared for him. But by closing himself off to those matters that could not be counted and measured—such as intangible feelings, like despair and lack of motivation, or confidence and long-range hopes—he was closed off to the factors that eventually counted most.

Then came crisis. To the world's horror, in June 1963 a Buddhist monk burned himself to death in protest against President Diem's oppressions—and the Diem regime simply scoffed. The American government pleaded with Diem to relent and allow them civil and political rights, but his response was to begin attacking pagodas where young Buddhists gathered to turn out leaflets, run their radio stations, and demand equality. A strong distaste for Diem began to build up in the United States. In the fall of 1963, President Kennedy broke relations with the Diem regime and gave tacit support to a plan for overthrowing Diem then brewing among South Vietnamese generals.

Robert Kennedy raised the question within the

Vietnam

* Major battles
△ U.S. bases
:: Areas of guerilla activity

Communist countries

Allied with U.S.

Neutral countries

administration whether the time had come for the United States to get out of Vietnam. President Kennedy, ruminating this issue, said in a television interview in September, "I don't think that unless a greater effort is made to win popular support that the war can be won out there. In the final analysis, it is their war. They are the ones who have to win it or lose it. We can help them, we can give them equipment, we can send our men out there as advisers, but they have to win it, the people of Vietnam, against the Communists." At the end of October 1963, the pressures in Saigon blew up. The generals gathered together, overthrew Diem, and captured him. While being taken to headquarters, he was shot and killed.

Lyndon Johnson takes over

Then, suddenly, John Kennedy was dead and Lyndon Johnson was president. Kennedy's death brought to the White House a man almost ten years older than Kennedy who had been reared in the simpler days of Franklin Roosevelt when the issues were clearer and the distinctions sharper. Primarily concerned with domestic issues, Johnson lacked the subtleties of Kennedy's outlook on foreign affairs. He was content with the older Cold War outlook that admired strong anti-Communists and condemned rebels who threatened to upset the Free World phalanx. Lyndon Johnson *liked* Chiang Kai-Shek, the Chinese Nationalist leader, Ngo Dinh Diem of South Vietnam, and other dogged Winston Churchill-type strong men like President Ayub Khan of Pakistan. He was not comfortable with Kennedy's warm treatment of reformist Third World politicians from Africa and Asia. As president, Johnson was brusque with countries receiving American economic aid and threatened withdrawal of such assistance if the recipients were too friendly toward China or Russia. He was genuinely worried about the Communists, often saying that their network in the United States was more powerful and effective than the public supposed. In 1954, when the North Vietnamese

inflicted the final defeat on the French at Dien Bien Phu, Johnson had said, "American foreign policy has never in all its history suffered such a stunning reversal. . . . We stand in clear danger of being left naked and alone in a hostile world." In 1961, after visiting Vietnam for President Kennedy, Johnson told him that "there is no alternative to United States leadership in Southern Asia." The American government must "attempt to meet the challenge of Communist expansion now in Southeast Asia by a major effort . . . or throw in the towel," by which he meant that the United States would have to "pull back [its] defenses to San Francisco and a 'Fortress America' concept. More important," he went on, "we would say to the world . . . that we don't live up to our treaties and don't stand by our friends. This is not my concept."

Lyndon Johnson was motivated also by grander visions. He dreamed of what might happen to the poor people of the world if their rivers were dammed and prosperous farms spread where now there was the terror of alternating floods and droughts. His own west Texas countryside had been transformed when the Pedernales River was controlled, and Tennessee's TVA project was the admiration of the world. Sitting on the porch of his ranch he rhapsodized about power lines running down the Mekong valley; about new kinds of crops, and the "green revolution" of hybrid rice strains; about clean villages, pure water, and an end to disease. Repeatedly he offered to North Vietnam the gift of immense funds to develop Indochinese TVAs, if they would but end the war. In 1966 he secured establishment of the Asian Development Bank, headquartered in Manila, whose capital of one billion dollars was designed to underwrite such ventures.

Johnson's "Alamo" syndrome

Johnson hated the thought of being a war leader. He distrusted the military, at first included no military men in his inner councils, and remarked that "all those generals want to do is bomb and spend." But more than this, he hated the thought that anyone would think him a coward. He wore proudly the decoration for bravery he had received during the Second World War (for his behavior under fire during a brief moment of aerial combat). Observers often remarked on Johnson's "Alamo syndrome," his belief that one must fight to achieve objectives, be tough, be capable of staring an adversary down. He was full of stories about indomitable Texas Rangers and Indian fighters, and stretched the truth on occasion to hint that he was connected by blood with the Alamo heroes. In his oversimplified imagery, the Vietcong were wicked gunslingers who had to be put down, after which the simple good folk of the Vietnamese countryside could build abundant lives.

Within days of Kennedy's assassination, President Johnson issued a policy document that stated the goal he would pursue for the next three-and-a-half years: assisting "the people and Government of [South Vietnam] to win their contest against the externally directed and supported Communist conspiracy." At the same time, he authorized the expansion of undercover "hit-and-run" raids against the North. More and more he leaned toward the view that, since things were going so badly in the South, the next step was to begin a program of gradually escalating pressure on the North. Meanwhile, in Saigon, the Americans watched helplessly as a succession of military coups led by South Vietnamese generals paraded one unpopular government after another before the indifferent populace. The Vietcong grew bolder and more powerful, taking over ever larger portions of the countryside.

The Gulf of Tonkin incident

On July 30, 1964, the American destroyer *Maddox* was approximately twenty miles off the North Vietnamese coast in the Gulf of Tonkin in waters claimed as territorial by North Vietnam, electronically gathering intelligence to support undercover operations, which included a raid on two North Vietnamese islands then being conducted by South Vietnamese units. Suddenly, three North Vietnamese torpedo boats appeared to attack the American ship. Brief gunfire ensued, primarily by the Maddox. A few nights later, the *Maddox* and another destroyer, the *Turner Joy* thought they were being subjected to torpedo attacks, later shown to have been misreading of instruments. President Johnson immediately ordered a "reprisal" aerial attack on North Vietnam, using a list of targets already prepared and naval air squadrons that had long since been placed in position near North Vietnam. He went on national television to inform the country of his actions, and then placed before Congress an authorizing resolution (which had also been earlier prepared by his staff and held in readiness). It read:

Resolved by the Senate and House of Representatives . . . in Congress assembled, that the Congress approve and support the determination of the President, as Commander in Chief, to take all necessary measures to repel any armed attack against the force of the United States *and to prevent further aggression* [*emphasis added*].

Some senators were worried about the last phrase: might it not be interpreted, they asked, to authorize an all-out war? Senator Fulbright, chairman of the Senate Foreign Relations Committee, remarked, "There is nothing in the resolution, as I read it, that contemplates it. I agree with the Senator that it is the last thing we would want to do. However, the language of the resolution would not prevent it." Senator John Sherman Cooper of Kentucky pushed the matter further: "Are we giving the President advance authority to take whatever action he may deem necessary respecting South Vietnam and its defense?" Senator Fulbright replied, "I think that is correct." Clearly, however, such doubts could not prevent passage of the resolution. The country still trusted the president, and it had become increasingly angry at North Vietnam for "causing" the seemingly endless warfare in the South. American public opinion was outraged at the North Vietnamese for their "unprovoked" attack: not even Congress had been informed of the provocative undercover operations the United States had been carrying on for months against North Vietnam. As always in the past, therefore, Congress swung behind the president and enacted the resolution. It was to be the *only* legal basis, thin as it was, for everything the American government did thereafter in Indochina.

With the one-time aerial strike over, the president concentrated on his 1964 election campaign. Senator Barry Goldwater, his antagonist, advocated all-out attacks against North Vietnam and massive American involvement, to include, perhaps, the use of atomic weapons. The frightened country and world were relieved to hear President Johnson say instead that the American role would remain a limited one, that he would not escalate the war, and that the conflict "is first and foremost a contest to be won by the government and the people of that country for themselves." He thus laid the basis for the later national loss of faith in his honesty that helped destroy his administration.

Massive aerial bombing begins

In February 1965 the Vietcong attacked American installations at Pleiku, killing seven men and wounding many more. The Pleiku attack imme-

Carrying her belongings in a bundle, a South Vietnamese woman walks around the body of a slain man sprawled on the curb. Her village was one of the many hit by Vietcong terrorists.

United Press International, photo by Dana Stone

diately triggered long-prepared plans. Within hours Seventh Fleet aircraft were loosing bombs and rockets upon Donghoi, forty miles north of the seventeenth parallel. Operation Rolling Thunder, the systematic air war against North Vietnam, had begun.

It went on uninterruptedly for three years, while the world watched in mounting horror. Very quickly it was clear that CIA warnings were correct: bombing alone would not halt North Vietnamese support for the warfare in the South. Indeed, at no time did it appreciably reduce Hanoi's ability to send arms and troops southward, even when the ground war had vastly escalated and North Vietnam was maintaining almost 100,000 of its own regular troops in the South. But the joint chiefs of staff continued adamantly to insist that the bombing must proceed, long after a chorus of protest against it had risen even within the Johnson administration. By 1968 the United States was dropping 1.2 million tons of bombs a year and flying 400,000 attack sorties (a sortie is one flight made by one aircraft) annually, with no significant effect on the war. Much of North Vietnam looked like the surface of the moon; tens of thousands of civilians were killed and wounded; the same places were bombed over and over again; and still the North Vietnamese fought on. They developed extremely effective antiaircraft fire. By the end of 1967, 1,000 American planes had been shot down over North Vietnam, and 500 more in the South. Including accidents, the United States had lost about 3,000 aircraft by that time, at a cost of almost three billion dollars and the lives of many hundreds of pilots. Meanwhile the world had come to look on the United States as it used to look on Nazi Germany: as a nation led by a government of war criminals.

Johnson sends in ground troops

Within two months after beginning Operation Rolling Thunder, President Johnson realized that bombing alone would not win the war. On

April 1, 1965, he decided to use American ground troops. The nation-building program begun by the Kennedy government, which involved working with the villages and stressed the need to avoid the massive destructiveness of all-out conventional military operations, now had few supporters in the government. Lyndon Johnson was faced with the inevitable collapse of the South Vietnamese government; he was determined not to become "the first American president to lose a war"; he was being given practically unanimous advice by his top advisers to get American troops in action against the Vietcong; and it seemed politically disastrous to do anything less. The American public was in no way prepared to accept defeat.

So, President Johnson vastly changed the character of America's involvement in the war by inundating Vietnam with American troops (from 21,000 at the beginning of 1965 to over 550,000 in 1968), aircraft, immense military installations, and astronomical sums of money (by 1969, total expenditures on the Vietnam War exceeded $100 billion). But from the beginning he insisted that this momentous change in policy was to be kept secret from the public. Troops were to be introduced piecemeal, with as little public notice as possible. It was all to be made to appear as if it flowed inexorably from decisions made by Eisenhower and Kennedy.

Johnson's great gamble, however, could be accepted by the American public only if a quick and decisive victory were won. Now, therefore, he began frantically urging the Pentagon to move faster, while he poured out troop authorizations with a lavish hand. By June 1965, there were 50,000 American troops in South Vietnam, and the fighting had begun. By midsummer, there were 170,000; by mid-1966, 270,000; at the end of that year, 380,000. In 1967, the American force rose another 100,000 and reached more than 500,000 in 1968. At the same time, by heavy diplomatic pressure the United States had gotten several of its Southeast Asia Treaty Organization (SEATO) allies to send troops: from South Korea,

Australia, Thailand (and a few from New Zealand and the Philippines), totaling 65,000 men. In addition, in 1968 there were almost 800,000 regular South Vietnamese troops under arms, joined by about 180,000 local militia. On the other side there were 35,000 Vietcong, 95,000 North Vietnamese regular troops, and about 100,000 Communist guerrillas in the fighting. The war had become a monstrously swollen holocaust.

"Search and destroy" tactics

President Johnson put General William C. Westmoreland in command and gave him complete freedom of action. Westmoreland depended on "search-and-destroy" tactics, sending his immense forces ranging about South Vietnam in search of Vietcong and North Vietnamese units. He was committed to the "body count" thesis, holding that the Communists could be defeated by killing so many of them that Hanoi would buckle under the pressure. He even stationed American units in exposed locations, hoping for an attack, and relying on helicopters and rapid reinforcement to win the battles. The butchery was sickening: the Communists lost tens of thousands of men, and American losses skyrocketed, from 147 in 1964 to 1,400 in 1965, 5,000 in 1966, over 9,000 in 1967, and almost 14,000 in 1968.

No matter: the North Vietnamese and the Vietcong continued fighting. Having sent relatively few men southward before 1964, Hanoi now simply matched every increase of American troops with more of its own. Its manpower was practically unlimited, since North Vietnam, being mainly a rural country, was not manufacturing its own war supplies, which came from China and Russia. General Giap was in command of the North Vietnamese forces, as he had been against the French, and he still relied confidently on his thesis that the domestic pressures within a democratic country, when faced by a limitless war, would eventually force the United States to pull out. The Pentagon continued to be fascinated by the floods of encouraging statistics sent back by

American generals in South Vietnam, and constantly claimed that victory was just around the corner.

Meanwhile, the South Vietnamese countryside was devastated. "Nation building" came to an end. American troops bombed and shelled villages at will, on the ground that they allegedly contained Vietcong. Vast areas were defoliated by the aerial spraying of plant-killing chemicals so as to uncover jungle trails or deny food to the rebels. Thousands of civilians were killed. By October 1967, almost a million of them had fled to the cities, thus gigantically enlarging South Vietnam's already grave urban problems. The military now completely dominated all policy arguments.

Johnson and the world

The president was absorbed by Vietnam, but he still had the rest of the world to think about. In April 1965, a revolt erupted in the Dominican Republic. The president had already decided that any chief executive who allowed the appearance of another Communist regime in the Caribbean (after Cuba) would be impeached. Worried that the Dominican rebels might be Communist-led, he immediately responded—without the formality of consulting with the Organization of American States or even securing congressional authorization—by sending in the incredible total of 22,000 troops. They remained until elections were held in 1966, elevating a man acceptable to the United States to the presidency. This brief intervention was praised in the United States but widely condemned in Latin America. In one swift action, Lyndon Johnson had demonstrated how weak was the United States' commitment to its pledges of nonintervention and to the use of the multilateral machinery of the Organization of American States.

President Johnson was too gigantic a personality to get along with France's president, the majestic, anti-American Charles de Gaulle, and relations with him soon deteriorated. In March 1966, de Gaulle capped his drive to break continental Europe away from what he called "Anglo-Saxon dominance" by taking France out of NATO. This action, which required a massive rearrangement of all United States military arrangements in Europe, symbolized the steady drawing apart of the transatlantic community, to be capped during Richard Nixon's presidency by Great Britain's entrance into the European Common Market.

Johnson's real concern in Europe, however, was with Soviet Russia. In 1966 he began seeking to establish better relations with Russia and eastern Europe by greatly easing trade, liberalizing travel regulations for Americans, and allowing the Export-Import Bank to make loans to eastern European countries in support of trade. Direct air service between Moscow and the United States was established by agreement in November 1966, and in December of that year a treaty was agreed to that prohibited the placing of nuclear arms or other such weapons in orbit around the earth.

Antiwar protests

Antiwar protests began as soon as American forces began fighting in Vietnam. Thousands of students attended the first "teach-in," held at the University of Michigan in late March 1965, and the idea swiftly spread across the country, culminating in a two-day gathering at the University of California at Berkeley. Stung, the administration announced publicly that it was ready for "unconditional discussions" with North Vietnam—but refused adamantly to admit the National Liberation Front, the Vietcong's official leadership, to the deliberations.

Protests continued. Peace marches, much condemned by the general public, which was still strongly behind the war, occurred in late 1965 in Oakland, California, only to be attacked by the police. A Quaker, Norman Morrison, burned himself to death on the steps of the Pentagon; other protestors began burning their draft cards, despite the passage of a federal law threatening five years in prison and heavy fines for doing so. As 1966 opened, prominent senators, among them William Fulbright of Arkansas, began to be called "doves," for they lent their voices to the criticism. In January, Fulbright's Foreign Relations Committee began holding televised hearings on Vietnam. These provided a platform on which Secretary of State Dean Rusk, implacable "hawk," could be grilled, and such eminent foreign policy analysts as the now-venerable George Kennan, author under President Truman of the containment policy, could state that Vietnam was of little importance to America's security. Now the antiwar movement could no longer be stigmatized as composed of a bunch of radicals and peacenik hippies. Stung by the widespread accusation that the president had gone far beyond his powers in launching a full-scale war, the Johnson administration actually claimed that, in the shrunken condition of the modern world, an attack on any country anywhere by anyone could be a direct threat to the United States, and that, therefore, under the Constitution the president had the power to wage "defensive" war anywhere in the world without congressional consent. By this astonishing theory, there were literally no bounds to the president's war-making powers. The "imperial presidency," as Arthur M. Schlesinger, Jr., has termed it (in his 1973 book so named) was being boldly proclaimed.

In April 1966 Senator William Fulbright spoke at Johns Hopkins University on what he called the arrogance of power: "The causes of the malady are a mystery but its recurrence is one of the uniformities of history: Power tends to confuse itself with virtue and a great nation is peculiarly susceptible to the idea that its power is a sign of God's favor, conferring upon it a special responsibility for other nations—to make them richer and happier and wiser, to remake them, that is, in its own shining image.

"Power also tends to take itself for omnipotence. Once imbued with the idea of a mission, a great nation easily assumes that it has the means as well as the duty to do God's work. The Lord, after all, surely would not choose you as His agent and then deny you the sword with which to work his will. German soldiers in the First World War wore belt buckles imprinted with the words 'Gott mit uns.' It was approximately under this kind of infatuation—an exaggerated sense of power and an imaginary sense of mission—that the Athenians attacked Syracuse and Napoleon and then Hitler invaded Russia. In plain words, they overextended their commitments and they came to grief.

"My question is whether America can overcome the fatal arrogance of power. . . . Gradually but unmistakably we are succumbing to [it]. In so doing we are not living up to our capacity and promise; the measure of our falling short is the measure of the patriot's duty of dissent. . . . There is a kind of voodoo about American foreign policy. Certain drums have to be beaten regularly to ward off evil spirits. . . . For example, we will never go back on a commitment no matter how unwise; we regard this alliance or that as absolutely 'vital' to the free world. . . . I see it as a mark of strength and maturity that an articulate minority have raised their voices against the Vietnamese war. . . ."

In Saigon, meanwhile, there was a merry-go-round of new governments and the reek of corruption. Premier Nguyen Cao Ky, a flashy former fighter pilot, was the dominant figure in 1966, but after the election of a constituent assembly in late 1966 and the adoption by popular vote of the constitution that body formulated, Nguyen Van Thieu emerged dominant. Another former general, he proved amazingly durable as president of South Vietnam, holding the post until North Vietnam's complete victory ended the war, and he fled from his country.

Unrestrained bombing

In 1967, the total number of American casualties passed 100,000 men. Jonathan Schell, a *New Yorker* reporter, observed that "we are destroying, seemingly by inadvertence, the very country we are supposedly protecting." American airplanes bombed villages apparently on the whim of their FAC (forward air controller). A helicopter pilot explained on American television that he had fired on a building simply because he saw footprints heading into it that showed the person making them had been running. Canadian television films showed American pilots cheering as if at a sporting event when they blew up structures whose occupancy could only be guessed at. Ambassador Henry Cabot Lodge, America's representative in Saigon, said, "I expect . . . the war to achieve very sensational results in 1967," but instead North Vietnam's fighting forces in the South swelled enormously, and American commanders called anxiously for more men. At home, Secretary of Defense Robert McNamara was revolted by the war he was running, fretted for months in silence, and then in August 1967 could restrain himself no longer. He publicly informed a Senate committee that the bombing campaign was totally useless. (Within three months, at Johnson's request, he left his post to become president of the World Bank.)

In April 1967, 125,000 people marched for peace in New York City, and 30,000 more did the same in San Francisco. Martin Luther King openly condemned the United States as "the greatest purveyor of violence in the world today." Thousands of young men refused to accept induction into the services as draftees, or fled to

American wounded, in a military encampment in the Vietnam jungles, which displays the conditions in which much of the fighting took place.

Larry Burrows, Time-Life Picture Agency

Canada. Thousands more went into the streets in the summer of 1967 to march in protest. They surrounded induction centers, clamored before war industries, and, in October 1967, organized a march of perhaps 70,000 demonstrators who picketed the Pentagon and clashed with its guards.

The beginning of the end

In late 1967 the administration was still pushing the war at full throttle and claiming victory. However, debate over the Vietnam War raged on in the public press, on television, and in political life. A Gallup poll in November 1967 showed that fifty-seven percent of the American public disapproved of the president's handling of the war, while only twenty-eight percent approved. The Senate seemed to be turning dove more and more each day, and even within the banking and business community important figures began privately communicating their alarm to the president. Everywhere rose a clamor that he end the bombing, for Hanoi had promised that in that event, the Communists would be willing to open peace negotiations. The *Saturday Evening Post,* long the voice of WASP America, said, "The war in Vietnam is Johnson's mistake, and through the power of his office, he has made it a national mistake." It was widely pointed out that the enemy forces in South Vietnam were now four times larger than when the bombing and ground fighting began, reaching more than a quarter of a million men.

Then, on January 31, 1968, during the Tet new year holidays in Vietnam, the Vietcong launched an immense nationwide offensive. They penetrated Saigon, devastating large areas of the city, captured (for a number of weeks) the old imperial capital of Hue, occupied many major towns, drove the South Vietnamese forces out of huge areas of countryside that they had slowly won back from the Vietcong, and killed thousands of Americans and South Vietnamese. Though suffering terrible losses themselves—perhaps 60,000 men—the Communists had demonstrated that even after almost three years of search-and-destroy campaigns, they had more power than ever to wreak enormous damage against the South Vietnam regime. The Tet offensive, in short, was a massive political defeat for the United States. It was now clear to all but the most hard-headed hawks that optimism was foolish. Even the *Wall Street Journal* observed in February 1968, "We think the American people should be getting ready to accept, if they haven't already, the prospect that the whole Vietnam effort may be doomed, that it may be falling apart beneath our feet." The last thin shreds of the president's credibility in the country were wearing away. Even so, in February 1968 he flew to Dallas to cry out to a Texas audience, "Persevere in Vietnam we will and we must [though] the weak will drop from the lines, their feet sore and their voices loud."

Days of crisis

Johnson's war had reached its days of crisis. After the Tet offensive the president asked General Westmoreland what more he needed in Vietnam to win the war. He received the stunning reply that the general would need 206,000 more men (in addition to the 500,000 already there), which, with the necessary support troops in the United States, would mean a total of 450,000 more men on active duty. Such an enormous call-up would massively disrupt every aspect of the nation's economic and social life. A shockwave ran through the government, setting off an immediate and drastic reappraisal of the entire Vietnam War policy. In March 1968, the Pentagon, the State Department, and the White House hummed with meetings. The new secretary of defense, Clark Clifford—for many years a powerful figure in Washington and a frequent aide to presidents—instructed his staff to work up fresh analyses of the Vietnam situation. Dean Rusk, W. W. Rostow, and the joint chiefs of staff continued to insist that no change in policy should be made, but a torrent of powerful criticisms poured in from high-ranking civilian officials throughout

the government. Secretary Clifford, formerly a hawk, began to turn against the bombing and unlimited ground war. He could see a fantastic national furor coming when the country learned of Westmoreland's request, and shortly, when the *New York Times* broke the story, the public was indeed horrified, and new waves of protest erupted.

Then came language that Lyndon Johnson, supreme politician, could understand: Senator Eugene McCarthy, who had been running a lonely race against him in the New Hampshire presidential primary on an anti-Vietnam platform, swept astonishingly close to victory in the balloting. The president was shocked. When Senator Robert Kennedy entered the presidential race too, enormous crowds turned out to hear his attacks on the war, and the polls quickly showed him leading the president. Once more, Senator Fulbright began public hearings, skewering Dean Rusk for two full days in the glare of television lights.

Advisers recommend de-escalation

At this point President Johnson turned to Dean Acheson, the very symbol of the hard-lining Cold Warriors. Always a hawk on Vietnam, a brilliant and gifted public figure, he was held in high regard by the president. Acheson stunned Johnson by telling him that the joint chiefs of staff did not know what they were talking about and were making a fool of the president. No one believed Lyndon Johnson anymore, he said; the war was a failure and could not be won. Johnson reacted almost hysterically by rushing off to the Midwest and, in a widely reported address, publicly appealing for "a total national effort to win the war, win the peace, and complete the job that must be done here at home. Make no mistake about it . . . we are going to win." Once more he called up the image of the Alamo—but as someone remarked, this was an ill-chosen example, for everyone there had died.

The end, indeed, was near. Clark Clifford persuaded the president to convene a meeting of what was called the Senior Advisory Group on Vietnam. It was composed of distinguished former public servants who had helped run the Cold War for twenty years. Every six months it gathered at the White House to counsel with the president on Vietnam. Among its members were Dean Acheson, McGeorge Bundy, Henry Cabot Lodge, General Omar Bradley from the Second World War, General Matthew Ridgway from the Korean War, John J. McCloy, head of the American occupation of Germany, and Cyrus Vance, veteran high government official. After two days of intensive discussions in the White House, they gave their verdict: military victory was impossible without a total war on the scale of World War II, which the American people would not accept. The president, they said, must make a major change in policy. Johnson was visibly shaken by the news. The men who had all along given him close support were turning against him. The only world that he really knew and understood, that of the ruling elite in the national capital, had told him that the war was hopeless. All those young men had died in pursuit of an impossible objective—and he, who had hoped to be one of America's greatest and most loved presidents, had become one of its most despised and unsuccessful. The national tragedy had become his own.

On the evening of March 31, 1968, the president revealed his decision to the nation: "Tonight I am taking the first step to de-escalate the conflict. We are reducing . . . the present level of hostilities . . . unilaterally and at once." All aerial bombing attacks, he went on, north of the twentieth parallel (that is, over some ninety percent of North Vietnam) would be halted. (Just before the November elections, the president extended this ban to include the whole of the country.) Johnson asked President Ho Chi Minh to "respond positively and favorably" to his action; i.e., come to the conference table. Then, he issued his last bombshell: "I shall not seek, and I will not accept the nomination of my party for another term as your President." Nine months later, Johnson came to the end of his term and left the presidency. With him went, perhaps forever, the no-

tion that there are no limits to what the United States can do. Gone, too, was the myth in which Americans had for so long confidently believed: that whatever their nation did in the world was morally good and proper. The Vietnam War was the true end of American innocence.

The Nixon revolution

When President Richard Nixon took office in January 1969, he profoundly changed American foreign policy. The new theme was withdrawal. Not only in Vietnam but around the world as well, the president pulled back from the old system of rigid and interlocked commitments, shook himself free of entanglements that had existed since the early days of the Cold War, and veered off in new directions almost as if he were a broken-field running halfback in his favorite game, football. His performance startled a world grown used to living within the crystallized patterns left behind by the Cold War, and it caused seismic tremors of mingled alarm and applause around the globe.

In a sense, Nixon's performance fell true to type, for these were traditionally Republican tactics. He simply revived the kind of nationalist, unilateral, "going it alone" foreign policy his party had always preferred. And he did it with great care and forethought. Few men in American politics knew more about foreign policy than he, had a longer experience in international relations, or were so fascinated by them. Meanwhile, in his long daily periods of seclusion and reflection, he and Dr. Henry Kissinger, his foreign affairs adviser and executive secretary of the National Security Council, discussed the nation's foreign policy, often for hours on end.

The fascinating Dr. Kissinger, who soon became a giant figure in world politics, was a German Jew whose family had fled from Hitler. He was a brilliant Harvard professor and a Republican intellectual of high stature. For years he had been urging presidents to be flexible in the conduct of American foreign relations. Kissinger admired Otto von Bismarck, towering German leader in the nineteenth century, who had skill-fully helped to keep Europe at peace for many years by shifting Germany's alignments around (and the weight of its powerful armies) in order to keep a balance of power in the world. In con-trast to what he regarded as the utopian idealists of the William Gladstone–Woodrow Wilson tra-dition, Kissinger had no faith that some form of international government, like the United Na-tions, would ever be able to provide a stable world order. Instead, like Bismarck and Theodore Roosevelt, Kissinger believed that international tensions would never disappear, and that the proper role for a big power was to stay well armed and keep itself free to move quickly and easily about in the constant flux of world politics (i.e., "speak softly and carry a big stick"). The "enemy" in such a system was likely, soon, to become a "friend," so the Nixon administration no longer talked loudly of the "Free World against totalitarian communism." Indeed, Nixon and Kissinger no longer conceived of the world as bipolar—divided between the Free World and the Communist bloc—but as pentagonal, with Eu-rope, the United States, Japan, Russia, and China standing each other off in an equilibrium of power maintained by the skillful movements of Washington, D.C. The Nixon administration did not feel itself irrevocably tied to any former rela-tionship, whether friendly or hostile.

Every nation, in the Nixon-Kissinger foreign policy, was to be watched carefully, particularly the powerful ones. Caution, a watchful distrust, an avoidance of any kind of deal that might weaken the United States' relative military and economic position—these were the hallmarks of the Nixon-Kissinger negotiating style. Thus, when the Russians at the outset of the Nixon administration proposed talks on limiting the number of missiles, Nixon remained unrespon-sive for many months while building a strong position. He authorized the start of a modified antiballistic missile system (leading to opposition in Congress), and the development of a frighten-ing hydra-headed missile weapon, the MIRV (multiple independently targeted reentry vehicle,

a kind of missile shotgun in which one rocket would carry many warheads that, at a certain point in flight, would head toward different tar-gets). With these steps, Nixon was ready to begin the Strategic Arms Limitation Talks (SALT) with Russia, which eventually produced encouraging but limited results.

Withdrawal from Vietnam

Dr. Kissinger came to his post convinced that the war in Vietnam was a *civil* war: it was not part of a worldwide Communist offensive. The United States should therefore *slowly* withdraw its forces while pouring huge funds into the South Viet-namese army to equip it to fight its own war. This "Vietnamization" policy was announced by the president in June 1969. The fighting died down, and American draft calls were greatly reduced. (A lottery was established in November 1969, and the draft, and the whole Selective Service system, were eventually shut down in 1974.) American battle deaths began dropping: to 8,250 in 1969, under 5,000 in 1970, and well under 2,000 in 1971. By the latter year, troop strength was under 200,000 in Vietnam, and the president announced in April that "American involvement in this war is coming to an end."

The last major burst of American ground fighting took place in April 1970 with a huge invasion of Cambodian territory. The stated ob-jective of this assault was to clear out Communist "sanctuaries" in that country, where massed sup-plies and large bodies of troops seemed prepared for a renewed campaign against South Vietnam. This action produced the last and most violent of all the campus protest movements in the United States, and rightly so, for Nixon's constitutional authority to invade a neutral bordering state was wholly lacking. Wrapping himself in the mantle of commander-in-chief, Nixon claimed unlimited powers never advanced by presidents before the 1960s (indeed, specifically rejected by them). Like his predecessor, Johnson, Nixon had broken loose from all traditional constitutional restraints governing his war-making authority. By the end of June 1970, all American and South Vietnamese troops had been withdrawn from Cambodia, their objectives apparently achieved, though critics worldwide scoffed at this assertion.

Global withdrawal

American withdrawal continued around the world. As President Nixon said in February 1970 in a formal statement of policy, the United States could not and would not "conceive *all* the plans, design *all* the programs, execute *all* the decisions and undertake *all* the defense of the free nations of the world." He waited for many months after his inauguration to make even a formal statement concerning Latin America, and rarely paid that part of the world much attention. In October 1969 he clearly intimated that the Alliance for Progress was a thing of the past, stating that a "more mature" relationship was needed between the United States and Latin America in which that region's social and economic progress would have to depend largely on its own efforts. As in prior Republican regimes, American business would be relied on to provide the kind of influence that, it was believed, helped the most.

In July 1969, while stopping at Guam on a journey to Southeast Asia, the president stated, in what was quickly called his Guam Doctrine, that there was need for "Asian solutions to Asian problems." The free Asian countries would need henceforth to take care of themselves more than they had in the past. The United States intended to maintain forces at key bases, but it would be altogether more reticent, keeping a low profile.

The year of surprises: 1971

President Nixon began 1971 with a long message to Congress analyzing the state of the world, remarking that "the postwar order of international relations—the configuration of power that emerged from the Second World War—is gone. With it are gone the conditions which have determined the assumptions and practice of United States foreign policy since 1945." The American people, the president observed, were "at the end of an era" in their relations with the other countries of the world.

As if to fulfill his own prophecy, Richard Nixon did indeed fill the year with surprising realignments, so fundamental in character as to change the nature of the world community. Most dramatically, he ended the long quarantine of China, opened the Peking door, and walked in to begin a new era. No development in world affairs was more ironic or startling. Here was the American president who had for years built his career on an almost fanatical anticommunism. In 1950 he had blamed treason in the State Department for the Communist victory in China; had afterward given his support to Senator Joseph McCarthy's carnival of hate and character assassination, which purged the State Department of practically all its trained experts in Far Eastern affairs; and had even talked of dropping atom bombs on Hanoi to halt the outward spread of an allegedly expansionist China. But in his years out of power, Nixon seemed to rethink his ideas and to conclude that it was absurd and dangerous for America, the world's most powerful nation, and China, its most populous one, not to be even on speaking terms. If he ever became president, he once observed, his greatest goal would be to begin a Chinese-American dialogue.

During the first two years of his presidency he gave the Chinese many public and private hints of his intentions. Then, in July 1971, Henry Kissinger suddenly disappeared from view while on a visit to Pakistan, and then reemerged after a secret visit to Peking with the startling news that he had arranged for President Nixon to visit China in February 1972 for general, wide-ranging discussions of all mutual affairs.

Crisis of the dollar

In August 1971 came a crisis of the American dollar, when world traders lost confidence in the sick United States economy and began swiftly exchanging American currency for gold. It was hardly coincidental that Nixon, a Republican president, responded by raising the American tariff against all foreign goods (installing a temporary surcharge of ten percent) and taking the American dollar off the international gold standard, making its exchange rate with other currencies subject to the American government's own *national* control. It was clearly an age of dying internationalism. The American people, worried about their swiftly rising trade deficit, warmly praised the president; but abroad, there was consternation. Euphoria swept the American stock market, but gloom struck America's trading partners, such as Japan, whose overseas sales were hurt by these unilateral actions.

In Europe, Anatole Shub, an American correspondent, wrote that since the mid-1960s, "European leaders have become increasingly dubious about the capacity of the United States either to govern itself or to protect its allies abroad. They have been disturbed by U.S. conduct of the Vietnam war. They are worried by an apparent revival of American isolationism and economic protectionism. They feel threatened by the seemingly insatiable appetites of U.S.-dominated multinational corporations. . . . Just a decade ago, European leaders envisioned an 'Atlantic Community.' . . . Nowadays the fashionable talk is all about greater European unity. . . . The more the U.S. draws back and turns inward, disregarding European interests, the more the Europeans will be drawn together. . . ." (*Harper's Magazine* [January 1972].)

The non-Communist nations of the world had no choice but to agree, and in December 1971, the American dollar was officially devalued (making American goods cheaper, and those of foreign countries more expensive to United States residents), and the gold standard for international commerce was permanently ended. Henceforth, the value of each nation's currency would be established by periodic negotiations between national governments, not set by a free internationally operating system of market exchange.

Nixon and Vietnam

By 1971, President Nixon had largely neutralized Vietnam as a political issue. The negotiations begun in Paris in late 1968 ground on without result, for the Communists demanded as a basic condition that all American troops be withdrawn immediately and the government of President Thieu be ended, which the Nixon administration refused to accept. But the continued removal of American troops and the absence of any major battles in South Vietnam drained away the sense of urgency—combined with the fact that, because of the draft lottery system, most American young men no longer had to fear being sent to Vietnam to fight in a hated war. The South Vietnamese army was now in charge of its own war.

Save from the air. The United States continued flying thousands of sorties a year to support ground operations. In November 1970, a brief heavy aerial attack was made on North Vietnam "in response to attacks on our unarmed reconnaissance aircraft" over that country; and in December 1971, there was another bombing attack designed to punish the North Vietnamese for building up large supplies of war materiel north of the seventeenth parallel. Congress had tried to halt the fighting by repealing the Tonkin Gulf Resolution in January 1971, thus stripping away the only legal justification for American military operations in Vietnam, but Nixon had brushed aside the action as "without binding force or effect." As commander-in-chief, he insisted, he had the right to do anything he thought necessary to protect the lives of the American troops already in Vietnam.

So, in the late months of 1971, the shape of the new world order emerged. Only the early years of the Cold War could match this startling year for the magnitude of transformations. Communist China was clearly moving swiftly back into the world community. In October, Great Britain ended years of agonized debate by deciding to enter the Common Market, thus opting for inclusion in the "New Europe" and leaving behind its ancient "special relationship" with the United States. In the same year, too, Great Britain withdrew the last of its troops from Asia; the Asians were indeed being placed on their own. Furthermore, the Russians, alarmed over the growing friendship between China and the United States and anxious to reduce tension on its western borders, finally came to a formal agreement with West Germany over Berlin, placing the former garrison city on a normalized relationship with the rest of Europe, guaranteeing open access and travel both to the east and west.

An English observer, Henry Brandon, wrote of the United States in 1972: "The new generation of Americans is coming to power with a different experience and different outlook [from that of the Cold War generation]. It is hardly aware of the Communist coup in Czechoslovakia in 1947; it has no memory of the Berlin blockade, the invasion of Korea, or the suppression of Hungary. Uppermost in its mind is the catastrophe of Vietnam. The poison from that war will circulate in the American body and the American conscience for some time to come; the war's character and conduct are bound to remain part of the American experience and may leave an imprint as lasting as that of the Civil War. To this new generation it is damning evidence that the far-flung responsibilities of the United States have been executed in a reckless manner, that the limitations of American power have not been correctly assessed, and that American domestic needs have been badly neglected. The aim of this new generation will be to change the priorities of the past. Between those who do not understand the game of world power politics and those who exaggerate the need for overkill capacity, a great political struggle is developing in the seventies. There are many eloquent spokesmen among this new generation for the urgent American domestic needs, but for internationalism there are as yet none who can command the re-

spect of this generation as well as of Congress." (*The Atlantic Monthly* [January 1973].)

Richard Nixon's year of triumph: 1972

The year 1972 was one of mounting triumph for the president. Inflation slowed as a price and wage control mechanism took hold, the national economy entered a slowly gathering boom that extended well through election day, and the president's political fortunes rose accordingly. The Democrats did not, as in 1970, have their favorite economic issues—slumping business activity and rising unemployment—to throw at the president. What shaped up, instead, was a campaign centered on the kinds of cultural issues that historically have aided Republicans.

At the same time, a series of dramatic achievements in foreign affairs sent Nixon's prestige soaring, mainly because it appeared he was successfully disengaging the United States from the war in Vietnam, while at the same time ending world tensions by bold gestures toward friendship with China and Russia. Nixon and Kissinger labored hard at firming up the new American foreign policy of breaking loose from old alliances and practicing a flexible, shifting game of balance of power. In February, in pursuance of the new policy, the president made his historic journey to China. Premier Chou En-lai was a gracious host, and the world was treated to a flood of stunning photographs showing Nixon striding along the Chinese Wall and exchanging pleasantries with the Communists. Little of substance came from the meeting save the crucially important opening up of a friendly relationship that could hopefully lead to a more peaceful world. Furthermore, in a milestone event that stunned Taiwan, President Nixon began to phase out America's protection of the Nationalist Chinese regime on that island. Henceforth, the United States would no longer interfere in relations between the Peking Communist government and Taiwan, and would pull out its military forces as soon as tensions in the area ceased.

George Ball, who had been under-secretary of state in the Kennedy and Johnson administrations, keenly summarized the Nixon-Kissinger foreign policy within a few weeks after President Nixon's reelection in 1972: The President, he said, had "replaced America's policy of alliance with a policy of maneuver. Instead of continuing to build an expanding circle of like-minded nations that would concert their strategies and combine their resources in seeking a détente with Moscow and Peking, we embarked on an intricate game of check and maneuver with what the President has identified as 'equal' players—the Soviet Union, China, Western Europe, and Japan. The object of this game is to try to maintain a precarious power equilibrium by playing one nation off against the other without distinction between ally and adversary. Essential to success are the exploitation of surprise and the quick reversal of positions—and these, in turn, require the maximum of secrecy and flexibility. . . . [The] hard question remains whether—though productive of successes in the short run—it is a game that can be effectively played by a democracy over the longer pull. Throughout history the best players have been . . . agents of authoritarian governments . . . who felt no obligation to Parliament or public opinion—and for the past year or so this has been the foreign-policy posture of the Nixon Administration. . . . [But] once the country catches on to the implications of the power-juggling act, it is not likely to be comfortable with it. What Americans like is to have a circle of identifiable friends, close allies, companions in a common endeavor—something other than the cold geometry of a shifting balance conducted in secret by alchemists at work somewhere under the stage." (*Newsweek*, November 20, 1972.)

Revived bombing in Vietnam

In April 1972 the war in Vietnam was suddenly ripped wide open as the Communists inexplicably launched a classic conventional invasion across the seventeenth parallel (as well as over the border in other locations) using hundreds of

President Nixon shakes hands with Chinese Communist leader Mao Tse-tung during his startling trip to China in 1972. By this act, he reversed decades of American policy.
Wide World Photos

tanks. While the South Vietnamese army slowly fought back this invasion, following initial headlong retreats, President Nixon revived aerial bombing over the north. Only this time the campaign did not cease after the initial crisis was over, but went on month after month, using new "smart bombs," which could be guided electronically to pin-point bridges and other locations. Using a force of at least 100,000 men, stationed at air bases in Thailand and Guam and on Seventh Fleet ships off the Vietnamese coast, the president devastated huge areas of North Vietnamese countryside.

There was worldwide condemnation of Nixon's bombing, which reached unimaginable and terrifying heights. The London *Times* called "the appalling destruction . . . out of all proportion to the end." The *Boston Globe* observed, "The total inhumanity of what Americans are doing on the orders of an American President devastates the spirit. America will be a long time recovering from what it has done not only to a land of peasants but to itself." The *New Yorker* agreed: "This latest form of intervention . . . represents a culmination of our century's tendency toward mechanized killing. The government has made the invaluable discovery that an air force will go on fighting long after ground troops have balked, especially when there is virtually no opposing air force in the sky." But the very abstractness and remoteness of this new assault seemed soon to remove it from public controversy.

Nixon and Russia

In May 1972, Richard Nixon became the first American president to consult with Soviet leaders in Moscow, leaving the Russian capital with a crammed bag of diplomatic achievements: fifteen major agreements relating to trade and cooperation in space, technology, and other fields, including one for a huge expansion in American-Russian trade, until now a largely untapped field for American producers. This was soon followed by an enormous purchase of American wheat by the Russians, who had been hard hit by crop failures. Then came other negotiations relating to the American purchase of such crucial Russian commodities as natural gas. Lastly, Moscow and the United States agreed to begin discussions on "mutual balanced force reductions" (troop and aircraft reductions) in Europe in January 1973.

These path-breaking steps aroused serious concern among America's former allies. Europe and Japan felt themselves ignored and harmed by this abrupt end to the longstanding United States policy of close cooperation with its traditional friends. The North Atlantic Assembly—the transatlantic consultative body for NATO—spoke with the grave authority of its fourteen member nations when it formally warned the United States that "divisive political effects . . . may arise if Western policies are not harmonized before the conference with [the Soviet bloc] on European security . . . [in January 1973]." Furthermore, the Assembly went on, there were "possible dangers for Western solidarity in the growth of strictly bilateral diplomacy between the United States and the Soviet Union, if there were not adequate consultation." Senator Edward Kennedy, speaking to the gathering, said that American policy-makers had, in fact, largely dis-

regarded the NATO alliance for six years. "We must restore the habits and procedures of consensus," he insisted, "if we are to avoid a slide into jungle politics and jungle economics." President Nixon, undeterred, continued playing his lone hand, preferring to continue his nationalist, unilateral diplomacy in the classic Disraelian style.

The election of 1972

During these events the Democrats had been slugging through a long series of bruising primary elections, seeking to find a winner among the group of men and women—Hubert Humphrey, Edmund Muskie, George McGovern, Henry Jackson, Shirley Chisholm, and George Wallace—who contended for the party's nomination. Wallace's role was crucial. As the American Independent party candidate in 1968 he had taken 13.5 percent of the popular vote, appealing primarily to those on the right wing of American politics who were most strongly hostile to blacks, intellectuals, and young radicals. Then on May 15, 1972, he was felled by an assassin's bullet and rendered paralyzed from the waist down. By default, his popular following swung behind Richard Nixon. Meanwhile, Senator George McGovern of South Dakota, who since the assassination of Robert Kennedy in 1968 had stood out courageously as an often lonely voice against the Vietnam War, began surging into the lead for the Democratic nomination. After a harsh battle with Humphrey in California he captured that state's huge convention delegation. By the time of the Democratic National Convention in July—held, like its Republican counterpart, in Miami—he had a commanding lead and quickly became the party's nominee.

It was a stunningly swift victory for a man who, until these events, had been given little chance. McGovern had long condemned the war with all the genuine moral passion of a Methodist minister's son who had himself briefly considered a career in the pulpit. A professor of history, then an important official in the Kennedy administration, he had emerged as the voice of all those forces that, in the late 1960s, called for a thoroughgoing transformation of American society, as well as of its policies abroad. After the calamitous 1968 convention of the Democratic party, when young protestors had been mercilessly clubbed outside the Chicago convention hall and the old guard of city bosses and union leaders had dominated proceedings, McGovern had chaired the committee that the party then appointed to rewrite its rules. The result was a group of policies that stated that, henceforth, convention delegates were to be selected by proceedings that ensured that youth, women, and minority groups would receive a sizable quota of votes. The discontented, disadvantaged, and alienated were to be given a voice.

Democrats offend traditional support groups

Thus, as the nation watched the 1972 Democratic National Convention on television, it was astonished to observe a screen that seemed filled with young people, women's libbers, and dashiki-clad black Americans. Fuming outside the hall and denied seats were the labor leaders and city bosses—most notably George Meany, head of the AFL-CIO and Irish Catholic Richard Daley, mayor of Chicago—who bitterly protested a convention that to them seemed to have forgotten the ancient sources of Democratic voting strength. George McGovern, with his flat South Dakota twang and his preacher's manner, came across as an honest and sincere patriot genuinely determined to aid the nation's poor and end the Vietnam War, but his personal style failed to ignite any mass enthusiasm among the millions of urbanites. As soon as the convention was over, a Gallup poll showed him trailing the president thirty-seven percent to fifty-six percent, and from then on the margin widened.

Everything went Richard Nixon's way. The economy continued to pick up, his foreign policy moved from success to success, and the Vietnam War seemed to be steadily winding down. In late October, indeed, the last shreds of the Vietnam

issue that George McGovern had fought for so many years appeared to vanish when Kissinger emerged from long negotiating sessions with the North Vietnamese in Paris and exultantly proclaimed, "Peace is at hand!" McGovern's more radical supporters called loudly for legalized abortion, marijuana, and homosexuality, and for amnesty for the thousands of Americans who had gone to Canada rather than be drafted to fight in Vietnam. These demands simply inflamed mass opinion against the Democratic candidate. At the same time, McGovern's sincere advocacy of major reforms in connection with other cultural matters—women's rights, black equality, and greater power and influence for the young—turned away millions of Americans for whom these causes, during the volcanic 1960s, had become hateful. In such a setting, President Nixon needed hardly to campaign at all, remaining secluded in the White House or at his regularly used retreats, Key Biscayne in Florida and San Clemente in California.

Behind the rhetoric and the bombast lay the fact that the United States had finally changed its view of Richard Nixon. After decades of being called "Tricky Dick," polls revealed that he was widely respected, though not loved. People regarded him as a principled, thoughtful, forward-looking president who had brought strength and fairness to the chief executive's post. At long last, Nixon was admired for himself, and not as a kind of surrogate-Eisenhower. In every age group, in all parts of the country, especially among white voters in the South, at every level of educational attainment, among both Protestants and Catholics and with women as well as men, Nixon led McGovern in public opinion polls.

Nixon landslide

When the balloting took place, even the young voters on whom McGovern had placed so much of his hopes were split evenly, and fewer than half of those newly enfranchised actually voted. Black and Latin Catholic voters comprised the only ethnic groups massively pro-McGovern, but their actual turnout at the polls continued to be gravely disappointing to Democrats. Only fifty-two percent of eligible black Americans cast a ballot, and only thirty-eight percent of the Latin Catholics. Jews remained two-thirds Democratic in the balloting, but this was a drop of almost twenty percentage points from their performance in 1968. For the first time a Republican candidate won a majority of both the Irish and Italian voters (fifty-three percent and fifty-eight percent, respectively), which meant that, overall, Nixon took the Catholic vote (fifty-three percent), a stunning reversal of a pattern as old as the nation itself. Since a whopping two-thirds of the immense Protestant voting group also supported him, Nixon achieved one of the great runaway presidential victories in American history.

When the ballots were counted up, Nixon was found to have taken every electoral vote save those of Massachusetts and the District of Columbia (520 electoral votes to McGovern's 17) and just under sixty-one percent of the popular vote, four percent more than the combined Nixon-Wallace vote in 1968. Two of every three white voters had cast their ballot for Nixon. While McGovern was massively rejected, the Democratic party itself still made a strong showing. In voting for congressional seats the Democrats took fifty-five percent of the vote; they actually won two additional seats in the Senate, and despite Nixon's runaway victory, lost only about a dozen seats in the House, thus keeping firm control of Congress. Of the eighteen governorships being voted on, ten went to their party, raising the nation's split in the governor's mansions to thirty-one Democratic and nineteen Republican. Nixon's victory, in short, was highly personal. He did very little campaigning to help his party, leading to bitterness among Republicans in Congress.

The end of the Vietnam War

The postelection days were filled with news. The apparent peace with the Communists in Vietnam broke down on a diplomatic impasse not clearly explained, and the president suddenly and with no public statement to the nation ordered massive aerial bombardment of North Vietnam, especially Hanoi. This heaviest concentrated bombing in the history of warfare horrified the nation and the world. The largest weekly publication in France, *L'Express,* observed bitingly, "In this poker game of life, Nixon is a master. By means of this nearly blind monster, the B-52, he has discarded forever an assumption. Mr. Nixon is no longer, and will never again be, a respectable man." *Die Zeit,* a liberal weekly in Hamburg, Germany, deplored the bombing as "nothing but terror and torture; torture with a method in order to make the North Vietnamese pliable. The bombs fall on military targets, but they also hit hospitals and schools, women and children. . . . Even allies must call this a crime against humanity. . . . The American credibility has been shattered." The president halted the bombing after two weeks, and negotiations began again, leading to a cease-fire and an exchange of prisoners announced in January 1973. There was worldwide relief. However, as Hamilton Fish Armstrong, former editor of the prestigious American publication *Foreign Affairs,* put the matter, "The President has a second chance now, but nothing will justify the bombing of the North. Millions of Americans are disgusted by it. . . ." And so, within weeks of his immense national victory, Richard Nixon had gravely harmed his moral authority.

At the least, however, the long and wasting American war in Vietnam was over. It had been almost twenty years since the United States had moved in as South Vietnam's protector, following the division of the country in 1954; almost eight years since Lyndon Johnson had decided to make it directly an American war by sending in American troops; and four since Richard Nixon had begun his slow and reluctant withdrawal. Little had been proved by the deaths of 56,000 Americans and over a million Vietnamese, and the expenditure of $150 billion, save that an unpopular government in the south of Vietnam could be at least temporarily propped up. It was not long before even that shallow achievement was nullified. Fighting within South Vietnam broke out again in 1975, swelling to a savage climax in which, in April, the Communists won a complete victory. More than 100,000 fled the country, most of them coming to the United States. After the Khmer Rouge—Communist-backed forces—finished taking over Cambodia, southeast Asia quieted. The dominoes did not fall very far.

The Vietnamese Communists were determinedly independent, furthermore, of either Red China or Moscow. The Communist victory that the United States had fought so hard to stave off in Vietnam made little impact, indeed, upon the world balance of forces. A savagely repressive regime took over in Cambodia, one whose subsequent violence against its own people appalled the world. Hanoi's rule over the South in Vietnam was less brutal, but, nevertheless, harsh. However, in American security that ensued in the succeeding years, not even Republicans of the most hawkish views ever mentioned, in their cataloguing of threats to American security, the existence of a unified Vietnam under Communist control. It was difficult, from any standpoint, to locate any particular benefit to the United States, or significant danger warded off, that resulted from this unnecessary war. The American people had learned a great lesson: this was perhaps all that can be said. But that it was in any calculation of human values right that the United States, or any nation, could claim the sacrifice of hundreds of thousands of lives so that it could gain a better understanding of the truths of life was a proposition to which few, certainly among those who suffered or died, would ever agree.

A puritan toughness of spirit, in the mode of the theologian Reinhold Niebuhr, helped set the mood in which, at the beginning of the Cold War, the American people took up the belief that they were guardians of the world's liberties; that they were empowered by the grandness of this cause to wage war even upon small countries if the enemy, as they believed it to be, were found there. There is a seemliness, therefore, in the fact that the outcome inescapably brought to mind, for many, one of those central human paradoxes which so absorbed Niebuhr's thoughts: that those who profess or aspire to the noblest motives are in that same impulse made perilously liable, through the sin of pride, to commit the gravest crimes.

Bibliography

Three books that were especially valuable to me in writing this chapter: Aside from *The Pentagon Papers,* the spectacular collection of inside documents published by the *New York Times* (1971), I also have drawn a great deal from Roger Hilsman's *To Move a Nation: The Politics of Foreign Policy in the Administration of John F. Kennedy** (1967), written by a man high in the State Department; and Townsend Hoopes's *The Limits of Intervention** (1969), prepared by the man who was undersecretary of the air force under Johnson. Arthur M. Schlesinger, Jr.'s *The Imperial Presidency* (1973) is an historical study of crucial value in gaining a perspective on the modern presidency.

How have historians looked at the topic?

"Vietnam has knocked us Americans off our pedestal," James William Fulbright said in 1969, extending the views expressed in his *The Arrogance of Power** (1967). "It was the moral presumption . . . that we are better than other people—that led us into this war in which we have largely destroyed Vietnamese society while brutalizing ourselves." In *The Roots of American Foreign Policy: An Analysis of Power and Purpose** (1969), Gabriel Kolko views the United States involvement in more diabolical terms. Emphasizing the importance of foreign policy decisions following World War II, Kolko sees the Vietnam intervention as a part of a global attempt of the "ruling class of American capitalism" to extend its hegemony over the world community. David Halberstam's *The Best and the Brightest* (1972) finds the reasons for United States involvement in the machismo and moral blindness of a select group of policy-makers. American intellectuals' roles in designing and implementing policy are criticized in Noam Chomsky's *American Power and the New Mandarins** (1969). Other perceptive views on Vietnam are advanced in Theodore Draper's *The Abuse of Power** (1967), A. M. Schlesinger, Jr.'s *Bitter Heritage: Vietnam and American Democracy** (1967), R. N. Goodwin's *Triumph or Tragedy: Reflections on Vietnam** (1966), and Chester L. Cooper's *The Lost Crusade: America in Vietnam* (1970), written by a former State Department official.

The theory of counterinsurgency, a popular idea with John Kennedy, is analyzed in *American Strategy: A New Perspective* (1966) by Urs Schwarz. Lyndon B. Johnson's decision to escalate—and the advisers who encouraged him—are discussed in Edward Weintal and Charles Bartlett's *Facing the Brink: An Intimate Study of Crisis Diplomacy* (1967). The progression of the war is followed in a notable work by Dennis Bloodworth, *An Eye for the Dragon: Southeast Asia Observed, 1954–1970* (1970). Frances FitzGerald's *Fire in the Lake: The Vietnamese and the Americans in Vietnam* (1972) is a powerful and graphic account. Jonathan Schell tells a chilling story in *The Military Half: An Account of Destruction in Quang Ngai and Quang Tin* (1968). Jon M. Van Dyke's *North Vietnam's Strategy for Survival* (1972) conveys the nation's determination. Frank Harvey's *Air War-Vietnam* (1967) is a compelling and utterly grim account of massive extermination.

The many abortive peace attempts are described in *The Secret Search for Peace in Vietnam* (1968) by David Kraslow and Stuart H. Loory. *Teach-ins USA* (1967), ed. Louis Menashe and Ronald Radosh, contains the early criticism of Johnson's escalation tactics. Kenneth Keniston's *Young Radicals* (1968) explains the importance of New Left activists in Johnson's change of policy. Ken Hurwitz's *Marching Nowhere* (1971) critiques the peace movement. The Vietnam War's impact in the American courts is discussed in Jack Nelson and Ronald J. Ostrow's *The FBI and the Berrigans* (1972).

Lyndon B. Johnson and the World (1966) by P. L. Geyelin is a good study of the president's foreign policy. The Dominican intervention is brilliantly analyzed in Theodore Draper's *The Dominican Revolt: A Case Study in American Policy* (1968) and in John B. Martin's *Overtaken by Events: The Dominican Crisis from the Fall of Trujillo to the Civil War* (1966). Robert Shaplen's *The Road from War: Vietnam, 1965–1971** (1971) provides keen insights on Nixon's policies. A wider perspective, including the years from 1957 to 1972, is W. W. Rostow's *The Diffusion of Power* (1972).

*Available in paperback.

CHAPTER 38

The Watergate Crisis and the Ford Presidency

TIME LINE

1969	Nixon authorizes illegal wiretaps on reporters
1970	Cambodia crisis; Nixon begins search for "foreign agents" causing uproar, authorizes surreptitious entries
1971	*Pentagon Papers* published; Nixon establishes Special Investigations Unit
1972	Watergate arrests
1973	McCord incriminates higher-ups; Ervin committee investigates; bugging revealed; Cox fired; Nixon ends price and wage controls; oil boycott; Congress ends military operations in Southeast Asia, passes War Powers Act; Vice President Spiro Agnew resigns, Ford appointed
1974	Indictments issued in Watergate case; tapes contents revealed; Nixon resigns, Ford becomes president, pardons Nixon; serious inflation and recession; large Democratic Congressional elections victory; Rockefeller appointed vice-president
1975	Cabinet shuffled; CIA and FBI investigated; fall of South Vietnam
1976	Presidential election year; Jimmy Carter elected thirty-ninth president

FTER his triumphant re-election in November, 1972, President Richard Nixon looked ahead with settled confidence. But before the year 1973 was out, his administration had fallen into the gravest scandal in American history. By March 1974, the stunning events of the Watergate crisis and associated villainies had led to the resignation of more than a dozen men from high national office—including the vice-presidency of the United States—and the indictment or conviction of thirty-five men for criminal acts that made Harding's Teapot Dome and the misdeeds of the Grant administration pale into insignificance: burglary, forgery, illegal wiretapping and electronic surveillance, perjury and the subornation of perjury, obstruction of justice, destruction of evidence, tampering with witnesses, misprision of felony, bribery and the acceptance of bribes, and conspiracies to involve government agencies in crimes.

These unprecedented events had their roots in the long Democratic years when, beginning with the election of Franklin Roosevelt, the American presidency rose in a kind of solitary majesty to become overwhelmingly the most powerful agency of government. In Roosevelt's time a great depression and then an enormous war gathered immense authority in the hands of a man who was also widely loved and admired. The White House and its occupant became for many Americans objects not only of veneration but of adoration as well. Television, and the charismatic personality of John F. Kennedy, introduced the impact of a direct visual presence into every American home. Even political parties seemed to fall away, by contrast, into relatively petty and unimportant organizations. The voice and image of the president filled the land.

Nixon's imperial presidency

All that was needed for grave events to occur was the appearance in the White House of men who would put this immense power to its full use. Lyndon Johnson was such a man, for he was driven by gargantuan dreams, and he conceived of the presidency in towering dimensions. The result was America's involvement in the Vietnam war. Richard Nixon believed also that the presidency was an office almost kingly in its authority to act entirely on its own. In the making of war, as earlier described, he claimed for himself unlimited powers over which, he insisted, Congress had no control. In domestic affairs he suddenly expanded a little-used and always doubtful presidential tactic—the impoundment of funds voted by Congress—into a major instrument of national government. In effect, he was assuming the right to an "item veto" (the unchecked vetoing of particular items within an appropriation), which the Constitution had not given to the president. As Franklin Roosevelt had earlier said, impoundment "should not be used to set aside or nullify the expressed will of Congress." But Richard Nixon believed he had the power to pick and choose which laws enacted by Congress he would execute, and by 1973 he had impounded some fifteen billion dollars, thus greatly reducing or wholly eliminating over a hundred federal programs concerning health, housing, urban needs, and environmental protection.

Similarly, he made executive privilege a vastly heightened barrier against the acquisition by Congress of any information whatever concerning the actions of various branches of the federal government. From a vague principle that the president should have the right to confidential conversation with his immediate advisers (so long as criminal activities were not being thereby protected), by April 1973 he had so broadened its outreach as to state, through then-Attorney General Richard Kleindienst, that none of the 2.5 million employees of the executive branch could give testimony on any matter to Congress if the president objected. Meanwhile as if to remind the nation of his imperial powers, in late March 1973, he reinstituted bombing operations in Cambodia, even though the United States was legally at peace with that country and had no right to violate its air space for the purpose of carrying on military operations within its borders. The Tonkin Gulf Resolution had long since been repealed, and American combat troops had departed Vietnam and were no longer in any conceivable danger, thus removing the justification that he had formerly advanced to excuse such actions. And now, as the Watergate investigations soon revealed, he had at least since 1969 operated on the belief that whenever he adjudged something to be a national security matter, at his direction members of the national government could violate the law.

Thus, in an irony of history, the nation witnessed Democrats and liberal intellectuals condemning the strong presidency, which they and their forebears had created. In truth, Richard Nixon's version of the strong presidency was not that of the "tribune of the people" model fashioned by Democratic chief executives—a role that involved working actively with Congress, going frequently to the people, being highly visible and accessible, and leading an assault against social ills and the privileged few. Rather, he revived conceptions reaching far back to the Tory governments of traditional Britain: a belief that legislative branches were quarrelsome bodies whose views could be set aside and ignored; a faith in the unchecked "prerogative" of the Crown to do largely what it felt was best for the nation, whatever the laws said; a conviction that criticism is the same as disloyalty; a preference for rulers who were remote and relatively inactive in social affairs, and almost divine; and an instinctive impulse to crush "disorder" and "rebelliousness" with a strong hand. Suddenly, very old events buried, for most Americans, in the dust of the past, became current. The American air was filled with a clamor of voices crying out the same things that Englishmen had hurled at Charles I three hundred years ago in their Civil War, and that Americans had flung at George III two hundred years ago in their Revolution. For the first time in a century, the venerable impeachment machinery of the Constitution began to rumble into motion. Richard Nixon had challenged the ancient system of democratic government at its core. For millions, therefore, he had become a tyrant who must be expelled from office.

The Watergate crisis

As early as 1969 the president illegally authorized the placing of wiretaps on the phones of newspaper reporters (the law required him to secure the approval of the courts in each instance), on the ground that their description of "secret" American bombing raids over Cambodia—secret only to the American people, certainly not to the Communists—endangered national security. Then, when the nation's campuses erupted in massive protest over the invasion of Cambodia, which he launched in April 1970, he set off a search for the "foreign agents" who were allegedly behind the turmoil. Failing to find any, in July 1970 he took the fateful step of authorizing surreptitious entry (burglary) into private homes and offices in searches for evidence, an action that was patently illegal. Then he issued a formal decision memorandum that called for a shocking array of measures: spying by the CIA on Americans abroad, monitoring of phone calls going out of the country, opening of mail, bugging of telephones, and the placement of undercover agents on college campuses.

J. Edgar Hoover refused to let the FBI engage in these activities though revelations in 1976 showed that for years the FBI had routinely burglarized private homes and offices whenever it chose. For a time the undertaking languished. Then, in June 1971, the *New York Times* began publishing *The Pentagon Papers*, having received them from former Defense Department official Dr. Daniel Ellsberg. This, the president later said, created "a threat so grave as to require extraordinary actions"—though nothing since then has demonstrated that this was so. Not trusting

J. Edgar Hoover, Nixon established, without any congressional knowledge or authorization, an extralegal Special Investigations Unit within his staff, headed by a young aide named Egil Krogh, to "find out all it could about Mr. Ellsberg's associates and motives." Securing a wig and other preposterous devices from the CIA, members of the unit then broke into the offices of Ellsberg's psychiatrist in a vain search for information. Following this, there emerged within the presidential staff a belief that the coming presidential election had to be fought as if against an enemy state. The Gestapolike investigations unit, now apparently financed by the Committee to Re-Elect the President, broadened its activities to include an assault on the nominating processes of the Democratic party. On June 17, 1972, several members of the unit were arrested while burglarizing the national offices of the Democratic party in the Watergate office and apartment complex in Washington, and installing bugs on the phones.

McCord revelations

In the ensuing trial, held after the election of 1972, seven men (two from the White House staff) were sentenced to long terms by Judge John Sirica who, convinced that crucial information concerning the involvement of others was being held back, offered reduced sentences if full confessions were made. In March 1973, one of the burglars, James McCord, made such a declaration, and the whole scandal was ripped wide open. As later recounted in the grand jury indictment issued in March 1974—after a year of national controversy and investigation—what had apparently happened immediately after the Watergate arrests was a frantic effort by members of the White House staff to cover up, by bribes and the subornation of perjury, links between the Watergate burglars and the executive branch. Since this constituted another criminal act, that of the obstruction of justice, and since the people

allegedly involved were not simply "overzealous" minor aides (as Nixon euphemistically described them) but such eminent public officials as former Attorney General John Mitchell—and, it was widely alleged, the president himself—the people of the United States found themselves catapulted into a stunning national scandal reaching the heart of the constitutional system.

"This is the greatest moral crisis of the Presidency," observed distinguished historian Arthur S. Link, biographer of Woodrow Wilson, when interviewed about the Watergate crisis. "It is unprecedented. There is nothing analogous to it in the past, nothing. . . . The peculations of the Harding and Grant administrations . . . were sores on the body politic but not cancers in the body itself. They didn't subvert democratic processes. They didn't corrupt entire administrations. [But] Watergate . . . makes it clear that at least the White House staff and part of the Nixon Administration set out deliberately, knowingly, in a systematic way to subvert and destroy the very processes through which the American democracy must operate. . . .

"Today we don't have congressional leadership that could move into a power vacuum. Our whole politics have become so institutionalized in the last 60 years since T. R. and Wilson that presidential leadership is the vital ingredient, the oil that keeps the machinery of government running. . . .

"The main lesson is there are bounds beyond which presidential power should not be permitted to go. The President himself has to consciously employ self-restraint on his own exercise of power. . . . Another lesson is that skullduggery, burglary, bugging, taping—all of this—simply won't work, at least as long as we are free people. . . . Let's face it, the President has already lost a tremendous amount of credibility with the responsible people of the country, not because they think he was involved but because he set the whole moral, or immoral, tone. He brought in amoral people without any principles or standards whatever. He trusted them. How can he escape responsibility for what they did?'' (*Los Angeles Times* [May 1973].)

Senate Watergate hearings

Millions of Americans watched in appalled fascination as, from May to August 1973, a special congressional committee under Senator Sam Ervin of North Carolina conducted televised hearings, bringing a steady stream of public officials and undercover men before the cameras to confess grave misdeeds. They learned of millions of dollars jammed into random office safes and sluiced about from hand to hand to finance shady dealings; of idealistic young men deluded into criminal activities to protect a president whom they honored; of elaborate procedures for covering tracks and destroying papers. In July 1973, came the incredible news that for years the president had bugged his own offices, so that all conversations that he had had with aides over the Watergate affair were available. Through the summer months Nixon and the Watergate committee jousted over the possession of these tapes. In September, Judge Sirica ordered that they be turned over to him for examination, but the pres-

ident refused, thus becoming the first chief executive ever to defy a formal court order to turn over evidence.

So much else, indeed, had been happening to dismay the United States and the world. In January 1973, Nixon had abruptly ended all price and wage controls, a decision that turned out to be shockingly misguided. Inflation exploded upward. Partial ceilings and freezes that the president later established did little good. By 1974 the cost of food and other living essentials was skyrocketing, and the national economy was teetering gravely close to recession. An Arab-Israeli war that broke out in October 1973, leading to a boycott of oil shipments to the United States by the Arab countries, triggered an energy crisis that caused hundreds of thousands of workers to lose their jobs, and put even greater pressure on the precarious economy. Henry Kissinger, now Nixon's secretary of state, was able in a brilliant display of juggernaut diplomacy to bring peace to the warring nations by early 1974, but the effects of the oil embargo continued.

With Watergate eroding Nixon's prestige, Congress finally began lashing back against his regal uses of power. It decreed that no further American funds were to be spent for military operations in Southeast Asia after August 15, thus bringing a final end to the longest war in American history. In November 1973, after extended debate and over the president's veto, Congress passed the War Powers Act, sharply limiting the executive branch's freedom of action. Henceforth, the president must inform Congress forty-eight hours after sending combat troops abroad for action; Congress would have power immediately to order their return by a majority vote in both houses, not subject to veto; and if that body did not formally give approval for such troops to remain abroad, after sixty days the president would have to withdraw them. Congress also passed a bill requiring that if any government agency involved in international affairs refused to furnish within thirty-five days information it had requested, all funds would be cutoff.

The Senate hearings into the Watergate conspiracy held the nation fascinated for months on end, revealing sordid maneuverings, widely violative of law, ordered from the President's oval office.
Wide World Photos

Agnew's resignation

Meanwhile, as a fitting commentary on the diseased state of American government, Vice-President Spiro Agnew pleaded no contest, on October 10, 1973, to one charge of income-tax evasion (for not reporting perhaps $100,000 in graft), was placed on three years' probation, and given a $10,000 fine. He then became the second man ever to resign from the vice-presidency (John C. Calhoun had done so for political reasons in 1832) and the first to leave office because of crimes committed. Almost immediately afterward, President Nixon selected Gerald R. Ford, veteran congressman from Michigan and minority leader in the House, as Agnew's successor. A forthright, honest, and thoroughly responsible man, Ford reflected, in his down-the-line conservatism on most social issues, the strong traditional Republicanism of his constituency—heavily Calvinist Dutch in ethnic composition—and was widely respected for his strength and solidarity of character.

Ten months later, on August 9, 1974, Richard Nixon was flying home to San Clemente a private citizen, and Gerald Ford was taking the oath as thirty-eighth president of the United States. This unprecedented event came as the stunning climax to a series of increasingly spectacular events that utterly destroyed the Nixon presidency. The root of the matter lay in the fact that in the disputed presidential tapes lay information so damning to Richard Nixon that he fought doggedly, month after month and through every delaying procedure available to him, to prevent their full disclosure. He fired Special Prosecutor Archibald Cox in late October 1973 for refusing to give up his efforts to gain access to the tapes, setting off an earthquake of shock and anger that shook the country. Thereafter, events moved inexorably to their climax. The final act began when, on March 1, 1974, a grand jury charged H. R. Haldeman, John D. Ehrlichman, John Mitchell, and five other close Nixon associates with various crimes in connection with the Watergate burglary and

cover-up, stated that the president was an unindicted co-conspirator, and delivered a mass of evidence to Judge Sirica. The House Judiciary Committee then subpoenaed a large group of tapes to further its impeachment inquiry, and from another direction Cox's successor as special prosecutor, Leon Jaworski, did the same.

On April 30, 1974, Nixon publicly turned over to the Judiciary Committee some 1,200 transcript pages of taped conversations, insisting that everything now was made public (thus refusing to submit the actual tapes). The transcripts, though severely edited to soften their impact, caused a national sensation. They revealed so sordid a moral atmosphere in the White House that the cry for Nixon's resignation erupted on every hand, even among conservative Republicans. In July, the United States Supreme Court ruled unanimously that Nixon must give the special prosecutor the tapes he had requested (after screening by Judge Sirica to remove irrelevant material). Then, in the last few days of that month, the House Judiciary Committee, in a carefully reasoned and widely praised televised debate, voted to recommend three articles of impeachment to the full House: for the president's involvement in the Watergate cover-up; for his abuse of the powers of his office (in the use of such devices as Internal Revenue Service harassment of political enemies); and for his refusal to abide by the committee's subpoenas. The bipartisan majorities behind these actions made it a foregone conclusion that the House of Representatives, for the second time in the nation's history, would vote to begin impeachment proceedings against a sitting president.

Nixon's resignation

On August 5, 1974, President Nixon finally released transcripts of conversations he had had with his aides immediately after the Watergate arrests in June 1972, which proved that he had indeed directly approved the cover-up, thus obstructing justice and committing a felony. Now his house of cards utterly collapsed. Informed by Republican congressional leaders that his conviction by the Senate in the coming impeachment proceedings was certain, he resigned, refusing to the end to admit to more than errors of judgment.

"So down he fell," as the poet Edmund Spenser had centuries before written on a similar occasion, "and like a heapéd mountain lay." Around the country went a vast sigh of relief, tinged perhaps equally with anger and compassion. The president who was so driven by hatred of his enemies that he would connive to violate the laws of the land to harass them, and to protect his followers guilty of illegal activities in his cause, was now gone. A subsequent poll revealed that, by a 4 to 1 margin, the American people approved of his resignation.

There was a widespread feeling that the nation's government had been given a long-overdue cleansing. An arrogance of power had become too much a part of daily life in the White House, and not only in the Nixon administration. "The Constitution works," said the new president, Gerald Ford, in his first remarks following the administration of his oath of office, and indeed Americans generally awakened to a growing sense of pleased surprise that this was so. Their Congress had executed its measured proceedings with great credit to the nation; the Supreme Court, with its large component of conservative Nixon appointees, had unanimously struck down his claim to unlimited executive privilege; and even so powerful a man as a president of the United States could be made to depart his great office in scenes, not of turmoil and revolution, but of quiet orderliness. The air of thoughtful dignity that surrounded these events gave them a majesty few had expected to witness in the affairs of the American republic.

President Gerald Ford's obvious goodness and simplicity of character immediately won him wide support. The columnists Rowland Evans, Jr., and Robert D. Novak had already speculated that he might be the "Eisenhower of the seventies." In these terms, Americans indulged in a hope that

the nightmare, as the new president said in his opening remarks, was indeed over; that the future might be a time of healing and quiet.

End of the honeymoon

Gerald Ford's honeymoon lasted only a month. On the ninth of September, 1974, he startled the nation by issuing an unconditional pardon to Richard Nixon for all federal crimes he may have "committed or taken part in" while in office—before the former president had even been indicted, let alone tried and convicted. This act shattered the nation's trust in Ford's judgment and credibility. The President said that Richard Nixon had already been punished enough by having to give up his great office, and that he wanted to clear the decks, thus saving the nation the ordeal that a trial of the former president would entail. Nonetheless, rumors rushed about that he had made a secret deal with Nixon to do this, in return for his being given the presidency. More than 70 percent of the nation had been positive toward Ford prior to this act. Now his popularity plummeted to below 40 percent, and generally remained there.

His faults, thereafter, were consistently ridiculed: his penchant for banging his head on obstructions; for fumbling his lines; for saying unfortunate things. He tried a few press conferences, then like Nixon largely gave them up. It was widely said that, though a fine and honest man, he was intellectually incapable of being president. His conservatism on social and economic policy had critics comparing him to other midwestern presidents of Republican lineage who had preceded him, such as Herbert Hoover, Warren Harding, William Howard Taft, and William McKinley. His closest friends were from the business, corporate community at the highest national levels, and in domestic affairs he gave the strongest support to his two most conservative cabinet members, William Simon of the Treasury, and Earl Butz of Agriculture.

Economic policy

He agreed with Simon that the most serious economic problem the nation faced was not unemployment, but inflation. This meant maintaining a tight control upon the money supply and keeping interest rates high, so as to cut back on demand. In truth, inflation did burst upward in 1974, raising the cost of living about 25 percent. At the same time, unemployment mounted rapidly from about five percent to over eight percent—a figure thought wholly unacceptable in earlier years—by 1975. The nation's business began winding down deeper and deeper into a recession which held through the rest of 1975 and well into 1976.

Secretary Butz's policies, established under Nixon, had a profound impact upon farming, and therefore upon food prices. Former administrations had kept prices relatively low by subsidizing farmers, keeping huge quantities of land in a "soil-bank"—unused for production and reserved for future needs—and maintaining an output keyed primarily to what the nation itself needed. Butz was profoundly opposed to any government intervention in farming. He negotiated huge food sales to foreign countries, chiefly Russia, and then urged farmers to turn to "wall to wall" agriculture to meet these demands. All available land was put to the plow, production sky-rocketed as heavy investments were made in agricultural machinery, and soil banks disappeared. However, since huge amounts of the food thus raised were committed to foreign purchasers, this left relatively little food to sell at home, creating a steep rise in food prices to consumers, and an end to most subsidies for farmers.

The sum result was a farming world which could not go backward, for it was too heavily committed to all-out production by large investments in equipment, and a cost of living which could not be pushed downward. Secretary Butz's response was for Americans to be more abstemious in their eating. He pointed to the food consumed by the millions of dogs, cats, and other pets that Americans had in their homes, and suggested reductions in this direction. In late 1974 the President abruptly embargoed all grain shipments abroad, in response to wide criticism of the grain deal with Russia, and a new agreement was negotiated which reserved more food for the home market. However, the basic policy remained.

Ford argued constantly with Congress over energy policy. He believed that price controls should be taken off petroleum and natural gas. Once their prices rose to what the open market would pay, each gallon of gas and cubic foot of natural gas would be more expensive to the consumer, and people would cut back in their usage, thus saving energy resources. Also, higher prices would stimulate oil men to search at deeper, more costly depths for new pools of petroleum, and to re-open fields then abandoned as insufficiently productive to be profitable. A heavy push to make the nation energy self-sufficient led to approval of the much-debated Alaska pipe line project, so as to bring down petroleum from the immense oil fields along the northern shore of that state. Ironically, as the extremely costly project got closer to completion in 1976, doubts surfaced that there would actually be a market for Alaskan oil in the relatively oil-rich western states.

Congressional elections and reforms

The Democrats won a large victory in the Congressional elections of November, 1974, increasing their seats in the house to a two-thirds majority, and adding several in the Senate. At the same time, there was a heavy retirement of older legislators, together with a marked liberal shift among Republicans elected, so that the Congress as a whole became younger and more reform-oriented. This led to constant argument with the President, who by the fall elections had vetoed 56 bills passed by Congress.

Reforms pushed through Congress over the previous two years, by a group of liberal Demo-

The incredibly difficult opening of the vast oil resources in the northern Alaska region of Prudhoe Bay showed the desperate straits to which the American national economy, now consuming oceans of oil daily, was reduced in the 1970s.
Alaska Pipeline Service Co.

crats, overhauled its ancient rules and drastically reduced the power of seniority. The party caucuses (the members of each party gathered together outside of Congress's halls to thrash things out among themselves), which shifted and changed in response to each national election, were given effective authority to choose the chairmen of congressional committees. This meant that an inner circle of senior committee chairmen, insulated from the national will by their long tenure in office, would no longer dominate the Congress as formerly.

Congress also pushed ahead to recapture the power that had slipped to the presidency. It centralized its own procedures in the making up of the national budget, and seized a much larger and more effective role in that process. It also prevented the president from frustrating duly enacted laws by impounding funds. A Freedom of Information Act threw open the files of the federal government to reasonable inquiry, and in fall, 1976, a so-called sunshine law was passed which required more than fifty federal agencies henceforth to conduct their deliberations in sessions open to the public.

Presidential appointments

On August 21, 1974, President Ford nominated Nelson A. Rockefeller, former long-time governor of New York, to be vice president. After lengthy hearings into the uses he had made of his great wealth while governor, his choice was approved. Since Ford had no basic changes to make in the policies of the Nixon regime, save to make his administration more open, accessible, and law-abiding, for more than a year he retained the Nixon cabinet. However, by the latter months of 1975 it was clear that he needed to take fundamental steps to re-build his low standing in public esteem, and place his own stamp on his administration. The cabinet, save for Butz, Simon, and Secretary of State Henry Kissinger, was swept clean, new faces appearing at every post. Of these, the most notable were Carla A. Hills of Housing and Urban Development, the third woman to hold a cabinet post, and William T. Coleman of Transportation, the second black person to be in such a position.

The CIA and FBI investigations

President Ford declared in his first address before Congress that his administration would never engage in the illegal wiretapping and other invasions of privacy that the Watergate crisis had unveiled. Investigations soon revealed that the CIA had for years been directly violating its charter (which specifically forbad it to carry on operations within the United States) by conducting massive, illegal domestic intelligence operations, during the Johnson and Nixon administrations, against anti-war and politically dissident groups. Then it was discovered that for thirty years the FBI had gathered political intelligence upon journalists, political opponents of sitting presidents, and critics of national policy, delivering this information to the White House. During the 1960s the FBI had even tried covertly to discredit Martin Luther King, and had sent him harassing letters. J. Edgar Hoover, in his near half-century as head of the Bureau, had become a law to himself long before his death in 1972.

The two agencies plummeted in national standing. Clarence M. Kelley, who became FBI director in 1974, was gravely embarrassed when his flat declarations that these operations had ceased in the early 1960s were shown to be untrue in light of new information, formerly unknown to him. The Socialist Workers party and other political dissidents suffered direct FBI efforts to disrupt their activities; indeed, not until September 1976, did the Attorney General, Edward Levi, announce that surveillance of the Socialist Workers party would cease.

Decline in prestige of government

Continued inflation, rising unemployment, the impasse in Washington, and the disturbing FBI and CIA revelations all combined to drive national respect for the federal government ever lower. In 1964 polls had shown that 76 percent of the people had a basic confidence in their government; by the early 1970s this had dropped to 52 percent; and after the Watergate crisis, only one out of every three Americans held such sentiments. By the spring of 1976, almost half of those polled said they wished to see someone come in from entirely outside the existing ranks of national politicians to take over the country's leadership. Only 23 percent of them had much trust in President Ford or his cabinet; only 19 percent were positive toward Congress. When a long list of Democratic politicians declared their intention of running for their party's presidential nomination, none of them created much public excitement.

The fall of Indochina

The milestone event in 1975 was the final collapse of the South Vietnamese government. In March, North Vietnamese forces, which had remained deeply implanted in the South after the Americans and North Vietnam signed peace agreements in January 1973, began assaulting Saigon's troops in the central highlands. The South Vietnamese army collapsed, and in a swift few weeks of confusion and bloodshed, it was all over. On the 29th of April, 1975, the last Americans evacuated Saigon by helicopter; more than 100,000 South Vietnamese fled their country; and peace finally came to Vietnam after thirty years of war. (Some 130,000 Vietnamese were given permanent residence in the United States.)

Meanwhile, Secretary of State Kissinger labored to bring peace to the Middle East. He secured an agreement between Israel and Egypt over the Sinai peninsula, in which American civilians would occupy a buffer strip between the forces of the two countries, and the Suez canal would finally open to world trade under Egyptian control. President Ford continued his policy of detente with Russia, as inaugurated under Nixon, though relations were strained over a Soviet-backed uprising in Angola, and over the fact that the Strategic Arms Limitation Talks bogged down. It was widely alleged by Ford's critics within and outside of his party that the Russians were using the prior agreement (SALT I) to gain an advantage in arms over the United States.

The Presidential campaign year

The United States entered 1976 at peace, with a stock market which in December 1975, began a long and sustained upward rise which wiped out its heavy losses of previous years, and with an economy which looked as if it might be recovering from recession. Unemployment remained high, over 8 percent, but during 1975 the con-

sumer price index had risen only 7.6 percent, a figure far lower than that in 1974.

President Ford's national standing remained low, for without a foreign war to take the country's attentions, the American people were able to concentrate upon their own internal ills, and they found them disturbing. Ronald Reagan, former governor of California, a man deeply respected by conservatives within the Republican party, announced formally in November 1975, that he was running for his party's presidential nomination. At first his campaign sputtered, but then it caught fire, bringing him victories in primaries in North Carolina and Indiana, then in Texas and many other western and southern states. Over and over he hammered at the president's detente with Russia and at the arms agreements, calling for a much more aggressive and truculent foreign policy. The Panama Canal, he asserted, was sovereign American territory (which it was not) and should never be relinquished to the Panamanians, whose government for years had been pressing for fundamental changes in this direction. He talked constantly of the classic cultural issues which, in one form or another, have been important to conservative Republicans: abortion, busing to achieve racial balance in public schools, crime in the streets, and alleged abuses in the huge welfare program. In an emotional national convention, Reagan came within sixty votes, out of more than two thousand cast, of winning the nomination. Once nominated, Ford sought to mollify conservatives by choosing Senator Robert Dole of Kansas, a man identical with Ford in political ideas, to be vice-presidential nominee. The Republicans would present a solidly conservative front.

Jimmy Carter emerges

The crowd of Democratic aspirants only confused voters early in the year. Including a dozen men, they numbered among them Senator Henry Jackson of Washington, Senator Frank Church of

Idaho, Congressman Morris Udall of Arizona, Governor Edmund Brown, Jr., of California, and Governor George Wallace of Alabama. However, one among them, the relatively unknown Jimmy Carter, former governor of Georgia, began to surge. For two years he had been shaking thousands of hands and talking to groups all over the nation. In Iowa this kind of campaign won him the largest group of delegates; then he won a plurality in the New Hampshire primary, defeated George Wallace in Florida—for which black Americans were grateful—and won a great victory in May when he took the Pennsylvania primary, demonstrating his appeal in a northern industrial, heavily ethnic state. In his speeches during this startling rise from obscurity he insisted that the nation must turn to someone from entirely outside Washington, and called for a politics of love for each other, compassion for the suffering, honesty, and truth. "I will never lie to you," he said, in clear reference to the disgraces of the Watergate and Vietnam years. Joined to his pietistic social moralism (as distinct from concerns for controlling private moral behavior more prominent among Republicans) was an insistence that government be reorganized to make it lean, efficient, and effective. Like Woodrow Wilson long before, whom among Democratic presidential predecessors he most resembled in his style and attitudes, he condemned secret government, secret diplomacy, and a government linked to the powerful and wealthy. It should once more be made open to the people and their ideas, not closed-in, arrogant, and elitist, as he described it to be.

What this all meant in terms of specific program was uncertain, but when Jimmy Carter took the Ohio primary, he had enough committed delegates to secure the nomination in the first ballot, and the Democratic race was over. In a peaceful and good-spirited Democratic convention, strikingly unlike those of 1968 and 1972, he was accorded that honor, choosing Senator Walter Mondale of Minnesota as his running mate.

After more than thirty state primaries, nine more than formerly, and some $70 million spent by the candidates (for the first time, using public funds), the nation had its nominees and its choice to make.

The campaign

The two men campaigned quite differently. Carter moved constantly about the country, speaking day and night. Ford sought to retain his presidential image by remaining at the White House, holding press conferences in which he took opportunities to condemn big spenders and activist government, and performed his executive duties. He was the underdog: after both men were nominated, the President was about ten percentage points behind the Democrat. But then Carter, with his habit of frank and candid statement on personal beliefs derived from his evangelical religious style, made a series of blunders. The most sensational was an interview in *Playboy* magazine in which he spoke explicitly of his own sexual impulses, and used bald language thought by many vulgar and demeaning. In ironic contrast, his tendency to make cautiously qualified statements on complex public issues gave him in that direction a reputation for evasiveness, ambiguity, and two-facedness. His liberal, even populist (the term he used) views turned many voters away from him, for there was a wide impatience with more government-led reformism. President Ford's standing began steadily rising in the polls, and a cliff-hanging race developed.

Then an unprecedented series of three televised debates between the candidates, the first ever between a sitting president and his opponent, dramatically changed the situation. An average of 70 million people, one in three Americans, watched the encounters. Unlike the situation in 1960, when Nixon and Kennedy debated, the electorate's interest remained as high at the end of these sessions as at the beginning. For the first time the American people en masse came to know Jimmy Carter as a person, for television is an intimate medium revealing every nuance of expression. Nervous in the first debate, he was more confident and effective with each succeeding meeting, while President Ford stumbled into errors, as when he decalred that the peoples of eastern Europe were free of Soviet domination. Carter's clarity of mind and his articulateness, as well as his mastery of public issues over a wide range, made him appear as "presidential" as Gerald Ford.

Carter wins

Thereafter, Carter's support firmed, holding at a bare majority of a few percentage points advantage over the President's. Election night saw Carter sweeping the South back into the Democratic fold, save for Virginia; Ford taking all of the West beyond the state of Missouri save for Texas and Hawaii; and the two candidates see-sawing until far into the morning hours in the crucial states of the Middle West and Northeast. When New York and Pennsylvania in the Middle Atlantic region, Massachusetts and Rhode Island in New England, and Ohio, Wisconsin, and Minnesota in the Middle West fell to the Democrat, the White House became Jimmy Carter's. In effect, he had recreated that ancient coalition of the South and the large Middle Atlantic states that since Jefferson's day had delivered the presidency to the Democratic party.

The popular vote stood at fifty percent (40,827,292) for Carter, and forty-eight percent (39,146,157) for Ford, a difference regarded as narrow, but in fact one that was wider than the winning margins gained by either Kennedy in 1960 or Nixon in 1968 (the only other non-incumbents to win since Eisenhower's landslide in 1952). Early studies of voting statistics demonstrated that, for the first time in many years, cultural issues no longer predominated in shaping the outcome. Jimmy Carter was himself the chief cultural issue, in his Deep South identity and accent, his "born again" Christianity, and his

habit of talking about intimate matters that made many nervous. But much stronger was a deep national sense of alarm over the economy—the classic Democratic issue since the Great Depression. Inflation and high unemployment were burdens Ford could never escape. More than a quarter of the voters described themselves as financially worse off than they had been a year before, and that quarter voted for Carter almost four to one. Millions of Democrats who had supported Nixon in 1972 returned to their party on economic grounds. Manual workers surged for Carter by about 64 percent, while in 1972 they had supported McGovern at only the 44 percent level. Indeed, Democrats in general voted four to one for their candidate, a return to the levels of support given Kennedy and Johnson.

Cultural analysis

Among culture groups, Catholics turned Democratic again, from their 50 percent support of McGovern to almost 60 percent for Carter, despite a widely reported unease among Catholics concerning his openly pietistic Baptist faith. Indeed, recent studies demonstrate that the heralded Catholic exodus to the Republican party, said to be the fruit of their movement to the suburbs and rise in wealth, has not occurred. They remain more politically liberal than Protestants, more desirous of an activist government. Even in the suburbs they hold on to their Democratic heritage.

The most striking voting performance, however, occurred among black Americans, who voted 15–1 for Jimmy Carter, sensing in him and his past record as governor an understanding of and sympathy for their cause. They provided his narrow victory in such battlegrounds as New York and Ohio, and it was their huge pro-Carter vote in the southern states that swung that region, save for Virginia, to the Democrat. (In the South as well as nationally, 51 percent of the whites voted Republican.) The Voting Rights Act of 1965, which effectively enfranchised southern blacks, won the election for Jimmy Carter by delivering to the Democratic party the last large low-status voting group which, to that point, had remained without political power. As at the nation's beginnings, the Democrats remained distinctively the party of the outgroups. In 1800 it had been the massive pro-Jefferson vote of the Scotch-Irish, feared and disliked by the then-English majority, that had delivered the Middle Atlantic states and the presidency to the Virginian. In 1976, it was the massive pro-Carter vote of the black Americans, the twentieth century's largest outgroup in politics and one widely feared by the white majority, that put the Georgian in the White House.

How could the Republican party, which could only claim about 20 percent of the American people as registered members, get so close to victory? Jimmy Carter was a deep southerner. For more than a hundred years, such people had been kept out of the presidency. It was clear from the beginning that perhaps his greatest problem lay in the instinctive recoiling of northerners, especially northern journalists and political figures, from the idea of a southerner in the White House. Many within his party, furthermore, could not forgive him his daring victory in the race for the nomination, pushing aside powerful Congressional figures in the process who also desired the prize. They clearly lagged in their

The election of 1976

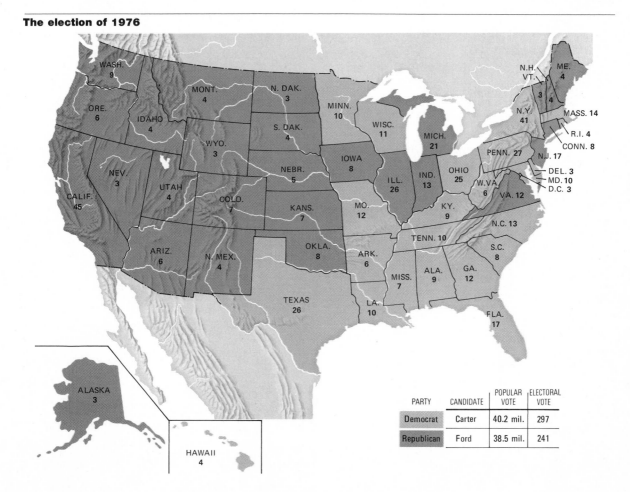

PARTY	CANDIDATE	POPULAR VOTE	ELECTORAL VOTE
Democrat	Carter	40.2 mil.	297
Republican	Ford	38.5 mil.	241

readiness to work hard for his election. Governor Jerry Brown of California refused until the very end to release his delegates at the convention to vote for Carter, he did almost nothing thereafter for the Carter campaign in California, and that state tipped for Ford in the balloting.

When Ford voters were asked why they disliked Carter, they responded most frequently that they did not know his position on the issues (i.e., he took ambiguous stands), and did not trust him. He had appealed to voters to elect him because he had not been part of the Washington Establishment that had got the country into such a mess, but this very lack of experience in the nation's capital worked against him. In fact, his candidacy revived a traditional national habit. Until Harry Truman, the country regularly had chosen state governors for the White House, men who had not had long experience in Washington. Indeed, Abraham Lincoln himself had only been a one-term congressman and a legislator in Illinois when he became president. Instinctively, the electorate periodically has wished to see fresh men from outside the Washington orbit govern the country. This historical fact, however, was little taken account of, and Carter's "inexperience" was widely commented upon as a grave and unusual weakness.

Gerald Ford came close—but not close enough. Perhaps the crucial influence causing his defeat lay in what he had done within a few days of becoming president: his pardon of Richard Nixon. Half of the voters, when asked after the election, said the pardon had been wrong. That half of the electorate voted eight out of ten for Jimmy Carter.

The Carter administration

At the opening of the year 1977, the Democratic party stood in command of the country, refreshed and cautiously hopeful, beginning what seemed a new, post-Vietnam and post-Watergate phase of power that could dominate American life for much of the rest of the century. It had a new

president ready to be inaugurated, youthful at 52 and possessed of a new mandate from the people. He had a young vice president of exceptional promise coming to power with him, and 37 Democratic governors in the states. While Gerald Ford had come near to victory, Republicans in Congress had done badly. That body remained dominated by the two-thirds Democratic majority that Watergate had produced in the congressional election of 1974, a sobering fact to Republicans who had expected to rebound from that low point. Their twenty-year effort to build an enduring new base of power in the South had failed. By inaugural day, furthermore, Jimmy Carter had behind him a strong surge of public support, 60 percent of polled Americans, after watching him build his new administration, saying they felt more favorable to him than at election time. By overwhelming margins, they expected him to introduce tax reform bills to make the system more equitable; to reduce unemployment; and to make the country more optimistic, unified, and idealistic. More citizens, indeed, said they had voted for him than could have possibly done so, given the closeness of the election.

On Inaugural Day, Jimmy Carter swept into Washington in classic Democratic form. Insisting upon being sworn in as "Jimmy," wearing a business suit bought from the rack instead of the formal attire of tradition, he gave an inaugural address in which he called for a "new spirit." Then he startled and excited the nation by taking his wife Rosalyn by the hand and walking the mile and a half to the White House, down the middle of Pennsylvania Avenue, smiling and waving to the hundreds of thousands who lined the route.

His first weeks were devoted to making many more such gestures designed to express his view that the government should be brought close to the people again. He began twice-monthly press conferences, his first one generally described by the press and political observers as a virtuoso performance of calm and informed articulateness, sprinkled with wit. Then he went before the nation's television audience in a cardigan sweatered fireside chat, speaking with reassuring steadiness and directness about the energy crisis, his plans for welfare and tax reform, and government reorganization. Abolishing the ruffles and flourishes that surrounded the presidency, he took steps to lay to rest the "imperial presidency," at least in its trappings and grandeur. Then he spent two hours in a televised call-a-thon, answering phoned-in questions from citizens around the country. Some 300,000 randomly selected Americans were invited to send in suggestions for a new national energy policy, and plans were laid for ten forays into the American countryside, in which the President would attend town meetings, spend evenings in private homes, and talk to government officials.

His cabinet had relatively few new faces, most of them—such as Cyrus Vance, his secretary of state—being well-known Washington figures. However, in the second-level cabinet positions, where the first rank leaders of future years are traditionally trained, persons exciting to liberal Democrats took up major posts, including many women, blacks, and young academics. At the same time, in his policies Carter moved strongly to take over the political center, proposing a moderate stimulus to the economy, and a measured pace in reforms. Like Democratic presidents in the past, he laid heavy stress on working closely with Congressional leaders, who found access to the Carter White House and ear readily available.

Carter's "human rights" foreign policy

Surprisingly, for a newly installed Democratic president who had spent most of his campaign talking about domestic problems, the President moved most boldly in foreign affairs. He sent Vice President Walter Mondale abroad for personal conversations with western European and Japanese leaders, thus signallizing a rebuilding of the special relationship with the democracies of the world that Democratic critics of Republican

In an historic event, former Georgia governor Jimmy Carter, though a Deep Southerner and evangelical Baptist, won both the Democratic nomination to the presidency and the election, and on January 20, 1977, was inaugurated the nation's thirty-ninth President.
Wide World Photos

foreign policies had urged. While control of nuclear weapons was his most important goal, Carter shelved Henry Kissinger's theory of "linkage": that criticism of Russian policies in regard to human rights had to be set aside in order to get Moscow, thus mollified, to negotiate meaningfully on nuclear arms control and other world problems. "I think we come out better," said Carter, "in dealing with the Soviet Union if I am consistently and completely dedicated to the enhancement of human rights." These words evoked the traditional Democratic urge in foreign policy to improve the world, to follow the "missionary diplomacy" strategy of Woodrow Wilson.

The nation watched in high interest, and western Europe was electrified. The emergence of a Wilsonian world leader in the person of Jimmy

Carter stimulated an agitated, continent-wide uprush in European countries of debate over human rights questions that for years had been tacitly ignored. To Moscow's expressed anger, the President met with Soviet dissident Vladimir Bukovsky, recently expelled from Russia, and sent a personal letter to Andrei Sakharov, Nobel Peace Prize winner and leader of the dissident movement in the Soviet Union. At the same time, he criticized Czechoslovakia and Uganda, and cut back on foreign aid to Argentina, Ethiopia, and Uruguay, on grounds that human rights were being violated in those countries. In such sensitive locations as South Korea and the Philippines, however, where autocratic governments were in charge, "we must balance," said Secretary of State Cyrus Vance, "a political concern for human rights against economic or security goals," and no measures were taken. "He obviously has no idea just how far up the wall the human-rights issue drives the Russians," said a critical Ford administration foreign policy expert of Carter's policies. "They are literally unable to tolerate the criticism and they're capable of almost anything to shut it off." But a cause of great importance to many Americans had been reawakened.

In his first two months of power, President Jimmy Carter had shown himself to be remarkably sure-footed. Apparently as adept as John Kennedy and Franklin Roosevelt in using the media to reach the American people; skillful in choosing gestures that dramatized his goals; and a formidably intelligent man, he seemed not simply comfortable in his great Presidential office, but well suited to it. The nation and the world, however, have a way of challenging good beginnings. A daily stream of great and difficult, often surprising, problems and crises arrive at the White House. The American people were clearly ready, after his first weeks in office, to regard Jimmy Carter with trust and approval, but his real testing was yet to come.

Bibliography

The narrative this chapter presents has been based primarily upon current sources: newspapers, periodicals, and direct observance. Particularly valuable, of course, is Arthur M. Schlesinger's *The Imperial Presidency* (Boston, 1973), a brilliant historical study, brought to the Watergate crisis, of the emergence of the kind of presidency to which, in this book, he gave the name which is now commonly in use. Carl Bernstein and Bob Woodward's *All the President's Men* (New York, 1974), written by the two Washington *Post* reporters who broke the Watergate affair, is fascinating. Arthur Schlesinger and Roger Bruns have together edited a volume, *Congress Investigates: A Documented History, 1792–1974* (New York, 1975), which gives a panoramic view. Jonathan Schell has published a valuable study of the Nixon era, *The Time of Illusion* (New York, 1974).

President Ford has so recently emerged as chief executive that the literature upon him is still quite thin. Useful are: Jerald F. TerHorst, *Gerald Ford and the Future of the Presidency* (N.Y., 1974); Richard Reeves, *A Ford, Not a Lincoln* (N.Y., 1975); Bud Vestal, *Jerry Ford, up Close: An Investigative Biography* (N.Y., 1974); and Congressional Quarterly, *President Ford: The Man and His Record* (Washington, D.C., 1974). For Jimmy Carter, see his own autobiographical book, *Why Not the Best?* (1975).

CHAPTER 39

The American Nation: A Comparison Across Time

E observe a familiar scene: a busy university full of controversy and argument. Major world events have produced an upheaval in the way men and women think about all the aspects of life. A flood of new books and ideas is pouring onto the scene, leading to skepticism and a questioning of old truths. Authority is being challenged on all sides; tradition is being scorned. Students and their more radical faculty reject God and religion, saying that people can be sure only of the world around them. Long-accepted ideals are being swept away. Education is in turmoil. People are saying that learning must be made more relevant to the here and now, more purposeful, more real. Others are advocating retreat from society and the living of simple lives of meditation. There is a widely expressed contempt for humanity's materialism and greed.

This scene, so filled with events and ideas that remind us of our own time, was not, however, at the University of California at Berkeley in 1964, or at Columbia University in 1968. It was at Oxford, and the time was almost 400 years ago. Copernicus and Galileo had transformed science; explorers had revealed strange new continents; gold and silver from Mexico and Peru were pouring wealth and turbulence into the European economy; wars and the threat of wars were everywhere. The colony of Virginia was being founded, and all the things recounted in this book were just beginning. The more things change, runs an ancient French proverb, the more they remain the same. The human predicament seems to be the same no matter what the time or circumstance. Ordinary citizens, little trained in history, feel that the time in which they live is uniquely revolutionary and turbulent, and yet historians are aware that throughout the modern centuries people have always thought of their own time as an age of upheaval. It is often said that no earlier era can compare with the present one since none had the atomic bomb confronting

it with the implied specter of civilization's complete annihilation. The destruction of which people are now capable dwarfs everything past into insignificance—until we read of the Thirty Years War, the medieval Black Death, the millions who died in China's nineteenth-century T'aiping rebellion; or consider what happened to the American Indian, reflect on the millions of black people who died while being brought to the New World to be slaves or while laboring in the fields, and look at almost an entire generation cut down by machine guns and artillery in the First World War. The past is choked with destroyed tribes, cities, nations, and empires. Our time has no monopoly on apocalypse.

A healthier people

By any reckoning, however, the way we live has drastically changed, and the changes are worth exploring. If a group of Americans who had been alive in the 1870s were somehow to appear among us now, a century later, they would be amazed. The surface changes would impress them at first, and then, the longer they looked, the more they would notice deeper considerations. They would be struck by the enormous numbers of people filling city streets like salmon crowding up a river, oceanic in their multitude; then by the comparative absence of mutilated people—people with open sores, stumps for limbs, ravaged faces, dropsy, filmed eyes—the human wreckage of a society in a premedical age. They would note with surprise that most people achieve a healthy adulthood and that chronically ill men and women are seldom seen in private homes. Death, birth, and wasting disease are banished to remote, aseptic hospitals, impersonal and bustling. Pain would seem gone, by their standards, from chronic disease, certainly from surgical operations.

And the cleanliness and orderliness everywhere: the lack of dirt, dust, awful smells; the absence of stinking privies outside homes and in great ranks outside hotels; the clean food and drink; the lack of rumpled clothes, tobacco spittle, stains and patches. Abraham Lincoln and his cabinet, next to the neatly pressed men of modern government, would look like refugees from a rummage sale. Walking about an American city, people from the 1870s would be struck also by the absence in the streets of thousands of animals used in past times for transportation and labor, and thus the lack of manure and great droning clouds of flies. There are neat roads, painted lines, smoothly riding automobiles, discreet curbs and gutters. The motor car was approved by most people when it appeared because it *cleaned up* the environment. They would observe cars and people waiting quietly at traffic lights, and orderly lines in stores and theaters. The water supplies, heating systems, food markets, flood control systems, communication networks, and vast departmentalized stores would all seem so logically and rationally arranged, measured, and centrally regulated.

There is the radically changed *appearance* of things. Floods of color—kaleidoscopic, rich, and bright—pour from buildings at night and are displayed in everyday clothes, buildings, and advertisements. The world of the 1870s, with its dull black leather, its dirt and smudges, has been replaced by a world of startling oranges, yellows, blues, and reds. And light is everywhere, blurring daytime and evening. Light in rooms, streets, on buildings; constantly glowing across the countryside, dotting the whole earth with vast spreads of many colored, darting, flashing, steadily burning light. People from the 1870s would think the typical home an industry in itself with its array of motorized aids and devices. The center of incoming communications systems that pour in floods of information, music, and visual stimulation by the hour, it would seem open, airy, clean.

Range of life style

They would note the enormous range in most people's style of life: the distances they travel for enjoyment or for business; the vast array of occupations, most of them unheard of a century ago; the many ways of recreation. They would be surprised by the extraordinary cosmopolitanism of taste in music, books, and art, and by the fact that America is no longer slavishly dependent on Europe for its cultural life; that it has itself become a source of cultural forms and standards, its influence flowing out to all the world. People living in the 1870s would have known a culture determinedly practical and little concerned with aesthetics, but in the 1970s they would see a widespread concern with beauty, styling, and urban beautification. Music is everywhere—in automobiles, offices, supermarkets, and homes. Thousands of local symphonies, play companies, and art programs have sprung to life in the past generation. Allied to this interest in aesthetics is a new attitude toward wilderness, which is considered no longer a howling savageness to be tamed and cut down, but a place of beauty and refuge.

In the midst of an orderly culture that is sensitive to the arts, however, persons from the 1870s would note a contrasting tendency: a disorderly fragmentation of accepted styles. They would be perplexed by the personalization of literature, the uniqueness of each writer's vision expressed in many changing forms; the personalization of dance, with people expressing their own emotions in their own pattern; the disappearance of clear social directives as to how one dresses, eats, behaves. Our society would seem paradoxical to them because in some ways it has become orderly and standardized and in others chaotic and individualized. American city streets, with their anarchic tangle of wires, illuminated signs, and fried chicken eateries, would seem, in their special squalor, an ironic foil for the remarkable islands of ordered architectural elegance which urban renewal is causing to spring up in the midst of most great cities.

Of course, the visitors from a century ago would be astonished by America's wealth. The average standard of living would seem incredible to them. Society's capacity, furthermore, to carry through vast projects using immense stores of public and private capital, the enormous social power of government and business corporations—these things would be almost appalling. The sight of soaring buildings and arabesques of concrete freeways circling and swooping through the cities would be breathtaking, quite aside from the endless, roaring streams of automobiles flowing everywhere like metallic rivers. The speed of transport would be a continual wonder to the people of the 1870s—not simply over long distances, for which the railway would have in part prepared them, but over the short distances of everyday life. The ease of going ten miles in one direction, five miles in another, and ten miles in still another all in the course of a morning; the fact that many people go 500 miles over the course of a weekend to ski, swim, mountain-climb, or carry on business—all would be amazing.

Would pollution surprise?

Produced by this power and affluence, of course, are the polluted skies, lakes, and rivers of present-day America. Would this also astonish Americans from the 1870s? Certainly the cities of their time were massively polluted with human excrement, noisome smells, disease, filthy water, rotten food, choking coal smoke, and the noise of traffic. Urban humanity had to live closely jammed together, since transportation facilities were meager and jobs had to be nearby. By the 1870s, London had been a polluted city for centuries. In the late nineteenth century, men and women staggered about through blinding fogs in that city because the air was choked with tiny particles of coal ash. Pittsburgh, Chicago, Boston, Philadelphia, and New York were black and grimy as a result of the pervasiveness of coal-fired industries and coal stoves in homes. Humanity has probably never lived in such polluted environments as those of the great cities of Europe and America a century ago.

Then, however, people had a different attitude toward pollution than they do now. The grimy steel workers of Pittsburgh liked coal smoke, for heavy plumes pouring out of steel plant chimneys meant jobs. Caught in a nationwide frenzy of development, people were heartened by the sight of factories springing up everywhere and of seemingly limitless mineral resources being mined. Environmental concern is a sophisticated state of mind. Its development depends on mass education, an instantaneous communication system, and the ability to look at the world at arm's length, so to speak, to become conscious of a polluted planet.

It is hard to believe, however, that the massiveness of the problem as it now exists would fail to affect someone from even so environmentally indifferent an era as the 1870s. The incredible rate at which resources are being gobbled up, the rendering of such huge bodies of water as Lake Erie unsafe for man or creature, the fact that 200 miles east—that is, generally downwind—of Los Angeles one can encounter smog so thick that it seems as if a huge forest fire must be nearby—all of this would certainly be alarming to someone from a century ago. The impending death of the biosphere, widely forecast, would be a chilling thought. The loss of blue skies and sparkling rivers outside the cities, as well as the sprawling invasion of streets and homes into vast areas of countryside, would also seem grievous to a visitor from the past.

Wealth and the masses

It is a safe guess, however, that the people of the 1870s, like anybody from a part of the contemporary world that is markedly less wealthy than the United States, would be more impressed and attracted by the tremendous change in the life style and income of the farming and laboring classes. They would note that farm protest, industrial warfare, and the widespread conviction that bankers and employers are cruelly exploiting the masses, have all died down. Protest now comes from culture groups—black Americans, youth, women, Mexican-Americans, and Indians—not from economic classes. Americans from the 1870s would be surprised at the relative power of workers in relation to their employers, at the safety of working conditions, and at the shorter working hours. Instead of the seventy-hour average workweek of the 1870s, the average today is forty hours or less. This decrease has opened up opportunities for leisure and recreation thought only visionary before. In 1976, though the nation's population was growing steadily older (the average person in that year could expect to live almost 72 years), the death rate was at its lowest-point in the country's 200 years (8.9 per thousand, as against 19.8 in even so advanced a state as Massachusetts in 1876). A national survey among 30-year-olds in the bicentennial year revealed that more than three out of four of those polled thought the quality of their life "quite good," in relation to their health, love lives, and jobs (though almost half were not happy with their intellectual development, i.e., their understanding of life). In 1976 another national study, made for the Ford Foundation, even revealed that Jews and European Catholics, for so many decades poor and exploited, actually outclassed Protestants in wealth and education, demonstrating how profoundly changed was American life from its condition a century before. (Jews averaged $13,340 in income; Irish Catholics $12,426, with Italian, German, and Polish Catholics just behind them; then Episcopalians, the highest income group among Protestants, followed with $11,032. Baptist whites were the poorest, with $8,693, a figure which was not improved when rural southerners were kept out of the computation. British Protestants, it should be noted, still had a higher rate of occupational mobility, securing higher prestige positions than other groups.)

Even more shocking to visitors from the 1870s, therefore, would be the intractable problem of poverty, created in good part by the virtual disappearance of any need for unskilled workers. They would see millions of people living outside the affluent economy, superfluous and apparently unneeded. In the South Bronx, in New York City, they would observe forty percent of its 400,000 residents on welfare, twenty percent of the homes without water, drugs and crime so prevalent that fear poisons the atmosphere, and a tuberculosis rate fifty times higher than the national average—in sum, a degradation probably unparalleled since eighteenth-century London.

Gentling of manners

Outside the slums, however, they would observe that social lines between classes have blurred since the 1870s; that there is a relative absence of haughtiness, overt arrogance, blatant pride of class. Associated with this is a gentling of manners and a sensitivity to the needs of unfortunate people unknown before. In the 1870s the unemployed, the blind and the crippled, the old, the children without fathers, the extremely poor, were ignored by government. There were no schools for the mentally retarded, no publicly provided medical care for the needy or the elderly, no old-age pensions. Vast areas of American cities went completely unpoliced and unregulated, for few cared about bad housing or violence and death among the poor. Indeed, street violence as a general phenomenon has steadily decreased since far back in the nineteenth century—except for an upsurge of drug-associated robberies, muggings, and burglaries that began to engulf the central cities in the late 1960s.

What the people of the 1870s would find interesting is the greater sensitivity now to levels of violence and crime formerly ignored—indeed, a rising sensitivity to every other indication of poor performance in the social system. In the 1870s, Americans expected trains to run erratically, water to smell, streets to be filled with garbage, politicians to take graft, hold-up men to endanger travelers, government to be massively ineffective, and epidemic diseases to sweep off thousands every year. Now, save in slums and urban enclaves, Americans expect everything to work well and are angered by inefficiencies that would formerly be thought near-perfection. They expect surgeons to perform open-heart surgery successfully; intricate mechanisms like their automobiles and their jet airliners always to work; food and water to be hygienically pure; government to be financially honest and relatively effective; and the streets to be not only well paved and lighted but also orderly. Social efficiency is a self-feeding mechanism: the more of it there is, the more of it is expected. It is a benign process that generates continual criticism and reform.

The information revolution

Although the Americans of the 1870s would be prepared for the telegraph, they would not be prepared for the extraordinary instantaneousness and pervasiveness of information from other sources. They would be dazzled by the speed not merely of public information about disasters or great events (in relation to which the nation has become a kind of electronic village, a non-stop town meeting) but of domestic information as well. The husband calling his wife, friends and extended family keeping in touch over long distances, the immense buzzing network of communication lines and radio signals that links business houses and directs government—all this creates far more complex and wider webs of communication than any individual in the 1870s ever maintained. Probably more from the information revolution than from any other cause, the visitor from the 1870s would feel surrounded by enormous physical power—in armaments, corporations, and technology, and in the extension of people's limbs and agility by electrical power and the automobile. Just as Americans in the 1970s move about in a bath of sound, so they are awash in a constant impouring of information about increasingly complicated national issues.

For this reason, too, visitors from the 1870s would be surprised by the sophistication of ordinary people about matters few, if any, understood in their day. Many average citizens today know more about the body and its ills and processes, about the natural world and the universe,

about psychology, society, politics, world affairs, and economics than even the most knowledgeable scholars did a century ago. The knowledge revolution has created an incredible number of intellectuals, whose power and prominence in modern society would stun their counterparts of a century ago, who were few in number and generally ignored. The learned professions extend to scores of skilled occupations that did not even exist before. While in the 1870s the average American was either illiterate or had at most three or four years of schooling, now almost everyone is educated at least through high school, and roughly half of the entire population above the age of eighteen will soon have all or part of a college education. The level of technological knowledge alone required to read and understand a modern newspaper is extraordinary when compared to that required in earlier times.

The changed sex roles and family

People from the 1870s would be astonished and embarrassed by the sexual revolution and surprised by the transformed position of women in society. To a degree unimagined in the 1870s, women work outside the home in gainful employment. The vote, styles of dress, public visibility—these and other aspects of women's lives would come as a shock. They would note, however, that despite all the changes, the authority structure in modern society is still dominated by men. Though the high divorce rate would be far beyond their experience—a phenomenon caused in good part by rising expectations—people from the 1870s would find Americans to be a child- and family-centered people, as they had been a century before. Indeed, there is today a stronger awareness of the importance of the family constellation in the development of personality. The observer from the past would immediately note, however, that the family as an economic unit has been replaced by the family as an emotional unit. Many hands are no longer needed to till the land or to labor in the factories so as to support the family. Children have almost no economic function at all except as consumers. Their adolescence (the period in which they have little or no responsibilities for the care of others) is greatly extended, for many into the middle and late twenties until college is finished. The task of the family in such a setting, therefore, has become the emotional nurturing of its members.

The visitors from a century ago would be astonished at the vast rebellion of youth that occurred in the 1960s, although they would expect young people to be bold and reckless. In the nineteenth century, Americans took pride in the impatience of youth, accounting it a major reason why progress was inevitable. The whole country was young: millions of young people poured in from abroad as immigrants, built factories, laid out railroad lines, led armies, attacked Indians, rushed westward to plow the Great Plains and mine gold, and founded state after state in the immense continental sweep to the Pacific. Furthermore, college youth (of whom there were few a hundred years ago) were traditionally known to be troublesome and unruly. Since the colleges then closely controlled their students both outside and inside of class, there were frequent eruptions of violent protest against the strict discipline. Dormitories were burned down and faculties were harassed.

Even so, Americans from the 1870s would be unprepared for the kind of nationwide upheaval against established authority that occurred on hundreds of college and university campuses in the 1960s. They would recognize the anticapitalist, proanarchy cry of the most radical of the protestors, for they would have heard it from young radicals in their own day. What would bewilder them, instead, would be the *multitudes* involved; the radicalization, so it seemed, of an entire generation. They would be observing, indeed, the first major rebellion of generation against generation in United States history, though not, of course, the first appearance of a fresh wave of young reformers determined to change things. That had happened almost in

waves, as in the Revolution, the Age of Jackson, and in the abolitionist crusade. But mass violence? Student radicals blowing up buildings, storming government offices, skirmishing with police and soldiers? It would seem like the French Revolution.

Optimism about America fades

The people of the 1870s would observe that the bountiful, almost childlike faith in a golden American future that inspired the country a century ago has faded. The sense of America as the example for all the world, the seat of democracy and equality, is little heard. Two immense world wars, like shattering thunderclaps, have revived an image of humankind held by the Puritans centuries ago: that we are corrupt, power-hungry, dangerous, and in need of God's help. Indeed, visitors from the 1870s would learn that in the 1950s and 1960s a great awakening occurred in the churches like those that surged through the eighteenth and nineteenth centuries. It is true that people do not think in terms of traditional religious concepts as a matter of course, as they did in the 1870s. The spread of scientific knowledge and the impact of skepticism has ended, for most Americans, the bitter argument over Darwinian evolution that was just beginning in the 1870s. Relatively few now accept the story of the Garden of Eden as an accurate account of human origins. But the search for transcendent meaning still goes on; millions of Americans either go regularly to religious services or pursue the search for meaning in other directions, such as in philosophy classes, communal movements, existentialism, encounter groups, mystical or astrological societies, and eastern religions. Four out of ten Christians are members of pietist, evangelical sects.

Personal and national problems are both more subtle and elusive now. Most public conversation in the 1870s dealt with tangible issues, such as jobs, the money system, or federal control over the southern states. In the 1970s, however, intangibles, such as the quality of the environment or feelings of anonymity and rootlessness in a computerized mass society, are prominent. The visitors from the 1870s would encounter a conviction that the problems of modern society have grown so complex, pervasive, and enormous that the handles to grab onto are no longer available. It is no longer possible even to damn specific public enemies—the John Rockefellers and Jay Goulds —but only the system, the huge corporation, the military-industrial complex. Interwoven with these unformed anxieties is a frightened sense of potential mass destruction created by the atom bomb and intercontinental missiles. A tragic sense of life, indeed, has become almost a national style. It is revealing that this more cynical people, more intellectual in its outlook, is given to a different kind of humor. Satire is now the style, not bellywhoppers and tall tales.

The more sophisticated and tempered society of today is less aroused than was nineteenth-century society by the style of political oratory and appeal popular a century ago and evidenced in campaigns glorying in American "superiority," shouts for territorial expansion, bellows of hatred of the Irish, Catholics, aliens, Orientals, or southerners, or calls for such alleged panaceas as free silver. At the same time, widespread affluence has meant a dwindling of class rivalry and the disappearance of the great issues that for so long agitated the country: the currency and tariff questions, the position of labor, and the conflicting needs of farmers, bankers, and consumers.

Corruption changes in form

The stink of old-style political corruption, which clung to government from top to bottom in the 1870s, has faded. The visitors from the 1870s would be surprised that governments could spend hundreds of billions of dollars annually without much of it being illegally siphoned into private pockets. The civil service revolution has occurred: in practical and concrete terms, government servants care honestly for public funds, are not beholden for their jobs to political manipulators, and are enabled to provide experienced and trained administration no matter which party is in power. But the billions spent on huge aircraft and complex armaments that fail to perform would look very much, to people of the 1870s, like the railroad-building scandals of the nineteenth century and the Tweed Ring's thievery in building New York City's city hall with millions where hundreds would have sufficed.

More disturbing, however, would be the political corruption displayed in the Watergate scandal. It was common a hundred years ago for Americans to warn that someday, if they were not vigilant, they might build a national government like those that existed then in continental Europe: so strong and militarized that they depended on secret police, spies, and undercover operations against their political critics to stay in power. Powerful government agencies and a mighty presidency were warned against in America precisely because of their potential for invasion of civil liberties. So, indeed, has it turned out. Watergate was not a simple affair, like the old search for money and contracts; it was, rather, a corruption of the heart of the American system of government itself, ideally a free and uncontrolled political process presided over by a national government that does not arrogantly regard itself as above the law.

The pervasiveness of government

Few things, indeed, would so astonish the people of the 1870s as the immensity and everyday *presentness* of government. Perhaps the most striking of their experiences would be to observe in the daily newspaper that almost nothing occurs in city, county, state, or nation that is not in some way linked to an agency of government. From decisions on how people are to build on land, pay employees, advertise goods, plant crops, minister to patients, set aside funds for retirement, wire a house, or cohabit with an unemployed husband, to negotiations between labor unions and employers, modes of power distribution, and the intricate mechanisms of international finance, government is involved.

Laissez-faire government has disappeared, gone with the passenger pigeon, the dime novel, and the dictatorial employer who ran his factory out of his back pocket. The search for order, which had its rudimentary beginnings in the middle of the nineteenth century, has produced an immense social machinery of centralized regulation and control. Bureaucracy, a new and pervasive force, now exists in business life as well as in public affairs. Born in the effort to make the railroad system efficient, it has proliferated like an incredibly gargantuan plant, sending its tendrils through the length and breadth of the social system. Vague and remote but ubiquitous, it presents contradictory aspects. Rigid, impersonal, self-serving, and self-perpetuated, the bureaucracies are also responsible for the creation of a society in which there is regularity of operation, predictability, orderliness, even-handed treatment for all, carefully made decisions, a diffusion of power, and a concern for the public interest. Capable of generating an irreversible momentum in one direction—as in, for example, the Vietnam War—and resistant to change in ways that frustrate congressmen and presidents alike, the bureaucracies also provide a steady accumulation of knowledge and rule by experts who are not subject to public whims. Once again, the people of the 1870s would be forced to reflect on the paradox of it all: the creation of great power, together with an ever wider spread of justice, or, at least, the possibility of achieving it. Who, in the 1870s, would have dreamed that the government would try, even fitfully, to regulate how foods are produced, products are advertised, and employees are treated by their employers?

Basic ideologies in politics persist

Americans from the 1870s would note, however, that the bureaucratic system has also created a great and continuing problem: now that the reg-

ulative state is here and the search for order as embodied in the powerful government and many independent commissions in Washington has reached some kind of apex, who controls the state, and to what end? Does it regulate the business community in a spirit of critical watchfulness? Or does it simply provide the aids to business efficiency that can flow from centralized decisions and common regulations? Here, in different form, the visitors from a century ago would find repeated the division in politics that rang through their own clamorous years. The Republicans still represent the business entrepreneur, the aggressive and self-reliant person inspired by notions of rugged individualism. The Republican outlook remains that espoused by James G. Blaine in the 1870s, Henry Clay in the 1830s, and Alexander Hamilton in the 1790s: when the government does anything with regard to the economy, it should be to help the businessman, who creates jobs and opportunity and develops the country. According to the Republican view, the agencies of federal and state government should be run by men sympathetic to his cause and inclined to grant him the railroad rate increase, the liberalization of regulations, or the license to drill for oil that he requests. Thus, in such hands, the regulative state has become a different institution than past reformers envisioned. Producers, not consumers, continue to be regarded with fostering care in a Republican White House.

So much else, indeed, would be familiar in politics to the visitors from the 1870s. The Democratic party, though clearly not a radical, anticapitalist organization, contains, as it always has, most of those politicians who worry about the consumer and advocate low prices and high wages, as well as those who are convinced that businessmen and bankers conspire behind the scenes to exploit the public. As did Andrew Jackson and Grover Cleveland, Democrats still deplore privilege and the power of great corporations, and brood about the harm being done to the country by those who advocate "development." Democrats in the 1870s condemned Republican policies of government aid to business as inherently corrupt, and they do so today. Still Jeffersonian in its aims, the Democratic party has nonetheless left far behind Jefferson's laissez-faire methods while building an ever stronger government through social reform. Their presidents maintain high public visibility, cooperate closely with Congress, work actively for social improvement, and seem to prefer the ferment of ideas over orderly administration. Watergate, leading to Nixon's resignation, showed that the Republican tradition has its own version of the "strong president," Tory in lineage, but it remains true that Republican administrations are little concerned with social reform, pay little attention to Congress, stress good management, and keep a low profile.

Cultural alignments in politics persist

The same cultural influences of a hundred years ago still suffuse American politics in the 1970s. The Republicans continue to be preeminently the party of Anglo-Saxon, Protestant America (though, of course, many WASPs are on the Democratic side as well). Thus, as the representatives of the huge "core" ethnic group that (among the whites) first arrived in America, created the national culture, and for generations provided its cultural, economic, and political leadership, they still think of themselves as guardians of traditional American life. The wealthy and established classes gravitate to the Republican party, which continues to symbolize the values of rule by an elite, and conservatism in life style. In most parts of the country, Democrats, as a century ago, make up the party of the outsiders, especially the non-WASP ethnic groups. For this reason, Catholics vote strongly Democratic, as they have been doing since the beginning of national history (though the proportion is declining, perhaps in response to their greater wealth), and so do Jews. Democrats are still stigmatized as radical intellectuals, lenient

coddlers of youth, and supporters of rebellion. On all these traditional cultural issues, Republicans gain heavily in votes. Horace Greeley, who was the Democratic and Liberal Republican candidate in 1872, was an advocate of women's rights, communal social reforms, and labor unions. Since these causes were much disliked by the "square majority," he was almost as thoroughly beaten by the Republican candidate, Ulysses Grant, as George McGovern in 1972, with his radical youth, women's liberation, and dashiki-clad Afro-American image, was beaten by Richard Nixon. In the 1870s, it was the Republicans who believed that government should enforce moral reforms—at that time the issues related to alcohol and Sunday laws—and today it is true that campaigns against pornography, drugs, and unusual sexual relationships tend to emanate from Republican ranks (although often with the aid, in this instance, of the strongly religious, whatever their party).

The black revolution

One great transformation in the ethnic alignment of the two major parties, however, has occurred. The Democrats of the 1870s were antiblack, but now, as between the two major parties, they are the principal advocates of black (and brown) America's cause in national affairs. The complicated coalition of out-groups that has traditionally made up the voting strength of the Democratic party has, therefore, been joined by yet another ethnic constituency. It was always an intricate business to hold together, say, the Irish, Jews, and Poles. Now black and brown Americans have arrived in party councils as well, making the task of party managers even more complex. How can they keep white Americans voting Democratic when racial tensions are high? Deeply sobering—and revealing—was the fact that in the presidential election of 1972, two-thirds of all white voters supported the Republican candidate.

In regard to racial discrimination, however, much would be familiar to the visitors from the 1870s. The Civil War and First Reconstruction would certainly prepare them for the fact that, in the Second Reconstruction of the 1950s and 1960s, the turmoil over Afro-Americans and their status in national life continues. They would observe that in the past twenty years the United States has been going through a transformation from a caste society, in which black Americans by law and practice were kept in a separate and depressed status, to one of legal equality. Of the four aspects of equality—civil, political, economic, and social—the Radical Republicans of their day had been concerned with only the first two, working (in the long run unsuccessfully) to guarantee fair trials and the vote to the black community. Since those had been lost in later years in the southern states, the Second Reconstruction had to labor all over again to achieve them once more. Furthermore, strong efforts were made in the 1960s to extend the concept of equality into economic and social spheres.

Americans from the 1870s would be surprised to see how markedly, in the face of great odds (and with the occasional and crucially important aid of government) black Americans have improved their life. They would be surprised, indeed, to see how strikingly the situation of all ethnic groups has changed. The fact that Irish Catholics are no longer reviled and segregated would be especially notable. They would see that the spread of black Americans across the length and breadth of the continent has made what their generation thought of as a southern problem a national one. They would, in fact, observe with a certain wry detachment that northern whites are drawing back from northern blacks in ways similar to the behavior of their white countrymen in the South over many generations, thus leading to a southernization of politics throughout the country. Black Americans have participated in all the sweeping changes described earlier in this chapter, but to what degree? Their share of the national standard of living is far less than that of

white Americans. Prejudice still exists, and it still fuels politics. Mexican-Americans, Puerto Ricans, and American Indians, in varying degrees, continue to experience the same exclusion as their black countrymen.

The sectional pattern of national politics, however, has been modified greatly. As communications, transportation, and the spread of industry, ethnic groups, and population increasingly makes American culture more homogeneous, the South now takes a new role. It is receding from its traditional "Solid South" Democratic voting pattern. Republicanism, because of the prowhite policies it has adopted in the last generation, is spreading into the South, which has thus become a two-party region for the first time since the 1840s. Indeed, in an important sense, the "sun states," which occupy a broad southern band across the United States from South Carolina and Florida to southern California, appear to be shaping up as the new heartland of Republicanism, though the advent of Jimmy Carter, who swept the South to his side, may change this. Furthermore, the northeastern states no longer dominate Washington as they did in the past. Of the seven presidents since 1945, four have come from the interior of the continent (Missouri, Michigan, Kansas, and Texas), a fifth from California, and a sixth from the Deep South. The whole balance of cultural, political, and economic power has tipped westward with the steady movement of population to the West in the last century, and southward in recent decades with the rise there of defense bases and industries. California contained only one out of every four hundred Americans in the 1870s; now it contains one out of every ten.

Party differences in foreign policy persist

The deep involvement of the United States in global politics would at first surprise the people of the 1870s, for in their day the United States had practically no foreign policy. But if they had lived ahead another twenty years to the 1890s, they would recognize present patterns. They would see the Republicans, as in the 1890s, leaning toward the nationalist side and the Democrats toward the internationalist. While Republican administrations tend to "go it alone" in world affairs, pulling back from multilateralism, Democrats have stressed the building of an ever widening circle of friends with whom a joint policy toward world events is maintained (though Lyndon Johnson veered strongly toward the Republican tradition in this regard). Among the Republicans in the 1890s were most of the strong voices that insisted that the world is a place of constant threat requiring the protection of strong military forces, a pattern that remains largely true, whereas among the Democrats, in both time periods, are to be found most of those who urge cooperation, coexistence, and the reduction of arms. Then as now there is a foreign policy elite, composed of newspaper editors, magazine publishers, scholars, bankers, and corporation presidents, which is seized by the notion that the United States must be a power in world affairs. Playing a leading role in taking the United States to war with Spain in 1898 and in the subsequent acquisition of an empire, in the 1960s this same confident group of men helped take the nation into the Vietnam disaster on the ground that America was steward and high guardian of liberty and freedom around the globe. In this destructive experience, which could only appall Americans from the 1870s, both Democrats and Republicans were deeply implicated. It was, however, within the former party that the strongest chorus rose condemning the involvement and calling for disengagement, while among the latter, with its greater inherent trust in military responses to world challenges, the disengagement was assented to most reluctantly. Visitors from the 1870s would recognize the dawning isolationism that is now, in gathering momentum, ending America's thirty-year adventure with international involvements.

The British parallel and relationships

What they would also see, however, is an America still seen by many in the world and in this country as unconsciously arrogant and unfeeling in its foreign policy, through the inescapable influence of its own success, power, and global influence. The United States' role in this past generation they would see as the same role that Britain was playing in world politics in their own day: powerful, ranging the seas with its great fleets, working most of the time for free trade and lowered tariffs, providing in the Bank of England (as the United States does now in Wall Street) the controlling center of world finances and investment, and holding off the "Russian menace." In this endeavor Britain's armed forces carried on wars around the globe at its imperial frontiers, as American troops have fought in Korea, occupied Lebanon, patrolled the China seas, garrisoned Berlin and West Germany, sailed the Mediterranean, and fought a seemingly endless war in Vietnam. The United States, too, like Britain then, has been carrying on this imperium as a proud nation, convinced of its superiority, infinitely capable of arousing dislike and hatred abroad and puzzled by these reactions. The habit of authority, bred into the British by generations of success and dominance—a habit that led them into such grave errors as those that set off the American Revolution—has been bred into the United States as well, though the Vietnam defeat has greatly reduced its itch for making interventions abroad.

By the 1970s, the transatlantic Anglo-American community within which for so long the American people had lived and worked had faded, or at least changed fundamentally. As late as the first World War the Americans were still looking to the British for cultural and political leadership. They watched British politics closely, read their books, drew inspiration from their great public leaders, examined their social reforms, and admired and disliked them as a powerful, wealthy, awe-inspiring people. The love-hate relationship, born in colonial times, remained alive. But in the era of Kennedy, Johnson, Nixon, and Ford, little of this remained. No one bothered to "twist the lion's tail" anymore. President Nixon might frequently refer to himself as a devotee of Benjamin Disraeli, thus demonstrating again how closely related in outlook and ideas are the British Conservatives and the American Republicans—just as his presidential style resembled that of traditional Tory governments—but the old vital connections were not there. Americans flood Britain as tourists, seeking out all the ancient landmarks, and mention of "the Queen" still needs no further description than that: everyone knows it means Elizabeth II of the United Kingdom. But now it would appear to be the British who read American books, watch American politics closely, examine American social reforms, and admire and dislike the Americans as a powerful, wealthy, and awe-inspiring people. American politicians of a reforming temperament in Woodrow Wilson's day liked being called Gladstonian, after the great nineteenth-century Liberal premier who battled Disraeli and the Conservatives, and now there are British politicians who would not be upset at being called Kennedyesque. Ironically, just as Americans spent generations pouring scorn on the "imperialistic" British, so in these times have many British done the same to the United States.

The comparison is instructive, and it would be well noted by the visitors from the 1870s. They would see a nation that, while idealizing peace, has frequently used violence to gain its ends; a nation that has labored to build a world community through such multilateral and cooperative devices as the United Nations, the Marshall Plan, the Peace Corps, the Alliance for Progress, joint reductions in tariffs, and billions of dollars in foreign aid—and yet is capable of turning away from such a vision and pursuing a nationalist, unilateral course in which it looks after its own interests in times of economic crisis by (in effect) raising its tariffs, and in diplomacy cutting loose from its venerable friendships. As Britain did a century ago, in the high days of its world supremacy and imperial rule, the United States now plays a paradoxical role: striving to aid liberty, yet standing forth as an enemy of revolution in order to protect law and order; advocating nonintervention and the rights of small nations, and then launching huge military interventions against small countries abroad to protect its client states.

The "taken for granted" syndrome

Perhaps more striking than anything else to a group of Americans from the 1870s, as they reflected upon the enormous changes their nation has undergone, would be the fact that few people now seem aware of these changes at all. The "world taken for granted" syndrome would mystify the visitors. Especially arresting would be the common tendency, among modern Americans, to idealize the past. They would find such misplaced nostalgia to be, at the least, amusing. Things that had seemed like visionary fantasies in their own day now actually exist. For most Americans life in the United States is much easier, more bountiful, and potentially more various and interesting than it ever was in earlier times. It is richer in its forms, more open, less hag-ridden by the limitations of ignorance, poverty, and social weakness. The possibility of experiencing life itself, in health, is incomparably greater. The opportunities for finding the particular way in which an individual can best express his or her nature are far greater in this pluralistic, many-doored society. The prospects of a lifetime of labor in brutalized conditions, of injury and death in factories built without concern for human safety, of deadening work for long hours and starvation wages, of having one's dignity violated by the arrogance and exploitation of superiors—these, for most Americans, have been vastly reduced.

The persistence of social sickness

The United States is a society that has realized so many of its dreams that it has lost count; in which evils that caused decades of bitter controversy seem largely to have disappeared, or at least to have lost their former virulence. But having realized their dreams, the American people have in truth found that this is not enough; that happiness still eludes them. The United States still struggles with social sickness, sometimes in gargantuan forms unknown a century ago. So much opulence exists that this continental society is choking on its wastes; such intricate mechanisms are so widely in use that only huge and virtually uncontrollable corporations can produce them. There is the constant presence of a military establishment bristling with doomsday weapons, and a presidency so enormously powerful and uncontrolled that its possessor can rain millions of tons of bombs on another country apparently at will. And America is still soured and twisted by social prejudice and unequal treatment. Millions live in wretched poverty, subsisting on welfare checks, frightened by inner-city crime, and surrounded by the wasting social disease of drug addiction. The country clubs and the comfortable suburbs are still overwhelmingly WASP; the slums are still predominantly black or brown. The inescapable question remains before us: how can all Americans, whatever their sex, ethnic membership, or class position, find an equal opportunity for self-fulfillment in this country?

The most appealing quality in the older American scene—the optimistic belief that life could be beautiful in the here and now if only certain problems were solved—seems vanished. As we lay each problem down, another, more subtle and elusive, rises in its place. Americans have always been a happiness-oriented people, the innocents in a grieving world, but now, in the latter decades of the twentieth century, they are coming ever more to the seasoned and rueful understanding that the ancient societies of Europe have long possessed: life can never be made serene; unease

lies in the human condition itself. And yet each generation cannot feel its humanity, cannot fulfill its own inner nature, unless it continues this unequal struggle, hoping somehow to leave its mark and make the world better than it has been.

The era of limits

In the bicentennial year of the American nation, its people shared a pervasive sense of subdued concern. The 200th birthday itself passed as a warming, folkish observance, but once it was over, a brooding conviction settled in again that the picnic was over. The American dream was in process of being slimmed down. The country's affluence was staggering, by comparison with practically all of the rest of the world (some countries in western Europe were richer on a per capita basis). Yet the quantum jump upward in energy and raw material costs was widely believed inevitably to cause a downward spiral in consumption: less automobile driving, everything more costly and fewer things bought, less lavish use of resources. Owning a home was becoming a luxury that fewer and fewer could afford as land and construction costs rose breathtakingly. Economic progress could no longer be taken for granted, certainly in the sense that each generation would get richer and live more bountifully.

Even the steady rise in physical height and weight of young people which had persisted for generations came to an end in the 1960s, hinting at the reaching of some natural limitation. One of the brightest flares in the politics of 1976 was the campaign of young Governor Edmund G. Brown, Jr., of California, who based his appeal to the electorate during the presidential primary on the assertion that the country had reached an "era of limits," and must begin making painful adjustments to that fact. Ominous warnings were being issued by leading scholars that the American economy was indeed in grave, long range trouble because of the ending of cheap raw materials and energy. The consensus of economists was that growth in productivity had been slowing substantially for a decade; that full employment would be impossible to reach again; and that the heavily urbanized and industrial regions of the Northeast and upper Middle West had entered a long stagnation and decline in which new jobs would be ever harder to generate. Joining these gloomy prognoses was the continuing loss of confidence by Americans in their government.

The first centennial's mood

This national state of mind would be familiar to those living a century ago. The nation's first centennial, 1876, was hardly a time of unmixed and gladsome self-pride. The economy was still suffering from the depression which began in 1873, and industrial warfare was beginning to rage between labor and capital, fatally sapping the long-held myth that America was the land of classless equality. The most violent labor outbreak in American history, the railway strike of 1877, was soon to devastate national morale; it was becoming ever more clear that the long and bloody effort to create racial justice in the South was failing; and at every level of government and in every state, corruption in politics made it almost impossible to move toward the solution of any social problem. Government had practically broken down; the whole democratic experiment seemed to be failing miserably.

Those devoted to the democratic experiment felt it all as a deep wound upon the spirit. "It is not necessary for me to attempt to paint the state of political corruption to which we have been reduced," said the reformer Henry George of California during the presidential election campaign of 1876. Corruption, he went on,

is the dark background to our national rejoicing, the skeleton which has stood by us at the feast. Our Fourth of July orators do not proclaim it; our newspapers do not announce it; we hardly whisper it to one another, but we all know, for we all feel, that beneath all our centennial rejoicing there exists in the public mind to-day a greater doubt of the success of Republican institutions than has existed within the memory of our oldest man.

This book has in part been written to make clear the fact that American cultural history is a record of oscillations in temper, characterized by broad swings from relative confidence to alarm and back again, not of movement in but one direction. This look backward a century demonstrates that feelings of stagnation and dismay have not arrived now for the first time in the American experience. As the psychologist Erik Erikson observes, mood swings from carnival to atonement seem to be the basic emotional rhythm in our nature. Human society is enormously volatile, able with startling suddenness to break from gloom into periods of astonishing intellectual excitement and creative response, especially in so open and libertarian a country as this one.

Perhaps Americans are to be denied any such revivals of spirit; perhaps a grey sterility is what lies ahead. But it would be at the least unhistorical to regard such forecasts as irresistibly persuasive to the reasonable mind. Life grows more complex and puzzling, in good part because our understanding of it grows more sophisticated and our knowledge of its difficulties more exact. Innocence lost is irretrievable. It is not likely that the nation's earlier buoyant optimism will ever return. This is not, however, the same as saying that Americans are fated permanently, henceforth, to suffer despair as an unrelieved state of mind; or that they are to be denied those tidal upwellings of fresh vision and renewed vigor which in the past have so persistently recurred in its public life and consciousness.

General Bibliography

The intent of the General Bibliography is to provide selected titles of general works useful in understanding and researching the scope of United States history.

Recent works in historiography

Bass, Herbert J. *The State of American History.* 1970.

Benson, Lee. *Toward the Scientific Study of History: Selected Essays.* 1972.

Bernstein, Barton J., ed. *Towards a New Past: Dissenting Essays in American History.* 1968.

Cunliffe, Marcus and Winks, Robin W., eds. *Pastmasters: Some Essays on American Historians.* 1969.

Grob, Gerald N. and Billias, George A., eds. *Interpretations of American History: Patterns and Perspectives.* 2 vols. 2nd ed. 1972.

Rapson, Richard L., ed. *Major Interpretations of the American Past.* 1971.

Woodward, C. Vann, ed., *The Comparative Approach to American History.* 1968.

Bibliographies and guides

Barrios, E., ed. *Bibliografía de Aztlán: An Annotated Chicano Bibliography.* 1971.

Fisher, Mary L. and Miller, Elizabeth, eds. *The Negro in America: A Bibliography.* Rev. ed. 1970.

Handlin, Oscar et al., *The Harvard Guide to American History.* 1972.

Krichmar, Albert et al. *The Women's Rights Movement in the United States, 1848–1970: A Bibliography and Sourcebook.* 1972.

Van Doren, Charles and McHenry, Robert, eds. *Webster's Guide to American History.* 1971. Features chronology, primary documents, maps, tables, biographies, and cross-referenced index.

Dictionaries and encyclopedias

James, Edward T. and James, Janet W., eds. *Notable American Women, 1607–1950: A Biographical Dictionary.* 3 vols. 1971.

Johnson, Allen and Malone, Dumas, eds. *Dictionary of American Biography.* 1928–1944.

Klein, Bernard and Icolari, Daniel, eds. *Reference Encyclopedia of the American Indian.* 1967.

Morris, Richard B. and Commager, Henry S., eds. *Encyclopedia of American History.* Rev. ed. 1970.

Statistics

The standard source for census and other data is *Historical Statistics of the United States, Colonial Times to 1957* (1960), now supplemented by *Continuation to 1962* (1965). This material is published by the Bureau of the Census, as are the annual volumes of *Statistical Abstract of the United States.*

Periodicals

The numerous periodicals devoted to history provide current information on what is going on among professional historians, reviews of the new books, and the results of contemporary research. Only a few can be listed here.

American Historical Review. 1895–.
American Political Science Review. 1906–.
American Quarterly. 1948–.
The Historian. 1938–.
Journal of American History (until 1965 the *Mississippi Valley Review.*) 1914–.
Political Science Quarterly. 1886–.

Cooperative histories

Cooperative histories usually span United States history from colonial to modern times with either a thematic or a chronological approach. Separate volumes are written by experts in the particular period or specialty.

Boorstin, Daniel J., ed. Chicago History of American Civilization Series. 1956–.

Commager, Henry S., ed. New American Nation Series. 1954–. A successor to The American Nation: A History, edited by Albert B. Hart, 28 vols. (1904–1918).

David, Henry et al., eds. Economic History of the United States. 9 vols. 1945–.

Handlin, Oscar, ed. The Library of American Biography. 1954–.

Schlesinger, Arthur M. and Fox, Dixon R., eds. A History of American Life. 13 vols. 1929–1948.

Stephenson, Wendell H. and Coulter, E. Merton, eds. History of the South. 10 vols. 1947–1967. This series supplants an older series, The South in the Building of the Nation, 13 vols. (1909–1913).

Pictorial and cartoon histories

Adams, James T., ed. *Album of American History.* 5 vols. 1944–1960.

Butterfield, Roger, ed. *The American Past.* 2nd rev. ed. 1966.

Davidson, Marshall B. *Life in America.* 2 vols. 1951.

Gabriel, Ralph H., ed. *Yale Pageant of America.* 15 vols. 1925–1929.

Horan, James D. *Matthew Brady: Historian with a Camera.* 1955.

Kouwenhoven, John A. *Adventures of America, 1857–1900: A Pictorial Record from Harper's Weekly,* 1938.

Longley, Marjorie; Silverstein, Louis; and Tower, Samuel A. *America's Taste: The Cultural Events of a Century Reported by Contemporary Observers in the Pages of the New York Times, 1851–1959.* 1960.

Murrell, William. *A History of American Graphic Humor.* 2 vols. 1938.

Nevins, Allan and Weitenkampf, Frank. *A Century of Political Cartoons, Caricatures in the United States: 1800–1900.* 1944.

Documents

The collections listed here include documents of a semiofficial and official nature. Every state has its own collection of records, documents, and statutes. University libraries are most often the source for important individuals' private and state papers.

American State Papers. 38 vols. 1832–1861. Executive and legislative papers in various categories.

Carter, Clarence E., ed. and comp. *Territorial Papers of the United States.* 1934–.

Commons, John R. et al., eds. *Documentary History of American Industrial Society.* 10 vols. 1909–1911.

Congressional Record. 1874–. Contains House and Senate debates. Before 1874, congressional debates were printed privately in *Congressional Globe, 1833–1873, Congressional Debates,* 1824–1837, and *Annals of Congress,* 1789–1824.

Fitzpatrick, John C. et al., eds. *Journal of the Continental Congress, 1744–1789.* 34 vols. 1904–1937.

Richardson, James D., ed. *Compilation of the Messages and Papers of the Presidents.* 10 vols. 1897. Reissued several times since with additions.

Statutes at Large. Contains all laws passed since the adoption of the Constitution. Issued at the end of each Congress or, after 1938, at the end of each calendar year.

United States Reports. 1790–. Contains Supreme Court decisions. Until 1874, decisions were cited by name of the Court reporter and the volume number. They were Dallas, vols. 1–4; Cranch, vols. 5–13; Wheaton, vols. 14–25; Peters, vols. 26–41; Howard, vols. 42–65; Black, vols. 66–67; and Wallace, vols. 68–90.

The Declaration of Independence

When in the Course of human events, it becomes necessary for one people to dissolve the political bands which have connected them with another, and to assume among the Powers of the earth, the separate and equal station to which the Laws of Nature and of Nature's God entitle them, a decent respect to the opinions of mankind requires that they should declare the causes which impel them to the separation.

We hold these truths to be self-evident, that all men are created equal, that they are endowed by their Creator with certain unalienable Rights, that among these are Life, Liberty and the pursuit of Happiness. That to secure these rights, Governments are instituted among Men, deriving their just powers from the consent of the governed, That whenever any Form of Government becomes destructive of these ends, it is the Right of the people to alter or to abolish it, and to institute new Government, laying its foundation on such principles and organizing its powers in such form, as to them shall seem most likely to effect their Safety and Happiness. Prudence, indeed, will dictate that Governments long established should not be changed for light and transient causes; and accordingly all experience hath shown, that mankind are more disposed to suffer, while evils are sufferable, than to right themselves by abolishing the forms to which they are accustomed. But when a long train of abuses and usurpations, pursuing invariably the same Object evinces a design to reduce them under absolute Despotism, it is their right, it is their duty, to throw off such Government, and to provide new Guards for their future security.—Such has been the patient sufferance of these Colonies; and such is now the necessity which constrains them to alter their former Systems of Government. The history of the present King of Great Britain is a history of repeated injuries and usurpations, all having in direct object the establishment of an absolute Tyranny over these States. To prove this, let Facts be summitted to a candid world.

He has refused his Assent to Laws, the most wholesome and necessary for the public good.

He has forbidden his Governors to pass Laws of immediate and pressing importance, unless suspended in their operation till his Assent should be obtained; and when so suspended, he has utterly neglected to attend to them.

He has refused to pass other Laws for the accommodation of large districts of people, unless those people would relinquish the right of Representation in the Legislature, a right inestimable to them and formidable to tyrants only.

He has called together legislative bodies at places unusual, uncomfortable, and distant from the depository of their public Records, for the sole purpose of fatiguing them into compliance with his measures.

He has dissolved Representative Houses repeatedly, for opposing with manly firmness his invasions on the rights of the people.

He has refused for a long time, after such dissolutions, to cause others to be elected; whereby the Legislative Powers, incapable of Annihilation, have returned to the People at large for their exercise; the State remaining in the mean time exposed to all the dangers of invasion from without, and convulsions within.

He has endeavoured to prevent the population of these States; for that purpose obstructing the Laws of Naturalization of Foreigners; refusing to pass others to encourage their migration hither, and raising the conditions of new Appropriations of Lands.

He has obstructed the Administration of Justice, by refusing his Assent to Laws for establishing Judiciary powers.

He has made Judges dependent on his Will alone, for the tenure of their offices, and the amount and payment of their salaries.

He has erected a multitude of New Offices, and sent hither swarms of Officers to harass our People, and eat out their substance.

He has kept among us in times of peace, Standing Armies without the Consent of our legislature.

He has affected to render the Military independent of and superior to the Civil power.

He has combined with others to subject us to a jurisdiction foreign to our constitution, and unacknowledged by our laws; giving his Assent to their acts of pretended Legislation:

For quartering large bodies of armed troops among us:

For protecting them, by a mock Trial, from punishment for any Murders which they should commit on the Inhabitants of these States:

For cutting off our Trade with all parts of the world:

For imposing taxes on us without our Consent:

For depriving us in many cases, of the benefits of Trial by Jury:

For transporting us beyond Seas to be tried for pretended offences:

For abolishing the free System of English Laws in a neighbouring Province, establishing therein an Arbitrary government, and enlarging its Boundaries so as to render it at once an example and fit instrument for introducing the same absolute rule into these Colonies:

For taking away our Charters, abolishing our most valuable Laws, and altering fundamentally the Forms of our Governments:

For suspending our own Legislature, and declaring themselves invested with Power to legislate for us in all cases whatsoever.

He has abdicated Government here, by declaring us out of his Protection and waging War against us.

He has plundered our seas, ravaged our Coasts, burnt our towns, and destroyed the lives of our people.

He is at this time transporting large Armies of foreign Mercenaries to compleat the works of death, desolation and tyranny, already begun with circumstances of Cruelty & perfidy scarcely paralleled in the most barbarous ages, and totally unworthy the Head of a civilized nation.

He has constrained our fellow Citizens taken Captive on the high Seas to bear Arms against their Country, to become the executioners of their friends and Brethren, or to fall themselves by their Hands.

He has excited domestic insurrections amongst us, and has endeavoured to bring on the inhabitants of our frontiers, the merciless Indian Savages, whose known rule of warfare, is an undistinguished destruction of all ages, sexes and conditions.

In every stage of these Oppressions We have Petitioned for Redress in the most humble terms: Our repeated Petitions have been answered only by repeated injury. A Prince, whose character is thus marked by every act which may define a Tyrant, is unfit to be the ruler of a free People.

Nor have We been wanting in attention to our British brethren. We have warned them from time to time of attempts by their legislature to extend an unwarrantable jurisdiction over us. We have reminded them of the circumstances of our emigration and settlement here. We have appealed to their native justice and magnanimity, and we have conjured them by the ties of our common kindred to disavow these usurpations, which, would inevitably interrupt our connections and correspondence. They too have been deaf to the voice of justice and of consanguinity. We must, therefore, acquiesce in the necessity, which denounces our Separation, and hold them, as we hold the rest of mankind, Enemies in War, in Peace Friends.

We, therefore, the Representatives of the United States of America, in General Congress, Assembled, appealing to the Supreme Judge of the world for the rectitude of our intentions, do, in the Name, and by Authority of the good People of these Colonies, solemnly publish and declare, That these United Colonies are, and of Right ought to be Free and Independent States; that they are Absolved from all Allegiance to the British Crown, and that all political connection between them and the State of Great Britain, is and ought to be totally dissolved; and that as Free and Independent States, they have full Power to levy War, conclude Peace, contract Alliances, establish Commerce, and to do all other Acts and Things which Independent States may of right do. And for the support of this Declaration, with a firm reliance on the protection of divine Providence, we mutually pledge to each other our Lives, our Fortunes and our sacred Honor.

The Constitution of the United States

We the people of the United States, in Order to form a more perfect Union, establish Justice, insure domestic Tranquility, provide for the common defense, promote the general Welfare, and secure the Blessings of Liberty to ourselves and our Posterity, do ordain and establish this CONSTITUTION for the United States of America.

Article I

Section 1. All legislative Powers herein granted shall be vested in a Congress of the United States, which shall consist of a Senate and House of Representatives.

Section 2. The House of Representatives shall be composed of Members chosen every second Year by the People of the several States, and the Electors in each State shall have the Qualifications requisite for Electors of the most numerous Branch of the State Legislature.

No Person shall be a Representative who shall not have attained to the Age of twenty-five Years, and been seven Years a Citizen of the United States, and who shall not, when elected, be an Inhabitant of that State in which he shall be chosen.

Representatives and direct Taxes shall be apportioned among the several States which may be included within this Union, according to their respective Numbers, which shall be determined by adding to the whole Number of Free Persons, including those bound to Service for a Term of Years, and excluding Indians not taxed, three fifths of all other Persons. The actual Enumeration shall be made within three Years after the first Meeting of the Congress of the United States, and within every subsequent Term of ten Years, in such Manner as they shall by Law direct. The Number of Representatives shall not exceed one for every thirty Thousand, but each State shall have at Least one Representative; and until such enumeration shall be made, the State of New Hampshire shall be entitled to chuse three, Massachusetts eight, Rhode Island and Providence Plantations one, Connecticut five, New York six, New Jersey four, Pennsylvania eight, Delaware one, Maryland six, Virginia ten, North Carolina five, South Carolina five, and Georgia three.

When vacancies happen in the Representation from any State, the Executive Authority thereof shall issue Writs of Election to fill such Vacancies.

The House of Representatives shall chuse their Speaker and other Officers; and shall have the sole Power of Impeachment.

Section 3. The Senate of the United States shall be composed of two Senators from each State, chosen by the Legislature thereof, for six Years; and each Senator shall have one Vote.

Immediately after they shall be assembled in Consequence of the first Election, they shall be divided as equally as may be into three Classes. The Seats of the Senators of the first Class shall be vacated at the Expiration of the second Year, of the second Class at the Expiration of the fourth Year, and of the third Class at the Expiration of the sixth Year, so that one-third may be chosen every second Year; and if Vacancies happen by Resignation, or otherwise during the Recess of the Legislature of any State, the Executive thereof may make temporary Appointments until the next Meeting of the Legislature, which shall then fill such Vacancies.

No Person shall be a Senator who shall not have attained to the Age of thirty Years, and been nine Years a Citizen of the United States, and who shall not, when elected, be an Inhabitant of that State in which he shall be chosen.

The Vice President of the United States shall be President of the Senate, but shall have no vote, unless they be equally divided.

The Senate shall choose their Officers, and also a President pro tempore, in the absence of the Vice President, or when he shall exercise the Office of the President of the United States.

The Senate shall have the sole Power to try all Impeachments. When sitting for that purpose, they shall be on Oath or Affirmation. When the President of the United States is tried, the Chief Justice shall preside: And no person shall be convicted without the Concurrence of two thirds of the Members present.

Judgment in Cases of Impeachment shall not extend further than to removal from Office, and disqualification to hold and enjoy any Office of honor, Trust, or Profit under the United States: but the Party convicted shall nevertheless be liable and subject to Indictment, Trial, Judgment, and Punishment, according to Law.

Section 4. The Times, Places and Manner of holding Elections for Senators and Representatives, shall be prescribed in each state by the Legislature thereof; but the Congress may at any time by Law make or alter such Regulations, except as to the Places of Chusing Senators.

The Congress shall assemble at least once in every Year, and such Meeting shall be on the first Monday in December, unless they shall by Law appoint a different Day.

Section 5. Each House shall be the Judge of the Elections, Returns and Qualifications of its own Members, and a Majority of each shall constitute a Quorum to do Business; but a smaller number may adjourn from day to day, and may be authorized to compel the Attendance of absent Members, in such Manner, and under such Penalties, as each House may provide.

Each House may determine the Rules of its Proceedings, punish its Members for disorderly Behaviour, and, with the Concurrence of two thirds, expel a Member.

Each House shall keep a Journal of its Proceedings, and from time to time publish the same, excepting such Parts as may in their Judgment require Secrecy; and the Yeas and Nays of the Members of either House on any question shall, at the Desire of one fifth of those Present, be entered on the Journal.

Neither House, during the Session of Congress, shall, without the Consent of the other, adjourn for more than three days, nor to any other Place than that in which the two Houses shall be sitting.

Section 6. The Senators and Representatives shall receive a Compensation for their Services, to be ascertained by Law, and paid out of the Treasury of the United States. They shall in all Cases, except Treason, Felony, and Breach of the Peace, be privileged from Arrest during their Attendance at the Session of their respective Houses, and in going to and returning from the same; and for any Speech or Debate in either House, they shall not be questioned in any other Place.

No Senator or Representative shall, during the Time for which he was elected, be appointed to any civil Office under the Authority of the United States, which shall have been created, or the Emoluments whereof shall have been increased, during such time; and no Person holding any Office under the United States shall be a Member of either House during his continuance in Office.

Section 7. All Bills for raising Revenue shall originate in the House of Representatives; but the Senate may propose or concur with Amendments as on other Bills.

Every Bill which shall have passed the House of Representatives and the Senate, shall, before it become a Law, be presented to the President of the United States; If he approve he shall sign it, but if not he shall return it, with his Objections, to that House in which it shall have originated, who shall enter the Objections at large on their Journal, and proceed to reconsider it. If after such Reconsideration two thirds of that House shall agree to pass the Bill, it shall be sent, together with the Objections, to the other House, by which it shall likewise be reconsidered, and if approved by two thirds of that House, it shall become a Law. But in all such Cases the Votes of both Houses shall be determined by Yeas and Nays, and the Names of the Persons voting for and against the Bill shall be entered on the Journal of each House respectively. If any Bill shall not be returned by the President within ten Days (Sundays excepted) after it shall have been represented to him, the Same shall be a Law, in like Manner as if he had signed it, unless the Congress by their Adjournment prevent its Return, in which Case it shall not be a Law.

Every Order, Resolution, or Vote to which the Concurrence of the Senate and House of Representatives may be necessary (except on a question of Adjournment) shall be presented to the President of the United States; and before the Same shall take Effect, shall be approved by him, or being disapproved by him, shall be repassed by two thirds of the Senate and House of Representatives, according to the Rules and Limitations prescribed in the Case of a Bill.

Section 8. The Congress shall have Power To lay and collect Taxes, Duties, Imposts and Excises, to pay the Debts and provide for the common Defense and general Welfare of the United

States; but all Duties, Imposts and Excises shall be uniform throughout the United States;

To borrow money on the credit of the United States;

To regulate Commerce with foreign Nations, and among the several States, and with the Indian Tribes;

To establish an uniform Rule of Naturalization, and uniform Laws on the subject of Bankruptcies throughout the United States;

To coin Money, regulate the Value thereof, and of foreign Coin, and fix the Standard of Weights and Measures;

To provide for the Punishment of counterfeiting the Securities and current Coin of the United States;

To establish Post Offices and post Roads;

To promote the Progress of Science and useful Arts, by securing for limited Times to Authors and Inventors the exclusive Right to their respective Writings and Discoveries;

To constitute Tribunals inferior to the Supreme Court;

To define and punish Piracies and Felonies committed on the high Seas, and Offenses against the Law of Nations;

To declare War, grant Letters of Marque and Reprisal, and make Rules concerning Captures on Land and Water;

To raise and support Armies, but no Appropriation of Money to that Use shall be for a longer Term than two Years;

To provide and maintain a Navy;

To make Rules for the Government and Regulation of the land and naval forces;

To provide for calling forth the Militia to execute the Laws of the Union, suppress Insurrections and repel Invasions;

To provide for organizing, arming, and disciplining the Militia, and for governing such Part of them as may be employed in the Service of the United States, reserving to the States respectively, the Appointment of the Officers, and the Authority of training the Militia according to the discipline prescribed by Congress;

To exercise exclusive Legislation in all Cases whatsoever, over such District (not exceeding ten Miles square) as may, by Cession of particular States, and the acceptance of Congress, become the Seat of Government of the United States, and to exercise like Authority over all Places purchased by the Consent of the Legislature of the State in which the Same shall be, for the Erection of Forts, Magazines, Arsenals, dock-Yards, and other needful Buildings;— And

To make all Laws which shall be necessary and proper for carrying into Execution the foregoing Powers, and all other Powers vested by this Constitution in the Government of the United States, or in any Department or Officer thereof.

Section 9. The Migration or Importation of such Persons as any of the States now existing shall think proper to admit, shall not be prohibited by the Congress prior to the Year one thousand eight hundred and eight, but a tax or duty may be imposed on such Importation, not exceeding ten dollars for each Person.

The privilege of the Writ of Habeas Corpus shall not be suspended, unless when in Cases of Rebellion or Invasion the public Safety may require it.

No Bill of Attainder or ex post facto Law shall be passed.

No Capitation, or other direct, Tax shall be laid unless in Proportion to the Census or Enumeration herein before directed to be taken.

No Tax or Duty shall be laid on Articles exported from any State.

No Preference shall be given by any Regulation of Revenue to the Ports of one State over those of another: nor shall Vessels bound to, or from, one State, be obliged to enter, clear, or pay Duties in another.

No Money shall be drawn from the Treasury, but in Consequence of Appropriations made by Law; and a regular Statement and Account of the Receipts and Expenditures of all public Money shall be published from time to time.

No Title of Nobility shall be granted by the United States: And no Person holding any Office of Profit or Trust under them, shall, without the Consent of the Congress, accept of any present, Emolument, Office, or Title, of any kind whatever, from any King, Prince, or foreign State.

Section 10. No State shall enter into any Treaty Alliance, or Confederation; grant Letters of Marque and Reprisal; coin Money; emit Bills of Credit; make any Thing but gold and silver Coin a Tender in Payment of Debts; pass any Bill of Attainder, ex post facto Law, or Law impairing the Obligation of Contracts, or grant any Title of Nobility.

No State shall, without the Consent of the Congress, lay any Imposts or Duties on Imports or Exports, except what may be absolutely necessary for exercising its inspection Laws: and the net Produce of all Duties and Imposts, laid by any State on Imports or Exports, shall be for the Use of the Treasury of the United States; and all such Laws shall be subject to the Revision and Control of the Congress.

No State shall, without the Consent of Congress, lay any duty of Tonnage, keep Troops, or Ships of War in time of Peace, enter into any Agreement or Compact with another State, or with a foreign Power, or engage in War, unless actually invaded, or in such imminent Danger as will not admit of delay.

Article II

Section 1. The executive Power shall be vested in a President of the United States of America. He shall hold his Office during the Term of four Years, and, together with the Vice President, chosen for the same term, be elected, as follows:

Each State shall appoint, in such Manner as the Legislature thereof may direct, a Number of Electors, equal to the whole Number of Senators and Representatives to which the State may be entitled in the Congress: but no Senator or Representative, or Person holding an Office of Trust or Profit under the United States, shall be appointed an Elector.

The Electors shall meet in their respective States, and vote by Ballot for two Persons, of whom one at least shall not be an Inhabitant of the same State with themselves. And they shall make a list of all the Persons voted for, and of the Number of Votes for each; which List they shall sign and certify, and transmit sealed to the Seat of the Government of the United States, directed to the President of the Senate. The President of the Senate shall, in the Presence of the Senate and House of Representatives, open all the Certificates, and the Votes shall then be counted. The Person having the greatest Number of Votes shall be the President, if such Number be a Majority of the whole Number of Electors appointed; and if there be more than one who have such Majority, and have an equal Number of Votes, then the House of Representatives shall immediately chuse by Ballot one of them for President; and if no Person have a Majority, then from the five highest on the List the said House shall in like Manner chuse the President. But in chusing the President, the Votes shall be taken by States, the Representation from each State having one Vote; a quorum for this Purpose shall consist of a Member or Members from two-thirds of the States, and a Majority of all the States shall be necessary to a Choice. In every Case, after the Choice of the President, the Person having the greatest Number of Votes of the Electors shall be the Vice President. But if there should remain two or more who have equal votes, the Senate shall chuse from them by Ballot the Vice President.

The Congress may determine the Time of chusing the Electors, and the Day on which they shall give their Votes; which Day shall be the same throughout the United States.

No person except a natural-born citizen, or a Citizen of the United States, at the time of the adoption of this Constitution, shall be eligible to the Office of President; neither shall any Person be eligble to that Office who shall not have attained to the Age of thirty-five Years, and been fourteen Years a Resident within the United States.

In case of the Removal of the President from Office, or of his Death, Resignation, or Inability to discharge the Powers and Duties of the said Office, the same shall devolve on the Vice President, and the Congress may by Law provide for the Case of Removal, Death, Resignation, or Inability, both of the President and Vice President, declaring what Officer shall then act as President, and such Officer shall act accordingly, until the Disability be removed, or a President shall be elected.

The President shall, at stated Times, receive for his Services a Compensation, which shall neither be increased nor diminished during the Period for which he shall have been elected, and he shall not receive within that Period any other Emolument from the United States, or any of them.

Before he enters on the Execution of his Office, he shall take the following Oath or Affirmation:— "I do solemnly swear (or affirm) that I will faithfully execute the Office of President of the United States, and will, to the best of my Ability, preserve, protect, and defend the Constitution of the United States."

Section 2. The President shall be Commander in Chief of the Army and Navy of the United States, and of the Militia of the several States, when called into the actual Service of the United States; he may require the Opinion, in writing, of the principal Officer in each of the executive Departments, upon any subject relating to the Duties of their respective Offices, and he shall have Power to Grant Reprieves and Pardons for Offenses against the United States, except in Cases of Impeachment.

He shall have Power, by and with the Advice and Consent of the Senate, to make Treaties, provided two thirds of the Senators present concur; and he shall nominate, and by and with the Advice and Consent of the Senate, shall appoint Ambassadors, other public Ministers and Consuls, Judges of the supreme Court, and all other Officers of the United States, whose Appointments are not herein otherwise provided for, and which shall be established by Law: but the Congress may by Law vest the Appointment of such inferior Officers, as they think proper, in the President alone, in the Courts of Law, or in the Heads of Departments.

The President shall have Power to fill up all Vacancies that may happen during the Recess of the Senate, by granting Commissions which shall expire at the end of their next Session.

Section 3. He shall from time to time give to the Congress Information of the State of the Union, and recommend to their Consideration such Measures as he shall judge necessary and expedient; he may, on extraordinary occasions, convene both Houses, or either of them, and in Case of Disagreement between them, with respect to the Time of Adjournment, he may adjourn them to such Time as he shall think proper; he shall receive Ambassadors and other public Ministers; he shall take Care that the Laws be faithfully executed, and shall Commission all the Officers of the United States.

Section 4. The President, Vice President and all civil Officers of the United States, shall be removed from Office on Impeachment for, and Conviction of, Treason, Bribery, or other high Crimes and Misdemeanors.

Article III

Section 1. The judicial Power of the United States, shall be vested in one supreme Court, and in such inferior Courts as the Congress may from time to time ordain and establish. The Judges, both of the supreme and inferior Courts shall hold their Offices during good Behaviour, and shall, at stated Times, receive for their Services, a Compensation, which shall not be diminished during their Continuance in Office.

Section 2. The judicial Power shall extend to all Cases, in Law and Equity, arising under this Constitution, the Laws of the United States, and Treaties made, or which shall be made, under their Authority;—to all Cases affecting Ambassadors, other public Ministers and Consuls;—to all Cases of admiralty and maritime Jurisdiction;—to Controversies to which the United States shall be a Party;—to Controversies between two or more States;—between a State and Citizens of another State;—between Citizens of the same State claiming Lands under Grants of different States, and between a State, or the Citizens thereof, and foreign States, Citizens or Subjects.

In all Cases affecting Ambassadors, other public Ministers and Consuls, and those in which a State shall be Party, the supreme Court shall have original Jurisdiction. In all the other Cases before mentioned, the supreme Court shall have appellate Jurisdiction, both as to Law and Fact, with such Exceptions, and under such Regulations as the Congress shall make.

The trial of all Crimes, except in Cases of Impeachment, shall be by Jury; and such Trial shall be held in the State where the said Crimes shall have been committed; but when not committed within any State, the Trial shall be at such Place or Places as the Congress may by Law have directed.

Section 3. Treason against the United States, shall consist only in levying War against them, or in adhering to their Enemies, giving them Aid and Comfort. No Person shall be convicted of Treason unless on the Testimony of two Witnesses to the same overt Act, or on Confession in open Court.

The Congress shall have power to declare the Punishment of Treason, but no Attainder of Treason shall work Corruption of Blood, or Forfeiture except during the Life of the Person attainted.

Article IV

Section 1. Full Faith and Credit shall be given in each State to the public Acts, Records, and judicial Proceedings of every other State. And the Congress may by general Laws prescribe the Manner in which such Acts, Records and Proceedings shall be proved, and the Effect thereof.

Section 2. The Citizens of each State shall be entitled to all Privileges and Immunities of Citizens in the several States.

A Person charged in any State with Treason, Felony, or other Crime, who shall flee from Justice, and be found in another State, shall on demand of the executive Authority of the State from which he fled, be delivered up, to be removed to the State having Jurisdiction of the crime.

No Person held to Service or Labour in one State, under the Laws thereof, escaping into another, shall, in Consequence of any Law or Regulation therein, be discharged from such Service or Labour, but shall be delivered up on Claim of the Party to whom such Service or Labour may be due.

Section 3. New States may be admitted by the Congress into this Union; but no new State shall be formed or erected within the Jurisdiction of any other State; nor any State be formed by the Junction of two or more States, or parts of States, without the Consent of the Legislatures of the States concerned as well as of the Congress.

The Congress shall have Power to dispose of and make all needful Rules and Regulations respecting the Territory or other Property belonging to the United States; and nothing in this Constitution shall be so construed as to Prejudice any Claims of the United States, or of any particular State.

Section 4. The United States shall guarantee to every State in this Union a Republican Form of Government, and shall protect each of them against Invasion; and on Application of the Legislature, or of the Executive (when the Legislature cannot be convened) against domestic Violence.

Article V

The Congress, whenever two thirds of both Houses shall deem it necessary, shall propose Amendments to this Constitution, or, on the Application of the Legislatures of two thirds of the several States, shall call a Convention for proposing Amendments, which, in either Case, shall be valid to all Intents and Purposes, as part of this Constitution, when ratified by the Legislatures of three fourths of the several States, or by Conventions in three fourths thereof, as the one or the other Mode of Ratification may be proposed by the Congress; Provided that no Amendment which may be made prior to the Year One thousand eight hundred and eight shall in any Manner affect the first and fourth Clauses in the Ninth Section of the first Article; and that no State, without its Consent, shall be deprived of its equal Suffrage in the Senate.

Article VI

All Debts contracted and Engagements entered into, before the Adoption of this Constitution, shall be as valid against the United States under this Constitution, as under the Confederation.

This Constitution, and the Laws of the United States which shall be made in Pursuance thereof: and all Treaties made, or which shall be made, under the Authority of the United States, shall be the supreme Law of the Land; and the Judges in every State shall be bound thereby, any Thing in the Constitution or laws of any State to the Contrary notwithstanding.

The Senators and Representatives before mentioned, and the Members of the several State Legislatures, and all executive and judicial Officers, both of the United States and of the several States, shall be bound by Oath or Affirmation to support this Constitution; but no religious Test shall ever be required as a qualification to any Office or public Trust under the United States.

Article VII

The Ratification of the Conventions of nine States shall be sufficient for the Establishment of this Constitution between the States so ratifying the same.

Done in Convention by the Unanimous Consent of the States present the Seventeenth Day of September in the Year of our Lord one thousand seven hundred and Eighty seven and of the Independence of the United States of America the Twelfth. In Witness whereof We have hereunto subscribed our Names.

Articles in Addition to, and Amendment of, the Constitution of the United States of America, Proposed by Congress, and Ratified by the Legislatures of the Several States, Pursuant to the Fifth Article of the Original Constitution.

Amendment I [1791]

Congress shall make no law respecting an establishment of religion, or prohibiting the free exercise thereof; or abridging the freedom of speech, or of the press; or the right of the people peaceably to assemble, and to petition the Government for a redress of grievances.

Amendment II [1791]

A well regulated Militia, being necessary to the security of a free State, the right of the people to keep and bear Arms, shall not be infringed.

Amendment III [1791]

No Soldier shall, in time of peace, be quartered in any house, without the consent of the Owner, nor in time of war, but in a manner to be prescribed by law.

Amendment IV [1791]

The right of the people to be secure in their persons, houses, papers, and effects, against unreasonable searches and seizures, shall not be violated, and no Warrants shall issue, but upon probable cause, supported by Oath or affirmation, and particularly describing the place to be searched, and the persons or things to be seized.

Amendment V [1791]

No person shall be held to answer for a capital or otherwise infamous crime, unless on a presentment or indictment of a Grand Jury, except in cases arising in the land or naval forces, or in the Militia, when in actual service in time of War or public danger; nor shall any person be subject for the same offence to be twice put in jeopardy of life or limb; nor shall be compelled in any criminal case to be a witness against himself, nor be deprived of life, liberty, or property, without due process of law; nor shall private property be taken for public use, without just compensation.

Amendment VI [1791]

In all criminal prosecutions, the accused shall enjoy the right to a speedy and public trial, by an impartial jury of the State and district wherein the crime shall have been committed, which district shall have been previously ascertained by law, and to be informed of the nature and cause of the accusation, to be confronted with the witnesses against him; to have compulsory process for obtaining witnesses in his favor, and to have the Assistance of Counsel for his defence.

Amendment VII [1791]

In Suits at common law, where the value in controversy shall exceed twenty dollars, the right of trial by jury shall be preserved, and no fact tried by a jury, shall be otherwise re-examined in any Court of the United States, than according to the rules of the common law.

Amendment VIII [1791]

Excessive bail shall not be required, nor excessive fines imposed, nor cruel and unusual punishments inflicted.

Amendment IX [1791]

The enumeration in the Constitution, of certain rights, shall not be construed to deny or disparage others retained by the people.

Amendment X [1791]

The powers not delegated to the United States by the Constitution,

nor prohibited by it to the States, are reserved to the States respectively, or to the people.

Amendment XI [1798]

The Judicial power of the United States shall not be construed to extend to any suit in law or equity, commenced or prosecuted against one of the United States by Citizens of another State, or by citizens or Subjects of any Foreign State.

Amendment XII [1804]

The Electors shall meet in their respective States and vote by ballot for President and Vice President, one of whom, at least, shall not be an inhabitant of the same State with themselves; they shall name in their ballots the person voted for as President, and in distinct ballots the person voted for as Vice-President, and they shall make distinct lists of all persons voted for as President, and of all persons voted for as Vice-President, and of the number of votes for each, which lists they shall sign and certify, and transmit sealed to the seat of the government of the United States, directed to the President of the Senate;—The President of the Senate shall, in the presence of the Senate and House of Representatives, open all the certificates and the votes shall then be counted;—The person having the greatest number of votes for President, shall be the President, if such number be a majority of the whole number of Electors appointed; and if no person have such majority, then from the persons having the highest numbers not exceeding three on the list of those voted for as President, the House of Representatives shall choose immediately, by ballot, the President. But in choosing the President, the votes

shall be taken by states, the representation from each state having one vote; a quorum for this purpose shall consist of a member or members from two-thirds of the states, and a majority of all the states shall be necessary to a choice. And if the House of Representatives shall not choose a President whenever the right of choice shall devolve upon them, before the fourth day of March next following, then the Vice-President shall act as President, as in the case of the death or other constitutional disability of the President.—The person having the greatest number of votes as Vice-President, shall be the Vice-President, if such number be a majority of the whole number of Electors appointed, and if no person have a majority, then from the two highest numbers on the list, the Senate shall choose the Vice-President; a quorum for the purpose shall consist of two-thirds of the whole number of Senators, and a majority of the whole number shall be necessary to a choice. But no person constitutionally ineligible to the office of the President shall be eligible to that of Vice-President of the United States.

Amendment XIII [1865]

Section 1. Neither slavery nor involuntary servitude, except as a punishment for crime whereof the party shall have been duly convicted, shall exist within the United States, or any place subject to their jurisdiction.

Section 2. Congress shall have the power to enforce this article by appropriate legislation.

Amendment XIV [1868]

Section 1. All persons born or naturalized in the United States, and subject to the jurisdiction thereof, are citizens of the United States and of the State wherein they reside. No state shall make or enforce any law which shall abridge the privileges or immunities of citizens of the United States; nor shall any State deprive any person of life, liberty, or property, without due process of law; nor deny to any person within its jurisdiction the equal protection of the laws.

Section 2. Representatives shall be apportioned among the several States according to their respective numbers, counting the whole number of persons in each State, excluding Indians not taxed. But when the right to vote at any election for the choice of electors for President and Vice President of the United States, Representatives in Congress, the Executive and Judicial officers of a State, or the members of the Legislature thereof, is denied to any of the male inhibitants of such State, being twenty-one years of age, and citizens of the United States, or in any way abridged, except for participation in rebellion, or other crime, the basis of representation therein shall be reduced in the proportion which the number of such male citizens shall bear to the whole number of male citizens twenty-one years of age in such State.

Section 3. No person shall be a Senator or Representative in Congress, or elector of President and Vice President, or hold any office, civil or military, under the United States, or under any State, who, having previously taken an oath, as a member of Congress, or as an officer of the United States, or as a member of any State legislature, or as an executive or judicial officer of any State, to support the Constitution of the United States, shall have engaged in insurrection or rebellion against the same, or given aid or comfort to the ene-

mies thereof. But Congress may by a vote of two-thirds of each House, remove such disability.

Section 4. The validity of the public debt of the United States, authorized by law, including debts incurred for payment of pensions and bounties for services in suppressing insurrection or rebellion, shall not be questioned. But neither the United States nor any State shall assume or pay any debt or obligation incurred in aid of insurrection or rebellion against the United States, or any claim for the loss or emancipation of any slave; but all such debts, obligations, and claims shall be held illegal and void.

Section 5. The Congress shall have the power to enforce, by appropriate legislation, the provisions of this article.

Amendment XV [1870]

Section 1. The right of citizens of the United States to vote shall not be denied or abridged by the United States or by any State on account of race, color, or previous condition of servitude—

Section 2. The Congress shall have the power to enforce this article by appropriate legislation.

Amendment XVI [1913]

The Congress shall have power to lay and collect taxes on incomes, from whatever source derived, without apportionment among the several States, and without regard to any census or enumeration.

Amendment XVII [1913]

The Senate of the United States shall be composed of two Senators from each State, elected by the people thereof, for six years; and each Senator shall have one vote. The electors in each State

shall have the qualifications requisite for electors of the most numerous branch of the State legislatures.

When vacancies happen in the representation of any State in the Senate, the executive authority of such State shall issue writs of election to fill such vacancies: *Provided,* That the legislature of any State may empower the executive thereof to make temporary appointments until the people fill the vacancies by election as the legislature may direct.

This amendment shall not be so construed as to affect the election or term of any Senator chosen before it becomes valid as part of the Constitution.

Amendment XVIII [1919]

Section 1. After one year from the ratification of this article the manufacture, sale, or transportation of intoxicating liquors within, the importation thereof into, or the exportation thereof from the United States and all territory subject to the jurisdiction thereof for beverage purposes is hereby prohibited.

Section 2. The Congress and the several States shall have concurrent power to enforce this article by appropriate legislation.

Section 3. This article shall be inoperative unless it shall have been ratified as an amendment to the Constitution by the legislatures of the several States, as provided in the Constitution, within seven years from the date of the submission hereof to the States by the Congress.

Amendment XIX [1920]

The right of citizens of the United States to vote shall not be denied or abridged by the United States or by any State on account of sex.

Congress shall have power to enforce this article by appropriate legislation.

Amendment XX [1933]

Section 1. The terms of the President and Vice President shall end at noon on the 20th day of January, and the terms of Senators and Representatives at noon on the 3rd day of January, of the years in which such terms would have ended if this article had not been ratified; and the terms of their successors shall then begin.

Section 2. The Congress shall assemble at least once in every year, and such meeting shall begin at noon on the 3d day of January, unless they shall by law appoint a different day.

Section 3. If, at the time fixed for the beginning of the term of the President, the President elect shall have died, the Vice President elect shall become President. If a President shall not have been chosen before the time fixed for the beginning of his term, or if the President elect shall have failed to qualify, then the Vice President elect shall act as President until a President shall have qualified; and the Congress may by law provide for the case wherein neither a President elect nor a Vice President elect shall have qualified, declaring who shall then act as President, or the manner in which one who is to act shall be selected, and such person shall act accordingly until a President or Vice President shall have qualified.

Section 4. The Congress may by law provide for the case of the death of any of the persons from whom the House of Representatives may choose a President whenever the right of choice shall have devolved upon them, and for the case of the death of any of the persons from whom the Senate may choose a Vice President whenever the right of choice shall have devolved upon them.

Section 5. Sections 1 and 2 shall take effect on the 15th day of October following the ratification of this article.

Section 6. This article shall be inoperative unless it shall have been ratified as an amendment to the Constitution by the legislatures of three-fourths of the several States within seven years from the date of its submission.

Amendment XXI [1933]

Section 1. The eighteenth article of amendment to the Constitution of the United States is hereby repealed.

Section 2. The transportation or importation into any State, Territory, or possession of the United States for delivery or use therein of intoxicating liquors, in violation of the laws thereof, is hereby prohibited.

Section 3. This article shall be inoperative unless it shall have been ratified as an amendment to the Constitution by conventions in the several States, as provided in the Constitution, within seven years from the date of the submission hereof to the States by the Congress.

Amendment XXII [1951]

No person shall be elected to the office of the President more than twice, and no person who has held the office of President, or acted as President, for more than two years of a term to which some other person was elected President shall be elected to the office of the President more than once.

But this Article shall not apply to any person holding the office of President when this Article was proposed by the Congress, and shall not prevent any person who may be holding the office of President, or acting as President, during the term within which this Article becomes operative from holding the office of President or acting as President during the remainder of such term.

Amendment XXIII [1961]

Section 1. The District constituting the seat of Government of the United States shall appoint in such manner as the Congress may direct:

A number of electors of President and Vice President equal to the whole number of Senators and Representatives in Congress to which the District would be entitled if it were a State, but in no event more than the least populous State; they shall be in addition to those appointed by the States, but they shall be considered, for the purposes of the election of President and Vice President, to be electors appointed by a State; and they shall meet in the District and perform such duties as provided by the twelfth article of amendment.

Section 2. The Congress shall have the power to enforce this article by appropriate legislation.

Amendment XXIV [1964]

Section 1. The right of citizens of the United States to vote in any primary or other election for President or Vice President, for electors for President or Vice President, or for Senator or Representative in Congress, shall not be denied or abridged by the United States or any State by reason of failure to pay any poll tax or other tax.

Section 2. The Congress shall have the power to enforce this article by appropriate legislation.

Amendment XXV [1967]

Section 1. In case of the removal of the President from office or his death or resignation, the Vice President shall become President.

Section 2. Whenever there is a vacancy in the office of the Vice President, the President shall nominate a Vice President who shall take the office upon confirmation by a majority vote of both houses of Congress.

Section 3. Whenever the President transmits to the President pro tempore of the Senate and the Speaker of the House of Representatives his written declaration that he is unable to discharge the powers and duties of his office, and until he transmits to them a written declaration to the contrary, such powers and duties shall be discharged by the Vice President as Acting President.

Section 4. Whenever the Vice President and a majority of either the principal officers of the executive departments, or of such other body as Congress may by law provide, transmit to the President pro tempore of the Senate and the Speaker of the House of Representatives their written declaration that the President is unable to discharge the powers and duties of his office, the Vice President shall immediately assume the powers and duties of the office as Acting President.

Thereafter, when the President transmits to the President pro tempore of the Senate and the Speaker of the House of Representatives his written declaration that no inability exists, he shall resume the powers and duties of his office unless the Vice President and a majority of either the principal officers of the executive departments, or of such other body as Congress may by law provide, transmit within four days to the President pro tempore of the Senate and the speaker of the House of Representatives their written declaration that the President is unable to discharge the powers and duties of his office. Thereupon Congress shall decide the issue, assembling within 48 hours for that purpose if not in session. If the Congress, within 21 days after receipt of the latter written declaration, or, if Congress is not in session, within 21 days after Congress is required to assemble, determines by two-thirds vote of both houses that the President is unable to discharge the powers and duties of his office, the Vice President shall continue to discharge the same as Acting President; otherwise, the President shall resume the powers and duties of his office.

Amendment XXVI [1971]

Section 1. The rights of citizens of the United States, who are 18 years of age or older, to vote shall not be denied or abridged by the United States or any state on account of age.

Section 2. The Congress shall have the power to enforce this article by appropriate legislation.

Presidential Elections

Year	Candidates	Party	Popular vote	Electoral vote
1789	**George Washington**			69
	John Adams			34
	Others			35
1792	**George Washington**			132
	John Adams			77
	George Clinton			50
	Others			5
1796	**John Adams**	Federalist		71
	Thomas Jefferson	Republican		68
	Thomas Pinckney	Federalist		59
	Aaron Burr	Republican		30
	Others			48
1800	**Thomas Jefferson**	Republican		73
	Aaron Burr	Republican		73
	John Adams	Federalist		65
	Charles C. Pinckney	Federalist		64
1804	**Thomas Jefferson**	Republican		162
	Charles C. Pinckney	Federalist		14
1808	**James Madison**	Republican		122
	Charles C. Pinckney	Federalist		47
	George Clinton	Independent-Republican		6
1812	**James Madison**	Republican		128
	DeWitt Clinton	Federalist		89
1816	**James Monroe**	Republican		183
	Rufus King	Federalist		34
1820	**James Monroe**	Democratic-Republican		231
	John Quincy Adams	Independent-Republican		1
1824	**John Quincy Adams**	Republican	108,740	84 (elected by the House of Representatives)
	Andrew Jackson	Republican	153,544	99
	Henry Clay	Republican	47,136	37
	William H. Crawford	Republican	46,618	41
1828	**Andrew Jackson**	Democratic	647,286	178
	John Quincy Adams	National Republican	508,064	83
1832	**Andrew Jackson**	Democratic	688,000	219
	Henry Clay	National Republican	530,000	49
	William Wirt	Anti-Masonic	255,000	7
	John Floyd	National Republican		11
1836	**Martin Van Buren**	Democratic	762,678	170
	William H. Harrison	Whig	549,000	73
	Hugh L. White	Whig	146,000	26
	Daniel Webster	Whig	41,000	14
1840	**William Harrison**	Whig	1,275,017	234
	Martin Van Buren	Democratic	1,128,702	60

Year	Candidates	Party	Popular vote	Electoral vote
1844	**James K. Polk**	Democratic	1,337,243	170
	Henry Clay	Whig	1,299,068	105
	James G. Birney	Liberty	62,300	
1848	**Zachary Taylor**	Whig	1,360,101	163
	Lewis Cass	Democratic	1,220,544	127
	Martin Van Buren	Free Soil	291,263	
1852	**Franklin Pierce**	Democratic	1,601,274	254
	Winfield Scott	Whig	1,386,580	42
1856	**James Buchanan**	Democratic	1,838,169	174
	John C. Fremont	Republican	1,335,264	114
	Millard Fillmore	American	874,534	8
1860	**Abraham Lincoln**	Republican	1,866,452	180
	Stephen A. Douglas	Democratic	1,375,157	12
	John C. Breckinridge	Democratic	847,953	72
	John Bell	Constitutional Union	592,631	39
1864	**Abraham Lincoln**	Republican	2,213,665	212
	George B. McClellan	Democratic	1,805,237	21
1868	**Ulysses S. Grant**	Republican	3,012,833	214
	Horatio Seymour	Democratic	2,703,249	80
1872	**Ulysses S. Grant**	Republican	3,596,745	286
	Horace Greeley	Democratic	2,843,446	66
1876	**Rutherford B. Hayes**	Republican	4,036,572	185
	Samuel J. Tilden	Democratic	4,284,020	184
1880	**James A. Garfield**	Republican	4,449,053	214
	Winfield S. Hancock	Democratic	4,442,032	155
	James B. Weaver	Greenback-Labor	308,578	
1884	**Grover Cleveland**	Democratic	4,874,986	219
	James G. Blaine	Republican	4,851,981	182
	Benjamin F. Butler	Greenback-Labor	175,370	
1888	**Benjamin Harrison**	Republican	5,444,337	233
	Grover Cleveland	Democratic	5,540,050	168
1892	**Grover Cleveland**	Democratic	5,554,414	277
	Benjamin Harrison	Republican	5,190,802	145
	James B. Weaver	People's	1,027,329	22
1896	**William McKinley**	Republican	7,104,779	271
	William J. Bryan	Democratic; Populist	6,502,925	176
1900	**William McKinley**	Republican	7,219,530	292
	William J. Bryan	Democratic; Populist	6,356,734	155
1904	**Theodore Roosevelt**	Republican	7,628,834	336
	Alton B. Parker	Democratic	5,084,401	140
	Eugene V. Debs	Socialist	402,460	
1908	**William H. Taft**	Republican	7,679,006	321
	William J. Bryan	Democratic	6,409,106	162
	Eugene V. Debs	Socialist	420,820	

Year	Candidates	Party	Popular vote	Electoral vote
1912	**Woodrow Wilson**	Democratic	6,293,454	435
	Theodore Roosevelt	Progressive	4,119,538	88
	William H. Taft	Republican	3,484,980	8
	Eugene V. Debs	Socialist	897,011	
1916	**Woodrow Wilson**	Democratic	9,129,606	277
	Charles E. Hughes	Republican	8,538,221	254
1920	**Warren G. Harding**	Republican	16,152,200	404
	James M. Cox	Democratic	9,147,353	127
	Eugene V. Debs	Socialist	919,799	
1924	**Calvin Coolidge**	Republican	15,725,016	382
	John W. Davis	Democratic	8,385,586	136
	Robert M. LaFollette	Progressive	4,822,856	13
1928	**Herbert C. Hoover**	Republican	21,392,190	444
	Alfred E. Smith	Democratic	15,016,443	87
1932	**Franklin D. Roosevelt**	Democratic	22,809,638	472
	Herbert C. Hoover	Republican	15,758,901	59
	Norman Thomas	Socialist	881,951	
1936	**Franklin D. Roosevelt**	Democratic	27,751,612	523
	Alfred M. Landon	Republican	16,618,913	8
	William Lemke	Union	891,858	
1940	**Franklin D. Roosevelt**	Democratic	27,243,466	449
	Wendell L. Willkie	Republican	22,304,755	82
1944	**Franklin D. Roosevelt**	Democratic	25,602,505	432
	Thomas E. Dewey	Republican	22,006,278	99
1948	**Harry S. Truman**	Democratic	24,105,812	303
	Thomas E. Dewey	Republican	21,970,065	189
	J. Strom Thurmond	States' Rights	1,169,063	39
	Henry A. Wallace	Progressive	1,157,172	
1952	**Dwight D. Eisenhower**	Republican	33,936,234	442
	Adlai E. Stevenson	Democratic	27,314,992	89
1956	**Dwight D. Eisenhower**	Republican	35,590,472	457
	Adlai E. Stevenson	Democratic	26,022,752	73
1960	**John F. Kennedy**	Democratic	34,227,096	303
	Richard M. Nixon	Republican	34,108,546	219
1964	**Lyndon B. Johnson**	Democratic	43,126,233	486
	Barry M. Goldwater	Republican	27,174,989	53
1968	**Richard M. Nixon**	Republican	31,783,783	301
	Hubert M. Humphrey	Democratic	31,271,839	191
	George C. Wallace	Amer. Independent	9,899,557	46
1972	**Richard M. Nixon**	Republican	47,168,963	520
	George S. McGovern	Democratic	29,169,615	17
	John Hospers	Republican (noncandidate)		1
1976	**Jimmy Carter**	Democratic	40,827,292	297
	Gerald R. Ford	Republican	39,146,157	240
	Ronald Reagan	Republican (noncandidate)		1

Date of Statehood

Delaware	December 7, 1787	Michigan	January 16, 1837
Pennsylvania	December 12, 1787	Florida	March 3, 1845
New Jersey	December 18, 1787	Texas	December 29, 1845
Georgia	January 2, 1788	Iowa	December 28, 1846
Connecticut	January 9, 1788	Wisconsin	May 29, 1848
Massachusetts	February 6, 1788	California	September 9, 1850
Maryland	April 28, 1788	Minnesota	May 11, 1858
South Carolina	May 23, 1788	Oregon	February 14, 1859
New Hampshire	June 21, 1788	Kansas	January 29, 1861
Virginia	June 25, 1788	West Virginia	June 19, 1863
New York	July 26, 1788	Nevada	October 31, 1864
North Carolina	November 21, 1789	Nebraska	March 1, 1867
Rhode Island	May 29, 1790	Colorado	August 1, 1876
Vermont	March 4, 1791	North Dakota	November 2, 1889
Kentucky	June 1, 1792	South Dakota	November 2, 1889
Tennessee	June 1, 1796	Montana	November 8, 1889
Ohio	March 1, 1803	Washington	November 11, 1889
Louisiana	April 30, 1812	Idaho	July 3, 1890
Indiana	December 11, 1816	Wyoming	July 10, 1890
Mississippi	December 10, 1817	Utah	January 4, 1896
Illinois	December 3, 1818	Oklahoma	November 16, 1907
Alabama	December 14, 1819	New Mexico	January 6, 1912
Maine	March 15, 1820	Arizona	February 14, 1912
Missouri	August 10, 1821	Alaska	January 3, 1959
Arkansas	June 15, 1836	Hawaii	August 21, 1959

Population of the United States

1790	3,929,214	1890	62,947,714
1800	5,308,483	1900	75,994,575
1810	7,239,881	1910	91,972,266
1820	9,638,453	1920	105,710,620
1830	12,860,692	1930	122,775,046
1840	17,063,353	1940	131,669,275
1850	23,191,876	1950	150,697,361
1860	31,443,321	1960	179,323,175
1870	38,558,371	1970	204,765,770
1880	50,155,783		

Presidents, Vice-Presidents, and Cabinet Members

President		Vice-President		Secretary of State		Secretary of Treasury	
1. George Washington	1789	John Adams	1789	T. Jefferson	1789	Alex. Hamilton	1789
				E. Randolph	1794	Oliver Wolcott	1795
				T. Pickering	1795		
2. John Adams, Federalist	1797	Thomas Jefferson	1797	T. Pickering	1797	Oliver Wolcott	1797
				John Marshall	1800	Samuel Dexter	1801
3. Thomas Jefferson, Republican	1801	Aaron Burr	1801	James Madison	1801	Samuel Dexter	1801
		George Clinton	1805			Albert Gallatin	1801
4. James Madison, Republican	1809	George Clinton	1809	Robert Smith	1809	Albert Gallatin	1809
		Elbridge Gerry	1813	James Monroe	1811	G. W. Campbell	1814
						A. J. Dallas	1814
						W. H. Crawford	1816
5. James Monroe, Republican	1817	D. D. Tompkins	1817	J. Q. Adams	1817	W. H. Crawford	1817
6. John Quincy Adams, Republican	1825	John C. Calhoun	1825	Henry Clay	1825	Richard Rush	1825
7. Andrew Jackson, Democrat	1829	John C. Calhoun	1829	M. Van Buren	1829	Sam D. Ingham	1820
		Martin Van Buren	1833	E. Livingston	1831	Louis McLane	1831
				Louis McLane	1833	W. J. Duane	1833
				John Forsyth	1834	Roger B. Taney	1833
						Levi Woodbury	1834
8. Martin Van Buren, Democrat	1837	Richard M. Johnson	1837	John Forsyth	1837	Levi Woodbury	1837
9. William H. Harrison, Whig	1841	John Tyler	1841	Daniel Webster	1841	Thos. Ewing	1841
10. John Tyler, Whig	1841			Daniel Webster	1841	Thos. Ewing	1841
				Hugh S. Legare	1843	Walter Forward	1841
				Abel P. Upshur	1843	John C. Spencer	1843
				John C. Calhoun	1844	Geo. M. Bibb	1844
11. James K. Polk, Democrat	1845	George M. Dallas	1845	James Buchanan	1845	Robt. J. Walker	1845
12. Zachary Taylor, Whig	1849	Millard Fillmore	1849	John M. Clayton	1849	Wm. M. Meredith	1849

Secretary of War		Attorney General		Postmaster General		Secretary of Navy		Secretary of Interior	
Henry Knox	1789	E. Randolph	1789	Samuel Osgood	1789				
T. Pickering	1795	Wm. Bradford	1794	Tom Pickering	1791				
Jas. McHenry	1796	Charles Lee	1795	Jos. Habersham	1795				
Jas. McHenry	1797	Charles Lee	1797	Jos. Habersham	1797	Benj. Stoddert	1798		
John Marshall	1800	Theo. Parsons	1801						
Sam'l Dexter	1800								
R. Griswold	1801								
H. Dearborn	1801	Levi Lincoln	1801	Jos. Habersham	1801	Benj. Stoddert	1801		
		Robert Smith	1805	Gideon Granger	1801	Robert Smith	1801		
		J. Breckinridge	1805			J. Crowninshield	1805		
		C. A. Rodney	1807						
Wm. Eustis	1809	C. A. Rodney	1809	Gideon Granger	1809	Paul Hamilton	1809		
J. Armstrong	1813	Wm. Pinkney	1811	R. J. Meigs. Jr.	1814	William Jones	1813		
James Monroe	1814	Richard Rush	1814			B. W. Crowninshield	1814		
W. H. Crawford	1815								
Isaac Shelby	1817	Richard Rush	1817	R. J. Meigs. Jr.	1817	B. W. Crowninshield	1817		
Geo. Graham	1817	William Wirt	1817	John McLean	1823	Smith Thompson	1818		
J. C. Calhoun	1817					S. L. Southard	1823		
Jas. Barbour	1825	William Wirt	1825	John McLean	1825	S. L. Southard	1825		
Peter B. Porter	1828								
John H. Eaton	1829	John M. Berrien	1829	Wm. T. Barry	1829	John Branch	1829		
Lewis Cass	1831	Roger R. Taney	1831	Amos Kendall	1835	Levi Woodbury	1831		
B. F. Butler	1837	B. F. Butler	1833			Mahlon Dickerson	1834		
Joel R. Poinsett	1837	B. F. Butler	1837	Amos Kendall	1837	Mahlon Dickerson	1837		
		Felix Grundy	1838	John M. Niles	1840	Jas. K. Paulding	1838		
		H. D. Gilpin	1840						
John Bell	1841	J. J. Crittenden	1841	Francis Granger	1841	George E. Badger	1841		
John Bell	1841	J. J. Crittenden	1841	Francis Granger	1841	George E. Badger	1841		
John McLean	1841	Hugh S. Legare	1841	C. A. Wickliffe	1841	Abel Upshur	1841		
J. C. Spencer	1841	John Nelson	1843			David Henshaw	1843		
Jas. M. Porter	1843					Thomas W. Gilmer	1844		
Wm. Wilkins	1844					John Y. Mason	1844		
Wm. L. Marcy	1845	John Y. Mason	1845	Cave Johnson	1845	George Bancroft	1845		
		Nathan Clifford	1846			John Y. Mason	1846		
		Isaac Toucey	1848						
G. W. Crawford	1849	Reverdy Johnson	1849	Jacob Collamer	1849	Wm. P. Preston	1849	Thomas Ewing	1849

President		Vice-President		Secretary of State		Secretary of Treasury		Secretary of War	
13. Millard Fillmore Whig	1850			Daniel Webster Edward Everett	1850 1852	Thomas Corwin	1850	C. M. Conrad	1850
14. Franklin Pierce Democrat	1853	William R. D. King	1853	W. L. Marcy	1853	James Guthrie	1853	Jefferson Davis	1853
15. James Buchanan Democrat	1857	John C. Breckinridge	1857	Lewis Cass J. S. Black	1857 1860	Howell Cobb Philip F. Thomas John A. Dix	1857 1860 1861	John B. Floyd Joseph Holt	1857 1861
16. Abraham Lincoln Republican	1861	Hannibal Hamlin Andrew Johnson	1861 1865	W. H. Seward	1861	Salmon P. Chase W. P. Fessenden Hugh McCulloch	1861 1864 1865	S. Cameron E. M. Stanton	1861 1862
17. Andrew Johnson Unionist	1865			Wm. H. Seward	1865	Hugh McCulloch	1865	E. M. Stanton U. S. Grant L. Thomas J. M. Schofield	1865 1867 1868 1868
18. Ulysses S. Grant Republican	1869	Schuyler Colfax Henry Wilson	1869 1873	E. B. Washburne Hamilton Fish	1869 1869	Geo. S. Boutwell W. A. Richardson Benj. H. Bristow Lot M. Morrill	1869 1873 1874 1876	J. A. Rawlins W. T. Sherman W. W. Belknap Alphonso Taft J. D. Cameron	1869 1869 1869 1876 1876
19. Rutherford B. Hayes Republican	1877	William A. Wheeler	1877	W. M. Evarts	1877	John Sherman	1877	G. W. McCrary Alex. Ramsey	1877 1879
20. James A. Garfield Republican	1881	Chester A. Arthur	1881	James G. Blaine	1881	Wm. Windom	1881	R. T. Lincoln	1881
21. Chester A. Arthur Republican	1881			F. T. Frelinghuysen	1881	Chas. J. Folger W. Q. Gresham Hugh McCulloch	1881 1884 1884	R. T. Lincoln	1881
22. Grover Cleveland Democrat	1885	T. A. Hendricks	1885	Thos. F. Bayard	1885	Daniel Manning Chas. S. Fairchild	1885 1887	W. C. Endicott	1885
23. Benjamin Harrison Republican	1889	Levi P. Morton	1889	James G. Blaine John W. Foster	1889 1892	Wm. Windom Charles Foster	1889 1891	R. Proctor S. B. Elkins	1889 1891
24. Grover Cleveland Democrat	1893	Adlai E. Stevenson	1893	W. Q. Gresham Richard Olney	1893 1895	John G. Carlisle	1893	D. S. Lamont	1893
25. William McKinley Republican	1897	Garret A. Hobart Theodore Roosevelt	1897 1901	John Sherman Wm. R. Day John Hay	1897 1897 1898	Lyman J. Gage	1897	R. A. Alger Elihu Root	1897 1899
26. Theodore Roosevelt Republican	1901	Chas. W. Fairbanks	1905	John Hay Elihu Root Robert Bacon	1901 1905 1909	Lyman J. Gage Leslie M. Shaw G. B. Cortelyou	1901 1902 1907	Elihu Root Wm. H. Taft Luke E. Wright	1901 1904 1908
27. William H. Taft Republican	1909	James S. Sherman	1909	P. C. Knox	1909	F. MacVeagh	1909	J. M. Dickinson H. L. Stimson	1909 1911
28. Woodrow Wilson Democrat	1913	Thomas R. Marshall	1913	Wm. J. Bryan Robert Lansing Bainbridge Colby	1913 1915 1920	W. G. McAdoo Carter Glass D. F. Houston	1913 1918 1920	L. M. Garrison N. D. Baker	1913 1916
29. Warren G. Harding Republican	1921	Calvin Coolidge	1921	Chas. E. Hughes	1921	Andrew W. Mellon	1921	John W. Weeks	1921
30. Calvin Coolidge Republican	1923	Charles G. Dawes	1925	Chas. E. Hughes Frank B. Kellogg	1923 1925	Andrew W. Mellon	1923	John W. Weeks Dwight F. Davis	1923 1925
31. Herbert Hoover Republican	1929	Charles Curtis	1929	H. L. Stimson	1929	Andrew W. Mellon Ogden L. Mills	1929 1932	James W. Good P. J. Hurley	1929 1929
32. Franklin D. Roosevelt Democrat	1933	John Nance Garner Henry A. Wallace Harry S. Truman	1933 1941 1945	Cordell Hull E. R. Stettinius, Jr.	1933 1944	Wm. H. Woodin Henry Morgenthau, Jr.	1933 1934	Geo. H. Dern H. A. Woodring H. L. Stimson	1933 1936 1940

Attorney General		Secretary of Navy		Secretary of Interior		Secretary of Agriculture	
J. J. Crittenden	1850	Wm. A. Graham	1850	A. H. Stuart	1850		
		John P. Kennedy	1852				
Caleb Cushing	1853	James C. Dobbin	1853	Rob't. McClelland	1853		
J. S. Black	1857	Isaac Toucey	1857	Jacob Thompson	1857		
Edw. M. Stanton	1860						
Edward Bates	1861	Gideon Welles	1861	Caleb B. Smith	1861		
Titian J. Coffey	1863			John P. Usher	1863		
James Speed	1864						
James Speed	1865	Gideon Welles	1865	John P. Usher	1865	Cabinet status, since 1889	
Henry Stanbery	1866			James Harlan	1865		
Wm. M. Evarts	1868			O. H. Browning	1866		
E. R. Hoar	1869	Adolph E. Borie	1869	Jacob D. Cox	1869		
A. T. Ackerman	1870	Geo. M. Robeson	1869	C. Delano	1870		
Geo. H. Williams	1871			Zach. Chandler	1875		
Edw. Pierrepont	1875						
Alphonso Taft	1876						
Chas. Devens.	1877	R. W. Thompson	1877	Carl Schurz	1877		
		Nathan Goff, Jr.	1881				
W. MacVeagh	1881	W. H. Hunt	1881	S. J. Kirkwood	1881		
B. H. Brewster	1881	W. E. Chandler	1881	Henry M. Teller	1881		
A. H. Garland	1885	W. C. Whitney	1885	L. Q. C. Lamar	1885	N. J. Colman	1889
				Wm. F. Vilas	1888		
W. H. H. Miller	1889	Benj. F. Tracy	1889	John W. Noble	1889	J. M. Rusk	1889
R. Olney	1893	Hilary A.		Hoke Smith	1893	J. S. Morton	1893
J. Harmon	1895	Herbert		D. R. Francis	1896		
J. McKenna	1897	John D. Long	1897	C. N. Bliss	1897	James Wilson	1897
J. W. Griggs	1897			E. A. Hitchcock	1899		
P. C. Knox	1901						
P. C. Knox	1901	John D. Long	1901	E. A. Hitchcock	1901	James Wilson	1901
W. H. Moody	1904	Wm. H. Moody	1902	J. R. Garfield	1907		
C. J. Bonaparte	1907	Paul Morton	1904				
		C. J. Bonaparte	1905				
		V. H. Metcalf	1907				
		T. H. Newberry	1908				
G. W. Wicker-sham	1909	G. von L. Meyer	1909	R. A. Ballinger	1909	James Wilson	1909
				W. L. Fisher	1911		
J. C. McReynolds	1913	Josephus Daniels	1913	F. K. Lane	1913	D. F. Houston	1913
T. W. Gregory	1914			J. B. Payne	1920	E. T. Meredith	1920
A. M. Palmer	1919						
H. M. Daugherty	1921	Edwin Denby	1921	Albert B. Fall	1921	H. C. Wallace	1921
				Hubert Work	1923		
H. M. Daugherty	1923	Edwin Denby	1923	Hubert Work	1923	H. M. Gore	1924
Harlan F. Stone	1924	Curtis D. Wilbur	1924	Roy O. West	1928	W. M. Jardine	1925
John G. Sargent	1925						
Wm. D. Mitchell	1929	Chas. F. Adams	1929	Ray L. Wilbur	1929	Arthur M. Hyde	1929
H. S. Cummings	1933	Claude A. Swanson	1933	Harold L. Ickes	1933	H. A. Wallace	1933
Frank Murphy	1939	Chas. Edison	1940			C. R. Wickard	1940
Robt. H. Jackson	1940	Frank Knox	1940				
Francis Biddle	1941	James V. Forrestal	1944				

Other Members

Postmaster General

Nathan K. Hall	1850
Sam D. Hubbard	1852
James Campbell	1853
Aaron V. Brown	1857
Joseph Holt	1859
Horatio King	1861
M'tgomery Blair	1861
Wm. Dennison	1864

Secretary of Commerce

W. C. Redfield	1913
J. W. Alexander	1919
H. C. Hoover	1921
H. C. Hoover	1925
W. F. Whiting	1928
R. P. Lamont	1929
R. D. Chapin	1932
D. C. Roper	1933
H. L. Hopkins	1939
Jesse Jones	1940
Henry A. Wallace	1945
W. Averell Harriman	1946
Charles W. Sawyer	1948
Sinclair Weeks	1953
Lewis L. Strauss	1958
Frederick H. Mueller	1959
Luther H. Hodges	1961
J. Thomas Connor	1964
A. B. Trowbridge	1967
C. R. Smith	1968
Maurice H. Stans	1969
Peter G. Peterson	1972
Frederick B. Dent	1972
Elliot Richardson	1975
Juanita Kreps	1977

Secretary of Labor

W. B. Wilson	1913
J. J. Davis	1921
W. N. Doak	1930
Frances Perkins	1933
L. B. Schellenbach	1945
M. J. Tobin	1948
M. P. Durkin	1953
James P. Mitchell	1953
Arthur J. Goldberg	1961
W. Willard Wirtz	1962
George P. Shultz	1969
James D. Hodgson	1970
Peter J. Brennan	1972
John T. Dunlop	1974
W. J. Usery, Jr.	1976
F. Ray Marshall	1977

Secretary of Defense

James V. Forrestal	1947
Louis A. Johnson	1949
George C. Marshall	1950
Robert A. Lovett	1951
Charles E. Wilson	1953
Neil McElroy	1957
Thomas Gates	1960
Robert S. McNamara	1961
Clark M. Clifford	1968
Melvin R. Laird	1969
E. L. Richardson	1972
James B. Schlesinger	1973
Donald Rumsfeld	1975
Harold Brown	1977

President		Vice-President		Secretary of State		Secretary of Treasury		Secretary of War	
33. **Harry S. Truman** Democrat	1945	Alben W. Barkley	1949	James F. Byrnes Geo. C. Marshall Dean G. Acheson	1945 1947 1949	Fred M. Vinson John W. Snyder	1945 1946	Robt. H. Patterson K. C. Royall*	1945 1947
34. **Dwight D. Eisenhower** Republican	1953	Richard M. Nixon	1953	John Foster Dulles Christian Herter	1953 1959	George C. Humphrey Robert B. Anderson	1953 1957		
35. **John F. Kennedy** Democrat	1961	Lyndon B. Johnson	1961	Dean Rusk	1961	C. Douglas Dillon	1961		
36. **Lyndon B. Johnson** Democrat	1963	Hubert H. Humphrey	1965			Henry H. Fowler	1965		
37. **Richard M. Nixon** Republican	1969	Spiro T. Agnew Gerald R. Ford	1969 1973	William P. Rogers Henry Kissinger	1969 1973	David M. Kennedy John B. Connally George P. Shultz William Simon	1969 1970 1972 1974		
38. **Gerald R. Ford** Republican	1974	Nelson A. Rockefeller	1974						
39. **Jimmy Carter** Democrat	1977	Walter F. Mondale	1977	Cyrus Vance	1977	W. Michael Blumenthal	1977		

*Lost Cabinet status in 1947.

Attorney General		Secretary of Navy		Secretary of Interior		Secretary of Agriculture		Other Members
								Secretary of Health, Education and Welfare
Tom C. Clark	1945	James V.		Harold L. Ickes	1945	C. P. Anderson	1945	Oveta Culp Hobby 1953
J. H. McGrath	1949	Forrestal	1945	Julius A. Krug	1946	C. F. Brannan	1948	Marion B. Folsom 1955
James P.		†		O. L. Chapman	1951			Arthur S. Flemming 1958
McGranery	1952							Abraham A. Ribicoff 1961
								A. J. Celebrezze 1962
Herbert				Douglas		Ezra T.		John W. Gardner 1965
Brownell, Jr.	1953			McKay	1953	Benson	1953	Wilbur J. Cohen 1968
William P.				Fred Seaton	1956			Robert H. Finch 1969
Rogers	1957							E. L. Richardson 1970
								Caspar W. Weinberger 1972
Robert F.				Stewart L.		Orville L.		F. David Matthews 1975
Kennedy	1961			Udall	1961	Freeman	1961	Joseph Califano 1977
Nicholas deB.								**Secretary of Housing and Urban Development**
Katzenbach	1965							Robert C. Weaver 1966
Ramsey Clark	1967			Walter J.		Clifford M.		George W. Romney 1969
John N. Mitchell	1969			Hickel	1969	Hardin	1969	James T. Lynn 1972
R. G. Kleindienst	1972			Rogers C. B.		Earl L. Butz	1971	Carla A. Hills 1975
E. L. Richardson	1973			Morton	1970			Patricia Harris 1977
William Saxbe	1973							**Secretary of Transportation**
								Alan S. Boyd 1967
Edward H.				Thomas S.				John A. Volpe 1969
Levi	1974			Kleppe	1975			Claude S. Brinegar 1972
Griffin				Cecil		Robert		William T. Coleman 1975
Bell	1977			Andrus	1977	Berglund	1977	Brock Adams 1977

† Lost Cabinet status in 1947.

INDEX